THE

CONSTITUTIONAL

HISTORY OF ENGLAND

FROM THE ACCESSION OF HENRY VII. TO
THE DEATH OF GEORGE II.

BY HENRY HALLAM, LL.D., F.R.A.S.,
FOREIGN ASSOCIATE OF THE INSTITUTE OF FRANCE.

IN THREE VOLUMES.

VOLUME I.

NEW YORK:
SHELDON AND COMPANY.
BOSTON:
WILLIAM VEAZIE.
1862.

RIVERSIDE, CAMBRIDGE:
STEREOTYPED AND PRINTED BY
H. O. HOUGHTON.

TO

HENRY MARQUIS OF LANSDOWNE,

IN TOKEN OF HIGH ESTEEM

AND SINCERE REGARD,

THIS WORK IS RESPECTFULLY INSCRIBED

BY

THE AUTHOR.

PREFACE.

The origin and progress of the English constitution, down to the extinction of the house of Plantagenet, formed a considerable portion of a work published by me some years since, on the history, and especially the laws and institutions, of Europe during the period of the middle ages. It had been my first intention to have prosecuted that undertaking in a general continuation; and when experience taught me to abandon a scheme projected early in life with very inadequate views of its magnitude, I still determined to carry forward the constitutional history of my own country, as both the most important to ourselves, and, in many respects, the most congenial to my own studies and habits of mind.

The title which I have adopted appears to exclude all matter not referrible to the state of government, or what is loosely denominated the constitution. I have, therefore, generally abstained from mentioning, except cursorily, either military or political transactions, which do not seem to bear on this primary subject. It must, however, be evident that the constitutional and general history of England, at some periods, nearly coincide; and I presume that a few occasional deviations of this nature will not be deemed unpardonable, especially where they tend, at least indirectly, to illustrate the main topic of inquiry. Nor will the reader, perhaps, be of opinion that I have forgotten my theme in those parts of the following work which relate to the establishment of the English church, and to the proceedings of the state with respect to those who have dissented from it; facts certainly belonging to the history of our constitution, in the large sense of the word, and most important in their application to modern times, for which all knowledge of the past is principally valuable. Still less apology can be required for a slight verbal inconsistency with the title of these volumes in the addition of two supplemental chapters on Scotland and Ireland. This indeed I mention less to obviate a criticism which possibly might not be suggested, than to express my regret that, on account of their brevity, if for no other reasons, they are both so disproportionate to the interest and importance of their subjects.

During the years that, amidst avocations of different kinds, have been occupied in the composition of this work, several others have been given to the world, and have attracted considerable attention, relating particularly to the periods of the Reformation and of the civil wars. It seems necessary to mention that I had read none of these till after I had written such of the following pages as treat of the same subjects. The three first chapters indeed were finished in 1820, before the appearance of those publications which have led to so much controversy as to the ecclesiastical history of the sixteenth century; and I was equally unacquainted with Mr. Brodie's "History of the British Empire from the Accession of Charles I. to the Restoration," while engaged myself on that period. I have, however, on a revision of the present work, availed myself of the valuable labors of recent authors, especially Dr. Lingard and Mr. Brodie; and in several of my notes I have sometimes supported myself by their authority, sometimes taken the liberty to express my dissent; but I have seldom thought it necessary to make more than a few verbal modifications in my text.

It would perhaps, not become me to offer any observations on these contemporaries; but I cannot refrain from bearing testimony to the work of a distinguished foreigner, M. Guizot, "Histoire de la Révolution d'Angleterre, depuis l'Avènement de Charles I. jusqu'à la Chute de Jacques II.," the first volume of which was published in 1826. The extensive knowledge of M. Guizot, and his remarkable impartiality, have already been displayed in his collection of memoirs illustrating that part of English history; and I am much disposed to believe that, if the rest of his present undertaking shall be completed in as satisfactory a manner as the first volume, he will be entitled to the preference above any one, perhaps, of our native writers, as a guide through the great period of the seventeenth century.

In terminating the Constitutional History of England at

the accession of George III. I have been influenced by unwillingness to excite the prejudices of modern politics, especially those connected with personal character, which extend back through at least a large portion of that reign. It is indeed vain to expect that any comprehensive account of the two preceding centuries can be given without risking the disapprobation of those parties, religious or political, which originated during that period; but as I shall hardly incur the imputation of being the blind zealot of any of these, I have little to fear, in this respect, from the dispassionate public, whose favor, both in this country and on the continent, has been bestowed on my former work, with a liberality less due to any literary merit it may possess than to a regard for truth, which will, I trust, be found equally characteristic of the present.

June, 1827.

ADVERTISEMENT TO THE THIRD EDITION.

The present edition has been revised, and some use made of recent publications. The note on the authenticity of the Icon Basilike, at the end of the second volume of the two former editions, has been withdrawn; not from the slightest doubt in the author's mind as to the correctness of its argument, but because a discussion of a point of literary criticism, as this ought to be considered, seemed rather out of its place in the Constitutional History of England.

April, 1832.

ADVERTISEMENT TO THE FIFTH EDITION.

Many alterations and additions have been made in this edition, as well as some in that published in 1842. They are distinguished, when more than verbal, by brackets and by the date.

January, 1846.

The following Editions have been used for the References in these Volumes.

STATUTES at Large, by Ruffhead, except where the late edition of Statutes of the Realm is expressly quoted.
State Trials, by Howell.
Rymer's Fœdera, London, 20 vols.
The paging of this edition is preserved in the margin of the Hague edition in 10 vols.
Parliamentary History, new edition.
Burnet's History of the Reformation, 3 vols. folio, 1681.
Strype's Ecclesiastical Memorials, Annals of Reformation, and Lives of Archbishops Cranmer, Parker, Grindal, and Whitgift, folio.
The paging of these editions is preserved in those lately published in 8vo.
Hall's Chronicles of England.
Holingshed's Chronicles of England, Scotland, and Ireland.
The edition in 4to. published in 1808.
Somers Tracts, by Sir Walter Scott, 13 vols. 4to.
Harleian Miscellany, 8 vols. 4to.
Neal's History of the Puritans, 2 vols. 4to.
Bacon's Works, by Mallet, 3 vols. folio, 1753.
Kennet's Complete History of England, 3 vols. folio, 1719.
Wood's History of University of Oxford, by Gutch, 4 vols. 4to.
Lingard's History of England, 10 vols. 8vo.
Butler's Memoirs of English Catholics, 4 vols. 1819.
Harris's Lives of James I., Charles I., Cromwell, and Charles II., 5 vols. 1814.
Clarendon's History of the Rebellion, 8 vols. 8vo. Oxf. 1826.
It is to be regretted that the editor has not preserved the paging of the folio in his margin, which is of great convenience in a book so frequently referred to; and still more so, that he has not thought the true text worthy of a better place than the bottom of the page, leaving to the spurious readings the post of honor.
Clarendon's Life, folio.
Rushworth Abridged, 6 vols. 8vo. 1703.
This edition contains many additions from works published since the folio edition in 1680.
Whitelock's Memorials, 1732.
Memoirs of Col. Hutchinson, 4to. 1806.
May's History of the Parliament, 4to. 1812.
Baxter's Life, folio.

Rapin's History of England, 3 vols. folio, 1732.

Burnet's History of his own Times, 2 vols. folio.

The paging of this edition is preserved in the margin of that printed at Oxford, 1823, which is sometimes quoted, and the text of which has always been followed.

Life of William Lord Russell, by Lord John Russell, 4to.

Temple's Works, 2 vols. folio, 1720.

Coxe's Life of Marlborough, 3 vols. 4to.

Coxe's Memoirs of Sir Robert Walpole, 3 vols. 4to.

Robertson's History of Scotland, 2 vols. 8vo. 1794.

Laing's History of Scotland, 4 vols. 8vo.

Dalrymple's Annals of Scotland, 2 vols. 4to.

Leland's History of Ireland, 3 vols. 4to.

Spenser's Account of State of Ireland, in 8th volume of Todd's edition of Spenser's Works.

These are, I believe, almost all the works quoted in the following volumes, concerning which any uncertainty could arise from the mode of reference.

CONTENTS

OF

THE FIRST VOLUME.

CHAPTER I.

ON THE ENGLISH CONSTITUTION FROM HENRY VII. TO MARY.

CHAPTER II.

ON THE ENGLISH CHURCH UNDER HENRY VIII., EDWARD VI., AND MARY.

CHAPTER III.

ON THE LAWS OF ELIZABETH'S REIGN RESPECTING THE ROMAN CATHOLICS.

CHAPTER IV.

ON THE LAWS OF ELIZABETH'S REIGN RESPECTING PROTESTANT NONCONFORMISTS.

CHAPTER V.

ON THE CIVIL GOVERNMENT OF ELIZABETH.

CHAPTER VI.

ON THE ENGLISH CONSTITUTION UNDER JAMES I.

CHAPTER VII.

ON THE ENGLISH CONSTITUTION FROM THE ACCESSION OF CHARLES I. TO THE DISSOLUTION OF HIS THIRD PARLIAMENT.

THE CONSTITUTIONAL HISTORY OF ENGLAND FROM HENRY VII. TO GEORGE II.

CHAPTER I.

ON THE ENGLISH CONSTITUTION FROM HENRY VII. TO MARY.

Ancient Government of England — Limitations of Royal Authority — Difference in the effective Operation of these — Sketch of the state of Society and Law — Henry VII. — Statute for the Security of the Subject under a King *de facto* — Statute of Fines — Discussion of its Effect and Motive — Exactions of Money under Henry VII. — Taxes demanded by Henry VIII. — Illegal Exactions of Wolsey in 1523 and 1525 — Acts of Parliament releasing the King from his Debts — A Benevolence again exacted — Oppressive Treatment of Reed — Severe and unjust Executions for Treason — Earl of Warwick — Earl of Suffolk — Duke of Buckingham — New Treasons created by Statute — Executions of Fisher and More — Cromwell — Duke of Norfolk — Anne Boleyn — Fresh Statutes enacting the Penalties of Treason — Act giving Proclamations the force of Law — Government of Edward VI.'s Counsellors — Attainder of Lord Seymour and Duke of Somerset — Violence of Mary's reign — The House of Commons recovers part of its independent power in these two Reigns — Attempt of the Court to strengthen itself by creating new Boroughs — Causes of the High Prerogative of the Tudors — Jurisdiction of the Council of Star-Chamber — This not the same with the Court erected by Henry VII. — Influence of the Authority of the Star-Chamber in enhancing the Royal Power — Tendency of Religious Disputes to the same end.

Ancient government of England.

THE government of England, in all times recorded by history, has been one of those mixed or limited monarchies which the Celtic and Gothic tribes appear universally to have established in preference to the coarse despotism of eastern nations, to the more artificial tyranny of Rome and Constantinople, or to the various models of republican polity which were tried upon the coasts of the Mediterranean Sea. It bore the same general features, it belonged, as it were, to the same family, as the governments of almost every European state, though less resembling, perhaps, that of France than any other. But, in the course of many centuries, the boundaries which determined the sovereign's prerogative and the people's liberty or power having seldom been very accurately defined by law, or at least by such law as was deemed fundamental and unchangeable, the forms and principles of political regimen in these different nations became more divergent from each other, according to their peculiar dispositions, the revolutions they underwent, or the influence of personal character. England, more fortunate than the rest, had acquired in the fifteenth century a just reputation for the goodness of her laws and the security of her citizens from oppression.

This liberty had been the slow fruit of ages, still waiting a happier season for its perfect ripeness, but already giving proof of the vigor and industry which had been employed in its culture. I have endeavored, in a work of which this may in a certain degree be reckoned a continuation, to trace the leading events and causes of its progress. It will be sufficient in this place briefly to point out the principal circumstances in the polity of England at the accession of Henry VII.

Limitations of royal authority.

The essential checks upon the royal authority were five in number. — 1. The king could levy no sort of new tax upon his people, except by the grant of his parliament, consisting as well of bishops and mitred abbots or lords spiritual, and of hereditary peers or temporal lords, who sat and voted promiscuously in the same chamber, as of representatives from the freeholders of each county, and from the burgesses of many towns and less considerable places, forming the lower or commons' house. 2. The previous assent and authority of the same assembly were necessary for every new law, whether of a general or temporary nature. 3. No man could be committed to prison but by a legal warrant specifying his offence; and by an usage nearly tantamount to constitutional right, he must be speedily brought to trial by means of regular sessions of jail-delivery. 4. The fact of guilt or innocence on a criminal charge was determined in a public court, and in the county where the offence was alleged to have occurred, by a jury of twelve men, from whose unanimous verdict no appeal could be made. Civil rights, so far as they depended on questions of fact, were subject to the same decision. 5. The officers and servants of the crown, violating the personal liberty or other right of the subject, might be sued in an action for damages to be assessed by a jury, or, in some cases, were liable to criminal process; nor could they plead any warrant or command in their justification, not even the direct order of the king.

These securities, though it would be easy to prove that they were all recognized in law, differed much in the degree of their effective operation. It may be said of the first, that it was now completely established. After a long contention, the kings of England had desisted for near a hundred years from every attempt to impose taxes without consent of parliament; and their recent device of demanding benevolences, or half-compulsory gifts, though very oppressive, and on that account just abolished by an act of the late usurper Richard, was in effect a recognition of the general principle, which it sought to elude rather than transgress.

Difference in the effective operation of these.

The necessary concurrence of the two houses of parliament in legislation, though it could not be more unequivocally established than the former, had in earlier times been more free from all attempt at encroachment. We know not of any laws that were ever enacted by our kings without the assent and advice of their great council; though it is justly doubted whether the representatives of the ordinary freeholders, or of the boroughs, had seats and suffrages in that assembly during seven or eight reigns after the conquest. They were then, however, ingrafted upon it with plenary legislative authority; and if the sanction of a statute were required for this fundamental axiom, we might refer to one in the 15th of Edward II. (1322), which declares that "the matters to be established for the estate of the king and of his heirs, and for the estate of the realm and of the people, should be treated, accorded, and established in parliament, by the king, and by the assent of the prelates, earls, and barons, and the commonalty of the realm, according as had been before accustomed."[1]

It may not be impertinent to remark in this place, that the

[1] This statute is not even alluded to in Ruffhead's edition, and has been very little noticed by writers on our law or history. It is printed in the late edition, published by authority, and is brought forward in the First Report of the Lords' Committee on the Dignity of a Peer (1819), p. 282. Nothing can be more evident than that it not only establishes by a legislative declaration the present constitution of parliament, but recognizes it as already standing upon a custom of some length of time.

opinion of such as have fancied the royal prerogative under the houses of Plantagenet and Tudor to have had no effectual or unquestioned limitations is decidedly refuted by the notorious fact that no alteration in the general laws of the realm was ever made, or attempted to be made, without the consent of parliament. It is not surprising that the council, in great exigency of money, should sometimes employ force to extort it from the merchants, or that servile lawyers should be found to vindicate these encroachments of power. Impositions, like other arbitrary measures, were particular and temporary, prompted by rapacity, and endured through compulsion. But if the kings of England had been supposed to enjoy an absolute authority, we should find some proofs of it in their exercise of the supreme function of sovereignty, the enactment of new laws. Yet there is not a single instance, from the first dawn of our constitutional history, where a proclamation, or order of council, has dictated any change, however trifling, in the code of private rights, or in the penalties of criminal offences. Was it ever pretended that the king could empower his subjects to devise their freeholds, or to levy fines of their entailed lands? Has even the slightest regulation, as to judicial procedure, or any permanent prohibition, even in fiscal law, been ever enforced without statute? There was, indeed, a period, later than that of Henry VII., when a control over the subject's free right of doing all things not unlawful was usurped by means of proclamations. These, however, were always temporary, and did not affect to alter the established law. But though it would be difficult to assert that none of this kind had ever been issued in rude and irregular times, I have not observed any under the kings of the Plantagenet name which evidently transgress the boundaries of their legal prerogative.

The general privileges of the nation were far more secure than those of private men. Great violence was often used by the various officers of the crown, for which no adequate redress could be procured; the courts of justice were not strong enough, whatever might be their temper, to chastise such aggressions; juries, through intimidation or ignorance, returned such verdicts as were desired by the crown; and, in general, there was perhaps little effective restraint upon the government, except in the two articles of levying money and enacting laws.

State of society and law.

The peers alone, a small body, varying from about fifty to eighty persons, enjoyed the privileges of aristocracy; which, except that of sitting in parliament, were not very considerable, far less oppressive. All below them, even their children, were commoners, and in the eye of the law equal to each other. In the gradation of ranks, which, if not legally recognized, must still subsist through the necessary inequalities of birth and wealth, we find the gentry or principal landholders, many of them distinguished by knighthood, and all by bearing coat armor, but without any exclusive privilege; the yeomanry, or small freeholders and farmers, a very numerous and respectable body, some occupying their own estates, some those of landlords; the burgesses and inferior inhabitants of trading towns; and, lastly, the peasantry and laborers. Of these, in earlier times, a considerable part, though not perhaps so very large a proportion as is usually taken for granted, had been in the ignominious state of villenage, incapable of possessing property but at the will of their lords. They had, however, gradually been raised above this servitude; many had acquired a stable possession of lands under the name of copyholders; and the condition of mere villenage was become rare.

The three courts at Westminster — the King's Bench, Common Pleas, and Exchequer — consisting each of four or five judges, administered justice to the whole kingdom; the first having an appellant jurisdiction over the second, and the third being in a great measure confined to causes affecting the crown's property. But as all suits relating to land, as well as most others, and all criminal indictments, could only be determined, so far as they depended upon oral evidence, by a jury of the county, it was necessary that justices of assize and jail-delivery, being in general the judges of the courts at Westminster, should travel into each county, commonly twice a year, in order to try issues of fact, so called in distinction from issues of law, where the suitors, admitting all essential facts, disputed the rule applicable to them.[1] By this device, which is as ancient as the reign of

[1] The pleadings, as they are called, or written allegations of both parties, which form the basis of a judicial inquiry, commence with the *declaration*, wherein the plaintiff states, either specially or in some established form, according to the nature of the case, that he has a debt to demand from, or an injury to be redressed by, the defendent. The latter, in return, puts in his *plea;* which, if it

Henry II., the fundamental privilege of trial by jury, and the convenience of private suitors, as well as accused persons, were made consistent with an uniform jurisprudence; and though the reference of every legal question, however insignificant, to the courts above must have been inconvenient and expensive in a still greater degree than at present, it had, doubtless, a powerful tendency to knit together the different parts of England, to check the influence of feudality and clanship, to make the inhabitants of distant counties better acquainted with the capital city and more accustomed to the course of government, and to impair the spirit of provincial patriotism and animosity. The minor tribunals of each county, hundred, and manor, respectable for their antiquity and for their effect in preserving a sense of freedom and justice, had in a great measure, though not probably so much as in modern times, gone into disuse. In a few counties

amount to a denial of the facts alleged in the declaration, must *conclude to the country*, that is, must refer the whole matter to a jury. But if it contain an admission of the fact, along with a legal justification of it, it is said to *conclude to the court;* the effect of which is to make it necessary for the plaintiff to reply; in which *replication* he may deny the facts pleaded in justification, and conclude to the country; or allege some new matter in explanation, to show that they do not meet all the circumstances, concluding to the court. Either party also may demur, that is, deny that, although true and complete as a statement of facts, the declaration or plea is sufficient according to law to found or repel the plaintiff's suit. In the last case it becomes an issue in law, and is determined by the judges, without the intervention of a jury; it being a principle that, by demurring, the party acknowledges the truth of all matters alleged on the pleadings. But in whatever stage of the proceedings either of the litigants concludes to the country, (which he is obliged to do whenever the question can be reduced to a disputed fact,) a jury must be impanelled to decide it by their verdict. These pleadings, together with what is called the *postea*, that is, an indorsement by the clerk of the court wherein the trial has been, reciting that *afterwards* the cause was so tried, and such a verdict returned, with the subsequent entry of the judgment itself, form the record.

This is merely intended to explain the phrase in the text, which common readers might not clearly understand. The theory of special pleading, as it is generally called, could not be further elucidated without lengthening this note beyond all bounds. But it all rests upon the ancient maxim: "De facto respondent juratores, de jure judices." Perhaps it may be well to add one observation — that in many forms of action, and those of most frequent occurrence in modern times, it is not required to state the legal justification on the pleadings, but to give it in evidence on the general issue; that is, upon a bare plea of denial. In this case the whole matter is actually in the power of the jury. But they are generally bound in conscience to defer, as to the operation of any rule of law, to what is laid down on that head by the judge; and when they disregard his directions, it is usual to annul the verdict, and grant a new trial. There seem to be some disadvantages in the annihilation, as it may be called, of written pleadings, by their reduction to an unmeaning form, which has prevailed in three such important and extensive forms of action as *ejectment*, *general assumpsit*, and *trover;* both as it throws too much power into the hands of the jury, and as it almost nullifies the appellant jurisdiction, which can only be exercised where some error is apparent on the face of the record. But great practical convenience, and almost necessity, has generally been alleged as far more than a compensation for these evils.— [1827.] [This note is left, but the last paragraph is no longer so near the truth as it was, in consequence of the alterations subsequently made by the judges in the rules of pleading.]

there still remained a palatine jurisdiction, exclusive of the king's courts; but in these the common rules of law and the mode of trial by jury were preserved. Justices of the peace, appointed out of the gentlemen of each county, inquired into criminal charges, committed offenders to prison, and tried them at their quarterly sessions, according to the same forms as the judges of jail-delivery. The chartered towns had their separate jurisdiction under the municipal magistracy.

The laws against theft were severe, and capital punishments unsparingly inflicted. Yet they had little effect in repressing acts of violence, to which a rude and licentious state of manners, and very imperfect dispositions for preserving the public peace, naturally gave rise. These were frequently perpetrated or instigated by men of superior wealth and power, above the control of the mere officers of justice. Meanwhile the kingdom was increasing in opulence; the English merchants possessed a large share of the trade of the north; and a woollen manufacture, established in different parts of the kingdom, had not only enabled the legislature to restrain the import of cloths, but had begun to supply foreign nations. The population may probably be reckoned, without any material error, at about three millions, but by no means distributed in the same proportions as at present; the northern counties, especially Lancashire and Cumberland, being very ill peopled, and the inhabitants of London and Westminster not exceeding sixty or seventy thousand.[1]

Such was the political condition of England when Henry Tudor, the only living representative of the house of Lancaster, though incapable, by reason of the illegitimacy of the ancestor who connected him with it, of asserting a just right of inheritance, became master of the throne by the defeat and death of his competitor at Bosworth, and by the general submission of the kingdom. He assumed the royal title immediately after his victory, and summoned a parliament to recognize or sanction his possession. The circumstances were by no means such as to offer

Henry VII.

[1] The population for 1485 is estimated by comparing a sort of census in 1378, when the inhabitants of the realm seem to have amounted to about 2,300,000, with one still more loose under Elizabeth, in 1588, which would give about 4,400,000. Making some allowance for the more rapid increase in the latter period, three millions at the accession of Henry VII. is probably not too low an estimate. — [I now incline to rate the population somewhat higher. — 1841.]

an auspicious presage for the future. A subdued party had risen from the ground, incensed by proscription and elated by success; the late battle had in effect been a contest between one usurper and another; and England had little better prospect than a renewal of that desperate and interminable contention which pretences of hereditary right have so often entailed upon nations.

A parliament called by a conqueror might be presumed to be itself conquered. Yet this assembly did not display so servile a temper, or so much of the Lancastrian spirit, as might be expected. It was "ordained and enacted by the assent of the lords, and at the request of the commons, that the inheritance of the crowns of England and France, and all dominions appertaining to them, should remain in Henry VII. and the heirs of his body forever, and in none other."[1] Words studiously ambiguous, which, while they avoid the assertion of an hereditary right that the public voice repelled, were meant to create a parliamentary title, before which the pretensions of lineal descent were to give way. They seem to make Henry the stock of a new dynasty. But, lest the spectre of indefeasible right should stand once more in arms on the tomb of the house of York, the two houses of parliament showed an earnest desire for the king's marriage with the daughter of Edward IV., who, if she should bear only the name of royalty, might transmit an undisputed inheritance of its prerogatives to her posterity.

Statute for the security of the subject under a king *de facto*.

This marriage, and the king's great vigilance in guarding his crown, caused his reign to pass with considerable reputation, though not without disturbance. He had to learn, by the extraordinary though transient success of two impostors, that his subjects were still strongly infected with the prejudice which had once overthrown the family he claimed to represent. Nor could those who served him be exempt from apprehensions of a change of dynasty, which might convert them into attainted rebels. The state of the nobles and gentry had been intolerable during the alternate proscriptions of Henry VI. and Edward IV. Such apprehensions led to a very important statute in

1 Rot. Parl. vi. 270. But the pope's bull of dispensation for the king's marriage speaks of the realm of England as "jure hæreditario ad te legitimum in illo prædecessorum tuorum successorem pertinens." Rymer, xii. 294. And all Henry's own instruments claim an hereditary right, of which many proofs appear in Rymer.

the eleventh year of this king's reign, intended, as far as law could furnish a prospective security against the violence and vengeance of factions, to place the civil duty of allegiance on a just and reasonable foundation, and indirectly to cut away the distinction between governments *de jure* and *de facto*. It enacts, after reciting that subjects by reason of their allegiance are bound to serve their prince for the time being against every rebellion and power raised against him, that "no person attending upon the king and sovereign lord of this land for the time being, and doing him true and faithful service, shall be convicted of high treason, by act of parliament or other process of law, nor suffer any forfeiture or punishment; but that every act made contrary to this statute should be void and of no effect."[1] The endeavor to bind future parliaments was of course nugatory; but the statute remains an unquestionable authority for the constitutional maxim that possession of the throne gives a sufficient title to the subject's allegiance, and justifies his resistance of those who may pretend to a better right. It was much resorted to in argument at the time of the revolution and in the subsequent period.[2]

It has been usual to speak of this reign as if it formed a great epoch in our constitution; the king having by his politic measures broken the power of the barons who had hitherto withstood the prerogative, while the commons had not yet risen from the humble station which they were supposed to have occupied. I doubt, however, whether the change was quite so precisely referable to the time of Henry VII., and whether his policy has not been somewhat overrated. In certain respects his reign is undoubtedly an era in our history. It began in revolution and a change in the line of descent. It nearly coincides, which is more material, with the commencement of what is termed modern history, as distinguished from the middle ages, and with the memorable events that have led us to make that leading distinction, especially the consolidation of the great European monarchies, among which England took a conspicuous station. But,

[1] Stat. 11 H. 7, c. 1.

[2] Blackstone (vol. iv. c. 6) has some rather perplexed reasoning on this statute, leaning a little towards the *de jure* doctrine, and at best confounding *moral* with *legal* obligations. In the latter sense, whoever attends to the preamble of the act will see that Hawkins, whose opinion Blackstone calls in question, is right; and that he is himself wrong in pretending that "the statute of Henry VII. does by no means command any opposition to a king *de jure*, but excuses the obedience paid to a king *de facto*."

relatively to the main subject of our inquiry, it is not evident that Henry VII. carried the authority of the crown much beyond the point at which Edward IV. had left it. The strength of the nobility had been grievously impaired by the bloodshed of the civil wars, and the attainders that followed them. From this cause, or from the general intimidation, we find, as I have observed in another work, that no laws favorable to public liberty, or remedial with respect to the aggressions of power, were enacted, or (so far as appears) even proposed in parliament, during the reign of Edward IV.; the first, since that of John, to which such a remark can be applied. The commons, who had not always been so humble and abject as smatterers in history are apt to fancy, were by this time much degenerated from the spirit they had displayed under Edward III. and Richard II. Thus the founder of the line of Tudor came, not certainly to an absolute, but a vigorous prerogative, which his cautious, dissembling temper and close attention to business were well calculated to extend.

Statute of Fines.

The laws of Henry VII. have been highly praised by Lord Bacon as "deep and not vulgar, not made upon the spur of a particular occasion for the present, but out of providence for the future, to make the estate of his people still more and more happy, after the manner of the legislators in ancient and heroical times." But when we consider how very few kings or statesmen have displayed this prospective wisdom and benevolence in legislation, we may hesitate a little to bestow so rare a praise upon Henry. Like the laws of all other times, his statutes seem to have had no further aim than to remove some immediate mischief, or to promote some particular end. One, however, has been much celebrated as an instance of his sagacious policy and as the principal cause of exalting the royal authority upon the ruins of the aristocracy; I mean the statute of Fines (as one passed in the fourth year of his reign is commonly called), which is supposed to have given the power of alienating entailed lands. But both the intention and effect of this seem not to have been justly apprehended.

Discussion of its effect and motive.

In the first place, it is remarkable that the statute of Henry VII. is merely a transcript, with very little variation, from one of Richard III., which is actually printed in most editions. It was reënacted, as we must presume, in order to obviate any doubt, however ill-grounded, which might hang upon the validity of Richard's laws. Thus vanish at once into air the deep policy of Henry VII. and his insidious schemes of leading on a prodigal aristocracy to its ruin. It is surely strange that those who have extolled this sagacious monarch for breaking the fetters of landed property (though many of them were lawyers) should never have observed that whatever credit might be due for the innovation should redound to the honor of the unfortunate usurper. But Richard, in truth, had no leisure for such long-sighted projects of strengthening a throne for his posterity which he could not preserve for himself. His law, and that of his successor, had a different object in view.

It would be useless to some readers, and perhaps disgusting to others, especially in the very outset of this work, to enter upon the history of the English law as to the power of alienation. But I cannot explain the present subject without mentioning that by a statute in the reign of Edward I., commonly called *de donis conditionalibus*, lands given to a man and the heirs of his body, with remainder to other persons, or reversion to the donor, could not be alienated by the possessor for the time being, either from his own issue or from those who were to succeed them. Such lands were also not subject to forfeiture for treason or felony; and more, perhaps, upon this account than from any more enlarged principle, these entails were not viewed with favor by the courts of justice. Several attempts were successfully made to relax their strictness; and finally, in the reign of Edward IV., it was held by the judges in the famous case of Taltarum, that a tenant in tail might, by what is called suffering a common recovery, that is, by means of a fictitious process of law, divest all those who were to come after him of their succession, and become owner of the fee simple. Such a decision was certainly far beyond the sphere of judicial authority. The legislature, it was probably suspected, would not have consented to infringe a statute which they reckoned the safeguard of their families. The law, however, was laid down by the judges; and in those days the appellant jurisdiction of the house of lords, by means of which the aristocracy might have indignantly reversed the insidious decision, had gone wholly into disuse. It became by degrees a fundamental principle, that an estate in tail can be barred by a common recovery; nor is it possible by any legal subtlety to deprive the tenant of this control over his estate. Schemes were, indeed, gradually devised, which to a limited extent have restrained the power of alienation; but these do not belong to our subject.

The real intention of these statutes of Richard and Henry was not to give the tenant in tail a greater power over his estate (for it is by no means clear that the words enable him to bar his issue by levying a fine; and when a decision to that effect took place long afterwards (19 H. 8), it was with such difference of opinion that it was thought necessary to confirm the interpretation by a new act of parliament;) but rather, by establishing a short term of prescription, to put a check on the suits for recovery of lands, which, after times of so much violence and disturbance, were naturally springing up in the courts. It is the usual policy of governments to favor possession; and on this principle the statute enacts that a fine levied with proclamations in a public court of justice shall after five years, except in particular circumstances, be a bar to all claims upon lands. This was its main scope; the liberty of alienation was neither necessary, nor probably intended to be given.[1]

Exactions of Henry VII.

The two first of the Tudors rarely experienced opposition but when they endeavored to levy money. Taxation, in the eyes of their subjects, was so far from being no tyranny, that it seemed the only species worth a complaint. Henry VII. obtained from his first parliament a grant of tonnage and poundage during life, according to several precedents of former reigns. But when general subsidies were granted, the same people, who would have seen an innocent man led to prison or the scaffold with little attention, twice broke out into dangerous rebellions; and as these, however arising from such immediate discontent, were yet a good

1 For these observations on the statute of Fines I am principally indebted to Reeves's History of the English Law (iv. 133), a work, especially in the latter volumes, of great research and judgment; a continuation of which, in the same spirit and with the same qualities, would be a valuable accession not only to the lawyer's but philosopher's library. That entails had been defeated by means of a common recovery before the statute, had been remarked by former writers, and is indeed obvious; but the subject was never put in so clear a light as by Mr. Reeves.

The principle of breaking down the statute *de donis* was so little established, or consistently acted upon, in this reign, that in 11 H. 7 the judges held that the donor of an estate-tail might restrain the tenant from suffering a recovery. Id. p. 159, from the Year-book.

deal connected with the opinion of Henry's usurpation and the claims of a pretender, it was a necessary policy to avoid too frequent imposition of burdens upon the poorer classes of the community.[1] He had recourse accordingly to the system of benevolences, or contributions apparently voluntary, though in fact extorted from his richer subjects. These, having become an intolerable grievance under Edward IV., were abolished in the only parliament of Richard III. with strong expressions of indignation. But in the seventh year of Henry's reign, when, after having with timid and parsimonious hesitation suffered the marriage of Anne of Brittany with Charles VIII., he was compelled by the national spirit to make a demonstration of war, he ventured to try this unfair and unconstitutional method of obtaining aid; which received afterwards too much of a parliamentary sanction by an act enforcing the payment of arrears of money which private men had thus been prevailed upon to promise.[2] The statute, indeed, of Richard is so expressed as not clearly to forbid the solicitation of voluntary gifts, which of course rendered it almost nugatory.

Archbishop Morton is famous for the dilemma which he proposed to merchants and others whom he solicited to contribute. He told those who lived handsomely that their opulence was manifest by their rate of expenditure. Those, again, whose course of living was less sumptuous, must have grown rich by their economy. Either class could well afford assistance to their sovereign. This piece of logic, unanswerable in the mouth of a privy councillor, acquired the name of Morton's fork. Henry doubtless reaped great profit from these indefinite exactions, miscalled benevolences. But, insatiate of accumulating treasure, he discovered other methods of extortion, still more odious, and possibly more lucrative.

[1] It is said by the biographer of Sir Thomas More that parliament refused the king a subsidy in 1502, which he demanded on account of the marriage of his daughter Margaret, at the advice of More, then but twenty-two years old. "Forthwith Mr. Tyler, one of the privy chamber, that was then present, resorted to the king, declaring that a beardless boy, called More, had done more harm than all the rest, for by his means all the purpose is dashed." This of course displeased Henry, who would not however, he says, "infringe the ancient liberties of that house, which would have been odiously taken." Wordsworth's Eccles. Biography, ii. 66. This story is also told by Roper.

[2] Stat. 11 H. 7, c. 10. Bacon says the benevolence was granted by act of parliament, which Hume shows to be a mistake. The preamble of 11 H. 7 recites it to have been "granted by divers of your subjects severally;" and contains a provision that no heir shall be charged on account of his ancestor's promise.

Many statutes had been enacted in preceding reigns, sometimes rashly or from temporary motives, sometimes in opposition to prevailing usages which they could not restrain, of which the pecuniary penalties, though exceedingly severe, were so little enforced as to have lost their terror. These his ministers raked out from oblivion; and, prosecuting such as could afford to endure the law's severity, filled his treasury with the dishonorable produce of amercements and forfeitures. The feudal rights became, as indeed they always had been, instrumental to oppression. The lands of those who died without heirs fell back to the crown by escheat. It was the duty of certain officers in every county to look after its rights. The king's title was to be found by the inquest of a jury, summoned at the instance of the escheator, and returned into the exchequer. It then became a matter of record, and could not be impeached. Hence the escheators taking hasty inquests, or sometimes falsely pretending them, defeated the right heir of his succession. Excessive fines were imposed on granting livery to the king's wards on their majority. Informations for intrusions, criminal indictments, outlawries on civil process, in short, the whole course of justice, furnished pretences for exacting money; while a host of dependents on the court, suborned to play their part as witnesses, or even as jurors, rendered it hardly possible for the most innocent to escape these penalties. Empson and Dudley are notorious as the prostitute instruments of Henry's avarice in the later and more unpopular years of his reign; but they dearly purchased a brief hour of favor by an ignominious death and perpetual infamy.[1] The avarice of Henry VII., as it rendered his government unpopular, which had always been penurious, must be deemed a drawback from the wisdom ascribed to him; though by his good fortune it answered the end of invigorating his power. By these fines and forfeitures he impoverished and intimidated the nobility. The earl of Oxford compounded, by the payment of 15,000 pounds, for the penalties he had incurred by keeping retainers in livery; a practice mischievous and illegal, but too customary to have been punished before this reign. Even the king's clemency seems to have been influenced by the sordid motive of selling pardons; and it has

[1] Hall, 502.

been shown that he made a profit of every office in his court, and received money for conferring bishoprics.[1]

It is asserted by early writers, though perhaps only on conjecture, that he left a sum, thus amassed, of no less than 1,800,000 pounds at his decease. This treasure was soon dissipated by his successor, who had recourse to the assistance of parliament in the very first year of his reign. The foreign policy of Henry VIII., far unlike that of his father, was ambitious and enterprising. No former king had involved himself so frequently in the labyrinth of continental alliances. And, if it were necessary to abandon that neutrality which is generally the most advantageous and laudable course, it is certain that his early undertakings against France were more consonant to English interests, as well as more honorable, than the opposite policy, which he pursued after the battle of Pavia. The campaigns of Henry in France and Scotland displayed the valor of our English infantry, seldom called into action for fifty years before, and contributed with other circumstances to throw a lustre over his reign which prevented most of his contemporaries from duly appreciating his character. But they naturally drew the king into heavy expenses, and, together with his profusion and love of magnificence, rendered his government very burdensome. At his accession, however, the rapacity of his father's administration had excited such universal discontent, that it was found expedient to conciliate the nation. An act was passed in his first parliament to correct the abuses that had prevailed in finding the king's title to lands by escheat.[2] The same parliament repealed the law of the late reign enabling justices of assize and of the peace to determine all offences, except treason and felony, against any statute in force, without a jury, upon information in the king's name.[3] This serious innovation had evidently been prompted by the spirit of rapacity, which probably some honest juries had shown courage enough to withstand. It was a much less laudable concession to the vindictive temper of an injured people, seldom unwilling to see bad methods employed in punishing bad men, that Empson and Dudley, who might

1 Turner's History of England, iii. 628, from a manuscript document. A vast number of persons paid fines for their share in the western rebellion of 1497, from 200*l*. down to 20*s*. Hall, 486. Ellis's Letters illustrative of English History, i. 38.

2 1 H. 8. c. 8.

3 11 H 7. c. 3. Rep. 1 H. 8. c. 6.

perhaps by stretching the prerogative have incurred the penalties of a misdemeanor, were put to death on a frivolous charge of high treason.[1]

Taxes demanded by Henry VIII.

The demands made by Henry VIII. on parliament were considerable, both in frequency and amount. Notwithstanding the servility of those times it sometimes attempted to make a stand against these inroads upon the public purse. Wolsey came into the house of commons in 1523, and asked for 800,000*l.*, to be raised by a tax of one fifth upon lands and goods, in order to prosecute the war just commenced against France. Sir Thomas More, then speaker, is said to have urged the house to acquiesce.[2] But the sum demanded was so much beyond any precedent that all the independent members opposed a vigorous resistance. A committee was appointed to remonstrate with the cardinal, and to set forth the impossibility of raising such a subsidy. It was alleged that it exceeded all the current coin of the kingdom. Wolsey, after giving an uncivil answer to the committee, came down again to the house, on pretence of reasoning with them, but probably with a hope of carrying his end by intimidation. They received him, at More's suggestion, with all the train of attendants that usually encircled the haughtiest subject who had ever been known in England. But they made no other answer to his harangue than that it was their usage to debate only among themselves. These debates lasted fifteen or sixteen days. A considerable part of the commons appears to have consisted of the king's household officers, whose influence, with the utmost difficulty, obtained a grant much inferior to the cardinal's requisition, and payable by instalments in four years. But Wolsey, greatly dissatisfied with this imperfect obe-

1 They were convicted by a jury, and afterwards attainted by parliament, but not executed for more than a year after the king's accession. If we may believe Holingshed, the council at Henry VIII.'s accession made restitution to some who had been wronged by the extortion of the late reign; — a singular contrast to their subsequent proceedings! This, indeed, had been enjoined by Henry VII.'s will. But he had excepted from this restitution "what had been done by the course and order of our laws;" which, as Mr. Astle observes, was the common mode of his oppressions.

2 Lord Herbert inserts an acute speech, which he seems to ascribe to More, arguing more acquaintance with sound principles of political economy than was usual in the supposed speaker's age, or even in that of the writer. But it is more probable that this is of his own invention. He has taken a similar liberty on another occasion, throwing his own broad notions of religion into an imaginary speech of some unnamed member of the commons, though manifestly unsuited to the character of the times. That More gave satisfaction to Wolsey by his conduct in the chair, appears by a letter of the latter to the king, in State Papers, temp. H. 8, p. 124.

dience, compelled the people to pay up the whole subsidy at once.[1]

No parliament was assembled for nearly seven years after this time. Wolsey had already resorted to more arbitrary methods of raising money by loans and benevolences.[2] The year before this debate in the commons he borrowed twenty thousand pounds of the city of London; yet so insufficient did that appear for the king's exigencies, that within two months commissioners were appointed throughout the kingdom to swear every man to the value of his possessions, requiring a ratable part according to such declaration. The clergy, it is said, were ex-

Illegal exactions of Wolsey in 1522 and 1525.

[1] Roper's Life of More. Hall, 656, 672. This chronicler, who wrote under Edward VI., is our best witness for the events of Henry's reign. Grafton is so literally a copyist from him, that it was a great mistake to republish this part of his chronicle in the late expensive, and therefore incomplete, collection; since he adds no one word, and omits only a few ebullitions of Protestant zeal which he seems to have considered too warm. Holinshed, though valuable, is later than Hall. Wolsey, the latter observes, gave offence to the commons by descanting on the wealth and luxury of the nation, "as though he had repined or disclaimed that any man should fare well, or be well clothed, but himself."

But the most authentic memorial of what passed on this occasion has been preserved in a letter from a member of the commons to the earl of Surrey (soon after duke of Norfolk), at that time the king's lieutenant in the north.

"Please it your good lordships to understand, that sithence the beginning of the parliament there hath been the greatest and sorest hold in the lower house, for the payment of two shillings of the pound, that ever was seen, I think, in any parliament. This matter hath been debated and beaten fifteen or sixteen days together. The highest necessity alleged on the king's behalf to us that ever was heard of; and on the contrary, the highest poverty confessed, as well by knights, esquires and gentlemen of every quarter, as by the commoners, citizens, and burgesses. There hath been such hold that the house was l ke to have been dissevered; that is to say, the knights being of the king's council, the king's servants and gentlemen of the one party; which in so long time were spoken with, and made to see, yea, it may fortune, contrary to their heart, will, and conscience. Thus hanging this matter, yesterday the more part being the king's servants, gentlemen, were there assembled; and so they, being the more part, willed and gave to the king two shillings of the pound of goods or lands, the best to be taken for the king. All lands to pay two shillings of the pound for the laity, to the highest. The goods to pay two shillings of the pound, for twenty pound upward; and from forty shillings of goods to twenty pound to pay sixteen pence of the pound; and under forty shillings, every person to pay eight pence. This to be paid in two years. I have heard no man in my life that can remember that ever there was given to any one of the king's áncestors half so much at one graunt. Nor, I think, there was never such a president seen before this time. I beseeke Almighty God it may be well and peaceably levied, and surely payd unto the king's grace, without grudge, and especially without loosing the good will and true hearts of his subjects, which I reckon a far greater treasure for the king than gold and silver. And the gentlemen that must take pains to levy this money among the king's subjects, I think, shall have no little business about the same." Strype's Eccles. Memorials, vol. i. p. 49. This is also printed in Ellis's Letters illustrative of English History, i. 220.

[2] I may notice here a mistake of Mr. Hume and Dr. Lingard. They assert Henry to have received tonnage and poundage several years before it was vested in him by the legislature. But it was granted by his first parliament, stat. 1 H. 8, c. 20, as will be found even in Ruffhead's table of contents, though not in the body of his volume; and the act is of course printed at length in the great edition of the statutes. That which probably by its title gave rise to the error, 6 H. 8, c. 13, has a different object.

pected to contribute a fourth; but I believe that benefices above ten pounds in yearly value were taxed at one third. Such unparalleled violations of the clearest and most important privilege that belonged to Englishmen excited a general apprehension.[1] Fresh commissioners, however, were appointed in 1525, with instructions to demand the sixth part of every man's substance, payable in money, plate, or jewels, according to the last valuation.[2] This demand Wolsey made

[1] Hall, 645. This chronicler says the laity were assessed at a tenth part. But this was only so for the smaller estates, namely, from 20*l.* to 300*l.*; for from 300*l.* to 1000*l.* the contribution demanded was twenty marks for each 100*l.*, and for an estate of 1000*l.* two hundred marks, and so in proportion upwards. — MS. Instructions to commissioners, penes auctorem. This was, "upon sufficient promise and assurance, to be repaid unto them upon such grants and contributions as shall be given and granted to his grace at his next parliament." Ib. — "And they shall practise by all the means to them possible that such sums as shall be so granted by the way of loan, be forthwith levied and paid, or the most part, or at the least the moiety thereof, the same to be paid in as brief time after as they can possibly persuade and induce them unto; showing unto them that, for the sure payment thereof, they shall have writings delivered unto them under the king's privy seal by such person or persons as shall be deputed by the king to receive the said loan, after the form of a minute to be shown unto them by the said commissioners, the tenor whereof is thus: We. Henry VIII., by the grace of God, King of England and of France, Defender of Faith, and Lord of Ireland, promise by these presents truly to content and repay unto our trusty and well-beloved subject, A. B., the sum of ——, which he hath lovingly advanced unto us by way of loan, for defence of our realm, and maintenance of our wars against France and Scotland: In witness whereof we have caused our privy seal hereunto to be set and annexed the —— day of ——, the fourteenth year of our reign." — Ib. The rate fixed on the clergy I collect by analogy from that imposed in 1525, which I find in another manuscript letter.

[2] A letter in my possession from the duke of Norfolk to Wolsey, without the date of the year, relates, I believe, to this commission of 1525, rather than that of 1522; it being dated on the 10th April, which appears from the contents to have been before Easter; whereas Easter did not fall beyond that day in 1523 or 1524, but did so in 1525; and the first commission, being of the fourteenth year of the king's reign, must have sat later than Easter, 1522. He informs the cardinal that from twenty pounds upwards there were not twenty in the county of Norfolk who had not consented. "So that I see great likelihood that this grant shall be much more than the loan was." It was done, however, very reluctantly, as he confesses; "assuring your grace that they have not granted the same without shedding of many salt tears, only for doubt how to find money to content the king's highness." The resistance went farther than the duke thought fit to suppose; for in a very short time the insurrection of the common people took place in Suffolk. In another letter from him and the duke of Suffolk to the cardinal, they treat this rather lightly, and seem to object to the remission of the contribution.

This commission issued soon after the news of the battle of Pavia arrived. The pretext was the king's intention to lead an army into France. Warham wrote more freely than the duke of Norfolk as to the popular discontent, in a letter to Wolsey, dated April 5. "It hath been showed me in a secret manner of my friends, the people sore grudgeth and murmureth, and speaketh cursedly among themselves, as far as they dare, saying that they shall never have rest of payments as long as some liveth, and that they had better die than to be thus continually handled, reckoning themselves, their children, and wives, as despoulit, and not greatly caring what they do, or what becomes of them. * * * Further I am informed that there is a grudge newly now resuscitate and revived in the minds of the people; for the loan is not repaid to them upon the first receipt of the grant of parliament, as it was promised them by the commissioners, showing them the king's grace's instructions, containing the same, signed with his grace's own hand in summer, that they fear not to speak, that they be continually beguiled, and no promise is kept

in person to the mayor and chief citizens of London. They attempted to remonstrate, but were warned to beware, lest "it might fortune to cost some their heads." Some were sent to prison for hasty words, to which the smart of injury excited them. The clergy, from whom, according to usage, a larger measure of contribution was demanded, stood upon their privilege to grant their money only in convocation, and denied the right of a king of England to ask any man's money without authority of parliament. The rich and poor agreed in cursing the cardinal as the subverter of their laws and liberties; and said, "if men should give their goods by a commission, then it would be worse than the taxes of France, and England should be bond, and not free."[1] Nor did their discontent terminate in complaints. The commissioners met with forcible opposition in several counties, and a serious insurrection broke out in Suffolk. So menacing a spirit overawed the proud tempers of Henry and his minister, who found it necessary not only to pardon all those

unto them; and thereupon some of them suppose that if this gift and grant be once levied, albeit the king's grace go not beyond the sea, yet nothing shall be restored again, albeit they be showed the contrary. And generally it is reported unto me, that for the most part every man saith he will be contented if the king's grace have as much as he can spare, but verily many say they be not able to do as they be required. And many denieth not but they will give the king's grace according to their power, but they will not anywise give at any other men's appointments, which knoweth not their needs. * * * * I have heard say, moreover, that when the people be commanded to make fires and tokens of joy for the taking of the French king, divers of them have spoken that they have more cause to weep than to rejoice thereat. And divers, as it hath been showed me secretly, have wished openly that the French king were at his liberty again, so as there were a good peace, and the king should not attempt to win France, the winning whereof should be more chargeful to England than profitable, and the keeping thereof much more chargeful than the winning. Also it hath been told me secretly that divers have recounted and repeated what infinite sums of money the king's grace hath spent already in invading of France, once in his own royal person, and two other sundry times by his several noble captains, and little or nothing in comparison of his costs hath prevailed; insomuch that the king's grace at this hour hath not one foot of land more in France than his most noble father had, which lacked no riches or wisdom to win the kingdom of France, if he had thought it expedient." The archbishop goes on to observe, rather oddly, that "he would that the time had suffered that this practising with the people for so great sums might have been spared till the cuckoo time and the hot weather (at which time mad brains be wont to be most busy) had been overpassed."

Warham dwells, in another letter, on the great difficulty the clergy had in making so large a payment as was required of them, and their unwillingness to be sworn as to the value of their goods. The archbishop seems to have thought it passing strange that people would be so wrongheaded about their money. "I have been," he says, "in this shire twenty years and above, and as yet I have not seen men but would be conformable to reason and would be induced to good order till this time; and what shall cause them now to fall into these wilful and indiscreet ways I cannot tell, except poverty and decay of substance be the cause of it."

[1] Hall, 696. These expressions, and numberless others might be found, show the fallacy of Hume's hasty assertion that the writers of the sixteenth century do not speak of our own government as more free than that of France.

concerned in these tumults, but to recede altogether upon some frivolous pretexts from the illegal exaction, revoking the commissions, and remitting all sums demanded under them. They now resorted to the more specious request of a voluntary benevolence. This also the citizens of London endeavored to repel, by alleging the statute of Richard III. But it was answered, that he was an usurper, whose acts did not oblige a lawful sovereign. It does not appear whether or not Wolsey was more successful in this new scheme; but, generally, rich individuals had no remedy but to compound with the government.

No very material attempt had been made since the reign of Edward III. to levy a general imposition without consent of parliament, and in the most remote and irregular times it would be difficult to find a precedent for so universal and enormous an exaction; since tallages, however arbitrary, were never paid by the barons or freeholders, nor by their tenants; and the aids to which they were liable were restricted to particular cases. If Wolsey, therefore, could have procured the acquiescence of the nation under this yoke, there would probably have been an end of parliaments for all ordinary purposes, though, like the states general of France, they might still be convoked to give weight and security to great innovations. We cannot, indeed, doubt that the unshackled condition of his friend, though rival, Francis I., afforded a mortifying contrast to Henry. Even under his tyrannical administration there was enough to distinguish the king of a people who submitted in murmuring to violations of their known rights from one whose subjects had almost forgotten that they ever possessed any. But the courage and love of freedom natural to the English commons, speaking in the hoarse voice of tumult, though very ill supported by their superiors, preserved us in so great a peril.[1]

Acts of parliament releasing the king from his debts.

If we justly regard with detestation the memory of those ministers who have aimed at subverting the liberties of their country, we shall scarcely approve the partiality of some modern historians towards cardinal Wolsey; a partiality, too, that contradicts the general opinion of his contemporaries. Haughty beyond comparison, negligent of the duties and de-

[1] Hall, 699.

corums of his station, profuse as well as rapacious, obnoxious alike to his own order and to the laity, his fall had long been secretly desired by the nation, and contrived by his adversaries. His generosity and magnificence seem rather to have dazzled succeeding ages than his own. But, in fact, his best apology is the disposition of his master. The latter years of Henry's reign were far more tyrannical than those during which he listened to the counsels of Wolsey; and though this was principally owing to the peculiar circumstances of the latter period, it is but equitable to allow some praise to a minister for the mischief which he may be presumed to have averted. Had a nobler spirit animated the parliament which met at the era of Wolsey's fall, it might have prompted his impeachment for gross violations of liberty. But these were not the offences that had forfeited his prince's favor, or that they dared bring to justice. They were not absent, perhaps, from the recollection of some of those who took a part in prosecuting the fallen minister. I can discover no better apology for Sir Thomas More's participation in impeaching Wolsey on articles so frivolous that they have served to redeem his fame with later times than his knowledge of weightier offences against the common weal which could not be alleged, and especially the commissions of 1525.[1] But in truth this parliament showed little outward disposition to object any injustice of such a kind to the cardinal. They professed to take upon themselves to give a sanction to his proceedings, as if in mockery of their own and their country's liberties. They passed a statute, the most extraordinary, perhaps, of those strange times, wherein "they do, for themselves and all the whole body of the realm which they represent, freely, liberally, and absolutely, give and grant unto the king's highness, by authority of this present parliament, all and every sum and sums of money which to them and every of them is, ought, or might be due, by reason of any money, or any other thing, to his grace at any time here-

[1] The word impeachment is not very accurately applicable to these proceedings against Wolsey; since the articles were first presented to the upper house, and sent down to the commons, where Cromwell so ably defended his fallen master that nothing was done upon them. "Upon this honest beginning," says lord Herbert, "Cromwell obtained his first reputation." I am disposed to conjecture, from Cromwell's character and that of the house of commons, as well as from some passages of Henry's subsequent behavior towards the cardinal, that it was not the king's intention to follow up this prosecution, at least for the present. This also I find to be Dr. Lingard's opinion.

tofore advanced or paid by way of trust or loan, either upon any letter or letters under the king's privy seal, general or particular, letter, missive, promise, bond, or obligation of repayment, or by any taxation or other assessing, by virtue of any commission or commissions, or by any other mean or means, whatever it be, heretofore passed for that purpose." [1] This extreme servility and breach of trust naturally excited loud murmurs; for the debts thus released had been assigned over by many to their own creditors, and, having all the security both of the king's honor and legal obligation, were reckoned as valid as any other property. It is said by Hall that most of this house of commons held offices under the crown. This illaudable precedent was remembered in 1544, when a similar act passed, releasing to the king all moneys borrowed by him since 1542, with the additional provision, that if he should have already discharged any of these debts, the party or his heirs should repay his majesty.[2]

A benevolence again exacted.

Henry had once more recourse, about 1545, to a general exaction, miscalled benevolence. The council's instructions to the commissioners employed in levying it leave no doubt as to its compulsory character. They were directed to incite all men to a loving contribution according to the rates of their substance, as they were assessed at the last subsidy, calling on no one whose lands were of less value than 40*s.* or whose chattels were less than 15*l.* It is intimated that the least which his majesty could reasonably accept would be twenty pence in the pound on the yearly value of land, and half that sum on movable goods. They are to summon but a few to attend at one time, and to commune with every one apart, "lest some one unreasonable man, amongst so many, forgetting his duty towards God, his sovereign lord, and his country, may go about by his malicious frowardness to silence all the

[1] Rot. Parl. vi. 164. Burnet, Appendix, No. 13. "When this release of the loan," says Hall, "was known to the commons of the realm, Lord! so they grudged and spake ill of the whole parliament; for almost every man counted on his debt, and reckoned surely of the payment of the same, and therefore some made their wills of the same, and some other did set it over to other for debt; and so many men had loss by it, which caused them sore to murmur, but there was no remedy." P. 767.

[2] Stat. 35 H. 8, c. 12. I find in a manuscript which seems to have been copied from an original in the exchequer that the moneys thus received by way of loan in 1543 amounted to 110,147*l.* 15*s.* 8*d.* There was also a sum called *devotion money*, amounting only to 1093*l.* 8*s.* 3*d.*, levied in 1544, "of the devotion of his highness's subjects for *Defence of Christendom against the Turk.*"

rest, be they never so well disposed." They were to use "good words and amiable behavior," to induce men to contribute, and to dismiss the obedient with thanks. But if any person should withstand their gentle solicitations, alleging either poverty or some other pretence which the commissioners should deem unfit to be allowed, then, after failure of persuasions and reproaches for ingratitude, they were to command his attendance before the privy council, at such time as they should appoint, to whom they were to certify his behavior, enjoining him silence in the mean time, that his evil example might not corrupt the better disposed.[1]

It is only through the accidental publication of some family papers that we have become acquainted with this document, so curiously illustrative of the government of Henry VIII. From the same authority may be exhibited a particular specimen of the consequences that awaited the refusal of this benevolence. One Richard Reed, an alderman of London, had stood alone, as is said, among his fellow-citizens, in refusing to contribute. It was deemed expedient not to overlook this disobedience; and the course adopted in punishing it is somewhat remarkable. The English army was then in the field on the Scots border. Reed was sent down to serve as a soldier at his own charge; and the general, sir Ralph Ewer, received intimations to employ him on the hardest and most perilous duty, and subject him, when in garrison, to the greatest privations, that he might feel the smart of his folly and sturdy disobedience. "Finally," the letter concludes, "you must use him in all things according to the sharpe disciplyne militar of the northern wars."[2] It is natural to presume that few would expose themselves to the treatment of this unfortunate citizen; and that the commissioners whom we find appointed two years afterwards in every county, to obtain from

Oppressive treatment of Reed.

1 Lodge's Illustrations of British History, i. 711. Strype's Eccles. Memorials, Appendix, n. 119. The sums raised from different counties for this benevolence afford a sort of criterion of their relative opulence. Somerset gave 6807*l.*; Kent, 6471*l.*; Suffolk, 4512*l.*; Norfolk, 4046*l.*; Devon, 4527*l.*; Essex, 5051*l.*; but Lancaster only 660*l.*, and Cumberland 574*l.* The whole produced 119,581*l.* 7*s.* 6*d.*, besides arrears. In Haynes's State Papers, p. 54, we find a curious minute of secretary Paget, containing reasons why it was better to get the money wanted by means of a benevolence than through parliament. But he does not hint at any difficulty of obtaining a parliamentary grant.

2 Lodge, p. 80. Lord Herbert mentions this story, and observes, that Reed having been taken by the Scots, was compelled to pay much more for his ransom than the benevolence required of him.

the king's subjects as much as they would willingly give, if they did not always find perfect readiness, had not to complain of many peremptory denials.[1]

Severe and unjust executions for treason.

Such was the security that remained against arbitrary taxation under the two Henries. Were men's lives better protected from unjust measures, and less at the mercy of a jealous court? It cannot be necessary to expatiate very much on this subject in a work that supposes the reader's acquaintance with the common facts of our history; yet it would leave the picture too imperfect, were I not to recapitulate the more striking instances of sanguinary injustice, that have cast so deep a shade over the memory of these princes.

Earl of Warwick.

The duke of Clarence, attainted in the reign of his brother Edward IV., left one son, whom his uncle restored to the title of earl of Warwick. This boy, at the accession of Henry VII., being then about twelve years old, was shut up in the Tower. Fifteen years of captivity had elapsed, when, if we trust to the common story, having unfortunately become acquainted with his fellow-prisoner Perkin Warbeck, he listened to a scheme for their escape, and would probably not have been averse to second the ambitious views of that young man. But it was surmised, with as much likelihood as the character of both parties could give it, that the king had promised Ferdinand of Aragon to remove the earl of Warwick out of the way, as the condition of his daughter's marriage with the prince of Wales, and the best means of securing their inheritance. Warwick accordingly was brought to trial for a conspiracy to overturn the government; which he was induced to confess, in the hope, as we must conceive, and perhaps with an assurance, of pardon, and was immediately executed.

Earl of Suffolk.

The nearest heir to the house of York, after the queen and her children and the descendants of the duke of Clarence, was a son of Edward IV.'s sister, the earl of Suffolk, whose elder brother, the earl of Lincoln, had joined in the rebellion of Lambert Simnel, and perished at the battle of Stoke. Suffolk, having killed a man in an affray, obtained a pardon, which the king compelled him to plead in open court at his arraignment. This laudable im-

1 Rymer, xv. 84. These commissions bear date 5th Jan. 1546.

partiality is said to have given him offence, and provoked his flight into the Netherlands; whence, being a man of a turbulent disposition, and partaking in the hatred of his family towards the house of Lancaster, he engaged in a conspiracy with some persons at home, which caused him to be attainted of treason. Some time afterwards, the archduke Philip, having been shipwrecked on the coast of England, found himself in a sort of honorable detention at Henry's court. On consenting to his departure, the king requested him to send over the earl of Suffolk; and Philip, though not insensible to the breach of hospitality exacted from him, was content to satisfy his honor by obtaining a promise that the prisoner's life should be spared. Henry is said to have reckoned this engagement merely personal, and to have left as a last injunction to his successor, that he should carry into effect the sentence against Suffolk. Though this was an evident violation of the promise in its spirit, yet Henry VIII., after the lapse of a few years, with no new pretext, caused him to be executed.

Duke of Buckingham.

The duke of Buckingham, representing the ancient family of Stafford, and hereditary high constable of England, stood the first in rank and consequence, perhaps in riches, among the nobility. But being too ambitious and arrogant for the age in which he was born, he drew on himself the jealousy of the king and the resentment of Wolsey. The evidence on his trial for high treason was almost entirely confined to idle and vaunting language, held with servants who betrayed his confidence, and soothsayers whom he had believed. As we find no other persons charged as parties with him, it seems manifest that Buckingham was innocent of any real conspiracy. His condemnation not only gratified the cardinal's revenge, but answered a very constant purpose of the Tudor government, that of intimidating the great families from whom the preceding dynasty had experienced so much disquietude.[1]

The execution, however, of Suffolk was at least not con-

[1] Hall, 622. Hume, who is favorable to Wolsey says, "There is no reason to think the sentence against Buckingham unjust." But no one who reads the trial will find any evidence to satisfy a reasonable mind; and Hume himself soon after adds, that his crime proceeded more from indiscretion than deliberate malice. In fact, the condemnation of this great noble was owing to Wolsey's resentment, acting on the savage temper of Henry.

New treason created by statutes.

trary to law; and even Buckingham was attainted on evidence which, according to the tremendous latitude with which the law of treason had been construed, a court of justice could not be expected to disregard. But after the fall of Wolsey, and Henry's breach with the Roman see, his fierce temper, strengthened by habit and exasperated by resistance, demanded more constant supplies of blood; and many perished by sentences which we can hardly prevent ourselves from considering as illegal, because the statutes to which they might be conformable seem, from their temporary duration, their violence, and the passiveness of the parliaments that enacted them, rather like arbitrary invasions of the law than alterations of it. By an act of 1534 not only an oath was imposed to maintain the succession in the heirs of the king's second marriage, in exclusion of the princess Mary, but it was made high treason to deny that ecclesiastical supremacy of the crown, which, till about two years before, no one had ever ventured to assert.[1] Bishop Fisher, the most inflexibly honest churchman who filled a high station in that age, was beheaded for this denial. Sir Thomas More, whose name can ask no epithet, underwent a similar fate. He had offered to take the oath to maintain the succession, which, as he justly said, the legislature was competent to alter; but prudently avoided to give an opinion as to the supremacy, till Rich, solicitor-general, and afterwards chancellor, elicited, in a private conversation, some expressions which were thought sufficient to bring him within the fangs of the recent statute. A considerable number of less distinguished persons, chiefly ecclesiastical, were afterwards executed by virtue of this law.

Executions of Fisher and More.

The sudden and harsh innovations made by Henry in religion, as to which every artifice of concealment and delay is required, his destruction of venerable establishments, his tyr-

1 [25 H. 8, c. 22. This is not accurately stated. This act does not make it treason to deny the ecclesiastical supremacy, which is not hinted in any part of it; but makes a refusal to take the oath to maintain the succession in the issue of the king's marriage with Anne Boleyn *misprision* of treason; and on this More and Fisher, who scrupled the preamble to the oath, denying the pope's right of dispensation, though they would have sworn to the succession itself, as a legislative enactment, were convicted and imprisoned. But a subsequent statute, 26 H. 8, c. 13, made it high treason to wish by words to deprive the king of his title, name, or dignity; and the appellation Supreme Head, being part of this title, not only More and Fisher, but several others, suffered death on this construction. See this fully explained in the 27th volume of the Archæologia, by Mr. Bruce. 1845.]

anny over the recesses of the conscience, excited so dangerous a rebellion in the north of England that his own general, the duke of Norfolk, thought it absolutely necessary to employ measures of conciliation.[1] The insurgents laid down their arms on an unconditional promise of amnesty. But another rising having occurred in a different quarter, the king made use of this pretext to put to death some persons of superior rank, who, though they had, voluntarily or by compulsion, partaken in the first rebellion, had no concern in the second, and to let loose military law upon their followers. Nor was his vengeance confined to those who had evidently been guilty of these tumults. It is, indeed, unreasonable to deny that there might be, nay, there probably were, some real conspirators among those who suffered on the scaffolds of Henry. Yet in the proceedings against the countess of Salisbury, an aged woman, but obnoxious as the daughter of the duke of Clarence and mother of Reginald Pole, an active instrument of the pope in fomenting rebellion,[2] against the abbots of Reading and Glastonbury, and others who were implicated in charges of treason at this period, we find so much haste, such neglect of judicial forms, and so bloodthirsty a determination to obtain convictions, that we are naturally tempted to reckon them among the victims of revenge or rapacity.

It was probably during these prosecutions that Cromwell, a man not destitute of liberal qualities, but who is liable to

[1] Several letters that passed between the council and duke of Norfolk (Hardwicke State Papers, i. 28, &c.) tend to confirm what some historians have hinted, that he was suspected of leaning too favorably towards the rebels. The king was most unwilling to grant a free pardon. Norfolk is told, "If you could, by any good means or possible dexterity, reserve a very few persons for punishments, you should assuredly administer the greatest pleasure to his highness that could be imagined, and much in the same advance your own honor." — P. 32. He must have thought himself in danger from some of these letters which indicate the king's distrust of him. He had recommended the employment of men of high rank as lords of the marches, instead of the rather inferior persons whom the king had lately chosen. This called down on him rather a warm reprimand (p. 39); for it was the natural policy of a despotic court to restrain the ascendency of great families; nor were there wanting very good reasons for this, even if the public weal had been the sole object of Henry's council. See also, for the subject of this note, the State Papers Hen. 8, p. 518 et alibi. They contain a good deal of interesting matter as to the northern rebellion, which gave Henry a pretext for great severities towards the monasteries in that part of England.

[2] Pole, at his own solicitation, was appointed legate to the Low Countries in 1537, with the sole object of keeping alive the flame of the northern rebellion, and exciting foreign powers, as well as the English nation, to restore religion by force, if not to dethrone Henry. It is difficult not to suspect that he was influenced by ambitious views in a proceeding so treasonable, and so little in conformity with his polished manners and temperate life. Phillips, his able and artful biographer, both proves and glories in the treason. Life of Pole, sect. 3.

Cromwell.

the one great reproach of having obeyed too implicitly a master whose commands were crimes, inquired of the judges whether, if parliament should condemn a man to die for treason without hearing him, the attainder could ever be disputed. They answered that it was a dangerous question, and that parliament should rather set an example to inferior courts by proceeding according to justice. But being pressed to reply by the king's express commandment, they said that an attainder in parliament, whether the party had been heard or not in his defence, could never be reversed in a court of law. No proceedings, it is said, took place against the person intended, nor is it known who he was.[1] But men prone to remark all that seems an appropriate retribution of Providence, took notice that he who had thus solicited the interpreters of the law to sanction such a violation of natural justice, was himself its earliest example. In the apparent zenith of favor this able and faithful minister, the king's vicegerent in his ecclesiastical supremacy, and recently created earl of Essex, fell so suddenly, and so totally without offence, that it has perplexed some writers to assign the cause. But there seems little doubt that Henry's dissatisfaction with his fourth wife, Anne of Cleves, whom Cromwell had recommended, alienated his selfish temper, and inclined his ear to the whisperings of those courtiers who abhorred the favorite and his measures. An act attainting him of treason and heresy was hurried through parliament, without hearing him in his defence.[2] The charges, indeed, were so ungrounded that had he been

1 Coke's 4th Institute, 37. It is however said by lord Herbert and others, that the countess of Salisbury and the marchioness of Exeter were not heard in their defence. The acts of attainder against them were certainly hurried through parliment; but whether without hearing the parties does not appear.

2 Burnet observes, that Cranmer was absent the first day the bill was read, 17th June, 1540; and by his silence leaves the reader to infer that he was so likewise on 19th June, when it was read a second and third time. But this, I fear, cannot be asserted. He is marked in the journal as present on the latter day: and there is the following entry: "Hodie lecta est pro secundo et tertio, billa attincturæ Thomæ Comitis Essex, et communi omnium procerum tunc præsentium concessu, nemine discrepante, expedita est." And at the close of the session we find a still more remarkable testimony to the unanimity of parliament in the following words: "Hoc animadvertendum est, quod in hâc sessione cum proceres darent suffragia, et dicerent sententias super actibus prædictis, ea erat concordia et sententiarum conformitas, ut singuli iis et eorum singulis assenserint, nemine discrepante. Thomas de Soulemont, Cleric. Parliamentorum." As far therefore as entries on the journals are evidence, Cranmer was placed in the painful and humiliating predicament of voting for the death of his innocent friend. He had gone as far as he dared in writing a letter to Henry, which might be construed into an apology for Cromwell, though it was full as much so for himself.

permitted to refute them, his condemnation, though not less certain, might, perhaps, have caused more shame. This precedent of sentencing men unheard, by means of an act of attainder, was followed in the case of Dr. Barnes, burned not long afterwards for heresy.

Duke of Norfolk.

The duke of Norfolk had been throughout Henry's reign one of his most confidential ministers. But as the king approached his end, an inordinate jealousy of great men rather than mere caprice appears to have prompted the resolution of destroying the most conspicuous family in England. Norfolk's son, too, the earl of Surrey, though long a favorite with the king, possessed more talents and renown, as well as a more haughty spirit, than were compatible with his safety. A strong party at court had always been hostile to the duke of Norfolk; and his ruin was attributed especially to the influence of the two Seymours. No accusations could be more futile than those which sufficed to take away the life of the noblest and most accomplished man in England. Surrey's treason seems to have consisted chiefly in quartering the royal arms in his escutcheon; and this false heraldry, if such it were, must have been considered as evidence of meditating the king's death. His father ignominiously confessed the charges against himself, in a vain hope of mercy from one who knew not what it meant. An act of attainder (for both houses of parliament were commonly made accessory to the legal murders of this reign) was passed with much haste, and perhaps irregularly; but Henry's demise ensuing at the instant prevented the execution of Norfolk. Continuing in prison during Edward's reign, he just survived to be released and restored in blood under Mary.

Anne Boleyn.

Among the victims of this monarch's ferocity, as we bestow most of our admiration on Sir Thomas More, so we reserve our greatest pity for Anne Boleyn. Few, very few, have in any age hesitated to admit her innocence.[1] But her discretion was by no means sufficient to

[1] Burnet has taken much pains with the subject, and set her innocence in a very clear light: — i. 197, and iii. 114. See also Strype, i. 280, and Ellis's Letters, ii. 52. But Anne had all the failings of a vain, weak woman raised suddenly to greatness. She behaved with unamiable vindictiveness towards Wolsey, and perhaps (but this worst charge is not fully authenticated) exasperated the king against More. A remarkable passage in Cavendish's Life of Wolsey, p. 103. edit. 1667, strongly displays her indiscretion.

A late writer, whose acuteness and industry would raise him to a very respectable place among our historians if he

preserve her steps on that dizzy height, which she had ascended with more eager ambition than feminine delicacy could approve. Henry was probably quicksighted enough to perceive that he did not possess her affections, and his own were soon transferred to another object. Nothing in this detestable reign is worse than her trial. She was indicted, partly upon the statute of Edward III., which, by a just though rather technical construction, has been held to extend the guilt of treason to an adulterous queen as well as to her paramour, and partly on the recent law for preservation of the succession, which attached the same penalties to anything done or said in slander of the king's issue. Her levities in discourse were brought within this strange act by a still more strange interpretation. Nor was the wounded pride of the king content with her death. Under the fear, as is most likely, of a more cruel punishment, which the law affixed to her offence, Anne was induced to confess a precontract with Lord Percy, on which her marriage with the king was annulled by an ecclesiastical sentence, without awaiting its certain dissolution by the axe.[1] Henry seems

could have repressed the inveterate partiality of his profession, has used every oblique artifice to lead his readers into a belief of Anne Boleyn's guilt, while he affects to hold the balance, and state both sides of the question without determining it. Thus he repeats what he must have known to be the strange and extravagant lies of Sanders about her birth; without vouching for them indeed, but without any reprobation of their absurd malignity. Lingard's Hist. of England, vi. 153, (8vo. edit.) Thus he intimates that "the records of her trial and conviction have perished, perhaps by the hands of those who respected her memory." p. 316, though the evidence is given by Burnet, and the record (in the technical sense) of a trial contains nothing from which a party's guilt or innocence can be inferred. Thus he says that those who were executed on the same charge with the queen, neither admitted nor denied the offence for which they suffered; though the best informed writers assert that Norris constantly declared the queen's innocence and his own.

Dr. Lingard can hardly be thought serious when he takes credit to himself, in the commencement of a note at the end of the same volume, for "not rendering his book more interesting by representing her as an innocent and injured woman, falling a victim to the intrigues of a religious faction." He well knows that he could not have done so without contradicting the tenor of his entire work, without ceasing, as it were, to be himself. All the rest of this note is a pretended balancing of evidence, in the style of a judge who can hardly bear to put for a moment the possibility of a prisoner's innocence.

I regret very much to be compelled to add the name of Mr. Sharon Turner to those who have countenanced the supposition of Anne Boleyn's guilt. But Mr. Turner, a most worthy and painstaking man, to whose earlier writings our literature is much indebted, has, in his history of Henry VIII., gone upon the strange principle of exalting that tyrant's reputation at the expense of every one of his victims, to whatever party they may have belonged. *Odit damnatos.* Perhaps he is the first, and will be the last, who has defended the attainder of Sir Thomas More. A verdict of a jury, an assertion of a statesman, a recital of an act of parliament, are, with him, satisfactory proofs of the most improbable accusations against the most blameless character.

[1] The lords pronounced a singular sentence, that she should be burned or beheaded at the king's pleasure. Burnet says, the judges complained of this

to have thought his honor too much sullied by the infidelity of a lawful wife. But for this destiny he was yet reserved. I shall not impute to him as an act of tyranny the execution of Catherine Howard, since it appears probable that the licentious habits of that young woman had continued after her marriage;[1] and though we might not in general applaud the vengeance of a husband who should put a guilty wife to death, it could not be expected that Henry VIII. should lose so reasonable an opportunity of shedding blood.[2] It was after the execution of this fifth wife that the celebrated law was enacted, whereby any woman whom the king should marry as a virgin incurred the penalties of treason if she did not previously reveal any failings that had disqualified her for the service of Diana.[3]

These parliamentary attainders, being intended rather as judicial than legislative proceedings, were violations of reason and justice in the application of law. But many general enactments of this reign bear the same character of servility. New politi-

Fresh statutes enacting the penalties of treason.

as unprecedented. Perhaps in strictness the king's right to *alter* a sentence is questionable; or rather would be so, if a few precedents were out of the way. In high treason committed by a man, the beheading was part of the sentence, and the king only remitted the more cruel preliminaries. Women, till 1791, were condemned to be burned. But the two queens of Henry, the countess of Salisbury, lady Rochford, lady Jane Grey, and, in later times, Mrs. Lisle were beheaded. Poor Mrs. Gaunt was not thought noble enough to be rescued from the fire. In felony, where beheading is no part of the sentence, it has been substituted by the king's warrant in the cases of the duke of Somerset and Lord Audley. I know not why the latter obtained this favor; for it had been refused to Lord Stourton, hanged for murder under Mary, as it was afterwards to Earl Ferrers.

1 [The letters published in State Papers, temp. Henry 8, vol. i. p. 689 et post, by no means increase this probability; Catherine Howard's post-nuptial guilt must remain very questionable, which makes her execution, and that of others who suffered with her, another of Henry's murders. There is too much appearance that Cranmer, by the king's order, promised that her life should be spared, with a view of obtaining a confession of a pre-contract with Derham. — 1845.]

2 It is often difficult to understand the grounds of a parliamentary attainder, for which any kind of evidence was thought sufficient; and the strongest proofs against Catherine Howard undoubtedly related to her behavior before marriage, which could be no legal crime. But some of the depositions extend farther.

Dr. Lingard has made a curious observation on this case: "A plot was woven by the industry of the reformers, which brought the young queen to the scaffold, and weakened the ascendency of the reigning party." — p. 407. This is a very strange assertion; for he proceeds to admit her antenuptial guilt, which indeed she is well known to have confessed, and does not give the slightest proof of any plot. Yet he adds, speaking of the queen and lady Rochford, "I fear [i. e. wish to insinuate] both were sacrificed to the manes of Anne Boleyn."

3 Stat. 26 H. 8, c. 13.

It may be here observed, that the act attainting Catherine Howard of treason proceeds to declare that the king's assent to bills by commission under the great seal is as valid as if he were personally present, any custom or use to the contrary notwithstanding. 33 H. 8, c. 21. This may be presumed, therefore, to be the earliest instance of the king's passing bills in this manner.

cal offences were created in every parliament, against which the severest penalties were denounced. The nation had scarcely time to rejoice in the termination of those long debates between the houses of York and Lancaster, when the king's divorce, and the consequent illegitimacy of his eldest daughter, laid open the succession to fresh questions. It was needlessly unnatural and unjust to bastardize the princess Mary, whose title ought rather to have had the confirmation of parliament. But Henry, who would have deemed so moderate a proceeding injurious to his cause in the eyes of Europe, and a sort of concession to the adversaries of the divorce, procured an act settling the crown on his children by Anne or any subsequent wife. Any person disputing the lawfulness of the king's second marriage might, by the sort of construction that would be put on this act, become liable to the penalties of treason. In two years more this very marriage was annulled by sentence; and it would, perhaps, have been treasonable to assert the princess Elizabeth's legitimacy. The same punishment was enacted against such as should marry without license under the great seal, or have a criminal intercourse with, any of the king's children "lawfully born, or otherwise commonly reputed to be his children, or his sister, aunt, or niece."[1]

Act giving proclamations the force of law.

Henry's two divorces had created an uncertainty as to the line of succession, which parliament endeavored to remove, not by such constitutional provisions in concurrence with the crown as might define the course of inheritance, but by enabling the king, on failure of issue by Jane Seymour, or any other lawful wife, to make over and bequeath the kingdom to any persons at his pleasure, not even reserving a preference to the descendants of former sovereigns.[2] By a subsequent statute, the princesses Mary and Elizabeth were nominated in the entail, after the king's male issue, subject, however, to such conditions as he should declare, by non-compliance with which their right was to cease.[3] This act still left it in his power to limit the remainder at his discretion. In execution of this authority, he devised the crown, upon failure of issue from his three children, to the heirs of the body of Mary duchess of Suffolk, the younger of his two sisters; postpon-

1 28 H. 8, c. 18. 2 28 H. 8, c. 7. 3 35 H. 8, c. 1.

ing at least, if not excluding, the royal family of Scotland, descended from his elder sister Margaret. In surrendering the regular laws of the monarchy to one man's caprice, this parliament became accessory, so far as in it lay, to dispositions which might eventually have kindled the flames of civil war. But it seemed to aim at inflicting a still deeper injury on future generations, in enacting that a king, after he should have attained the age of twenty-four years, might repeal any statutes made since his accession.[1] Such a provision not only tended to annihilate the authority of a regency, and to expose the kingdom to a sort of anarchical confusion during its continuance, but seemed to prepare the way for a more absolute power of abrogating all acts of the legislature. Three years afterwards it was enacted that proclamations made by the king and council, under penalty of fine and imprisonment, should have the force of statutes, so that they should not be prejudicial to any person's inheritance, offices, liberties, goods and chattels, nor infringe the established laws. This has been often noticed as an instance of servile compliance. It is, however, a striking testimony to the free constitution it infringed, and demonstrates that the prerogative could not soar to the heights it aimed at, till thus impeded by the perfidious hand of parliament. It is also to be observed, that the power given to the king's proclamations is considerably limited.[2]

A government administered with so frequent violations not only of the chartered privileges of Englishmen, but of those still more sacred rights which natural law has established, must have been regarded, one would imagine, with just abhorrence, and earnest longings for a change. Yet

[1] 28 H. 8, c. 17.

[2] 31 H. 8, c. 8. Burnet, i. 263, explains the origin of this act. Great exceptions had been taken to some of the king's ecclesiastical proclamations, which altered laws, and laid taxes on spiritual persons. He justly observes that the restrictions contained in it gave great power to the judges, who had the power of expounding in their hands. The preamble is full as offensive as the body of the act; reciting the contempt and disobedience of the king's proclamations by some "who did not consider *what a king by his royal power might do*," which, if it continued, would tend to the disobedience of the laws of God, and the dishonor of the king's majesty, "who might full ill bear it," &c. See this act at length in the great edition of the statutes. There was one singular provision: the clause protecting all persons as mentioned, in their inheritance or other property, proceeds, "nor shall by virtue of the said act suffer any pains of death." But an exception is afterwards made for "such persons which shall offend against any proclamation to be made by the king's highness, his heirs or successors, for or concerning any kind of heresies against Christian doctrine." Thus it seems that the king claimed a power to declare heresy by proclamation, under penalty of death.

contemporary authorities by no means answer to this expectation. Some mention Henry after his death in language of eulogy; and, if we except those whom attachment to the ancient religion had inspired with hatred towards his memory, very few appear to have been aware that his name would descend to posterity among those of the many tyrants and oppressors of innocence, whom the wrath of Heaven has raised up, and the servility of men has endured. I do not indeed believe that he had really conciliated his people's affection. That perfect fear which attended him must have cast out love. But he had a few qualities that deserve esteem, and several which a nation is pleased to behold in a sovereign. He wanted, or at least did not manifest in any eminent degree, one usual vice of tyrants, dissimulation: his manners were affable, and his temper generous. Though his schemes of foreign policy were not very sagacious, and his wars, either with France or Scotland, productive of no material advantage, they were uniformly successful, and retrieved the honor of the English name. But the main cause of the reverence with which our forefathers cherished this king's memory was the share he had taken in the Reformation. They saw in him, not indeed the proselyte of their faith, but the subverter of their enemies' power, the avenging minister of Heaven, by whose giant arm the chain of superstition had been broken, and the prison gates burst asunder.[1]

Government of Edward VI.'s councillors.

The ill-assorted body of councillors who exercised the functions of regency by Henry's testament were sensible that they had not sinews to wield his iron sceptre, and that some sacrifice must be made to a nation exasperated as well as overawed by the violent measures of his reign. In the first session, accordingly, of Edward's parliament, the new treasons and felonies

[1] Gray has finely glanced at this bright point of Henry's character, in that beautiful stanza where he has made the founders of Cambridge pass before our eyes, like shadows over a magic glass:

—— the majestic lord
Who broke the bonds of Rome.

In a poet, this was a fair employment of his art; but the partiality of Burnet towards Henry VIII. is less warrantable; and he should have blushed to excuse, by absurd and unworthy sophistry, the punishment of those who refused to swear to the king's supremacy. p. 351.

After all, Henry was every whit as good a king and man as Francis I., whom there are still some, on the other side of the Channel, servile enough to extol; not in the least more tyrannical and sanguinary, and of better faith towards his neighbors.

which had been created to please his father's sanguinary disposition were at once abrogated.[1]

The statute of Edward III. became again the standard of high treason, except that the denial of the king's supremacy was still liable to its penalties. The same act, which relieves the subject from these terrors, contains also a repeal of that which had given legislative validity to the king's proclamations. These provisions appear like an elastic recoil of the constitution after the extraordinary pressure of that despotic reign. But, however they may indicate the temper of parliament, we must consider them but as an unwilling and insincere compliance on the part of the government. Henry, too arrogant to dissemble with his subjects, had stamped the law itself with the print of his despotism. The more wily courtiers of Edward's council deemed it less obnoxious to violate than to new-mould the constitution. For, although proclamations had no longer the legal character of statutes, we find several during Edward's reign enforced by penalty of fine and imprisonment. Many of the ecclesiastical changes were first established by no other authority, though afterwards sanctioned by parliament. Rates were thus fixed for the price of provisions; bad money was cried down, with penalties on those who should buy it under a certain value, and the melting of the current coin prohibited on pain of forfeiture.[2] Some of these might possibly have a sanction from precedent, and from the acknowledged prerogative of the crown in regulating the coin. But no legal apology can be made for a proclamation in April, 1549, addressed to all justices of the peace, enjoining them to arrest sowers and tellers abroad of vain and forged tales and lies, and to commit them to the galleys, there to row in chains as slaves during the king's pleasure.[3] One would imagine that the late

[1] 1 Edw. 6, c. 12. By this act it is provided that a lord of parliament shall have the benefit of clergy though he cannot read. Sect. 14. Yet one can hardly believe that this provision was necessary at so late an era.

[2] 2 Strype, 147, 341, 491.

[3] Id. 149. Dr. Lingard has remarked an important change in the coronation ceremony of Edward VI. Formerly the king had taken an oath to preserve the liberties of the realm, and especially those granted by Edward the Confessor, &c., before the people were asked whether they would consent to have him as their king. See the form observed at Richard the Second's cononation in Rymer, vii. 158. But at Edward's coronation the archbishop presented the king to the people, as rightful and undoubted inheritor by the laws of God and man to the royal dignity and crown imperial of this realm, &c., and asked if they would serve him and assent to his coronation, as by their duty of allegiance they were bound to do. All this was before the oath. 2 Burnet, Appendix, p. 93.

Few will pretend that the coronation, or the coronation oath, was essential to

statute had been repealed, as too far restraining the royal power, rather than as giving it an unconstitutional extension.

Attainder of lord Seymour.

It soon became evident that if the new administration had not fully imbibed the sanguinary spirit of their late master, they were as little scrupulous in bending the rules of law and justice to their purpose in cases of treason. The duke of Somerset, nominated by Henry as one only of his sixteen executors, obtained almost immediately afterwards a patent from the young king, constituting him sole regent under the name of protector, with the assistance, indeed, of the rest as his councillors, but with the power of adding any others to their number. Conscious of his own usurpation, it was natural for Somerset to dread the aspiring views of others; nor was it long before he discovered a rival in his brother, lord Seymour, of Sudeley, whom, according to the policy of that age, he thought it necessary to destroy by a bill of attainder. Seymour was apparently a dangerous and unprincipled man; he had courted the favor of the young king by small presents of money, and appears beyond question to have entertained a hope of marrying the princess Elizabeth, who had lived much in his house during his short union with the queen dowager. It was surmised that this lady had been poisoned to make room for a still nobler consort.[1] But in this there could be no treason; and it is not likely that any evidence was given which could have brought him within the statute of Edward III. In this prosecution against lord Seymour it was thought expedient to follow the very worst of Henry's precedents, by not hearing the accused in his defence. The bill passed through the upper house, the natural guardian of a peer's life and honor, without one dissenting voice. The

the legal succession of the crown, or the exercise of its prerogatives. But this alteration in the form is a curious proof of the solicitude displayed by the Tudors, as it was much more by the next family, to suppress every recollection that could make their sovereignty appear to be of popular origin.

1 Haynes's State Papers contain many curious proofs of the incipient amour between lord Seymour and Elizabeth, and show much indecent familiarity on one side, with a little childish coquetry on the other. These documents also rather tend to confirm the story of our elder historians, which I have found attested by foreign writers of that age (though Burnet has thrown doubts upon it), that some differences between the queen-dowager and the duchess of Somerset aggravated at least those of their husbands. P. 61, 69. It is alleged with absurd exaggeration, in the articles against lord Seymour, that, had the former proved immediately with child after her marriage with him, it might have passed for the king's. This marriage, however, did not take place before June, Henry having died in January. Ellis's Letters, ii. 150.

commons addressed the king that they might hear the witnesses, and also the accused. It was answered that the king did not think it necessary for them to hear the latter; but that those who had given their depositions before the lords might repeat their evidence before the lower house. It rather appears that the commons did not insist on this any further; but the bill of attainder was carried with a few negative voices.[1] How striking a picture it affords of the sixteenth century, to behold the popular and well-natured duke of Somerset, more estimable at least than any other statesman employed under Edward, not only promoting this unjust condemnation of his brother, but signing the warrant under which he was beheaded!

Attainder of duke of Somerset.

But it was more easy to crush a single competitor than to keep in subjection the subtle and daring spirits trained in Henry's councils, and jealous of the usurpation of an equal. The protector, attributing his success, as is usual with men in power, rather to skill than fortune, and confident in the two frailest supports that a minister can have, the favor of a child and of the lower people, was stripped of his authority within a few months after the execution of lord Seymour, by a confederacy which he had neither the discretion to prevent nor the firmness to resist. Though from this time but a secondary character upon the public stage, he was so near the throne as to keep alive the suspicions of the duke of Northumberland, who, with no ostensible title, had become not less absolute than himself. It is not improbable that Somerset was innocent of the charge imputed to him, namely, a conspiracy to murder some of the privy councillors, which had been erected into felony by a recent statute; but the evidence, though it may have been false, does not seem legally insufficient. He demanded on his trial to be confronted with the witnesses, a favor rarely granted in that age to state criminals, and which he could not very decently solicit after causing his brother to be condemned unheard. Three lords, against whom he was charged to have conspired, sat upon his trial; and it was thought a sufficient reply to his complaints of this breach of a known principle that no challenge could be allowed in the case of a peer.

[1] Journals, Feb. 27, March 4, 1548–9. From these I am led to doubt whether the commons actually heard witnesses against Seymour, which Burnet and Strype have taken for granted.

From this designing and unscrupulous oligarchy no measure conducive to liberty and justice could be expected to spring. But among the commons there must have been men, although their names have not descended to us, who, animated by a purer zeal for these objects, perceived on how precarious a thread the life of every man was suspended, when the private deposition of one suborned witness, unconfronted with the prisoner, could suffice to obtain a conviction in cases of treason. In the worst period of Edward's reign we find inserted in a bill creating some new treasons one of the most important constitutional provisions which the annals of the Tudor family afford. It is enacted that "no person shall be indicted for any manner of treason except on the testimony of two lawful witnesses, who shall be brought in person before the accused at the time of his trial, to avow and maintain what they have to say against him, unless he shall willingly confess the charges."[1] This salutary provision was strengthened, not taken away, as some later judges ventured to assert, by an act in the reign of Mary. In a subsequent part of this work I shall find an opportunity for discussing this important branch of constitutional law.

Violence of Mary's reign.

It seems hardly necessary to mention the momentary usurpation of lady Jane Grey, founded on no pretext of title which could be sustained by any argument. She certainly did not obtain that degree of actual possession which might have sheltered her adherents under the statute of Henry VII.; nor did the duke of Northumberland allege this excuse on his trial, though he set up one of a more technical nature, that the great seal was a sufficient protection for acts done by its authority.[2] The reign that im-

1 Stat. 5 & 6 Edw. 6, c. 11, s. 12.

2 Burnet, ii. 243. An act was made to confirm deeds of private persons, dated during Jane's ten days, concerning which some doubt had arisen. 1 Mary, sess. 2, c. 4. It is said in this statute, "her highness's most lawful possession was for a time disturbed and disquieted by traitorous rebellion and usurpation."

It appears that the young king's original intention was to establish a modified Salic law, excluding females from the crown, but not their male heirs. In a writing drawn by himself, and entitled "My Device for the Succession," it is entailed on the heirs male of the lady queen, if she have any before his death; then to the *lady Jane and her heirs male;* then to the heirs male of lady Katharine; and in every instance, except Jane, excluding the female herself. Strype's Cranmer, Append. 164. A late author, on consulting the original MS., in the king's handwriting, found that it had been at first written "the lady Jane's heirs male," but that the words "and her" had been interlined. Nares's Memoirs of Lord Burghley, i. 451. Mr. Nares does not seem to doubt but that this was done by Edward himself: the change, however, is remarkable, and should probably be ascribed to Northumberland's influence.

mediately followed is chiefly remembered as a period of sanguinary persecution; but though I reserve for the next chapter all mention of ecclesiastical disputes, some of Mary's proceedings in reëstablishing popery belong to the civil history of our constitution. Impatient under the existence, for a moment, of rights and usages which she abhorred, this bigoted woman anticipated the legal authority which her parliament was ready to interpose for their abrogation; the Latin liturgy was restored, the married clergy expelled from their livings, and even many protestant ministers thrown into prison for no other crime than their religion, before any change had been made in the established laws.[1] The queen, in fact, and those around her, acted and felt as a legitimate government restored after an usurpation, and treated the recent statutes as null and invalid. But even in matters of temporal government the stretches of prerogative were more violent and alarming than during her brother's reign. It is due, indeed, to the memory of one who has left so odious a name, to remark that Mary was conscientiously averse to encroach upon what she understood to be the privileges of her people. A wretched book having been written to exalt her prerogative, on the ridiculous pretence that, as a queen, she was not bound by the laws of former kings, she showed it to Gardiner, and on his expressing indignation at the sophism, threw it herself into the fire. An act passed, however, to settle such questions, which declares the queen to have all the lawful prerogatives of the crown.[2] But she was surrounded by wicked councillors, renegades of every faith, and ministers of every tyranny. We must, in candor, attribute to their advice her arbitrary measures, though not her persecution of heresy, which she counted for virtue. She is said to have extorted loans from the citizens of London, and others of her subjects.[3] This, indeed, was not more than had been usual with her predecessors. But we find one clear in-

[1] Burnet. Strype, iii. 50, 53. Carte, 290. I doubt whether we have anything in our history more like conquest than the administration of 1553. The queen, in the month only of October, presented to 256 livings, restoring all those turned out under the acts of uniformity. Yet the deprivation of the bishops might be justified probably by the terms of the commission they had taken out in Edward's reign, to hold their sees during the king's pleasure, for which was afterwards substituted "during good behavior." Burnet, App. 257. Collier, 218.

[2] Burnet, ii. 278. Stat. 1 Mary, sess. 3, c. 1. Dr. Lingard rather strangely tells this story on the authority of father Persons, whom his readers probably do not esteem quite as much he does. If he had attended to Burnet, he would have found a more sufficient voucher.

[3] Carte, 330.

stance during her reign of a duty upon foreign cloth, imposed without assent of parliament; an encroachment unprecedented since the reign of Richard II. Several proofs might be adduced from records of arbitrary inquests for offences and illegal modes of punishment. The torture is, perhaps, more frequently mentioned in her short reign than in all former ages of our history put together, and, probably from that imitation of foreign governments, which contributed not a little to deface our constitution in the sixteenth century, seems deliberately to have been introduced as part of the process in those dark and uncontrolled tribunals which investigated offences against the state.[1] A commission issued in 1557, authorizing the persons named in it to inquire, by any means they could devise, into charges of heresy or other religious offences, and in some instances to punish the guilty, in others of a graver nature to remit them to their ordinaries, seems (as Burnet has well observed) to have been meant as a preliminary step to bringing in the inquisition. It was at least the germ of the high-commission court in the next reign.[2] One proclamation in the last year of her inauspicious administration may be deemed a flight of tyranny beyond her father's example, which, after denouncing the importation of books filled with heresy and treason from beyond sea, proceeds to declare that whoever should be found to have such books in his possession should be reputed and taken for a rebel, and executed according to martial law.[3] This had been provoked as well by a violent libel written at Geneva by Goodman, a refugee, exciting the people to dethrone the queen, as by the recent attempt of one Stafford, a descendant of the house of Buckingham, who, having landed with a small force at Scarborough, had vainly hoped that the general disaffection would enable him to overthrow her government.[4]

1 Haynes, 195. Burnet, ii. Appendix, 256. iii. 243.

2 Burnet, ii. 347. Collier, ii. 404, and Lingard, vii. 266 (who, by the way, confounds this commission with something different two years earlier), will not hear of this allusion to the inquisition. But Burnet has said nothing that is not perfectly just.

3 Strype, iii. 459.

4 See Stafford's proclamation from Scarborough castle, Strype, iii. Appendix, No. 71. It contains no allusion to religion, both parties being weary of Mary's Spanish counsels. The important letters of Noailles, the French ambassador, to which Carte had access, and which have since been printed, have afforded information to Dr. Lingard, and with those of the imperial ambassador, Renard, which I have not had an opportunity of seeing, throw much light on this reign. They certainly appear to justify the restraint put on Elizabeth, who, if not herself privy to the conspiracies planned in her behalf (which is, however, very probable),

The house of commons recovers part of its independent power in these two reigns.

Notwithstanding, however, this apparently uncontrolled career of power, it is certain that the children of Henry VIII. did not preserve his almost absolute dominion over parliament. I have only met with one instance in his reign where the commons refused to pass a bill recommended by the crown. This was in 1532; but so unquestionable were the legislative rights of parliament, that, although much displeased, even Henry was forced to yield.[1] We find several instances during the reign of Edward, and still more in that of Mary, where the commons rejected bills sent down from the upper house; and though there was always a majority of peers for the government, yet the dissent of no small number is frequently recorded in the former reign. Thus the commons not only threw out a bill creating several new treasons, and substituted one of a more moderate nature, with that memorable clause for two witnesses to be produced in open court, which I have already mentioned;[2] but rejected one attainting Tunstal bishop of Durham for misprision of treason, and were hardly brought to grant a subsidy.[3] Their conduct in the two former instances, and probably in the third, must be attributed to the indignation that was generally felt at the usurped power of Northumberland, and the untimely fate of Somerset. Several cases of similar unwillingness to go along with court measures occurred under Mary. She dissolved, in fact, her two first parliaments on this account. But the third was far from obsequious, and rejected several of her favorite bills.[4] Two

was at least too dangerous to be left at liberty. Noailles intrigued with the malecontents, and instigated the rebellion of Wyatt, of which Dr. Lingard gives a very interesting account. Carte, indeed, differs from him in many of these circumstances, though writing from the same source, and particularly denies that Noailles gave any encouragement to Wyatt. It is, however, evident from the tenor of his despatches that he had gone great lengths in fomenting the discontent, and was evidently desirous of the success of the insurrection, iii. 36, 43, &c. This critical state of the government may furnish the usual excuse for its rigor. But its unpopularity was brought on by Mary's breach of her word as to religion, and still more by her obstinacy in forming her union with Philip, against the general voice of the nation, and the opposition of Gardiner; who, however, after her resolution was taken, became its strenuous supporter in public. For the detestation in which the queen was held, see the letters of Noailles, passim; but with some degree of allowance for his own antipathy to her.

1 Burnet, i. 117. The king refused his assent to a bill which had passed both houses, but apparently not of a political nature. Lords' Journals, p. 162.

2 Burnet, 190.

3 Id. 195, 215. This was the parliament, in order to secure favorable elections for which the council had written letters to the sheriffs. These do not appear to have availed so much as they might hope.

4 Carte, 311, 322. Noailles, v. 252. He says that she committed some knights to the Tower for their language in the house. Id. 247. Burnet, p. 324, mentions the same.

reasons principally contributed to this opposition: the one, a fear of entailing upon the country those numerous exactions of which so many generations had complained, by reviving the papal supremacy, and more especially of a restoration of abbey lands; the other, an extreme repugnance to the queen's Spanish connection.[1] If Mary could have obtained the consent of parliament, she would have settled the crown on her husband, and sent her sister, perhaps, to the scaffold.[2]

Attempt of the court to strengthen itself by creating new boroughs.

There cannot be a stronger proof of the increased weight of the commons during these reigns than the anxiety of the court to obtain favorable elections. Many ancient boroughs, undoubtedly, have at no period possessed sufficient importance to deserve the elective franchise on the score of their riches or population; and it is most likely that some temporary interest or partiality, which cannot now be traced, first caused a writ to be addressed to them. But there is much reason to conclude that the councillors of Edward VI., in erecting new boroughs, acted upon a deliberate plan of strengthening their influence among the commons. Twenty-two boroughs were created or restored in this short reign; some of them, indeed, places of much consideration, but not less than seven in Cornwall, and several others that appear to have been insignificant. Mary added fourteen to the number; and as the same course was pursued under Elizabeth, we in fact owe a great part of that irregularity in our popular representation, the advantages or evils of which we need not here discuss, less to changes wrought by time, than to deliberate and not very constitutional policy. Nor did the government scruple a direct and avowed interference with elections. A circular letter of Edward to all the sheriffs commands them to give notice to the freeholders, citizens, and burgesses, within their respective counties, "that our

1 Burnet, 322. Carte, 296. Noailles says that a third part of the commons in Mary's first parliament was hostile to the repeal of Edward's laws about religion, and that the debates lasted a week, ii. 247. The Journals do not mention any division; though it is said in Strype, iii. 204, that one member, sir Ralph Bagnal, refused to concur in the act abolishing the supremacy. The queen, however, in her letter to cardinal Pole, says of this repeal: "quod non sine contentione, disputatione acri, et summo labore fidelium factum est." Lingard, Carte, Philips's Life of Pole. Noailles speaks repeatedly of the strength of the protestant party, and of the enmity which the English nation, as he expressed it, bore to the pope. But the aversion to the marriage with Philip, and dread of falling under the yoke of Spain, were common to both religions, with the exception of a few mere bigots to the church of Rome.

2 Noailles, vol. v. passim.

pleasure and commandment is, that they shall choose and appoint, as nigh as they possibly may, men of knowledge and experience within the counties, cities, and boroughs;" but nevertheless, that where the privy council should "recommend men of learning and wisdom, in such case their directions be regarded and followed." Several persons accordingly were recommended by letters to the sheriffs, and elected as knights for different shires; all of whom belonged to the court, or were in places of trust about the king.[1] It appears probable that persons in office formed at all times a very considerable portion of the house of commons. Another circular of Mary before the parliament of 1554, directing the sheriffs to admonish the electors to choose good catholics and "inhabitants, as the old laws require," is much less unconstitutional; but the earl of Sussex, one of her most active councillors, wrote to the gentlemen of Norfolk, and to the burgesses of Yarmouth, requesting them to reserve their voices for the person he should name.[2] There is reason to believe that the court, or rather the imperial ambassador, did homage to the power of the commons, by presents of money, in order to procure their support of the unpopular marriage with Philip;[3] and if Noailles, the ambassador of Henry II., did not make use of the same means to thwart the grants of subsidy and other measures of the administration, he was at least very active in promising the succor of France, and animating the patriotism of those unknown leaders of that assembly, who withstood the design of a besotted woman and her unprincipled councillors to transfer this kingdom under the yoke of Spain.[4]

Causes of the high prerogative of the Tudors.

It appears to be a very natural inquiry, after beholding the course of administration under the Tudor line, by what means a government so violent in itself, and so plainly inconsistent with the acknowledged laws, could be maintained; and what had become of that English spirit which had not only controlled such injudicious princes as John and Richard II., but withstood the first and third Edward in the fulness of their

[1] Strype, ii. 394.
[2] Id. iii. 155. Burnet, ii. 228.
[3] Burnet, ii. 262, 277.
[4] Noailles, v. 190. Of the truth of this plot there can be no rational ground to doubt; even Dr. Lingard has nothing to advance against it but the assertion of Mary's counsellors, the Pagets and Arundels, the most worthless of mankind. We are, in fact, greatly indebted to Noailles for his spirited activity, which contributed, in a high degree, to secure both the protestant religion and the national independence of our ancestors.

pride and glory. Not, indeed, that the excesses of prerogative had ever been thoroughly restrained, or that, if the memorials of earlier ages had been as carefully preserved as those of the sixteenth century, we might not possibly find in them equally flagrant instances of oppression; but still the petitions of parliament and frequent statutes remain on record, bearing witness to our constitutional law, and to the energy that gave it birth. There had evidently been a retrograde tendency towards absolute monarchy between the reigns of Henry VI. and Henry VIII. Nor could this be attributed to the common engine of despotism, a military force. For, except the yeomen of the guard, fifty in number, and the common servants of the king's household, there was not, in time of peace, an armed man receiving pay throughout England.[1] A government that ruled by intimidation was absolutely destitute of force to intimidate. Hence risings of the mere commonalty were sometimes highly dangerous, and lasted much longer than ordinary. A rabble of Cornishmen, in the reign of Henry VII., headed by a blacksmith, marched up from their own county to the suburbs of London without resistance. The insurrections of 1525 in consequence of Wolsey's illegal taxation, those of the north ten years afterwards, wherein, indeed, some men of higher quality were engaged, and those which broke out simultaneously in several counties under Edward VI., excited a well-grounded alarm in the country, and in the two latter instances were not quelled without much time and exertion. The reproach of servility and patient acquiescence under usurped power falls not on the English people, but on its natural leaders. We have seen, indeed, that the house of commons now and then gave signs of an independent spirit, and occasioned more trouble, even to Henry VIII., than his compliant nobility. They yielded to every mandate of his imperious will; they bent with every breath of his capricious humor; they are responsible for the illegal trial, for the iniquitous attainder, for the sanguinary statute, for the tyranny which they sanctioned by law, and for that which they permitted to subsist without law. Nor was this selfish and pusillanimous subserviency more characteristic of the

[1] Henry VII. first established a band of fifty archers to wait on him. Henry VIII. had fifty horse-guards, each with an archer, demilance, and couteiller, like the gendarmerie of France; but on account, probably, of the expense it occasioned, their equipment being too magnificent, this soon was given up.

minions of Henry's favor, the Cromwells, the Riches, the Pagets, the Russells, and the Powletts, than of the representatives of ancient and honorable houses, the Howards, the Fitz-Allans, and the Talbots. We trace the noble statesmen of those reigns concurring in all the inconsistencies of their revolutions, supporting all the religions of Henry, Edward, Mary, and Elizabeth; adjudging the death of Somerset to gratify Northumberland, and of Northumberland to redeem their participation in his fault, setting up the usurpation of lady Jane, and abandoning her on the first doubt of success, constant only in the rapacious acquisition of estates and honors, from whatever source, and in adherence to the present power.

Jurisdiction of the council of star-chamber.

I have noticed in a former work that illegal and arbitrary jurisdiction exercised by the council, which, in despite of several positive statutes, continued in a greater or less degree, through all the period of the Plantagenet family, to deprive the subject, in many criminal charges, of that sacred privilege, trial by his peers.[1] This usurped jurisdiction, carried much further, and exercised more vigorously, was the principal grievance under the Tudors; and the forced submission of our forefathers was chiefly owing to the terrors of a tribunal which left them secure from no infliction but public execution, or actual dispossession of their freeholds. And, though it was beyond its direct province to pass sentence on capital charges, yet, by intimidating jurors, it procured convictions which it was not authorized to pronounce. We are naturally astonished at the easiness with which verdicts were sometimes given against persons accused of treason, on evidence insufficient to support the charge in point of law, or in its nature not competent to be received, or unworthy of belief. But this is explained by the peril that hung over the jury in case of acquittal. "If," says Sir Thomas Smith, in his Treatise on the Commonwealth of England, "they do pronounce not guilty upon the prisoner, against whom manifest witness is brought in, the petitioner escapeth, but the twelve are not only rebuked by the judges, but also threatened of punishment, and many times commanded to appear in the star-

[1] View of Middle Ages, ch. 8. I must here acknowledge that I did not make the requisite distinction between the concilium secretum, or privy council of state, and the concilium ordinarium, as lord Hale calls it, which alone exercised jurisdiction.

chamber, or before the privy council, for the matter. But this threatening chanceth oftener than the execution thereof; and the twelve answer with most gentle words, they did it according to their consciences, and pray the judges to be good unto them; they did as they thought right, and as they accorded all; and so it passeth away for the most part. Yet I have seen in my time, but not in the reign of the king now [Elizabeth], that an inquest, for pronouncing one not guilty of treason contrary to such evidence as was brought in, were not only imprisoned for a space, but a large fine set upon their heads, which they were fain to pay; another inquest, for acquitting another, beside paying a fine, were put to open ignominy and shame. But these doings were even then accounted of many for violent, tyrannical, and contrary to the liberty and custom of the realm of England."[1] One of the instances to which he alludes was probably that of the jury who acquitted Sir Nicholas Throckmorton in the second year of Mary. He had conducted his own defence with singular boldness and dexterity. On delivering their verdict, the court committed them to prison. Four, having acknowledged their offence, were soon released; but the rest, attempting to justify themselves before the council, were sentenced to pay some a fine of two thousand pounds, some of one thousand marks; a part of which seems ultimately to have been remitted.[2]

This not the same with the court erected by Henry VII.

It is here to be observed that the council of which we have just heard, or as lord Hale denominates it (though rather, I believe, for the sake of distinction than upon any ancient authority), the king's ordinary council, was something different from the privy council, with which several modern writers are apt to confound it; that is, the court of jurisdiction is to be distinguished from the deliberative body, the advisers of the

1 Commonwealth of England, book 3, c. 1. The statute 26 H. 8, c. 4, enacts that if a jury in Wales acquit a felon, contrary to good and pregnant evidence, or otherwise misbehave themselves, the judge may bind them to appear before the president and council of the Welsh marches. The partiality of Welsh jurors was notorious in that age; and the reproach has not quite ceased.

2 State Trials, i. 901. Strype, ii. 120. In a letter to the Duke of Norfolk (Hardwicke Papers, i. 46) at the time of the Yorkshire rebellion in 1536, he is directed to question the jury who had acquitted a particular person, in order to discover their motive. Norfolk seems to have objected to this for a good reason, "least the fear thereof might trouble others in the like case." But it may not be uncandid to ascribe this rather to a leaning towards the insurgents than a constitutional principle.

crown. Every privy councillor belonging to the concilium ordinarium; but the chief justices, and perhaps several others who sat in the latter (not to mention all temporal and spiritual peers, who, in the opinion at least of some, had a right of suffrage therein), were not necessarily of the former body.[1] This cannot be called in question, without either charging lord Coke, lord Hale, and other writers on the subject, with ignorance of what existed in their own age, or gratuitously supposing that an entirely novel tribunal sprang up in the sixteenth century, under the name of the star-chamber. It has indeed been often assumed, that a statute enacted early in the reign of Henry VII, gave the first legal authority to the criminal jurisdiction exercised by that famous court, which in reality was nothing else but another name for the ancient concilium regis, of which our records are full, and whose encroachments so many statutes had endeavored to repress; a name derived from the chamber wherein it sat, and which is found in many precedents before the time of Henry VII., though not so specially applied to the council of judicature as afterwards.[2] The statute of this reign has a much more limited operation. I have

[1] Hale's Jurisdiction of the Lords' House, p. 5. Coke, 4th Inst. 65, where we have the following passage: — "So this court, [the court of star-chamber, as the concilium was then called,] being holden coram rege et concilio, it is, or may be, compounded of three several councils; that is to say, of the lords and others of his majesty's privy council, always judges without appointment, as before it appeareth. 2. The judges of either bench and barons of the exchequer are of the king's council, for matters of law, &c.; and the two chief justices, or in their absence other two justices, are standing judges of this court. 3. The lords of parliament are properly de magno concilio regis; but neither those, not being of the king's privy council, nor any of the rest of the judges or barons of the exchequer, are standing judges of the court." But Hudson, in his Treatise of the Court of Star-Chamber, written about the end of James's reign, inclines to think that all peers had a right of sitting in the court of star-chamber; there being several instances where some who were not of the council of state were present and gave judgment as in the case of Mr. Davison, "and how they were complete judges unsworn, if not by their native right, I cannot comprehend; for surely the calling of them in that case was not made legitimate by any act of parliament; neither without their right were they more apt to be judges than any other inferior persons in the kingdom; and yet I doubt not but it resteth in the king's pleasure to restrain any man from that table, as well as he may any of his council from the board." Collectanea Juridica, ii. p. 24. He says also, that it was demurrable for a bill to pray process against the defendant, to appear before the king and his privy council. Ibid.

[2] The privy council sometimes met in the star-chamber, and made orders. See one in 18 H. 6. Harl. MSS. Catalogue, N. 1878, fol. 20. So the statute 21 H. 8, c. 16, recites a decree *by the king's council in his star-chamber*, that no alien artificer shall keep more than two alien servants, and other matters of the same kind. This could no way belong to the court of star-chamber, which was a judicial tribunal.

It should be remarked, though not to our immediate purpose, that this decree was supposed to require an act of parliament for its confirmation; so far was the government of Henry VIII. from arrogating a legislative power in matters of private right.

observed in another work, that the coercive jurisdiction of the council had great convenience, in cases where the ordinary course of justice was so much obstructed by one party, through writs, combinations of maintenance, or overawing influence, that no inferior court would find its process obeyed; and that such seem to have been reckoned necessary exceptions from the statutes which restrain its interference. The act of 3 H. 7, c. 1, appears intended to place on a lawful and permanent basis the jurisdiction of the council, or rather a part of the council, over this peculiar class of offences; and after reciting the combinations supported by giving liveries, and by indentures or promises, the partiality of sheriffs in making panels, and in untrue returns, the taking of money by juries, the great riots and unlawful assemblies, which almost annihilated the fair administration of justice, empowers the chancellor, treasurer, and keeper of the privy seal, or any two of them, with a bishop and temporal lord of the council, and the chief justices of king's bench and common pleas, or two other justices in their absence, to call before them such as offended in the before-mentioned respects, and to punish them after examination in such manner as if they had been convicted by course of law. But this statute, if it renders legal a jurisdiction which had long been exercised with much advantage, must be allowed to limit the persons in whom it should reside, and certainly does not convey by any implication more extensive functions over a different description of misdemeanors. By a later act, 21 H. 8, c. 20, the president of the council is added to the judges of this court; a decisive proof that it still existed as a tribunal perfectly distinct from the council itself. But it is not styled by the name of star-chamber in this, any more than in the preceding statute. It is very difficult, I believe, to determine at what time the jurisdiction legally vested in this new court, and still exercised by it forty years afterwards, fell silently into the hands of the body of the council, and was extended by them so far beyond the boundaries assigned by law, under the appellation of the court of star-chamber. Sir Thomas Smith, writing in the early part of Elizabeth's reign, while he does not advert to the former court, speaks of the jurisdiction of the latter as fully established, and ascribes the whole praise (and to a certain degree it was matter of praise) to Cardinal Wolsey.

The celebrated statute of 31 H. 8, c. 8, which gives the king's proclamations, to a certain extent, the force of acts of parliament, enacts that offenders convicted of breaking such proclamations before certain persons enumerated therein (being apparently the usual officers of the privy council, together with some bishops and judges), "in the star-chamber or elsewhere," shall suffer such penalties of fine and imprisonment as they shall adjudge. "It is the effect of this court," Smith says, "to bridle such stout noblemen or gentlemen which would offer wrong by force to any manner of men, and cannot be content to demand or defend the right by order of the law. It began long before, but took augmentation and authority at that time that cardinal Wolsey, archbishop of York, was chancellor of England, who of some was thought to have first devised that court, because that he, after some intermission, by negligence of time, augmented the authority of it,[1] which was at that time marvellous ne-

[1] Lord Hale thinks that the jurisdiction of the council was gradually "brought into great disuse, though there remain some straggling footsteps of their proceedings till near 3 H. 7," p. 38. "The continual complaints of the commons against the proceedings before the council in causes civil or criminal, although they did not always attain their concession, yet brought a disreputation upon the proceedings of the council, as contrary to Magna Charta and the known laws," p. 39. He seems to admit afterwards, however, that many instances of proceedings before them in criminal causes might be added to those mentioned by lord Coke, p. 43.

The paucity of records about the time of Edward IV. renders the negative argument rather weak: but from the expression of sir Thomas Smith in the text, it may perhaps be inferred that the council had intermitted in a considerable degree, though not absolutely disused, their exercise of jurisdiction for some time before the accession of the house of Tudor.

Mr. Brodie, in his History of the British Empire under Charles I., i. 158, has treated at considerable length, and with much acuteness, this subject of the antiquity of the star-chamber. I do not coincide in all his positions; but the only one very important is that wherein we fully agree that its jurisdiction was chiefly usurped, as well as tyrannical.

I will here observe that this part of our ancient constitutional history is likely to be elucidated by a friend of my own, who has already given evidence to the world of his singular competence for such an undertaking, and who unites, with all the learning and diligence of Spelman, Prynne, and Maddox, an acuteness and vivacity of intellect which none of those writers possessed. — [1827.] [This has since been done in "An Essay upon the Original Authority of the King's Council, by sir Francis Palgrave, K. H.," 1834. The "Proceedings and Ordinances of the Privy Council of England," published by sir Harris Nicolas, contain the transactions of that body from 10 Ric. II. (1387) to 13 Hen. VI. (1435), with some scattered entries for the rest of the latter reign. They recommence in 1540. And a material change appears to have occurred, doubtless through Wolsey, in the latter years of the interval; the privy council exercising the same arbitrary and penal jurisdiction, or nearly such, as the concilium ordinarium had done with so much odium under Edw. III. and Ric. II. There may possibly be a very few instances of this before, to be traced in the early volumes of the Proceedings; but from 1540 to 1547 the course of the privy council is just like that of the star-chamber, as sir Thomas Smith intimates in the passage above quoted (p. 48); and in fact considerably more unconstitutional and dangerous, from there being no admixture of the judges to keep up some regard to law. — 1845.]

cessary to do to repress the insolency of the noblemen and gentlemen in the north parts of England, who being far from the king and the seat of justice, made almost, as it were, an ordinary war among themselves, and made their force their law, binding themselves, with their tenants and servants, to do or revenge an injury one against another as they listed. This thing seemed not supportable to the noble prince Henry VIII.; and sending for them one after another to his court, to answer before the persons before named, after they had remonstrance showed them of their evil demeanor, and been well disciplined, as well by words as by *fleeting* [confinement in the Fleet prison] a while, and thereby their pride and courage somewhat assuaged, they began to range themselves in order, and to understand that they had a prince who would rule his subjects by his law and obedience. Since that time this court has been in more estimation, and is continued to this day in manner as I have said before." [1] But, as the court erected by the statute of Henry VII. appears to have been in activity as late as the fall of cardinal Wolsey, and exercised its jurisdiction over precisely that class of offences which Smith here describes, it may perhaps be more likely that it did not wholly merge in the general body of the council till the minority of Edward, when that oligarchy became almost independent and supreme. It is obvious that most, if not all, of the judges in the court held under that statute were members of the council; so that it might, in a certain sense, be considered as a committee from that body, who had long before been wont to interfere with the punishment of similar misdemeanors. And the distinction was so soon forgotten, that the judges of the king's bench in the 13th of Elizabeth cite a case from the year-book of 8 H. 7, as "concerning the star-chamber," which related to the limited court erected by the statute.[2]

In this half-barbarous state of manners we certainly discover an apology, as well as motive, for the council's inter-

1 Commonwealth of England, book 3, c. 4. We find sir Robert Sheffield in 1517 "put into the Tower again for the complaint he made to the king of my lord Cardinal." Lodge's Illustrations, i., p. 27. See also Hall, p. 585, for Wolsey's strictness in punishing the "lords, knights and men of all sorts, for riots, bearing and maintenance."

2 Plowden's Commentaries, 393. In the year-book itself, 8 H. 7, pl. ult., the word star-chamber is not used. It is held in this case, that the chancellor, treasurer, and privy seal were the only judges, and the rest but assistants. Coke, 4 Inst. 62, denies this to be law; but on no better grounds than that the practice of the star-chamber, that is, of a different tribunal, was not such.

ference; for it is rather a servile worshipping of names than a rational love of liberty to prefer the forms of trial to the attainment of justice, or to fancy that verdicts obtained by violence or corruption are at all less iniquitous than the violent or corrupt sentences of a court. But there were many cases wherein neither the necessity of circumstances nor the legal sanction of any statute could excuse the jurisdiction habitually exercised by the court of star-chamber. Lord Bacon takes occasion from the act of Henry VII. to descant on the sage and noble institution, as he terms it, of that court whose walls had been so often witnesses to the degradation of his own mind. It took cognizance principally, he tells us, of four kinds of causes, "forces, frauds, crimes, various of stellionate, and the inchoations or middle acts towards crimes, capital or heinous, not actually committed or perpetrated."[1] Sir Thomas Smith uses expressions less indefinite than these last; and specifies scandalous reports of persons in power, and seditious news, as offences which they were accustomed to punish. We shall find abundant proofs of this department of their functions in the succeeding reigns. But this was in violation of many ancient laws, and not in the least supported by that of Henry VII.[2]

Influence of the authority of the star-chamber in enhancing the royal power.

A tribunal so vigilant and severe as that of the star-chamber, proceeding by modes of interrogatory unknown to the common law, and possessing a discretionary power of fine and imprisonment, was easily able to quell any private opposition or contumacy. We have seen how the council dealt with those who refused to lend money by way of benevolence, and with the juries who found verdicts that they disapproved. Those that did not yield obedience to their proclamations were not likely to fare better. I know not whether menaces were used towards members of the commons who took part against the crown; but it would not be unreasonable to believe it, or at least that a man of moderate

[1] Hist. of Henry VII. in Bacon's Works, ii. p. 290.

[2] The result of what has been said in the last pages may be summed up in a few propositions. 1. The court erected by the statute of 3 Henry VII., was not the court of star-chamber. 2. This court by the statute subsisted in full force till beyond the middle of Henry VIII.'s reign, but not long afterwards went into disuse. 3. The court of star-chamber was the old concilium ordinarium, against whose jurisdiction many statutes had been enacted from the time of Edward III. 4. No part of the jurisdiction exercised by the star-chamber could be maintained on the authority of the statute of Henry VII.

courage would scarcely care to expose himself to the resentment which the council might indulge after a dissolution. A knight was sent to the Tower by Mary for his conduct in parliament;[1] and Henry VIII. is reported, not, perhaps, on very certain authority, to have talked of cutting off the heads of refractory commoners.

In the persevering struggles of earlier parliaments against Edward III., Richard II., and Henry IV., it is a very probable conjecture that many considerable peers acted in union with, and encouraged the efforts of, the commons. But in the period now before us the nobility were precisely the class most deficient in that constitutional spirit which was far from being extinct in those below them. They knew what havoc had been made among their fathers by multiplied attainders during the rivalry of the two roses. They had seen terrible examples of the danger of giving umbrage to a jealous court, in the fate of lord Stanley and the duke of Buckingham, both condemned on slight evidence of treacherous friends and servants, from whom no man could be secure. Though rigor and cruelty tend frequently to overturn the government of feeble princes, it is unfortunately too true that, steadily employed and combined with vigilance and courage, they are often the safest policy of despotism. A single suspicion in the dark bosom of Henry VII., a single cloud of wayward humor in his son, would have been sufficient to send the proudest peer of England to the dungeon and the scaffold. Thus a life of eminent services in the field, and of unceasing compliance in council, could not rescue the duke of Norfolk from the effects of a dislike which we cannot even explain. Nor were the nobles of this age more held in subjection by terror than by the still baser influence of gain. Our law of forfeiture was well devised to stimulate as well as to deter; and Henry VIII., better pleased to slaughter the prey than to gorge himself with the carcass, distributed the spoils it brought him among those who had helped in the chase. The dissolution of monasteries opened a more abundant source of munificence; every courtier, every peer, looked for an increase of wealth from grants of ecclesiastical estates, and naturally thought that the king's favor would most readily be gained by an implicit conformity to his will. Nothing, how-

[1] Burnet, ii. 324.

ever, seems more to have sustained the arbitrary rule of Henry VIII. than the jealousy of the two religious parties formed in his time, and who, for all the latter years of his life, were maintaining a doubtful and emulous contest for his favor. But this religious contest, and the ultimate establishment of the reformation are events far too important, even in a constitutional history, to be treated in a cursory manner; and as, in order to avoid transitions, I have purposely kept them out of sight in the present chapter, they will form the proper subject of the next.

Tendency of religious disputes to the same end.

CHAPTER II.

ON THE ENGLISH CHURCH UNDER HENRY VIII., EDWARD VI., AND MARY.

State of Public Opinion as to Religion — Henry VIII.'s Controversy with Luther — His Divorce from Catherine — Separation from the Church of Rome — Dissolution of Monasteries — Progress of the Reformed Doctrine in England — Its Establishment under Edward — Sketch of the chief points of Difference between the two Religions — Opposition made by part of the Nation — Cranmer — His Moderation in introducing changes not acceptable to the Zealots — Mary — Persecution under her — Its effect rather favorable to Protestantism.

State of public opinion as to religion.

No revolution has ever been more gradually prepared than that which separated almost one half of Europe from the communion of the Roman see; nor were Luther and Zwingle any more than occasional instruments of that change, which, had they never existed, would at no great distance of time have been effected under the names of some other reformers. At the beginning of the sixteenth century the learned doubtfully and with caution, the ignorant with zeal and eagerness, were tending to depart from the faith and rites which authority prescribed. But probably not even Germany was so far advanced on this course as England. Almost a hundred and fifty years before Luther nearly the same doctrines as he taught had been maintained by Wicliffe, whose disciples, usually called Lollards, lasted as a numerous, though obscure and proscribed sect, till, aided by the confluence of foreign streams, they swelled into the Protestant Church of England. We hear, indeed, little of them during some part of the fifteenth century, for they generally shunned persecution; and it is chiefly through records of persecution that we learn the existence of heretics. But immediately before the name of Luther was known they seem to have become more numerous, or to have attracted more attention; since several persons were burned for heresy, and others abjured their errors, in the first years of Henry VIII.'s reign. Some of these (as usual among ignorant men engaging in religious speculations) are charged with very absurd notions; but it is not so material to observe their particular tenets as the general fact that an inquisitive and sectarian spirit had begun to prevail.

Those who took little interest in theological questions, or who retained an attachment to the faith in which they had been educated, were in general not less offended than the Lollards themselves with the inordinate opulence and encroaching temper of the clergy. It had been for two or three centuries the policy of our lawyers to restrain these within some bounds. No ecclesiastical privilege had occasioned such dispute or proved so mischievous as the immunity of all tonsured persons from civil punishment for crimes. It was a material improvement in the law under Henry VI. that, instead of being instantly claimed by the bishop on their arrest for any criminal charge, they were compelled to plead their privilege at their arraignment, or after conviction. Henry VII. carried this much farther, by enacting that clerks convicted of felony should be burned in the hand. And in 1513 (4 H. 8), the benefit of clergy was entirely taken away from murderers and highway robbers. An exemption was still preserved for priests, deacons, and subdeacons. But this was not sufficient to satisfy the church, who had been accustomed to shield under the mantle of her immunity a vast number of persons in the lower degrees of orders, or without any orders at all; and had owed no small part of her influence to those who derived so important a benefit from her protection. Hence, besides violent language in preaching against this statute, the convocation attacked one Dr. Standish, who had denied the divine right of clerks to their exemption from temporal jurisdiction. The temporal courts naturally defended Standish; and the parliament addressed the king to support him against the malice of his persecutors. Henry, after a full debate between the opposite parties in his presence, thought his prerogative concerned in taking the same side, and the clergy sustained a mortifying defeat. About the same time a citizen of London, named Hun, having been confined on a charge of heresy in the bishop's prison, was found hanged in his chamber; and though this was asserted to be his own act, yet the bishop's chancellor was indicted for the murder on such vehement presumptions that he would infallibly have been convicted, had the attorney-general thought fit to proceed in the trial. This occurring at the same time with the affair of Standish, furnished each party with an argument; for the clergy maintained that they should have no chance of justice in a temporal court; one of the bishops declaring that the London juries were so prejudiced against the church that they would find Abel guilty of the murder of Cain. Such an admission is of more consequence than whether Hun died by his own hands or those of a clergyman; and the story is chiefly worth remembering, as it illustrates the popular disposition towards those who had once been the objects of reverence.[1]

Henry VIII.'s controversy with Luther.

Such was the temper of England when Martin Luther threw down his gauntlet of defiance against the ancient hierarchy of the Catholic church. But, ripe as a great portion of the people might be to applaud the efforts of this reformer, they were viewed with no approbation by their sovereign. Henry had acquired a fair portion of theological learning, and on reading one of Luther's treatises, was not only shocked at its tenets, but undertook to refute them in a formal answer.[2] Kings who divest themselves of their robes to mingle among polemical writers have not perhaps a claim to much deference from strangers; and Luther, intoxicated with arrogance, and deeming himself a more prominent individual among the human species than any monarch, treated Henry, in replying to his book, with the rudeness that characterized his temper. A few years afterwards indeed he thought proper to write a letter of apology for the language he had held towards the king; but this letter, a strange medley of abjectness and impertinence, excited only contempt in Henry, and was published by him with a severe commentary.[3] Whatever

[1] Burnet, Reeves's History of the Law, iv. p. 308. The contemporary authority is Keilwey's Reports. Collier disbelieves the murder of Hun on the authority of sir Thomas More; but he was surely a prejudiced apologist of the clergy, and this historian is hardly less so. An entry on the journals, 7 H. 8, drawn of course by some ecclesiastic, particularly complains of Standish as the author of periculosissimæ seditiones inter clericam et secularem potestatem.

[2] Burnet is confident that the answer to Luther was not written by Henry (vol. iii. 171), and others have been of the same opinion. The king, however, in his answer to Luther's apologetical letter, where this was insinuated, declares it to be his own. From Henry's general character and proneness to theological disputation, it may be inferred that he had at least a considerable share in the work, though probably with the assistance of some who had more command of the Latin language. Burnet mentions in another place, that he had seen a copy of the Necessary Erudition of a Christian Man, full of interlineations by the king.

[3] Epist. Lutheri ad Henricum regem missa, &c. Lond. 1526. The letter bears

apprehension, therefore, for the future might be grounded on the humor of the nation, no king in Europe appeared so steadfast in his allegiance to Rome as Henry VIII. at the moment when a storm sprang up that broke the chain forever.

His divorce from Catherine.

It is certain that Henry's marriage with his brother's widow was unsupported by any precedent, and that although the pope's dispensation might pass for a cure of all defects, it had been originally considered by many persons in a very different light from those unions which are merely prohibited by the canons. He himself, on coming to the age of fourteen, entered a protest against the marriage which had been celebrated more than two years before, and declared his intention not to confirm it; an act which must naturally be ascribed to his father.[1] It is true that in this very instrument we find no mention of the impediment on the score of affinity; yet it is hard to suggest any other objection, and possibly a common form had been adopted in drawing up the protest. He did not cohabit with Catherine during his father's lifetime. Upon his own accession he was remarried to her; and it does not appear manifest at what time his scruples began, nor whether they preceded his passion for Anne Boleyn.[2]

date at Wittenberg, Sept. 1, 1525. It had no relation, therefore, to Henry's quarrel with the pope, though probably Luther imagined that the king was becoming more favorably disposed. After saying that he had written against the king, "stultus ac præceps," which was true, he adds, "invitantibus iis qui majestati tuæ parum favebant," which was surely a pretence; since who, at Wittenberg, in 1521, could have any motive to wish that Henry should be so scurrilously treated? He then bursts out into the most absurd attack on Wolsey; "illud monstrum et publicum odium Dei et hominum, Cardinalis Eboracensis, pestis illa regni tui." This was a singular style to adopt in writing to a king, whom he affected to propitiate; Wolsey being nearer than any man to Henry's heart. Thence relapsing into his tone of abasement, he says, "ita ut vehementer nunc pudefactus, metuam oculos coram majestate tuâ levare, qui passus sim levitate istâ me moveri in talem tantumque regem per malignos istos operarios; præsertim cum sim fæx et vermis, quem solo contemptu oportuit victum aut neglectum esse," &c. Among the many strange things which Luther said and wrote, I know not one more extravagant than this letter, which almost justifies the supposition that there was a vein of insanity in his very remarkable character.

[1] Collier, vol. ii. Appendix, No. 2. In the Hardwicke Papers, i. 13, we have an account of the ceremonial of the first marriage of Henry with Catherine in 1503. It is remarkable that a person was appointed to object publicly in Latin to the marriage as unlawful, for reasons he should there exhibit; "whereunto Mr. Doctor Barnes shall reply, and declare solemnly, also in Latin, the said marriage to be good and effectual in the law of Christ's church, by virtue of a dispensation, which he shall have then to be openly read." There seems to be something in this of the tortuous policy of Henry VII.; but it shows that the marriage had given offence to scrupulous minds.

[2] See Burnet, Lingard, Turner, and the letters lately printed in State Papers, temp. Henry VIII. pp. 194, 196

This, however, seems the more probable supposition; yet there can be little doubt that weariness of Catherine's person, a woman considerably older than himself, and unlikely to bear more children, had a far greater effect on his conscience than the study of Thomas Aquinas or any other theologian. It by no means follows from hence that, according to the casuistry of the Catholic church and the principles of the canon law, the merits of that famous process were so much against Henry, as, out of dislike to him and pity for his queen, we are apt to imagine, and as the writers of that persuasion have subsequently assumed.

It would be unnecessary to repeat what is told by so many historians, the vacillating and evasive behavior of Clement VII., the assurances he gave the king, and the arts with which he receded from them, the unfinished trial in England before his delegates, Campeggio and Wolsey, the opinions obtained from foreign universities in the king's favor, not always without a little bribery,[1] and those of the same import at home, not given without a little intimidation, or the tedious continuance of the process after its adjournment to Rome. More than five years had elapsed from the first application to the pope, before Henry, though by nature the most uncontrollable of mankind, though irritated by perpetual chicanery and breach of promise, though stimulated by impatient love, presumed to set at nought the jurisdiction to which he had submitted, by a marriage with Anne. Even this was a furtive step; and it was not till compelled by the consequences that he avowed her as his wife, and was finally divorced from Catherine by a sentence of nullity, which would more decently no doubt have preceded his second marriage.[2] But, determined as his mind had become, it was

1 Burnet wishes to disprove the bribery of these foreign doctors. But there are strong presumptions that some opinions were got by money (Collier, ii. 58); and the greatest difficulty was found, where corruption perhaps had least influence, in the Sorbonne. Burnet himself proves that some of the cardinals were bribed by the king's ambassador, both in 1528 and 1532. Vol. i. Append. pp. 30, 110. See, too, Strype, i. Append. No. 40.

The same writer will not allow that Henry menaced the university of Oxford in case of non-compliance; yet there are three letters of his to them, a tenth part of which, considering the nature of the writer, was enough to terrify his readers. Vol. iii. Append. p. 25. These probably Burnet did not know when he published his first volume.

2 The king's marriage is related by the earlier historians to have taken place Nov. 14, 1532. Burnet, however, is convinced by a letter of Cranmer, who, he says, could not be mistaken, though he was not apprised of the fact till some time afterwards, that it was not solemnized till about the 25th of January (vol. iii. p. 70). This letter has since been published in the Archæologia, vol. xviii., and in Ellis's Letters, ii. 34. Elizabeth was born September 7, 1533,

plainly impossible for Clement to have conciliated him by anything short of a decision which he could not utter without the loss of the emperor's favor, and the ruin of his own family's interests in Italy. And even for less selfish reasons it was an extremely embarrassing measure for the pope, in the critical circumstances of that age, to set aside a dispensation granted by his predecessor; knowing that, however some erroneous allegations of fact contained therein might serve for an outward pretext, yet the principle on which the divorce was commonly supported in Europe went generally to restrain the dispensing power of the holy see. Hence it may seem very doubtful whether the treaty which was afterwards partially renewed through the mediation of Francis I., during his interview with the pope at Nice about the end of 1533, could have led to a restoration of amity through the only possible means; when we consider the weight of the imperial party in the conclave, the discredit that so notorious a submission would have thrown on the church, and, above all, the precarious condition of the Medici at Florence in case of a rupture with Charles V. It was more probably the aim of Clement to delude Henry once more by his promises; but this was prevented by the more violent measure into which the cardinals forced him, of a definitive sentence in favor of Catherine, whom the king was required under pain of excommunication to take back as his wife. This sentence of the 23d of March, 1534, proved a declaration of interminable war; and the king, who, in consequence of the hopes held out to him by Francis, had already despatched an envoy to Rome with his submission to what the pope should decide, now resolved to break off all intercourse forever, and trust to his own prerogative and power over his subjects for

for though Burnet, on the authority, he says, of Cranmer, places her birth on Sept. 14, the former date is decisively confirmed by letters in Harl. MSS. vol. CCLXXXIII. 22, and vol. DCCLXXXVII. 1. (both set down incorrectly in the catalogue). If a late historian therefore had contented himself with commenting on these dates and the clandestine nature of the marriage, he would not have gone beyond the limits of that character of an advocate for one party which he has chosen to assume. It may not be unlikely, though by no means evident, that Anne's prudence, though, as Fuller says of her, "she was cunning in her chastity," was surprised at the end of this long courtship. I think a prurient curiosity about such obsolete scandal very unworthy of history. But when this author asserts Henry to have cohabited with her for three years, and repeatedly calls her his mistress, when he attributes Henry's patience with the pope's chicanery to "the infecundity of Anne," and all this on no other authority than a letter of the French ambassador, which amounts hardly to evidence of a transient rumor, we cannot but complain of a great deficiency in historical candor.

securing the succession to the crown in the line which he designed. It was doubtless a regard to this consideration that put him upon his last overtures for an amicable settlement with the court of Rome.[1]

But long before this final cessation of intercourse with that court, Henry had entered upon a course of measures which would have opposed fresh obstacles to a renewal of the connection. He had found a great part of his subjects in a disposition to go beyond all he could wish in sustaining his quarrel, not in this instance from mere terror, but because a jealousy of ecclesiastical power and of the Roman court had long been a sort of national sentiment in England. The pope's avocation of the process to Rome, by which his duplicity and alienation from the king's side were made evident, and the disgrace of Wolsey, took place in the summer of 1529. The parliament which met soon afterwards was continued through several sessions (an unusual circumstance), till it completed the separation of this kingdom from the supremacy of Rome. In the progress of ecclesiastical usurpation, the papal and episcopal powers had lent mutual support to each other; both consequently were involved in the same

[1] The principal authority on the story of Henry's divorce from Catherine is Burnet, in the first and third volumes of his History of the Reformation; the latter correcting the former from additional documents. Strype, in his Ecclesiastical Memorials, adds some particulars not contained in Burnet, especially as to the negotiations with the pope in 1528; and a very little may be gleaned from Collier, Carte, and other writers. There are few parts of history, on the whole, that have been better elucidated. One exception perhaps may yet be made. The beautiful and affecting story of Catherine's behavior before the legates at Dunstable is told by Cavendish and Hall, from whom later historians have copied it. Burnet, however, in his third volume, p. 46, disputes its truth, and on what should seem conclusive authority, that of the original register, from which it appears that the queen never came into court but once, June 18, 1529, to read a paper protesting against the jurisdiction, and that the king never entered it. Carte accordingly treated the story as a fabrication. Hume of course did not choose to omit so interesting a circumstance; but Dr. Lingard has pointed out a letter of the king, which Burnet himself had printed, vol. i. Append. 78, mentioning the queen's presence as well as his own, on June 21, and greatly corroborating the popular account. To say the truth, there is no small difficulty in choosing between two authorities so considerable, if they cannot be reconciled, which seems impossible; but, upon the whole, the preference is due to Henry's letter, dated June 23, as he could not be mistaken, and had no motive to misstate.

This is not altogether immaterial; for Catherine's appeal to Henry, de integritate corporis usque ad secundas nuptias servatâ, without reply on his part, is an important circumstance as to that part of the question. It is, however, certain, that, whether on this occasion or not, she did constantly declare this; and the evidence adduced to prove the contrary is very defective, especially as opposed to the assertion of so virtuous a woman. Dr. Lingard says that all the favorable answers which the king obtained from foreign universities went upon the supposition that the former marriage had been consummated, and were of no avail unless that could be proved. See a letter of Wolsey to the king, July 1, 1527, printed in State Papers, temp. Henry VIII. p. 194; whence it appears that the queen had been consistent in her denial.

odium, and had become the object of restrictions in a similar spirit. Warm attacks were made on the clergy by speeches in the commons, which bishop Fisher severely reprehended in the upper house. This provoked the commons to send a complaint to the king by their speaker, demanding reparation; and Fisher explained away the words that had given offence. An act passed to limit the fees on probates of wills, a mode of ecclesiastical extortion much complained of, and upon mortuaries.[1] The next proceeding was of a far more serious nature. It was pretended that Wolsey's exercise of authority as papal legate contravened a statute of Richard II., and that both himself and the whole body of the clergy, by their submission to him, had incurred the penalties of a præmunire, that is, the forfeiture of their movable estate, besides imprisonment at discretion. These old statutes in restraint of the papal jurisdiction had been so little regarded, and so many legates had acted in England without objection, that Henry's prosecution of the church on this occasion was extremely harsh and unfair. The clergy, however, now felt themselves to be the weaker party. In convocation they implored the king's clemency, and obtained it by paying a large sum of money. In their petition he was styled the protector and supreme head of the church and clergy of England. Many of that body were staggered at the unexpected introduction of a title that seemed to strike at the supremacy they had always acknowledged in the Roman see. And in the end it passed only with a very suspicious qualification, "so far as is permitted by the law of Christ." Henry had previously given the pope several intimations that he could proceed in his divorce without him. For, besides a strong remonstrance by letter from the temporal peers as well as bishops against the procrastination of sentence in so just a suit, the opinions of English and foreign universities had been laid before both houses of parliament and of convocation, and the divorce approved without difficulty in the former, and by a great majority in the latter. These proceedings took place in the first months of 1531, while the king's ambassadors at Rome were still pressing for a favorable sentence, though with diminished hopes. Next year the annates,

[1] Stat. 21 Hen. 8, cc. 5, 6; Strype, i. 73; Burnet, 83. It cost a thousand marks to prove Sir William Compton's will in 1528. These exactions had been much augmented by Wolsey, who interfered, as legate, with the prerogative court.

or first fruits of benefices, a constant source of discord between the nations of Europe and their spiritual chief, were taken away by act of parliament; but with a remarkable condition, that if the pope would either abolish the payment of annates, or reduce them to a moderate burden, the king might declare before the next session, by letters patent, whether this act, or any part of it, should be observed. It was accordingly confirmed by letters patent more than a year after it received the royal assent.

It is difficult for us to determine whether the pope, by conceding to Henry the great object of his solicitude, could in this stage have not only arrested the progress of the schism, but recovered his former ascendency over the English church and kingdom. But probably he could not have done so in its full extent. Sir Thomas More, who had rather complied than concurred with the proceedings for a divorce (though his acceptance of the great seal on Wolsey's disgrace would have been inconsistent with his character, had he been altogether opposed in conscience to the king's measures), now thought it necessary to resign, when the papal authority was steadily, though gradually, assailed.[1] In the next session an act was passed to take away all appeals to Rome from ecclesiastical courts, which annihilated at one stroke the jurisdiction built on long usage and on the authority of the false decretals. This law rendered the king's second marriage, which had preceded it, secure from being annulled by the papal court. Henry, however, still advanced very cautiously, and on the death of Warham, archbishop of Canterbury, not long before this time, applied to Rome for the usual bulls in behalf of Cranmer, whom he

1 It is hard to say what were More's original sentiments about the divorce. In a letter to Cromwell (Strype, i. 183, and App. No. 48; Burnet, App. p. 280) he speaks of himself as always doubtful. But if his disposition had not been rather favorable to the king, would he have been offered, or have accepted, the great seal? We do not indeed find his name in the letter of remonstrance to the pope, signed by the nobility and chief commoners in 1530, which Wolsey, though then in disgrace, very willingly subscribed. But in March, 1531, he went down to the house of commons, attended by several lords, to declare the king's scruples about his marriage, and to lay before them the opinions of universities. In this he perhaps thought himself acting ministerially. But there can be no doubt that he always considered the divorce as a matter wholly of the pope's competence, and which no other party could take out of his hands, though he had gone along cheerfully, as Burnet says, with the prosecution against the clergy, and wished to cut off the illegal jurisdiction of the Roman see. The king did not look upon him as hostile; for even so late as 1532, Dr. Bennet, the envoy at Rome, proposed to the pope that the cause should be tried by four commissioners, of whom the king should name one, either sir Thomas More, or Stokesly, bishop of London. Burnet, i. 126.

nominated to the vacant see. These were the last bulls obtained, and probably the last instance of any exercise of the papal supremacy in this reign. An act followed in the next session, that bishops elected by their chapter on a royal recommendation should be consecrated, and archbishops receive the pall, without suing for the pope's bulls. All dispensations and licenses hitherto granted by that court were set aside by another statute, and the power of issuing them in lawful cases transferred to the archbishop of Canterbury. The king is in this act recited to be the supreme head of the church of England, as the clergy had two years before acknowledged in convocation. But this title was not formally declared by parliament to appertain to the crown till the ensuing session of parliament.[1]

Separation from the Church of Rome.

By these means was the church of England altogether emancipated from the superiority of that of Rome. For as to the pope's merely spiritual primacy and authority in matters of faith, which are, or at least were, defended by Catholics of the Gallican or Cisalpine school on quite different grounds from his jurisdiction or his legislative power in points of discipline, they seem to have attracted little peculiar attention at the time, and to have dropped off as a dead branch, when the axe had lopped the fibres that gave it nourishment. Like other momentous revolutions this divided the judgment and feelings of the nation. In the previous affair of Catherine's divorce, generous minds were more influenced by the rigor and indignity of her treatment than by the king's inclinations, or the venal opinions of foreign doctors in law. Bellay, bishop of Bayonne, the French ambassador at London, wrote home in 1528 that a revolt was apprehended from the general unpopularity of the divorce.[2] Much difficulty was found in procuring the judgments of Oxford and Cambridge against the marriage; which was effected in the former case, as is said,

[1] Dr. Lingard has pointed out, as Burnet had done less distinctly, that the bill abrogating the papal supremacy was brought into the commons in the beginning of March, and received the royal assent on the 30th; whereas the determination of the conclave at Rome against the divorce was on the 23d; so that the latter could not have been the cause of this final rupture. Clement VII. might have been outwitted in his turn by the king, if, after pronouncing a decree in favor of the divorce, he had found it too late to regain his jurisdiction in England. On the other hand, so flexible were the parliaments of this reign, that if Henry had made terms with the pope, the supremacy might have revived again as easily as it had been extinguished.

[2] Burnet, iii. 44, and App. 24.

by excluding the masters of arts, the younger and less worldly part of the university, from their right of suffrage. Even so late as 1532, in the pliant house of commons a member had the boldness to move an address to the king that he would take back his wife. [And this temper of the people seems to have been the great inducement with Henry to postpone any sentence by a domestic jurisdiction, so long as a chance of the pope's sanction remained.]

The aversion entertained by a large part of the community, and especially of the clerical order, towards the divorce, was not perhaps so generally founded upon motives of justice and compassion as on the obvious tendency which its prosecution latterly manifested to bring about a separation from Rome. Though the principal Lutherans of Germany were far less favorably disposed to the king in their opinions on this subject than the catholic theologians, holding that the prohibition of marrying a brother's widow in the Levitical law was not binding on Christians, or at least that the marriage ought not to be annulled after so many years' continuance,[1] yet in England the interests of Anne Boleyn and of the Reformation were considered as the same. She was herself strongly suspected of an inclination to the new tenets; and her friend Cranmer had been the most active person both in promoting the divorce and the recognition of the king's supremacy. [The latter was, as I imagine, by no

[1] Conf. Burnet, i. 94, and App. No. 35; Strype, i. 230; Sleidan, Hist. de la Réformation, par Courayer, l. 10. The notions of these divines, as here stated, are not very consistent or intelligible. The Swiss reformers were in favor of the divorce, though they advised that the princess Mary should not be declared illegitimate. Luther seems to have inclined towards compromising the difference by the marriage of a secondary wife. Lingard, p. 172. Melancthon, this writer says, was of the same opinion. Burnet indeed denies this; but it is rendered not improbable by the well-authenticated fact that these divines, together with Bucer, signed a permission to the landgrave of Hesse to take a wife or concubine, on account of the drunkenness and disagreeable person of his landgravine. Bossuet, Hist. des Var. des Egl. Protest. vol. i., where the instrument is published. [Cranmer, it is just to say, remonstrated with Osiander on this permission, and on the general laxity of the Lutherans in matrimonial questions. Jenkins's edition, i. 303.] Clement VII., however, recommended the king to marry immediately, and then prosecute his suit for a divorce, which it would be easier for him to obtain in such circumstances. This was as early as January, 1528. (Burnet, i. App. p. 27.) But at a much later period, September, 1530, he expressly suggested the expedient of allowing the king to retain two wives. Though the letter of Cassali, the king's ambassador at Rome, containing this proposition, was not found by Burnet, it is quoted at length by an author of unquestionable veracity, lord Herbert. Henry had himself, at one time, favored this scheme, according to Burnet, who does not, however, produce any authority for the instructions to that effect said to have been given to Brian and Vannes, despatched to Rome at the end of 1528. But at the time when the pope made this proposal, the king had become exasperated against Catherine, and little inclined to treat either her or the holy see with any respect.

means unacceptable to the nobility and gentry, who saw in it the only effectual method of cutting off the papal exactions that had so long impoverished the realm; nor yet to the citizens of London and other large towns, who, with the same dislike of the Roman court, had begun to acquire some taste for the Protestant doctrine.] But the common people, especially in remote countries, had been used to an implicit reverence for the holy see, and had suffered comparatively little by its impositions. They looked up also to their own teachers as guides in faith; and the main body of the clergy were certainly very reluctant to tear themselves at the pleasure of a disappointed monarch, in the most dangerous crisis of religion, from the bosom of catholic unity.[1] They complied indeed with all the measures of government far more than men of rigid conscience could have endured to do; but many, who wanted the courage of More and Fisher, were not far removed from their way of thinking.[2] This repugnance to so great an alteration showed itself above all in the monastic orders, some of whom by wealth, hospitality, and long-established dignity, others by activity in preaching and confessing, enjoyed a very considerble influence over the poorer class. But they had to deal with a sovereign whose policy as well as temper dictated that he had no safety but in advancing; and their disaffection to his government, while it overwhelmed them in ruin, produced a second grand innovation in the ecclesiastical polity of England.

Dissolution of monasteries.

The enormous, and in a great measure ill-gotten, opulence of the regular clergy had long since excited jealousy in every part of Europe. Though the statutes of mortmain under Edward I. and Edward III. had put some obstacle to its increase, yet, as these were eluded by licenses of alienation, a larger proportion of landed wealth was constantly accumulating in hands which lost nothing that they had grasped.[3] A writer much inclined to partiality tow-

[1] Strype, i. 151 et alibi.

[2] Strype, passim. Tunstal, Gardiner, and Bonner wrote in favor of the royal supremacy; all of them, no doubt, insincerely. The first of these has escaped severe censure by the mildness of his general character, but was full as much a temporizer as Cranmer. But the history of this period has been written with such undisguised partiality by Burnet and Strype on the one hand, and lately by Dr. Lingard on the other, that it is almost amusing to find the most opposite conclusions and general results from nearly the same premises. Collier, though with many prejudices of his own, is, all things considered, the fairest of our ecclesiastical writers as to this reign.

[3] Burnet, 188. For the methods by which the regulars acquired wealth, fair

ards the monasteries says that they held not one fifth part of the kingdom; no insignificant patrimony! He adds, what may probably be true, that through granting easy leases they did not enjoy more than one tenth in value.[1] These vast possessions were very unequally distributed among four or five hundred monasteries. Some abbots, as those of Reading, Glastonbury, and Battle, lived in princely splendor, and were in every sense the spiritual peers and magnates of the realm. In other foundations the revenues did little more than afford a subsistence for the monks, and defray the needful expenses. As they were in general exempted from episcopal visitation, and intrusted with the care of their own discipline, such abuses had gradually prevailed and gained strength by connivance, as we may naturally expect in corporate bodies of men leading almost of necessity useless and indolent lives, and in whom very indistinct views of moral obligations were combined with a great facility of violating them. The vices that for many ages had been supposed to haunt the monasteries had certainly not left their precincts in that of Henry VIII. Wolsey, as papal legate, at the instigation of Fox, bishop of Hereford, a favorer of the Reformation, commenced a visitation of the professed as well as secular clergy in 1523, in consequence of the general complaint against their manners.[2] This great minister, though not perhaps very rigid as to the morality of the church, was the first who set an example of reforming monastic foundations in the most efficacious manner, by converting their revenues to different purposes. Full of anxious zeal for promoting education, the noblest part of his character, he obtained bulls from Rome suppressing many convents (among which was that of St. Frideswide at Oxford), in order to erect and endow a new college in that university, his favorite work, which after his fall was more completely established by the name of Christ Church.[3] A few more were afterwards extinguished through his instigation; and thus the prejudice against interference with this species of property was somewhat worn off, and men's minds gradually

and unfair, I may be allowed to refer to the View of the Middle Ages, ch. 7, or rather to the sources from which the sketch there given was derived.

1 Harmer's Specimens of Errors in Burnet.

2 Strype, i. App. 19.

3 Burnet; Strype. Wolsey alleged as the ground for this suppression, the great wickedness that prevailed therein. Strype says the number was twenty; but Collier, ii. 19, reckons them at forty.

prepared for the sweeping confiscations of Cromwell. The king indeed was abundantly willing to replenish his exchequer by violent means, and to avenge himself on those who gainsayed his supremacy; but it was this able statesman who, prompted both by the natural appetite of ministers for the subject's money, and, as has been generally surmised, by a secret partiality towards the Reformation, devised and carried on with complete success, if not with the utmost prudence, a measure of no inconsiderable hazard and difficulty. For such it surely was under a system of government which rested so much on antiquity, and in spite of the peculiar sacredness which the English attach to all freehold property, to annihilate so many prescriptive baronial tenures, the possessors whereof composed more than a third part of the house of lords, and to subject so many estates which the law had rendered inalienable, to maxims of escheat and forfeiture that had never been held applicable to their tenure. But for this purpose it was necessary, by exposing the gross corruptions of monasteries, both to intimidate the regular clergy and to excite popular indignation against them. It is not to be doubted that in the visitation of these foundations under the direction of Cromwell, as lord vicegerent of the king's ecclesiastical supremacy, many things were done in an arbitrary manner, and much was unfairly represented.[1] Yet the reports of these visitors are so minute and specific that it is rather a preposterous degree of incredulity to reject their testimony whenever it bears hard on the regulars. It is always to be remembered that the vices to which they bear witness are not only probable from the nature of such foundations, but are imputed to them by the most respectable writers of preceding ages. Nor do I find that the reports of this visitation were impeached for general falsehood in that age, whatever exaggeration there might be in particular cases. And surely the commendation bestowed on some religious houses as pure and unexceptionable, may afford a presumption that the censure of others was not an indiscriminate prejudging of their merits.[2]

[1] Collier, though not implicitly to be trusted, tells some hard truths, and charges Cromwell with receiving bribes from several abbeys, in order to spare them, p. 159. This is repeated by Lingard, on the authority of some Cottonian manuscripts. Even Burnet speaks of the violent proceedings of a doctor Loudon towards the monasteries. This man was of infamous character, and became afterwards a conspirator against Cranmer and a persecutor of protestants.

[2] Burnet, 190; Strype, i. ch. 35, see especially p. 257; Ellis's Letters, ii. 71.

The dread of these visitors soon induced a number of abbots to make surrenders to the king; a step of very questionable legality. But in the next session the smaller convents whose revenues were less than 200*l.* a year, were suppressed by act of parliament to the number of three hundred and seventy-six, and their estates vested in the crown. This summary spoliation led to the great northern rebellion soon afterwards. It was, in fact, not merely to wound the people's strongest impressions of religion, and especially those connected with their departed friends for whose souls prayers were offered in the monasteries, but to deprive the indigent in many places of succor, and the better rank of hospitable reception. This of course was experienced in a far greater degree at the dissolution of the larger monasteries, which took place in 1540. But, Henry having entirely subdued the rebellion, and being now exceedingly dreaded by both the religious parties, this measure produced no open resistance, though there seems to have been less pretext for it on the score of immorality and neglect of discipline than was found for abolishing the smaller convents.[1] These great foundations were all surrendered; a few excepted, which, against every principle of received law, were held to fall by the attainder of their abbots for high treason.

We should be on our guard against the Romanizing high-church men, such as Collier, and the whole class of antiquaries, Wood, Hearne, Drake, Browne, Willis, &c., &c., who are, with hardly an exception, partial to the monastic orders, and sometimes scarce keep on the mask of protestantism. No one fact can be better supported by current opinion, and that general testimony which carries conviction, than the relaxed and vicious state of those foundations for many ages before their fall. Ecclesiastical writers had not then learned, as they have since, the trick of suppressing what might excite odium against their church, but speak out boldly and bitterly. Thus we find in Wilkins, iii. 630, a bull of Innocent VIII. for the reform of monasteries in England, charging many of them with dissoluteness of life. And this is followed by a severe monition from archbishop Morton to the abbot of St. Alban's, imputing all kinds of scandalous vices to him and his monks. Those who reject at once the reports of Henry's visitors, will do well to consider this. See also Fosbrook's British Monachism, passim. [The "Letters relating to the Suppression of Monasteries," published by the Camden Society, and edited by Mr. Thomas Wright, 1843, contain a part only of extant documents illustrative of this great transaction. There seems no reason for setting aside their evidence as wholly false, though some lovers of monachism raised a loud clamor at their publication. 1845.]

[1] The preamble of 27 H. 8, c. 28, which gives the smaller monasteries to the king, after reciting that "manifest sin, vicious, carnal and abominable living, is daily used and committed commonly in such little and small abbeys, priories, and other religious houses of monks, canons, and nuns, where the congregation of such religious persons is under the number of twelve persons," bestows praise on many of the greater foundations, and certainly does not intimate that their fate was so near at hand. Nor is any misconduct alleged or insinuated against the greater monasteries in the act 31 H. 8, c. 13, that abolishes them; which is rather more remarkable, as in some instances the religious had been induced to confess their evil lives and ill deserts. Burnet, 236.

Parliament had only to confirm the king's title arising out of these surrenders and forfeitures. Some historians assert the monks to have been turned adrift with a small sum of money. But it rather appears that they generally received pensions not inadequate, and which are said to have been pretty faithfully paid.[1] These however were voluntary gifts on the part of the crown. For the parliament which dissolved the monastic foundations, while it took abundant care to preserve any rights of property which private persons might enjoy over the estates thus escheated to the crown, vouchsafed not a word towards securing the slightest compensation to the dispossessed owners.

The fall of the mitred abbots changed the proportions of the two estates which constitute the upper house of parliament. Though the number of abbots and priors to whom writs of summons were directed varied considerably in different parliaments, they always, joined to the twenty-one bishops, preponderated over the temporal peers.[2] It was no longer possible for the prelacy to offer an efficacious opposition to the reformation they abhorred. Their own baronial tenure, their high dignity as legislative councillors of the land, remained; but, one branch as ancient and venerable as their own thus lopped off, the spiritual aristocracy was reduced to play a very secondary part in the councils of the nation. Nor could the Protestant religion have easily been

1 Id. ibid. and Append. p. 151; Collier, 167. The pensions to the superiors of the dissolved greater monasteries, says a writer not likely to spare Henry's government, appear to have varied from 266*l.* to 6*l.* per annum. The priors of cells received generally 13*l.* A few, whose services had merited the distinction, obtained 20*l.* To the other monks were allotted pensions of six, four, or two pounds, with a small sum to each at his departure, to provide for his immediate wants. The pensions to nuns averaged about 4*l.* Lingard, vi. 341. He admits that these were ten times their present value in money; and surely they were not unreasonably small. Compare them with those, generally and justly thought munificent, which this country bestows on her veterans of Chelsea and Greenwich. The monks had no right to expect more than the means of that hard fare to which they ought by their rules to have been confined in the convents. The whole revenues were not to be shared among them as private property. It cannot of course be denied that the compulsory change of life was to many a severe and an unmerited hardship; but no great revolution, and the Reformation as little as any, could be achieved without much private suffering.

2 The abbots sat till the end of the first session of Henry's sixth parliament, the act extinguishing them not having passed till the last day. In the next session they do not appear, the writ of summons not being supposed to give them personal seats. There are indeed so many parallel instances among spiritual lords, and the principle is so obvious, that it would not be worth noticing, but for a strange doubt said to be thrown out by some legal authorities, near the beginning of George III.'s reign, in the case of Pearce, bishop of Rochester, whether, after resigning his see, he would not retain his seat as a lord of parliament; in consequence of which his resignation was not accepted.

established by legal methods under Edward and Elizabeth without this previous destruction of the monasteries. Those who, professing an attachment to that religion, have swollen the clamor of its adversaries against the dissolution of foundations that existed only for the sake of a different faith and worship, seem to me not very consistent or enlightened reasoners. In some the love of antiquity produces a sort of fanciful illusion; and the very sight of those buildings, so magnificent in their prosperous hour, so beautiful even in their present ruin, begets a sympathy for those who founded and inhabited them. In many, the violent courses of confiscation and attainder which accompanied this great revolution excite so just an indignation, that they either forget to ask whether the end might not have been reached by more laudable means, or condemn that end itself either as sacrilege, or at least as an atrocious violation of the rights of property. Others again, who acknowledge that the monastic discipline cannot be reconciled with the modern system of religion, or with public utility, lament only that these ample endowments were not bestowed upon ecclesiastical corporations, freed from the monkish cowl, but still belonging to that spiritual profession to whose use they were originally consecrated. And it was a very natural theme of complaint at the time, that such abundant revenues as might have sustained the dignity of the crown and supplied the means of public defence without burdening the subject, had served little other purpose than that of swelling the fortunes of rapacious courtiers, and had left the king as necessitous and craving as before.

Notwithstanding these various censures, I must own myself of opinion, both that the abolition of monastic institutions might have been conducted in a manner consonant to justice as well as policy, and that Henry's profuse alienation of the abbey lands, however illaudable in its motive, has proved upon the whole more beneficial to England than any other disposition would have turned out. I cannot, until some broad principle is made more obvious than it ever has yet been, do such violence to all common notions on the subject, as to attach an equal inviolability to private and corporate property. The law of hereditary succession, as ancient and universal as that of property itself, the law of testamentary disposition, the complement of the former, so long established in most countries as to seem a natural right, have invested the individual possessor of the soil with such a fictitious immortality, such anticipated enjoyment, as it were, of futurity, that his perpetual ownership could not be limited to the term of his own existence, without what he would justly feel as a real deprivation of property. Nor are the expectancies of children, or other probable heirs, less real possessions, which it is a hardship, if not an absolute injury, to defeat. Yet even this hereditary claim is set aside by the laws of forfeiture, which have almost everywhere prevailed. But in estates held, as we call it, in mortmain, there is no intercommunity, no natural privity of interest, between the present possessor and those who may succeed him; and as the former cannot have any pretext for complaint, if, his own rights being preserved, the legislature should alter the course of transmission after his decease, so neither is any hardship sustained by others, unless their succession has been already designated or rendered probable. Corporate property therefore appears to stand on a very different footing from that of private individuals; and while all infringements of the established privileges of the latter are to be sedulously avoided, and held justifiable only by the strongest motives of public expediency, we cannot but admit the full right of the legislature to new-mould and regulate the former, in all that does not involve existing interests, upon far slighter reasons of convenience. If Henry had been content with prohibiting the profession of religious persons for the future, and had gradually diverted their revenues instead of violently confiscating them, no Protestant could have found it easy to censure his policy.

It is indeed impossible to feel too much indignation at the spirit in which these proceedings were conducted. Besides the hardship sustained by so many persons turned loose upon society, for whose occupations they were unfit, the indiscriminate destruction of convents produced several public mischiefs. The visitors themselves strongly interceded for the nunnery of Godstow, as irreproachably managed, and an excellent place of education; and no doubt some other foundations should have been preserved for the same reason. Latimer, who could not have a prejudice on that side, begged earnestly that the priory of Malvern might be spared for the maintenance of preaching and hospitality. It was urged for Hexham abbey that, there not being a house for many miles in that part of England, the country would be in danger of going to waste.[1] And the total want of inns in many parts of the kingdom must have rendered the loss of these hospitable places of reception a serious grievance. These, and probably other reasons, ought to have checked the destroying spirit of reform in its career, and suggested to Henry's counsellors, that a few years would not be ill consumed in contriving new methods of attaining the beneficial effects which monastic institutions had not failed to produce, and in preparing the people's minds for so important an innovation.

The suppression of monasteries poured in an instant such a torrent of wealth upon the crown as has seldom been equalled in any country by the confiscations following a subdued rebellion. The clear yearly value was rated at 131,607*l.*; but was in reality, if we believe Burnet, ten times as great; the courtiers undervaluing those estates in order to obtain grants or sales of them more easily. It is certain, however, that Burnet's supposition errs extravagantly on the other side.[2] The movables of the smaller monasteries alone were reckoned at 100,000*l.*; and as the rents of these were less than a fourth of the whole, we may calculate the aggregate value of movable wealth in the same proportion. All this was enough to dazzle a more prudent mind than that of Henry, and to inspire those sanguine dreams of inexhaustible affluence with which private men are so often filled by sudden prosperity.

The monastic rule of life being thus abrogated, as neither conformable to pure religion nor to policy, it is to be considered to what uses these immense endowments ought to have been applied. [There are some, perhaps, who may be of opinion that the original founders of monasteries, or those who had afterwards bestowed lands on them, having annexed to their grants an implied condition of the continuance of

[1] Burnet, i.; Append. 96.

[2] P. 268. Dr. Lingard, on the authority of Nasmith's edition of Tanner's Notitia Monastica, puts the annual revenue of all the monastic houses at 142,914*l.* This would only be one twentieth part of the rental of the kingdom, if Hume were right in estimating that at three millions. But this is certainly by much too high. The author of Harmer's Observations on Burnet, as I have mentioned above, says the monks will be found not to have possessed above one fifth of the kingdom; and in value, by reason of their long leases, not one tenth. But, on this supposition, the crown's gain was enormous.

According to a valuation in Speed's Catalogue of Religious Houses, apud Collier, Append. p. 34, sixteen mitred abbots had revenues above 1000*l.* per annum. St. Peter's, Westminster, was the richest, and valued at 3977*l.*, Glastonbury at 3508*l.*, St. Alban's at 2510*l.*, &c.

certain devotional services, and especially of prayers for the repose of their souls, it were but equitable that, if the legislature rendered the performance of this condition impossible, their heirs should reënter upon the lands that would not have been alienated from them on any other account. But, without adverting to the difficulty in many cases of ascertaining the lawful heir, it might be answered that the donors had absolutely divested themselves of all interest in their grants, and that it was more consonant to the analogy of law to treat these estates as escheats or vacant possessions, devolving to the sovereign, than to imagine a right of reversion that no party had ever contemplated. There was indeed a class of persons very different from the founders of monasteries, to whom restitution was due. A large proportion of conventual revenues arose out of parochial tithes, diverted from the legitimate object of maintaining the incumbent to swell the pomp of some remote abbot. These impropriations were in no one instance, I believe, restored to the parochial clergy, and have passed either into the hands of laymen, or of bishops and other ecclesiastical persons, who were frequently compelled by the Tudor princes to take them in exchange for lands.[1] It was not in the spirit of Henry's policy, or in that of the times, to preserve much of these revenues to the church, though he had designed to allot 18,000*l.* a year for eighteen new sees, of which he only erected six with far inferior endowments. Nor was he much better inclined to husband them for public exigencies, although more than sufficient to make the crown independent of parliamentary aid. It may perhaps be reckoned a providential circumstance, that his thoughtless humor should have rejected the obvious means of establishing an uncontrollable despotism, by rendering unnecessary the only exertion of power which his subjects were likely to withstand. Henry VII. would probably have followed a very different course. Large sums, however, are said to have been expended in the repair of highways, and in fortifying ports in

[1] An act entitling the queen to take into her hands, on the avoidance of any bishopric, so much of the lands belonging to it as should be equal in value to the impropriate rectories, &c. within the same, belonging to the crown, and to give the latter in exchange, was made (1 Eliz. c. 19). This bill passed on a division in the commons by 104 to 90, and was ill taken by some of the bishops, who saw themselves reduced to live on the lawful subsistence of the parochial clergy. Strype's Annals, i. 68. 97.

the channel.[1] But the greater part was dissipated in profuse grants to the courtiers, who frequently contrived to veil their acquisitions under cover of a purchase from the crown. It has been surmised that Cromwell, in his desire to promote the Reformation, advised the king to make this partition of abbey lands among the nobles and gentry, either by grant, or by sale on easy terms, that, being thus bound by the sure ties of private interest, they might always oppose any return towards the dominion of Rome.[2] In Mary's reign, accordingly, her parliament, so obsequious in all matters of religion, adhered with a firm grasp to the possession of church lands; nor could the papal supremacy be reëstablished until a sanction was given to their enjoyment. And we may ascribe part of the zeal of the same class in bringing back and preserving the reformed church under Elizabeth to a similar motive; not that these gentlemen were hypocritical pretenders to a belief they did not entertain, but that, according to the general laws of human nature, they gave a readier reception to truths which made their estates more secure.

But, if the participation of so many persons in the spoils of ecclesiastical property gave stability to the new religion, by pledging them to its support, it was also of no slight advantage to our civil constitution, strengthening, and as it were infusing new blood into, the territorial aristocracy, who were to withstand the enormous prerogative of the crown. For if it be true, as surely it is, that wealth is power, the distribution of so large a portion of the kingdom among the nobles and gentry, the elevation of so many new families, and the increased opulence of the more ancient, must have sensibly affected their weight in the balance. Those families indeed, within or without the bounds of the peerage, which are now deemed the most considerable, will be found, with no great number of exceptions, to have first become conspicuous under the Tudor line of kings; and if we could

[1] Burnet, 268, 339. In Strype, i. 211, we have a paper drawn up by Cromwell for the king's inspection, setting forth what might be done with the revenues of the lesser monasteries. Among a few other particulars are the following: — "His grace may furnish 200 gentlemen to attend on his person, every one of them to have 100 marks yearly — 20,000 marks. His highness may assign to the yearly reparation of highways in sundry parts, or the doing of other good deeds for the commonwealth, 5000 marks." In such scant proportion did the claims of public utility come after those of selfish pomp, or rather perhaps, looking more attentively, of cunning corruption.

[2] Burnet, i. 223.

trace the titles of their estates, to have acquired no small portion of them, mediately or immediately, from monastic or other ecclesiastical foundations. And better it has been that these revenues should thus from age to age have been expended in liberal hospitality, in discerning charity, in the promotion of industry and cultivation, in the active duties or even generous amusements of life, than in maintaining a host of ignorant and inactive monks, in deceiving the populace by superstitious pageantry, or in the encouragement of idleness and mendicity.[1]

A very ungrounded prejudice had long obtained currency, and notwithstanding the contradiction it has experienced in our more accurate age, seems still not eradicated, that the alms of monasteries maintained the indigent throughout the kingdom, and that the system of parochial relief, now so much the topic of complaint, was rendered necessary by the dissolution of those beneficent foundations. There can be no doubt that many of the impotent poor derived support from their charity. But the blind eleemosynary spirit inculcated by the Romish church is notoriously the cause, not the cure, of beggary and wretchedness. The monastic foundations, scattered in different counties, but by no means at regular distances, and often in sequestered places, could never answer the end of local and limited succor, meted out

[1] It is a favorite theory with many who regret the absolute secularization of conventual estates, that they might have been rendered useful to learning and religion by being bestowed on chapters and colleges. Thomas Whitaker has sketched a pretty scheme for the abbey of Whalley, wherein, besides certain opulent prebendaries, he would provide for schoolmasters and physicians. I suppose this is considered an adherence to the donor's intention, and no sort of violation of property; somewhat on the principle called *cy près*, adopted by the court of chancery in cases of charitable bequests; according to which, that tribunal, if it holds the testator's intention unfit to be executed, carries the bequest into effect by doing what it presumes to come next in his wishes though sometimes very far from them. It might be difficult indeed to prove that a Norman baron, who, not quite easy about his future prospects, took comfort in his last hours from the anticipation of daily masses for his soul, would have been better satisfied that his lands should maintain a grammar-school than that they should escheat to the crown. But to waive this, and to revert to the principle of public utility, it may possibly be true that, in one instance, such as Whalley, a more beneficial disposition could have been made in favor of a college than by granting away the lands. But the question is, whether all, or even a great part, of the monastic estates could have been kept in mortmain with advantage. We may easily argue that the Derwentwater property, applied as it has been, has done the state more service than if it had gone to maintain a race of Ratcliffes, and been squandered at White's or Newmarket. But does it follow that the kingdom would be the more prosperous if all the estates of the peerage were diverted to similar endowments? And can we seriously believe that, if such a plan had been adopted at the suppression of monasteries, either religion or learning would have been the better for such an inundation of prebendaries and schoolmasters?

in just proportion to the demands of poverty. Their gates might indeed be open to those who knocked at them for alms, and came in search of streams that must always be too scanty for a thirsty multitude. Nothing could have a stronger tendency to promote that vagabond mendicity, which unceasing and very severe statutes were enacted to repress. It was and must always continue a hard problem, to discover the means of rescuing those whom labor cannot maintain from the last extremities of helpless suffering. The regular clergy were in all respects ill fitted for this great office of humanity. Even while the monasteries were yet standing, the scheme of a provision for the poor had been adopted by the legislature, by means of regular collections, which in the course of a long series of statutes, ending in the 43d of Elizabeth, were almost insensibly converted into compulsory assessments.[1] It is by no means probable that, however some in particular districts may have had to lament the cessation of hospitality in the convents, the poor in general, after some time, were placed in a worse condition by their dissolution; nor are we to forget that the class to whom the abbey lands have fallen have been distinguished at all times, and never more than in the first century after that transference of property, for their charity and munificence.

These two great political measures — the separation from the Roman see, and the suppression of monasteries — so broke the vast power of the English clergy, and humbled their spirit, that they became the most abject of Henry's vassals, and dared not offer any steady opposition to his caprice, even when it led him to make innovations in the essential parts of their religion. It is certain that a large majority of that order would gladly have retained their allegiance to Rome, and that they viewed with horror the downfall of the monasteries. In rending away so much that had been incorporated with the public faith Henry seemed to prepare the road for the still more radical changes of the reformers. These, a numerous and increasing sect, exulted by turns in the innovations he promulgated, lamented their dilatoriness and im-

[1] The first act for the relief of the impotent poor passed in 1535 (27 H. 8, c. 25). By this statute no alms were allowed to be given to beggars, on pain of forfeiting ten times the value; but a collection was to be made in every parish. The compulsory contributions, properly speaking, began in 1572 (14 Eliz. c. 5). But by an earlier statute, i. Edw. 6. c. 3, the bishop was empowered to proceed in his court against such as should refuse to contribute, or dissuade others from doing so.

perfection, or trembled at the reaction of his bigotry against themselves. Trained in the school of theological controversy, and drawing from those bitter waters fresh aliment for his sanguinary and imperious temper, he displayed the impartiality of his intolerance by alternately persecuting the two conflicting parties. We all have read how three persons convicted of disputing his supremacy, and three deniers of transubstantiation, were drawn on the same hurdle to execution. But the doctrinal system adopted by Henry in the latter years of his reign, varying, indeed, in some measure from time to time, was about equally removed from popish and protestant orthodoxy. The corporal presence of Christ in the consecrated elements was a tenet which no one might dispute without incurring the penalty of death by fire; and the king had a capricious partiality to the Romish practice in those very points where a great many real catholics on the Continent were earnest for its alteration, the communion of the laity by bread alone, and the celibacy of the clergy. But in several other respects he was wrought upon by Cranmer to draw pretty near to the Lutheran creed, and to permit such explications to be given in the books set forth by his authority, the Institution, and the Erudition of a Christian Man, as, if they did not absolutely proscribe most of the ancient opinions, threw at best much doubt upon them, and gave intimations which the people, now become attentive to these questions, were acute enough to interpret.[1]

Progress of the reformed doctrine in England.

It was natural to suspect, from the previous temper of the nation, that the revolutionary spirit which blazed out in Germany would spread rapidly over England. The enemies of ancient superstition at home, by frequent communication with the Lutheran and Swiss reformers, acquired not only more enlivening confidence, but a surer and more definite system of belief. Books printed in Germany or in the Flemish provinces, where at first the administration connived at the new religion, were imported and read with that eagerness and delight which always compensate the risk of forbidden studies.[2]

[1] The Institution was printed in 1537; the Erudition, according to Burnet, in 1540; but in Collier and Strype's opinion, not till 1543. They are both artfully drawn, probably in the main by Cranmer, but not without the interference of some less favorable to the new doctrine, and under the eye of the king himself. Collier. 137, 189. The doctrinal variations in these two summaries of royal faith are by no means inconsiderable.

[2] Strype. i. 165. A statute enacted in 1534 (25 H. 8, c. 15), after reciting

Wolsey, who had no turn towards persecution, contented himself with ordering heretical writings to be burned, and strictly prohibiting their importation. But to withstand the course of popular opinion is always like a combat against the elements in commotion; nor is it likely that a government far more steady and unanimous than that of Henry VIII. could have effectually prevented the diffusion of protestantism. And the severe punishment of many zealous reformers in the subsequent part of this reign tended, beyond a doubt, to excite a favorable prejudice for men whose manifest sincerity, piety, and constancy in suffering, were as good pledges for the truth of their doctrine, as the people had been always taught to esteem the same qualities in the legends of the early martyrs. Nor were Henry's persecutions conducted upon the only rational principle, that of the inquisition, which judges from the analogy of medicine, that a deadly poison cannot be extirpated but by the speedy and radical excision of the diseased part; but falling only upon a few of a more eager and officious zeal, left a well-grounded opinion among the rest, that by some degree of temporizing prudence they might escape molestation till a season of liberty should arrive.

One of the books originally included in the list of proscription among the writings of Luther and the foreign Protestants was a translation of the New Testament into English by Tyndale, printed at Antwerp in 1526. A complete version of the Bible, partly by Tyndale, and partly by Coverdale, appeared, perhaps at Hamburg, in 1535; a second edition, under the name of Matthews, following in 1537; and as Cranmer's influence over the king became greater, and his aversion to the Roman church more inveterate, so material a change was made in the ecclesiastical policy of this reign as to direct the Scriptures in this translation (but with corrections in many places) to be set up in parish churches, and permit them to be publicly sold.[1] This measure had a strong tendency to promote the

that "at this day there be within this realm a great number cunning and expert in printing, and as able to execute the said craft as any stranger," proceeds to forbid the sale of bound books imported from the Continent. A terrible blow was thus levelled both against general literature and the reformed religion; but, like many other bad laws, produced very little effect.

[1] The accounts of early editions of the English Bible in Burnet, Collier, Strype, and an essay by Johnson in Watson's Theological Tracts, vol. iii., are erroneous or defective. A letter of Strype, in Harleian MSS. 3782, which has been printed, is better; but the most complete enumeration is in Cotton's list of editions, 1821. The dispersion of the Scriptures, with full liberty to read them, was

Reformation, especially among those who were capable of reading; not, surely, that the controverted doctrines of the Romish church are so palpably erroneous as to bear no sort of examination, but because such a promulgation of the Scriptures at that particular time seemed both tacitly to admit the chief point of contest, that they were the exclusive standard of Christian faith, and to lead the people to interpret them with that sort of prejudice which a jury would feel in considering evidence that one party in a cause had attempted to suppress; a danger which those who wish to restrain the course of free discussion without very sure means of success will in all ages do well to reflect upon.

The great change of religious opinions was not so much effected by reasoning on points of theological controversy, upon which some are apt to fancy it turned, as on a persuasion that fraud and corruption pervaded the established church. The pretended miracles, which had so long held the understanding in captivity, were wisely exposed to ridicule and indignation by the government. Plays and interludes were represented in churches, of which the usual subject was the vices and corruptions of the monks and clergy. These were disapproved of by the graver sort, but no doubt served a useful purpose.[1] The press sent forth its light hosts of libels;

greatly due to Cromwell, as is shown by Burnet. Even after his fall, a proclamation, dated May 6, 1542, referring to the king's former injunctions for the same purpose, directs a large Bible to be set up in every parish church. But, next year the duke of Norfolk and Gardiner prevailing over Cranmer, Henry retraced a part of his steps; and the act 34 H. 8, c. 1, forbids the sale of Tyndale's "false translation," and the reading of the Bible in churches, or by yeomen, women, and other incapable persons. The popish bishops, well aware how much turned on this general liberty of reading the Scriptures, did all in their power to discredit the new version. Gardiner made a list of about one hundred words which he thought unfit to be translated, and which, in case of an authorized version (whereof the clergy in convocation had reluctantly admitted the expediency), ought, in his opinion, to be left in Latin. Tyndale's translation may, I apprehend, be reckoned the basis of that now in use, but has undergone several corrections before the last. It has been a matter of dispute whether it were made from the original languages or from the Vulgate. Hebrew and even Greek were very little known in England at that time.

The edition of 1537, called Matthews's Bible, printed by Grafton, contains marginal notes reflecting on the corruptions of popery. These it was thought expedient to suppress in that of 1539, commonly called Cranmer's Bible as having been revised by him, and in later editions. In all these editions of Henry's reign, though the version is properly Tyndale's, there are, as I am informed, considerable variations and amendments. Thus, in Cranmer's Bible, the word *ecclesia* is always rendered congregation, instead of church; either as the primary meaning, or, more probably, to point out that the laity had a share in the government of a Christian society.

[1] Burnet, 318; Strype's Life of Parker, 18. Collier (187) is of course much scandalized. In his view of things, it had been better to give up the Reformation entirely than to suffer one reflection on the clergy. These dramatic satires on that order had also an effect in promoting the Reformation in Holland. Brandt's History of Reformation in Low Countries, vol. i. p. 128.

and though the catholic party did not fail to try the same means of influence, they had both less liberty to write as they pleased, and fewer readers than their antagonists.[1]

Its establishment under Edward.

In this feverish state of the public mind on the most interesting subject ensued the death of Henry VIII., who had excited and kept it up. More than once, during the latter part of his capricious reign, the popish party, headed by Norfolk and Gardiner, had gained an ascendant, and several persons had been burned for denying transubstantiation. But at the moment of his decease Norfolk was a prisoner attainted of treason, Gardiner in disgrace, and the favor of Cranmer at its height. It is said that Henry had meditated some further changes in religion. Of his executors, the greater part, as their subsequent conduct evinces, were nearly indifferent to the two systems, except so far as more might be gained by innovation. But Somerset, the new protector, appears to have inclined sincerely towards the Reformation, though not wholly uninfluenced by similar motives. His authority readily overcame all opposition in the council; and it was soon perceived that Edward, whose singular precocity gave his opinions in childhood an importance not wholly ridiculous, had imbibed a steady and ardent attachment to the new religion, which probably, had he lived longer, would have led him both to diverge farther from what he thought an idolatrous superstition, and to have treated its adherents with severity.[2] Under his reign, accordingly, a series of alterations in the

1 ["In place of the ancient reverence which was entertained for the pope and the Romish chair, there was not a masquerade or other pastime in which some one was not to be seen going about in the dress of a pope or cardinal. Even the women jested incessantly at the pope and his servants, and thought they could do no greater disgrace to any man than by calling him priest of the pope, or papist." Extract from an anonymous French MS. by a person resident at the English court, about 1540, in Raumer's History of 16th and 17th centuries illustrated, vol. ii. p. 66. 1845.]

2 I can hardly avoid doubting whether Edward VI.'s Journal, published in the second volume of Burnet, be altogether his own; because it is strange for a boy of ten years old to write with the precise brevity of a man of business. Yet it is hard to say how far an intercourse with able men on serious subjects may force a royal plant of such natural vigor; and his letters to his young friend Barnaby Fitzpatrick, published by H. Walpole in 1774, are quite unlike the style of a boy. One could wish this journal not to be genuine; for the manner in which he speaks of both his uncles' executions does not show a good heart. Unfortunately, however, there is a letter extant of the king to Fitzpatrick, which must be genuine, and is in the same strain. He treated his sister Mary harshly about her religion, and had, I suspect, too much Tudor blood in his veins. It is certain that he was a very extraordinary boy, or, as Cardan calls him, monstrificus puellus; and the reluctance with which he yielded, on the solicitations of Cranmer, to sign the warrant for burning Joan Boucher, is as much to his honor as it is against the archbishop's. [But see p. 106.]

tenets and homilies of the English church were made, the principal of which I shall point out, without following a chronological order, or adverting to such matters of controversy as did not produce a sensible effect on the people.

Sketch of the chief points of difference between the two religions

I. It was obviously among the first steps required in order to introduce a mode of religion at once more reasonable and more earnest than the former, that the public services of the church should be expressed in the mother tongue of the congregation. The Latin ritual had been unchanged ever since the age when it was vernacular; partly through a sluggish dislike of innovation, but partly also because the mysteriousness of an unknown dialect served to impose on the vulgar, and to throw an air of wisdom around the priesthood. Yet what was thus concealed would have borne the light. Our own liturgy, so justly celebrated for its piety, elevation, and simplicity, is in great measure a translation from the catholic services, or more properly from those which had been handed down from a more primitive age; those portions, of course, being omitted which had relation to different principles of worship. In the second year of Edward's reign, the reformation of the public service was accomplished, and an English liturgy compiled, not essentially different from that in present use.[1]

II. No part of exterior religion was more prominent or more offensive to those who had imbibed a protestant spirit than the worship, or at least veneration, of images, which in remote and barbarous ages had given excessive scandal both in the Greek and Latin churches, though long fully established in the practice of each. The populace in towns where the reformed tenets prevailed began to pull them down in the very first days of Edward's reign; and after a little pretence at distinguishing those which had not been abused, orders were given that all images should be taken away from churches. It was, perhaps, necessary thus to hinder the zealous protestants from abating them as nuisances, which had already caused several disturbances.[2] But this order

[1] The litany had been translated into English in 1542. Burnet, i. 331; Collier, 111; where it may be read, not much differing from that now in use. It was always held out by our church, when the object was conciliation, that the liturgy was essentially the same with the mass-book. Strype's Annals, ii. 39; Hollingshed, iii. 921. (4to. edition.)

[2] "It was observed," says Strype, ii. 79, "that where images were left there was most contest, and most peace where they were all sheer pulled down, as they were in some places."

was executed with a rigor which lovers of art and antiquity have long deplored. Our churches bear witness to the devastation committed in the wantonness of triumphant reform by defacing statues and crosses on the exterior of buildings intended for worship, or windows and monuments within. Missals and other books dedicated to superstition perished in the same manner. Altars were taken down, and a great variety of ceremonies abrogated, such as the use of incense, tapers, and holy water; and though more of these were retained than eager innovators could approve, the whole surface of religious ordinances, all that is palpable to common minds, underwent a surprising transformation.

III. But this change in ceremonial observances and outward show was trifling when compared to that in the objects of worship, and in the purposes for which they were addressed. Those who have visited some catholic temples, and attended to the current language of devotion, must have perceived, what the writings of apologists or decrees of councils will never enable them to discover, that the saints, but more especially the Virgin, are almost exclusively the *popular* deities of that religion. All this polytheism was swept away by the reformers; and in this may be deemed to consist the most specific difference of the two systems. Nor did they spare the belief in purgatory, that unknown land which the hierarchy swayed with so absolute a rule, and to which the earth had been rendered a tributary province. Yet in the first liturgy put forth under Edward the prayers for departed souls were retained; whether out of respect to the prejudices of the people or to the immemorial antiquity of the practice. But such prayers, if not necessarily implying the doctrine of purgatory (which yet in the main they appear to do), are at least so closely connected with it that the belief could never be eradicated while they remained. Hence, in the revision of the liturgy, four years afterwards, they were laid aside;[1] and several other changes made, to eradicate the vestiges of the ancient superstition.

IV. Auricular confession, as commonly called, or the pri-

[1] Collier, p. 257, enters into a vindication of the practice, which appears to have prevailed in the church from the second century. It was defended in general by the nonjurors and the whole school of Andrews. But, independently of its wanting the authority of Scripture, which the reformers set up exclusively of all tradition, it contradicted the doctrine of justification by mere faith, in the strict sense which they affixed to that tenet. See preamble of the act for dissolution of chantries, 1 Edw. 6, c. 14.

vate and special confession of sins to a priest for the purpose of obtaining his absolution, an imperative duty in the church of Rome, and preserved as such in the statute of the six articles, and in the religious codes published by Henry VIII., was left to each man's discretion in the new order; a judicious temperament, which the reformers would have done well to adopt in some other points. And thus, while it has never been condemned in our church, it went without dispute into complete neglect. Those who desire to augment the influence of the clergy regret, of course, its discontinuance; and some may conceive that it would serve either for wholesome restraint or useful admonition. It is very difficult, or, perhaps, beyond the reach of any human being, to determine absolutely how far these benefits, which cannot be reasonably denied to result in some instances from the rite of confession, outweigh the mischiefs connected with it. There seems to be something in the Roman catholic discipline (and I know nothing else so likely) which keeps the balance, as it were of moral influence pretty even between the two religions, and compensates for the ignorance and superstition which the elder preserves; for I am not sure that the protestant system in the present age has any very sensible advantage in this respect; or that in countries where the comparison can fairly be made, as in Germany or Switzerland, there is more honesty in one sex, or more chastity in the other, when they belong to the reformed churches. Yet, on the other hand, the practice of confession is at the best of very doubtful utility, when considered in its full extent and general bearings. The ordinary confessor, listening mechanically to hundreds of penitents, can hardly preserve much authority over most of them. But in proportion as his attention is directed to the secrets of conscience, his influence may become dangerous; men grow accustomed to the control of one perhaps more feeble and guilty than themselves, but over whose frailties they exercise no reciprocal command; and, if the confessors of kings have been sometimes terrible to nations, their ascendency is probably not less mischievous, in proportion to its extent, within the sphere of domestic life. In a political light, and with the object of lessening the weight of the ecclesiastical order in temporal affairs, there cannot be the least hesitation as to the expediency of discontinuing the usage.[1]

[1] Collier, p. 248, descants, in the true spirit of a high churchman, on the im-

V. It has very rarely been the custom of theologians to measure the importance of orthodox opinions by their effect on the lives and hearts of those who adopt them; nor was this predilection for speculative above practical doctrines ever more evident than in the leading controversy of the sixteenth century, that respecting the Lord's Supper. No errors on this point could have had any influence on men's moral conduct, nor indeed much on the general nature of their faith; yet it was selected as the test of heresy; and most, if not all, of those who suffered death upon that charge, whether in England or on the Continent, were convicted of denying the corporal presence, in the sense of the Roman church. It had been well if the reformers had learned, by abhorring her persecution, not to practise it in a somewhat less degree upon each other; or, by exposing the absurdities of transubstantiation, not to contend for equal nonsense of their own. Four principal theories, to say nothing of subordinate varieties, divided Europe at the accession of Edward VI. about the sacrament of the Eucharist. The church of Rome would not depart a single letter from transubstantiation, or the change at the moment of consecration of the substances of bread and wine into those of Christ's body and blood; the accidents, in school language, or sensible qualities of the former remaining, or becoming inherent in the new substance. This doctrine does not, as vulgarly supposed, contradict the evidence of our senses; since our senses can report nothing as to the unknown being, which the schoolmen denominated substance, and which alone was the subject of this conversion. But metaphysicians of later ages might inquire whether material substances, abstractedly considered, exist at all, or, if they exist, whether they can have any specific distinction except their sensible qualities. This, perhaps, did not suggest itself in the sixteenth century; but it was strongly objected that the simultaneous existence of a body in many places, which the Romish doctrine implied, was inconceivable, and even contradictory. Luther, partly, as it seems, out of his determination to multiply differences with the church, invented a theory somewhat different, usually called consubstantiation, which was adopted in the confession of Augsburg, and to which, at least down to the

portance of confession. This also, as is well known, is one of the points on which his party disagreed with the generality of protestants.

middle of the eighteenth century, the divines of that communion were much attached. They imagined the two substances to be united in the sacramental elements, so that they might be termed bread and wine, or the body and blood, with equal propriety.[1] But it must be obvious that there is little more than a metaphysical distinction between this doctrine and that of Rome; though, when it suited the Lutherans to magnify rather than dissemble their deviations from the mother church, it was raised into an important difference. A simpler and more rational explication occurred to Zwingle and Œcolampadius, from whom the Helvetian protestants imbibed their faith. Rejecting every notion of a real presence, and divesting the institution of all its mystery, they saw only figurative symbols in the elements which Christ had appointed as a commemoration of his death. But this novel opinion excited as much indignation in Luther as in the Romanists. It was indeed a rock on which the Reformation was nearly shipwrecked; since the violent contests which it occasioned, and the narrow intolerance which one side at least displayed throughout the controversy, not only weakened on several occasions the temporal power of the protestant churches, but disgusted many of those who might have inclined towards espousing their sentiments. Besides these three hypotheses, a fourth was promulgated by Martin Bucer of Strasburg, a man of much acuteness, but prone to metaphysical subtilty, and not, it is said, of a very ingenuous character.[2] Bucer, as I apprehend, though his expressions are unusually confused, did not acknowledge a local presence of Christ's body and blood in the elements after consecration — so far concurring with the Helvetians; while he contended that they were really, and without figure, received by the worthy communicant through faith, so as to preserve the belief of a mysterious union, and of what was sometimes

[1] Nostra sententia est, says Luther, apud Burnet, 111, Appendix, 194, corpus ita cum pane, seu in pane esse, ut revera cum pane manducetur, et quemcunque motum vel actionem panis habet, eundem et corpus Christi.

[2] "Bucer thought, that for avoiding contention, and for maintaining peace and quietness in the church, somewhat more ambiguous words should be used, that might have a respect to both persuasions concerning the presence. But Martyr was of another judgment, and affected to speak of the sacrament with all plainness and perspicuity." Strype, ii. 121. The truth is, that there were but two opinions at bottom as to this main point of the controversy; nor in the nature of things was it possible that there should be more; for what can be predicated concerning a body, in its relation to a given space, but presence and absence?

called a real presence. Bucer himself came to England early in the reign of Edward, and had a considerable share in advising the measures of reformation. But Peter Martyr, a disciple of the Swiss school, had also no small influence. In the forty-two articles set forth by authority, the real or corporal presence, using these words as synonymous, is explicitly denied. This clause was omitted on the revision of the articles under Elizabeth.[1]

VI. These various innovations were exceedingly inimical to the influence and interests of the priesthood. But that order obtained a sort of compensation in being released from its obligation to celibacy. This obligation, though unwarranted by Scripture, rested on a most ancient and universal rule of discipline; for though the Greek and Eastern churches have always permitted the ordination of married persons, yet they do not allow those already ordained to take wives. No very good reason, however, could be given for this distinction; and the constrained celibacy of the Latin clergy had given rise to mischiefs, of which their general practice of retaining concubines might be reckoned among the smallest.[2] The German protestants soon rejected this burden, and encouraged regular as well as secular priests to marry. Cranmer had himself taken a wife in Germany, whom Henry's law of the six articles, one of which made the marriage of priests felony, compelled him to send away. In the reign of Edward this was justly reckoned an indispensable part of the new Reformation. But the bill for that purpose passed the lords with some little difficulty, nine bishops and four peers dissenting; and its preamble cast such an imputation on the practice it allowed, treating the marriage of priests as ignominious and a tolerated evil, that another act was thought necessary a few years afterwards, when the Reformation was better established, to vindicate this right of the protestant church.[3] A great number of the clergy availed themselves of their liberty; which may probably have had as extensive an effect in conciliating the eccle-

[1] Burnet, ii. 105, App. 216; Strype, ii. 121, 208; Collier, &c. The Calvinists certainly did not own a local presence in the elements.

[2] It appears to have been common for the clergy, by license from their bishops, to retain concubines, who were, Collier says, for the most part their wives, p. 262. But I do not clearly understand in what the distinction could have consisted; for it seems unlikely that marriages of priests were ever solemnized at so late a period; or if they were, they were invalid.

[3] Stat. 2 & 3 Edw. 6, c. 21; 5 & 6 Edw. 6, c. 12; Burnet, 89.

siastical profession, as the suppression of monasteries had in rendering the gentry favorable to the new order of religion.

But great as was the number of those whom conviction or self-interest enlisted under the protestant banner, it appears plain that the Reformation moved on with too precipitate a step for the majority. The new doctrines prevailed in London, in many large towns, and in the eastern counties. But in the north and west of England the body of the people were strictly catholics. The clergy, though not very scrupulous about conforming to the innovations, were generally averse to most of them.[1] And, in spite of the church lands, I imagine that most of the nobility, if not the gentry, inclined to the same persuasion; not a few peers having sometimes dissented from the bills passed on the subject of religion in this reign, while no sort of disagreement appears in the upper house during that of Mary. In the western insurrection of 1549, which partly originated in the alleged grievance of enclosures, many of the demands made by the rebels go to the entire reëstablishment of popery. Those of the Norfolk insurgents, in the same year, whose political complaints were the same, do not, as far as I perceive, show any such tendency. But an historian, whose bias was certainly not unfavorable to protestantism, confesses that all endeavors were too weak to overcome the aversion of the people towards Reformation, and even intimates that German troops were sent for from Calais on account of the bigotry with which the bulk of the nation adhered to the old superstition.[2] This is somewhat an humiliating admission, that the protestant faith was imposed upon our ancestors by a foreign army. And as the reformers, though still the fewer, were undeniably a great and increasing party, it may be natural to inquire whether a

Opposition made by part of the nation.

[1] 2 Strype, 53. Latimer pressed the necessity of expelling these temporizing conformists, — "out with them all! I require it in God's behalf; make them *quondams*, all the pack of them." Id. 204; 2 Burnet, 143.

[2] Burnet, iii. 190, 196. "The use of the old religion," says Paget, in remonstrating with Somerset on his rough treatment of some of the gentry and partiality to the commons, "is forbidden by a law, and the use of the new is not yet printed in the stomachs of eleven out of twelve parts of the realm, whatever countenance men make outwardly to please them in whom they see the power resteth." Strype, ii.; Appendix, H. H. This seems rather to refer to the upper classes than to the whole people. But at any rate it was an exaggeration of the fact, the protestants being certainly in a much greater proportion. Paget was the adviser of the scheme of sending for German troops in 1549, which, however, was in order to quell a seditious spirit in the nation, not by any means wholly founded upon religious grounds. Strype, xi. 169.

regard to policy as well as equitable considerations should not have repressed still more, as it did in some measure, the zeal of Cranmer and Somerset? It might be asked whether, in the acknowledged coexistence of two religions, some preference were not fairly claimed for the creed which all had once held, and which the greater part yet retained; whether it were becoming that the councillors of an infant king should use such violence in breaking up the ecclesiastical constitution; whether it were to be expected that a free-spirited people should see their consciences thus transferred by proclamation, and all that they had learned to venerate not only torn away from them, but exposed to what they must reckon blasphemous contumely and profanation? The demolition of shrines and images, far unlike the speculative disputes of theologians, was an overt insult on every catholic heart. Still more were they exasperated at the ribaldry which vulgar protestants uttered against their most sacred mystery. It was found necessary in the very first act of the first protestant parliament to denounce penalties against such as spoke irreverently of the sacrament, an indecency not unusual with those who held the Zwinglian opinion in that age of coarse pleasantry and unmixed invective.[1] Nor could the people repose much confidence in the judgment and sincerity of their governors, whom they had seen submitting without outward repugnance to Henry's various schemes of religion, and whom they saw every day enriching themselves with the plunder of the church they affected to reform. There was a sort of endowed colleges or fraternities, called chantries, consisting of secular priests, whose duty was to say daily masses for the founders. These were abolished and given to the king by acts of parliament in the last year of Henry and the first of Edward. It was intimated in the preamble of the latter statute that their revenues should be converted to the erection of schools, the augmentation of the universities, and the sustenance of the indigent.[2] But this was entirely neglected, and the estates fell into the hands of the courtiers. Nor did they content themselves with this escheated wealth of the church. Almost every bishopric was spoiled by their

[1] 2 Edw. 6, c. 1; Strype, xi. 81.

[2] 37 H. 8, c. 2; 1 Edw. 6, c. 14; Strype, ii. 63; Burnet, &c. Cranmer, as well as the catholic bishops, protested against this act, well knowing how little regard would be paid to its intention. In the latter part of the young king's reign, as he became more capable of exerting his own power, he endowed, as is well known, several excellent foundations.

ravenous power in this reign, either through mere alienations, or long leases, or unequal exchanges. Exeter and Llandaff, from being among the richest sees, fell into the class of the poorest. Lichfield lost the chief part of its lands to raise an estate for lord Paget. London, Winchester, and even Canterbury, suffered considerably. The duke of Somerset was much beloved; yet he had given no unjust offence by pulling down some churches in order to erect Somerset House with the materials. He had even projected the demolition of Westminster Abbey, but the chapter averted this outrageous piece of rapacity, sufficient of itself to characterize that age, by the usual method, a grant of some of their estates.[1]

Tolerance in religion, it is well known, so unanimously admitted (at least verbally) even by theologians in the present century, was seldom considered as practicable, much less as a matter of right, during the period of the Reformation. The difference in this respect between the catholics and protestants was only in degree, and in degree there was much less difference than we are apt to believe. Persecution is the deadly original sin of the reformed churches; that which cools every honest man's zeal for their cause in proportion as his reading becomes more extensive. The Lutheran princes and cities in Germany constantly refused to tolerate the use of the mass as an idolatrous service;[2] and this name of idolatry, though adopted in retaliation for that of heresy,

[1] Strype, Burnet, Collier, passim; Harmer's specimens, 100. Sir Philip Hobby, our minister in Germany, writes to the protector, in 1548, that the foreign protestants thought our bishops too rich, and advises him to reduce them to a competent living; he particularly recommends his taking away all the prebends in England. Strype, 88. These counsels, and the acts which they prompted, disgust us, from the spirit of rapacity they breathe. Yet it might be urged, with some force, that the enormous wealth of the superior ecclesiastics had been the main cause of those corruptions which it was sought to cast away, and that most of the dignitaries were very averse to the new religion. Even Cranmer had written some years before to Cromwell, deprecating the establishment of any prebends out of the conventual estates, and speaking of the collegiate clergy as an idle, ignorant, and gormandizing race, who might, without any harm, be extinguished along with the regulars. Burnet, iii. 141. But the gross selfishness of the great men in Edward's reign justly made him anxious to save what he could for the church, that seemed on the brink of absolute ruin. Collier mentions a characteristic circumstance. So great a quantity of church plate had been stolen, that a commission was appointed to inquire into the facts, and compel its restitution. Instead of this, the commissioners found more left than they thought sufficient, and seized the greater part to the king's use.

[2] They declared in the famous protestation of Spire, which gave them the name of protestants, that their preachers having confuted the mass by passages in Scripture, they could not permit their subjects to go thither; since it would afford a bad example to suffer two sorts of service, directly opposite to each other, in their churches. Schmidt, Hist. des Allemands, vi. 394, vii. 24.

answered the same end as the other, of exciting animosity and uncharitableness. The Roman worship was equally proscribed in England. Many persons were sent to prison for hearing mass, and similar offences.[1] The princess Mary supplicated in vain to have the exercise of her own religion at home, and Charles V. several times interceded in her behalf; but though Cranmer and Ridley, as well as the council, would have consented to this indulgence, the young king, whose education had unhappily infused a good deal of bigotry into his mind, could not be prevailed upon to connive at such idolatry.[2] Yet in one memorable instance he had shown a milder spirit, struggling against Cranmer to save a fanatical woman from the punishment of heresy.[3] This is a stain upon Cranmer's memory which nothing but his own death could have lightened. In men hardly escaped from a similar peril, in men who had nothing to plead but the right of private judgment, in men who had defied the prescriptive authority of past ages and of established power, the crime of persecution assumes a far deeper hue, and is capable of far less extenuation, than in a Roman inquisitor. Thus the death of Servetus has weighed down the name and memory of Calvin. And though Cranmer was incapable of the rancorous malignity of the Genevan lawgiver, yet I regret to say that there is a peculiar circumstance of aggravation in his pursuing to death this woman, Joan Boucher, and a Dutchman that had been convicted of Arianism. It is said that he had been accessory in the preceding reign to the condemnation of Lambert, and perhaps some others, for opinions

1 Stat. 2 & 3 Edw. 6, c. 1; Strype's Cranmer, p. 233.

2 Burnet, 192. Somerset had always allowed her to exercise her religion, though censured for this by Warwick, who died himself a papist, but had pretended to fall in with the young king's prejudices. Her ill treatment was subsequent to the protector's overthrow. It is to be observed that, in her father's life, she had acknowledged his supremacy, and the justice of her mother's divorce. 1 Strype, 285; 2 Burnet, 241; Lingard, vi. 326. It was, of course, by intimidation; but that excuse might be made for others. Cranmer is said to have persuaded Henry not to put her to death, which we must in charity hope she did not know.

3 [It has been pointed out to me by a correspondent, that Mr. Bruce, in his edition of Roger Hutchinson's works (Parker Society, 1842, preface, p. 8), has given strong reasons for questioning this remonstrance of Edward with Cranmer, which rests originally on no authority but that of Fox. In some of its circumstances the story told by Fox is certainly disproved; but it is not impossible that the young king may have expressed his reluctance to have the sentence carried into execution, though his signature of the warrant was not required. This, however, is mere conjecture; and perhaps it may be better that the whole anecdote should vanish from history. This, of course, mitigates the censure on Cranmer in the text to an indefinite degree. 1845.]

concerning the Lord's Supper which he had himself afterwards embraced.[1] Such an evidence of the fallibility of human judgment, such an example that persecutions for heresy, how conscientiously soever managed, are liable to end in shedding the blood of those who maintain truth, should have taught him, above all men, a scrupulous repugnance to carry into effect those sanguinary laws. Compared with these executions for heresy, the imprisonment and deprivation of Gardiner and Bonner appear but measures of ordinary severity towards political adversaries under the pretext of religion; yet are they wholly unjustifiable, particularly in the former instance; and if the subsequent retaliation of those bad men was beyond all proportion excessive, we should remember that such is the natural consequence of tyrannical aggressions.[2]

The person most conspicuous, though Ridley was perhaps the most learned divine, in moulding the faith and discipline of the English church, which has not

Cranmer.

1 When Joan Boucher was condemned, she said to her judges, "It was not long ago since you burned Anne Askew for a piece of bread, and yet came yourselves soon after to believe and profess the same doctrine for which you burned her; and now you will needs burn me for a piece of flesh, and in the end you will come to believe this also, when you have read the Scriptures and understand them." Strype, ii. 214.

2 Gardiner had some virtues, and entertained sounder notions of the civil constitution of England than his adversaries. In a letter to Sir John Godsalve, giving his reasons for refusing compliance with the injunctions issued by the council to the ecclesiastical visitors (which, Burnet says, does him more honor than anything else in his life), he dwells on the king's wanting power to command anything contrary to common law, or to a statute, and brings authorities for this. Burnet, ii. Append. 112. See also Lingard, vi. 387, for another instance. Nor was this regard to the constitution displayed only when out of the sunshine; for in the next reign he was against despotic counsels, of which an instance has been given in the last chapter. His conduct, indeed, with respect to the Spanish connection is equivocal. He was much against the marriage at first, and took credit to himself for the securities exacted in the treaty with Philip, and established by statute. Burnet, ii. 267. But afterwards, if we may trust Noailles, he fell in with the Spanish party in the council, and even suggested to parliament that the queen should have the same power as her father to dispose of the succession by will. Ambassades de Noailles, iii. 153, &c., &c. Yet, according to Dr. Lingard, on the imperial ambassador's authority, he saved Elizabeth's life against all the council. The article GARDINER, in the Biographia Britannica, contains an elaborate and partial apology, at great length; and the historian just quoted has of course said all he could in favor of one who labored so strenuously for the extirpation of the northern heresy. But he was certainly not an honest man, and had been active in Henry's reign against his real opinions.

Even if the ill treatment of Gardiner and Bonner by Edward's council could be excused (and the latter by his rudeness might deserve some punishment), what can be said for the imprisonment of the bishops Heath and Day, worthy and moderate men, who had gone a great way with the Reformation, but objected to the removal of altars, an innovation by no means necessary, and which should have been deferred till the people had grown ripe for further change? Mr. Southey says, "Gardiner and Bonner were deprived of their sees, and imprisoned; but *no rigor was used towards them*." Book of the Church, ii. 111. Liberty and property being trifles!

been very materially altered since his time, was archbishop Cranmer.[1] Few men, about whose conduct there is so little room for controversy upon facts, have been represented in more opposite lights. We know the favoring colors of protestant writers; but turn to the bitter invective of Bossuet, and the patriarch of our reformed church stands forth as the most abandoned of time-serving hypocrites. No political factions affect the impartiality of men's judgment so grossly or so permanently as religious heats. Doubtless, if we should reverse the picture, and imagine the end and scope of Cranmer's labor to have been the establishment of the Roman catholic religion in a protestant country, the estimate formed of his behavior would be somewhat less favorable than it is at present. If, casting away all prejudice on either side, we weigh the character of this prelate in an equal balance, he will appear far indeed removed from the turpitude imputed to him by his enemies, yet not entitled to any extraordinary veneration. Though it is most eminently true of Cranmer, that his faults were always the effect of circumstances, and not of intention, yet this palliating consideration is rather weakened when we recollect that he consented to place himself in a station where those circumstances occurred. At the time of Cranmer's elevation to the see of Canterbury, Henry, though on the point of separating forever from Rome, had not absolutely determined upon so strong a measure; and his policy required that the new archbishop should solicit the usual bulls from the pope, and take the oath of canonical obedience to him. Cranmer, already a rebel from that dominion in his heart, had recourse to the disingenuous shift of a protest, before his consecration, that "he did not intend to restrain himself thereby from anything to which he was

[1] The doctrines of the English church were set forth in forty-two articles, drawn up, as is generally believed, by Cranmer and Ridley, with the advice of Bucer and Martyr, and perhaps of Cox. The three last of these, condemning some novel opinions, were not renewed under Elizabeth, and a few other variations were made; but upon the whole there is little difference, and none perhaps in those tenets which have been most the object of discussion. See the original Articles in Burnet, ii., App. N. 55. They were never confirmed by a convocation or a parliament, but imposed by the king's supremacy on all the clergy, and on the universities. His death, however, ensued before they could be actually subscribed. [The late editor of Cranmer's works thinks him mainly responsible for the forty-two articles: he probably took the advice of Ridley. A considerable portion of them, including those of chief importance, is taken, almost literally, either from the Augsburg Confession or a set of articles agreed upon by some German and English divines at a conference in 1538. Jenkins's Cranmer, preface, xxiii. 3, c. vii., also vol. iv. 273, where these articles are printed at length. 1845.]

bound by his duty to God or the king, or from taking part in any reformation of the English church which he might judge to be required." [1] This first deviation from integrity, as is almost always the case, drew after it many others, and began that discreditable course of temporizing and undue compliance to which he was reduced for the rest of Henry's reign. Cranmer's abilities were not perhaps of a high order, or at least they were unsuited to public affairs; but his principal defect was in that firmness by which men of more ordinary talents may insure respect. Nothing could be weaker than his conduct in the usurpation of lady Jane, which he might better have boldly sustained, like Ridley, as a step necessary for the conservation of protestantism, than given into against his conscience, overpowered by the importunities of a misguided boy. Had the malignity of his enemies been directed rather against his reputation than his life, had he been permitted to survive his shame as a prisoner in the Tower, it must have seemed a more arduous task to defend the memory of Cranmer, but his fame has brightened in the fire that consumed him.[2]

His moderation in introducing changes not acceptable to the zealots.

Those who, with the habits of thinking that prevail in our times, cast back their eyes on the reign of Edward VI., will generally be disposed to censure the precipitancy, and still more the exclusive spirit, of our principal reformers. But relatively to the course that things had taken in Germany, and to the feverish zeal of that age, the moderation of Cranmer and Ridley, the only ecclesiastics who took a prominent share

1 Strype's Cranmer, Appendix, p. 9.—I am sorry to find a respectable writer inclining to vindicate Cranmer in this protestation, which Burnet admits to agree better with the maxims of the casuists than with the prelate's sincerity: Todd's Introduction to Cranmer's Defence of the True Doctrine of the Sacrament (1825), p. 40. It is of no importance to inquire whether the protest were made publicly or privately. Nothing can possibly turn upon this. It was, on either supposition, unknown to the promisee, the pope at Rome. The question is, whether, having obtained the bulls from Rome on an express stipulation that he should take a certain oath, he had a right to offer a limitation, not explanatory, but utterly inconsistent with it? We are sure that Cranmer's views and intentions, which he very soon carried into effect, were irreconcilable with any sort of obedience to the pope; and if, under all the circumstances, his conduct was justifiable, there would be an end of all promissory obligations whatever.

2 The character of Cranmer is summed up in no unfair manner by Mr. C. Butler, Memoirs of English Catholics, vol. i. p 139; except that his obtaining from Anne Boleyn an acknowledgment of her supposed pre-contract of marriage, having proceeded from motives of humanity, ought not to incur much censure, though the sentence of nullity was a mere mockery of law.—Poor Cranmer was compelled to subscribe not less than six recantations. Strype (iii. 232) had the integrity to publish all these, which were not fully known before.

in these measures, was very conspicuous, and tended above everything to place the Anglican church in that middle position which it has always preserved between the Roman hierarchy and that of other protestant denominations. It is manifest, from the history of the Reformation in Germany, that its predisposing cause was the covetous and arrogant character of the superior ecclesiastics, founded upon vast temporal authority; a yoke long borne with impatience, and which the unanimous adherence of the prelates to Rome in the period of separation gave the Lutheran princes a good excuse for entirely throwing off. Some of the more temperate Reformers, as Melanchthon, would have admitted a limited jurisdiction of the episcopacy; but in general the destruction of that order, such as it then existed, may be deemed as fundamental a principle of the new discipline as any theological point could be of the new doctrine. But besides that the subjection of ecclesiastical to civil tribunals, and possibly other causes, had rendered the superior clergy in England less obnoxious than in Germany, there was this important difference between the two countries, that several bishops from zealous conviction, many more from pliability to self-interest, had gone along with the new modelling of the English church by Henry and Edward; so that it was perfectly easy to keep up that form of government in the regular succession which had usually been deemed essential; though the foreign reformers had neither the wish, nor possibly the means, to preserve it. Cranmer himself, indeed, during the reign of Henry, had bent, as usual, to the king's despotic humor, and favored a novel theory of ecclesiastical authority, which resolved all its spiritual as well as temporal powers into the royal supremacy. Accordingly, at the accession of Edward, he himself, and several other bishops, took out commissions to hold their sees during pleasure.[1] But when the necessity of compliance had passed by, they showed a disposition not only to oppose the continual spoliation of church property, but to maintain the jurisdiction which the canon law had conferred upon them.[2] And though, as this

[1] Burnet, ii. 6.

[2] There are two curious entries in the Lords' Journ. 14th and 18th of Nov. 1549, which point out the origin of the new code of ecclesiastical law mentioned in the next note: "Hodie questi sunt episcopi, contemni se a plebe, audere autem nihil pro potestate suâ administrare, eo quod per publicas quasdam denuntiationes quas proclamationes vocant, sublata esset penitus sua jurisdictio, adeo ut neminem judicio sistere, nullum scelus punire, neminem ad ædem sacram cogere, neque cætera id genus munia ad eos pertinentia

papal code did not appear very well adapted to a protestant church, a new scheme of ecclesiastical laws was drawn up, which the king's death rendered abortive, this was rather calculated to strengthen the hands of the spiritual courts than to withdraw any matter from their cognizance.[1]

exequi auderent. Hæc querela ab omnibus proceribus non sine mœrore audita est; et ut quam citissimè huic malo subveniretur, injunctum est episcopis ut formulam aliquam statuti hâc de re scriptam traderent: quæ si concilio postea prælecta omnibus ordinibus probaretur, pro lege omnibus sententiis sanciri posset.

"18 Nov. Hodie lecta est billa pro jurisdictione episcoporum et aliorum ecclesiasticorum, quæ cum proceribus, *eo quod episcopi nimis sibi arrogare viderentur*, non placeret, visum est deligere prudentes aliquot viros utriusque ordinis, qui habitâ maturâ tantæ rei inter se deliberatione, referrent toti consilio quid pro ratione temporis et rei necessitate in hac causa agi expediret." Accordingly, the lords appoint the archbishop of Canterbury, the bishops of Ely, Durham, and Lichfield, lords Dorset, Wharton, and Stafford, with chief justice Montague.

[1] It had been enacted, 3 Edw. 6. c. 11, that thirty-two commissioners, half clergy, half lay, should be appointed to draw up a collection of new canons. But these, according to Strype, ii. 303 (though I do not find it in the act), might be reduced to eight, without preserving the equality of orders; and of those nominated in Nov. 1551, five were ecclesiastics, three laymen. The influence of the former shows itself in the collection, published with the title of Reformatio Legum Ecclesiasticûm, and intended as a complete code of protestant canon law. This was referred for revisal to a new commission; but the king's death ensued, and the business was never again taken up. Burnet, ii. 197. Collier, 326. The Latin style is highly praised; Cheke and Haddon, the most elegant scholars of that age, having been concerned in it. This, however, is of small importance. The canons are founded on a principle current among the clergy, that a rigorous discipline enforced by church censures and the aid of the civil power is the best safeguard of a Christian commonwealth against vice. But it is easy to perceive that its severity would never have been endured in this country, and that this was the true reason why it was laid aside: not, according to the improbable refinement with which Warburton has furnished Hurd, because the old canon law was thought more favorable to the prerogative of the crown. Compare Warburton's Letters to Hurd, p. 192, with the latter's Moral and Political Dialogues, p. 308, 4th edit.

The canons trench in several places on the known province of the common law, by assigning specific penalties and forfeitures to offences, as in the case of adultery; and though it is true that this was all subject to the confirmation of parliament, yet the lawyers would look with their usual jealousy on such provisions in ecclesiastical canons. But the great sin of this protestant legislation is its extension of the name and penalties of heresy to the wilful denial of any part of the authorized articles of faith. This is clear from the first and second titles. But it has been doubted whether capital punishments for this offence were intended to be preserved. Burnet, always favorable to the reformers, asserts that they were laid aside. Collier and Lingard, whose bias is the other way, maintain the contrary. There is, it appears to me, some difficulty in determining this. That all persons denying any one of the articles might be turned over to the secular power is evident. Yet it rather seems by one passage in the title, de judiciis contra hæreses, c. 10, that infamy and civil disability were the only punishments intended to be kept up, except in case of the denial of the Christian religion. For if a heretic were, as a matter of course, to be burned, it seems needless to provide, as in this chapter, that he should be incapable of being a witness, or of making a will. Dr. Lingard, on the other hand, says, "It regulates the delivery of the obstinate heretic to the civil magistrate, that he may *suffer death* according to law." The words to which he refers are these: Cum sic penitus insederit error, et tam alte radices egerit, ut nec sententiâ quidem excommunicationis ad veritatem reus inflecti possit, tum consumptis omnibus aliis remediis, ad extremum ad civiles magistratus ablegetur *puniendus*. Id. tit. c. 4.

It is generally best, where the words are at all ambiguous, to give the reader the power of judging for himself. But I by no means pretend that Dr. Lingard is mistaken. On the contrary, the language of this passage leads to a strong

The policy, or it may be the prejudices, of Cranmer induced him also to retain in the church a few ceremonial usages, which the Helvetic, though not the Lutheran, reformers had swept away, such as the copes and rochets of bishops, and the surplice of officiating priests. It should seem inconceivable that any one could object to these vestments, considered in themselves; far more, if they could answer in the slightest degree the end of conciliating a reluctant people. But this motive unfortunately was often disregarded in that age; and indeed in all ages an abhorrence of concession and compromise is a never-failing characteristic of religious factions. The foreign reformers then in England, two of whom, Bucer and Peter Martyr, enjoyed a deserved reputation, expressed their dissatisfaction at seeing these habits retained, and complained, in general, of the backwardness of the English reformation. Calvin and Bullinger wrote from Switzerland in the same strain.[1] Nor was this sentiment by any means confined to strangers. Hooper,

suspicion that the rigor of popish persecution was intended to remain, especially as the writ de hæretico comburendo was in force by law, and there is no hint of taking it away. Yet it seems monstrous to conceive that the denial of predestination (which by the way is asserted in this collection, tit. de hæresibus, c. 22, with a shade more of Calvinism than in the articles) was to subject any one to be burned alive. And on the other hand there is this difficulty, that Arianism, Pelagianism, popery, anabaptism, are all put on the same footing; so that, if we deny that the papist or free-willer was to be burned, we must deny the same of the anti-trinitarian, which contradicts the principle and practice of that age. Upon the whole, I cannot form a decided opinion as to this matter. Dr. Lingard does not hesitate to say, "Cranmer and his associates perished in the flames which they had prepared to kindle for the destruction of their opponents."

Upon further consideration, I incline to suspect that the temporal punishment of heresy was intended to be fixed by act of parliament; and probably with various degrees, which will account for the indefinite word "puniendus." [A manuscript of the Reformatio Legum in the British Museum (Harl. 426) has the following clause after the word puniendus: "Vel ut in perpetuum pellatur exilium, vel ad æternas carceris deprimatur tenebras, vel alioqui pro magistratûs prudenti consideratione plectendus, ut maxime illius conversioni expedire videntur.' Jenkins's edition of Cranmer, vol. i. preface, cx. This seems to prove that capital penalties were not designed by the original compilers of this ecclesiastical code. 1845.]

The language of Dr. Lingard, as I have since observed, about "suffering death," is taken from Collier, who puts exactly the same construction on the canon.

Before I quit these canons, one mistake of Dr. Lingard's may be corrected. He says that divorces were allowed by them not only for adultery, but cruelty, desertion, and *incompatibility of temper*. But the contrary may be clearly shown, from tit. de matrimonio, c. 11, and tit. de divortiis, c. 12. Divorce was allowed for something more than incompatibility of temper, namely, *capitales inimicitiæ*, meaning, as I conceive, attempts by one party on the other's life. In this respect their scheme of a very important branch of social law seems far better than our own. Nothing can be more absurd than our modern *privilegia*, our acts of parliament to break the bond between an adulteress and her husband. Nor do I see how we can justify the denial of redress to women in every case of adultery and desertion. It does not follow that the marriage tie ought to be dissolved as easily as it is in the Lutheran states of Germany.

[1] Strype, passim. Burnet, ii. 154; iii. Append. 200. Collier, 294, 303.

an eminent divine, having been elected bishop of Gloucester, refused to be consecrated in the usual dress. It marks, almost ludicrously, the spirit of those times, that, instead of permitting him to decline the station, the council sent him to prison for some time. until by some mutual concessions the business was adjusted.[1] These events it would hardly be worth while to notice in such a work as the present if they had not been the prologue to a long and serious drama.

Mary. Persecution under her.

It is certain that the reëstablishment of popery on Mary's accession must have been acceptable to a large part, or perhaps to the majority, of the nation. There is reason, however, to believe that the reformed doctrine had made a real progress in the few years of her brother's reign. The counties of Norfolk and Suffolk, which placed Mary on the throne as the lawful heir, were chiefly protestant, and experienced from her the usual gratitude and good faith of a bigot.[2] Noailles bears witness, in many of his despatches, to the unwillingness which great numbers of the people displayed to endure the restoration of popery, and to the queen's excessive unpopularity, even before her marriage with Philip had been resolved upon.[3] As for the higher classes, they partook far less than their inferiors in the religious zeal of that age. Henry, Edward, Mary, Elizabeth, found almost an equal compliance with their varying schemes of faith. Yet the larger proportion of the nobility and gentry appear to have preferred the catholic religion. Several peers opposed the bills for reformation under Edward; and others, who had gone along with the current, became active counsellors of Mary. Not a few persons of family emigrated in the latter reign; but with the exception of the second earl of Bedford, who suffered a short imprisonment on account of religion, the protestant martyrology contains no confessor of superior rank.[4] The

[1] Strype, Burnet. The former is the more accurate.

[2] Burnet, 237, 246. 3 Strype, 10, 341. No part of England suffered so much in the persecution.

[3] Ambassades de Noailles, v. ii. passim. 3 Strype, 100.

[4] Strype, iii. 107. He reckons the emigrants at 800. Life of Cranmer, 314. Of these the most illustrious was the duchess of Suffolk, — not the first cousin of the queen, but, as has been suggested to me, the sister of Charles Brandon, whose first wife was sister to Henry VIII. In the parliament of 1555, a bill sequestering the property of "the duchess of Suffolk and others, contemptuously gone over the seas," was rejected by the commons on the third reading. Journals, 6th Dec.

It must not be understood that all the aristocracy were supple hypocrites, though they did not expose themselves voluntarily to prosecution. Noailles tells us that the earls of Oxford and Westmoreland, and lord Willoughby, were

same accommodating spirit characterized, upon the whole, the clergy; and would have been far more general, if a considerable number had not availed themselves of the permission to marry granted by Edward; which led to their expulsion from their cures on his sister's coming to the throne.[1] Yet it was not the temper of Mary's parliaments, whatever pains had been taken about their election, to second her bigotry in surrendering the temporal fruits of their recent schism. The bill for restoring first fruits and impropriations in the queen's hands to the church passed not without difficulty; and it was found impossible to obtain a repeal of the act of supremacy without the pope's explicit confirmation of the abbey lands to their new proprietors. Even this confirmation, though made through the legate cardinal Pole, by virtue of a full commission, left not unreasonably an apprehension that, on some better opportunity, the imprescriptible nature of church property might be urged against the possessors.[2] With these selfish considerations others of a more generous nature conspired to render the old religion more obnoxious than it had been at the queen's accession. Her marriage with Philip, his encroaching disposition, the arbitrary turn of his counsels, the insolence imputed to the Spaniards who accompanied him, the unfortunate loss of Calais through that alliance, while it thoroughly alienated the kingdom from Mary, created a prejudice against the

censured by the council *for religion;* and it was thought that the former would lose his title (more probably his hereditary office of chamberlain), which would be conferred on the earl of Pembroke, v. 319. Michele, the Venetian ambassador, in his Relazione del Stato d' Inghilterra, Lansdowne MSS. 840, does not speak favorably of the general affection towards popery. "The English in general," he says, "would turn Jews or Turks if their sovereign pleased; but the restoration of the abbey lands by the crown keeps alive a constant fear among those who possess them." Fol. 176. This restitution of church lands in the hands of the crown cost the queen 60,000*l.* a year of revenue.

[1] Parke had extravagantly reckoned the number of these at 12,000, which Burnet reduces to 3000, vol. iii. 226. But upon this computation they formed a very considerable body on the protestant side. Burnet's calculation, however, is made by assuming the ejected ministers of the diocese of Norwich to have been in the ratio of the whole; which, from the eminent protestantism of that district, is not probable; and Dr. Lingard, on Wharton's authority, who has taken his ratio from the diocese of Canterbury, thinks they did not amount to more than about 1500.

[2] Burnet, ii. 298, iii. 245. But see Philips's Life of Pole, sect. ix., *contra;* and Ridley's answer to this, p. 272. In fact no scheme of religion would on the whole have been so acceptable to the nation as that which Henry left established, consisting chiefly of what was called catholic in doctrine, but free from the grosser abuses and from all connection with the see of Rome. Arbitrary and capricious as that king was, he carried the majority along with him, as I believe, in all great points, both as to what he renounced and what he retained. Michele (Relazione, &c.) is of this opinion.

religion which the Spanish court so steadily favored.[1] So violent indeed was the hatred conceived by the English nation against Spain during the short period of Philip's marriage with their queen, that it diverted the old channel of public feelings, and almost put an end to that dislike and jealousy of France which had so long existed. For at least a century after this time we rarely find in popular writers any expressions of hostility towards that country; though their national manners, so remote from our own, are not unfrequently the object of ridicule. The prejudices of the populace, as much as the policy of our councillors, were far more directed against Spain.

Its effect rather favorable to protestantism.

But what had the greatest efficacy in disgusting the English with Mary's system of faith, was the cruelty by which it was accompanied. Though the privy council were in fact continually urging the bishops forward in this prosecution,[2] the latter bore the chief blame, and the abhorrence entertained for them naturally extended to the doctrine they professed. A sort of instinctive reason told the people, what the learned on neither side had been able to discover, that the truth of a religion begins to be very suspicious when it stands in need of prisons and scaffolds to eke out its evidences. And as the English were constitutionally humane, and not hardened by continually witnessing the infliction of barbarous punish-

[1] No one of our historians has been so severe on Mary's reign, except on a religious account, as Carte, on the authority of the letters of Noailles. Dr. Lingard, though with these before him, has softened and suppressed, till this queen appears honest and even amiable. But, admitting that the French ambassador had a temptation to exaggerate the faults of a government wholly devoted to Spain, it is manifest that Mary's reign was inglorious, her capacity narrow, and her temper sanguinary; that, although conscientious in some respects, she was as capable of dissimulation as her sister, and of breach of faith as her husband; that she obstinately and wilfully sacrificed her subjects' affections and interests to a misplaced and discreditable attachment; and that the words with which Carte has concluded the character of this unlamented sovereign, though little pleasing to men of Dr. Lingard's profession, are perfectly just: — "Having reduced the nation to the brink of ruin, she left it, by her seasonable decease, to be restored by her admirable successor to its ancient prosperity and glory." I fully admit, at the same time, that Dr. Lingard has proved Elizabeth to have been as dangerous a prisoner as she afterwards found the queen of Scots.

[2] Strype, ii. 17; Burnet, iii. 263, and Append. 285, where there is a letter from the king and queen to Bonner, as if even he wanted excitement to prosecute heretics. The number who suffered death by fire in this reign is reckoned by Fox at 284, by Speed at 277, and by Lord Burghley at 290. Strype, iii. 473. These numbers come so near to each other, that they may be presumed also to approach the truth. But Carte, on the authority of one of Noailles's letters, thinks many more were put to death than our martyrologists have discovered. And the prefacer to Ridley's Treatise de Cœnâ Domini, supposed to be bishop Grindal, says that 800 suffered in this manner for religion. Burnet, ii. 364. I incline, however, to the lower statements.

ments, there arose a sympathy for men suffering torments with such meekness and patience, which the populace of some other nations were perhaps less apt to display, especially in executions on the score of heresy.[1] The theologian indeed and the philosopher may concur in deriding the notion that either sincerity or moral rectitude can be the test of truth; yet among the various species of authority to which recourse had been had to supersede or to supply the deficiencies of argument, I know not whether any be more reasonable, and none certainly is so congenial to unsophisticated minds. Many are said to have become protestants under Mary, who, at her coming to the throne, had retained the contrary persuasion.[2] And the strongest proof of this may be drawn from the acquiescence of the great body of the kingdom in the reëstablishment of protestantism by Elizabeth, when compared with the seditions and discontent on that account under Edward. The course which this famous princess steered in ecclesiastical concerns, during her long reign, will form the subject of the two ensuing chapters.

1 Burnet makes a very just observation on the cruelties of this period, that "they raised that horror in the whole nation, that there seems ever since that time such an abhorrence to that religion to be derived down from father to son, that it is no wonder an aversion so deeply rooted, and raised upon such grounds, does, upon every new provocation or jealousy of returning to it, break out in most violent and convulsive symptoms," p. 388. "Delicta majorum immeritus luis, *Romane.*" But those who would diminish this aversion and prevent these convulsive symptoms will do better by avoiding for the future either such panegyrics on Mary and her advisers, or such insidious extenuations of her persecution, as we have lately read, and which do not raise a favorable impression of their sincerity in the principles of toleration to which they profess to have been converted.

Noailles, who, though an enemy to Mary's government, must, as a catholic, be reckoned an unsuspicious witness, remarkably confirms the account given by Fox, and since by all our writers, of the death of Rogers, the proto-martyr, and its effect on the people. "Ce jour d'huy a esté faite la confirmation de l'alliance entre le pape et ce royaume par un sacrifice publique et solemnel d'un docteur prédicant nommé Rogerus, lequel a été brulé tout vif pour estre Lutherien; mais il est mort persistant en son opinion. A quoy le plus grand partie de ce peuple a pris tel plaisir, qu'ils n'ont eu crainte de luy faire plusieurs acclamations pour comforter son courage; et même ses enfans y ont assisté, le consolant de telle façon qu'il semblait qu'on le menait aux noces." V. 173.

[The execration with which Mary's bishops were met in the next reign is attested in a letter of Parkhurst to Conrad Gesner. "Jam et Deo et hominibus sunt exosi, nec usquam nisi inviti prorepunt, ne forte fiat tumultus in populo. Multi coram eos vocant carnifices." Zurich Letters, by Parker Society, p. 18. 1845.]

2 Strype, iii. 295.

CHAPTER III.

ON THE LAWS OF ELIZABETH'S REIGN RESPECTING THE ROMAN CATHOLICS.

Change of Religion on the Queen's Accession — Acts of Supremacy and Uniformity — Restraint of Roman Catholic Worship in the first years of Elizabeth — Statute of 1562 — Speech of Lord Montague against it — This Act not fully enforced — Application of the Emperor in behalf of the English Catholics — Persecution of this Body in the ensuing Period — Uncertain Succession of the Crown between the Families of Scotland and Suffolk — the Queen's unwillingness to decide this, or to marry — Imprisonment of Lady Catherine Grey — Mary Queen of Scotland — Combination in her Favor — Bull of Pious V. — Statutes for the Queen's Security — Catholics more rigorously treated — Refugees in the Netherlands — Their Hostility to the Government — Fresh Laws against the Catholic Worship — Execution of Campian and others — Defence of the Queen by Burleigh — Increased Severity of the Government — Mary — Plot in her Favor — Her Execution — Remarks upon it — Continued Persecution of Roman Catholics — General Observations.

THE accession of Elizabeth, gratifying to the whole nation on account of the late queen's extreme unpopularity, infused peculiar joy into the hearts of all well-wishers to the Reformation. Child of that famous marriage which had severed the connection of England with the Roman see, and trained betimes in the learned and reasoning discipline of protestant theology, suspected and oppressed for that very reason by a sister's jealousy, and scarcely preserved from the death which at one time threatened her, there was every ground to be confident, that, notwithstanding her forced compliance with the catholic rites during the late reign, her inclinations had continued steadfast to the opposite side.[1] Nor was she long in manifesting this disposition sufficiently to alarm one party, though not entirely to satisfy the other. Her great prudence, and that of her advisers, which taught her to move slowly,

Change of religion on the queen's accession.

[1] Elizabeth was much suspected of a concern in the conspiracy of 1554, which was more extensive than appeared from Wyatt's insurrection, and had in view the placing her on the throne, with the earl of Devonshire for her husband. Wyatt indeed at his execution acquitted her; but as he said as much for Devonshire, who is proved by the letters of Noailles to have been engaged, his testimony is of less value. Nothing, however, appears in these letters, I believe, to criminate Elizabeth. Her life was saved, against the advice of the imperial court, and of their party in the cabinet, especially lord Paget, by the influence of Gardiner,

while the temper of the nation was still uncertain, and her government still embarrassed with a French war and a Spanish alliance, joined with a certain tendency in her religious sentiments not so thoroughly protestant as had been expected, produced some complaints of delay from the ardent reformers just returned from exile. She directed sir Edward Carne, her sister's ambassador at Rome, to notify her accession to Paul IV. Several catholic writers have laid stress on this circumstance as indicative of a desire to remain in his communion; and have attributed her separation from it to his arrogant reply, commanding her to lay down the title of royalty, and to submit her pretensions to his decision.[1] But she

according to Dr. Lingard, writing on the authority of Renard's despatches. Burnet, who had no access to that source of information, imagines Gardiner to have been her most inveterate enemy. She was even released from prison for the time, though soon afterwards detained again, and kept in custody, as is well known, for the rest of this reign. Her inimitable dissimulation was all required to save her from the penalties of heresy and treason. It appears by the memoir of the Venetian ambassador, in 1557 (Lansdowne MSS. 840), as well as from the letters of Noailles, that Mary was desirous to change the succession, and would have done so, had it not been for Philip's reluctance, and the impracticability of obtaining the consent of parliament. Though herself of a dissembling character, she could not conceal the hatred she bore to one who brought back the memory of her mother's and her own wrongs; especially when she saw all eyes turned towards the successor, and felt that the curse of her own barrenness was to fall on her beloved religion. Elizabeth had been not only forced to have a chapel in her house, and to give all exterior signs of conformity, but to protest on oath her attachment to the catholic faith; though Hume, who always loves a popular story, gives credence to the well-known verses ascribed to her, in order to elude a declaration of her opinion on the sacrament. The inquisitors of that age were not so easily turned round by an equivocal answer. Yet Elizabeth's faith was constantly suspected. "Accresce oltro questo l' odio," says the Venetian, "il sapere che sia aliena dalla religione presente, per essere non pur nata, ma dotta ed allevata nell' altra, che se bene con la esteriore ha mostrato, e mostra di essersi ridotta, vivendo cattolicamente, pure è opinione che dissimuli e nell' interiore la ritenga più che mai."

1 [This remarkable fact, which runs through all domestic and foreign histories, has been disputed, and, as far as appears, disproved, by the late editor of Dodd's Church History of England, vol. iv. preface, on the authority of Carne's own letters in the State Paper Office. It is at least highly probable, not to say evident, from these, that Elizabeth never contemplated so much intercourse with the pope, even as a temporal sovereign, or to notify her accession to him; and it had before been shown by Strype, that, on Dec. 1, 1558, an order was despatched to Carne, forbidding him to proceed in an ecclesiastical suit, wherein, as English ambassador, he had been engaged. Strype's Annals, i. 34. Carne, on his own solicitation, was recalled, Feb. 10; though the pope would not suffer him, nor, when he saw what was going forward at home, was he willing, to return. Mr. Tierney, the editor of Dodd, conceives the story of Paul IV.'s intemperate language to have been coined by "the inventive powers of Paul Sarpi," who first published it in his History of the Council of Trent, in 1619. From him Mr. T. supposes Spondanus and Pallavicino to have taken it; and from them it has passed to a multitude of catholic as well as protestant historians. It may, however, seem rather doubtful whether Spondanus would have taken this simply on the authority of Sarpi; and we may perhaps conjecture that the anecdote had been already in circulation, even if it had never appeared in print, (a negative hard to establish,) before the publication of the History of the Council of Trent. Nor is it improbable that Paul, according to the violence of his disposition, had uttered some such language, and even to Carne himself,

had begun to make alterations, though not very essential, in the church service, before the pope's behavior could have become known to her; and the bishops must have been well aware of the course she designed to pursue, when they adopted the violent and impolitic resolution of refusing to officiate at her coronation.[1] Her council was formed of a very few catholics, of several pliant conformists with all changes, and of some known friends to the protestant interest. But two of these, Cecil and Bacon, were so much higher in her confidence, and so incomparably superior in talents to the other councillors, that it was evident which way she must incline.[2] The parliament met about two months after her accession. The creed of parliament from the time of Henry VIII. had been always that of the court; whether it were that elections had constantly been influenced, as we know was sometimes the case, or that men of adverse principles, yielding to the torrent, had left the way clear to the partisans of power. This first, like all subsequent parliaments, was to the full as favorable to protestantism as the queen could desire: the first-fruits of benefices, and, what was far more important, the supremacy in ecclesiastical affairs, were restored to the crown; the laws made concerning religion in Edward's time were reënacted. These acts did not pass without considerable opposition among the lords; nine temporal peers, beside all the bishops, having protested against the bill of uniformity establishing the Anglican liturgy, though some pains had been taken to soften the passages most obnoxious to cath-

though not, as the story represents it, in reply to an official communication. But it is chiefly material to observe, that Elizabeth displayed her determination to keep aloof from Rome in the very beginning of her reign. 1845.]

1 Elizabeth ascended the throne November 17, 1558. On the 5th of December Mary was buried; and on this occasion White, bishop of Winchester, in preaching her funeral sermon, spoke with virulence against the protestant exiles, and expressed apprehension of their return. Burnet, iii. 272. Directions to read part of the service in English, and forbidding the elevation of the host, were issued prior to the proclamation of December 27, against innovations without authority. The great seal was taken from archbishop Heath early in January, and given to sir Nicholas Bacon. Parker was pitched upon to succeed Pole at Canterbury in the preceding month. From the dates of these and other facts, it may be fairly inferred that Elizabeth's resolution was formed independently of the pope's behavior towards sir Edward Carne; though that might probably exasperate her against the adherents of the Roman see, and make their religion appear more inconsistent with their civil allegiance. If, indeed, the refusal of the bishops to officiate at her coronation (Jan. 14, 1558-9) were founded in any degree on Paul IV.'s denial of her title, it must have seemed in that age within a hair's breadth of high treason. But it more probably arose from her order that the host should not be elevated, which in truth was not legally to be justified.

2 See a paper by Cecil on the best means of reforming religion, written at this time with all his cautious wisdom, in Burnet, or in Strype's Annals of the Reformation, or in the Somers Tracts.

olics.[1] But the act restoring the royal supremacy met with less resistance; whether it were that the system of Henry retained its hold over some minds, or that it did not encroach, like the former, on the liberty of conscience, or that men not over-scrupulous were satisfied with the interpretation which the queen caused to be put upon the oath.

Several of the bishops had submitted to the Reformation under Edward VI. But they had acted, in general, so conspicuous a part in the late restoration of popery, that, even amidst so many examples of false profession, shame restrained them from a second apostasy. Their number happened not to exceed sixteen, one of whom was prevailed on to conform; while the rest, refusing the oath of supremacy, were deprived of their bishoprics by the court of ecclesiastical high commission. In the summer of 1559 the queen appointed a general ecclesiastical visitation, to compel the observance of the protestant formularies. It appears from their reports that only about one hundred dignitaries, and eighty parochial priests, resigned their benefices, or were deprived.[2] Men eminent for their zeal in the protestant cause, and most of them exiles during the persecution, occupied the vacant sees. And thus, before the end of 1559, the English church, so long contended for as a prize by the two religions, was lost forever to that of Rome.

Acts of Supremacy and Uniformity.

These two statutes, commonly denominated the Acts of Supremacy and Uniformity, form the basis of that restrictive code of laws, deemed by some one of the fundamental bulwarks, by others the reproach of our constitution, which pressed so heavily for

[1] Parl. Hist. vol. i. p. 394. In the reign of Edward a prayer had been inserted in the liturgy to deliver us "from the bishop of Rome and all his detestable enormities." This was now struck out; and, what was more acceptable to the nation, the words used in distributing the elements were so contrived, by blending the two forms successively adopted under Edward, as neither to offend the popish or Lutheran, nor the Zuinglian communicant. A rubric directed against the doctrine of the real or corporal presence was omitted. This was replaced after the Restoration. Burnet owns that the greater part of the nation still adhered to this tenet, though it was not the opinion of the rulers of the church. ii. 390, 406.

[2] Burnet; Strype's Annals, 169. Pensions were reserved for those who quitted their benefices on account of religion. Burnet, ii. 398. This was a very liberal measure, and at the same time a politic check on their conduct. Lingard thinks the number must have been much greater; but the visitors' reports seem the best authority. It is, however, highly probable that others resigned their preferments afterwards, when the casuistry of their church grew more scrupulous. It may be added, that the visitors restored the married clergy who had been dispossessed in the preceding reign; which would of course considerably augment the number of sufferers for popery.

more than two centuries upon the adherents to the Romish church. By the former all beneficed ecclesiastics, and all laymen holding office under the crown, were obliged to take the oath of supremacy, renouncing the spiritual as well as temporal jurisdiction of every foreign prince or prelate, on pain of forfeiting their office or benefice; and it was rendered highly penal, and for the third offence treasonable, to maintain such supremacy by writing or advised speaking.[1] The

[1] 1 Eliz. c. 1. The oath of supremacy was expressed as follows: — "I, A. B., do utterly testify and declare, that the queen's highness is the only supreme governor of this realm, and all other her highness's dominions and countries, as well in all spiritual and ecclesiastical things or causes as temporal; and that no foreign prince, person, prelate, state, or potentate, hath or ought to have any jurisdiction, power, superiority, preëminence, or authority, ecclesiastical or spiritual, within this realm; and therefore I do utterly renounce and forsake all foreign jurisdictions, powers, superiorities, and authorities, and do promise that from henceforth I shall bear faith and true allegiance to the queen's highness, her heirs and lawful successors, and to my power shall assist and defend all jurisdictions, preëminences, privileges, and authorities, granted or belonging to the queen's highness, her heirs and successors, or united and annexed to the imperial crown of this realm."

A remarkable passage in the injunctions to the ecclesiastical visitors of 1559, which may be reckoned in the nature of a contemporaneous exposition of the law, restrains the royal supremacy established by this act, and asserted in the above oath, in the following words: "Her majesty forbiddeth all manner her subjects to give ear or credit to such perverse and malicious persons, which most sinisterly and maliciously labor to notify to her loving subjects how by words of the said oath it may be collected that the kings or queens of this realm, possessors of the crown, may challenge authority and power of ministry of divine service in the church; wherein her said subjects be much abused by such evil disposed persons. For certainly her majesty neither doth, nor ever will, challenge any other authority than that was challenged and lately used by the said noble kings of famous memory, king Henry VIII. and king Edward VI., which is, and was of ancient time, due to the imperial crown of this realm; that is, under God to have the sovereignty and rule over all manner of persons born within these her realms, dominions, and countries, of what estate, either ecclesiastical or temporal, soever they be, so as no other foreign power shall or ought to have any superiority over them. And if any person that hath conceived any other sense of the form of the said oath shall accept the same with this interpretation, sense or meaning, her majesty is well pleased to accept every such in that behalf, as her good and obedient subjects, and shall acquit them of all manner of penalties contained in the said act, against such as shall peremptorily or obstinately refuse to take the same oath." 1 Somers Tracts, edit. Scott, 73.

This interpretation was afterwards given in one of the thirty-nine articles, which having been confirmed by parliament, it is undoubtedly to be reckoned the true sense of the oath. Mr. Butler, in his Memoirs of English Catholics, vol. i. p. 157, enters into a discussion of the question, whether Roman catholics might concientiously take the oath of supremacy in this sense. It appears that in the seventeenth century some contended for the affirmative; and this seems to explain the fact that several persons of that persuasion, besides peers, from whom the oath was not exacted, did actually hold offices under the Stuarts, and even enter into parliament, and that the test act and declaration against transubstantiation were thus rendered necessary to make their exclusion certain. Mr. B. decides against taking the oath, but on grounds by no means sufficient; and oddly overlooks the decisive objection, that it denies in toto the jurisdiction and ecclesiastical authority of the pope. No writer, as far as my slender knowledge extends, of the Gallican or German school of discipline, has gone to this length; certainly not Mr. Butler himself, who in a modern publication, Book of the Roman Catholic Church, p. 120, seems to consider even the appellant jurisdiction in ecclesiastical causes as vested in the holy see by divine right.

As to the exposition before given of the oath of supremacy, I conceive that it was

latter statute trenched more on the natural rights of conscience; prohibiting, under pain of forfeiting goods and chattels for the first offence, of a year's imprisonment for the second, and of imprisonment during life for the third, the use by a minister, whether beneficed or not, of any but the established liturgy; and imposed a fine of one shilling on all who should absent themselves from church on Sundays and holydays.[1]

Restraint of Roman catholic worship in the first years of Elizabeth.

This act operated as an absolute interdiction of the catholic rites, however privately celebrated. It has frequently been asserted, that the government connived at the domestic exercise of that religion during these first years of Elizabeth's reign. This may possibly have been the case with respect to some persons of very high rank whom it was inexpedient to irritate. But we find instances of severity towards catholics, even in that early period; and it is evident that their solemn rites were only performed by stealth, and at much hazard. Thus sir Edward Waldgrave and his lady were sent to the Tower in 1561, for hearing mass and having a priest in their house. Many others about the same time were punished for the like offence.[2] Two bishops, one of whom, I regret to say, was Grindal, write to the council in 1562, concerning a priest apprehended in a lady's house, that neither he nor the servants would be sworn to answer to articles, saying they would not accuse themselves; and, after a wise remark on this, that "papistry is like to end in anabaptistry," proceed to hint, that "some think that if this priest might be put to some kind of torment, and so driven to confess what he knoweth, he might gain the queen's majesty a good mass of money by the masses that he hath said; but this we refer to your lordships' wisdom."[3] This commencement of persecution induced many catholics to fly beyond sea, and gave rise to those reunions of disaffected

intended not only to relieve the scruples of catholics, but of those who had imbibed from the school of Calvin an apprehension of what is sometimes, though rather improperly, called Erastianism,—the merging of all spiritual powers, even those of ordination and of preaching, in the paramount authority of the state, towards which the despotism of Henry, and obsequiousness of Cranmer, had seemed to bring the church of England.

[1] 1 Eliz. c. 2.

[2] Strype's Annals, i. 233, 241.

[3] Haynes, 395. The penalty for causing mass to be said, by the act of uniformity, was only 100 marks for the first offence. These imprisonments were probably in many cases illegal, and only sustained by the arbitrary power of the High Commission court.

exiles, which never ceased to endanger the throne of Elizabeth.

It cannot, as far as appears, be truly alleged that any greater provocation had as yet been given by the catholics than that of pertinaciously continuing to believe and worship as their fathers had done before them. I request those who may hesitate about this, to pay some attention to the order of time, before they form their opinions. The master mover, that became afterwards so busy, had not yet put his wires into action. Every prudent man at Rome (and we shall not at least deny that there were such) condemned the precipitate and insolent behavior of Paul IV. towards Elizabeth, as they did most other parts of his administration. Pius IV., the successor of that injudicious old man, aware of the inestimable importance of reconciliation, and suspecting probably that the queen's turn of thinking did not exclude all hope of it, despatched a nuncio to England, with an invitation to send ambassadors to the council at Trent, and with powers, as is said, to confirm the English liturgy, and to permit double communion; one of the few concessions which the more indulgent Romanists of that age were not very reluctant to make.[1] But Elizabeth had taken her line as to the court of Rome; the nuncio received a message at Brussels, that he must not enter the kingdom; and she was too wise to countenance the impartial fathers of Trent, whose labors had nearly drawn to a close, and whose decisions on the controverted points it had never been very difficult to foretell. I have not found that Pius IV., more moderate than most other pontiffs of the sixteenth century, took any measures hostile to the temporal government of this realm: but the deprived ecclesiastics were not unfairly anxious to keep alive the faith of their former hearers, and to prevent them from sliding into conformity, through indifference and disuse of their ancient rites.[2] The means taken were chiefly the same as had been adopted against themselves, the dispersion of small papers either in a serious or lively strain; but the remarkable position in which the queen was placed rendering

[1] Strype, 220.

[2] Questions of conscience were circulated, with answers all tending to show the unlawfulness of conformity. Strype, 228. There was nothing more in this than the catholic clergy were bound in consistency with their principles to do, though it seemed very atrocious to bigots. Mr. Butler says, that some theologians at Trent were consulted as to the lawfulness of occasional conformity to the Anglican rites, who pronounced against it. Mem. of Catholics, i. 171.

her death a most important contingency, the popish party made use of pretended conjurations and prophecies of that event, in order to unsettle the people's minds, and to dispose them to anticipate another reaction.[1] Partly through these political circumstances, but far more from the hard usage they experienced for professing their religion, there seems to have been an increasing restlessness among the catholics about 1562, which was met with new rigor by the parliament of that year.[2]

Statute of 1562.

The act entitled, "for the assurance of the queen's royal power over all estates and subjects within her dominions," enacts, with an iniquitous and sanguinary retrospect, that all persons, who had ever taken holy orders or any degree in the universities, or had been admitted to the practice of the laws, or held any office in their execution, should be bound to take the oath of supremacy, when tendered to them by a bishop, or by commissioners appointed under the great seal. The penalty for the first refusal of this oath was that of a præmunire; but any person who, after the space of three months from the first tender, should again refuse it when in like manner tendered, incurred the pains of high treason. The oath of supremacy was imposed by the statute on every member of the House of Commons, but could not be tendered to a peer; the queen declaring her full confidence in those hereditary councillors. Several peers of great weight and dignity were still catholics.[3]

Speech of lord Montagu against it.

This harsh statute did not pass without opposition. Two speeches against it have been preserved; one by lord Montagu in the House of Lords, the other by Mr. Atkinson in the Commons, breathing such generous abhorrence of persecution as some erro-

[1] The trick of conjuration about the queen's death began very early in her reign (Strype, i. 7), and led to a penal statute against "fond and fantastical prophecies." 5 Eliz. c. 15.

[2] I know not how to charge the catholics with the conspiracy of the two Poles, nephews of the cardinal, and some others, to obtain five thousand troops from the duke of Guise, and proclaim Mary queen. This seems however to have been the immediate provocation for the statute 5 Eliz.; and it may be thought to indicate a good deal of discontent in that party upon which the conspirators relied. But as Elizabeth spared the lives of all who were arraigned, and we know no details of the case, it may be doubted whether their intentions were altogether so criminal as was charged. Strype, i. 333; Camden, 388 (in Kennet).

Strype tells us (i. 374) of resolutions adopted against the queen in a consistory held by Pius IV. in 1563; one of these is a pardon to any cook, brewer, vintner, or other, that would poison her. But this is so unlikely, and so little in that pope's character, that it makes us suspect the rest, as false information of a spy.

[3] 5 Eliz. c. 1.

neously imagine to have been unknown to that age, because we rarely meet with it in theological writings. "This law," said lord Montagu, "is not necessary; forasmuch as the catholics of this realm disturb not, nor hinder the public affairs of the realm, neither spiritual nor temporal. They dispute not, they preach not, they disobey not the queen; they cause no trouble nor tumults among the people; so that no man can say that thereby the realm doth receive any hurt or damage by them. They have brought into the realm no novelties in doctrine and religion. This being true and evident, as it is indeed, there is no necessity why any new law should be made against them. And where there is no sore nor grief, medicines are superfluous, and also hurtful and dangerous. I do entreat," he says afterwards, "whether it be just to make this penal statute to force the subjects of this realm to receive and believe the religion of protestants on pain of death. This I say to be a thing most unjust; for that it is repugnant to the natural liberty of men's understanding. For understanding may be persuaded but not forced." And farther on: "It is an easy thing to understand that a thing so unjust, and so contrary to all reason and liberty of man, cannot be put in execution but with great incommodity and difficulty. For what man is there so without courage and stomach, or void of all honor, that can consent or agree to receive an opinion and new religion by force and compulsion; or will swear that he thinketh the contrary to what he thinketh? To be still, or dissemble, may be borne and suffered for a time—to keep his reckoning with God alone: but to be compelled to lie and to swear, or else to die therefore, are things that no man ought to suffer and endure. And it is to be feared rather than to die they will seek how to defend themselves; whereby should ensue the contrary of what every good prince and well advised commonwealth ought to seek and pretend, that is, to keep their kingdom and government in peace."[1]

I am never very willing to admit as an apology for unjust

[1] Strype, Collier, Parliament. History. The original source is the manuscript collections of Fox the martyrologist, a very unsuspicious authority; so that there seems every reason to consider this speech, as well as Mr. Atkinson's authentic. The following is a specimen of the sort of answer given to these arguments: "They say it touches conscience, and it is a thing wherein a man ought to have a scruple; but if any hath a conscience in it, these four years' space might have settled it. Also, after his first refusal, he hath three months' respite for conference and settling of his conscience."—Strype, 270.

Statute of 1562 not fully enforced.

or cruel enactments, that they are not designed to be generally executed; a pretext often insidious, always insecure, and tending to mask the approaches of arbitrary government. But it is certain that Elizabeth did not wish this act to be enforced in its full severity. And archbishop Parker, by far the most prudent churchman of the time, judging some of the bishops too little moderate in their dealings with the papists, warned them privately to use great caution in tendering the oath of supremacy according to the act, and never to do so the second time, on which the penalty of treason might attach, without his previous approbation.[1] The temper of some of his colleagues was more narrow and vindictive. Several of the deprived prelates had been detained in a sort of honorable custody in the palaces of their successors.[2] Bonner, the most justly obnoxious of them all, was confined in the Marshalsea. Upon the occasion of this new statute, Horn, bishop of Winchester, indignant at the impunity of such a man, proceeded to tender him the oath of supremacy, with an evident intention of driving him to high treason. Bonner, however, instead of evading this attack, intrepidly denied the other to be a lawful bishop; and, strange as it may seem, not only escaped all further molestation, but had the pleasure of seeing his adversaries reduced to pass an act of parliament, declaring the present bishops to have been legally consecrated.[3] This statute, and especially its preamble, might lead a hasty reader to suspect that the celebrated story of an irregular consecration of the first protestant bishops at the Nag's-head tavern was not wholly undeserving of credit. That tale, however, has been satisfactorily refuted; the only irregularity which gave rise to this statute consisted in the use of an ordinal, which had not been legally reëstablished.

It was not long after the act imposing such heavy penalties on catholic priests for refusing the oath of supremacy, that the emperor Ferdinand addressed two letters to Eliza-

1 Strype's Life of Parker, 125.

2 Strype's Annals, 149. Tunstall was treated in a very handsome manner by Parker, whose guest he was. But Feckenham, abbot of Westminster, met with rather unkind usage, though he had been active in saving the lives of protestants under Mary, from bishops Horn and Cox, (the latter of whom seems to have been an honest but narrow-spirited and peevish man,) and at last was sent to Wisbeach jail for refusing the oath of supremacy. Strype, i. 457, ii. 526; Fuller's Church History, 178.

3 8 Eliz. c. 1. Eleven peers dissented, all noted catholics except the earl of Sussex. Strype, i. 492.

beth, interceding for the adherents to that religion, both with respect to those new severities to which they might become liable by conscientiously declining that oath, and to the prohibition of the free exercise of their rites. He suggested that it might be reasonable to allow them the use of one church in every city. And he concluded with an expression, which might possibly be designed to intimate that his own conduct towards the protestants in his dominions would be influenced by her concurrence in his request.[1] Such considerations were not without great importance. The protestant religion was gaining ground in Austria, where a large proportion of the nobility as well as citizens had for some years earnestly claimed its public toleration. Ferdinand, prudent and averse from bigoted counsels, and for every reason solicitous to heal the wounds which religious differences had made in the empire, while he was endeavoring, not absolutely without hope of success, to obtain some concessions from the pope, had shown a disposition to grant further indulgences to his protestant subjects. His son Maximilian, not only through his moderate temper, but some real inclination towards the new doctrine, bade fair to carry much farther the liberal policy of the reigning emperor.[2] It was consulting very little the general interests of protestantism, to disgust persons so capable and so well disposed to befriend it. But our queen, although free from the fanatical spirit of persecution which actuated part of her subjects, was too deeply imbued with arbitrary principles to endure any public deviation from the mode of worship she should prescribe. And it must perhaps be admitted that experience alone could fully demonstrate the safety of toleration, and show the fallacy of apprehensions that unprejudiced men might have entertained. In her answer to Ferdinand, the queen declares that she cannot grant churches to those who disagree from her religion, being

Application of the emperor in behalf of the English catholics.

1 Nobis vero factura est rem adeo gratam, ut omnem simus daturi operam, quo possimus eam rem serenitati vestræ mutuis benevolentiæ et fraterni animi studiis cumulatissimè compensare. See the letter in the additions to the first volume of Strype's Annals, prefixed to the second, p. 67. It has been erroneously referred by Camden, whom many have followed, to the year 1559, but bears date 24th Sept. 1563.

2 For the dispositions of Ferdinand and Maximilian towards religious toleration in Austria, which indeed for a time existed, see F. Paul, Concile de Trente (par Courayer), ii. 72, 197, 220, &c.; Schmidt, Hist. des Allemands, viii. 120, 179, &c. Flechier, Vie de Commendom, 388; or Coxe's House of Austria. [To these we may now add Ranke's excellent History of the Popes of the 16th and 17th centuries.]

against the laws of her parliament, and highly dangerous to the state of her kingdom; as it would sow various opinions in the nation to distract the minds of honest men, and would cherish parties and factions that might disturb the present tranquillity of the commonwealth. Yet enough had already occurred in France to lead observing men to suspect that severities and restrictions are by no means an infallible specific to prevent or subdue religious factions.

Camden and many others have asserted that by systematic connivance the Roman catholics enjoyed a pretty free use of their religion for the first fourteen years of Elizabeth's reign. But this is not reconcilable to many passages in Strype's collections. We find abundance of persons harassed for recusancy, that is, for not attending the protestant church, and driven to insincere promises of conformity. Others were dragged before ecclesiastical commissioners for harboring priests, or for sending money to those who had fled beyond sea.[1] Students of the inns of court, where popery had a strong hold at this time, were examined in the star-chamber as to their religion, and on not giving satisfactory answers were committed to the Fleet.[2] The catholic party were not always scrupulous about the usual artifices of an oppressed people, meeting force by fraud, and concealing their heartfelt wishes under the mask of ready submission, or even of zealous attachment. A great majority both of clergy and laity yielded to the times; and of these temporizing conformists it cannot be doubted that many lost by degrees all thought of returning to their ancient fold. But others, while they complied with exterior ceremonies, retained in their private devotions their accustomed mode of worship. It is an admitted fact, that the catholics generally attended the church, till it came to be reckoned a distinctive sign of their having renounced their own religion. They persuaded themselves (and the English priests, uninstructed and accustomed to a temporizing conduct, did not discourage the notion) that the private observance of their own rites would excuse a formal obedience to the civil power.[3] The Romish scheme

1 Strype, 513, et alibi.

2 Strype, 522. He says the lawyers in most eminent places were generally favorers of popery, p. 269. But if he means the judges, they did not long continue so.

3 Cum regina Maria moreretur, et religio in Angliâ mutaret, post episcopos et prælatos catholicos captos et fugatos, populus velut ovium grex sine pastore in magnis tenebris et caligine animarum suarum oberravit. Unde etiam factum est multi ut catholicorum superstitionibus impiis dissimulationibus et gravibus

of worship, though it attaches more importance to ceremonial rites, has one remarkable difference from the protestant, that it is far less social; and consequently the prevention of its open exercise has far less tendency to weaken men's religious associations, so long as their individual intercourse with a priest, its essential requisite, can be preserved. Priests therefore travelled the country in various disguises, to keep alive a flame which the practice of outward conformity was calculated to extinguish. There was not a county throughout England, says a Catholic historian, where several of Mary's clergy did not reside, commonly called the old priests. They served as chaplains in private families.[1] By stealth, at the dead of night, in private chambers, in the secret lurking-places of an ill-peopled country, with all the mystery that subdues the imagination, with all the mutual trust that invigorates constancy, these proscribed ecclesiastics celebrated their solemn rites, more impressive in such concealment than if surrounded by all their former splendor. The strong predilection indeed of mankind for mystery, which has probably led many to tamper in political conspiracies without much further motive, will suffice to preserve secret associations, even where their purposes are far less interesting than those of religion. Many of these itinerant priests assumed the character of protestant preachers; and it has been said, with some truth, though not probably without exaggeration, that, under the directions of their crafty court, they fomented the division then springing

juramentis contra sanctæ sedis apostolicæ auctoritatem, cum admodum parvo aut plane nullo conscientiarum suarum scrupulo assuescerent. Frequentabant ergo hæreticorum synagogas, intererant eorum concionibus, atque ad easdem etiam audiendas filios et familiam suam compellabant. Videbatur illis ut catholici essent, sufficere una cum hæreticis eorum templa non adire, ferri autem posse si ante vel post illos eadem intrassent. Communicabatur de sacrilegâ Calvini cœnâ, vel secreto et clanculum intra privatos parietes. Missam qui audiverant, ac postea Calvinianos se haberi volebant, sic se de præcepto satisfecisse existimabant. Deferebantur filii catholicorum ad baptisteria hæreticorum, ac inter illorum manus matrimonia contrahebant. Atque hæc omnia sine omni scrupulo fiebant, facta propter catholicorum sacerdotum ignorantiam, qui talia vel licere credebant, vel timore quodam præpediti dissimulabant. Nunc autem per Dei misericordiam omnes catholici intelligunt, ut salventur non satis esse corde fidem catholicam credere, sed eandem etiam ore oportere confiteri. Ribadeneira de Schismate, p. 53. See also Butler's English Catholics, vol. iii. p. 156. [There is nothing in this statement of the fact, which serves to countenance the very unfair misrepresentations lately given, as if the Roman catholics generally had acquiesced in the Anglican worship, believing it to be substantially the same as their own. They frequented our churches, because the law compelled them by penalties so to do, not out of a notion that very little change had been made by the Reformation. It is true, of course, that many became real protestants, by habitual attendance on our rites, and by disuse of their own. But these were not the recusants of a later period. — 1845.]

[1] Dodd's Church Hist. vol. ii. p. 8.

up, and mingled with the anabaptists and other sectaries, in the hope both of exciting dislike to the establishment, and of instilling their own tenets, slightly disguised, into the minds of unwary enthusiasts.[1]

Persecution of the catholics in the ensuing period.

It is my thorough conviction that the persecution, for it can obtain no better name,[2] carried on against the English catholics, however it might serve to delude the government by producing an apparent conformity, could not but excite a spirit of disloyalty in many adherents of that faith. Nor would it be safe to assert that a more conciliating policy would have altogether disarmed their hostility, much less laid at rest those busy hopes of the future, which the peculiar circumstances of Elizabeth's reign had a tendency to produce. This remarkable posture of affairs affected all her civil, and still more her ecclesiastical policy. Her own title to the crown depended absolutely on a parliamentary recognition. The act of 35 H. 8, c. 1, had settled the crown upon her, and thus far restrained the previous statute, 28 H. 8, c. 7, which had empowered her father to regulate the succession at his pleasure. Besides this legislative authority, his testament had bequeathed the kingdom to Elizabeth after her sister Mary; and the common consent of the nation had ratified her possession. But the queen of Scots, niece of Henry by Mar-

[1] Thomas Heath, brother to the late archbishop of York, was seized at Rochester about 1570, well provided with anabaptist and Arian tracts for circulation. Strype, i. 521. For other instances, see pp. 281, 484; Life of Parker, 244; Nalson's Collections, vol. i. Introduction, p. 39, &c., from a pamphlet, written also by Nalson, entitled Foxes and Firebrands. It was surmised that one Henry Nicolas, chief of a set of fanatics, called the Family of Love, of whom we read a great deal in this reign, and who sprouted up again about the time of Cromwell, was secretly employed by the popish party. Strype, ii. 37, 589, 595. But these conjectures were very often ill founded, and possibly so in this instance, though the passages quoted by Strype (589) are suspicious. Brandt, however (Hist. of Reformation in Low Countries, vol. i. p. 105), does not suspect Nicolas of being other than a fanatic. His sect appeared in the Netherlands about 1555.

[2] "That church [of England] and the queen, its re-founder, are clear of persecution, as regards the catholics. No church, no sect, no individual even, had yet professed the principle of toleration." Southey's Book of the Church, vol. ii. p. 285. If the second of these sentences is intended as a proof of the first, I must say it is little to the purpose. But it is not true in this broad way of assertion. Not to mention Sir Thomas More's Utopia, the principle of toleration had been avowed by the chancellor l'Hospital, and many others in France. I mention him as on the stronger side; for in fact the weaker had always professed the general principle, and could demand toleration from those of different sentiments on no other plea. And as to *capital* inflictions for heresy, which Mr. S. seems chiefly to have in his mind, there is reason to believe that many protestants never approved them. Sleidan intimates, vol. iii. p. 263, that Calvin incurred odium by the death of Servetus. And Melanchthon says expressly the same thing, in the letter which he unfortunately wrote to the reformer of Geneva, declaring his own approbation of the crime; and which I am willing to ascribe rather to his constitutional fear of giving offence, than to sincere conviction.

garet, his elder sister, had a prior right to the throne during Elizabeth's life, in the eyes of such catholics as preferred an hereditary to a parliamentary title, and was reckoned by the far greater part of the nation its presumptive heir after her decease. There could indeed be no question of this, had the succession been left to its natural course. But Henry had exercised the power with which his parliament, in too servile a spirit, yet in the plenitude of its sovereign authority, had invested him, by settling the succession in remainder upon the house of Suffolk, descendants of his second sister Mary, to whom he postponed the elder line of Scotland. Mary left two daughters, Frances and Eleanor. The former became wife of Grey, marquis of Dorset, created duke of Suffolk by Edward; and had three daughters, — Jane, whose fate is well known, Catherine, and Mary. Eleanor Brandon, by her union with the earl of Cumberland, had a daughter, who married the earl of Derby. At the beginning of Elizabeth's reign, or rather after the death of the duchess of Suffolk, lady Catherine Grey was by statute law the presumptive heiress of the crown; but according to the rules of hereditary descent, which the bulk of mankind do not readily permit an arbitrary and capricious enactment to disturb, Mary queen of Scots, grand-daughter of Margaret, was the indisputable representative of her royal progenitors, and the next in succession to Elizabeth.

Uncertain succession of the crown between the families of Scotland and Suffolk.

This reversion, indeed, after a youthful princess, might well appear rather an improbable contingency. It was to be expected that a fertile marriage would defeat all speculations about her inheritance; nor had Elizabeth been many weeks on the throne, before this began to occupy her subjects' minds.[1] Among several who were named, two very soon became the prominent candidates for her favor, the archduke Charles, son of the emperor Ferdinand, and lord Robert Dudley, some time after created earl of Leicester; one recommended by his dignity and alliances, the other by her own evident partiality. She gave at the outset so little encouragement to the former proposal, that Leicester's ambition did not appear extravagant.[2] But her ablest councillors, who knew his

Elizabeth's unwillingness to decide the succession, or to marry.

[1] The address of the house of commons, begging the queen to marry, was on Feb. 6, 1559.

[2] Haynes, 233.

vices, and her greatest peers, who thought his nobility recent and ill acquired, deprecated so unworthy a connection.[1] Few will pretend to explore the labyrinths of Elizabeth's heart; yet we may almost conclude that her passion for this favorite kept up a struggle against her wisdom for the first seven or eight years of her reign. Meantime she still continued unmarried; and those expressions she had so early used, of her resolution to live and die a virgin, began to appear less like coy affectation than at first. Never had a sovereign's marriage been more desirable for a kingdom. Cecil, aware how important it was that the queen should marry, but dreading her union with Leicester, contrived, about the end of 1564, to renew the treaty with the archduke Charles.[2] During this negotiation, which lasted from two to three years, she showed not a little of that evasive and dissembling coquetry which was to be more fully displayed on subsequent occasions.[3] Leicester deemed himself so much interested as to quarrel with those who manifested any zeal for the Aus-

[1] See particularly two letters in the Hardwicke State Papers, i. 122 and 163, dated in October and November, 1560, which show the alarm excited by the queen's ill-placed partiality.

[2] Cecil's earnestness for the Austrian marriage appears plainly in Haynes, 430; and still more in a remarkable minute, where he has drawn up in parallel columns, according to a rather formal but perspicuous method he much used, his reasons in favor of the archduke, and against the earl of Leicester. The former chiefly relate to foreign politics, and may be conjectured by those acquainted with history. The latter are as follows: 1. Nothing is increased by marriage of him, either in riches, estimation, or power. 2. It will be thought that the slanderous speeches of the queen with the earl have been true. 3. He shall study nothing but to enhance his own particular friends to wealth, to offices, to lands; and to offend others. 4. He is infamed by death of his wife. 5. He is far in debt. 6. He is likely to be unkind, and jealous of the queen's majesty. Id. 444. These suggestions, and especially the second, if actually laid before the queen, show the plainness and freedom which this great statesman ventured to use towards her. The allusion to the death of Leicester's wife, which had occurred in a very suspicious manner, at Cumnor near Oxford, and is well known as the foundation of the novel of Kenilworth, though related there with great anachronism and confusion of persons, may be frequently met with in contemporary documents. By the above-quoted letters in the Hardwicke Papers it appears that those who disliked Leicester had spoken freely of this report to the queen.

[3] Elizabeth carried her dissimulation so far as to propose marriage articles, which were formally laid before the imperial ambassador. These, though copied from what had been agreed on Mary's marriage with Philip, now seemed highly ridiculous, when exacted from a younger brother without territories or revenues. Jura et leges regni conserventur, neque quicquam mutetur in religione aut in statu publico. Officia et magistratus exerceantur per naturales. Neque regina, neque liberi sui educantur ex regno sine concensu regni, &c. Haynes, 438.

Cecil was not too wise a man to give some credit to astrology. The stars were consulted about the queen's marriage; and those veracious oracles gave response that she should be married in the thirty-first year of her age to a *foreigner*, and have one son, who would be a great prince, and a daughter, &c. &c. Strype, ii. 16, and Appendix 4, where the nonsense may be read at full length. Perhaps, however, the wily minister was no dupe, but meant that his mistress should be. [See, as to Elizabeth's intentions to marry at this time, the extracts from despatches of the French ambassador, in Raumer, vol. ii. p. 85.]

trian marriage; but his mistress gradually overcame her misplaced inclinations; and from the time when that connection was broken off, his prospects of becoming her husband seem rapidly to have vanished away. The pretext made for relinquishing this treaty with the archduke was Elizabeth's constant refusal to tolerate the exercise of his religion; a difficulty which, whether real or ostensible, recurred in all her subsequent negotiations of a similar nature.[1]

In every parliament of Elizabeth the house of commons was zealously attached to the protestant interest. This, as well as an apprehension of disturbance from a contested succession, led to those importunate solicitations that she would choose a husband, which she so artfully evaded. A determination so contrary to her apparent interest, and to the earnest desire of her people, may give some countenance to the surmises of the time, that she was restrained from marriage by a secret consciousness that it was unlikely to be fruitful.[2] Whether these conjectures were well founded, of which I know no evidence; or whether the risk of experiencing that ingratitude which the husbands of sovereign princesses have often displayed, and of which one glaring example was immediately before her eyes, outweighed in her judgment that of remaining single; or whether she might not even apprehend a more desperate combination of the catholic party at home and abroad if the birth of any

[1] The council appear in general to have been as resolute against tolerating the exercise of the catholic religion in any husband the queen might choose, as herself. We find however that several divines were consulted on two questions: 1. Whether it were lawful to marry a papist. 2. Whether the queen might permit mass to be said. To which answers were given, not agreeing with each other. Strype, ii. 150; and Appendix 31, 33. When the earl of Worcester was sent over to Paris in 1571, as proxy for the queen, who had been made sponsor for Charles IX.'s infant daughter, she would not permit him, though himself a catholic, to be present at the mass on that occasion. ii. 171.

[2] "The people," Camden says, "cursed Huic, the queen's physician, as having dissuaded the queen from marrying on account of some impediment and defect in her." Many will recollect the allusion to this in Mary's scandalous letter to Elizabeth, wherein, under pretence of repeating what the countess of Shrewsbury had said, she utters everything that female spite and ungovernable malice could dictate. But in the long and confidential correspondence of Cecil, Walsingham, and sir Thomas Smith, about the queen's marriage with the duke of Anjou, in 1571, for which they were evidently most anxious, I do not perceive the slightest intimation that the prospect of her bearing children was at all less favorable than in any other case. The council seem, indeed, in the subsequent treaty with the other duke of Anjou, in 1579, when she was forty-six, to have reckoned on something rather beyond the usual laws of nature in this respect; for in a minute by Cecil of the reasons for and against this marriage, he sets down the probability of issue on the favorable side. "By marrying with Monsieur she is likely to have children, *because of his youth;*" as if her age were no objection.

issue from her should shut out their hopes of Mary's succession, it is difficult for us to decide.

Though the queen's marriage were the primary object of these addresses, as the most probable means of securing an undisputed heir to the crown, yet she might have satisfied the parliament in some degree by limiting the succession to one certain line. But it seems doubtful whether this would have answered the proposed end. If she had taken a firm resolution against matrimony, which, unless on the supposition already hinted, could hardly be reconciled with a sincere regard for her people's welfare, it might be less dangerous to leave the course of events to regulate her inheritance. Though all parties seem to have conspired in pressing her to some decisive settlement on this subject, it would not have been easy to content the two factions, who looked for a successor to very different quarters.[1] It is evident that any confirmation of the Suffolk title would have been regarded by the queen of Scots and her numerous partisans as a flagrant injustice, to which they would not submit but by compulsion; and on the other hand, by reëstablishing the hereditary line, Elizabeth would have lost her check on one whom she had reason to consider as a rival and competitor, and whose influence was already alarmingly extensive among her subjects.

1 Camden, after telling us that the queen's disinclination to marry raised great clamors, and that the earls of Pembroke and Leicester had professed their opinion that she ought to be obliged to take a husband, or that a successor should be declared by act of parliament even against her will, asserts some time after, as inconsistently as improperly, that "very few but malecontents and traitors appeared very solicitous in the business of a successor." P. 401, (in Kennet's Complete Hist. of England, vol. ii.) This, however, from Camden's known proneness to flatter James, seems to indicate that the Suffolk party were more active than the Scots upon this occasion. Their strength lay in the house of commons, which was wholly protestant, and rather puritan.

At the end of Murden's State Papers is a short journal kept by Cecil, containing a succinct and authentic summary of events in Elizabeth's reign. I extract as a specimen such passages as bear on the present subject.

"Oct 6, 1566. Certain lewd bills thrown abroad against the queen's majesty for not assenting to have the matter of succession proved in parliament; and bills also to charge sir W. Cecil the secretary with the occasion thereof.

"27. Certain lords, viz. the earls of Pembroke and Leicester, were excluded the presence-chamber, for furthering the proposition of the succession to be declared by parliament without the queen's allowance.

"Nov. 12. Messrs. Bell and Monson moved trouble in the parliament about the succession.

"14. The queen had before her thirty lords and thirty commoners to receive her answer concerning their petition for the succession and for marriage. Dalton was blamed for speaking in the commons' house.

"24. Command given to the parliament not to treat of the succession.

"Nota: in this parliament time the queen's majesty did remit a part of the offer of a subsidy to the commons, who offered largely, to the end to have had the succession established." P. 762.

Imprisonment of lady Catherine Grey.

She had, however, in one of the first years of her reign, without any better motive than her own jealous and malignant humor, taken a step not only harsh and arbitrary, but very little consonant to policy, which had almost put it out of her power to defeat the queen of Scots' succession. Lady Catherine Grey, who has been already mentioned as next in remainder of the house of Suffolk, proved with child by a private marriage, as they both alleged, with the earl of Hertford. The queen, always envious of the happiness of lovers, and jealous of all who could entertain any hopes of the succession, threw them both into the Tower. By connivance of their keepers, the lady bore a second child during this imprisonment. Upon this, Elizabeth caused an inquiry to be instituted before a commission of privy councillors and civilians; wherein, the parties being unable to adduce proof of their marriage, archbishop Parker pronounced that their cohabitation was illegal, and that they should be censured for fornication. He was to be pitied if the law obliged him to utter so harsh a sentence, or to be blamed if it did not. Even had the marriage never been solemnized, it was impossible to doubt the existence of a contract, which both were still desirous to perform. But there is reason to believe that there had been an actual marriage, though so hasty and clandestine that they had not taken precautions to secure evidence of it. The injured lady sank under this hardship and indignity;[1] but the legitimacy of her children was acknowledged by general consent, and, in a distant age, by a legislative declaration. These proceedings excited much dissatisfaction; generous minds revolted from their severity, and many lamented to see the reformed branch of the royal stock thus bruised by the queen's unkind and impolitic jealousy.[2] Hales, clerk of

[1] Catherine, after her release from the Tower, was placed in the custody of her uncle lord John Grey, but still suffering the queen's displeasure, and separated from her husband. Several interesting letters from her and her uncle to Cecil are among the Lansdowne MSS., vol. vi. They cannot be read without indignation at Elizabeth's unfeeling severity. Sorrow killed this poor young woman the next year, who was never permitted to see her husband again. Strype, i. 391. The earl of Hertford underwent a long imprisonment, and continued in obscurity during Elizabeth's reign; but had some public employments under her successor. He was twice afterwards married, and lived to a very advanced age, not dying till 1621, near sixty years after his ill-starred and ambitious love. It is worth while to read the epitaph on his monument in the S.E. aisle of Salisbury cathedral, an affecting testimony to the purity and faithfulness of an attachment rendered still more sacred by misfortune and time. Quo desiderio veteres revocavit amores! I shall revert to the question of this marriage in a subsequent chapter.

[2] Haynes, 396.

the hanaper, a zealous protestant, having written in favor of lady Catherine's marriage, and of her title to the succession, was sent to the Tower.[1] The lord keeper, Bacon himself, a known friend to the house of Suffolk, being suspected of having prompted Hales to write this treatise, lost much of his mistress's favor. Even Cecil, though he had taken a share in prosecuting lady Catherine, perhaps in some degree from an apprehension that the queen might remember he had once joined in proclaiming her sister Jane, did not always escape the same suspicion;[2] and it is probable that he felt the imprudence of entirely discountenancing a party from which the queen and religion had nothing to dread. There is reason to believe that the house of Suffolk was favored in parliament; the address of the commons in 1563, imploring the queen to settle the succession, contains several indications of a spirit unfriendly to the Scottish line;[3] and a speech is extant, said to have been made as late as 1571, expressly vindicating the rival pretension.[4] If indeed we consider with attention the statute of 13 Eliz. c. 1, which renders it treasonable to deny that the sovereigns of this kingdom, with consent of parliament, might alter the line of succession, it will appear little short of a confirmation of that title which the descendants of Mary Brandon derived from a parliamentary settlement. But the doubtful birth of lord Beauchamp and his brother, as well as an ignoble marriage, which

1 Id. 413. Strype, 410. Hales's treatise in favor of the authenticity of Henry's will is among the Harleian MSS., n. 537 and 555, and has also been printed in the Appendix to Hereditary Right Asserted, fol. 1713.

2 Camden, p. 416, ascribes the powerful coalition formed against him in 1569, wherein Norfolk and Leicester were combined with all the catholic peers, to his predilection for the house of Suffolk. But it was more probably owing to their knowledge of his integrity and attachment to his sovereign, which would steadfastly oppose their wicked design of bringing about Norfolk's marriage with Mary, as well as to their jealousy of his influence. Carte reports, on the authority of the despatches of Fenelon, the French ambassador, that they intended to bring him to account for breaking off the ancient league with the house of Burgundy, or, in other words, for maintaining the protestant interest. Vol. iii. p. 483. A papist writer, under the name of Andreas Philopater, gives an account of this confederacy against Cecil at some length. Norfolk and Leicester belonged to it; and the object was to defeat the Suffolk succession, which Cecil and Bacon favored. Leicester betrayed his associates to the queen. It had been intended that Norfolk should accuse the two councillors before the lords, eâ ratione ut è senatu regiâque abreptos ad curiæ januas in crucem agi præciperet, eoque perfecto rectè deinceps ad forum progressus explicaret populo tum hujus facti rationem, tum successionis etiam regnandi legitimam seriem, si quid forte reginæ humanitus accideret. P. 43.

3 D' Ewes, 81.

4 Strype, 11. Append. This speech seems to have been made while Catherine Grey was living; perhaps therefore it was in a former parliament, for no account that I have seen represents her as having been alive so late as 1571.

Frances, the younger sister of lady Catherine Grey, had thought it prudent to contract, deprived this party of all political consequence much sooner, as I conceive, than the wisest of Elizabeth's advisers could have desired; and gave rise to various other pretensions, which failed not to occupy speculative or intriguing tempers throughout this reign.

Mary, queen of Scotland.

We may well avoid the tedious and intricate paths of Scottish history, where each fact must be sustained by a controversial discussion. Every one will recollect that Mary Stuart's retention of the arms and style of England gave the first, and, as it proved, inexpiable provocation to Elizabeth. It is indeed true that she was queen consort of France, a state lately at war with England, and that, if the sovereigns of the latter country, even in peace, would persist in claiming the French throne, they could hardly complain of this retaliation. But, although it might be difficult to find a diplomatic answer to this, yet every one was sensible of an important difference between a title retained through vanity, and expressive of pretensions long since abandoned, from one that several foreign powers were prepared to recognize, and a great part of the nation might perhaps only want opportunity to support.[1] If, however, after the death of Francis II. had set the queen of Scots free from all adverse connections, she had with more readiness and apparent sincerity renounced a pretension

[1] There was something peculiar in Mary's mode of blazonry. She bore Scotland and England quarterly, the former being first; but over all was a half-scutcheon of pretence with the arms of England, the sinister half being as it were obscured, in order to intimate that she was kept out of her right. Strype, vol. i. p. 8.

The despatches of Throckmorton, the English ambassador in France, bear continual testimony to the insulting and hostile manner in which Francis II. and his queen displayed their pretensions to our crown. Forbes's State Papers, vol. i. passim. The following is an instance. At the entrance of the king and queen into Chatelherault, 23d Nov. 1559, these lines formed the inscription over one of the gates: —

Gallia perpetuis pugnaxque Britannia bellis
Olim odio inter se dimicuere pari.
Nunc Gallos totoque remotos orbe Britannos
Unum dos Mariæ cogit imperium.
Ergo pace potes, Francisce quod omnibus armis,
Mille patres annis non potuere tui.

This offensive behavior of the French court is the apology of Elizabeth's intrigues during the same period with the malecontents, which to a certain extent cannot be denied by any one who has read the collection above quoted; though I do not think Dr. Lingard warranted in asserting her privity to the conspiracy of Amboise as a proved fact. Throckmorton was a man very likely to exceed his instructions; and there is much reason to believe that he did so. It is remarkable that no modern French writers that I have seen, Anquetil, Garnier, Lacretelle, or the editors of the General Collection of Memoirs, seem to have been aware of Elizabeth's secret intrigues with the king of Navarre and other protestant chiefs in 1559, which these letters, published by Forbes in 1740, demonstrate.

which could not be made compatible with Elizabeth's friendship, she might perhaps have escaped some of the consequences of that powerful neighbor's jealousy. But, whether it were that female weakness restrained her from unequivocally abandoning claims which she deemed well founded, and which future events might enable her to realize even in Elizabeth's lifetime, or whether she fancied that to drop the arms of England from her scutcheon would look like a dereliction of her right of succession, no satisfaction was fairly given on this point to the English court. Elizabeth took a far more effective revenge, by intriguing with all the malecontents of Scotland. But while she was endeavoring to render Mary's throne uncomfortable and insecure, she did not employ that influence against her in England, which lay more fairly in her power. She certainly was not unfavorable to the queen of Scots' succession, however she might decline compliance with importunate and injudicious solicitations to declare it. She threw both Hales and one Thornton into prison for writing against that title. And when Mary's secretary, Lethington, urged that Henry's testament, which alone stood in their way, should be examined, alleging that it had not been signed by the king, she paid no attention to this imprudent request.[1]

The circumstances wherein Mary found herself placed on her arrival in Scotland were sufficiently embarrassing to divert her attention from any regular scheme against Elizabeth, though she may sometimes have indulged visionary hopes; nor is it probable that, with the most circumspect management, she could so far have mitigated the rancor of some, or checked the ambition of others, as to find leisure for hostile intrigues. But her imprudent marriage with Darnley, and the far greater errors of her subsequent behavior, by lowering both her resources and reputation as far as possible, seemed to be pledges of perfect security from that quarter. Yet it was precisely when Mary was

[1] Burnet, i. Append. 266. Many letters, both of Mary herself and of her secretary, the famous Maitland of Lethington, occur in Haynes's State Papers, about the end of 1561. In one of his to Cecil, he urges, in answer to what had been alleged by the English court, that a collateral successor had never been declared in any prince's lifetime, that, whatever reason there might be for that, "if the succession had remained untouched according to the law, yet, where by a limitation men had gone about to prevent the providence of God, and shift one into the place due to another, the offended party could not but seek the redress thereof." P. 373.

become most feeble and helpless that Elizabeth's apprehensions grew most serious and well-founded.

At the time when Mary, escaped from captivity, threw herself on the protection of a related, though rival queen, three courses lay open to Elizabeth, and were discussed in her councils. To restore her by force of arms, or rather, by a mediation which would certainly have been effectual, to the throne which she had compulsorily abdicated, was the most generous, and would perhaps have turned out the most judicious, proceeding. Reigning thus with tarnished honor and diminished power, she must have continually depended on the support of England, and become little better than a vassal of its sovereign. Still it might be objected by many, that the queen's honor was concerned not to maintain too decidedly the cause of one accused by common fame, and even by evidence that had already been made public, of adultery and the assassination of her husband. To have permitted her retreat into France would have shown an impartial neutrality; and probably that court was too much occupied at home to have afforded her any material assistance. Yet this appeared rather dangerous; and policy was supposed, as frequently happens, to indicate a measure absolutely repugnant to justice, that of detaining her in perpetual custody.[1] Whether this policy had no other fault than its want of justice may reasonably be called in question.

The queen's determination neither to marry nor limit the succession had inevitably turned every one's thoughts towards the contingency of her death. She was young indeed; but had been dangerously ill, once in 1562,[2] and again in 1568. Of all possible competitors for the throne, Mary was incomparably the most powerful, both among the nobility and the people. Besides the undivided attachment of all who retained any longings for the ancient religion, and many such

Combination in favor of Mary.

[1] A very remarkable letter of the earl of Sussex, Oct. 22, 1568, contains these words: "I think surely no end can be made good for England, except the person of the Scottish queen be detained, by one means or other, in England." The whole letter manifests the spirit of Elizabeth's advisers, and does no great credit to Sussex's sense of justice, but a great deal to his ability. Yet he afterwards became an advocate for the duke of Norfolk's marriage with Mary. Lodge's Illustrations, vol. ii. p. 4.

[2] Hume and Carte say, this first illness was the small-pox. But it appears by a letter from the queen to lord Shrewsbury, Lodge, 279, that her attack in 1571 was suspected to be that disorder.

were to be found at Elizabeth's court and chapel, she had the stronghold of hereditary right, and the general sentiment that revolts from acknowledging the omnipotency of a servile parliament. Cecil, whom no one could suspect of partiality towards her, admits, in a remarkable minute on the state of the kingdom in 1569, that "the queen of Scots' strength standeth by the universal opinion of the world for the justice of her title, as coming of the ancient line."[1] This was no doubt in some degree counteracted by a sense of the danger which her accession would occasion to the protestant church, and which, far more than its parliamentary title, kept up a sort of party for the house of Suffolk. The crimes imputed to her did not immediately gain credit among the people; and some of higher rank were too experienced politicians to turn aside for such considerations. She had always preserved her connections among the English nobility, of whom many were catholics, and others adverse to Cecil, by whose councils the queen had been principally directed in all her conduct with regard to Scotland and its sovereign.[2] After the unfinished process of inquiry to which Mary submitted at York and Hampton Court, when the charge of participation in Darnley's murder had been substantiated by evidence at least that she did not disprove, and the whole course of which proceedings created a very unfavorable impression both in England and on the Continent, no time was to be lost by those who considered her as the object of their dearest hopes. She was in the kingdom; she might, by a bold rescue, be placed at their head; every hour's delay increased the danger of her being delivered up to the rebel Scots; and doubtless some eager protestants had already begun to demand her exclusion by an absolute decision of the legislature.

Elizabeth must have laid her account, if not with the disaffection of the catholic party, yet at least with their attachment to the queen of Scots. But the extensive combination

[1] Haynes, 580.

[2] In a conversation which Mary had with one Rooksby, a spy of Cecil's, about the spring of 1566, she imprudently named several of her friends, and of others whom she hoped to win, such as the duke of Norfolk, the earls of Derby, Northumberland, Westmoreland, Cumberland, Shrewsbury. "She had the better hope of this, for that she thought them to be all of the old religion, which she meant to restore again with all expedition, and thereby win the hearts of the common people." The whole passage is worth notice. Haynes, 447. See also Melvil's Memoirs, for the dispositions of an English party towards Mary in 1566.

that appeared, in 1569, to bring about by force the duke of Norfolk's marriage with that princess, might well startle her cabinet. In this combination Westmoreland and Northumberland, avowed catholics, Pembroke and Arundel, suspected ones, were mingled with Sussex and even Leicester, unquestioned protestants. The duke of Norfolk himself, greater and richer than any English subject, had gone such lengths in this conspiracy, that his life became the just forfeit of his guilt and folly. It is almost impossible to pity this unhappy man, who, lured by the most criminal ambition, after proclaiming the queen of Scots a notorious adulteress and murderer, would have compassed a union with her at the hazard of his sovereign's crown, of the tranquillity and even independence of his country, and of the reformed religion.[1] There is abundant proof of his intrigues with the duke of Alva, who had engaged to invade the kingdom. His trial was not indeed conducted in a manner that we can approve (such was the nature of state proceedings in that age); nor can it, I think, be denied that it formed a precedent of constructive treason not easily reconcilable with the statute; but much evidence is extant that his prosecutors did not adduce, and no one fell by a sentence more amply merited, or the execution of which was more indispensable.[2]

Norfolk was the dupe throughout all this intrigue of more artful men: first of Murray and Lethington, who had filled his mind with ambitious hopes, and afterwards of Italian agents employed by Pius V. to procure a combination of the catholic party. Collateral to Norfolk's conspiracy, but doubtless connected with it, was that of the northern earls of Northumberland and Westmoreland, long prepared, and perfectly foreseen by the government, of which the ostensible and manifest aim was the reëstablishment of popery.[3]

[1] Murden's State Papers, 134, 180, Norfolk was a very weak man, the dupe of some very cunning ones. We may observe that his submission to the queen, id. 153, is expressed in a style which would now be thought most pusillanimous in a man of much lower station; yet he died with great intrepidity. But such was the tone of those times; an exaggerated hypocrisy prevailed in everything.

[2] State Trials, i. 957. He was interrogated by the queen's counsel with the most insidious questions. All the material evidence was read to the lords from written depositions of witnesses who might have been called, contrary to the statute of Edward VI. But the Burghley Papers, published by Haynes and Murden, contain a mass of documents relative to this conspiracy, which leave no doubt as to the most heinous charge, that of inviting the duke of Alva to invade the kingdom. There is reason to suspect that he feigned himself a catholic in order to secure Alva's assistance. — Murden, p. 10.

[3] The northern counties were at this time chiefly catholic. "There are not," says Sadler, writing from thence, "ten

Bull of Pius V.

Pius V., who took a far more active part than his predecessor in English affairs, and had secretly instigated this insurrection, now published his celebrated bull, excommunicating and deposing Elizabeth, in order to second the efforts of her rebellious subjects.[1] This is, perhaps, with the exception of that issued by Sixtus V. against Henry IV. of France, the latest blast of that trumpet which had thrilled the hearts of monarchs. Yet there was nothing in the sound that bespoke declining vigor; even the illegitimacy of Elizabeth's birth is scarcely alluded to; and the pope seems to have chosen rather to tread the path of his predecessors, and absolve her subjects from their allegiance, as the just and necessary punishment of her heresy.

Since nothing so much strengthens any government as an unsuccessful endeavor to subvert it, it may be thought that the complete failure of the rebellion under the earls of Northumberland and Westmoreland, with the detection and punishment of the duke of Norfolk, rendered Elizabeth's throne more secure. But those events revealed the number of her enemies, or at least of those in whom no confidence could be reposed. The rebellion, though provided against by the ministry, and headed by two peers of great family but no personal weight, had not only assumed for a time a most formidable aspect in the north, but caused many to waver in other parts of the kingdom.[2] Even in Norfolk, an eminently protestant county, there was a slight insurrection in 1570, out of attachment to the duke.[3] If her greatest subject could thus be led astray from his faith and loyalty, if others not less near to her councils could unite with him in measures so contrary to her wishes and interests, on whom was she firmly to rely? Who, especially, could be trusted, were she to be snatched away from the world, for the maintenance of the protestant establishment under a yet unknown successor? This was the manifest and principal danger that her coun-

gentlemen in this country who do favor and allow of her majesty's proceedings in the cause of religion." Lingard, vii. 54. It was consequently the great resort of the priests from the Netherlands, and in the feeble state of the protestant church there wanted sufficient ministers to stand up in its defence. Strype, i. 509, et post; ii. 183. Many of the gentry indeed were still disaffected in other parts towards the new religion. A profession of conformity was required in 1569 from all justices of the peace, which some refused, and others made against their consciences. Id. i. 567.

1 Camden has quoted a long passage from Hieronymo Catena's Life of Pius V., published at Rome in 1578, which illustrates the evidence to the same effect contained in the Burghley Papers, and partly adduced on the duke of Norfolk's trial.

2 Strype, i. 546, 553, 556.

3 Strype, i. 578; Camden, 428; Lodge, ii. 45.

cillors had to dread. Her own great reputation, and the respectful attachment of her people, might give reason to hope that no machinations would be successful against her crown; but let us reflect in what situation the kingdom would have been left by her death in a sudden illness such as she had more than once experienced in earlier years, and again in 1571. "You must think," lord Burleigh writes to Walsingham on that occasion, "such a matter would drive me to the end of my wits." And sir Thomas Smith expresses his fears in equally strong language.[1] Such statesmen do not entertain apprehensions lightly. Whom, in truth, could her privy council, on such an event, have resolved to proclaim? The house of Suffolk, had its right been more generally recognized than it was (lady Catherine being now dead), presented no undoubted heir. The young king of Scotland, an alien and an infant, could only have reigned through a regency; and it might have been difficult to have selected from the English nobility a fit person to undertake that office, or at least one in whose elevation the rest would have acquiesced. It appears most probable that the numerous and powerful faction who had promoted Norfolk's union with Mary would have conspired again to remove her from her prison to the throne. Of such a revolution the disgrace of Cecil and Elizabeth's wisest ministers must have been the immediate consequence; and it is probable that the restoration of the catholic worship would have ensued. These apprehensions prompted Cecil, Walsingham, and Smith to press the queen's marriage with the duke of Anjou far more earnestly than would otherwise have appeared consistent with her interest. A union with any member of that perfidious court was repugnant to genuine protestant sentiments. But the queen's absolute want of foreign alliances, and the secret hostility both of France and Spain, impressed Cecil with that deep sense of the perils of the time which his private letters so strongly bespeak. A treaty was believed to have been concluded in 1567, to which the two last-mentioned powers, with the emperor Maximilian and some other catholic princes, were parties, for the extirpation of the protestant religion.[2] No alliance that the court of Charles IX.,

[1] Strype, ii. 88. Life of Smith, 152.

[2] Strype, i. 502. I do not give any credit whatever to this league, as printed in Strype, which seems to have been fabricated by some of the queen's emissaries. There had been, not perhaps a

could have formed with Elizabeth was likely to have diverted it from pursuing this object; and it may have been fortunate that her own insincerity saved her from being the dupe of those who practised it so well. Walsingham himself, sagacious as he was, fell into the snares of that den of treachery, giving credit to the young king's assurances almost on the very eve of St. Bartholomew.[1]

The bull of Pius V., far more injurious in its consequences to those it was designed to serve than to Elizabeth, forms a leading epoch in the history of our English catholics. It rested upon a principle never universally acknowledged, and regarded with much jealousy by temporal governments, yet maintained in all countries by many whose zeal and ability rendered them formidable, — the right vested in the supreme pontiff to depose kings for heinous crimes against the church. One Felton affixed this bull to the gates of the bishop of London's palace, and suffered death for the offence. So audacious a manifestation of disloyalty was imputed with little justice to the catholics at large, but might more reasonably lie at the door of those active instruments of Rome, the English refugee priests and jesuits dispersed over Flanders, and lately established at Douay, who were continually passing into the kingdom, not only to keep alive the precarious faith of the laity, but, as was generally surmised, to excite them against their sovereign.[2] This produced the act of 13 Eliz. c. 2; which, after reciting these mischiefs, enacts that all persons publishing any bull from Rome, or absolving and reconciling any one to the Romish church, or being so reconciled, should incur the penalties of high treason; and such as brought into the realm any crosses, pictures, or superstitious things consecrated by the pope or under his authority, should be liable to a præmunire. Those who should conceal or connive at the offenders were to

Statutes for the queen's security.

treaty, but a verbal agreement between France and Spain at Bayonne some time before; but its object was apparently confined to the suppression of protestantism in France and the Netherlands. Had they succeeded however in this, the next blow would have been struck at England. It seems very unlikely that Maximilian was concerned in such a league.

1 Strype, vol. ii.

2 The college of Douay for English refugee priests was established in 1568 or 1569. Lingard, 374. Strype seems, but I believe through inadvertence, to put this event several years later. Annals, ii. 630. It was dissolved by Requesens, while governor of Flanders, but revived at Rheims in 1575, under the protection of the cardinal of Lorrain, and returned to Douay in 1593. Similar colleges were founded at Rome in 1579, at Valladolid in 1589, at St. Omer in 1596, and at Louvain in 1606.

be held guilty of misprision of treason. This statute exposed the catholic priesthood, and in great measure the laity, to the continual risk of martyrdom; for so many had fallen away from their faith through a pliant spirit of conformity with the times, that the regular discipline would exact their absolution and reconciliation before they could be reinstated in the church's communion. Another act of the same session, manifestly levelled against the partisans of Mary, and even against herself, makes it high treason to affirm that the queen ought not to enjoy the crown, but some other person; or to publish that she is a heretic, schismatic, tyrant, infidel, or usurper of the crown; or to claim right to the crown, or to usurp the same during the queen's life; or to affirm that the laws and statutes do not bind the right of the crown, and the descent, limitation, inheritance, or governance thereof. And whosoever should, during the queen's life, by any book or work written or printed, expressly affirm, before the same had been established by parliament, that any one particular person was or ought to be heir and successor to the queen, except the same be the natural issue of her body, or should print or utter any such book or writing, was for the first offence to be imprisoned a year, and to forfeit half his goods; and for the second to incur the penalties of a præmunire.[1]

It is impossible to misunderstand the chief aim of this statute. But the house of commons, in which the zealous protestants, or, as they were now rather denominated, puritans, had a predominant influence, were not content with these demonstrations against the unfortunate captive. Fear, as often happens, excited a sanguinary spirit amongst them; they addressed the queen upon what they called the great cause, that is, the business of the queen of Scots, presenting by their committee reasons gathered out of the civil law to prove that "it standeth not only with justice, but also with the queen's majesty's honor and safety, to proceed criminally against the pretended Scottish queen."[2] Elizabeth, who could not really dislike these symptoms of hatred towards her rival,

[1] 13 Eliz. c. 1. This act was made at first retrospective, so as to affect every one who had at any time denied the queen's title. A member objected to this in debate "as a precedent most perilous." But sir Francis Knollys, Mr. Norton, and others, defended it. D'Ewes, 162. It seems to have been amended by the lords. So little notion had men of observing the first principles of equity towards their enemies! There is much reason from the debate to suspect that the ex post facto words were levelled at Mary.

[2] Strype, ii. 133. D'Ewes, 207.

took the opportunity of simulating more humanity than the commons; and when they sent a bill to the upper house attainting Mary of treason, checked its course by proroguing the parliament. Her backwardness to concur in any measures for securing the kingdom, as far as in her lay, from those calamities which her decease might occasion, could not but displease lord Burleigh. "All that we labored for," he writes to Walsingham in 1572, "and had with full consent brought to fashion, I mean a law to make the Scottish queen unable and unworthy of succession to the crown, was by her majesty neither assented to nor rejected, but deferred." Some of those about her, he hints, made herself her own enemy, by persuading her not to countenance these proceedings in parliament.[1] I do not think it admits of much question that, at this juncture, the civil and religious institutions of England would have been rendered more secure by Mary's exclusion from the throne, which indeed, after all that had occurred, she could not be endured to fill without national dishonor. But the violent measures suggested against her life were hardly, under all the circumstances of her case, to be reconciled with justice; even admitting her privity to the northern rebellion and to the projected invasion by the duke of Alva. These, however, were not approved merely by an eager party in the commons: archbishop Parker does not scruple to write about her to Cecil—"If that only [one] desperate person were taken away, as by justice soon it might be, the queen's majesty's good subjects would be in better hope, and the papists' daily expectation vanquished."[2] And Walsingham, during his embassy at Paris, desires that "the queen should see how much they (the papists) built upon the possibility of that dangerous woman's coming to the crown of England, whose life was a step to her majesty's death;" adding that "she was bound, for her own safety and that of her subjects, to add to God's providence her own policy, so far as might stand with justice."[3]

We cannot wonder to read that these new statutes increased the dissatisfaction of the Roman catholics, who perceived a systematic determination to extirpate their religion. Governments ought always to remember that the intimidation of a few disaffected persons

Catholics more rigorously treated.

[1] Strype, ii. 135. [2] Life of Parker, 354.
[3] Strype's Annals, ii. 48.

is dearly bought by alienating any large portion of the community.[1] Many retired to foreign countries, and, receiving for their maintenance pensions from the court of Spain, became unhappy instruments of its ambitious enterprises. Those who remained at home could hardly think their oppression much mitigated by the precarious indulgences which Elizabeth's caprice, or rather the fluctuation of different parties in her councils, sometimes extended to them. The queen indeed, so far as we can penetrate her dissimulation, seems to have been really averse to extreme rigor against her catholic subjects; and her greatest minister, as we shall more fully see afterwards, was at this time in the same sentiments. But such of her advisers as leaned towards the puritan faction, and too many of the Anglican clergy, whether puritan or not, thought no measure of charity or compassion should be extended to them. With the divines they were idolaters; with the council they were a dangerous and disaffected party; with the judges they were refractory transgressors of statutes; on every side they were obnoxious and oppressed. A few aged men having been set at liberty, Sampson, the famous puritan, himself a sufferer for conscience' sake, wrote a letter of remonstrance to lord Burleigh. He urged in this that they should be compelled to hear sermons, though he would not at first oblige them to communicate.[2] A bill having been introduced in the session of 1571, imposing a penalty for not receiving the communion, it was objected that consciences ought not to be forced. But Mr. Strickland entirely denied this principle, and quoted authori-

1 Murden's Papers, p. 43, contain proofs of the increased discontent among the catholics in consequence of the penal laws.

2 Strype, ii. 330. See too, in vol. iii. Appendix 68, a series of petitions intended to be offered to the queen and parliament about 1583. These came from the puritanical mint, and show the dread that party entertained of Mary's succession, and of a relapse into popery. It is urged in these that no toleration should be granted to the popish worship in private houses. Nor, in fact, had they much cause to complain that it was so. Knox's famous intolerance is well known.

"One mass," he declared in preaching against Mary's private chapel at Holyrood house, "was more fearful unto him than if ten thousand armed enemies were landed in any part of the realm, on purpose to suppress the whole religion." M'Crie's Life of Knox, vol. ii. p. 24. In a conversation with Maitland he asserted most explicitly the duty of putting idolaters to death. Id. p. 120. Nothing can be more sanguinary than the reformer's spirit in this remarkable interview. St. Dominic could not have surpassed him. It is strange to see men, professing all the while our modern creed of charity and toleration, extol these sanguinary spirits of the sixteenth century. The English puritans, though I cannot cite any passages so strong as the foregoing, were much the bitterest enemies of the catholics. When we read a letter from any one, such as Mr. Topcliffe, very fierce against the latter, we may expect to find him put in a word in favor of silenced ministers.

ties against it.[1] Even Parker, by no means tainted with puritan bigotry, and who had been reckoned moderate in his proceedings towards catholics, complained of what he called "a Machiavel government;" that is, of the queen's lenity in not absolutely rooting them out.[2]

This indulgence, however, shown by Elizabeth, the topic of reproach in those times, and sometimes of boast in our own, never extended to any positive toleration, nor even to any general connivance at the Romish worship in its most private exercise. She published a declaration in 1570, that she did not intend to sift men's consciences, provided they observed her laws by coming to church; which, as she well knew, the strict catholics deemed inconsistent with their integrity.[3] Nor did the government always abstain from an inquisition into men's private thoughts. The inns of court were more than once purified of popery by examining their members on articles of faith. Gentlemen of good families in the country were harassed in the same manner.[4] One sir Richard Shelley, who had long acted as a sort of spy for Cecil on the Continent, and given much useful information, requested only leave to enjoy his religion without hindrance; but the queen did not accede to this without much reluctance and delay.[5] She had indeed assigned no other ostensible pretext for breaking off her own treaty of marriage with the archduke Charles, and subsequently with the dukes of Anjou and Alençon, than her determination not to suffer the mass to be celebrated even in her husband's private chapel. It is worthy to be repeatedly inculcated on the reader, since so false a color has been often employed to disguise the ecclesiastical tyranny of this reign, that the most clandestine exercise of the Romish worship was severely punished. Thus we read in the Life of Whitgift, that, on information given that some ladies and others heard mass in the house of one Edwards by night, in the county of Denbigh, he, being then bishop of Worcester and vice-president of Wales, was directed to make inquiry into the facts; and finally was instructed to commit Edwards to close prison; and as for another person implicated, named Morice, "if he remained obstinate he might cause some kind of torture to be used upon him; and the like

1 D'Ewes, 161, 177.

2 Strype's Life of Parker, 354.

3 Strype's Annals, i. 582. Honest old Strype, who thinks church and state never in the wrong, calls this "a notable piece of favor."

4 Strype's Annals, ii. 110, 408.

5 Id. iii. 127.

order they prayed him to use with the others."[1] But this is one of many instances, the events of every day, forgotten on the morrow, and of which no general historian takes account. Nothing but the minute and patient diligence of such a compiler as Strype, who thinks no fact below his regard, could have preserved this from oblivion.[2]

It will not surprise those who have observed the effect of

[1] Life of Whitgift, 83. See too p. 99; and Annals of Reformation, ii. 631, &c.; also Hollingshed, ann. 1574, ad init.

[2] An almost incredible specimen of ungracious behavior towards a Roman catholic gentleman is mentioned in a letter of Topcliffe, a man whose daily occupation was to hunt out and molest men for popery. "The next good news, but in account the highest, her majesty hath served God with great zeal and comfortable examples; for by her council two notorious papists, young Rockwood, the master of Euston-hall, where her majesty did lie upon Sunday now a fortnight, and one Downes, a gentleman, were both committed, the one to the town prison at Norwich, the other to the county prison there, for obstinate papistry; and seven more gentlemen of worship were committed to several houses in Norwich as prisoners; two of the Lovels, another Downes, one Beningfield, one Parry, and two others not worth memory, for badness of belief.

"This Rockwood is a papist of kind [family] newly crept out of his late wardship. Her majesty, by some means I know not, was lodged at his house, Euston, far unmeet for her highness; nevertheless, the gentleman brought into her presence by like device, her majesty gave him ordinary thanks for his bad house, and her fair hand to kiss: but my lord chamberlain, nobly and gravely understanding that Rockwood was excommunicated for papistry, called him before him, demanded of him how he durst presume to attempt her royal presence, he, unfit to accompany any Christian person; forthwith said he was fitter for a pair of stocks, commanded him out of the court, and yet to attend her council's pleasure at Norwich he was committed. And to dissyffer [sic] the gentleman to the full, a piece of plate being missed in the court, and searched for in his hay-house, in the hay-rick, such an image of our lady was there found, as for greatness, for gayness, and workmanship, I did never see a match; and after a sort of country dances ended, in her majesty's sight the idol was set behind the people who avoided; she rather seemed a beast raised upon a sudden from hell by conjuring, than the picture for whom it had been so often and so long abused. Her majesty commanded it to the fire, which in her sight by the country folks was quickly done, to her content, and unspeakable joy of every one but some one or two who had sucked of the idol's poisoned milk.

"Shortly after, a great sort of good preachers, who had been long commanded to silence for a little niceness, were licensed, and again commanded to preach; a greater and more universal joy to the countries, and the most of the court, than the disgrace of the papists: and the gentlemen of those parts, being great and hot protestants, almost before by policy discredited and disgraced, were greatly countenanced.

"I was so happy lately, amongst other good graces, that her majesty did tell me of sundry lewd papist beasts that have resorted to Buxton," &c. Lodge, ii. 188. 30 Aug. 1578.

This Topcliffe was the most implacable persecutor of his age. In a letter to lord Burleigh (Strype, iv. 39) he urges him to imprison all the principal recusants, and especially women, "the farther off from their own family and friends the better." The whole letter is curious, as a specimen of the prevalent spirit, especially among the puritans, whom Topcliffe favored. Instances of the ill-treatment experienced by respectable families (the Fitzherberts and Foljambes), and even aged ladies, without any other provocation than their recusancy, may be found in Lodge, ii. 372, 462; iii. 22. [See also Dodd's Church History, vol. iii. passim, with the additional facts contributed by the last editor.] But those farthest removed from puritanism partook sometimes of the same tyrannous spirit. Aylmer, bishop of London, renowned for his persecution of nonconformists, is said by Rishton, de Schismate, p. 319, to have sent a young catholic lady to be whipped in Bridewell for refusing to conform. If the authority is suspicious (and yet I do not perceive that Rishton is a liar like Sanders), the fact is rendered hardly improbable by Aylmer's harsh character.

all persecution for matters of opinion upon the human mind, that during this period the Romish party continued such in numbers and in zeal as to give the most lively alarm to Elizabeth's administration. One cause of this was beyond doubt the connivance of justices of the peace, a great many of whom were secretly attached to the same interest, though it was not easy to exclude them from the commission, on account of their wealth and respectability.[1] The facility with which catholic rites can be performed in secret, as before observed, was a still more important circumstance. Nor did the voluntary exiles established in Flanders remit their diligence in filling the kingdom with emissaries. The object of many at least among them, it cannot for a moment be doubted, from the era of the bull of Pius V., if not earlier, was nothing less than to subvert the queen's throne. They were closely united with the court of Spain, which had passed from the character of an ally and pretended friend, to that of a cold and jealous neighbor, and at length of an implacable adversary. Though no war had been declared between Elizabeth and Philip, neither party had scrupled to enter into leagues with the disaffected subjects of the other. Such sworn vassals of Rome and Spain as an Allen or a Persons were just objects of the English government's distrust; it is the extension of that jealousy to the peaceful and loyal which we stigmatize as oppressive, and even as impolitic.[2]

Refugees in the Netherlands. Their hostility to the government.

1 Strype's Life of Smith, 171; Annals, ii. 631, 636, iii. 479, and Append. 170. The last reference is to a list of magistrates sent up by the bishops from each diocese, with their characters. Several of these, but the wives of many more, were inclined to popery.

2 Allen's Admonition to the Nobility and People of England, written in 1588, to promote the success of the Armada, is full of gross lies against the queen. See an analysis of it in Lingard, note B B. Mr. Butler fully acknowledges, what indeed the whole tenor of historical documents for this reign confirms, that Allen and Persons were actively engaged in endeavoring to dethrone Elizabeth by means of a Spanish force. But it must, I think, be candidly confessed by protestants, that they had very little influence over the superior catholic laity. And an argument may be drawn from hence against those who conceive the political conduct of catholics to be entirely swayed by their priests, when even in the sixteenth century the efforts of these able men, united with the head of their church, could produce so little effect. Strype owns that Allen's book gave offence to many catholics: iii. 560. Life of Whitgift, 505. One Wright of Douay answered a case of conscience, whether catholics might take up arms to assist the king of Spain against the queen, in the negative. Id. 251. Annals, 565. This man, though a known loyalist, and actually in the employment of the ministry, was afterwards kept in a disagreeable sort of confinement in the dean of Westminster's house, of which he complains with much reason. Birch's Memoirs, vol. ii. p. 71, et alibi. Though it does not fall within the province of a writer on the constitution to enlarge on Elizabeth's foreign policy, I must observe, in consequence of the labored attempts of Dr. Lingard to represent it as perfectly Machiavelian, and without any motive

Fresh laws against the catholic worship.

In concert with the directing powers of the Vatican and Escurial, the refugees redoubled their exertions about the year 1580. Mary was now wearing out her years in hopeless captivity; her son, though they did not lose hope of him, had received a strictly protestant education; while a new generation had grown up in England, rather inclined to diverge more widely from the ancient religion than to suffer its restoration. Such were they who formed the house of commons that met in 1581, discontented with the severities used against the puritans, but ready to go beyond any measures that the court might propose to subdue and extirpate popery. Here an act was passed, which, after repeating the former provisions that had made it high treason to reconcile any of her majesty's subjects, or to be reconciled, to the church of Rome, imposes a penalty of 20*l.* a month on all persons absenting themselves from church, unless they shall hear the English service at home: such as could not pay the same within three months after judgment were to be imprisoned until they should conform. The queen, by a subsequent act, had the power of seizing two thirds of the party's land, and all his goods, for default of payment.[1] These grievous penalties on recusancy, as the wilful absence of catholics from church came now to be denominated, were doubtless founded on the extreme difficulty of proving an actual celebration of their own rites. But they established a persecution which fell not at all short in principle of that for which the inquisition had become so odious. Nor were the statutes merely designed for terror's sake, to keep a check over the disaffected, as some would pretend. They were executed in the most sweeping and indiscriminating manner, unless perhaps a few families of high rank might enjoy a connivance.[2]

Execution of Campian and others.

It had certainly been the desire of Elizabeth to abstain from capital punishments on the score of religion. The first instance of a priest suffering death by her statutes was in 1577, when one Mayne was hanged at Launceston, without any charge against him except his religion; and a gentleman who had harbored him

but wanton malignity, that, with respect to France and Spain, and even Scotland, it was strictly defensive, and justified by the law of self-preservation; though, in some of the means employed, she did not always adhere more scrupulously to good faith than her enemies.

1 23 Eliz. c. 1, and 29 Eliz. c. 6.

2 Strype's Whitgift, p. 117, and other authorities, passim.

was sentenced to imprisonment for life.[1] In the next year, if we may trust the zealous catholic writers, Thomas Sherwood, a boy of fourteen years, was executed for refusing to deny the temporal power of the pope, when urged by his judges.[2] But in 1581, several seminary priests from Flanders having been arrested, whose projects were supposed (perhaps not wholly without foundation) to be very inconsistent with their allegiance, it was unhappily deemed necessary to hold out some more conspicuous examples of rigor. Of those brought to trial, the most eminent was Campian, formerly a protestant, but long known as the boast of Douay for his learning and virtues.[3] This man, so justly respected, was put to the rack, and revealed through torture the names of some catholic gentlemen with whom he had conversed.[4] He appears to have been indicted along with several other priests, not on the recent statutes, but on that of 25 Edw. III., for compassing and imagining the queen's death. Nothing that I have read affords the slightest proof of Campian's concern in treasonable practices, though his connections, and profession as a Jesuit, render it by no means unlikely. If we may confide in the published trial, the prosecution was as unfairly conducted, and supported by as slender evidence, as any perhaps which can be found in our books.[5] But as this account, wherein Campian's language is full of a dignified eloquence, rather seems to have been compiled by a partial hand, its faithfulness may not be above suspicion. For the same reason I hesitate to admit his alleged declarations at the place of execution, where, as well as at his trial, he is represented to have expressly acknowledged Elizabeth, and to have prayed for her as his queen *de facto* and *de jure*. For this was one of the questions propounded to him before his trial, which he refused to answer, in such a manner as betrayed his way of thinking. Most of those interrogated at the same time, on being pressed whether the queen was their

1 Camden. Lingard. Two others suffered at Tyburn not long afterwards for the same offence. Hollingshed, 344. See in Butler's Mem. of Catholics, vol. iii. p. 382, an affecting narrative from Dodd's Church History, of the sufferings of Mr. Tregian and his family, the gentleman whose chaplain Mayne had been. I see no cause to doubt its truth.

2 Ribadeneira, Continuatio Sanderi et Rishtoni de Schismate Anglicano, p. 111. Philopater, p. 247. This circumstance of Sherwood's age is not mentioned by Stowe; nor does Dr. Lingard advert to it. No woman was put to death under the penal code, so far as I remember; which of itself distinguishes the persecution from that of Mary, and of the house of Austria in Spain and the Netherlands.

3 Strype's Parker, 375.

4 Strype's Annals, ii. 644.

5 State Trials, i. 1050; from the Phœnix Britannicus.

lawful sovereign, whom they were bound to obey, notwithstanding any sentence of deprivation that the pope might pronounce, endeavored, like Campian, to evade the snare. A few, who unequivocally disclaimed the deposing power of the Roman see, were pardoned.[1] It is more honorable to Campian's memory that we should reject these pretended declarations than imagine him to have made them at the expense of his consistency and integrity. For the pope's right to deprive kings of their crowns was in that age the common creed of the jesuits, to whose order Campian belonged; and the Continent was full of writings published by the English exiles, by Sanders, Bristow, Persons, and Allen, against Elizabeth's unlawful usurpation of the throne. But many availed themselves of what was called an explanation of the bull of Pius V., given by his successor Gregory XIII., namely, that the bull should be considered as always in force against Elizabeth and the heretics, but should only be binding on catholics when due execution of it could be had.[2]

[1] State Trials, i. 1078. Butler's English Catholics, i. 184, 244. Lingard, vii. 182; whose remarks are just and candid. A tract, of which I have only seen an Italian translation, printed at Macerata in 1585, entitled Historia del glorioso martirio di diciotto sacerdoti e un secolare, fatti morire in Inghilterra per la confessione e difensione della fede cattolica, by no means asserts that he acknowledged Elizabeth to be queen de jure, but rather that he refused to give an opinion as to her right. He prayed however for her as a queen. "Io ho pregato, e prego per lei. All' ora il Signor Howardo li domandò per qual regina egli pregasse, se per Elisabetta? Al quale rispose, Si, per Elisabetta." Mr. Butler quotes this tract in English.

The trials and deaths of Campian and his associates are told in the continuation of Hollingshed with a savageness and bigotry which, I am very sure, no scribe for the Inquisition could have surpassed. — p. 456. But it is plain, even from this account, that Campian owned Elizabeth as queen. See particularly p. 448, for the insulting manner in which this writer describes the pious fortitude of these butchered ecclesiastics.

[2] Strype, ii. 637. Butler's Eng. Catholics, i. 196. The earl of Southampton asked Mary's ambassador, bishop Lesley, whether, after the bull, he could in conscience obey Elizabeth. Lesley answered, that as long as she was the stronger he ought to obey her. Murden, p. 30. The writer quoted before by the name of Andreas Philopater (Persons, translated by Cresswell, according to Mr. Butler, vol. iii. p. 236), after justifying at length the resistance of the League to Henry IV., adds the following remarkable paragraph: "Hinc etiam infert universa theologorum et jurisconsultorum schola, et est certum et de fide, quemcunque principem christianum, si a religione catholicâ manifestè deflexerit, et alios avocare voluerit, excidere statim omni potestate et dignitate, ex ipsâ vi juris tum divini tum humani, hocque ante omnem sententiam supremi pastoris ac judicis contra ipsum prolatam; et subditos quoscunque liberos esse ab omni juramenti obligatione, quod ei de obedientiâ tanquam principi legitimo præstitissent; posseque et debere (si vires habeant) istiusmodi hominem, tanquam apostatam, hæreticum, ac Christi domini desertorem, et inimicum reipublicæ suæ, hostemque ex hominum christianorum dominatu ejicere, ne alios inficiat, vel suo exemplo aut imperio a fide avertat." — p. 149. He quotes four authorities for this in the margin, from the works of divines or canonists.

This broad duty, however, of expelling a heretic sovereign, he qualifies by two conditions; first, that the subjects should have the power, "ut vires habeant idoneas ad hoc subditi;" secondly, that the heresy be undeniable. There can, in truth, be no doubt that the allegiance professed to the

This was designed to satisfy the consciences of some papists in submitting to her government, and taking the oath of allegiance. But in thus granting a permission to dissemble, in hope of better opportunity for revolt, this interpretation was not likely to tranquillize her council, or conciliate them towards the Romish party. The distinction, however, between a king by possession and one by right was neither heard for the first nor for the last time in the reign of Elizabeth. It is the lot of every government that is not founded on the popular opinion of legitimacy to receive only a precarious allegiance. Subject to this reservation, which was pretty generally known, it does not appear that the priests or other Roman catholics, examined at various times during this reign, are more chargeable with insincerity or dissimulation than accused persons generally are.

The public executions, numerous as they were, scarcely form the most odious part of this persecution. The common law of England has always abhorred the accursed mysteries of a prison-house, and neither admits of torture to extort confession, nor of any penal infliction not warranted by a judicial sentence. But this law, though still sacred in the courts of justice, was set aside by the privy council under the Tudor line. The rack seldom stood idle in the Tower for all the latter part of Elizabeth's reign.[1] To those who remember the annals of their country, that dark and gloomy pile affords associations not quite so numerous and recent as the Bastile once did, yet enough to excite our hatred and horror. But standing as it does in such striking contrast to the fresh and flourishing constructions of modern wealth, the proofs and the rewards of civil and religious liberty, it seems like a captive tyrant, reserved to grace the triumph of a vic-

queen by the seminary priests and jesuits, and, as far as their influence extended, by all catholics, was with this reservation — till they should be strong enough to throw it off. See the same tract, p. 229. But, after all, when we come fairly to consider it, is not this the case with every disaffected party in every state? a good reason for watchfulness, but none for extermination.

1 Rishton and Ribadeneira. See in Lingard, note U, a specification of the different kinds of torture used in this reign.

The government did not pretend to deny the employment of torture. But the puritans, eager as they were to exert the utmost severity of the law against the professors of the old religion, had more regard to civil liberty than to approve such a violation of it. Beal, clerk of the council, wrote, about 1585, a vehement book against the ecclesiastical system, from which Whitgift picks out various enormous propositions, as he thinks them; one of which is, "that he condemns, without exception of any cause, racking of grievous offenders, as being cruel, barbarous, contrary to law, and unto the liberty of English subjects." Strype's Whitgift, p. 212.

torious republic, and should teach us to reflect in thankfulness how highly we have been elevated in virtue and happiness above our forefathers.

Such excessive severities under the pretext of treason, but sustained by very little evidence of any other offence than the exercise of the catholic ministry, excited indignation throughout a great part of Europe. The queen was held forth in pamphlets, dispersed everywhere from Rome and Douay, not only as a usurper and heretic, but a tyrant more ferocious than any heathen persecutor, for inadequate parallels to whom they ransacked all former history.[1] These exaggerations, coming from the very precincts of the Inquisition, required the unblushing forehead of bigotry; but the charge of cruelty stood on too many facts to be passed over, and it was thought expedient to repel it by two remarkable pamphlets, both ascribed to the pen of lord Burleigh. One of these, entitled "The Execution of Justice in England for Maintenance of public and private Peace," appears to have been published in 1583. It contains an elaborate justification of the late prosecutions for treason, as no way connected with religious tenets, but grounded on the ancient laws for protection of the queen's person and government from conspiracy.

Defence of the queen, by Burleigh.

[1] The persecution of catholics in England was made use of as an argument against permitting Henry IV. to reign in France, as appears by the title of a tract published in 1586: Avertissement des catholiques Anglois aux François catholiques, du danger où ils sont de perdre leur religion, et d'expérimenter, comme en Angleterre, la cruauté des ministres, s'ils reçoivent à la couronne un roy qui soit hérétique. It is in the British Museum.

One of the attacks on Elizabeth deserves some notice, as it has lately been revived. In the statute 13 Eliz. an expression is used, "her majesty, and the natural issue of her body," instead of the more common legal phrase, "lawful issue." This probably was adopted by the queen out of prudery, as if the usual term implied the possibility of her having unlawful issue. But the papistical libellers, followed by an absurd advocate of Mary in later times, put the most absurd interpretation on the word "natural," as if it were meant to secure the succession for some imaginary bastards by Leicester. And Dr. Lingard is not ashamed to insinuate the same suspicion, vol. viii. p. 81, note. Surely what was congenial to the dark malignity of Persons, and the blind frenzy of Whitaker, does not become the good sense, I cannot say the candor, of this writer.

It is true that some, not prejudiced against Elizabeth, have doubted whether "Cupid's fiery dart" was as effectually "quenched in the chaste beams of the watery moon" as her poet intimates. This I must leave to the reader's judgment. She certainly went strange lengths of indelicacy. But, if she might sacrifice herself to the queen of Cnidus and Paphos, she was unmercifully severe to those about her, of both sexes, who showed any inclination to that worship, though under the escort of Hymen. Miss Aikin, in her well-written and interesting Memoirs of the Court of Elizabeth, has collected several instances from Harrington and Birch. It is by no means true, as Dr. Lingard asserts, on the authority of one Faunt, an austere puritan, that her court was dissolute, comparatively at least with the general character of courts; though neither was it so virtuous as the enthusiasts of the Elizabethan period suppose.

It is alleged that a vast number of catholics, whether of the laity or priesthood, among whom the deprived bishops are particularly enumerated, had lived unmolested on the score of their faith, because they paid due temporal allegiance to their sovereign. Nor were any indicted for treason but such as obstinately maintained the pope's bull depriving the queen of her crown. And even of these offenders, as many as after condemnation would renounce their traitorous principles had been permitted to live; such was her majesty's unwillingness, it is asserted, to have any blood spilled without this just and urgent cause proceeding from themselves. But that any matter of opinion not proved to have ripened into an overt act, and extorted only, or rather conjectured, through a compulsive inquiry, could sustain in law or justice a conviction for high treason, is what the author of this pamphlet has not rendered manifest.[1]

A second and much shorter paper bears for title, "A Declaration of the favorable dealing of her Majesty's Commissioners appointed for the examination of certain traitors, and of tortures unjustly reported to be done upon them for matter of religion." Its scope was to palliate the imputation of excessive cruelty with which Europe was then resounding. Those who revere the memory of lord Burleigh must blush for this pitiful apology. "It is affirmed for truth," he says, "that the forms of torture in their severity or rigor of execution have not been such and in such manner performed as the slanderers and seditious libellers have published. And that even the principal offender, Campian himself, who was sent and came from Rome, and continued here in sundry corners of the realm, having secretly wandered in the greater part of the shires of England in a disguised suit, to the intent to make special preparation of treasons, was never so racked but that he was perfectly able to walk and to write, and did presently write and subscribe all his confessions. The queen's servants, the warders, whose office and act it is to handle the rack, were ever by those that attended the examinations specially charged to use it in so charitable a man-

1 Somers Tracts, i. 189. Strype, iii. 205, 265, 480. Strype says that he had seen the manuscript of this tract in lord Burleigh's handwriting. It was answered by cardinal Allen, to whom a reply was made by poor Stubbe after he had lost his right hand. An Italian translation of the Execution of Justice was published at London in 1584. This shows how anxious the queen was to repel the charges of cruelty, which she must have felt to be not wholly unfounded.

ner as such a thing might be. None of those who were at any time put to the rack," he proceeds to assert, "were asked, during their torture, any question as to points of doctrine, but merely concerning their plots and conspiracies, and the persons with whom they had had dealings, and what was their own opinion as to the pope's right to deprive the queen of her crown. Nor was any one so racked until it was rendered evidently probable, by former detections or confessions, that he was guilty; nor was the torture ever employed to wring out confessions at random; nor unless the party had first refused to declare the truth at the queen's commandment." Such miserable excuses serve only to mingle contempt with our detestation.[1] But it is due to Elizabeth to observe that she ordered the torture to be disused; and upon a subsequent occasion, the quartering of some concerned in Babington's conspiracy having been executed with unusual cruelty, gave directions that the rest should not be taken down from the gallows until they were dead.[2]

I should be reluctant, but for the consent of several authorities, to ascribe this little tract to lord Burleigh for his honor's sake. But we may quote with more satisfaction a memorial addressed by him to the queen about the same year, 1583, full not only of sagacious, but just and tolerant advice. "Considering," he says, "that the urging of the oath of supremacy must needs, in some degree, beget despair, since, in the taking of it, he [the papist] must either think he doth an unlawful act, as without the special grace of God he cannot think otherwise, or else, by refusing it, must become a traitor, which before some hurt done seemeth hard; I humbly submit this to your excellent consideration, whether, with as much security of your majesty's person and state, and more satisfaction for them, it were not better to leave the oath to this sense, that whosoever would not bear arms against all foreign princes, and namely the pope, that should any way invade your majesty's dominions, he should be a traitor. For hereof this commodity will ensue, that those papists, as I think most papists would, that should take this oath, would be divided from the great mutual confidence which is now between the pope and them, by reason of their afflictions for him; and such priests as would refuse that oath,

[1] Somers Tracts, p. 209.

[2] State Trials, i. 1160.

then no tongue could say for shame that they suffer for religion, if they did suffer.

"But here it may be objected, they would dissemble and equivocate with this oath, and that the pope would dispense with them in that case. Even so may they with the present oath both dissemble and equivocate, and also have the pope's dispensation for the present oath as well as for the other. But this is certain, that whomsoever the conscience, or fear of breaking an oath, doth bind, him would that oath bind. And that they make conscience of an oath, the trouble, losses, and disgraces that they suffer for refusing the same do sufficiently testify; and you know that the perjury of either oath is equal."

These sentiments are not such as bigoted theologians were then, or have been since, accustomed to entertain. "I account," he says afterwards, "that putting to death does no ways lessen them; since we find by experience that it worketh no such effect, but, like hydra's heads, upon cutting off one, seven grow up, persecution being accounted as the badge of the church: and therefore they should never have the honor to take any pretence of martyrdom in England, where the fulness of blood and greatness of heart is such that they will even for shameful things go bravely to death, much more when they think themselves to climb heaven; and this vice of obstinacy seems to the common people a divine constancy; so that for my part I wish no lessening of their number but by preaching and by education of the younger under schoolmasters." And hence the means he recommends for keeping down popery, after the encouragement of diligent preachers and schoolmasters, are, "the taking order that, from the highest counsellor to the lowest constable, none shall have any charge or office but such as will really pray and communicate in their congregation according to the doctrine received generally into this realm;" and next the protection of tenants against their popish landlords, "that they be not put out of their living for embracing the established religion." "This," he says, "would greatly bind the commons' hearts unto you, in whom indeed consisteth the power and strength of your realm; and it will make them less, or nothing at all, depend on their landlords. And, although there may hereby grow some wrong, which the tenants upon that confidence may offer to their landlords, yet those wrongs are very easily, even with one wink of your majesty's, redressed; and are nothing comparable to the danger of having many thousands depending on the adverse party."[1]

Increased severity of the government.

The strictness used with recusants, which much increased from 1579 or 1580, had the usual consequence of persecution, that of multiplying hypocrites. For, in fact, if men will once bring themselves to comply, to take all oaths, to practise all conformity, to oppose simulation and dissimulation to arbitrary inquiries, it is hardly possible that any government should not be baffled. Fraud becomes an over-match for power. The real danger meanwhile, the internal disaffection, remains as before or is aggravated. The laws enacted against popery were precisely calculated to produce this result. Many indeed, especially of the female sex, whose religion, lying commonly more in sentiment than reason, is less ductile to the sophisms of worldly wisdom, stood out and endured the penalties. But the oath of supremacy was not refused, the worship of the church was frequented by multitudes who secretly repined for a change; and the council, whose fear of open enmity had prompted their first severities, were led on by the fear of dissembled resentment to devise yet further measures of the same kind. Hence, in 1584 a law was enacted, enjoining all jesuits, seminary priests, and other priests, whether ordained within or without the kingdom, to depart from it within forty days, on pain of being adjudged traitors. The penalty of fine and imprisonment at the queen's pleasure was inflicted on such as, knowing any priest to be within the realm, should not discover it to a magistrate. This seemed to fill up the measure of persecution, and to render the longer preservation of this obnoxious religion absolutely impracticable. Some of its adherents presented a petition against this bill, praying that they might not be suspected of disloyalty on account of refraining from the public worship, which they did to avoid sin; and that their priests might not be banished from the kingdom.[2] And they all very justly complained of this determined oppression. The queen, without any fault of theirs, they alleged, had been

[1] Somers Tracts, 164.

[2] Strype, iii. 298. Shelley, though notoriously loyal, and frequently employed by Burleigh, was taken up and examined before the council for preparing this petition.

alienated by the artifices of Leicester and Walsingham. Snares were laid to involve them unawares in the guilt of treason; their steps were watched by spies; and it was become intolerable to continue in England. Camden indeed asserts that counterfeit letters were privately sent in the name of the queen of Scots or of the exiles, and left in papists' houses.[1] A general inquisition seems to have been made about this time; but whether it was founded on sufficient grounds of previous suspicion we cannot absolutely determine. The earl of Northumberland, brother of him who had been executed for the rebellion of 1570, and the earl of Arundel, son of the unfortunate duke of Norfolk, were committed to the Tower, where the former put an end to his own life (for we cannot charge the government with an unproved murder); and the second, after being condemned for a traitorous correspondence with the queen's enemies, died in that custody. But whether or no some conspiracies (I mean more active than usual, for there was one perpetual conspiracy of Rome and Spain during most of the queen's reign) had preceded these severe and unfair methods by which her ministry counteracted them, it was not long before schemes more formidable than ever were put in action against her life. As the whole body of catholics was irritated and alarmed by the laws of proscription against their clergy, and by the heavy penalties on recusancy, which, as they alleged, showed a manifest purpose to reduce them to poverty;[2] so some desperate men saw no surer means to rescue their cause than the queen's assassination. One Somerville, half a lunatic, and Parry, a man who, long em-

[1] P. 591. Proofs of the text are too numerous for quotation, and occur continually to a reader of Strype's 2d and 3d volumes. In vol. iii. Append. 158, we have a letter to the queen from one Antony Tyrrel, a priest, who seems to have acted as an informer, wherein he declares all his accusations of catholics to be false. This man had formerly professed himself a protestant, and returned afterwards to the same religion; so that his veracity may be dubious. So, a little further on, we find in the same collection, p. 250, a letter from one Bennet, a priest, to lord Arundel, lamenting the false accusations he had given in against him, and craving pardon. It is always possible, as I have just hinted, that these retractations may be more false than the charges. But ministers who employ spies, without the utmost distrust of their information, are sure to become their dupes, and end by the most violent injustice and tyranny.

[2] The rich catholics compounded for their recusancy by annual payments, which were of some consideration in the queen's rather scanty revenue. A list of such recusants, and of the annual fines paid by them in 1594, is published in Strype, iv. 197; but is plainly very imperfect. The total was 3323*l*. 1*s*. 10*d* A few paid as much as 140*l*. per annum. The average seems however to have been about 20*l*. Vol. iii. Append. 153; see also p. 258. Probably these compositions, though oppressive, were not quite so serious as the catholics pretended.

ployed as a spy upon the papists, had learned to serve with sincerity those he was sent to betray, were the first who suffered death for unconnected plots against Elizabeth's life.[1] More deep-laid machinations were carried on by several catholic laymen at home and abroad, among whom a brother of lord Paget was the most prominent.[2] These had in view two objects, the deliverance of Mary and the death of her enemy. Some perhaps who were engaged in the former project did not give countenance to the latter. But few,

[1] Parry seems to have been privately reconciled to the church of Rome about 1580; after which he continued to correspond with Cecil, but generally recommending some catholics to mercy. He says, in one letter, that a book printed at Rome, De Persecutione Anglicanâ, had raised a barbarous opinion of our cruelty; and that he could wish that in those cases it might please her majesty to pardon the dismembering and drawing. Strype, iii. 260. He sat afterwards in the parliament of 1584, taking of course the oath of supremacy, where he alone opposed the act against catholic priests. Parl. Hist. 822. Whether he were actually guilty of plotting against the queen's life (for this part of his treason he denied at the scaffold), I cannot say; but his speech there made contained some very good advice to her. The ministry garbled this before its publication in Hollingshed and other books; but Strype has preserved a genuine copy; vol. iii. Append. 102. It is plain that Parry died a catholic; though some late writers of that communion have tried to disclaim him. Dr. Lingard, it may be added, admits that there were many schemes to assassinate Elizabeth, though he will not confess any particular instance. "There exist," he says, "in the archives at Simancas several notices of such offers." P. 384.

[2] It might be inferred from some authorities that the catholics had become in a great degree disaffected to the queen about 1584, in consequence of the extreme rigor practised against them. In a memoir of one Crichton, a Scots jesuit, intended to show the easiness of invading England, he says that "all the catholics without exception favor the enterprise; first, for the sake of the restitution of the catholic faith; secondly, for the right and interest which the queen of Scots has to the kingdom, and to deliver her out of prison; thirdly, for the great trouble and misery they endured more and more, being kept out of all employments, and dishonored in their own countries, and treated with great injustice and partiality when they have need to recur to law; and also for the execution of the laws touching the confiscation of their goods in such sort as in so short time would reduce the catholics to extreme poverty." Strype, iii. 415. And in the report of the earl of Northumberland's treasons, laid before the star-chamber, we read that "Throckmorton said that the bottom of this enterprise, which was not to be known to many, was, that if a toleration of religion might not be obtained without alteration of the government, that then the government should be altered, and the queen removed." Somers Tracts, vol. i. p. 206. Further proofs that the rigor used towards the catholics was the great means of promoting Philip's designs, occur in Birch's Memoirs of Elizabeth, i. 82, et alibi.

We have also a letter from Persons in England to Allen in 1586, giving a good account of the zeal of the catholics, though a very bad one of their condition through severe imprisonment and other ill-treatment. Strype, iii. 412, and Append. 151. Rishton and Ribadeneira bear testimony that the persecution had rendered the laity more zealous and sincere. De Schismate, 1, iii. 320, and 1, iv. 53.

Yet to all this we may oppose their good conduct in the year of the Spanish Armada, and in general during the queen's reign; which proves that the loyalty of the main body was more firm than their leaders wished, or their enemies believed. However, if any of my readers should incline to suspect that there was more disposition among this part of the community to throw off their allegiance to the queen altogether than I have admitted, he may possibly be in the right; and I shall not impugn his opinion, provided he concurs in attributing the whole, or nearly the whole, of this disaffection to her unjust aggressions on the liberty of conscience.

if any, ministers have been better served by their spies than Cecil and Walsingham. It is surprising to see how every letter seems to have been intercepted, every thread of these conspiracies unravelled, every secret revealed to these wise councillors of the queen. They saw that, while one lived whom so many deemed the presumptive heir, and from whose succession they anticipated, at least in possibility, an entire reversal of all that had been wrought for thirty years, the queen was as a mark for the pistol or dagger of every zealot. And fortunate, no question, they thought it, that the detection of Babington's conspiracy enabled them with truth, or a semblance of truth, to impute a participation in that crime to the most dangerous enemy whom, for their mistress, their religion, or themselves, they had to apprehend.

Mary.

Mary had now consumed the best years of her life in custody, and, though still the perpetual object of the queen's vigilance, had perhaps gradually become somewhat less formidable to the protestant interest. Whether she would have ascended the throne if Elizabeth had died during the latter years of her imprisonment must appear very doubtful when we consider the increasing strength of the puritans, the antipathy of the nation to Spain, the prevailing opinion of her consent to Darnley's murder, and the obvious expedient of treating her son, now advancing to manhood, as the representative of her claim. The new projects imputed to her friends, even against the queen's life, exasperated the hatred of the protestants against Mary. An association was formed in 1584, the members of which bound themselves by oath "to withstand and pursue, as well by force of arms as by all other means of revenge, all manner of persons, of whatsoever state they shall be, and their abettors, that shall attempt any act, or counsel or consent to anything, that shall tend to the harm of her majesty's royal person; and never to desist from all manner of forcible pursuit against such persons, to the utter extermination of them, their counsellors, aiders, and abettors. And if any such wicked attempt against her most royal person shall be taken in hand or procured, whereby any that have, may, or shall pretend title to come to this crown by the untimely death of her majesty so wickedly procured (which God of his mercy forbid!), that the same may be avenged, we do not only bind ourselves both jointly and severally never to allow, accept, or favor any such pretended successor, by whom or for whom any such detestable act shall be attempted or committed, as unworthy of all government in any Christian realm or civil state, but do also further vow and promise, as we are most bound, and that in the presence of the eternal and everlasting God, *to prosecute such person or persons to death* with our joint and particular forces, and to act the utmost revenge upon them that by any means we or any of us can devise and do, or cause to be devised and done, for their utter overthrow and extirpation."[1]

The pledge given by this voluntary association received the sanction of parliament in an act "for the security of the queen's person and continuance of the realm in peace." This statute enacts, that if any invasion or rebellion should be made by or for any person pretending title to the crown after her majesty's decease, or if anything be confessed or imagined tending to the hurt of her person, with the privity of any such person, a number of peers, privy councillors, and judges, to be commissioned by the queen, should examine and give judgment on such offences, and all circumstances relating thereto; after which judgment all persons against whom it should be published should be disabled forever to make any such claim.[2] I omit some further provisions to the same effect for the sake of brevity. But we may remark that this statute differs from the associators' engagement in omitting the outrageous threat of pursuing to death any person, whether privy or not to the design, on whose behalf an attempt against the queen's life should be made. The main intention of the statute was to procure, in the event of any rebellious movements, what the queen's councillors had long ardently desired to obtain from her, an absolute exclusion of Mary from the succession. But if the scheme of assassination devised by some of her desperate partisans had taken effect, however questionable might be her concern in it, I have little doubt that the rage of the nation would, with or without some process of law, have instantly avenged it in her blood. This was, in the language of parliament, their great cause; an expression which, though it may have an

[1] State Trials, i. 1162.

[2] 27 Eliz. c. i.

ultimate reference to the general interest of religion, is never applied, so far as I remember, but to the punishment of Mary, which they had demanded in 1572, and now clamored for in 1586. The addresses of both houses to the queen to carry the sentence passed by the commissioners into effect, her evasive answers and feigned reluctance, as well as the strange scenes of hypocrisy which she acted afterwards, are well-known matters of history upon which it is unnecessary to dwell. No one will be found to excuse the hollow affectation of Elizabeth; but the famous sentence that brought Mary to the scaffold, though it has certainly left in popular opinion a darker stain on the queen's memory than any other transaction of her life, if not capable of complete vindication has at least encountered a disproportioned censure.

Execution of Mary.

It is of course essential to any kind of apology for Elizabeth in this matter that Mary should have been assenting to a conspiracy against her life. For it could be no real crime to endeavor at her own deliverance; nor, under the circumstances of so long and so unjust a detention, would even a conspiracy against the aggressor's power afford a moral justification for her death. But though the proceedings against her are by no means exempt from the shameful breach of legal rules almost universal in trials for high treason during that reign (the witnesses not having been examined in open court), yet the depositions of her two secretaries, joined to the confessions of Babington and other conspirators, form a body of evidence, not indeed irresistibly convincing, but far stronger than we find in many instances where condemnation has ensued. And Hume has alleged sufficient reasons for believing its truth, derived from the great probability of her concurring in any scheme against her oppressor, from the certainty of her long correspondence with the conspirators (who, I may add, had not made any difficulty of hinting to her their designs against the queen's life),[1] and from the deep guilt that the falsehood of the

Remarks upon it.

[1] In Murden's State Papers we have abundant evidence of Mary's acquaintance with the plots going forward in 1585 and 1586 against Elizabeth's government, if not with those for her assassination. But Thomas Morgan, one of the most active conspirators, writes to her, 9th July, 1586, — "There be some good members that attend opportunity to do the queen of England a piece of service, which I trust will quiet many things, if it shall please God to lay his assistance to the cause, for the which I pray daily." p. 530. In her answer to this letter she does not

charge must inevitably attach to sir Francis Walsingham.[1] Those at least who cannot acquit the queen of Scots of her husband's murder, will hardly imagine that she would scruple to concur in a crime so much more capable of extenuation, and so much more essential to her interests. But as the proofs are not perhaps complete, we must hypothetically assume her guilt, in order to set this famous problem in the casuistry of public law upon its proper footing.

It has been said so often that few perhaps wait to reflect whether it has been said with reason that Mary, as an independent sovereign, was not amenable to any English jurisdiction. This, however, does not appear unquestionable. By one of those principles of law which may be called natural, as forming the basis of a just and rational jurisprudence, every independent government is supreme within its own territory. Strangers, voluntarily resident within a state, owe a temporary allegiance to its sovereign, and are amenable to the jurisdiction of its tribunals; and this principle, which is perfectly conformable to natural law, has been extended by positive usage even to those who are detained in it by force. Instances have occurred very recently in England when prisoners of war have suffered death for criminal offences; and, if some have doubted the propriety of carrying such sentences into effect, where a penalty of unusual severity has been inflicted by our municipal law, few, I believe, would dispute the fitness of punishing a prisoner of war for wilful murder in such a manner as the general practice of civil societies and the prevailing sentiments of man-

advert to this hint, but mentions Babington as in correspondence with her. At her trial she denied all communication with him. [In a letter from Persons to a Spanish nobleman, in 1597, it is said that Mary had reproved the duke of Guise and archbishop of Glasgow for omitting to supply a sum of money to a young English gentleman who had promised to murder Elizabeth. This, however, rests only on Person's authority. Dodd's Church History of Catholics, by Tierney: the editor gives the letter from a manuscript in his own possession. Vol. iii. Append. lix. — 1845.]

[1] It may probably be answered to this, that if the letter signed by Walsingham as well as Davison to sir Amias Paulet, urging him "to find out some way to shorten the life of the Scots queen," be genuine, which cannot perhaps be justly questioned (though it is so in the Biog. Brit., art. WALSINGHAM, note O), it will be difficult to give him credit for any scrupulousness with respect to Mary. But, without entirely justifying this letter, it is proper to remark, what the Marian party choose to overlook, that it was written after the sentence, during the queen's odious scenes of grimace, when some might argue, though erroneously, that, a legal trial having passed, the formal method of putting the prisoner to death might, in so peculiar a case, be dispensed with. This was Elizabeth's own wish, in order to save her reputation, and enable her to throw the obloquy on her servants; which, by Paulet's prudence and honor in refusing to obey her by privately murdering his prisoner, she was reduced to do in a very bungling and scandalous manner.

kind agree to point out. It is certainly true that an exception to this rule, incorporated with the positive law of nations, and established no doubt before the age of Elizabeth, has rendered the ambassadors of sovereign princes exempt, in all ordinary cases at least, from criminal process. Whether, however, an ambassador may not be brought to punishment for such a flagrant abuse of the confidence which is implied by receiving him, as a conspiracy against the life itself of the prince at whose court he resides, has been doubted by those writers who are most inclined to respect the privileges with which courtesy and convenience have invested him.[1] A sovereign, during a temporary residence in the territories of another, must of course possess as extensive an immunity as his representative; but that he might, in such circumstances, frame plots for the prince's assassination with impunity, seems to take for granted some principle that I do not understand.

But whatever be the privilege of inviolability attached to sovereigns, it must, on every rational ground, be confined to those who enjoy and exercise dominion in some independent territory. An abdicated or dethroned monarch may preserve his title by the courtesy of other states, but cannot rank with sovereigns in the tribunals where public law is administered. I should be rather surprised to hear any one assert that the parliament of Paris was incompetent to try Christina for the murder of Monaldeschi. And, though we must admit that Mary's resignation of her crown was compulsory, and retracted on the first occasion; yet, after a twenty years' loss of possession, when not one of her former subjects avowed allegiance to her, when the king of Scotland had been so long acknowledged by England and by all Europe, is it possible to consider her as more than a titular queen, divested of every substantial right to which a sovereign tribunal could

[1] Questions were put to civilians by the queen's order in 1570 concerning the extent of Lesley bishop of Ross's privilege as Mary's ambassador. Murden Papers, p. 18. Somers Tracts, i. 186. They answered, first, that an ambassador that raises rebellion against the prince to whom he is sent, by the law of nations and the civil law of the Romans, has forfeited the privileges of an ambassador, and is liable to punishment; secondly, that, if a prince be lawfully deposed from his public authority, and another substituted in his stead, the agent of such a prince cannot challenge the privileges of an ambassador; since none but absolute princes, and such as enjoy a royal prerogative, can constitute ambassadors. These questions are so far curious, that they show the jus gentium to have been already reckoned a matter of science, in which a particular class of lawyers was conversant.

have regard? She was styled accordingly, in the indictment, "Mary, daughter and heir of James the Fifth, late king of Scots, otherwise called Mary queen of Scots, dowager of France." We read even that some lawyers would have had her tried by a jury of the county of Stafford, rather than by the special commission; which Elizabeth noticed as a strange indignity. The commission, however, was perfectly legal under the recent statute.[1]

But while we can hardly pronounce Mary's execution to have been so wholly iniquitous and unwarrantable as it has been represented, it may be admitted that a more generous nature than that of Elizabeth would not have exacted the law's full penalty. The queen of Scots' detention in England was in violation of all natural, public, and municipal law; and if reasons of state policy or precedents from the custom of princes are allowed to extenuate this injustice, it is to be asked whether such reasons and such precedents might not palliate the crime of assassination imputed to her. Some might perhaps allege, as was so frequently urged at the time, that, if her life could be taken with justice, it could not be spared in prudence; and that Elizabeth's higher duty to preserve her people from the risks of civil commotion must silence every feeling that could plead for mercy. Of this necessity different judgments may perhaps be formed. It is evident that Mary's death extinguished the best hope of popery in England: but the relative force of the two religions was greatly changed since Norfolk's conspiracy; and it appears to me that an act of parliament explicitly cutting her off from the crown, and at the same time entailing it on her son, would have afforded a very reasonable prospect of securing the succession against all serious disturbance. But this neither suited the inclination of Elizabeth nor of some among those who surrounded her.

Continued persecution of Roman catholics.

As the catholics endured without any open murmuring the execution of her on whom their fond hopes had so long rested, so for the remainder of the queen's reign they by no means appear, when considered as a body, to have furnished any specious pretexts for severity. In that memorable year, when the dark cloud gathered around our coasts, when Europe

[1] Strype, 360, 362. Civilians were consulted about the legality of trying Mary. Idem, Append. 138.

stood by in fearful suspense to behold what should be the result of that great cast in the game of human politics, what the craft of Rome, the power of Philip, the genius of Farnese, could achieve against the island-queen with her Drakes and Cecils, — in that agony of the protestant faith and English name, they stood the trial of their spirits without swerving from their allegiance. It was then that the catholics in every county repaired to the standard of the lord-lieutenant, imploring that they might not be suspected of bartering the national independence for their religion itself. It was then that the venerable lord Montague brought a troop of horse to the queen at Tilbury, commanded by himself, his son, and grandson.[1] It would have been a sign of gratitude if the laws depriving them of the free exercise of their religion had been, if not repealed, yet suffered to sleep, after these proofs of loyalty. But the execution of priests and of other catholics became on the contrary more frequent, and the fines for recusancy were exacted as rigorously as before.[2] A statute was enacted, restraining popish recusants, a distinctive name now first imposed by law, to particular places of residence, and subjecting them to other vexatious provisions.[3] All persons were forbidden by proclamation to harbor any of whose conformity they were not assured.[4] Some indulgence was doubtless shown during all Elizabeth's reign to particular persons, and it was not unusual to release

[1] Butler's English Catholics, i. 259; Hume. This is strongly confirmed by a letter printed not long after, and republished in the Harleian Miscellany, vol. i. p. 142, with the name of one Leigh, a seminary priest, but probably the work of some protestant. He says, "for contributions of money, and for all other warlike actions, there was no difference between the catholic and the heretic. But in this case [of the Armada], to withstand the threatened conquest, yea, to defend the person of the queen, there appeared such a sympathy, concourse, and consent of all sorts of persons, without respect of religion, as they all appeared to be ready to fight against all strangers, as it were with one heart and one body." Notwithstanding this, I am far from thinking that it would have been safe to place the catholics, generally speaking, in command. Sir William Stanley's recent treachery in giving up Deventer to the Spaniards made it unreasonable for them to complain of exclusion from trust. Nor do I know that they did so. But trust and toleration are two different things. And even with respect to the former, I believe it far better to leave the matter in the hands of the executive government, which will not readily suffer itself to be betrayed, than to proscribe, as we have done, whole bodies by a legislative exclusion. Whenever, indeed, the government itself is not to be trusted, there arises a new condition of the problem.

[2] Strype, vols. iii. and iv. passim. Life of Whitgift, 401, 505. Murden, 667. Birch's Memoirs of Elizabeth. Lingard, &c. One hundred and ten catholics suffered death between 1588 and 1603. Lingard, 513.

[3] 23 Eliz. c. 2.

[4] Camden, 566. Strype, iv. 56. This was the declaration of October, 1591, which Andreas Philopater answered. Ribadeneira also inveighs against it. According to them, its publication was delayed till after the death of Hatton, when the persecuting part of the queen's council gained the ascendency.

priests from confinement; but such precarious and irregular connivance gave more scandal to the puritans than comfort to the opposite party.

General observations.

The catholic martyrs under Elizabeth amount to no inconsiderable number. Dodd reckons them at 191; Milner has raised the list to 204. Fifteen of these, according to him, suffered for denying the queen's supremacy, 126 for exercising their ministry, and the rest for being reconciled to the Romish church. Many others died of hardships in prison, and many were deprived of their property.[1] There seems nevertheless to be good reason for doubting whether any one who was executed might not have saved his life by explicitly denying the pope's power to depose the queen. It was constantly maintained by her ministers that no one had been executed for his religion. This would be an odious and hypocritical subterfuge if it rested on the letter of these statutes, which adjudge the mere manifestation of a belief in the Roman catholic religion, under certain circumstances, to be an act of treason. But both lord Burleigh, in his Execution of Justice, and Walsingham, in a letter published by Burnet,[2] positively assert the contrary; and I am not aware that their assertion has been disproved. This certainly furnishes a distinction between the persecution under Elizabeth (which, unjust as it was in its operation, yet, as far as it extended to capital inflictions, had in view the security of the government) and that which the protestants had sustained in her sister's reign, springing from mere bigotry and vindictive rancor, and not even shielding itself at the time with those shallow pretexts of policy which

[1] Butler, 178. In Coke's famous speech in opening the case of the Powder-plot, he says that not more than thirty priests and five receivers had been executed in the whole of the queen's reign, and for religion not any one. State Trials, ii. 179.

Dr. Lingard says of those who were executed between 1588 and the queen's death, "the butchery, with a few exceptions, was performed on the victim while he was in full possession of his senses." Vol. viii. p. 356. I should be glad to think that the few exceptions were the other way. Much would depend on the humanity of the sheriff, which one might hope to be stronger in an English gentleman than his zeal against popery. But I cannot help acknowledging that there is reason to believe the disgusting cruelties of the legal sentence to have been frequently inflicted. In an anonymous memorial among lord Burleigh's papers, written about 1586, it is recommended that priests persisting in their treasonable opinion should be hanged, "and the manner of drawing and quartering forborne." Strype, iii. 620. This seems to imply that it had been usually practised on the living. And lord Bacon, in his observations on a libel written against lord Burleigh in 1592, does not deny the "bowellings" of catholics; but makes a sort of apology for it, as "less cruel than the wheel of forcipation, or even simple burning." Bacon's Works, vol. i. p. 534.

[2] Burnet, ii. 418.

it has of late been attempted to set up in its extenuation. But that which renders these condemnations of popish priests so iniquitous is, that the belief in, or rather the refusal to disclaim, a speculative tenet, dangerous indeed, and incompatible with loyalty, but not coupled with any overt act, was construed into treason; nor can any one affect to justify these sentences who is not prepared to maintain that a refusal of the oath of abjuration, while the pretensions of the house of Stuart subsisted, might lawfully or justly have incurred the same penalty.[1]

An apology was always deduced for these measures, whether of restriction or punishment, adopted against all adherents to the Roman church, from the restless activity of that new militia which the Holy See had lately organized. The mendicant orders established in the thirteenth century had lent former popes a powerful aid towards subjecting both the laity and the secular priesthood, by their superior learning and ability, their emulous zeal, their systematic concert, their implicit obedience. But, in all these requisites for good and faithful janizaries of the church, they were far excelled by the new order of Ignatius Loyola. Rome, I believe, found in their services what has stayed her fall. They contributed in a very material degree to check the tide of the Reforma-

[2] "Though no papists were in this reign put to death purely on account of their religion, as numberless protestants had been in the woful days of queen Mary, yet many were executed for treason." Churton's Life of Nowell, p. 147. Mr. Southey, whose abandonment of the oppressed side I sincerely regret, holds the same language; and a later writer, Mr. Townsend, in his Accusations of History against the Church of Rome, has labored to defend the capital, as well as other punishments, of catholics under Elizabeth, on the same pretence of their treason.

Treason, by the law of England, and according to the common use of language, is the crime of rebellion or conspiracy against the government. If a statute is made, by which the celebration of certain religious rites is subjected to the same penalties as rebellion or conspiracy, would any man, free from prejudice, and not designing to impose upon the uninformed, speak of persons convicted on such a statute as guilty of treason, without expressing in what sense he uses the words, or deny that they were as truly punished for their religion as if they had been convicted of heresy? A man is punished for religion when he incurs a penalty for its profession or exercise to which he was not liable on any other account.

This is applicable to the great majority of capital convictions on this score under Elizabeth. The persons convicted could not be traitors in any fair sense of the word, because they were not charged with anything properly denominated treason. It certainly appears that Campian and some other priests about the same time were indicted on the statute of Edward III. for compassing the queen's death, or intending to depose her. But the only evidence, so far as we know or have reason to suspect, that could be brought against them, was their own admission, at least by refusing to abjure it, of the pope's power to depose heretical princes. I suppose it is unnecessary to prove that, without some overt act to show a design of acting upon this principle, it could not fall within the statute.

tion. Subtle alike and intrepid, pliant in their direction, unshaken in their aim, the sworn, implacable, unscrupulous enemies of protestant governments, the jesuits were a legitimate object of jealousy and restraint. As every member of that society enters into an engagement of absolute, unhesitating obedience to its superior, no one could justly complain that he was presumed capable at least of committing any crimes that the policy of his monarch might enjoin. But if the jesuits by their abilities and busy spirit of intrigue promoted the interests of Rome, they raised up enemies by the same means to themselves within the bosom of the church; and became little less obnoxious to the secular clergy, and to a great proportion of the laity, than to the protestants whom they were commissioned to oppose. Their intermeddling character was shown in the very prisons occupied by catholic recusants, where a schism broke out between the two parties, and the secular priests loudly complained of their usurping associates.[1] This was manifestly connected with the great problem of allegiance to the queen, which the one side being always ready to pay, did not relish the sharp usage it endured on account of the other's disaffection. The council indeed gave some signs of attending to this distinction, by a proclamation issued in 1602, ordering all priests to depart from the kingdom, unless they should come in and acknowledge their allegiance, with whom the queen would take further order.[2] Thirteen priests came forward on this, with a declaration of allegiance as full as could be devised. Some of the more violent papists blamed them for this; and the Louvain divines concurred in the censure.[3] There were now two parties among the English catholics; and those who, goaded by the sense of long persecution, and inflamed by obstinate bigotry, regarded every heretical government as unlawful or unworthy of obedience, used every machination to deter the rest from giving any test of their loyalty. These were the more busy, but by much the less numerous class;

[1] Watson's Quodlibets. True Relation of the Faction begun at Wisbech, 1601. These tracts contain rather an uninteresting account of the squabbles in Wisbech castle among the prisoners, but cast heavy reproaches on the jesuits, as the "fire-brands of all sedition, seeking by right or wrong simply or absolutely the monarchy of all England, enemies to all secular priests, and the causes of all the discord in the English nation." P. 74. I have seen several other pamphlets of the time relating to this difference. Some account of it may be found in Camden, 648, and Strype, iv. 194, as well as in the catholic historians, Dodd and Lingard.

[2] Rymer, xv. 473, 488.

[3] Butler's Engl. Catholics, p. 261.

and their influence was mainly derived from the laws of severity, which they had braved or endured with fortitude. It is equally candid and reasonable to believe that, if a fair and legal toleration, or even a general connivance at the exercise of their worship, had been conceded in the first part of Elizabeth's reign, she would have spared herself those perpetual terrors of rebellion which occupied all her later years. Rome would not indeed have been appeased, and some desperate fanatic might have sought her life; but the English catholics collectively would have repaid her protection by an attachment which even her rigor seems not wholly to have prevented.

It is not to be imagined that an entire unanimity prevailed in the councils of this reign as to the best mode of dealing with the adherents of Rome. Those temporary connivances or remissions of punishment which, though to our present view they hardly lighten the shadows of this persecution, excited loud complaints from bigoted men, were owing to the queen's personal humor, or the influence of some advisers more liberal than the rest. Elizabeth herself seems always to have inclined rather to indulgence than extreme severity. Sir Christopher Hatton, for some years her chief favorite, incurred odium for his lenity towards papists, and was, in their own opinion, secretly inclined to them.[1] Whitgift found enough to do with an opposite party. And that too noble and high-minded spirit, so ill fitted for a servile and dissembling court, the earl of Essex, was the consistent friend of religious liberty, whether the catholic or the puritan were to enjoy it. But those councillors, on the other hand, who favored the more precise reformers, and looked coldly on the established church, never failed to demonstrate their protestantism by excessive harshness towards the old religion's adherents. That bold, bad man, whose favor is the great reproach of Elizabeth's reign, the earl of Leicester, and the sagacious, disinterested, inexorable Walsingham, were deemed the chief advisers of sanguinary punishments. But, after their deaths, the catholics were mortified to discover

1 Ribadeneira says that Hatton "animo Catholicus, nihil perinde quam innocentem illorum sanguinem adeo crudeliter perfundi dolebat." He prevented Cecil from promulgating a more atrocious edict than any other, which was published after his death in 1591. De Schismate Anglic. c. 9. This must have been the proclamation of 29th Nov. 1591, forbidding all persons to harbor any one of whose conformity they should not be well assured.

that lord Burleigh, from whom they had hoped for more moderation, persisted in the same severities; contrary, I think, to the principles he had himself laid down in the paper from which I have above made some extracts.[1]

The restraints and penalties by which civil governments have at various times thought it expedient to limit the religious liberties of their subjects may be arranged in something like the following scale. The first and slightest degree is the requisition of a test of conformity to the established religion, as the condition of exercising offices of civil trust. The next step is to restrain the free promulgation of opinions, especially through the press. All prohibitions of the open exercise of religious worship appear to form a third and more severe class of restrictive laws. They become yet more rigorous when they afford no indulgence to the most private and secret acts of devotion or expressions of opinion. Finally, the last stage of persecution is to enforce by legal penalties a conformity to the established church, or an abjuration of heterodox tenets.

The first degree in this classification, or the exclusion of dissidents from trust and power, though it be always incumbent on those who maintain it to prove its necessity, may, under certain rare circumstances, be conducive to the political well-being of a state; and can then only be reckoned an encroachment on the principles of toleration when it ceases to produce a public benefit sufficient to compensate for the privation it occasions to its objects. Such was the English test act during the interval between 1672 and 1688. But, in my judgment, the instances which the history of mankind affords, where even these restrictions have been really consonant to the soundest policy, are by no means numerous. Cases may also be imagined where the free discussion of controverted doctrines might, for a time, at least, be subjected to some limitation for the sake of public tranquillity. I can scarcely conceive the necessity of restraining an open exercise of religious rites in any case, except that of glaring immorality. In no possible case can it be justifiable for the temporal power to intermeddle with the private devotions or doctrines of any man. But least of all can it carry its inquisition into the heart's recesses, and bend the reluctant con-

1 Birch, i. 84.

science to an insincere profession of truth, or extort from it an acknowledgment of error, for the purpose of inflicting punishment. The statutes of Elizabeth's reign comprehend every one of these progressive degrees of restraint and persecution. And it is much to be regretted that any writers worthy of respect should, either through undue prejudice against an adverse religion, or through timid acquiescence in whatever has been enacted, have offered for this odious code the false pretext of political necessity. That necessity, I am persuaded, can never be made out: the statutes were, in many instances, absolutely unjust; in others, not demanded by circumstances; in almost all, prompted by religious bigotry, by excessive apprehension, or by the arbitrary spirit with which our government was administered under Elizabeth.

CHAPTER IV.

ON THE LAWS OF ELIZABETH'S REIGN RESPECTING PROTESTANT NONCONFORMISTS.

Origin of the Differences among the English Protestants — Religious Inclinations of the Queen — Unwillingness of many to comply with the established Ceremonies — Conformity enforced by the Archbishop — Against the Disposition of others — A more determined Opposition, about 1570, led by Cartwright — Dangerous Nature of his Tenets — Puritans supported in the Commons — and in some measure by the Council — Prophesyings — Archbishops Grindal and Whitgift — Conduct of the latter in enforcing Conformity — High Commission Court — Lord Burleigh averse to Severity — Puritan Libels — Attempt to set up Presbyterian System — House of Commons averse to Episcopal Authority — Independents liable to severe Laws — Hooker's Ecclesiastical Polity — Its Character — Spoliation of Church Revenues — General Remarks — Letter of Walsingham in Defence of the Queen's Government.

Puritans.

THE two statutes, enacted in the first year of Elizabeth, commonly called the acts of supremacy and uniformity, are the main links of the Anglican church with the temporal constitution, and establish the subordination and dependency of the former; the first abrogating all jurisdiction and legislative power of ecclesiastical rulers, except under the authority of the crown; and the second prohibiting all changes of rites and discipline without the approbation of parliament. It was the constant policy of this queen to maintain her ecclesiastical prerogative and the laws she had enacted. But in following up this principle she found herself involved in many troubles, and had to contend with a religious party quite opposite to the Romish, less dangerous indeed and inimical to her government, but full as vexatious and determined.

Origin of the differences among the English protestants.

I have in another place slightly mentioned the differences that began to spring up under Edward VI. between the moderate reformers who established the new Anglican church, and those who accused them of proceeding with too much forbearance in casting off superstitions and abuses. These diversities of opinion were not without some relation to those which distinguished the two great families of protestantism in Europe. Luther, intent on his own system of dogmatic theology, had shown much indifference about retrenching exterior ceremonies, and had even favored, especially in the first years of his preaching, that specious worship which some ardent reformers were eager to reduce to simplicity.[1] Crucifixes and images, tapers and priestly vestments, even for a time the elevation of the host and the Latin mass-book, continued in the Lutheran churches; while the disciples of Zuingle and Calvin were carefully eradicating them as popish idolatry and superstition. Cranmer and Ridley, the founders of the English Reformation, justly deeming themselves independent of any foreign master, adopted a middle course between the Lutheran and Calvinistic ritual. The general tendency however of protestants, even in the reign of Edward VI., was towards the simpler forms; whether through the influence of those foreign divines who coöperated in our Reformation, or because it was natural in the heat of religious animosity to recede as far as possible, especially in such exterior distinctions, from the opposite denomination. The death of Edward seems to have prevented a further approach to the scheme of Geneva in our ceremonies, and perhaps in our church-government. During the persecution of Mary's reign the most eminent protestant clergymen took refuge in various cities of Germany and Switzerland. They were received by the Calvinists with hospitality and fraternal kindness; while the Lutheran divines, a narrow-minded intolerant faction, both neglected and insulted them.[2] Divisions soon arose among themselves about the use of the English service, in which a pretty considerable party was disposed to make alterations. The chief scene of these disturbances was Frankfort, where Knox, the famous reformer of Scotland, headed the innovators; while Cox, an eminent divine, much concerned in the establishment of Edward VI., and afterwards bishop of Ely, stood up for the original liturgy. Cox succeeded (not quite fairly, if we may rely on the only narrative we possess) in driving his opponents from the city; but these disagreements were by no means healed when the accession of Elizabeth recalled both parties to their own country, neither of them very likely to display more mutual

1 Sleidan, Hist. de la Réformation, par Courayer, ii. 74.
2 Strype's Cranmer, 354.

charity in their prosperous hour than they had been able to exercise in a common persecution.[1]

The first mortification these exiles endured on their return was to find a more dilatory advance towards public reformation of religion, and more of what they deemed lukewarmness, than their sanguine zeal had anticipated. Most part of this delay was owing to the greater prudence of the queen's councillors, who felt the pulse of the nation before they ventured on such essential changes. But there was yet another obstacle, on which the reformers had not reckoned. Elizabeth, though resolute against submitting to the papal supremacy, was not so averse to all the tenets abjured by protestants, and loved also a more splendid worship than had prevailed in her brother's reign; while many of those returned from the Continent were intent on copying a still simpler model. She reproved a divine who preached against the real presence, and is even said to have used prayers to the Virgin.[2] But her great struggle with the reformers was about images, and particularly the crucifix, which she retained, with lighted tapers before it, in her chapel; though in the injunctions to the ecclesiastical visitors of 1559 they are directed to have them taken away from churches.[3] This concession she must have made very reluctantly, for we find proofs the next year of her inclination to restore them; and the question of their lawfulness was debated, as Jewell writes word to Peter Martyr,

Religious inclinations of the queen.

1 These transactions have been perpetuated by a tract, entitled Discourse of the Troubles at Frankfort, first published in 1575, and reprinted in the well-known collection entitled the Phœnix. It is fairly and temperately written, though with an avowed bias towards the puritan party. Whatever we read in any historian on the subject is derived from this authority; but the refraction is of course very different through the pages of Collier and of Neal.

2 Strype's Annals, ii. 1. There was a Lutheran party at the beginning of her reign, to which the queen may be said to have inclined, not altogether from religion, but from policy. Id. i. 53. Her situation was very hazardous; and, in order to connect herself with sincere allies, she had thoughts of joining the Smalcaldic league of the German princes, whose bigotry would admit none but members of the Augsburg Confession. Jewell's letters to Peter Martyr, in the appendix to Burnet's third volume, and lately published more accurately, with many of other reformers, by the Parker Society [1845], throw considerable light on the first two years of Elizabeth's reign; and show that famous prelate to have been what afterwards would have been called a precisian or puritan. He even approved a scruple Elizabeth entertained about her title of head of the church, as appertaining only to Christ. But the unreasonableness of the discontented party, and the natural tendency of a man who has joined the side of power to deal severely with those he has left, made him afterwards their enemy.

3 Roods and relics accordingly were broken to pieces and burned throughout the kingdom, of which Collier makes loud complaint. This, Strype says gave much offence to the catholics; and it was not the most obvious method of inducing them to conform.

by himself and Grindal on one side, against Parker and Cox, who had been persuaded to argue in their favor.[1] But the strenuous opposition of men so distinguished as Jewell, Sandys, and Grindal, of whom the first declared his intention of resigning his bishopric in case this return towards superstition should be made, compelled Elizabeth to relinquish her project.[2] The crucifix was even for a time removed from her own chapel, but replaced about 1570.[3]

There was, however, one other subject of dispute between the old and new religions upon which her majesty could not be brought to adopt the protestant side of the question. This was the marriage of the clergy, to which she expressed so great an aversion, that she would never consent to repeal the statute of her sister's reign against it.[4] Accordingly the bishops and clergy, though they married by connivance, or rather by an ungracious permission,[5] saw with very just dissatisfaction their children treated by the law as the offspring

1 Burnet, iii. Appendix, 290. Strype's Parker, 46.

2 Quantum auguror, non scribam ad te posthac episcopus. Eo enim jam res pervenit, ut aut cruces argenteæ et stanneæ, quas nos ubique confregimus, restituendæ sint, aut episcopatus relinquendi. Burnet, 294. I conceive that by *cruces* we are to understand crucifixes, not mere crosses; though I do not find the word, even in Du Cange, used in the former sense. Sandys writes that he had nearly been deprived for expressing himself warmly against images. Id. 296. Other proofs of the text may be found in the same collection, as well as in Strype's Annals, and his Life of Parker. Even Parker seems, on one occasion, to have expected the queen to make such a retrograde movement in religion as would compel them all to disobey her. Life of Parker, Appendix, 29; a very remarkable letter.

3 Strype's Parker, 310. The archbishop seems to disapprove this as inexpedient, but rather coldly: he was far from sharing the usual opinions on this subject. A puritan pamphleteer took the liberty to name the queen's chapel as "the pattern and precedent of all superstition." Strype's Annals, i. 471.

4 Burnet, ii. 395.

5 One of the injunctions to the visitors of 1559, reciting the offence and slander to the church that had arisen by lack of discreet and sober behavior in many ministers, both in choosing of their wives and in living with them, directs that no priest or deacon shall marry without the allowance of the bishops, and two justices of the peace dwelling near the woman's abode, nor without the consent of her parents or kinsfolk, or, for want of these, of her master or mistress, on pain of not being permitted to exercise the ministry or hold any benefice; and that the marriages of bishops should be approved by the metropolitan, and also by commissioners appointed by the queen. Somers Tracts, i. 65. Burnet, ii. 398. It is reasonable to suppose that when a host of low-bred and illiterate priests were at once released from the obligation to celibacy, many of them would abuse their liberty improvidently, or even scandalously; and this probably had increased Elizabeth's prejudice against clerical matrimony. But I do not suppose that this injunction was ever much regarded. Some time afterwards (Aug. 1561) she put forth another extraordinary injunction, that no member of a college or cathedral should have his wife living within its precincts, under pain of forfeiting all his preferments. Cecil sent this to Parker, telling him at the same time that it was with great difficulty he had prevented the queen from altogether forbidding the marriage of priests. Life of P. 107. And the archbishop himself says, in the letter above mentioned, "I was in a horror to hear such words to come from her mild nature and Christianly learned conscience as she spake concerning God's holy ordinance and institution of matrimony."

of concubinage.[1] This continued, in legal strictness, till the first year of James, when the statute of Mary was explicitly repealed; though I cannot help suspecting that clerical marriages had been tacitly recognized, even in courts of justice, long before that time. Yet it appears less probable to derive Elizabeth's prejudice in this respect from any deference to the Roman discipline, than from that strange dislike to the most lawful union between the sexes which formed one of the singularities of her character.

Such a reluctance as the queen displayed to return in every point even to the system established under Edward was no slight disappointment to those who thought that too little had been effected by it. They had beheld at Zurich and Geneva the simplest and, as they conceived, the purest form of worship. They were persuaded that the vestments still worn by the clergy, as in the days of popery, though in themselves indifferent, led to erroneous notions among the people, and kept alive a recollection of former superstitions, which would render their return to them more easy in the event of another political revolution.[2] They disliked some other ceremonies for the same reason. These objections were by no means confined, as is perpetually insinuated, to a few discontented persons. Except archbishop Parker, who had remained in England during the late reign, and Cox, bishop of Ely, who had taken a strong part at Frankfort against innovation, all the most eminent churchmen, such as Jewell, Grindal, Sandys, Nowell, were in favor of leaving off the surplice and what were called the popish ceremonies.[3]

[1] Sandys writes to Parker, April, 1559, "The queen's majesty will wink at it, but not stablish it by law, which is nothing else but to bastard our children." And decisive proofs are brought by Strype that the marriages of the clergy were not held legal in the first part, at least, of the queen's reign. Elizabeth herself, after having been sumptuously entertained by the archbishop at Lambeth, took leave of Mrs. Parker with the following courtesy: "*Madam* (the style of a married lady) I may not call you; *mistress* (the appellation at that time of an unmarried woman) I am loath to call you; but however I thank you for your good cheer." This lady is styled, in deeds made while her husband was archbishop, *Parker* alias *Harleston*, which was her maiden name. And she dying before her husband, her brother is called her heir-at-law, though she left children. But the archbishop procured letters of legitimation, in order to render them capable of inheritance. Life of Parker, p. 511. Others did the same. Annals, i. 8. Yet such letters were, I conceive, beyond the queen's power to grant, and could not have obtained any regard in a court of law.

In the diocese of Bangor it was usual for the clergy, some years after Elizabeth's accession, to pay the bishop for a license to keep a concubine. Strype's Parker, 203.

[2] Burnet, iii. 305.

[3] Jewell's letters to Bullinger, in Burnet, are full of proofs of his dissatisfaction; and those who feel any doubts may easily satisfy themselves from the same collection, and from Strype as to the others. The current opinion, that

Whether their objections are to be deemed narrow and frivolous or otherwise, it is inconsistent with veracity to dissemble that the queen alone was the cause of retaining those observances to which the great separation from the Anglican establishment is ascribed. Had her influence been withdrawn, surplices and square caps would have lost their steadiest friend ; and several other little accommodations to the prevalent dispositions of protestants would have taken place. Of this it seems impossible to doubt, when we read the proceedings of the convocation in 1562, when a proposition to abolish most of the usages deemed objectionable was lost only by a vote, the numbers being 59 to 58.[1]

In thus restraining the ardent zeal of reformation, Elizabeth may not have been guided merely by her own prejudices, without far higher motives of prudence and even of equity. It is difficult to pronounce in what proportion the two conflicting religions were blended on her coming to the throne. The reformed occupied most large towns, and were no doubt a more active and powerful body than their opponents. Nor did the ecclesiastical visitors of 1559 complain of any resistance, or even unwillingness, among the people.[2]

these scruples were imbibed during the banishment of our reformers, must be received with great allowance. The dislike to some parts of the Anglican ritual had begun at home; it had broken out at Frankfort; it is displayed in all the early documents of Elizabeth's reign by the English divines, far more warmly than by their Swiss correspondents. Grindal, when first named to the see of London, had his scruples about wearing the episcopal habits removed by Peter Martyr. Strype's Grindal, 29.

1 It was proposed on this occasion to abolish all saints' days, to omit the cross in baptism, to leave kneeling at the communion to the ordinary's discretion, to take away organs, and one or two more of the ceremonies then chiefly in dispute. Burnet, iii. 303, and Append. 319. Strype, i. 297, 299. Nowell voted in the minority. It can hardly be going too far to suppose that some of the majority were attached to the old religion.

2 Jewell, one of these visitors, writes afterwards to Martyr, "Invenimus ubique animos multitudinis satis propensos ad religionem ; ibi etiam, ubi omnia putabantur fore difficillima. . . . . Si quid erat obstinatæ malitiæ, id totum erat in presbyteris, illis præsertim, qui aliquando stetissent à nostrâ sententiâ." Burnet, iii. Append. 289. The common people in London and elsewhere, Strype says, took an active part in demolishing images ; the pleasure of destruction, I suppose, mingling with their abhorrence of idolatry. And during the conferences held in Westminster Abbey, Jan. 1559, between the catholic and protestant divines, the populace, who had been admitted as spectators, testified such disapprobation of the former, that they made it a pretext for breaking off the argument. There was indeed such a tendency to anticipate the government in reformation as necessitated a proclamation, Dec. 28, 1558, silencing preachers on both sides.

Mr. Butler says, from several circumstances it is evident that a great majority of the nation then inclined to the Roman catholic religion. Mem. of English Catholics, i. 146. But his proofs of this are extremely weak. The attachment he supposes to have existed in the laity towards their pastors may well be doubted; it could not be founded on the natural grounds of esteem; and if Rishton, the continuator of Sanders de Schismate, whom he quotes, says that one third of the nation was protestant, we may surely double the calculation of so determined a papist. As to the in-

Still the Romish party was extremely numerous: it comprehended the far greater portion of the beneficed clergy, and all those who, having no turn for controversy, clung with pious reverence to the rites and worship of their earliest associations. It might be thought perhaps not very repugnant to wisdom or to charity that such persons should be won over to the reformed faith by retaining a few indifferent usages, which gratified their eyes, and took off the impression, so unpleasant to simple minds, of religious innovation. It might be urged that, should even somewhat more of superstition remain awhile than rational men would approve, the mischief would be far less than to drive the people back into the arms of popery, or to expose them to the natural consequences of destroying at once all old landmarks of reverence, — a dangerous fanaticism, or a careless irreligion. I know not in what degree these considerations had weight with Elizabeth; but they were such as it well became her to entertain.

We live, however, too far from the period of her accession

fluence which Mr. B. alleges the court to have employed in elections for Elizabeth's first parliament, the argument would equally prove that the majority was protestant under Mary, since she had recourse to the same means. The whole tenor of historical documents in Elizabeth's reign proves that the catholics soon became a minority, and still more among the common people than the gentry. The north of England, where their strength lay, was in every respect the least important part of the kingdom. Even according to Dr. Lingard, who thinks fit to claim half the nation as catholic in the middle of this reign, the number of recusants certified to the council under 23 Eliz. c. 1, amounted only to fifty thousand; and, if we can trust the authority of other lists, they were much fewer before the accession of James. This writer, I may observe in passing, has, through haste and thoughtlessness, misstated a passage he cites from Murden's State Papers, p. 605, and confounded the persons suspected for religion in the city of London, about the time of the Armada, with the whole number of men fit for arms; thus making the former amount to seventeen thousand and eighty-three.

Mr. Butler has taken up so paradoxical a notion on this subject, that he literally maintains the catholics to have been at least one half of the people at the epoch of the Gunpowder-plot. Vol. i. p. 295. We should be glad to know at what time he supposes the grand apostasy to have been consummated. Cardinal Bentivoglio gives a very different account; reckoning the real catholics, such as did not make profession of heresy, at only a thirtieth part of the whole; though he supposes that four fifths might become such, from secret inclination or general indifference, if it were once established. Opere di Bentivoglio, p. 83, edit. Paris, 1645. But I presume neither Mr. Butler nor Dr. Lingard would own these *adiaphorists*.

The latter writer, on the other hand, reckons the Hugonots of France, soon after 1560, at only one hundredth part of the nation, quoting for this Castelnau, an useful memoir-writer, but no authority on a matter of calculation. The stern spirit of Coligni, *atrox animus Catonis*, rising above all misfortune, and unconquerable except by the darkest treachery, is sufficiently admirable without reducing his party to so miserable a fraction. The Calvinists at this time are reckoned by some at one fourth, but more frequently at one tenth, of the French nation. Even in the beginning of the next century, when proscription and massacre, lukewarmness and self-interest, had thinned their ranks, they are estimated by Bentivoglio (*ubi supra*) at one fifteenth.

to pass an unqualified decision on the course of policy which it was best for the queen to pursue. The difficulties of effecting a compromise between two intolerant and exclusive sects were perhaps insuperable. In maintaining or altering a religious establishment, it may be reckoned the general duty of governments to respect the wishes of the majority. But it is also a rule of human policy to favor the more efficient and determined, which may not always be the more numerous, party. I am far from being convinced that it would not have been practicable, by receding a little from that uniformity which governors delight to prescribe, to have palliated in a great measure, if not put an end for a time to, the discontent that so soon endangered the new establishment. The frivolous usages, to which so many frivolous objections were raised, such as the tippet and surplice, the sign of the cross in baptism, the ring in matrimony, the posture of kneeling at the communion, might have been left to private discretion, not possibly without some inconvenience, but with less, as I conceive, than resulted from rendering their observance indispensable. Nor should we allow ourselves to be turned aside by the common reply, that no concessions of this kind would have ultimately prevented the disunion of the church upon more essential differences than these litigated ceremonies; since the science of policy, like that of medicine, must content itself with devising remedies for immediate danger, and can at best only retard the progress of that intrinsic decay which seems to be the law of all things human, and through which every institution of man, like his earthly frame, must one day crumble into ruin.

Unwillingness of many to comply with the established ceremonies.

The repugnance felt by a large part of the protestant clergy to the ceremonies with which Elizabeth would not consent to dispense, showed itself in irregular transgressions of the uniformity prescribed by statute. Some continued to wear the habits, others laid them aside; the communicants received the sacrament sitting, or standing, or kneeling, according to the minister's taste; some baptized in the font, others in a basin; some with the sign of the cross, others without it. The people in London and other towns, siding chiefly with the malecontents, insulted such of the clergy as observed the prescribed order.[1] Many of the bishops readily con-

[1] Strype's Parker, 152, 153. Collier, 508. In the Lansdowne Collection, vol.

nived at deviations from ceremonies which they disapproved. Some, who felt little objection to their use, were against imposing them as necessary.[1] And this opinion, which led to very momentous inferences, began so much to prevail, that we soon find the objections to conformity more grounded on the unlawfulness of compulsory regulations in the church prescribed by the civil power, than on any special impropriety in the usages themselves. But this principle, which perhaps the scrupulous party did not yet very fully avow, was altogether incompatible with the supremacy vested in the queen, of which fairest flower of her prerogative she was abundantly tenacious. One thing was evident, that the puritan malecontents were growing every day more numerous, more determined, and more likely to win over the generality of those who sincerely favored the protestant cause. There were but two lines to be taken; either to relax and modify the regulations which gave offence, or to enforce a more punctual observation of them. It seems to me far more probable that the former course would have prevented a great deal of that mischief which the second manifestly aggravated. For in this early stage the advocates of a simpler ritual had by no means assumed the shape of an embodied faction, which concessions, it must be owned, are not apt to satisfy, but numbered the most learned and distinguished portion of the hierarchy. Parker stood nearly alone on the other side, but alone more than an equipoise in the balance, through his high station, his judgment in matters of policy, and his knowledge of the queen's disposition. He had possibly reason to apprehend that Elizabeth, irritated by the prevalent humor for alteration, might burst entirely away from the protestant side, or stretch her supremacy to reduce the church into a slavish subjection to her caprice.[2] This might induce a man of his sagacity, who took a far wider view of civil affairs than his brethren, to exert himself according to her peremptory command for universal conformity. But it is not easy to reconcile the whole of his conduct to this supposition; and in the copious memorials of Strype we find the archbishop rather exciting the queen to rigorous meas-

viii. 47, is a letter from Parker, April, 1565, complaining of Turner, dean of Wells, for having made a man do penance for adultery in a square cap.

[1] Strype's Parker, 157, 173.

[2] This apprehension of Elizabeth's taking a disgust to protestantism is intimated in a letter of bishop Cox, Strype's Parker, 229.

ures against the puritans than standing in need of her admonition.[1]

The unsettled state of exterior religion which has been mentioned lasted till 1565. In the beginning of that year a determination was taken by the queen, or rather perhaps the archbishop, to put a stop to all irregularities in the public service. He sent forth a book called Advertisements, containing orders and regulations for the discipline of the clergy. This modest title was taken in consequence of the queen's withholding her sanction of its appearance, through Leicester's influence.[2] The primate's next step was to summon before the ecclesiastical commission Sampson, dean of Christchurch, and Humphrey, president of Magdalen college, Oxford, men of signal nonconformity, but at the same time of such eminent reputation that, when the law took its course against them, no other offender could hope for indulgence. On refusing to wear the customary habits, Sampson was deprived of his deanery; but the other seems to have been tolerated.[3] This instance of severity, as commonly happens, rather irritated than intimidated the puritan clergy, aware of their numbers, their popularity, and their powerful friends, but above all sustained by their own sincerity and earnestness. Parker had taken his resolution to proceed in the vigorous course he had begun. He obtained from the queen a proclamation, peremptorily requiring a conformity in the use of the clerical vestments and other matters of discipline. The London ministers, summoned before himself and their bishop Grindal, who did not very willingly coöperate with his metropolitan, were called upon for a promise to comply with the legal ceremonies, which thirty-seven out of ninety-eight refused to make. They were in consequence suspended from

Conformity enforced by the archbishop against the disposition of others.

1 Parker sometimes declares himself willing to see some indulgence as to the habits and other matters; but the queen's commands being peremptory, he had thought it his duty to obey them, though forewarning her that the puritan ministers would not give way: 225, 227. This, however, is not consistent with other passages, where he appears to importune the queen to proceed. Her wavering conduct, partly owing to caprice, partly to insincerity, was naturally vexatious to a man of his firm and ardent temper. Possibly he might dissemble a little in writing to Cecil, who was against driving the puritans to extremities. But, on the review of his whole behavior, he must be reckoned, and always has been reckoned, the most severe disciplinarian of Elizabeth's first hierarchy, though more violent men came afterwards.

2 Strype's Annals, 416. Life of Parker, 159. Some years after these Advertisements obtained the queen's sanction, and got the name of Articles and Ordinances. Id. 160.

3 Strype's Annals, 416, 430. Life of Parker, 184. Sampson had refused a bishopric on account of these ceremonies. Burnet, iii. 292.

their ministry, and their livings put in sequestration. But these unfortunately, as was the case in all this reign, were the most conspicuous both for their general character and for their talent in preaching.[1]

Whatever deviations from uniformity existed within the pale of the Anglican church, no attempt had hitherto been made to form separate assemblies; nor could it be deemed necessary while so much indulgence had been conceded to the scrupulous clergy. But they were now reduced to determine whether the imposition of those rites they disliked would justify, or render necessary, an abandonment of their ministry. The bishops of that school had so far overcome their repugnance, as not only to observe the ceremonies of the church, but, in some instances, to employ compulsion towards others.[2] A more unexceptionable, because more disinterested, judgment was pronounced by some of the Swiss reformers, to whom our own paid great respect—Beza, Gualter, and Bullinger; who, while they regretted the continuance of a few superfluous rites, and still more the severity used towards good men, dissuaded their friends from deserting their vocation on that account. Several of the most respectable opponents of the ceremonies were equally adverse to any open schism.[3] But the animosities springing from heated zeal, and the smart of what seemed oppression, would not suffer the English puritans generally to acquiesce in such temperate counsels. They began to form separate conventicles in London, not ostentatiously indeed, but of course without the possibility of eluding notice. It was doubtless worthy of much consideration whether an established church-government could wink at the systematic disregard of its discipline by those who were subject to its jurisdiction and partook of

[1] Life of Parker, 214. Strype says, p. 223, that the suspended ministers preached again after a little time by connivance.

[2] Jewell is said to have become strict in enforcing the use of the surplice. Annals, 421.

[3] Strype's Annals, i. 423, ii. 316; Life of Parker, 243, 348. Burnet, iii. 310, 325, 337. Bishops Grindal and Horn wrote to Zurich, saying plainly it was not their fault that the habits were not laid aside, with the cross in baptism, the use of organs, baptism by women, &c., p. 314. This last usage was much inveighed against by the Calvinists, because it involved a theological tenet differing from their own, as to the necessity of baptism. In Strype's Annals, 501, we have the form of an oath taken by all midwives to exercise their calling without sorcery or superstition, and to baptize with the proper words. It was abolished by James I.

Beza was more dissatisfied than the Helvetic divines with the state of the English church — Annals, i. 452; Collier 503 — but dissuaded the puritans from separation, and advised them rather to comply with the ceremonies. Id. 511.

its revenues. And yet there were many important considerations, derived from the posture of religion and of the state, which might induce cool-headed men to doubt the expediency of too much straitening the reins. But there are few, I trust, who can hesitate to admit that the puritan clergy, after being excluded from their benefices, might still claim from a just government a peaceful toleration of their particular worship. This it was vain to expect from the queen's arbitrary spirit, the imperious humor of Parker, and that total disregard of the rights of conscience which was common to all parties in the sixteenth century. The first instance of actual punishment inflicted on protestant dissenters was in June, 1567, when a company of more than one hundred were seized during their religious exercises at Plummer's Hall, which they had hired on pretence of a wedding, and fourteen or fifteen of them were sent to prison.[1] They behaved on their examination with a rudeness, as well as self-sufficiency, that had already begun to characterize the puritan faction. But this cannot excuse the fatal error of molesting men for the exercise of their own religion.

These coercive proceedings of the archbishop were feebly seconded, or directly thwarted, by most leading men both in church and state. Grindal and Sandys, successively bishops of London and archbishops of York, were naturally reckoned at this time somewhat favorable to the nonconforming ministers, whose scruples they had partaken. Parkhurst and Pilkington, bishops of Norwich and Durham, were openly on their side.[2] They had still more effectual support in the queen's council. The earl of Leicester, who possessed more power than any one to sway her wavering and capricious temper, the earls of Bedford, Huntingdon, and Warwick, regarded as the steadiest protestants among the aristocracy, the wise and grave lord keeper Bacon, the sagacious Walsingham, the experienced Sadler, the zealous Knollys, considered these objects of Parker's severity either as demanding a purer worship than had been established in the church, or at least as worthy by their virtues and services of more indulgent treatment.[3] Cecil himself, though on intimate terms

1 Strype's Life of Parker, 242. Life of Grindal, 114.

2 Burnet, iii. 316. Strype's Parker, 155, et alibi.

3 Id. 226. The church had but two or three friends, Strype says, in the council about 1572, of whom Cecil was the chief. Id. 388.

with the archbishop, and concurring generally in his measures, was not far removed from the latter way of thinking, if his natural caution and extreme dread at this juncture of losing the queen's favor had permitted him more unequivocally to express it. Those whose judgment did not incline them towards the puritan notions respected the scruples of men in whom the reformed religion could so implicitly confide. They had regard also to the condition of the church. The far greater part of its benefices were supplied by conformists of very doubtful sincerity, who would resume their mass-books with more alacrity than they had cast them aside.[1] Such a deficiency of protestant clergy had been experienced at the queen's accession, that for several years it was a common practice to appoint laymen, usually mechanics, to read the service in vacant churches.[2] These were not always wholly illiterate; or if they were, it was no more than might be said of the popish clergy, the vast majority of whom were destitute of all useful knowledge, and could read little Latin.[3]

[1] Burnet says, on the authority of the visitors' reports, that, "out of 9400 beneficed clergymen, not more than about 200 refused to conform. This caused for some years just apprehensions of the danger into which religion was brought by their retaining their affections to the old superstition; so that," he proceeds, "if queen Elizabeth had not lived so long as she did, till all that generation was dead and a new set of men better educated and principled were grown up and put in their rooms; and if a prince of another religion had succeeded before that time, they had probably turned about again to the old superstition as nimbly as they had done before in queen Mary's days." Vol. ii. p. 401. It would be easy to multiply testimonies out of Strype to the papist inclinations of a great part of the clergy in the first part of this reign. They are said to have been sunk in superstition and looseness of living. Annals, i. 166.

[2] Strype's Annals, 138, 177. Collier, 436, 465. This seems to show that more churches were empty by the desertion of popish incumbents than the foregoing note would lead us to suppose. I believe that many went off to foreign parts from time to time who had complied in 1559, and others were put out of their livings. The Roman catholic writers make out a longer list than Burnet's calculation allows.

It appears from an account sent in to the privy council by Parkhurst, bishop of Norwich, in 1562, that in his diocese more than one third of the benefices were vacant. Annals, i. 323. But in Ely, out of 152 cures, only 52 were served in 1560. L. of Parker, 72.

[3] Parker wrote in 1561 to the bishops of his province, enjoining them to send him certificates of the names and qualities of all their clergy; one column, in the form of certificate, was for learning: "And this," Strype says, "was commonly set down — Latinè aliqua verba intelligit, Latinè utcunque intelligit, Latinè pauca intelligit," &c. Sometimes, however, we find doctus. L. of Parker, 95. But if the clergy could not read the language in which their very prayers were composed, what other learning or knowledge could they have? Certainly none; and even those who had gone far enough to study the school logic and divinity do not deserve a much higher place than the wholly uninstructed. The Greek tongue was never *generally* taught in the universities or public schools till the Reformation, and perhaps not so soon.

Since this note was written, a letter of Gibson has been published in Pepys' Memoirs, vol. ii. p. 154, mentioning a catalogue he had found of the clergy in the archdeaconry of Middlesex, A.D. 1563, with their qualifications annexed. Three only are described as docti Latinè et Græcè; twelve are called docti simply; nine Latinè docti; thirty-one Latinè mediocriter intelligentes; forty-two La-

Of the two universities, Oxford had become so strongly attached to the Romish side during the late reign, that, after the desertion or expulsion of the most zealous of that party had almost emptied several colleges, it still for many years abounded with adherents to the old religion.[1] But at Cambridge, which had been equally popish at the queen's accession, the opposite faction soon acquired the ascendant. The younger students, imbibing ardently the new creed of ecclesiastical liberty, and excited by puritan sermons, began to throw off their surplices, and to commit other breaches of discipline, from which it might be inferred that the generation to come would not be less apt for innovation than the present.[2]

tinè perperam, utcunque aliquid, pauca verba, &c., intelligentes: seventeen are non docti or indocti. If this was the case in London, what can we think of more remote parts?

1 In the struggle made for popery at the queen's accession, the lower house of convocation sent up to the bishops five articles of faith, all strongly Roman catholic. These had previously been transmitted to the two universities, and returned with the hands of the greater part of the doctors to the first four. The fifth they scrupled, as trenching too much on the queen's temporal power. Burnet, ii. 388, iii. 269.

Strype says the universities were so addicted to popery, that for some years few educated in them were ordained. Life of Grindal, p. 50. And Wood's Antiquities of the University of Oxford contains many proofs of its attachment to the old religion. In Exeter College, as late as 1578, there were not above four protestants out of eighty, "all the rest secret or open Roman affectionaries." These chiefly came from the west, "where popery greatly prevailed, and the gentry were bred up in that religion." Strype's Annals, ii. 539. But afterwards Wood complains, "through the influence of Humphrey and Reynolds (the latter of whom became divinity lecturer on secretary Walsingham's foundation in 1586), the disposition of the times, and the long continuance of the earl of Leicester, the principal patron of the puritanical faction, in the place of chancellor of Oxford, the face of the university was so much altered that there was little to be seen in it of the church of England, according to the principles and positions upon which it was first reformed." Hist. of Oxford, vol. ii. p. 228. Previously, however, to this change towards puritanism, the university had not been Anglican, but popish; which Wood liked much better than the first, and nearly as well as the second.

A letter from the university of Oxford to Elizabeth on her accession (Herne's edition of Roper's Life of More, p. 173) shows the accommodating character of these academies. They extol Mary as an excellent queen, but are consoled by the thought of her excellent successor. One sentence is curious: "Cum *patri*, *fratri*, *sorori*, nihil fuerit republicâ carius, *religione optatius*, verâ gloriâ dulcius; cum in hâc familiâ hæ laudes floruerint vehementer confidimus, &c., quæ ejusdem stirpis sis, easdem cupidissime prosecuturam." It was a singular train of complaisance to praise Henry's, Edward's, and Mary's religious sentiments in the same breath; but the queen might at least learn this from it, that, whether she fixed on one of their creeds, or devised a new one for herself, she was sure of the acquiescence of this ancient and learned body. A preceding letter to cardinal Pole, in which the times of Henry and Edward are treated more cavalierly, seems by the style, which is very elegant, to have been the production of the same pen.

2 The fellows and scholars of St. John's College, to the number of three hundred, threw off their hoods and surplices, in 1565, without any opposition from their master, till Cecil, as chancellor of the university, took up the matter, and insisted on their conformity to the established regulations. This gave much dissatisfaction to the university; not only the more intemperate party, but many heads of colleges and grave men, among whom we are rather surprised to find the name of Whitgift, interceding with their chancellor for

The first period in the history of puritanism includes the time from the queen's accession to 1570, during which the retention of superstitious ceremonies in the church had been the sole avowed ground of complaint. But when these obnoxious rites came to be enforced with unsparing rigor, and even those who voluntarily renounced the temporal advantages of the establishment were hunted from their private conventicles, they began to consider the national system of ecclesiastical regimen as itself in fault, and to transfer to the institution of episcopacy that dislike which they felt for some of the prelates. The ostensible founder of this new school (though probably its tenets were by no means new to many of the sect) was Thomas Cartwright, the Lady Margaret's professor of divinity at Cambridge. He began about 1570 to inculcate the unlawfulness of any form of church-government, except what the apostles had instituted, namely, the presbyterian. A deserved reputation for virtue, learning, and acuteness, an ardent zeal, an inflexible self-confidence, a vigorous, rude, and arrogant style, marked him as the formidable leader of a religious faction.[1] In 1572 he published his celebrated Admonition to the Parliament, calling on that assembly to reform the various abuses subsisting in the church. In this treatise such a hardy spirit of innovation was displayed, and schemes of ecclesiastical policy so novel and extraordinary were developed, that it made a most important epoch in the contest, and rendered its termination far more improbable. The hour for liberal concessions had been suffered to pass away; the archbishop's intolerant temper had taught men to question the authority that oppressed them, till the battle was no longer to be fought for a tippet and a surplice, but for the whole ecclesiastical hierarchy, interwoven as it was with the temporal constitution of England.

A more determined opposition, about 1570, led by Cartwright.

Dangerous nature of his tenets.

It had been the first measure adopted in throwing off the yoke of Rome to invest the sovereign with an absolute con-

some mitigation as to these unpalatable observances. Strype's Annals, i. 441. Life of Parker, 194. Cambridge had, however her catholics, as Oxford had her puritans, of whom Dr. Caius, founder of the college that bears his name, was among the most remarkable. Id. 200. The chancellors of Oxford and Cambridge, Leicester and Cecil, kept a very strict hand over them, especially the latter, who seems to have acted as paramount visitor over every college, making them reverse any act which he disapproved. Strype, passim.

[1] Strype's Annals, i. 583. Life of Parker, 312, 347. Life of Whitgift, 27.

trol over the Anglican church; so that no part of its coercive discipline could be exercised but by his authority, nor any laws enacted for its governance without his sanction. This supremacy, indeed, both Henry VIII. and Edward VI. had carried so far, that the bishops were reduced almost to the rank of temporal officers taking out commissions to rule their dioceses during the king's pleasure; and Cranmer had prostrated at the feet of Henry those spiritual functions which have usually been reckoned inherent in the order of clergy. Elizabeth took some pains to soften, and almost explain away, her supremacy, in order to conciliate the catholics; while, by means of the High Commission court, established by statute in the first year of her reign, she was practically asserting it with no little despotism. But the avowed opponents of this prerogative were hitherto chiefly those who looked to Rome for another head of their church. The disciples of Cartwright now learned to claim an ecclesiastical independence, as unconstrained as any that the Romish priesthood in the darkest ages had usurped. "No civil magistrate in councils or assemblies for church matters," he says in his Admonition, "can either be chief-moderator, overruler, judge, or determiner; nor has he such authority as that, without his consent, it should not be lawful for ecclesiastical persons to make any church orders or ceremonies. Church matters ought ordinarily to be handled by church officers. The principal direction of them is by God's ordinance committed to the ministers of the church and to the ecclesiastical governors. As these meddle not with the making civil laws, so the civil magistrate ought not to ordain ceremonies, or determine controversies in the church, as long as they do not intrench upon his temporal authority. 'Tis the prince's province to protect and defend the councils of his clergy, to keep the peace, to see their decrees executed, and to punish the contemners of them; but to exercise no spiritual jurisdiction."[1] "It must be remembered," he says in another place, "that civil magistrates must govern the church according to the rules of God, prescribed in his word; and that, as they are nurses, so they be servants unto the church; and as they rule in the church, so they must remember to submit themselves unto the church, to submit

[1] Cartwright's Admonition, quoted in Neal's Hist. of Puritans, i. 88.

their sceptres, to thrown down their crowns before the church, yea, as the prophet speaketh, to lick the dust off the feet of the church."[1] It is difficult to believe that I am transcribing the words of a protestant writer; so much does this passage call to mind the tones of infatuated arrogance which had been heard from the lips of Gregory VII. and of those who trod in his footsteps.[2]

The strength of the protestant party had been derived, both in Germany and in England, far less from their superiority in argument, however decisive this might be, than from that desire which all classes, and especially the higher, had long experienced to emancipate themselves from the thraldom of ecclesiastical jurisdiction. For it is ever found that the generality of mankind do not so much as give a hearing to novel systems in religion, till they have imbibed, from some cause or other, a secret distaste to that in which they have been educated. It was therefore rather alarming to such as had an acquaintance with ecclesiastical history, and knew the encroachments formerly made by the hierarchy throughout Europe, encroachments perfectly distinguishable from those of the Roman see, to perceive the same pretensions urged, and the same ambition and arrogance at work, which had imposed a yoke on the necks of their fathers. With whatever plausibility it might be maintained that a connection with temporal magistrates could only corrupt the purity and shackle the liberties of a Christian church, this argument was not for them to urge who called on those magistrates to do the church's bidding, to enforce its decrees, to

1 Madox's Vindication of Church of England against Neal, p. 122. This writer quotes several very extravagant passages from Cartwright, which go to prove irresistibly that he would have made no compromise short of the overthrow of the established church (p. 111, &c.) "As to you, dear brethren," he said in a puritan tract of 1570, "whom God hath called into the brunt of the battle, the Lord keep you constant, that ye yield neither to toleration, neither to any other subtle persuasions of dispensations and licenses, which were to fortify their Romish practices; but, as you fight the Lord's fight, be valiant." Madox, p. 287.

2 These principles had already been broached by those who called Calvin master; he had himself become a sort of prophet-king at Geneva. And Collier quotes passages from Knox's Second Blast inconsistent with any government, except one slavishly subservient to the church. P. 444. The non-juring historian holds out the hand of fellowship to the puritans he abhors, when they preach up ecclesiastical independence. Collier liked the royal supremacy as little as Cartwright; and in giving an account of Bancroft's attack on the nonconformists for denying it, enters upon a long discussion in favor of an absolute emancipation from the control of laymen. P. 610. He does not even approve the determination of the judges in Cawdrey's case (5 Coke's Reports), though against the nonconformists, as proceeding on a wrong principle of setting up the state above the church. P. 634.

punish its refractory members; and while they disdained to accept the prince's coöperation as their ally, claimed his service as their minister. The protestant dissenters since the revolution, who have almost unanimously, and, I doubt not, sincerely, declared their averseness to any religious establishment, especially as accompanied with coercive power, even in favor of their own sect, are by no means chargeable with these errors of the early puritans. But the scope of Cartwright's declaration was not to obtain a toleration for dissent; not even, by abolishing the whole ecclesiastical polity, to place the different professions of religion on an equal footing; but to substitute his own model of government, the one, exclusive, unappealable standard of obedience, with all the endowments, so far as applicable to its frame, of the present church, and with all the support to its discipline that the civil power could afford.[1]

We are not however to conclude that every one, or even the majority, of those who might be counted on the puritan side in Elizabeth's reign, would have subscribed to these extravagant sentences of Cartwright, or desired to take away the legal supremacy of the crown.[2] That party acquired strength by the prevailing hatred and dread of popery, and by the disgust which the bishops had been unfortunate enough to excite. If the language which I have quoted from the puritans breathed a spirit of ecclesiastical usurpation that might one day become dangerous, many were of opinion that a spirit not less mischievous in the present hierarchy, under

1 The school of Cartwright were as little disposed as the episcopalians to see the laity fatten on church property. Bancroft, in his famous sermon preached at Paul's Cross in 1588 (p. 24), divides the puritans into the clergy factious and the lay factious. The former, he says, contend and lay it down in their supplication to parliament in 1585, that things once dedicated to a sacred use ought so to remain forever, and not to be converted to any private use. The lay, on the contrary, think it enough for the clergy to fare as the apostles did. Cartwright did not spare those who longed to pull down bishoprics for the sake of plundering them, and charged those who held impropriations with sin. Bancroft takes delight in quoting his bitter phrases from the Ecclesiastical Discipline.

2 The old friends and protectors of our reformers at Zurich, Bullinger and Gualter, however they had favored the principles of the first nonconformists, write in strong disapprobation of the innovators of 1574. Strype's Annals, ii. 316. And Fox, the martyrologist, a refuser to conform, speaks, in a remarkable letter quoted by Fuller in his Church History, p. 107, of factiosa illa Puritanorum capita, saying that he is totus ab iis alienus, and unwilling perbacchari in episcopos. The same is true of Bernard Gilpin, who disliked some of the ceremonies, and had subscribed the articles with a reservation, "so far as agreeable to the word of God;" but was wholly opposed to the new reform of church discipline. Carleton's Life of Gilpin, and Wordsworth's Ecclesiastical Biography, vol. iv. Neal has not reported the matter faithfully.

the mask of the queen's authority, was actually manifesting itself in deeds of oppression. The upper ranks among the laity, setting aside courtiers, and such as took little interest in the dispute, were chiefly divided between those attached to the ancient church and those who wished for further alterations in the new. I conceive the church of England party, that is the party adverse to any species of ecclesiastical change, to have been the least numerous of the three during this reign; still excepting, as I have said, the neutrals, who commonly make a numerical majority, and are counted along with the dominant religion.[1] But by the act of the fifth of Elizabeth, Roman catholics were excluded from the house of commons; or, if some that way affected might occasionally creep into it, yet the terror of penal laws impending over their heads would make them extremely cautious of betraying their sentiments. This contributed, with the prevalent tone of public opinion, to throw such a weight into the puritanical scale in the commons, as it required all the queen's energy to counterbalance.

Puritans supported in the Commons;

In the parliament that met in April, 1571, a few days only after the commencement of the session, Mr. Strickland, "a grave and ancient man of great zeal," as the reporter styles him, began the attack by a long but apparently temperate speech on the abuses of the church, tending only to the retrenchment of a

[1] "The puritan," says Persons the jesuit, in 1594, "is more generally favored throughout the realm with all those which are not of the Roman religion than is the protestant, upon a certain general persuasion that his profession is the more perfect, especially in great towns, where preachers have made more impression in the artificers and burghers than in the country people. And among the protestants themselves, all those that were less interested in ecclesiastical livings, or other preferments depending on the state, are more affected commonly to the puritans, or easily are to be induced to pass that way for the same reason." Doleman's Conference about the next Succession to the Crown of England, p. 242. And again: "The puritan party at home, in England, is thought to be most vigorous of any other, that is to say, most ardent, quick, bold, resolute, and to have a great part of the best captains and soldiers on their side, which is a point of no small moment." P. 244. I do not quote these passages out of trust in father Persons, but because they coincide with much besides that has occurred to me in reading, and especially with the parliamentary proceedings of this reign. The following observation will confirm (what may startle some readers) that the puritans, or at least those who rather favored them, had a majority among the protestant gentry in the queen's days. It is agreed on all hands, and is quite manifest, that they predominated in the house of commons. But that house was composed, as it has ever been, of the principal landed proprietors, and as much represented the general wish of the community when it demanded a further reform in religious matters as on any other subject. One would imagine, by the manner in which some express themselves, that the discontented were a small faction, who by some unaccountable means, in despite of the government and the nation, formed a majority of all parliaments under Elizabeth and her two successors.

few superstitions, as they were thought, in the liturgy, and to some reforms in the disposition of benefices. He proceeded to bring in a bill for the reformation of the common prayer, which was read a first time. Abuses in respect to benefices appear to have been a copious theme of scandal. The power of dispensation, which had occasioned so much clamor in former ages, instead of being abolished or even reduced into bounds at the Reformation, had been transferred entire from the pope to the king and archbishop. And, after the council of Trent had effected such considerable reforms in the catholic discipline, it seemed a sort of reproach to the protestant church of England that she retained all the dispensations, the exemptions, the pluralities, which had been deemed the peculiar corruptions of the worst times of popery.[1] In the reign of Edward VI., as I have already mentioned, the canon law being naturally obnoxious from its origin and character, a commission was appointed to draw up a code of ecclesiastical laws. This was accordingly compiled, but never obtained the sanction of parliament: and though some attempts were made, and especially in the commons at this very time, to bring it again before the legislature, our ecclesiastical tribunals have been always compelled to borrow a great part of their principles from the canon law: one important consequence of which may be mentioned by way of illustration; that they are incompetent to grant a divorce from the bond of marriage in cases of adultery, as had been provided in the reformation of ecclesiastical laws compiled under Edward VI. A disorderly state of the church, arising partly from the want of any fixed rules of discipline, partly from the negligence of some bishops and simony of others, but above all from the rude state of manners and general ignorance of the clergy, is the common theme of complaint in this period, and aggravated the increasing disaffection towards the prelacy. A bill was brought into the commons to take away the granting of licenses and dispensations by the

[1] Burnet, iii. 335. Pluralities are still the great abuse of the church of England; and the rules on this head are so complicated and unreasonable that scarce any one can remember them. It would be difficult to prove that, with a view to the interests of religion among the people, or of the clergy themselves, taken as a body, any pluralities of benefices with cure of souls ought to remain, except of small contiguous parishes. But with a view to the interests of some hundred well-connected ecclesiastics, the difficulty is none at all. [1827.] The case is now far from the same.—1845.

archbishop of Canterbury. But the queen's interference put a stop to this measure.[1]

The house of commons gave, in this session, a more forcible proof of its temper in ecclesiastical concerns. The articles of the English church, originally drawn up under Edward VI., after having undergone some alteration, were finally reduced to their present form by the convocation of 1562. But it seems to have been thought necessary that they should have the sanction of parliament, in order to make them binding on the clergy. Of these articles the far greater portion relate to matters of faith, concerning which no difference of opinion had as yet appeared. Some few, however, declare the lawfulness of the established form of consecrating bishops and priests, the supremacy of the crown, and the power of the church to order rites and ceremonies. These involved the main questions at issue; and the puritan opposition was strong enough to withhold the approbation of the legislature from this part of the national symbol. The act of 13 Eliz. c. 12, accordingly enacts that every priest or minister shall subscribe to all the articles of religion which *only* concern the confession of the true Christian faith, and the doctrines of the sacraments, comprised in a book entitled "Articles whereupon it was agreed," &c. That the word *only* was inserted for the sake of excluding the articles which established church authority and the actual discipline, is evident from a remarkable conversation which Mr. Wentworth, the most distinguished asserter of civil liberty in this reign, relates himself in a subsequent session (that of 1575) to have held on the subject with archbishop Parker. "I was," he says, "among others, the last parliament, sent for unto the archbishop of Canterbury, for the articles of religion that then passed this house. He asked us, 'Why we did put out of the book the articles for the homilies, consecration of bishops, and such like?' 'Surely, sir,' said I, 'because we were so occupied in other matters that we had no time to examine them how they agreed with the word of God.' 'What!' said he, 'surely you mistake the matter; you will refer yourselves wholly to us therein!' 'No; by the faith I bear to God,' said I, 'we will pass nothing before we understand what it is; for that were but to make you popes: make you popes who list,' said

[1] D'Ewes, p. 156. Parliament. Hist. i. 733, &c.

I, 'for we will make you none.' And sure, Mr. Speaker, the speech seemed to me to be a pope-like speech, and I fear least our bishops do attribute this of the pope's canons unto themselves; Papa non potest errare." [1] The intrepid assertion of the right of private judgment on one side, and the pretension to something like infallibility on the other, which have been for more than two centuries since so incessantly repeated are here curiously brought into contrast. As to the reservation itself, obliquely insinuated rather than expressed in this statute, it proved of little practical importance, the bishops having always exacted a subscription to the whole thirty-nine articles.[2]

[1] D'Ewes, p. 239. Parl. Hist. 790. Strype's Life of Parker, 394.

In a debate between cardinal Carvajal and Rockisane, the famous Calixtin archbishop of Prague, at the council of Basle, the former said he would reduce the whole argument to two syllables — Crede. The latter replied he would do the same, and confine himself to two others — Proba. Lenfant makes a very just observation on this: "Si la gravité de l'histoire le permettoit, on diroit avec le comique, C'est tout comme ici. Il y a long tems que le premier de ces mots est le langage de ce qu'on appelle *l'Eglise*, et que le second est le langage de ce qu'on appelle *l'hérésie*." Concile de Basle, p. 193.

[2] Several ministers were deprived, in 1572, for refusing to subscribe the articles. Strype, ii. 186. Unless these were papist, which indeed is possible, their objection must have been to the articles touching discipline; for the puritans liked the rest very well. [The famous dispute about the first clause of the 20th article, which was idly alleged by the puritans to have been interpolated by Laud, is settled conclusively enough in Cardwell's Synodalia, vol. i. p. 38, 53. — The questions are, 1, Whether this clause was formally accepted by convocation; and, 2, Whether it was confirmed by parliament. It is not found in the manuscript, being a rough draft of the articles bequeathed by Parker to Corpus Christi College, Cambridge, signed by all the convocation of 1562; which, notwithstanding the interlineations, must be taken as a final document, so far as their intentions prevailed. Nor is it found in the first English edition, that of 1563. It is found, however, in a Latin edition of the same year, of which one copy exists in the Bodleian Library, which belonged to Selden, and is said to have been obtained by him from Laud's library; though I am not aware how this is proved. To this copy is appended a parchment, with the signatures of the lower house of convocation in 1571, "but not in such a manner," says Dr. C., "as to prove that it originally belonged to the book." This would of course destroy its importance in evidence; but I must freely avow that my own impression on inspection was different, though it is very possible that I was deceived. It seems certainly strange that the lower house of convocation should have thus attested a single copy of a printed book.

The supposition of Dr. Lamb, dean of Bristol, which Dr. Cardwell seems to adopt, is that the queen, by her own authority, caused this clause to be inserted after the dissolution of the convocation, and, probably, to be entered on the register of that assembly, to which Laud refers in his speech in the Star-Chamber, 1637, but which was burned in the fire of London. We may conjecture that Parker had urged the adoption of it upon the convocation without success, and had therefore recourse to the supremacy of his sovereign. But, according to any principles which have been recognized in the church of England, the arbitrary nature of that ecclesiastical supremacy, so as to enact laws without consent either of convocation or of parliament, cannot be admitted; and this famous clause may be said to have wanted legal authority as a constitution of the church.

But there seems no doubt that it wanted still more the confirmation of the temporal legislature. The statute establishing the articles (13 Eliz. c. 12) refers to "a book imprinted, intituled Articles, whereupon it was agreed by the archbishops and bishops of both provinces, &c," following the title of the English edition of 1563, the only one

It was not to be expected that the haughty spirit of Parker, which had refused to spare the honest scruples of Sampson and Coverdale, would abate of its rigor towards the daring paradoxes of Cartwright. His disciples, in truth, from dissatisfied subjects of the church, were become her downright rebels, with whom it was hardly practicable to make any compromise that would avoid a schism, except by sacrificing the splendor and jurisdiction of an established hierarchy. The archbishop continued, therefore, to harass the puritan ministers, suppressing their books, silencing them in churches, prosecuting them in private meetings.[1] Sandys and Grindal, the moderate reformers of our spiritual aristocracy, not only withdrew their countenance from a party who aimed at improvement by subversion, but fell, according to the unhappy temper of their age, into courses of undue severity. Not merely the preachers, to whom, as regular ministers, the rules of canonical obedience might apply, but plain citizens, for listening to their sermons, were dragged before the high commission, and imprisoned upon any refusal to conform.[2] Strange that these prelates should not have remembered their own magnanimous readiness to encounter suffering for conscience' sake in the days of Mary, or should have fondly arrogated to their particular church that elastic force of resolution which disdains to acknowledge tyrannous power within the sanctuary of the soul, and belongs to the martyrs of every opinion without attesting the truth of any!

The puritans meanwhile had not lost all their friends in the council, though it had become more difficult to protect them. One powerful reason undoubtedly operated on Walsingham and other ministers of Elizabeth's court against crushing their party; namely, the

and in some measure by the council.

which then existed, besides the Latin of the same year. And from this we may infer that the commons either knew of no such clause, or did not mean to confirm it; which is consonant to the temper they showed on this subject, as may be seen in the text.

In a great majority of editions subsequent to 1571 the clause was inserted; and it had doubtless obtained universal reception long before Laud. The act of uniformity, 13 & 14 Car. 2, c. 4, merely refers to 13 Eliz., and leaves the legal operation as before.

It is only to be added that the clause contains little that need alarm any one, being in one part no more than the 34th article, and in the other being sufficiently secured from misinterpretation by the context, as well as by other articles. — 1845.]

[1] Neal, 187. Strype's Parker, 325. Parker wrote to Lord Burleigh (June, 1573), exciting the council to proceed against some of those men who had been called before the star-chamber. "He knew them," he said, "to be cowards" — a very great mistake — "and if they of the privy council gave over, they would hinder her majesty's government more than they were aware, and much abate the estimation of their own authorities," &c. Id. p. 421. Cartwright's Admonition was now prohibited to be sold. Ibid.

[2] Neal, 210.

precariousness of the queen's life, and the unsettled prospects of succession. They had already seen in the duke of Norfolk's conspiracy that more than half the superior nobility had committed themselves to support the title of the queen of Scots. That title was sacred to all who professed the catholic religion, and respectable to a large proportion of the rest. But deeming, as they did, that queen a convicted adulteress and murderer, the determined enemy of their faith, and conscious that she could never forgive those who had counselled her detention and sought her death, it would have been unworthy of their prudence and magnanimity to have gone as sheep to the slaughter, and risked the destruction of protestantism under a second Mary, if the intrigues of ambitious men, the pusillanimity of the multitude, and the specious pretext of hereditary right, should favor her claims on a demise of the crown. They would have failed perhaps in attempting to resist them; but upon resistance I make no question that they had resolved. In so awful a crisis, to what could they better look than to the stern, intrepid, uncompromising spirit of puritanism; congenial to that of the Scottish reformers, by whose aid the lords of the congregation had overthrown the ancient religion in despite of the regent Mary of Guise? Of conforming churchmen, in general, they might well be doubtful, after the oscillations of the three preceding reigns; but every abhorrer of ceremonies, every rejecter of prelatical authority, might be trusted as protestant to the heart's core, whose sword would be as ready as his tongue to withstand idolatry. Nor had the puritans admitted, even in theory, those extravagant notions of passive obedience which the church of England had thought fit to mingle with her homilies. While the victory was yet so uncertain, while contingencies so incalculable might renew the struggle, all politic friends of the Reformation would be anxious not to strengthen the enemy by disunion in their own camp. Thus sir Francis Walsingham, who had been against enforcing the obnoxious habits, used his influence with the scrupulous not to separate from the church on account of them; and again, when the schism had already ensued, thwarted, as far as his credit in the council extended, that harsh intolerance of the bishops which aggravated its mischiefs.[1]

[1] Strype's Annals, i. 433.

We should reason in as confined a manner as the puritans themselves, by looking only at the captious frivolousness of their scruples, and treating their sect either as wholly contemptible or as absolutely mischievous. We do injustice to these wise councillors of the maiden queen when we condemn (I do not mean on the maxims only of toleration, but of civil prudence) their unwillingness to crush the nonconforming clergy by an undeviating rigor. It may justly be said that, in a religious sense, it was a greater good to possess a well-instructed pious clergy, able to contend against popery, than it was an evil to let some prejudices against mere ceremonies gain a head. The old religion was by no means, for at least the first half of Elizabeth's reign, gone out of the minds of the people. The lurking priests had great advantages from the attractive nature of their faith, and some, no doubt, from its persecution. A middle system, like the Anglican, though it was more likely to produce exterior conformity, and for that reason was, I think, judiciously introduced at the outset, did not afford such a security against relapse, nor draw over the heart so thoroughly, as one which admitted of no compromise. Thus the sign of the cross in baptism, one of the principal topics of objection, may well seem in itself a very innocent and decorous ceremony. But if the perpetual use of that sign is one of the most striking superstitions in the church of Rome, it might be urged, in behalf of the puritans, that the people were less likely to treat it with contempt when they saw its continuance, even in one instance, so strictly insisted upon. I do not pretend to say that this reasoning is right, but that it is at least plausible, and that we must go back and place ourselves, as far as we can, in those times before we determine upon the whole of this controversy in its manifold bearings. The great object of Elizabeth's ministers, it must be kept in mind, was the preservation of the protestant religion, to which all ceremonies of the church, and even its form of discipline, were subordinate. An indifferent passiveness among the people, a humble trust in authority, however desirable in the eyes of churchmen, was not the temper which would have kept out the right heir from the throne, or quelled the generous ardor of the catholic gentry on the queen's decease.

A matter very much connected with the present subject will illustrate the different schemes of ecclesiastical policy pursued by the two parties that divided Elizabeth's council.

Prophesyings.

The clergy in several dioceses set up, with encouragement from their superiors, a certain religious exercise, called prophesyings. They met at appointed times to expound and discuss together particular texts of Scripture, under the presidency of a moderator appointed by the bishop, who finished by repeating the substance of their debate, with his own determination upon it. These discussions were in public, and it was contended that this sifting of the grounds of their faith and habitual argumentation would both tend to edify the people, very little acquainted as yet with their religion, and supply in some degree the deficiencies of learning among the pastors themselves. These deficiencies were indeed glaring, and it is not unlikely that the prophesyings might have had a salutary effect if it had been possible to exclude the prevailing spirit of the age. It must, however, be evident to any one who had experience of mankind, that the precise clergy, armed not only with popular topics, but with an intrinsic superiority of learning and ability to support them, would wield these assemblies at their pleasure, whatever might be the regulations devised for their control. The queen entirely disliked them, and directed Parker to put them down. He wrote accordingly to Parkhurst, bishop of Norwich, for that purpose. The bishop was unwilling to comply; and some privy-councillors interfered by a letter, enjoining him not to hinder those exercises so long as nothing contrary to the church was taught therein. This letter was signed by sir Thomas Smith, sir Walter Mildmay, bishop Sandys, and sir Francis Knollys. It was, in effect, to reverse what the archbishop had done. Parker, however, who was not easily daunted, wrote again to Parkhurst, that, understanding he had received instructions in opposition to the queen's orders and his own, he desired to be informed what they were. This seems to have checked the councillors, for we find that the prophesyings were now put down.[1]

Though many will be of opinion that Parker took a statesmanlike view of the interests of the church of England in discouraging these exercises, they were generally regarded as so conducive to instruction that he seems to have stood almost alone in his opposition to them. Sandys's name appears

[1] Strype's Annals, ii. 219, 322; Life of Parker, 461.

to the above-mentioned letter of the council to Parkhurst. Cox, also, was inclined to favor the prophesyings; and Grindal, who in 1575 succeeded Parker in the see of Canterbury, bore the whole brunt of the queen's displeasure rather than obey her commands on this subject. He conceived that, by establishing strict rules with respect to the direction of those assemblies, the abuses, which had already appeared, of disorderly debate and attacks on the discipline of the church, might be got rid of without entirely abolishing the exercise. The queen would hear of no middle course, and insisted both that the prophesyings should be discontinued and that fewer licenses for preaching should be granted. For no parish priest could, without a license, preach any discourse except the regular homilies; and this was one of the points of contention with the puritans.[1] Grindal steadily refused to comply with this injunction, and was in consequence sequestered from the exercise of his jurisdiction for the space of about five years, till, on his making a kind of submission, the sequestration was taken off not long before his death. The queen, by circular letters to the bishops, commanded them to put an end to the prophesyings, which were never afterwards renewed.[2]

Grindal.

[1] [In one of the canons enacted by convocation in 1571, and on which rather an undue stress has been laid in late controversies, we find a restraint laid on the teaching of the clergy in their sermons, who were enjoined to preach nothing but what was agreeable to scripture, and had been collected out of scripture by the catholic fathers and ancient bishops. Imprimis videbunt concionatores, ne quid unquam doceant pro concione, quod a populo religiosè teneri et credi velint, nisi quod consentaneum sit doctrinæ veteris aut novi testamenti, quodque ex illâ ipsâ doctrinâ Catholici patres et veteris episcopi collegerint. This appears to have been directed, in the first place, against those who made use of scholastic authorities and the doctors of the last four or five ages, to whom the church of Rome was fond of appealing; and, secondly, against those who, with little learning or judgment, set up their own interpretations of scripture. Against both these it seemed wise to guard, by directing preachers to the early fathers, whose authority was at least better than that of Romish schoolmen or modern sciolists. It is to be remembered that the exegetical part of divinity was not in the state in which it is at present. Most of the writers to whom a modern preacher has recourse were unborn. But that the contemporary reformers were not held in low estimation as guides in scriptural interpretation, appears by the injunction given some years afterwards that every clergyman should provide himself with a copy of Bullinger's decades. The authority given in the above canon to the fathers was certainly but a presumptive one; and, such as it was, it was given to each individually, not to the whole body, on any notion of what has been called catholic consent: since how was a poor English preacher to ascertain this? The real question as to the authority of the fathers in our church is not whether they are not copiously quoted, but whether our theologians surrendered their own opinion, or that of their side, in deference to such authority when it made against them. — 1845.]

[2] Strype's Life of Grindal, 219, 230, 272. The archbishop's letter to the queen, declaring his unwillingness to obey her requisition, is in a far bolder strain than the prelates were wont to use in this reign, and perhaps contributed to the severity she showed towards him. Grindal was a very honest, conscientious man, but too little of a courtier or statesman

Whitgift, bishop of Worcester, a person of a very opposite disposition, was promoted, in 1583, to the primacy on Grindal's decease. He had distinguished himself some years before by an answer to Cartwright's Admonition, written with much ability, but not falling short of the work it undertook to confute in rudeness and asperity.[1] It is seldom good policy to confer such eminent stations in the church on the gladiators of theological controversy, who, from vanity and resentment, as well as the course of their studies, will always be prone to exaggerate the importance of the disputes wherein they have been engaged, and to turn whatever authority the laws or the influence of their place may give them against their adversaries. This was fully illustrated by the conduct of archbishop Whitgift, whose elevation the wisest of Elizabeth's counsellors had ample reason to regret. In a few months after his promotion he gave an earnest of the rigor he had determined to adopt by promulgating articles for the observance of discipline. One of these prohibited all preaching, reading, or catechising in private houses, whereto any not of the same family should resort, "seeing the same was never permitted as lawful under any Christian magistrate." But that which excited the loudest complaints was the subscription to three points, the queen's supremacy, the lawfulness of the common prayer and ordination service, and the truth of the whole thirty-nine articles, exacted from every minister of the church.[2] These indeed were so far from novelties that it might seem rather supererogatory to demand them (if in fact the law required subscription to all the articles); yet it is highly probable that many had hitherto eluded the legal subscriptions, and that others had conceived their scruples after having conformed to the prescribed order. The archbishop's peremptory requisition passed, perhaps justly, for an illegal stretch of power.[3] It encountered the resistance of

Whitgift.

His conduct in enforcing conformity.

for the place he filled. He was on the point of resigning the archbishopric when he died; there had at one time been some thoughts of depriving him.

1 Strype's Whitgift, 27, et alibi. He did not disdain to reflect on Cartwright for his poverty, the consequence of a scrupulous adherence to his principles. But the controversial writers of every side in the sixteenth century display a want of decency and humanity which even our anonymous libellers have hardly matched. Whitgift was not of much learning, if it be true, as the editors of the Biographia Britannica intimate, that he had no acquaintance with the Greek language. This must seem strange to those who have an exaggerated notion of the scholarship of that age.

2 Strype's Whitgift, 115.

3 Neal, 266. Birch's Memoirs of Elizabeth, vol. i. p. 42, 47, &c

men pertinaciously attached to their own tenets, and ready to suffer the privations of poverty rather than yield a simulated obedience. To suffer, however, in silence has at no time been a virtue with our protestant dissenters. The kingdom resounded with the clamor of those who were suspended or deprived of their benefices and of their numerous abettors.[1] They appealed from the archbishop to the privy council. The gentry of Kent and other counties strongly interposed in their behalf. They had powerful friends at court, especially Knollys, who wrote a warm letter to the archbishop.[2] But, secure of the queen's support, who was now chiefly under the influence of Sir Christopher Hatton, a decided enemy to the puritans, Whitgift relented not a jot of his resolution, and went far greater lengths than Parker had ever ventured, or perhaps had desired, to proceed.

High commission court.

The act of supremacy, while it restored all ecclesiastical jurisdiction to the crown, empowered the queen to execute it by commissioners appointed under the great seal, in such manner and for such time as she should direct, whose power should extend to visit, correct, and amend all heresies, schisms, abuses, and offences whatever, which fall under the cognizance and are subject to the correction of spiritual authority. Several temporary commissions had sat under this act with continually augmented powers before that appointed in 1583, wherein the jurisdiction of this anomalous court almost reached its zenith. It consisted of forty-four commissioners, twelve of whom were bishops, many more privy-councillors, and the rest either

1 According to a paper in the appendix to Strype's Life of Whitgift, p. 60, the number of conformable ministers in eleven dioceses, not including those of London and Norwich, the strongholds of puritanism, was 786; that of noncompliers, 49. But Neal says that 233 ministers were suspended in only six counties, 64 of whom in Norfolk, 60 in Suffolk, 38 in Essex: p. 268. The puritans formed so much the more learned and diligent part of the clergy, that a great scarcity of preachers was experienced throughout this reign, in consequence of silencing so many of the former. Thus in Cornwall, about the year 1578, out of 140 clergymen, not one was capable of preaching. Neal, p. 245. And, in general, the number of those who could not preach, but only read the service, was to the others nearly as four to one — the preachers being a majority only in London. Id. p. 320.

This may be deemed by some an instance of Neal's prejudice. But that historian is not so ill-informed as they suppose; and the fact is highly probable. Let it be remembered that there existed few books of divinity in English; that all books were, comparatively to the value of money, far dearer than at present; that the majority of the clergy were nearly illiterate, and many of them addicted to drunkenness and low vices; above all, that they had no means of supplying their deficiencies by preaching the discourses of others; and we shall see little cause for doubting Neal's statement, though founded on a puritan document.

2 Life of Whitgift, 137, et alibi; Annals, iii. 183.

clergymen or civilians. This commission, after reciting the acts of supremacy, uniformity, and two others, directs them to inquire from time to time, as well by the oaths of twelve good and lawful men as by witnesses and all other means they can devise, of all offences, contempts, or misdemeanors done and committed contrary to the tenor of the said several acts and statutes; and also to inquire of all heretical opinions, seditious books, contempts, conspiracies, false rumors or talks, slanderous words and sayings, &c., contrary to the aforesaid laws. Power is given to any three commissioners, of whom one must be a bishop, to punish all persons absent from church, according to the act of uniformity, or to visit and reform heresies and schisms according to law; to deprive all beneficed persons holding any doctrine contrary to the thirty-nine articles; to punish incests, adulteries, and all offences of the kind; to examine all suspected persons on their oaths, and to punish all who should refuse to appear or to obey their orders by spiritual censure, or by discretionary fine or imprisonment; to alter and amend the statutes of colleges, cathedrals, schools, and other foundations, and to tender the oath of supremacy according to the act of parliament.[1]

Master of such tremendous machinery, the archbishop proceeded to call into action one of its powers, contained for the first time in the present commission, by tendering what was technically styled the oath ex officio to such of the clergy as were surmised to harbor a spirit of puritanical disaffection. This procedure, which was wholly founded on the canon law, consisted in a series of interrogations, so comprehensive as to embrace the whole scope of clerical uniformity, yet so precise and minute as to leave no room for evasion, to which the

1 Neal, 274; Strype's Annals, iii. 180. The germ of the high commission court seems to have been a commission granted by Mary (Feb. 1557) to certain bishops and others to inquire after all heresies, punish persons misbehaving at church, and such as refused to come thither, either by means of presentments by witness, or any other politic way they could devise; with full power to proceed as their discretions and consciences should direct them; and to use all such means as they could invent for the searching of the premises, to call witnesses, and force them to make oath of such things as might discover what they sought after. Burnet, ii. 347. But the primary model was the inquisition itself.

It was questioned whether the power of deprivation for not reading the common prayer, granted to the high commissioners, were legal — the act of uniformity having annexed a much smaller penalty. But it was held by the judges in the case of Cawdrey (5 Coke's Reports) that the act did not take away the ecclesiastical jurisdiction and supremacy which had ever appertained to the crown, and by virtue of which it might erect courts with as full spiritual jurisdiction as the archbishops and bishops exercised.

suspected party was bound to answer upon oath.[1] So repugnant was this to the rules of our English law and to the principles of natural equity, that no species of ecclesiastical tyranny seems to have excited so much indignation. Lord Burleigh, who, though at first rather friendly to Whitgift, was soon disgusted by his intolerant and arbitrary behavior, wrote in strong terms of remonstrance against these articles of examination, as "so curiously penned, so full of branches and circumstances, as he thought the inquisitors of Spain used not so many questions to comprehend and to trap their preys." The primate replied by alleging reasons in behalf of the mode of examination, but very frivolous, and such as a man determined to persevere in an unwarrantable course of action may commonly find.[2] They had little effect on the calm and sagacious mind of the treasurer, who continued to express his dissatisfaction, both individually and as one of the privy council.[3] But the extensive jurisdiction improvidently granted to the ecclesiastical commissioners, and which the queen was not at all likely to recall, placed Whitgift beyond the control of the temporal administration.

Lord Burleigh averse to severity.

The archbishop, however, did not stand alone in this impracticable endeavor to overcome the stubborn sectaries by dint of hard usage. Several other bishops were engaged in the same uncharitable course,[4] but especially Aylmer of London, who has left a worse name in this respect than any prelate of Elizabeth's reign.[5] The violence of Aylmer's temper was not redeemed by many virtues; it is impossible to exonerate his character from the imputations of covetousness and of plundering the revenues of his see: faults very prevalent among the bishops of that period. The privy council wrote sometimes to expostulate with Aylmer in a tone which could hardly have been employed towards a man in his station who had not forfeited the general esteem. Thus, upon occasion of one Benison, whom he had imprisoned without cause, we find a letter signed by Burleigh, Leicester, Walsingham, and even Hatton, besides several others, urging the

[1] Strype's Whitgift, 135; and Appendix, 49.

[2] Strype's Whitgift, 157, 160.

[3] Id. 163, 166, et alibi; Birch's Memoirs, i. 62. There was said to be a scheme on foot, about 1590, to make all persons in office subscribe a declaration that episcopacy was lawful by the word of God, which Burleigh prevented.

[4] Neal, 325, 385.

[5] Id. 290; Strype's Life of Aylmer, p. 59, &c. His biographer is here, as in all his writings, *too partial to condemn, but too honest to conceal.*

bishop to give the man a sum of money, since he would recover damages at law, which might hurt his lordship's credit. Aylmer, however, who was of a stout disposition, especially when his purse was interested, objected strongly to this suggestion, offering rather to confer on Benison a small living, or to let him take his action at law. The result does not appear, but probably the bishop did not yield.[1] He had worse success in an information laid against him for felling his woods, which ended not only in an injunction but a sharp reprimand from Cecil in the star-chamber.[2]

What lord Burleigh thought of these proceedings may be seen in the memorial to the queen on matters of religion and state, from which I have, in the last chapter, made an extract to show the tolerance of his disposition with respect to catholics. Protesting that he was not in the least addicted to the preciser sort of preachers, he declares himself "bold to think that the bishops, in these dangerous times, take a very ill and unadvised course in driving them from their cures;" first, because it must discredit the reputation of her majesty's power, when foreign princes should perceive that even among her protestant subjects, in whom consisted all her force, strength, and power, there was so great a heart-burning and division; and secondly, "because," he says, "though they were over-squeamish and nice in their opinions, and more scrupulous than they need, yet, with their careful catechising and diligent preaching, they bring forth that fruit which your most excellent majesty is to desire and wish, namely, the lessening and diminishing the papistical numbers."[3] But this great minister's knowledge of the queen's temper, and excessive anxiety to retain her favor, made him sometimes fearful to act according to his own judgment. "It is well known," lord Bacon says of him, in a treatise published in 1591, "that, as to her majesty, there was never a counsellor of his lordship's long continuance that was so appliable to her majesty's princely resolutions, endeavoring always after faithful propositions and remonstrances, and these in

1 Neal, 294.

2 Strype's Aylmer, 71. When he grew old, and reflected that a large sum of money would be due from his family for dilapidations of the palace at Fulham, &c., he literally proposed to sell his bishopric to Bancroft. Id. 169. The other, however, waited for his death, and had above 4000*l.* awarded to him; but the crafty old man having laid out his money in land, this sum was never paid. Bancroft tried to get an act of parliament in order to render the real estate liable, but without success. P. 194.

3 Somers Tracts, i. 166.

the best words and the most graceful manner, to rest upon such conclusions as her majesty in her own wisdom determineth, and them to execute to the best; so far hath he been from contestation, or drawing her majesty into any of his own courses."[1] Statesmen who betray this unfortunate infirmity of clinging too fondly to power become the slaves of the princes they serve. Burleigh used to complain of the harshness with which the queen treated him.[2] And though, more lucky than most of his class, he kept the white staff of treasurer down to his death, he was reduced in his latter years to court a rising favorite more submissively than became his own dignity.[3] From such a disposition we could not expect any decided resistance to those measures of severity towards the puritans which fell in so entirely with Elizabeth's temper.

There is no middle course, in dealing with religious sectaries, between the persecution that exterminates and the toleration that satisfies. They were wise in their generation, the Loaisas and Valdes of Spain, who kindled the fires of the inquisition, and quenched the rising spirit of protestantism in the blood of a Seso and a Cazalla. But, sustained by the favoring voice of his associates, and still more by that firm persuasion which bigots never know how to appreciate in their adversaries, a puritan minister set at nought the vexatious and arrogant tribunal before which he was summoned. Exasperated, not overawed, the sectaries threw off what little respect they had hitherto paid to the hierarchy. They had learned, in the earlier controversies of the Reformation, the use, or, more truly, the abuse, of that powerful lever of human bosoms, the press. He who in Saxony had sounded the first trumpet-peal against the battlements of Rome had often turned aside from his graver labors to excite the rude passions of the populace by low ribaldry and exaggerated invective; nor had the English reformers ever scrupled to win proselytes by the same arts. What had been accounted holy zeal in the mitred Bale and martyred Latimer, might plead some apology from example in the aggrieved puritan. Pamphlets, chiefly anonymous, were rapidly circulated throughout the kingdom, inveighing

Puritan libels.

1 Bacon's Works, i. 532.

2 Birch's Memoirs, ii. 146.

3 Id. ib. Burleigh does not shine much in these memoirs; but most of the letters they contain are from the two Bacons, then engaged in the Essex faction, though nephews of the treasurer.

against the prelacy. Of these libels the most famous went under the name of Martin Mar-prelate, a vizored knight of those lists, behind whose shield a host of sturdy puritans were supposed to fight. These were printed at a movable press, shifted to different parts of the country as the pursuit grew hot, and contained little serious argument, but the unwarrantable invectives of angry men, who stuck at no calumny to blacken their enemies.[1] If these insults upon authority are apt sometimes to shock us even now, when long usage has rendered such licentiousness of seditious and profligate libellers almost our daily food, what must they have seemed in the reign of Elizabeth, when the press had no acknowledged liberty, and while the accustomed tone in addressing those in power was little better than servile adulation?

A law had been enacted some years before, levelled at the books dispersed by the seminary priests, which rendered the publication of seditious libels against the queen's government a capital felony.[2] This act, by one of those strained constructions which the judges were commonly ready to put upon any political crime, was brought to bear on some of these puritanical writings. The authors of Martin Mar-prelate could not be traced with certainty; but strong suspicions having fallen on one Penry, a young Welshman, he was tried some time after for another pamphlet, containing sharp reflections on the queen herself, and received sentence of death, which it was thought proper to carry into execution.[3] Udal, a puritan minister, fell into the grasp of the same statute for an alleged libel on the bishops, which had surely a very indirect reference to the queen's administration. His trial, like most other political trials of the age, disgraces the name of English justice. It consisted mainly in a pitiful attempt by the court to entrap him into a confession that the

[1] The first of Martin Mar-prelate's libels were published in 1588. In the month of November of that year the archbishop is directed by a letter from the council to search for and commit to prison the authors and printers. Strype's Whitgift, 288. These pamphlets are scarce; but a few extracts from them may be found in Strype and other authors. The abusive language of the puritan pamphleteers had begun several years before. Strype's Annals, ii. 193. See the trial of Sir Richard Knightley of Northamptonshire, for dispersing puritanical libels. State Trials, i. 1263.

[2] 23 Eliz. c. 2.

[3] Penry's protestation at his death is in a style of the most affecting and simple eloquence. Life of Whitgift, 409; and Appendix, 176. It is a striking contrast to the coarse abuse for which he suffered. The authors of Martin Marprelate were never fully discovered; but Penry seems not to deny his concern in it.

imputed libel was of his writing, as to which their proof was deficient. Though he avoided this snare, the jury did not fail to obey the directions they received to convict him. So far from being concerned in Martin's writings, Udal professed his disapprobation of them, and his ignorance of the author. This sentence appeared too iniquitous to be executed even in the eyes of Whitgift, who interceded for his life; but he died of the effects of confinement.[1]

If the libellous pen of Martin Mar-prelate was a thorn to the rulers of the church, they had still more cause to take alarm at an overt measure of revolution which the discontented party began to effect about the year 1590. They set up, by common agreement, their own platform of government by synods and classes; the former being a sort of general assemblies, the latter held in particular shires or dioceses, agreeably to the presbyterian model established in Scotland. In these meetings debates were had, and determinations usually made, sufficiently unfavorable to the established system. The ministers composing them subscribed to the puritan book of discipline. These associations had been formed in several counties, but chiefly in those of Northampton and Warwick, under the direction of Cartwright, the legislator of their republic, who possessed, by the earl of Leicester's patronage, the mastership of a hospital in the latter town.[2] It would be

Attempt to set up a presbyterian system.

1 State Trials, 1271. It may be remarked, on this as on other occasions, that Udal's trial is evidently published by himself; and a defendant, especially in a political proceeding, is apt to give a partial color to his own case. Life of Whitgift, 314; Annals of Reformation, iv. 21; Fuller's Church History, 122; Neal, 340. This writer says—"Among the divines who *suffered death* for the libels above mentioned, was the Rev. Mr. Udal." This is no doubt a splenetic mode of speaking. But Warburton, in his short notes on Neal's history, treats it as a wilful and audacious attempt to impose on the reader—as if the ensuing pages did not let him into all the circumstances. I will here observe that Warburton, in his self-conceit, has paid a much higher compliment to Neal than he intended, speaking of his own comments as a "full confutation (I quote from memory) of that historian's false facts and misrepresentations." But when we look at these, we find a good deal of wit and some pointed remarks, but hardly anything that can be deemed a material correction of facts.

Neal's History of the Puritans is almost wholly compiled, as far as this reign is concerned, from Strype, and from a manuscript written by some puritan about the time. It was answered by Madox, afterwards bishop of Worcester, in a Vindication of the Church of England, published anonymously in 1733. Neal replied with tolerable success; but Madox's book is still an useful corrective. Both however were, like most controversialists, prejudiced men, loving the interests of their respective factions better than truth, and not very scrupulous about misrepresenting an adversary. But Neal had got rid of the intolerant spirit of the puritans, while Madox labors to justify every act of Whitgift and Parker.

2 Life of Whitgift, 328.

unjust to censure the archbishop for interfering to protect the discipline of his church against these innovators, had but the means adopted for that purpose been more consonant to equity. Cartwright with several of his sect were summoned before the ecclesiastical commission; where, refusing to inculpate themselves by taking the oath ex officio, they were committed to the Fleet. This punishment not satisfying the rigid churchmen, and the authority of the ecclesiastical commission being incompetent to inflict any heavier judgment, it was thought fit the next year to remove the proceedings into the court of star-chamber. The judges, on being consulted, gave it as their opinion, that, since far less crimes had been punished by condemnation to the galleys or perpetual banishment, the latter would be fittest for their offence. But several of the council had more tender regards to sincere though intractable men; and in the end they were admitted to bail upon a promise to be quiet, after answering some interrogatories respecting the queen's supremacy and other points, with civility and an evident wish to avoid offence.[1] It may be observed that Cartwright explicitly declared his disapprobation of the libels under the name of Martin Mar-prelate.[2] Every political party, however honorable may be its objects and character, is liable to be disgraced by the association of such unscrupulous zealots. But though it is an uncandid sophism to charge the leaders with the excesses they profess to disapprove in their followers, it must be confessed that few chiefs of faction have had the virtue to condemn with sufficient energy the misrepresentations which are intended for their benefit.

It was imputed to the puritan faction with more or less of truth, that, not content with the subversion of episcopacy and of the whole ecclesiastical polity established in the kingdom, they maintained principles that would essentially affect its civil institutions. Their denial, indeed, of the queen's supremacy, carried to such lengths as I have shown above, might justly be considered as a derogation of her temporal sovereignty. Many of them asserted the obligation of the judicial law of Moses, at least in criminal cases; and deduced from this the duty of putting idolaters (that is, papists), adulterers, witches, and demoniacs, sabbath-breakers, and several other

[1] Id. 336, 360, 366; Append. 142, 159.
[2] Id.; Append. 135; Annals, iv. 52.

classes of offenders, to death.[1] They claimed to their ecclesiastical assemblies the right of determining "all matters wherein breach of charity may be, and all matters of doctrine and manners, so far as appertaineth to conscience." They took away the temporal right of patronage to churches, leaving the choice of ministers to general suffrage.[2] There are even passages in Cartwright's Admonition which intimate that the commonwealth ought to be fashioned after the model of the church.[3] But these it would not be candid to press against the more explicit declarations of all the puritans in favor of a limited monarchy, though they grounded its legitimacy on the republican principles of popular consent.[4] And with respect to the former opinions, they appear to have been by no means common to the whole puritan body; some of the deprived and imprisoned ministers ever acknowledging the queen's supremacy in as full a manner as the law conferred it on her, and as she professed to claim it.[5]

The pretensions advanced by the school of Cartwright did not seem the less dangerous to those who cast their eyes upon what was passing in Scotland, where they received a practical illustration. In that kingdom a form of polity very nearly conforming to the puritanical platform had become established at the reformation in 1560; except that the office of bishop or superintendent still continued, but with no paramount, far less arbitrary dominion, and subject even to the

1 This predilection for the Mosaic polity was not uncommon among the reformers. Collier quotes passages from Martin Bucer as strong as could well be found in the puritan writings. P. 303.

2 Life of Whitgift, p. 61, 333, and Append. 138; Annals, iv. 140. As I have not seen the original works in which these tenets are said to be promulgated, I cannot vouch for the fairness of the representation made by hostile pens, though I conceive it to be not very far from the truth.

3 Ibid; Madox's Vindication of the Ch. of Eng. against Neal, p. 212; Strype's Annals, iv. 142.

4 The large views of civil government entertained by the puritans were sometimes imputed to them as a crime by their more courtly adversaries, who reproached them with the writings of Buchanan and Languet. Life of Whitgift, 258; Annals, iv. 142.

5 See a declaration to this effect, at which no one could cavil, in Strype's Annals, iv. 85. The puritans, or at least some of their friends, retaliated this charge of denying the queen's supremacy on their adversaries. Sir Francis Knollys strongly opposed the claims of episcopacy as a divine institution, which had been covertly insinuated by Bancroft, on the ground of its incompatibility with the prerogative, and urged lord Burleigh to make the bishops acknowledge they had no superiority over the clergy, except by statute, as the only means to save her majesty from the extreme danger into which she was brought by the machinations of the pope and king of Spain. Life of Whitgift, p. 350, 361, 389. He wrote afterwards to lord Burleigh in 1591, that, if he might not speak his mind freely against the power of the bishops, and prove it unlawful, by the laws of this realm, and not by the canon law, he hoped to be allowed to become a private man. This bold letter he desires to have shown to the queen. Catalogue of Lansdowne MSS., British Museum, lxviii. 84.

provincial synod, much more to the general assembly of the Scottish church. Even this very limited episcopacy was abolished in 1592. The presbyterian clergy, individually and collectively, displayed the intrepid, haughty, and untractable spirit of the English puritans. Though Elizabeth had from policy abetted the Scottish clergy in their attacks upon the civil administration, this connection itself had probably given her such an insight into their temper as well as their influence that she must have shuddered at the thought of seeing a republican assembly substituted for those faithful satraps her bishops, so ready to do her bidding, and so patient under the hard usage sometimes bestowed on them.

House of commons averse to episcopal authority.

These prelates did not, however, obtain so much support from the house of commons as from their sovereign. In that assembly a determined band of puritans frequently carried the victory against the courtiers. Every session exhibited proofs of their dissatisfaction with the state of the church. The crown's influence would have been too weak without stretches of its prerogative. The commons in 1575 received a message forbidding them to meddle with religious concerns. For five years afterwards the queen did not convoke parliament, of which her dislike to their puritanical temper might in all probability be the chief reason. But, when they met again in 1580, the same topic of ecclesiastical grievances, which had by no means abated during the interval, was revived. The commons appointed a committee, formed only of the principal officers of the crown who sat in the house, to confer with some of the bishops, according to the irregular and imperfect course of parliamentary proceedings in that age, "touching the griefs of this house for some things very requisite to be reformed in the church, as the great number of unlearned and unable ministers, the great abuse of excommunications for every matter of small moment, the commutation of penances, and the great multitude of dispensations and pluralities, and other things very hurtful to the church."[1] The committee reported that they found some of the bishops desirous of a remedy for the abuses they confessed, and of joining in a petition for that purpose to her majesty; which had accordingly been done, and a gracious answer, promising all conven-

[1] D'Ewes, 302; Strype's Whitgift, 92, Append. 32.

ient reformation, but laying the blame of remissness upon some prelates, had been received. This the house took with great thankfulness. It was exactly the course which pleased Elizabeth, who had no regard for her bishops, and a real anxiety that her ecclesiastical as well as temporal government should be well administered, provided her subjects would intrust the sole care of it to herself, or limit their interference to modest petitioning.

A new parliament having been assembled, soon after Whitgift on his elevation to the primacy had begun to enforce an universal conformity, the lower house drew up a petition in sixteen articles, to which they requested the lords' concurrence, complaining of the oath ex officio, the subscription to the three new articles, the abuses of excommunication, licenses for non-residence, and other ecclesiastical grievances. The lords replied coolly that they conceived many of those articles which the commons had proposed to be unnecessary, and that others of them were already provided for; and that the uniformity of the common prayer, the use of which the commons had requested to leave in certain respects to the minister's discretion, had been established by parliament. The two archbishops, Whitgift and Sandys, made a more particular answer to each article of the petition, in the name of their brethren.[1] But, in order to show some willingness towards reformation, they proposed themselves, in convocation, a few regulations for redress of abuses, none of which, however, on this occasion, though they received the royal assent, were submitted to the legislature;[2] the queen in fact maintaining an insuperable jealousy of all intermeddling on the part of parliament with her exclusive supremacy over the church. Excluded by Elizabeth's jealousy from entertaining these religious innovations, which would probably have met with no unfavorable reception from a free parliament, the commons vented their ill-will towards the dominant hierarchy in complaints of ecclesiastical grievances, and measures to redress them; as to which, even with the low notions of parliamentary right prevailing at court, it was impossible to deny their competence. Several bills were introduced this session of 1584–5 into the lower house, which, though they had little chance of receiving the queen's assent, manifest the sense of

[1] D'Ewes, 339, et post; Strype's Whitgift, 176, &c.; Append. 70.
[2] Strype's Annals, iii. 228.

that assembly, and in all likelihood of their constituents. One of these imported that bishops should be sworn in one of the courts of justice to do nothing in their office contrary to the common law. Another went to restrain pluralities, as to which the prelates would very reluctantly admit of any limitation.[1] A bill of the same nature passed the commons in 1589, though not without some opposition. The clergy took so great alarm at this measure that the convocation addressed the queen in vehement language against it; and the archbishop throwing all the weight of his advice and authority into the same scale, the bill expired in the upper house.[2] A similar proposition in the session of 1601 seems to have miscarried in the commons.[3] In the next chapter will be found other instances of the commons' reforming temper in ecclesiastical concerns, and the queen's determined assertion of her supremacy.

The oath ex officio, binding the taker to answer all questions that should be put to him, inasmuch as it contravened the generous maxim of English law, that no one is obliged to criminate himself, provoked very just animadversion. Morice, attorney of the court of wards, not only attacked its legality with arguments of no slight force, but introduced a bill to take it away. This was on the whole well received by the house; and sir Francis Knollys, the stanch enemy of episcopacy, though in high office, spoke in its favor. But the queen put a stop to the proceeding, and Morice lay some time in prison for his boldness. The civilians, of whom several sat in the lower house, defended a mode of procedure that had been borrowed from their own jurisprudence. This revived the ancient animosity between them and the common lawyers. The latter had always manifested a great jealousy of the spiritual jurisdiction, and had early learned to restrain its exorbitances by writs of prohibition from the temporal courts. Whitgift, as tenacious of power as the most ambitious of his predecessors, murmured like them at this subordination, for such it evidently was, to a lay tribunal.[4] But the judges,

1 Strype's Annals, iii. 186, 192. Compare Append. 35.

2 Strype's Whitgift, 279; Annals, i. 543.

3 Parl. Hist. 921.

4 Strype's Whitgift, 521, 537; App. 130. The archbishop could not disguise his dislike to the lawyers. "The temporal lawyer," he says in a letter to Cecil, "*whose learning is no learning anywhere but here at home*, being born to nothing, doth by his labor and travel in that barbarous knowledge purchase to himself and his heirs forever a thou-

who found as much gratification in exerting their power as the bishops, paid little regard to the remonstrances of the latter. We find the law reports of this and the succeeding reign full of cases of prohibitions. Nor did other abuses imputed to these obnoxious judicatures fail to provoke censure, such as the unreasonable fees of their officers, and the usage of granting licenses and commuting penances for money.[1] The ecclesiastical courts indeed have generally been reckoned more dilatory, vexatious, and expensive than those of the common law. But in the present age that part of their jurisdiction which, though coercive, is professedly spiritual, and wherein the greatest abuses have been alleged to exist, has gone very much into disuse. In matrimonial and testamentary causes their course of proceeding may not be open to any censure, so far as the essential administration of justice is concerned; though in the latter of these a most inconvenient division of jurisdictions, following not only the unequal boundaries of episcopal dioceses, but the various peculiars or exempt districts which the church of England has continued to retain, is productive of a good deal of trouble and needless expense. [1827.]

Independents liable to severe laws.

Notwithstanding the tendency towards puritanism which the house of commons generally displayed, the court succeeded in procuring an act which eventually pressed with very great severity upon that class. This passed in 1593, and enacted the penalty of imprisonment against any person above the age of sixteen who should forbear for the space of a month to repair to some church, until he should make such open submission and declaration of conformity as the act appoints. Those who refused to submit to these conditions were to abjure the realm, and if they should return without the queen's license to suffer death as felons.[2] As this, on the one hand, like so many former statutes, helped to crush the unfortunate adherents to the Romish faith, so too did it bear an obvious application to such protestant sectaries as had professedly

sand pounds per annum, and oftentimes much more, whereof there are at this day many examples." P. 215.

[1] Strype's Whitgift and D'Ewes, passim. In a convocation held during Grindal's sequestration (1580), proposals for reforming certain abuses in the spiritual courts were considered; but nothing was done in it. Strype's Grindal, p. 259, and Append. p. 97. And in 1594 a commission to inquire into abuses in the spiritual courts was issued; but whether this were intended bonâ fide or not, it produced no reformation. Strype's Whitgift, 419.

[2] 35 Eliz. c. 1; Parl. Hist 863.

separated from the Anglican church. But it is here worthy of remark, that the puritan ministers throughout this reign disclaimed the imputation of schism, and acknowledged the lawfulness of continuing in the established church, while they demanded a further reformation of her discipline.[1] The real separatists, who were also a numerous body, were denominated Brownists or Barrowists, from the names of their founders, afterwards lost in the more general appellation of Independents. These went far beyond the puritans in their aversion to the legal ministry, and were deemed in consequence still more proper subjects for persecution. Multitudes of them fled to Holland from the rigor of the bishops in enforcing this statute.[2] But two of this persuasion, Barrow and Greenwood, experienced a still severer fate. They were indicted on that perilous law of the 23d of the queen, mentioned in the last chapter, for spreading seditious writings, and executed at Bury. They died, Neal tells us, with such expressions of piety and loyalty that Elizabeth regretted the consent she had given to their deaths.[3]

But while these scenes of pride and persecution on one hand, and of sectarian insolence on the other, were deforming the bosom of the English church, she found a defender of her institutions in one who mingled in these vulgar controversies like a knight of romance among caitiff brawlers,

1 Neal asserts in his summary of the controversy, as it stood in this reign, that the puritans did not object to the office of bishop, provided he was only the head of the presbyters, and acted in conjunction with them. P. 398. But this was in effect to demand everything. For if the office could be so far lowered in eminence, there were many waiting to clip the temporal revenues and dignity in proportion.

In another passage Neal states clearly, if not quite fairly, the main points of difference between the church and nonconforming parties under Elizabeth. P. 147. He concludes with the following remark, which is very true. "Both parties agreed too well in asserting the necessity of an uniformity of public worship, and of calling in the sword of the magistrate for the support and defence of the several principles, which they made an ill use of in their turns, as they could grasp the power into their hands. The standard of uniformity, according to the bishops, was the queen's supremacy and the laws of the land; according to the puritans, the decrees of provincial and national synods, allowed and enforced by the civil magistrate; but neither party were for admitting that liberty of conscience and freedom of profession which is every man's right, as far as is consistent with the peace of the government he lives under."

2 Neal, 253. 386.

3 Strype's Whitgift, 414; Neal, 373. Several years before, in 1583, two men called anabaptists, Thacker and Copping, were hanged at the same place on the same statute for denying the queen's ecclesiastical supremacy; the proof of which was their dispersion of Brown's tracts, wherein that was only owned in civil cases. Strype's Annals, iii. 186. This was according to the invariable practice of Tudor times: an oppressive and sanguinary statute was first made; and next, as occasion might serve, a construction was put on it contrary to all common sense, in order to take away men's lives.

with arms of finer temper and worthy to be proved in a nobler field. Richard Hooker, master of the Temple, published the first four books of his Ecclesiastical Polity in 1594; the fifth, three years afterwards; and, dying in 1600, left behind three which did not see the light till 1647. This eminent work may justly be reckoned to mark an era in our literature; for if passages of much good sense and even of a vigorous eloquence are scattered in several earlier writers in prose, yet none of these, except perhaps Latimer and Ascham, and sir Philip Sidney in his Arcadia, can be said to have acquired enough reputation to be generally known even by name, much less are read in the present day; and it is, indeed, not a little remarkable that England until near the end of the sixteenth century had given few proofs in literature of that intellectual power which was about to develop itself with such unmatchable energy in Shakspeare and Bacon. We cannot, indeed, place Hooker (but whom dare we to place?) by the side of these master-spirits; yet he has abundant claims to be counted among the luminaries of English literature. He not only opened the mine, but explored the depths, of our native eloquence. So stately and graceful is the march of his periods, so various the fall of his musical cadences upon the ear, so rich in images, so condensed in sentences, so grave and noble his diction, so little is there of vulgarity in his racy idiom, of pedantry in his learned phrase, that I know not whether any later writer has more admirably displayed the capacities of our language, or produced passages more worthy of comparison with the splendid monuments of antiquity. If we compare the first book of the Ecclesiastical Polity with what bears, perhaps, most resemblance to it of anything extant, the treatise of Cicero de Legibus, it will appear somewhat, perhaps, inferior, through the imperfection of our language, which, with all its force and dignity, does not equal the Latin in either of these qualities, and certainly more tedious and diffuse in some of its reasonings, but by no means less high-toned in sentiment, or less bright in fancy, and far more comprehensive and profound in the foundations of its philosophy.

Hooker's Ecclesiastical Polity. Its character.

The advocates of a presbyterian church had always thought it sufficient to prove that it was conformable to the apostolical scheme as deduced merely from the scriptures.

A pious reverence for the sacred writings, which they made almost their exclusive study, had degenerated into very narrow views on the great themes of natural religion and the moral law, as deducible from reason and sentiment. These, as most of the various families of their descendants continue to do, they greatly slighted, or even treated as the mere chimeras of heathen philosophy. If they looked to the Mosaic law as the standard of criminal jurisprudence, if they sought precedents from Scripture for all matters of temporal policy, much more would they deem the practice of the Apostles an unerring and immutable rule for the discipline of the Christian church.[1] To encounter these adversaries, Hooker took a far more original course than the ordinary controvertists, who fought their battles with conflicting interpretations of Scriptural texts or passages from the fathers. He inquired into the nature and foundation of law itself, as the rule of operation to all created beings, yielding thereto obedience by unconscious necessity, or sensitive appetite, or reasonable choice; reviewing especially those laws that regulate human agency, as they arise out of moral relations, common to our species, or the institutions of political societies, or the intercommunity of independent nations; and having thoroughly established the fundamental distinction between laws natural and positive, eternal and temporary, immutable and variable, he came with all this strength of moral philosophy to discriminate by the same criterion the various rules and precepts contained in the Scriptures. It was a kind of maxim among the puritans that Scripture was so much the exclusive rule of human actions that whatever, in matters at least concerning religion, could not be found to have its authority, was unlawful. Hooker devoted the whole second book of his work to the refutation of this principle. He proceeded afterwards to attack its application more particularly to the episcopal scheme of church government, and to the various ceremonies or usages which those sectaries

1 "The discipline of Christ's church," said Cartwright, "that is necessary for all times, is delivered by Christ, and set down in the Holy Scriptures. Therefore the true and lawful discipline is to be fetched from thence, and from thence alone. And that which resteth upon any other foundation ought to be esteemed unlawful and counterfeit." Whitgift, in his answer to Cartwright's Admonition, rested the controversy in the main, as Hooker did, on the indifferency of church discipline and ceremony. It was not till afterwards that the defenders of the established order found out that one claim of divine right was best met by another.

treated as either absolutely superstitious, or at least as impositions without authority. It was maintained by this great writer, not only that ritual observances are variable according to the discretion of ecclesiastical rulers, but that no certain form of polity is set down in Scripture as generally indispensable for a Christian church. Far, however, from conceding to his antagonists the fact which they assumed, he contended for episcopacy as an apostolical institution, and always preferable, when circumstances would allow its preservation, to the more democratical model of the Calvinistic congregations. "If we did seek," he says, "to maintain that which most advantageth our own cause, the very best way for us and the strongest against them were to hold, even as they do, that in Scripture there must needs be found some particular form of church polity which God hath instituted, and which for that very cause belongeth to all churches at all times. But with any such partial eye to respect ourselves, and by cunning to make those things seem the truest which are the fittest to serve our purpose, is a thing which we neither like nor mean to follow."

The richness of Hooker's eloquence is chiefly displayed in his first book; beyond which, perhaps, few who want a taste for ecclesiastical reading are likely to proceed. The second and third, however, though less brilliant, are not inferior in force and comprehensiveness of reasoning. The eighth and last returns to the subject of civil government, and expands, with remarkable liberality, the principles he had laid down as to its nature in the first book. Those that intervene are mostly confined to a more minute discussion of the questions mooted between the church and puritans; and in these, as far as I have looked into them, though Hooker's argument is always vigorous and logical, and he seems to be exempt from that abusive insolence to which polemical writers were then even more prone than at present, yet he has not altogether the terseness or lucidity which long habits of literary warfare, and, perhaps, a natural turn of mind, have given to some expert dialecticians. In respect of language, the three posthumous books, partly from having never received the author's last touches, and partly, perhaps, from his weariness of the labor, are beyond comparison less elegantly written than the preceding.

The better parts of the Ecclesiastical Polity bear a resemblance to the philosophical writings of antiquity, in their defects as well as their excellences. Hooker is often too vague in the use of general terms, too inconsiderate in the admission of principles, too apt to acquiesce in the scholastic pseudo-philosophy, and, indeed, in all received tenets; he is comprehensive rather than sagacious, and more fitted to sift the truth from the stores of accumulated learning than to seize it by an original impulse of his own mind; somewhat also impeded, like many other great men of that and the succeeding century, by too much acquaintance with books, and too much deference for their authors. It may be justly objected to some passages that they elevate ecclesiastical authority, even in matters of belief, with an exaggeration not easily reconciled to the protestant right of private judgment, and even of dangerous consequence in those times; as when he inclines to give a decisive voice in theological controversies to general councils; not, indeed, on the principles of the church of Rome, but on such as must end in the same conclusion, the high probability that the aggregate judgment of many grave and learned men should be well founded.[1] Nor would it be difficult to point out several other subjects, such as religious toleration, as to which he did not emancipate himself from the trammels of prejudice. But, whatever may be the imperfections of his Ecclesiastical Polity, they are far more than compensated by its eloquence and its reasoning, and above all by that deep pervading sense of the relation between man and his Creator, as the groundwork of all eternal law, which rendered the first book of this work a rampart, on the one hand, against the puritan school who shunned the light of nature as a deceitful meteor; and, on

1 "If the natural strength of men's wit may by experience and study attain unto such ripeness in the knowledge of things human, that men in this respect may presume to build somewhat upon their judgment, what reason have we to think but that, even in matters divine, the like wits, furnished with necessary helps, exercised in Scripture with like diligence, and assisted with the grace of Almighty God, may grow unto so much perfection of knowledge, that men shall have just cause, when anything pertinent unto faith and religion is doubted of, the more willingly to incline their minds towards that which the sentence of so grave, wise, and learned in that faculty shall judge most sound? For the controversy is of the weight of such men's judgment," &c. But Hooker's mistake was to exaggerate the weight of such men's judgment, and not to allow enough for their passions and infirmities, the imperfection of their knowledge, their connivance with power, their attachment to names and persons, and all the other drawbacks to ecclesiastical authority.

It is well known that the preface to the Ecclesiastical Polity was one of the two books to which James II. ascribed his return into the fold of Rome; and it is not difficult to perceive by what course of reasoning on the positions it contains this was effected.

the other, against that immoral philosophy which, displayed in the dark precepts of Machiavel, or lurking in the desultory sallies of Montaigne, and not always rejected by writers of more apparent seriousness, threatened to destroy the sense of intrinsic distinctions in the quality of actions, and to convert the maxims of state-craft and dissembling policy into the rule of life and manners.

Nothing, perhaps, is more striking to a reader of the Ecclesiastical Polity than the constant and even excessive predilection of Hooker for those liberal principles of civil government which are sometimes so just and always so attractive. Upon these subjects his theory absolutely coincides with that of Locke. The origin of government, both in right and in fact, he explicitly derives from a primary contract; "without which consent there were no reason that one should take upon him to be lord or judge over another; because, although there be, according to the opinion of some very great and judicious men, a kind of natural right in the noble, wise, and virtuous, to govern them which are of servile disposition, nevertheless, for manifestation of this their right, and men's more peaceable contentment on both sides, the assent of them who are to be governed seemeth necessary." "The lawful power," he observes elsewhere, "of making laws to command whole politic societies of men, belongeth so properly unto the same entire societies, that for any prince or potentate of what kind soever upon earth to exercise the same of himself, and not either by express commission immediately and personally received from God, or else by authority received at first from their consent upon whose persons they impose laws, it is no better than mere tyranny. Laws they are not, therefore, which public approbation hath not made so. But approbation not only they give, who personally declare their assent by voice, sign, or act; but also when others do it in their names, by right originally, at the least, derived from them. As in parliaments, councils, and the like assemblies, although we be not personally ourselves present, notwithstanding our assent is by reason of other agents there in our behalf. And what we do by others, no reason but that it should stand as our deed, no less effectually to bind us than if ourselves had done it in person." And in another place still more peremptorily: "Of this thing no man doubteth, namely, that in all societies, companies, and corporations, what severally each shall be bound unto, it must be with all their assents ratified. Against all equity it were that a man should suffer detriment at the hands of men for not observing that which he never did either by himself or others mediately or immediately agree unto."

These notions respecting the basis of political society, so far unlike what prevailed among the next generation of churchmen, are chiefly developed and dwelt upon in Hooker's concluding book, the eighth; and gave rise to a rumor, very sedulously propagated soon after the time of its publication, and still sometimes repeated, that the posthumous portion of his work had been interpolated or altered by the puritans.[1] For this surmise, however, I am persuaded that there is no foundation. The three latter books are doubtless imperfect, and it is possible that verbal changes may have been made by their transcribers or editors; but the testimony that has been brought forward to throw a doubt over their authenticity consists in those vague and self-contradictory stories which gossiping compilers of literary anecdote can easily accumulate; while the intrinsic evidence arising from the work itself, on which in this branch of criticism I am apt chiefly to rely, seems altogether to repel every suspicion. For not only the principles of civil government, presented in a more expanded form by Hooker in the eighth book, are precisely what he laid down in the first; but there is a peculiar chain

1 In the Life of Hooker, prefixed to the edition I use, fol. 1671, I find an assertion of Dr. Barnard, chaplain to Usher, that he had seen a manuscript of the last books of Hooker, containing many things omitted in the printed volume. One passage is quoted, and seems in Hooker's style. But the question is rather with respect to interpolations than omissions. And of the former I see no evidence or likelihood. If it be true, as is alleged, that different manuscripts of the three last books did not agree, if even these disagreements were the result of fraud, why should we conclude that they were corrupted by the puritans rather than the church? In Zouch's edition of Walton's Life of Hooker the reader will find a long and ill-digested note on this subject, the result of which has been to convince me that there is no reason to believe any other than verbal changes to have been made in the loose draught which the author left, but that, whatever changes were made, it does not appear that the manuscript was ever in the hands of the puritans. The strongest probability, however, of their authenticity is from internal evidence. [But it has been proved by Mr. Keble, the last editor of the Ecclesiastical Polity, that the sixth book, as we now possess it, though written by Hooker, did not belong to this work, and consequently that the real sixth book has been lost. — 1841.]

A late writer has produced a somewhat ridiculous proof of the carelessness with which all editions of the Ecclesiastical Polity have been printed — a sentence having slipped into the text of the seventh book, which makes nonsense, and which he very probably conjectures to have been a marginal memorandum of the author for his own use on revising the manuscript. M'Crie's Life of Melvil, vol. i. p. 471. [But it seems on the whole a more plausible conjecture that the memorandum was by one of those who, after Hooker's death, had the manuscript to revise.— 1841.]

of consecutive reasoning running through it, wherein it would be difficult to point out any passages that could be rejected without dismembering the context. It was his business in this part of the Ecclesiastical Polity to vindicate the queen's supremacy over the church; and this he has done by identifying the church with the commonwealth; no one, according to him, being a member of the one who was not also a member of the other. But as the constitution of the Christian church, so far as the laity partook in its government, by choice of pastors or otherwise, was undeniably democratical, he labored to show, through the medium of the original compact of civil society, that the sovereign had received this, as well as all other powers, at the hands of the people. "Laws being made among us," he affirms, "are not by any of us so taken or interpreted as if they did receive their force from power which the prince doth communicate unto the parliament, or unto any other court under him, but from power which the whole body of the realm being naturally possessed with hath by free and deliberate assent derived unto him that ruleth over them so far forth as hath been declared; so that our laws made concerning religion do take originally their essence from the power of the whole realm and church of England."

In this system of Hooker and Locke, for it will be obvious to the reader that their principles were the same, there is much, if I am not mistaken, to disapprove. That no man can be justly bound by laws which his own assent has not ratified appears to me a position incompatible with the existence of society in its literal sense, or illusory in the sophistical interpretations by which it is usual to evade its meaning. It will be more satisfactory and important to remark the views which this great writer entertained of our own constitution, to which he frequently and fearlessly appeals, as the standing illustration of a government restrained by law. "I cannot choose," he says, "but commend highly their wisdom, by whom the foundation of the commonwealth hath been laid; wherein, though no manner of person or cause be unsubject unto the king's power, yet so is the power of the king over all, and in all, limited, that unto all his proceedings the law itself is a rule. The axioms of our regal government are these: 'Lex facit regem'— the king's grant of any favor made contrary to the law is void;—'Rex nihil potest nisi quod jure potest' — what power the king hath he hath it by law; the bounds and limits of it are known, the entire community giveth general order by law how all things publicly are to be done; and the king as the head thereof, the highest in authority over all, causeth, according to the same law, every particular to be framed and ordered thereby. The whole body politic maketh laws, which laws give power unto the king; and the king having bound himself to use according to law that power, it so falleth out that the execution of the one is accomplished by the other." These doctrines of limited monarchy recur perpetually in the eighth book; and though Hooker, as may be supposed, does not enter upon the perilous question of resistance and even intimates that he does not see how the people can limit the extent of power once granted, unless where it escheats to them, yet he positively lays it down that usurpers of power, that is, lawful rulers arrogating more than the law gives to them, cannot in conscience bind any man to obedience.

It would, perhaps, have been a deviation from my subject to enlarge so much on these political principles in a writer of any later age, when they had been openly sustained in the councils of the nation. But as the reigns of the Tudor family were so inauspicious to liberty that some have been apt to imagine its recollection to have been almost effaced, it becomes of more importance to show that absolute monarchy was, in the eyes of so eminent an author as Hooker, both pernicious in itself and contrary to the fundamental laws of the English commonwealth. Nor would such sentiments, we may surely presume, have been avowed by a man of singular humility, and whom we might charge with somewhat of an excessive deference to authority, unless they had obtained more currency, both among divines and lawyers, than the complaisance of courtiers in these two professions might lead us to conclude; Hooker being not prone to deal in paradoxes, nor to borrow from his adversaries that sturdy republicanism of the school of Geneva which had been their scandal. I cannot, indeed, but suspect that his whig principles in the last book are announced with a temerity that would have startled his superiors; and that its authenticity, however called in question, has been better preserved by the circumstance of a posthumous publication than if he had lived to give it to the world. Whitgift would probably have induced him to suppress a few passages incompatible with the servile theories already in vogue. It is far more usual that an author's genuine sentiments are perverted by means of his friends and patrons than of his adversaries.

The prelates of the English church, while they inflicted so many severities on others, had not always cause to exult in their own condition. From the time when Henry taught his courtiers to revel in the spoil of monasteries there had been a perpetual appetite for ecclesiastical possessions. Endowed by a prodigal superstition with pomp and wealth beyond all reasonable measure, and far beyond what the new system of religion appeared to prescribe, the church of England still excited the covetousness of the powerful and the scandal of the austere.[1] I have mentioned in another place how the bishoprics were impoverished in the first reformation under Edward VI. The catholic bishops who followed made haste to plunder, from a consciousness that the goods of their church were speedily to pass into the hands of heretics.[2] Hence the alienation of their estates had gone so far that in the beginning of Elizabeth's reign statutes were made disabling ecclesiastical proprietors from granting away their lands except on leases for three lives, or twenty-one years.[3] But an unfortunate reservation was introduced in favor of the crown. The queen, therefore, and her courtiers, who obtained grants from her, continued to prey upon their succulent victim. Few of her council imitated the noble disinterestedness of Walsingham, who spent his own estate in her service, and left not sufficient to pay his debts. The documents of that age contain ample proofs of their rapacity. Thus Cecil surrounded his mansion-house at Burleigh with estates once belonging to the see of Peterborough. Thus Hatton built his house in Holborn, on the bishop of Ely's garden. Cox, on making resistance to this spoliation, received a singular

Spoliation of church revenues.

1 The puritans objected to the title of lord bishop. Sampson wrote a peevish letter to Grindal on this, and received a very good answer. Strype's Parker, Append. 178. Parker, in a letter to Cecil, defends it on the best ground; that the bishops hold their lands by barony, and therefore the giving them the title of lords was no irregularity, and nothing more than a consequence of the tenure. Collier, 544. This will not cover our modern *colonial* bishops, on some of whom the same title has, without any good reason, been conferred.

2 Strype's Annals, i. 159.

3 1 Eliz. c. 19; 13 Eliz. c. 10; Blackstone's Commentaries, vol. ii. c. 28. The exception in favor of the crown was repealed in the first year of James.

epistle from the queen.[1] This bishop, in consequence of such vexations, was desirous of retiring from the see before his death. After that event Elizabeth kept it vacant eighteen years. During this period we have a petition to her from lord keeper Puckering that she would confer it on Scambler, bishop of Norwich, then eighty-eight years old, and notorious for simony, in order that he might give him a lease of part of the lands.[2] These transactions denote the mercenary and rapacious spirit which leavened almost all Elizabeth's courtiers.

The bishops of this reign do not appear, with some distinguished exceptions, to have reflected so much honor on the established church as those who attach a superstitious reverence to the age of the Reformation are apt to conceive. In the plunder that went forward they took good care of themselves. Charges against them of simony, corruption, covetousness, and especially destruction of their church estates for the benefit of their families, are very common, — sometimes no doubt unjust, but too frequent to be absolutely without foundation.[3] The council often wrote to them, as well as concerning them, with a sort of asperity which would astonish one of their successors. And the queen never restrained herself in treating them on any provocation with a good deal of rudeness, of which I have just mentioned an egregious example.[4] In her speech to parliament on closing the ses-

[1] It was couched in the following terms:—

"Proud Prelate,

"You know what you were before I made you what you are: if you do not immediately comply with my request by G— I will unfrock you.

"ELIZABETH."

Poor Cox wrote a very good letter before this, printed in Strype's Annals, vol. ii. Append. 84. The names of Hatton Garden and Ely Place (Mantua væ miseræ nimium vicina Cremonæ) still bear witness to the encroaching lord keeper and the elbowed bishop.

[2] Strype, iv. 246. See also p. 15 of the same volume. By an act in the first year of James, c. 3, conveyances of bishops' lands to the crown are made void — a concession much to the king's honor.

[3] Harrington's State of the Church, in Nugæ Antiquæ, vol. ii. passim; Wilkins's Concilia, iv. 256; Strype's Annals, iii. 620, et alibi; Life of Parker, 454; of Whitgift, 220; of Aylmer, passim. Observe the preamble of 13 Eliz. c. 10. It must be admitted, on the other hand, that the gentry, when popishly or puritanically affected, were apt to behave exceedingly ill towards the bishops. At Lambeth and Fulham they were pretty safe; but at a distance they found it hard to struggle with the rudeness and iniquity of the territorial aristocracy; as Sandys twice experienced.

[4] Birch's Memoirs, i. 48. Elizabeth seems to have fancied herself entitled by her supremacy to dispose of bishops as she pleased, though they did not hold commissions durante bene placito, as in her brother's time. Thus she suspended Fletcher, bishop of London, of her own authority, only for marrying "a fine lady and a widow." Strype's Whitgift, 458. And Aylmer having preached too vehemently against female vanity in dress, which came home to the queen's conscience, she told her ladies that, if the bishop held more discourse on such matters, she would fit him for heaven; but

sion of 1584, when many complaints against the rulers of the church had rung in her ears, she told the bishops that, if they did not amend what was wrong, she meant to depose them.[1] For there seems to have been no question in that age but that this might be done by virtue of the crown's supremacy.

The church of England was not left by Elizabeth in circumstances that demanded applause for the policy of her rulers. After forty years of constantly aggravated molestation of the nonconforming clergy, their numbers were become greater, their popularity more deeply rooted, their enmity to the established order more irreconcilable. It was doubtless a problem of no slight difficulty by what means so obstinate and opinionated a class of sectaries could have been managed; nor are we, perhaps, at this distance of time altogether competent to decide upon the fittest course of policy in that respect.[2] But it is manifest that the obstinacy of bold and sincere men is not to be quelled by any punishments that do not exterminate them, and that they were not likely to entertain a less conceit of their own reason when they found no arguments so much relied on to refute it as that of force. Statesmen invariably take a better view of such questions than churchmen; and we may well believe that Cecil and Walsingham judged more sagaciously than Whitgift and Aylmer. The best apology that can be made for Elizabeth's tenaciousness of those ceremonies which produced this fatal contention I have already suggested, without much express authority from the records of that age; namely, the justice and expediency of winning over the catholics to conformity, by retaining as much as possible of their accustomed rites. But in the latter period of the queen's reign this policy had lost a great deal of its application, or rather the same principle of policy would have dictated numerous concessions in order to satisfy the people. It appears by no means unlikely

he should walk thither without a staff, and leave his mantle behind him. Harrington's State of the Church, in Nugæ Antiquæ, i. 170; see too p. 217. It will of course not appear surprising that Hutton, archbishop of York, an exceedingly honest prelate, having preached a bold sermon before the queen, urging her to settle the succession, and pointing strongly towards Scotland, received a sharp message. p. 250.

[1] D'Ewes, 328.

[2] Collier says, p. 586, on Heylin's authority, that Walsingham offered the puritans, about 1583, in the queen's name, to give up the ceremony of kneeling at the communion, the cross in baptism, and the surplice; but that they answered, "ne ungulam quidem esse relinquendam." But I am not aware of any better testimony to the fact; and it is by no means agreeable to the queen's general conduct.

that, by reforming the abuses and corruption of the spiritual courts, by abandoning a part of their jurisdiction, so heterogeneous and so unduly obtained, by abrogating obnoxious and at best frivolous ceremonies, by restraining pluralities of benefices, by ceasing to discountenance the most diligent ministers, and by more temper and disinterestedness in their own behavior, the bishops would have palliated, to an indefinite degree, that dissatisfaction with the established scheme of polity, which its want of resemblance to that of other protestant churches must more or less have produced. Such a reformation would at least have contented those reasonable and moderate persons who occupy sometimes a more extensive ground between contending factions than the zealots of either are willing to believe or acknowledge.

General remarks.

I am very sensible that such freedom as I have used in this chapter cannot be pleasing to such as have sworn allegiance to either the Anglican or the puritan party; and that even candid and liberal minds may be inclined to suspect that I have not sufficiently admitted the excesses of one side to furnish an excuse for those of the other. Such readers I would gladly refer to lord Bacon's Advertisement touching the Controversies of the Church of England; a treatise written under Elizabeth, in that tone of dispassionate philosophy which the precepts of Burleigh sown in his own deep and fertile mind had taught him to apply. This treatise, to which I did not turn my attention in writing the present chapter, appears to coincide in every respect with the views it displays. If he censures the pride and obstinacy of the puritan teachers, their indecent and libellous style of writing, their affected imitation of foreign churches, their extravagance of receding from everything formerly practised, he animadverts with no less plainness on the faults of the episcopal party, on the bad example of some prelates, on their peevish opposition to every improvement, their unjust accusations, their contempt of foreign churches, their persecuting spirit.[1]

[1] Bacon, ii. 375. See also another paper concerning the pacification of the church, written under James, p. 387. "The wrongs," he says, "of those which are possessed of the government of the church towards the other, may hardly be dissembled or excused." p. 382. Yet Bacon was never charged with affection for the puritans. In truth, Elizabeth and James were personally the great support of the high-church interest; it had few real friends among their councillors.

Letter of Walsingham in defence of the queen's government.

Yet, that we may not deprive this great queen's administration, in what concerned her dealings with the two religious parties opposed to the established church, of what vindication may best be offered for it, I will refer the reader to a letter of sir Francis Walsingham, written to a person in France, after the year 1580.[1] It is a very able apology for her government; and if the reader should detect, as he doubtless may, somewhat of sophistry in reasoning, and of misstatement in matter of fact, he will ascribe both one and the other to the narrow spirit of the age with respect to civil and religious freedom, or to the circumstances of the writer, an advocate whose sovereign was his client.

[1] Burnet, ii. 418; Cabala, part ii. 38 (4to edition). Walsingham grounds the queen's proceedings upon two principles: the one, that "consciences are not to be forced, but to be won and reduced by force of truth, with the aid of time, and use of all good means of instruction and persuasion;" the other, that "cases of conscience, when they exceed their bounds, and grow to be matter of faction, lose their nature; and that sovereign princes ought distinctly to punish their practices and contempt, though colored with the pretence of conscience and religion." Bacon has repeated the same words, as well as some more of Walsingham's letter, in his observations on the libel on Lord Burleigh, i. 522. And Mr. Southey (Book of the Church, ii. 291) seems to adopt them as his own.

Upon this it may be observed — first, that they take for granted the fundamental sophism of religious intolerance, namely, that the civil magistrate, or the church he supports, is not only in the right, but so clearly in the right, that no honest man, if he takes time and pains to consider the subject, can help acknowledging it; secondly, that, according to the principles of Christianity as admitted on each side, it does not rest in an esoteric persuasion, but requires an exterior profession, evinced both by social worship and by certain positive rites; and that the marks of this profession, according to the form best adapted to their respective ways of thinking, were as incumbent upon the catholic and puritan as they had been upon the primitive church; nor were they more chargeable with faction, or with exceeding the bounds of conscience, when they persisted in the use of them, notwithstanding any prohibitory statute, than the early Christians.

The generality of statesmen, and churchmen themselves not unfrequently, have argued upon the principles of what, in the seventeenth century, was called Hobbism, towards which the Erastian system, which is that of the church of England, though excellent in some points of view, had a tendency to gravitate, namely, that civil and religious allegiance are so necessarily connected, that it is the subject's duty to follow the dictates of the magistrate in both alike. And this received some countenance from the false and mischievous position of Hooker, that the church and commonwealth are but different denominations of the same society. Warburton has sufficiently exposed the sophistry of this theory, though I do not think him equally successful in what he substitutes for it.

CHAPTER V.

ON THE CIVIL GOVERNMENT OF ELIZABETH.

General Remarks — Defective Security of the Subject's Liberty — Trials for Treason and other Political Offences unjustly conducted — Illegal Commitments — Remonstrance of Judges against them — Proclamations unwarranted by Law — Restrictions on Printing — Martial Law — Loans of Money not quite voluntary — Character of Lord Burleigh's Administration — Disposition of the House of Commons — Addresses concerning the Succession — Difference on this between the Queen and Commons in 1566 — Session of 1571 — Influence of the Puritans in Parliament — Speech of Mr. Wentworth in 1576 — The Commons continue to seek Redress of Ecclesiastical Grievances — Also of Monopolies, especially in the Session of 1601 — Influence of the Crown in Parliament — Debate on Election of non-resident Burgesses — Assertion of Privileges by Commons — Case of Ferrers, under Henry VIII. — Other Cases of Privilege — Privilege of determining contested Elections claimed by the House — The English Constitution not admitted to be an absolute Monarchy — Pretensions of the Crown.

General remarks.

THE subject of the two last chapters, I mean the policy adopted by Elizabeth for restricting the two religious parties which from opposite quarters resisted the exercise of her ecclesiastical prerogatives, has already afforded us many illustrations of what may more strictly be reckoned the constitutional history of her reign. The tone and temper of her administration have been displayed in a vigilant execution of severe statutes, especially towards the catholics, and sometimes in stretches of power beyond the law. And as Elizabeth had no domestic enemies or refractory subjects who did not range under one or other of these two sects, and little disagreement with her people on any other grounds, the ecclesiastical history of this period is the best preparation for our inquiry into the civil government. In the present chapter I shall first offer a short view of the practical exercise of government in this reign, and then proceed to show how the queen's high assumptions of prerogative were encountered by a resistance in parliament, not quite uniform, but insensibly becoming more vigorous.

Elizabeth ascended the throne with all the advantages of a very extended authority. Though the jurisdiction actually exerted by the court of star-chamber could not be vindicated according to statute law, it had been so well established as to pass without many audible murmurs. Her progenitors had intimidated the nobility; and if she had something to fear at one season from this order, the fate of the duke of Norfolk and of the rebellious earls in the north put an end forever to all apprehension from the feudal influence of the aristocracy. There seems no reason to believe that she attempted a more absolute power than her predecessors; the wisdom of her councillors, on the contrary, led them generally to shun the more violent measures of the late reigns; but she certainly acted upon many of the precedents they had bequeathed her, with little consideration of their legality. Her own remarkable talents, her masculine intrepidity, her readiness of wit and royal deportment, which the bravest men unaffectedly dreaded, her temper of mind, above all, at once fiery and inscrutably dissembling, would in any circumstances have insured her more real sovereignty than weak monarchs, however nominally absolute, can ever enjoy or retain. To these personal qualities was added the cöperation of some of the most diligent and circumspect, as well as the most sagacious councillors that any prince has employed; men as unlikely to loose from their grasp the least portion of that authority which they found themselves to possess, as to excite popular odium by an unusual or misplaced exertion of it. The most eminent instances, as I have remarked, of a high-strained prerogative in her reign have some relation to ecclesiastical concerns; and herein the temper of the predominant religion was such as to account no measures harsh or arbitrary that were adopted towards its conquered but still formidable enemy. Yet when the royal supremacy was to be maintained against a different foe by less violent acts of power, it revived the smouldering embers of English liberty. The stern and exasperated puritans became the depositaries of that sacred fire; and this manifests a second connection between the temporal and ecclesiastical history of the present reign.

Civil liberty in this kingdom has two direct guarantees; the open administration of justice according to known laws truly interpreted, and fair constructions of evidence; and the right of parliament, without let or interruption, to inquire into and obtain the redress of public grievances. Of these the first is by far the most indispensable; nor can the subjects of any state be reckoned to enjoy a real freedom where this condition is not found both in its judicial institutions and in their constant exercise. In this, much more than in positive law, our ancient constitution, both under the Plantagenet and Tudor line, had ever been failing; and it is because one set of writers have looked merely to the letter of our statutes or other authorities, while another have been almost exclusively struck by the instances of arbitrary government they found on record, that such incompatible systems have been laid down with equal positiveness on the character of that constitution.

Trials for treason and other political offences unjustly conducted.

I have found it impossible not to anticipate, in more places than one, some of those glaring transgressions of natural as well as positive law that rendered our courts of justice in cases of treason little better than the caverns of murderers. Whoever was arraigned at their bar was almost certain to meet a virulent prosecutor, a judge hardly distinguishable from the prosecutor except by his ermine, and a passive pusillanimous jury. Those who are acquainted only with our modern decent and dignified procedure can form little conception of the irregularity of ancient trials; the perpetual interrogation of the prisoner, which gives most of us so much offence at this day in the tribunals of a neighboring kingdom; and the want of all evidence except written, perhaps unattested, examinations or confessions. Habington, one of the conspirators against Elizabeth's life in 1586, complained that two witnesses had not been brought against him, conformably to the statute of Edward VI. But Anderson the chief justice told him that, as he was indicted on the act of Edward III., that provision was not in force.[1] In the case of captain Lee, a partisan of Essex and Southampton, the court appear to have denied the right of peremptory challenge.[2] Nor was more equal measure dealt to the noblest prisoners by their equals. The earl of Arundel was convicted of imagining the queen's death, on evidence which at the utmost would only have supported an indictment for reconciliation to the church of Rome.[3]

The integrity of judges is put to the proof as much by

[1] State Trials, i. 1148. [2] Id. i. 1256. [3] Id., i. 1403.

prosecutions for seditious writings as by charges of treason. I have before mentioned the convictions of Udal and Penry for a felony created by the 23d of Elizabeth; the former of which especially must strike every reader of the trial as one of the gross judicial iniquities of this reign. But, before this sanguinary statute was enacted, a punishment of uncommon severity had been inflicted upon one Stubbe, a puritan lawyer, for a pamphlet against the queen's intended marriage with the duke of Anjou. It will be in the recollection of most of my readers that, in the year 1579, Elizabeth exposed herself to much censure and ridicule, and inspired the justest alarm in her most faithful subjects, by entertaining, at the age of forty-six, the proposals of this young scion of the house of Valois. Her council, though several of them in their deliberations had much inclined against the preposterous alliance, yet in the end, displaying the compliance usual with the servants of self-willed princes, agreed, "conceiving," as they say, "her earnest disposition for this her marriage," to further it with all their power. Sir Philip Sidney, with more real loyalty, wrote her a spirited remonstrance, which she had the magnanimity never to resent.[1] But she poured her indignation on Stubbe, who, not entitled to use a private address, had ventured to arouse a popular cry in his 'Gaping Gulph, in which England will be swallowed up by the French Marriage.' This pamphlet is very far from being, what some have ignorantly or unjustly called it, a virulent libel, but is written in a sensible manner, and

[1] Murden, 337. Dr. Lingard has fully established, what indeed no one could reasonably have disputed, Elizabeth's passion for Anjou; and says very truly, "the writers who set all this down to policy cannot have consulted the original documents." p. 149. It was altogether repugnant to sound policy. Persons, the jesuit, indeed says in his famous libel, Leicester's Commonwealth, written not long after this time, that it would have been "honorable, convenient, profitable, and needful;" which every honest Englishman would interpret by the rule of contraries. Sussex wrote indeed to the queen in favor of the marriage (Lodge, ii. 177); and Cecil undoubtedly professed to favor it; but this must have been out of obsequiousness to the queen. It was a habit of this minister to set down briefly the arguments on both sides of a question, sometimes in parallel columns, sometimes successively; a method which would seem too formal in our age, but tending to give himself and others a clearer view of the case. He has done this twice in the present instance — Murden, 322, 331; and it is evident that he does not, and cannot, answer his own objections to the match. When the council waited on her with this resolution in favor of the marriage, she spoke sharply to those whom she believed to be against it. Yet the treaty went on for two years: her coquetry in this strange delay breeding her, as Walsingham wrote from Paris, "greater dishonor than I dare commit to paper." Strype's Annals, iii. 2. That she ultimately broke it off must be ascribed to the suspiciousness and irresolution of her character, which, acting for once conjointly with her good understanding, overcame a disgraceful inclination.

with unfeigned loyalty and affection towards the queen. But, besides the main offence of addressing the people on state affairs, he had, in the simplicity of his heart, thrown out many allusions proper to hurt her pride, such as dwelling too long on the influence her husband would acquire over her, and imploring that she would ask her physicians whether to bear children at her years would not be highly dangerous to her life. Stubbe, for writing this pamphlet, received sentence to have his right hand cut off. When the penalty was inflicted, taking off his hat with his left, he exclaimed, "Long live queen Elizabeth!" Burleigh, who knew that his fidelity had borne so rude a test, employed him afterwards in answering some of the popish libellers.[1]

There is no room for wonder at any verdict that could be returned by a jury, when we consider what means the government possessed of securing it. The sheriff returned a panel, either according to express directions, of which we have proofs, or to what he judged himself of the crown's intention and interest.[2] If a verdict had gone against the prosecution in a matter of moment, the jurors must have laid their account with appearing before the star-chamber; lucky if they should escape, on humble retractation, with sharp words, instead of enormons fines and indefinite imprisonment. The control of this arbitrary tribunal bound down and rendered impotent all the minor jurisdictions. That primæval institution, those inquests by twelve true men, the unadulterated voice of the people, responsible alone to God and their conscience, which should have been heard in the sanctuaries of justice, as fountains springing fresh from the lap of earth, became, like waters constrained in their course by art, stagnant and impure. Until this weight that hung upon the constitution should be taken off, there was literally no prospect of enjoying with security those civil privileges which it held forth.[3]

1 Strype, iii. 480. Stubbe always signed himself Scæva in these left-handed productions.

2 Lodge, ii. 412; iii. 49.

3 Several volumes of the Harleian MSS. illustrate the course of government under Elizabeth. The copious analysis in the catalogue, by Humphrey Wanley and others, which I have in general found accurate, will, for most purposes, be sufficient. See particularly vol. 703. A letter, inter alia, in this (folio 1), from Lord. Hunsdon and Walsingham to the sheriff of Sussex, directs him not to assist the creditors of John Ashburnham in molesting him "till such time as our determination touching the premises shall be known," Ashburnham being to attend the council to prefer his complaint. See also vols. 6995, 6996, 6997, and many others. The Lansdowne catalogue will furnish other evidences.

It cannot be too frequently repeated that no power of arbitrary detention has ever been known to our constitution since the charter obtained at Runnymede. The writ of habeas corpus has always been a matter of right. But, as may naturally be imagined, no right of the subject, in his relation to the crown, was preserved with greater difficulty. Not only the privy council in general arrogated to itself a power of discretionary imprisonment, into which no inferior court was to inquire, but commitments by a single councillor appear to have been frequent. These abuses gave rise to a remarkable complaint of the judges, which, though an authentic recognition of the privilege of personal freedom against such irregular and oppressive acts of individual ministers, must be admitted to leave by far too great latitude to the executive government, and to surrender, at least by implication from rather obscure language, a great part of the liberties which many statutes had confirmed.[1] This is contained in a passage from Chief Justice Anderson's Reports. But as there is an original manuscript in the British Museum, differing in some material points from the print, I shall follow it in preference.[2]

Illegal commitments.

"To the Rt: hon: our very good lords Sir Chr. Hatton, of the honourable order of the garter knight, and chancellor of England, and Sir W. Cecill of the hon: order of the garter knight, Lord Burleigh, lord high treasurer of England,— We her majesty's justices, of both benches, and barons of the exchequer, do desire your lordships that by your good means such order may be taken that her highness's subjects may not be committed or detained in prison, by commandment of any nobleman or councillor, against the laws of the realm, to the grievous charges and oppression of her majesty's said subjects: Or else help us to have access to her majesty, to be suitors unto her highness for the same; for divers have been imprisoned for suing ordinary actions, and suits at the common law, until they will leave the same, or against their wills put their matter to order, although some time it be after judgment and accusation.

Remonstrances of judges against them.

1 Anderson's Reports, i. 297. It may be found also in the Biographia Britannica, and the Biographical Dictionary, art. ANDERSON.

2 Lansdowne MSS. lviii. 87. The Harleian MS. 6846 is a mere transcript from Anderson's Reports, and consequently of no value. There is another in the same collection, at which I have not looked.

"Item: Others have been committed and detained in prison upon such commandment against the law; and upon the queen's writ in that behalf, no cause sufficient hath been certified or returned.

"Item: Some of the parties so committed and detained in prison after they have, by the queen's writ, been lawfully discharged in court, have been eftsoones recommitted to prison in secret places, and not in common and ordinary known prisons, as the Marshalsea, Fleet, King's Bench, Gatehouse, nor the custodie of any sheriff, so as, upon complaint made for their delivery, the queen's court cannot learn to whom to award her majesty's writ, without which justice cannot be done.

"Item: Divers serjeants of London and officers have been many times committed to prison for lawful execution of her majesty's writs out of the King's Bench, Common Pleas, and other courts, to their great charges and oppression, whereby they are put in such fear as they dare not execute the queen's process.

"Item: Divers have been sent for by pursuivants for private causes, some of them dwelling far distant from London, and compelled to pay to the pursuivants great sums of money against the law, and have been committed to prison till they would release the lawful benefit of their suits, judgments, or executions for remedie, in which behalf we are almost daily called upon to minister justice according to law, whereunto we are bound by our office and oath.

"And whereas it pleased your lordships to will divers of us to set down when a prisoner sent to custody by her majesty, her council, or some one or two of them, is to be detained in prison, and not to be delivered by her majesty's courts or judges:

"We think that, if any person shall be committed by her majesty's special commandment, or by order from the council-board, or for treason touching her majesty's person [a word of five letters follows, illegible to me], which causes being generally returned into any court, is good cause for the same court to leave the person committed in custody.

"But if any person shall be committed for any other cause, then the same ought specially to be returned."

This paper bears the original signatures of eleven judges. It has no date, but is indorsed 5 June, 1591. In the printed report it is said to have been delivered in Easter term 34 Eliz., that is, in 1592. The chancellor Hatton, whose name is mentioned, died in November, 1591; so that, if there is no mistake, this must have been delivered a second time, after undergoing the revision of the judges. And in fact the differences are far too material to have proceeded from accidental carelessness in transcription. The latter copy is fuller, and on the whole more perspicuous, than the manuscript I have followed; but in one or two places it will be better understood by comparison with it.

Proclamations unwarranted by law.

It was a natural consequence, not more of the high notions entertained of prerogative than of the very irregular and infrequent meeting of parliament, that an extensive and somewhat indefinite authority should be arrogated to proclamations of the king in council. Temporary ordinances, bordering at least on legislative authority, grow out of the varying exigencies of civil society, and will by very necessity be put up with in silence, wherever the constitution of the commonwealth does not directly or in effect provide for frequent assemblies of the body in whom the right of making or consenting to laws has been vested. Since the English constitution has reached its zenith, we have endeavored to provide a remedy by statute for every possible mischief or inconvenience; and if this has swollen our code to an enormous redundance, till, in the labyrinth of written law, we almost feel again the uncertainties of arbitrary power, it has at least put an end to such exertions of prerogative as fell at once on the persons and properties of whole classes. It seems, by the proclamations issued under Elizabeth, that the crown claimed a sort of supplemental right of legislation, to perfect and carry into effect what the spirit of existing laws might require, as well as a paramount supremacy, called sometimes the king's absolute or sovereign power, which sanctioned commands beyond the legal prerogative, for the sake of public safety, whenever the council might judge that to be in hazard. Thus we find anabaptists, without distinction of natives or aliens, banished the realm; Irishmen commanded to depart into Ireland; the culture of woad,[1] and the exportation of corn, money, and

[1] Hume says "that the queen had taken a dislike to the smell of this useful plant." But this reason, if it existed, would hardly have induced her to prohibit its cultivation throughout the kingdom. The real motive appears in several letters of the Lansdowne collection. By the domestic culture of woad the cus-

various commodities prohibited; the excess of apparel restrained. A proclamation in 1580 forbids the erection of houses within three miles of London, on account of the too great increase of the city, under the penalty of imprisonment and forfeiture of the materials.[1] This is repeated at other times, and lastly (I mean during her reign) in 1602, with additional restrictions.[2] Some proclamations in this reign hold out menaces which the common law could never have executed on the disobedient. To trade with the French king's rebels, or to export victuals into the Spanish dominions (the latter of which might possibly be construed into assisting the queen's enemies), incurred the penalty of treason. And persons having in their possession goods taken on the high seas, which had not paid customs, are enjoined to give them up, on pain of being punished as felons and pirates.[3] Notwithstanding these instances, it cannot perhaps be said on the whole that Elizabeth stretched her authority very outrageously in this respect. Many of her proclamations, which may at first sight appear illegal, are warrantable by statutes then in force, or by ancient precedents. Thus the council is empowered by an act, 28 H. 8, c. 14, to fix the prices of wines; and abstinence from flesh in Lent, as well as on Fridays and Saturdays (a common subject of Elizabeth's proclamations), is enjoined by several statutes of Edward VI. and of her own.[4] And it has been argued by some not at all inclined to diminish any popular rights, that the king did possess a prerogative by common law of restraining the export of corn and other commodities.[5]

Restrictions on printing.

It is natural to suppose that a government thus arbitrary and vigilant must have looked with extreme jealousy on the diffusion of free inquiry through the press. The trades of printing and bookselling, in fact, though not absolutely licensed, were always subject to a sort of peculiar superintendence. Besides protecting the copy-

toms on its importation were reduced; and this led to a project of levying a sort of excise upon it at home. Catalogue of Lansdowne MSS. xlix. 32–60. The same principle has since caused the prohibition of sowing tobacco.

1 Camden, 476.

2 Rymer, xvi. 448.

3 Many of these proclamations are scattered through Rymer; and the whole have been collected in a volume.

4 By a proclamation in 1560, butchers killing flesh in Lent are made subject to a specific penalty of 20*l.*; which was levied upon one man. Strype's Annals, i. 235. This seems to have been illegal.

5 Lord Camden, in 1766. See Hargrave's preface to Hale de Jure Coronæ, in Law Tracts, vol. i.

right of authors,[1] the council frequently issued proclamations to restrain the importation of books, or to regulate their sale.[2] It was penal to utter, or so much as to possess, even the most learned works on the catholic side; or if some connivance was usual in favor of educated men, the utmost strictness was used in suppressing that light infantry of literature, the smart and vigorous pamphlets with which the two parties arrayed against the church assaulted her opposite flanks.[3] Stow, the well-known chronicler of England, who lay under suspicion of an attachment to popery, had his library searched by warrant, and his unlawful books taken away; several of which were but materials for his history.[4] Whitgift, in this, as in every other respect, aggravated the rigor of preceding times. At his instigation the star-chamber, 1585, published ordinances for the regulation of the press. The preface to these recites "enormities and abuses of disorderly persons professing the art of printing and selling books" to have more and more increased in spite of the ordinances made against them, which it attributes to the inadequacy of the penalties hitherto inflicted. Every printer therefore is enjoined to certify his presses to the Stationers' Company, on pain of having them defaced, and suffering a year's imprisonment. None to print at all, under similar penalties, except in London, and one in each of the two universities. No printer who has only set up his trade within six months to exercise it any longer, nor any to begin it in future until the excessive multitude of printers be diminished and brought to such a number as the archbishop of Canterbury and bishop of London for the time being shall think convenient; but whenever any addition to the number of master printers shall be required, the Stationers' Company shall select proper persons to use that calling with the approbation of the ec-

1 We find an exclusive privilege granted in 1563 to Thomas Cooper, afterwards bishop of Winchester, to print his Thesaurus, or Latin dictionary, for twelve years—Rymer, xv. 620; and to Richard Wright to print his translation of Tacitus during his natural life; any one infringing this privilege to forfeit 40*s*. for every printed copy. Id. xvi. 97.

2 Strype's Parker 221. By the 51st of the queen's injunctions, in 1559, no one might print any book or paper whatsoever unless the same be first licensed by the council or ordinary.

3 A proclamation, dated Feb. 1589, against seditious and schismatical books and writings, commands all persons who shall have in their custody any such libels against the order and government of the church of England, or the rites and ceremonies used in it, to bring and deliver up the same with convenient speed to their ordinary. Life of Whitgift, Appendix, 126. This has probably been one cause of the extreme scarcity of the puritanical pamphlets.

4 Strype's Grindal, 124, and Append. 48, where a list of these books is given.

clesiastical commissioners. None to print any book, matter, or thing whatsoever, until it shall have been first seen, perused, and allowed by the archbishop of Canterbury or bishop of London, except the queen's printer, to be appointed for some special service, or law-printers, who shall require the license only of the chief justices. Every one selling books printed contrary to the intent of this ordinance to suffer three months' imprisonment. The Stationers' Company empowered to search houses and shops of printers and booksellers, and to seize all books printed in contravention of this ordinance, to destroy and deface the presses, and to arrest and bring before the council those who shall have offended therein.[1]

The forms of English law, however inadequate to defend the subject in state prosecutions, imposed a degree of seeming restraint on the crown, and wounded that pride which is commonly a yet stronger sentiment than the lust of power with princes and their counsellors. It was possible that juries might absolve a prisoner; it was always necessary that they should be the arbiters of his fate. Delays too were interposed by the regular process; not such, perhaps, as the life of man should require, yet enough to weaken the terrors of summary punishment. Kings love to display the divinity with which their flatterers invest them in nothing so much as the instantaneous execution of their will, and to stand revealed, as it were, in the storm and thunderbolt, when their power breaks through the operation of secondary causes, and awes a prostrate nation without the intervention of law. There may indeed be times of pressing danger, when the conservation of all demands the sacrifice of the legal rights of a few; there may be circumstances that not only justify, but compel, the temporary abandonment of constitutional forms. It has been usual for all governments, during an actual rebellion, to proclaim martial law, or the suspension of civil jurisdiction. And this anomaly, I must admit, is

[1] Strype's Whitgift, 222, and Append. 94. The archbishop exercised his power over the press, as may be supposed, with little moderation. Not confining himself to the suppression of books favoring the two parties adverse to the church, he permitted nothing to appear that interfered in the least with his own notions. Thus we find him seizing an edition of some works of Hugh Broughton, an eminent Hebrew scholar. This learned divine differed from Whitgift about Christ's descent to hell. It is amusing to read that ultimately the primate came over to Broughton's opinion: which, if it proves some degree of candor, is also a glaring evidence of the advantages of that free inquiry he had sought to suppress. P. 384, 431.

very far from being less indispensable at such unhappy seasons, in countries where the ordinary mode of trial is by jury, than where the right of decision resides in the judge. But it is of high importance to watch with extreme jealousy the disposition towards which most governments are prone, to introduce too soon, to extend too far, to retain too long, so perilous a remedy. In the fourteenth and fifteenth centuries the court of the constable and marshal, whose jurisdiction was considered as of a military nature, and whose proceedings were not according to the course of the common law, sometimes tried offenders by what was called martial law, but only, I believe, either during, or not long after, a serious rebellion. This tribunal fell into disuse under the Tudors. But Mary had executed some of those taken in Wyatt's insurrection without regular process, though their leader had his trial by a jury. Elizabeth, always hasty in passion and quick to punish, would have resorted to this summary course on a slighter occasion. One Peter Burchell, a fanatical puritan, and perhaps insane, conceiving that sir Christopher Hatton was an enemy to true religion, determined to assassinate him. But by mistake he wounded instead a famous seaman, captain Hawkins. For this ordinary crime the queen could hardly be prevented from directing him to be tried instantly by martial law. Her council, however (and this it is important to observe), resisted this illegal proposition with spirit and success.[1] We have indeed a proclamation some years afterwards, declaring that such as brought into the kingdom or dispersed papal bulls, or traitorous libels against the queen, should with all severity be proceeded against by her majesty's lieutenants or their deputies by martial law, and suffer such pains and penalties as they should inflict; and that none of her said lieutenants or their deputies be any wise impeached, in body, lands, or goods, at any time hereafter, for anything to be done or executed in the punishment of any such offender, according to the said

[1] Camden, 449; Strype's Annals, ii. 288. The queen had been told, it seems, of what was done in Wyatt's business, a case not at all parallel; though there was no sufficient necessity even in that instance to justify the proceeding by martial law. But bad precedents always beget "progeniem vitiosiorem."

There was a difficulty how to punish Burchell capitally, which probably suggested to the queen this strange expedient. It is said, which is full as strange, that the bishops were about to pass sentence on him for heresy, in having asserted that a papist might lawfully be killed. He put an end, however, to this dilemma, by cleaving the skull of one of the keepers in the Tower, and was hanged in a common way.

martial law, and the tenor of this proclamation, any law or statute to the contrary in any wise notwithstanding.[1] This measure, though by no means constitutional, finds an apology in the circumstances of the time. It bears date the 1st of July, 1588, when within the lapse of a few days the vast armament of Spain might effect a landing upon our coasts; and prospectively to a crisis when the nation, struggling for life against an invader's grasp, could not afford the protection of law to domestic traitors. But it is an unhappy consequence of all deviations from the even course of law, that the forced acts of overruling necessity come to be distorted into precedents to serve the purposes of arbitrary power.

Martial law.

No other measure of Elizabeth's reign can be compared, in point of violence and illegality, to a commission in July, 1595, directed to sir Thomas Wilford, whereby, upon no other allegation than that there had been of late "sundry great unlawful assemblies of a number of base people in riotous sort, both in the city of London and the suburbs, for the suppression whereof (for that the insolency of many desperate offenders is such that they care not for any ordinary punishment by imprisonment) it was found necessary to have some such notable rebellious persons to be speedily suppressed by execution to death, according to the justice of martial law," he is appointed provost-marshal, with authority, on notice by the magistrates, to attach and seize such notable rebellious and incorrigible offenders, and in the presence of the magistrates to execute them openly on the gallows. The commission empowers him also "to repair to all common highways near to the city which any vagrant persons do haunt, and, with the assistance of justices and constables, to apprehend all such vagrant and suspected persons, and them to deliver to the said justices, by them to be committed and examined of the causes of their wandering, and, finding them notoriously culpable in their unlawful manner of life, as incorrigible, and so certified by the said justices, to cause to be executed upon the gallows or gibbet some of them that are so found most notorious and incorrigible offenders; and some such also of them as have manifestly broken the peace since they have been adjudged and condemned to death for former offences, and had the queen's pardon for the same."[2]

1 Strype's Annals, iii. 570; Life of Whitgift, Append. 126.
2 Rymer, xvi. 279.

This peremptory style of superseding the common law was a stretch of prerogative without an adequate parallel, so far as I know, in any former period. It is to be remarked that no tumults had taken place of any political character or of serious importance, some riotous apprentices only having committed a few disorders.[1] But rather more than usual suspicion had been excited about the same time by the intrigues of the jesuits in favor of Spain, and the queen's advanced age had begun to renew men's doubts as to the succession. The rapid increase of London gave evident uneasiness, as the proclamations against new buildings show, to a very cautious administration, environed by bold and inveterate enemies, and entirely destitute of regular troops to withstand a sudden insurrection. Circumstances of which we are ignorant, I do not question, gave rise to this extraordinary commission. The executive government in modern times has been invested with a degree of coercive power to maintain obedience of which our ancestors, in the most arbitrary reigns, had no practical experience. If we reflect upon the multitude of statutes enacted since the days of Elizabeth in order to restrain and suppress disorder, and, above all, on the prompt and certain aid that a disciplined army affords to our civil authorities, we may be inclined to think that it was rather the weakness than the vigor of her government which led to its inquisitorial watchfulness and harsh measures of prevention. We find in an earlier part of her reign an act of state somewhat of the same character, though not perhaps illegal. Letters were written to the sheriffs and justices of divers counties in 1569, directing them to apprehend, on a certain night, all vagabonds and idle persons having no master nor means of living, and either to commit them to prison or pass them to their proper homes. This was repeated several times and no less than 13,000 persons were thus apprehended, chiefly in the north, which, as Strype says, very much broke the rebellion attempted in that year.[2]

Amidst so many infringements of the freedom of commerce, and with so precarious an enjoyment of personal liberty, the English subject continued to pride himself in his immunity from taxation without consent of parliament. This

[1] Carte, 693, from Stow. [2] Strype's Annals, i. 535.

privilege he had asserted, though not with constant success, against the rapacity of Henry VII. and the violence of his son. Nor was it ever disputed in theory by Elizabeth. She retained, indeed, notwithstanding the complaints of the merchants at her accession, a custom upon cloths, arbitrarily imposed by her sister, and laid one herself upon sweet wines. But she made no attempt at levying internal taxes, except that the clergy were called upon, in 1586, for an aid not granted in convocation, but assessed by the archdeacon according to the value of their benefices, to which they naturally showed no little reluctance.[1] By dint of singular frugality she continued to steer the true course, so as to keep her popularity undiminished and her prerogative unimpaired — asking very little of her subjects' money in parliaments, and being hence enabled both to have long breathing times between their sessions, and to meet them without coaxing or wrangling, till, in the latter years of her reign, a foreign war and a rebellion in Ireland, joined to a rapid depreciation in the value of money, rendered her demands somewhat higher. But she did not abstain from the ancient practice of sending privy-seals to borrow money of the wealthy. These were not considered as illegal, though plainly forbidden by the statute of Richard III.; for it was the fashion to set aside the authority of that act, as having been passed by an usurper. It is impossible to doubt that such loans were so far obtained by compulsion, that any gentleman or citizen of sufficient ability refusing compliance would have discovered that it were far better to part with his money than to incur the council's displeasure. We have indeed a letter from a lord mayor to the council, informing them that he had committed to prison some citizens for refusing to pay the money demanded of them.[2] But the

Loans of money not quite voluntary.

[1] Strype, iii. Append. 147. This was exacted in order to raise men for service in the Low Countries. But the beneficed clergy were always bound to furnish horses and armor, or their value, for the defence of the kingdom in peril of invasion or rebellion. An instance of their being called on for such a contingent occurred in 1569. Strype's Parker, 273; and Rymer will supply many others in earlier times.

The magistrates of Cheshire and Lancashire had imposed a charge of eightpence a week on each parish of those counties for the maintenance of recusants in custody. This, though very nearly borne out by the letter of a recent statute, 14th Eliz. c. 5, was conceived by the inhabitants to be against law. We have, in Strype's Annals, vol. iii. Append. 56, a letter from the privy-council, directing the charge to be taken off. It is only worth noticing as it illustrates the jealousy which the people entertained of anything approaching to taxation without consent of parliament, and the caution of the ministry, in not pushing any exertion of prerogative farther than would readily be endured.

[2] Murden, 632. That some degree of

queen seems to have been punctual in their speedy repayment according to stipulation, a virtue somewhat unusual with royal debtors. Thus we find a proclamation in 1571, that such as had lent the queen money in the last summer should receive repayment in November and December.[1] Such loans were but an anticipation of her regular revenue, and no great hardship on rich merchants, who, if they got no interest for their money, were recompensed with knighthoods and gracious words. And as Elizabeth incurred no debt till near the conclusion of her reign, it is probable that she never had borrowed more than she was sure to repay.

A letter quoted by Hume from Lord Burleigh's papers, though not written by him, as the historian asserts, and somewhat obscure in its purport, appears to warrant the conclusion that he had revolved in his mind some project of raising money by a general contribution or benevolence from persons of ability, without purpose of repayment. This was also amidst the difficulties of the year 1569, when Cecil

intimidation was occasionally made use of may be inferred from the following letter of sir Henry Cholmley to the mayor and aldermen of Chester in 1597. He informs them of letters received by him from the council, "whereby I am commanded in all haste to require you that you and every of you send in your several sums of money unto Torpley (Tarporly) on Friday next the 23d December, or else that you and every of you give me meeting there, the said day and place, to enter severally into bond to her highness for your appearance forthwith before their lordships, to show cause wherefore you and every of you should refuse to pay her majesty loan according to her highness' several privy-seals by you received letting you wit that I am now directed by other letters from their lordships to pay over the said money to the use of her majesty, and to send and certify the said bonds so taken; which praying you heartily to consider of as the last direction of the service, I heartily bid you farewell." Harl. MSS. 2173, 10.

[1] Strype, ii. 102. In Haynes, p. 518, is the form of a circular letter or privy-seal, as it was called from passing that office, sent in 1569, a year of great difficulty, to those of whose aid the queen stood in need. It contains a promise of repayment at the expiration of twelve months. A similar application was made, through the lord-lieutenants in their several counties, to the wealthy and well-disposed, in 1588, immediately after the destruction of the Armada. The loans are asked only for the space of a year, "as heretofore has been yielded unto her majesty in times of less need and danger, and yet always fully repaid." Strype, iii. 535. Large sums of money are said to have been demanded of the citizens of London in 1599. Carte, 675. It is perhaps to this year that we may refer a curious fact mentioned in Mr. Justice Hutton's judgment in the case of ship-money. "In the time of queen Elizabeth (he says), who was a gracious and a glorious queen, yet in the end of her reign, whether through covetousness or by reason of the wars that came upon her, I know not by what council she desired benevolence, the statute of 2d Richard III, was pressed, yet it went so far that by commission and direction money was gathered in every inn of court; and I myself for my part paid twenty shillings. But when the queen was informed by her judges that this kind of proceeding was against law, she gave directions to pay all such sums as were collected back; and so I (as all the rest of our house, and as I think of other houses too) had my twenty shillings repaid me again; and privy councillors were sent down to all parts, to tell them that it was for the defence of the realm, and it should be repaid them again." State Trials, iii. 1199.

perhaps might be afraid of meeting parliament, on account of the factions leagued against himself. But as nothing further was done in this matter, we must presume that he perceived the impracticability of so unconstitutional a scheme.[1]

Character of lord Burleigh's adminis-tration.

Those whose curiosity has led them to somewhat more acquaintance with the details of English history under Elizabeth than the pages of Camden or Hume will afford, cannot but have been struck with the perpetual interference of men in power with matters of private concern. I am far from pretending to know how far the solicitations for a prime minister's aid and influence may extend at present. Yet one may think that he would hardly be employed, like Cecil, where he had no personal connection, in reconciling family quarrels, interceding with a landlord for his tenant, or persuading a rich citizen to bestow his daughter on a young lord. We are sure, at least, that he would not use the air of authority upon such occasions. The vast collection of lord Burleigh's letters in the Museum is full of such petty matters, too insignificant for the most part to be mentioned even by Strype.[2] They exhibit, however, collectively, a curious view of the manner in which England was managed, as if it had been the household and estate of a nobleman under a strict and prying steward. We are told that the relaxation of this minister's mind was to study the state of England and the pedigrees of its nobility and gentry; of these last he drew whole books with his own hands, so that he was better versed in descents and families than most of the heralds, and would often surprise persons of distinction at his table by appearing better acquainted with their manors, parks, and woods, than themselves.[3] Such

[1] Haynes, 518. Hume has exaggerated this, like other facts, in his very able, but partial, sketch of the constitution in Elizabeth's reign.

[2] The following are a few specimens, copied from the Lansdowne catalogue: "Sir Antony Cooke to Sir William Cecil, that he would move Mr. Peters to recommend Mr. Edward Stanhope to a certain young lady of Mr. P.'s acquaintance, whom Mr. Stanhope was desirous to marry." Jan. 25, 1563, lxxi. 73. "Sir John Mason to Sir William Cecil, that he fears his young landlord, Spelman, has intentions of turning him out of his house, which will be disagreeable; hopes therefore Sir William C. will speak in his behalf." Feb. 4, 1566. Id. 74. "Lord Stafford to lord Burleigh, to further a match between a certain rich citizen's daughter and his son; he requests lord B. to appoint the father to meet him (lord Stafford) some day at his house, 'where I will in few words make him so reasonable an offer as I trust he will not disallow.'" lxviii. 20. "Lady Zouch to lord Burleigh, for his friendly interposition to reconcile lord Zouch, her husband, who had forsaken her through jealousy." 1593, lxxiv. 72.

[3] Biographia Britannica, art. CECIL.

knowledge was not sought by the crafty Cecil for mere diversion's sake. It was a main part of his system to keep alive in the English gentry a persuasion that his eye was upon them. No minister was ever more exempt from that false security which is the usual weakness of a court. His failing was rather a bias towards suspicion and timidity; there were times, at least, in which his strength of mind seems to have almost deserted him through sense of the peril of his sovereign and country. But those perils appear less to us, who know how the vessel outrode them, than they could do to one harassed by continual informations of those numerous spies whom he employed both at home and abroad. The one word of Burleigh's policy was prevention; and this was dictated by a consciousness of wanting an armed force or money to support it, as well as by some uncertainty as to the public spirit in respect at least of religion. But a government that directs its chief attention to prevent offences against itself is in its very nature incompatible with that absence of restraint, that immunity from suspicion, in which civil liberty, as a tangible possession, may be said to consist. It appears probable that Elizabeth's administration carried too far, even as a matter of policy, this precautionary system upon which they founded the penal code against popery; and we may surely point to a contrast very advantageous to our modern constitution in the lenient treatment which the Jacobite faction experienced from the princes of the house of Hanover. She reigned, however, in a period of real difficulty and danger. At such seasons few ministers will abstain from arbitrary actions, except those who are not strong enough to practise them.

Disposition of the house of commons.

I have traced, in another work, the acquisition by the house of commons of a practical right to inquire into and advise upon the public administration of affairs during the reigns of Edward III., Richard II., and the princes of the line of Lancaster. This energy of parliament was quelled by the civil wars of the fifteenth century; and, whatever may have passed in debates within its walls that have not been preserved, did not often display itself in any overt act under the first Tudors. To grant subsidies which could not be raised by any other course, to propose statutes which were not binding without their consent, to consider of public grievances, and procure their redress either by law or petition to the crown, were their acknowledged constitutional privileges, which no sovereign or minister ever pretended to deny. For this end liberty of speech and free access to the royal person were claimed by the speaker as customary privileges (though not quite, in his modern language, as undoubted rights) at the commencement of every parliament. But the house of commons in Elizabeth's reign contained men of a bold and steady patriotism, well read in the laws and records of old time, sensible to the dangers of their country and abuses of government, and conscious that it was their privilege and their duty to watch over the common weal. This led to several conflicts between the crown and parliament, wherein, if the former often asserted the victory, the latter sometimes kept the field, and was left on the whole a gainer at the close of the campaign.

It would surely be erroneous to conceive that many acts of government in the four preceding reigns had not appeared at the time arbitrary and unconstitutional. If indeed we are not mistaken in judging them according to the ancient law, they must have been viewed in the same light by contemporaries, who were full as able to try them by that standard. But, to repeat what I have once before said, the extant documents from which we draw our knowledge of constitutional history under those reigns are so scanty, that instances even of a successful parliamentary resistance to measures of the crown may have left no memorial. The debates of parliament are not preserved, and very little is to be gained from such histories as the age produced. The complete barrenness indeed of Elizabeth's chroniclers, Hollingshed and Thin, as to every parliamentary or constitutional information, speaks of itself the jealous tone of her administration. Camden, writing to the next generation, though far from an ingenuous historian, is somewhat less under restraint. This forced silence of history is much more to be suspected after the use of printing and the Reformation than in the ages when monks compiled annals in their convents, reckless of the censure of courts, because independent of their permission. Grosser ignorance of public transactions is undoubtedly found in the chronicles of the middle ages; but far less of that deliberate mendacity, or of that insidious suppression, by which fear, and flattery, and hatred, and the thirst of gain, have, since the invention of printing, corrupted so much of historical literature throughout Europe. We begin, however, to find in Elizabeth's reign more copious and unquestionable documents for parliamentary history. The regular journals indeed are partly lost; nor would those which remain give us a sufficient insight into the spirit of parliament without the aid of other sources. But a volume called Sir Simon D'Ewes's Journal, part of which is copied from a manuscript of Heywood Townsend, a member of all parliaments from 1580 to 1601, contains minutes of the most interesting debates as well as transactions, and for the first time renders us acquainted with the names of those who swayed an English house of commons.[1]

Addresses concerning the succession.

There was no peril more alarming to this kingdom during the queen's reign that the precariousness of her life — a thread whereon its tranquillity, if not its religion and independence, was suspended. Hence the commons felt it an imperious duty not only to recommend her to marry, but, when this was delayed, to solicit that some limitations of the crown might be enacted in failure of her issue. The former request she evaded without ever manifesting much displeasure, though not sparing a hint that it was a little beyond the province of parliament. Upon the last occasion indeed that it was preferred, namely, by the speaker in 1575, she gave what from any other woman must have appeared an assent, and almost a promise. But about declaring the succession she was always very sensible. Through a policy not perhaps entirely selfish, and certainly not erroneous on selfish principles, she was determined never to pronounce among the possible competitors for the throne. Least of all could she brook the intermeddling of parliament in such a concern. The commons first took up this business in 1562, when there had begun to be much debate in the nation about the opposite titles of the queen of Scots and lady Catherine Grey: and especially in consequence of a dangerous sickness the queen had just experienced, and which is said to have been the cause of summoning parliament. Their language is wary, praying her only by "proclamation of certainty already provided, if any such be," alluding to the will of Henry

[1] Townsend's manuscript has been separately published; but I do not find that D'Ewes has omitted anything of consequence.

VIII., "or else by limitations of certainty, if none be, to provide a most gracious remedy in this great necessity;"[1] offering at the same time to concur in provisions to guarantee her personal safety against any one who might be limited in remainder. Elizabeth gave them a tolerably courteous answer, though not without some intimation of her dislike to this address.[2] But at their next meeting, which was not till 1566, the hope of her own marriage having grown fainter, and the circumstances of the kingdom still more powerfully demanding some security, both houses of parliament united, with a boldness of which there had perhaps been no example for more than a hundred years, to overcome her repugnance. Some of her own council among the peers are said to have asserted in their places that the queen ought to be obliged to take a husband, or that a successor should be declared by parliament against her will. She was charged with a disregard to the state and to posterity. She would prove, in the uncourtly phrase of some sturdy members of the lower house, a stepmother to her country, as being seemingly desirous that England, which lived as it were in her, should rather expire with than survive her; that kings can only gain the affections of their subjects by providing for their welfare both while they live and after their deaths; nor did any but princes hated by their subjects, or faint-hearted women, ever stand in fear of their successors.[3] But this great princess wanted not skill and courage to resist this unusual importunity of parliament. The peers, who had forgotten their customary respectfulness, were excluded the presence-chamber till they made their submission. She prevailed on the commons, through her ministers who sat there, to join a request for her marriage with the more unpalatable alternative of naming her successor; and when this request was presented, gave them fair words and a sort of assurance that their desires should by some means be fulfilled.[4] When

Difference on this between the queen and commons in 1566.

[1] D'Ewes, p. 82; Strype, i. 258; from which latter passage it seems that Cecil was rather adverse to the proposal.

[2] D'Ewes, p. 85. The speech which Hume, on D'Ewes's authority, has put into the queen's mouth at the end of this session, is but an imperfect copy or abridgment of one which she made in 1566; as D'Ewes himself afterwards confesses. Her real answer to the speaker in 1563 is in Harrington's Nugæ Antiquæ, vol. i. p. 80.

[3] Camden, p. 400.

[4] The courtiers told the house that the queen intended to marry, in order to divert them from their request that they would name her successor. Strype, vol. i. p. 494.

they continued to dwell on the same topic in their speeches, she sent messages through her ministers, and at length a positive injunction through the speaker, that they should proceed no further in the business. The house, however, was not in a temper for such ready acquiescence as it sometimes displayed. Paul Wentworth, a bold and plain-spoken man, moved to know whether the queen's command and inhibition that they should no longer dispute of the matter of succession, were not against their liberties and privileges. This caused, as we are told, long debates, which do not appear to have terminated in any resolution.[1] But, more probably having passed than we know at present, the queen, whose haughty temper and tenaciousness of prerogative were always within check of her discretion, several days after announced through the speaker that she revoked her two former commandments; "which revocation," says the journal, "was taken by the house most joyfully, with hearty prayer and thanks for the same." At the dissolution of this parliament, which was perhaps determined upon in consequence of their steadiness, Elizabeth alluded, in addressing them, with no small bitterness to what had occurred.[2]

This is the most serious disagreement on record between the crown and the commons since the days of Richard II. and Henry IV. Doubtless the queen's indignation was excited by the nature of the subject her parliament ventured to discuss, still more than by her general disapprobation of their interference in matters of state. It was an endeavor to penetrate the great secret of her reign, in preserving which she conceived her peace, dignity, and personal safety to be bound up. There were, in her opinion, as she intimates in her speech at closing the session, some underhand movers of this intrigue (whether of the Scots or Suffolk faction does not appear), who were more to blame than even the speakers in parliament. And if, as Cecil seems justly to have thought, no limitations of the crown could at that time have been effected without much peril and inconvenience, we may find some apology for her warmth about their precipitation in a business which, even according to our present constitutional usage, it would naturally be for the government to bring forward. It is to be collected from

1 D'Ewes, p. 128.
2 Id. p. 116. Journals, 8th Oct., 25th Nov., 2d Jan.

Wentworth's motion, that to deliberate on subjects affecting the commonwealth was reckoned, by at least a large part of the house of commons, one of their ancient privileges and liberties. This was not one which Elizabeth, however she had yielded for the moment in revoking her prohibition, ever designed to concede to them. Such was her frugality, that, although she had remitted a subsidy granted in this session, alleging the very honorable reason that, knowing it to have been voted in expectation of some settlement of the succession, she would not accept it when that implied condition had not been fulfilled, she was able to pass five years without again convoking her people. A parliament met in April, 1571, when the lord keeper Bacon,[1] in answer to the speaker's customary request for freedom of speech in the commons, said that "her majesty having experience of late of some disorder and certain offences, which, though they were not punished, yet were they offences still, and so must be accounted, they would therefore do well to meddle with no matters of state but such as should be propounded unto them, and to occupy themselves in other matters concerning the commonwealth."

Session of 1571.

The commons so far attended to this intimation that no proceedings about the succession appear to have taken place in this parliament, except such as were calculated to gratify the queen. We may perhaps except a bill attainting the queen of Scots, which was rejected in the upper house. But they entered for the first time on a new topic, which did not cease for the rest of this reign to furnish matter of contention with their sovereign. The party called puritan, including such as charged abuses on the actual government of the church, as well as those who objected to part of its lawful discipline, had, not a little in consequence of the absolute exclusion of the catholic gentry, obtained a very considerable strength in the commons. But the queen valued her ecclesiastical supremacy more than any part of her prerogative. Next to the succession of the crown, it was the point she could least endure to be touched. The house had indeed resolved, upon reading a bill the first time for reformation of the Common Prayer, that petition be made to the queen's majesty for

Influence of the puritans in parliament.

[1] D'Ewes, p. 141.

her license to proceed in it before it should be farther dealt in. But Strickland, who had proposed it, was sent for to the council, and restrained from appearing again in his place, though put under no confinement. This was noticed as an infringement of their liberties. The ministers endeavored to excuse his detention, as not intended to lead to any severity, nor occasioned by anything spoken in that house, but on account of his introducing a bill against the prerogative of the queen, which was not to be tolerated. And instances were quoted of animadversion on speeches made in parliament. But Mr. Yelverton maintained that all matters not treasonable, nor too much to the derogation of the imperial crown, were tolerable there, where all things came to be considered, and where there was such fulness of power as even the right of the crown was to be determined, which it would be high treason to deny. Princes were to have their prerogatives, but yet to be confined within reasonable limits. The queen could not of herself make laws, neither could she break them. This was the true voice of English liberty, not so new to men's ears as Hume has imagined, though many there were who would not forfeit the court's favor by uttering it. Such speeches as the historian has quoted of sir Humphrey Gilbert, and many such may be found in the proceedings of this reign, are rather directed to intimidate the house by exaggerating their inability to contend with the crown, than to prove the law of the land to be against them. In the present affair of Strickland it became so evident that the commons would at least address the queen to restore him, that she adopted the course her usual prudence indicated, and permitted his return to his house. But she took the reformation of ecclesiastical abuses out of their hands, sending word that she would have some articles for that purpose executed by the bishops under her royal supremacy, and not dealt in by parliament. This did not prevent the commons from proceeding to send up some bills in the upper house, where, as was natural to expect, they fell to the ground.[1]

This session is also remarkable for the first marked complaints against some notorious abuses which defaced the civil government of Elizabeth.[2] A member having rather

[1] D'Ewes, 156, &c. There is no mention of Strickland's business in the Journal.

[2] Something of this sort seems to have occurred in the session of 1566, as may be inferred from the lord keeper's

prematurely suggested the offer of a subsidy, several complaints were made of irregular and oppressive practices, and Mr. Bell said that licenses granted by the crown and other abuses galled the people, intimating also that the subsidy should be accompanied by a redress of grievances.[1] This occasion of introducing the subject, though strictly constitutional, was likely to cause displeasure. The speaker informed them a few days after of a message from the queen to spend little time in motions, and make no long speeches.[2] And Bell, it appears, having been sent for by the council, came into the house "with such an amazed countenance, that it daunted all the rest," who for many days durst not enter on any matter of importance.[3] It became the common whisper, that no one must speak against licenses, lest the queen and council should be angry. And, at the close of the session, the lord keeper severely reprimanded those audacious, arrogant, and presumptuous members, who had called her majesty's grants and prerogatives in question, meddling with matters neither pertaining to them, nor within the capacity of their understanding.[4]

The parliament of 1572 seemed to give evidence of their inheriting the spirit of the last by choosing Mr. Bell for their speaker.[5] But very little of it appeared in their proceedings. In their first short session, chiefly occupied by the business of the queen of Scots, the most remarkable circumstances are the following. The commons were desirous of absolutely excluding Mary from inheriting the crown, and even of taking away her life, and had prepared bills with this intent. But Elizabeth, constant to her mysterious policy, made one of her ministers inform them that she would neither have the queen of Scots enabled nor disabled to succeed, and willed that the bill respecting her should be drawn by her council: and that in the mean time the house should not enter on any speeches or arguments on that matter.[6] Another circumstance worthy of note in this session is a signification, through the speaker,

reproof to the speaker for calling her majesty's letters patent in question. D'Ewes, 115.

1 Id. 158. Journals, 7 Apr.

2 Journals, 9 and 10 Apr.

3 D'Ewes, 159.

4 Id. 151.

5 Bell, I suppose, had reconciled himself to the court, which would have approved no speaker chosen without its recommendation. There was always an understanding between this servant of the house and the government. Proofs or presumptions of this are not unfrequent. In Strype's Annals, vol. iv. p. 124, we find instructions for the speaker's speech in 1592, drawn up by lord Burleigh, as might very likely be the case on other occasions.

6 D'Ewes, 219.

of her majesty's pleasure that no bills concerning religion should be received, unless they should be first considered and approved by the clergy, and requiring to see certain bills touching rites and ceremonies that had been read in the house. The bills were accordingly ordered to be delivered to her, with a humble prayer that, if she should dislike them, she would not conceive an ill opinion of the house, or of the parties by whom they were preferred.[1]

Speech of Mr. Wentworth in 1576.

The submissiveness of this parliament was doubtless owing to the queen's vigorous dealings with the last. At their next meeting, which was not till February 1575–6, Peter Wentworth, brother I believe of the person of that name before-mentioned, broke out, in a speech of uncommon boldness, against her arbitrary encroachments on their privileges. The liberty of free speech, he said, had in the two last sessions been so many ways infringed, that they were in danger, while they contented themselves with the name, of losing and foregoing the thing. It was common for a rumor to spread through that house, "the queen likes or dislikes such a matter; beware what you do." Messages were even sometimes brought down either commanding or inhibiting, very injurious to the liberty of debate. He instanced that in the last session restraining the house from dealing in matters of religion; against which and against the prelates he inveighed with great acrimony. With still greater indignation he spoke of the queen's refusal to assent to the attainder of Mary; and, after surprising the house by the bold words, "none is without fault, no, not our noble queen, but has committed great and dangerous faults to herself," went on to tax her with ingratitude and unkindness to her subjects, in a strain perfectly free indeed from disaffection, but of more rude censure than any kings would put up with.[2]

This direct attack upon the sovereign in matters relating to her public administration seems no doubt unparliamentary; though neither the rules of parliament in this respect, nor even the constitutional principle, were so strictly understood as at present. But it was part of Elizabeth's character to render herself extremely prominent, and, as it were, responsible in public esteem for every important measure of her

[1] D'Ewes, 213, 214.

[2] Id. 236.

government. It was difficult to consider a queen as acting merely by the advice of ministers who protested in parliament that they had labored in vain to bend her heart to their counsels. The doctrine that some one must be responsible for every act of the crown was yet perfectly unknown; and Elizabeth would have been the last to adopt a system so inglorious to monarchy. But Wentworth had gone to a length which alarmed the house of commons. They judged it expedient to prevent an unpleasant interference by sequestering their member, and appointing a committee of all the privy councillors in the house to examine him. Wentworth declined their authority, till they assured him that they sat as members of the commons and not as councillors. After a long examination, in which he not only behaved with intrepidity, but, according to his own statement, reduced them to confess the truth of all he advanced, they made a report to the house, who committed him to the Tower. He had lain there a month when the queen sent word that she remitted her displeasure towards him, and referred his enlargement to the house, who released him upon a reprimand from the speaker, and an acknowledgment of his fault upon his knees.[1] In this commitment of Wentworth it can hardly be said that there was anything, as to the main point, by which the house sacrificed its acknowledged privileges. In later instances, and even in the reign of George I., members have been committed for much less indecent reflections on the sovereign. The queen had no reason upon the whole to be ill-pleased with this parliament, nor was she in haste to dissolve it, though there was a long intermission of its sessions. The next was in 1581, when the chancellor, on confirming a new speaker, did not fail to admonish him that the house of commons should not intermeddle in anything touching her majesty's person or estate, or church government. They were supposed to disobey this injunction, and fell under the queen's displeasure, by appointing a public fast on their own authority, though to be enforced on none but themselves. This trifling resolution, which showed indeed a little of the puritan spirit, passed for an encroachment on the supremacy, and was only expiated by a humble apology.[2] It is not till the month of February, 1587–8, that the zeal for ecclesias-

[1] D'Ewes, 260.

[2] Id. 282.

tical reformation overcame in some measure the terrors of power, but with no better success than before. A Mr. Cope offered to the house, we are informed, a bill and a book, the former annulling all laws respecting ecclesiastical government then in force, and establishing a certain new form of common prayer contained in the latter. The speaker interposed to prevent this bill from being read, on the ground that her majesty had commanded them not to meddle in this matter. Several members however spoke in favor of hearing it read, and the day passed in debate on this subject. Before they met again the queen sent for the speaker, who delivered up to her the bill and book. Next time that the house sat Mr. Wentworth insisted that some questions of his proposing should be read. These queries were to the following purport: "Whether this council was not a place for any member of the same, freely and without control, by bill or speech, to utter any of the griefs of this commonwealth? Whether there be any council that can make, add, or diminish from the laws of the realm, but only this council of parliament? Whether it be not against the orders of this council to make any secret or matter of weight, which is here in hand, known to the prince or any other, without consent of the house? Whether the speaker may overrule the house in any matter or cause in question? Whether the prince and state can continue and stand, and be maintained, without this council of parliament, not altering the government of the state?" These questions sergeant Pickering, the speaker, instead of reading them to the house, showed to a courtier, through whose means Wentworth was committed to the Tower. Mr. Cope, and those who had spoken in favor of his motion, underwent the same fate; and, notwithstanding some notice taken of it in the house, it does not appear that they were set at liberty before its dissolution, which ensued in three weeks.[1] Yet the commons were so set on displaying an ineffectual hankering after reform, that they appointed a committee to address the queen for a learned ministry.

The commons continue to seek redress of ecclesiastical grievances.

At the beginning of the next parliament, which met in 1588–9, the speaker received an admonition that the house were not to extend their privileges to any irreverent or misbecoming speech. In this session Mr. Damport, we are informed by

1 D'Ewes, 410.

D'Ewes,[1] moved "neither for making of any new laws, nor for abrogating of any old ones, but for a due course of proceeding in laws already established, but executed by some ecclesiastical governors contrary both to their purport and the intent of the legislature, which he proposed to bring into discussion." So cautious a motion saved its author from the punishment which had attended Mr. Cope for his more radical reform; but the secretary of state, reminding the house of the queen's express inhibition from dealing with ecclesiastical causes, declared to them by the chancellor at the commencement of the session (in a speech which does not appear), prevented them from taking any further notice of Mr. Damport's motion. They narrowly escaped Elizabeth's displeasure in attacking some civil abuses. Sir Edward Hobby brought in a bill to prevent certain exactions made for their own profit by the officers of the exchequer. Two days after he complained that he had been very sharply rebuked by some great personage, not a member of the house, for his speech on that occasion. But instead of testifying indignation at this breach of their privileges, neither he nor the house thought of any further redress than by exculpating him to this great personage, apparently one of the ministers, and admonishing their members not to repeat elsewhere anything uttered in their debates.[2] For the bill itself, as well as one intended to restrain the flagrant abuses of purveyance, they both were passed to the lords. But the queen sent a message to the upper house, expressing her dislike of them, as meddling with abuses which, if they existed, she was both able and willing to repress; and this having been formally communicated to the commons, they appointed a committee to search for precedents in order to satisfy her majesty about their proceedings. They received afterwards a gracious answer to their address, the queen declaring her willingness to afford a remedy for the alleged grievances.[3]

Elizabeth, whose reputation for consistency, which haughty princes overvalue, was engaged in protecting the established hierarchy, must have experienced not a little vexation at the perpetual recurrence of complaints which the unpopularity of that order drew from every parliament. The speaker of

1 P. 438. Townsend calls this gentleman Davenport, which no doubt was his true name.

2 D'Ewes, 433.

3 Id. 440, et post.

that summoned in 1593 received for answer to his request of liberty of speech, that it was granted, "but not to speak every one what he listeth, or what cometh into his brain to utter; their privilege was ay or no. Wherefore, Mr. Speaker," continues the lord keeper Pickering, himself speaker in the parliament of 1588, "her majesty's pleasure is, that if you perceive any idle heads which will not stick to hazard their own estates, which will meddle with reforming the church and transforming the commonwealth, and do exhibit such bills to such purpose, that you receive them not, until they be viewed and considered by those who it is fitter should consider of such things, and can better judge of them." It seems not improbable that this admonition, which indeed is in no unusual style for this reign, was suggested by the expectation of some unpleasing debate. For we read that the very first day of the session, though the commons had adjourned on account of the speaker's illness, the unconquerable Peter Wentworth, with another member, presented a petition to the lord keeper, desiring "the lords of the upper house to join with them of the lower in imploring her majesty to entail the succession of the crown, for which they had already prepared a bill." This step, which may seem to us rather arrogant and unparliamentary, drew down, as they must have expected, the queen's indignation. They were summoned before the council, and committed to different prisons.[1] A few days afterwards a bill for reforming the abuses of ecclesiastical courts was presented by Morice, attorney of the court of wards, and underwent some discussion in the house.[2] But the queen sent for the speaker, and expressly commanded that no bill touching matters of state or reformation of causes ecclesiastical should be exhibited; and if any such should be offered, enjoining him on his allegiance not to read it.[3] It was the custom at that time for the speaker to read and expound to the house all the bills that any member offered. Morice himself was committed to safe custody, from which he wrote a spirited letter to lord Burleigh, expressing his sorrow for having offended the queen, but at the same time his resolution "to strive," he says, "while his life should last, for freedom of conscience, public justice, and the liberties of his country."[4] Some days

[1] D'Ewes, 470.
[2] Id. 474; Townsend, 60.
[3] Id. 62.
[4] See the letter in Lodge's Illustra

after, a motion was made that, as some places might complain of paying subsidies, their representatives not having been consulted nor been present when they were granted, the house should address the queen to set their members at liberty. But the ministers opposed this, as likely to hurt those whose good was sought, her majesty being more likely to release them if left to her own gracious disposition. It does not appear however that she did so during the session, which lasted above a month.[1] We read, on the contrary, in an undoubted authority, namely a letter of Antony Bacon to his mother, that "divers gentlemen who were of the parliament, and thought to have returned into the country after the end thereof, were stayed by her majesty's commandment, for being privy, as it is thought, and consenting to Mr. Wentworth's motion."[2] Some difficulty was made by this house of commons about their grant of subsidies, which was uncommonly large, though rather in appearance than truth, so great had been the depreciation of silver for some years past.[3]

Also of monopolies, especially in the session of 1601.

The admonitions not to abuse freedom of speech, which had become almost as much matter of course as the request for it, were repeated in the ensuing parliaments of 1597 and 1601. Nothing more remarkable occurs in the former of these sessions than an address to the queen against the enormous abuse of monopolies. The crown either possessed or assumed the prerogative of regulating almost all matters of commerce at its discretion. Patents to deal exclusively in particular articles, generally of foreign growth, but reaching in some instances to such important necessaries of life as salt, leather, and coal, had been lavishly granted to the courtiers, with little direct advantage to the revenue. They sold them to companies of merchants, who of course enhanced the price to the utmost ability of the purchaser. This business seems to have been purposely protracted by the ministers and the speaker, who, in this reign, was usually in the court's interests, till the last day of the session; when, in answer to

tions, vol. iii. 34. Townsend says he was committed to Sir John Fortescue's keeping, a gentler sort of imprisonment. P. 61.

[1] D'Ewes, 470.

[2] Birch's Memoirs of Elizabeth, i. 96.

[3] Strype has published, from lord Burleigh's manuscripts, a speech made in the parliament of 1589 against the subsidy then proposed. Annals, vol. iii. Append. 238. Not a word about this occurs in D'Ewes's Journal; and I mention it as an additional proof how little we can rely on negative inferences as to proceedings in parliament at this period.

his mention of it, the lord keeper said that the queen "hoped her dutiful and loving subjects would not take away her prerogative, which is the choicest flower in her garden, and the principal and head pearl in her crown and diadem; but would rather leave that to her disposition, promising to examine all patents, and to abide the touchstone of the law." [1] This answer, though less stern than had been usual, was merely evasive: and in the session of 1601 a bolder and more successful attack was made on the administration than this reign had witnessed. The grievance of monopolies had gone on continually increasing; scarce any article was exempt from these oppressive patents. When the list of them was read over in the house, a member exclaimed, "Is not bread among the number?" The house seemed amazed: "Nay," said he, "if no remedy is found for these, bread will be there before the next parliament." Every tongue seemed now unloosed; each as if emulously descanting on the injuries of the place he represented. It was vain for the courtiers to withstand this torrent. Raleigh, no small gainer himself by some monopolies, after making what excuse he could, offered to give them up. Robert Cecil the secretary, and Bacon, talked loudly of the prerogative, and endeavored at least to persuade the house that it would be fitter to proceed by petition to the queen than by a bill. But it was properly answered that nothing had been gained by petitioning in the last parliament. After four days of eager debate, and more heat than had ever been witnessed, this ferment was suddenly appeased by one of those well-timed concessions by which skilful princes spare themselves the mortification of being overcome. Elizabeth sent down a message that she would revoke all grants that should be found injurious by fair trial at law: and Cecil rendered the somewhat ambiguous generality of this expression more satisfactory by an assurance that the existing patents should all be repealed, and no more be granted. This victory filled the commons with joy, perhaps the more from being rather unexpected.[2] They addressed the queen with rapturous and hyperbolical acknowledgments, to which she answered in an affectionate strain, glancing only with an oblique irony at some of those movers

1 D'Ewes, 547.

2 Their joy and gratitude were rather premature, for her majesty did not revoke all of them; as appears by Rymer, xvi. 540, and Carte, iii. 712. A list of them, dated May, 1603, Lodge, iii. 159, seems to imply that they were still existing.

in the debate, whom in her earlier and more vigorous years she would have keenly reprimanded. She repeated this a little more plainly at the close of the session, but still with commendation of the body of the commons. So altered a tone must be ascribed partly to the growing spirit she perceived in her subjects, but partly also to those cares which clouded with listless melancholy the last scenes of her illustrious life.[1]

The discontent that vented itself against monopolies was not a little excited by the increasing demands which Elizabeth was compelled to make upon the commons in all her latter parliaments. Though it was declared, in the preamble to the subsidy bill of 1593, that "these large and unusual grants, made to a most excellent princess on a most pressing

[1] D'Ewes, 619, 644, &c.

The speeches made in this parliament are reported more fully than usual by Heywood Townsend, from whose journal those of most importance have been transcribed by D'Ewes. Hume has given considerable extracts, for the sole purpose of inferring, from this very debate on monopolies, that the royal prerogative was, according to the opinion of the house of commons itself, hardly subject to any kind of restraint. But the passages he selects are so unfairly taken (some of them being the mere language of courtiers, others separated from the context in order to distort their meaning), that no one who compares them with the original can acquit him of extreme prejudice. The adulatory strain in which it was usual to speak of the sovereign often covered a strong disposition to keep down his authority. Thus when a Mr. Davies says in this debate, "God hath given that power to absolute princes which he attributes to himself — Dixi quod dii estis," it would have been seen, if Hume had quoted the following sentence, that he infers from hence, that, justice being a divine attribute, the king can do nothing that is unjust, and consequently cannot grant licenses to the injury of his subjects. Strong language was no doubt used in respect of the prerogative. But it is erroneous to assert, with Hume, that it came equally from the courtiers and country gentlemen, and was admitted by both. It will chiefly be found in the speeches of secretary Cecil, the official defender of prerogative, and of some lawyers. Hume, after quoting an extravagant speech ascribed to sergeant Heyle, that "all we have is her majesty's, and she may lawfully at any time take it from us; yea, she hath as much right to all our lands and goods as to any revenue of her crown," observes that Heyle was an eminent lawyer, a man of character. That Heyle was high in his profession is beyond doubt; but in that age, as has since, though from the change of times less grossly, continued to be the case, the most distinguished lawyers notoriously considered the court and country as plaintiff and defendant in a great suit, and themselves as their retained advocates. It is not likely however that Heyle should have used the exact words imputed to him. He made, no doubt, a strong speech for prerogative, but so grossly to transcend all limits of truth and decency seems even beyond a lawyer seeking office. Townsend and D'Ewes write with a sort of sarcastic humor, which is not always to be taken according to the letter. D'Ewes, 433; Townsend, 205.

Hume proceeds to tell us that it was asserted this session that the speaker might either admit or reject bills in the house; and remarks that the very proposal of it is a proof at what a low ebb liberty was at that time in England. There cannot be a more complete mistake. No such assertion was made; but a member suggested that the speaker might, as the consuls in the Roman senate used, appoint the order in which bills should be read; at which speech, it is added, some hissed. D'Ewes, 677. The present regularity of parliamentary forms, so justly valued by the house, was yet unknown; and the members called confusedly for the business they wished to have brought forward.

and extraordinary occasion, should not at any time hereafter be drawn into a precedent," yet an equal sum was obtained in 1597, and one still greater in 1601, but money was always reluctantly given, and the queen's early frugality had accustomed her subjects to very low taxes; so that the debates on the supply in 1601, as handed down to us by Townsend, exhibit a lurking ill-humor which would find a better occasion to break forth.

Influence of the crown in parliament.

The house of commons, upon a review of Elizabeth's reign, was very far, on the one hand from exercising those constitutional rights which have long since belonged to it, or even those which by ancient precedent it might have claimed as its own; yet, on the other hand, was not quite so servile and submissive an assembly as an artful historian has represented it. If many of its members were but creatures of power, if the majority was often too readily intimidated, if the bold and honest, but not very judicious, Wentworths were but feebly supported, when their impatience hurried them beyond their colleagues, there was still a considerable party, sometimes carrying the house along with them, who with patient resolution and inflexible aim recurred in every session to the assertion of that one great privilege which their sovereign contested, the right of parliament to inquire into and suggest a remedy for every public mischief or danger. It may be remarked that the ministers, such as Knollys, Hatton, and Robert Cecil, not only sat among the commons, but took a very leading part in their discussions: a proof that the influence of argument could no more be dispensed with than that of power. This, as I conceive, will never be the case in any kingdom where the assembly of the estates is quite subservient to the crown. Nor should we put out of consideration the manner in which the commons were composed. Sixty-two members were added at different times by Elizabeth to the representation, as well from places which had in earlier times discontinued their franchise, as from those to which it was first granted;[1] a very large proportion of them

[1] Parl. Hist. 958. In the session of 1571 a committee was appointed to confer with the attorney and solicitor-general about the return of burgesses from nine places which had not been represented in the last parliament. But in the end it was "ordered, by Mr. Attorney's assent, that the burgesses shall remain according to their returns; for that the validity of the charters of their towns is elsewhere to be examined, if cause be" D'Ewes, p. 156, 159.

D'Ewes observes that it was very common in former times, in order to

petty boroughs, evidently under the influence of the crown or peerage. This had been the policy of her brother and sister, in order to counterbalance the country gentlemen, and find room for those dependents who had no natural interest to return them to parliament. The ministry took much pains with elections, of which many proofs remain.[1] The house accordingly was filled with placemen, civilians, and common lawyers grasping at preferment. The slavish tone of these persons, as we collect from the minutes of

avoid the charge of paying wages to their burgesses, that a borough which had fallen into poverty or decay either got license of the sovereign for the time being to be discharged from electing members, or discontinued it of themselves; but that of late, the members for the most part bearing their own charges, many of those towns which had thus discontinued their privilege renewed it, both in Elizabeth's reign and that of James. P. 80. This could only have been, it is hardly necessary to say, by obtaining writs out of chancery for that purpose. As to the payment of wages, the words of D'Ewes intimate that it was not entirely disused. In the session of 1586 the borough of Grantham complained that Arthur Hall (whose name now appears for the last time) had sued them for wages due to him as their representative in the preceding parliament; alleging that, as well by reason of his negligent attendance and some other offences by him committed in some of its sessions, as of his promise not to require any such wages, they ought not to be charged; and a committee, having been appointed to inquire into this, reported that they had requested Mr. Hall to remit his claim for wages, which he had freely done. D'Ewes, p. 417.

1 Strype mentions letters from the council to Mildmay, sheriff of Essex, in 1559, about the choice of knights. Annals, vol. i. p. 32. And other instances of interference may be found in the Lansdowne and Harleian collections. Thus we read that a Mr. Copley used to nominate burgesses for Gatton, "for that there were no burgesses in the borough." The present proprietor being a minor in custody of the court of wards, lord Burleigh directs the sheriff of Surrey to make no return without instructions from himself; and afterwards orders him to cancel the name of Francis Bacon in his indenture, he being returned for another place, and to substitute Edward Brown. Harl. MSS. DCCIII. 16.

I will introduce in this place, though not belonging to the present reign, a proof that Henry VIII. did not trust altogether to the intimidating effects of his despotism for the obedience of parliament, and that his ministers looked to the management of elections, as their successors have always done. Sir Robert Sadler writes to some one whose name does not appear, to inform him that the duke of Norfolk had spoken to the king, who was well content he should be a burgess of Oxford; and that he should "order himself in the said *room* according to such instructions as the said duke of Norfolk should give him from the king;" if he is not elected at Oxford, the writer will recommend him to some of "my lord's towns of his bishopric of Winchester." Cotton MSS. Cleopatra E. iv. 178. Thus we see that the practice of our government has always been alike: and we may add the same of the nobility, who interfered with elections full as continually, and far more openly, than in modern times. The difference is, that a secretary of the treasury, or peer's agent, does that with some precaution of secrecy, which the council-board, or peer himself, under the Tudors, did by express letters to the returning officer; and that the operating motive is the prospect of a good place in the excise or customs for compliance, rather than that of lying some months in the Fleet for disobedience.

A late writer has asserted, as an undoubted fact, which "historic truth requires to be mentioned," that for the first parliament of Elizabeth "five candidates were nominated by the court for each borough, and three for each county; and by the authority of the sheriffs the members were chosen from among the candidates." Butler's Book of the Roman Catholic Church, p. 225. I never met with any tolerable authority for this, and believe it to be a mere fabrication; not certainly of Mr. Butler, who is utterly incapable of a wilful deviation from truth, but of some of those whom he too implicitly follows.

D'Ewes, is strikingly contrasted with the manliness of independent gentlemen. And as the house was by no means very fully attended, the divisions, a few of which are recorded, running from 200 to 250 in the aggregate, it may be perceived that the court, whose followers were at hand, would maintain a formidable influence. But this influence, however pernicious to the integrity of parliament, is distinguishable from that exertion of almost absolute prerogative which Hume has assumed as the sole spring of Elizabeth's government, and would never be employed till some deficiency of strength was experienced in the other.

Debate on election of non-resident burgesses.

D'Ewes has preserved a somewhat remarkable debate on a bill presented in the session of 1571, in order to render valid elections of non-resident burgesses. According to the tenor of the king's writ, confirmed by an act passed under Henry V., every city and borough was required to elect none but members of their own community. To this provision, as a seat in the commons' house grew more an object of general ambition, while many boroughs fell into comparative decay, less and less attention had been paid; till, the greater part of the borough representatives having become strangers, it was deemed, by some, expedient to repeal the ancient statute, and give a sanction to the innovation that time had wrought; while others contended in favor of the original usage, and seemed anxious to restore its vigor. It was alleged on the one hand, by Mr. Norton, that the bill would take away all pretence for sending unfit men, as was too often seen, and remove any objection that might be started to the sufficiency of the present parliament, wherein, for the most part, against positive law strangers to their several boroughs had been chosen: that persons able and fit for so great an employment ought to be preferred without regard to their inhabitancy; since a man could not be presumed to be the wiser for being a resident burgess: and that the whole body of the realm, and the service of the same, was rather to be respected than any private regard of place or person. This is a remarkable, and perhaps the earliest assertion, of an important constitutional principle, that each member of the house of commons is deputed to serve, not only for his constituents, but for the whole kingdom; a principle which marks the distinction between a modern English parliament and such deputations of the estates as were assembled in several continental kingdoms; a principle to which the house of commons is indebted for its weight and dignity, as well as its beneficial efficiency, and which none but the servile worshippers of the populace are ever found to gainsay. It is obvious that such a principle could never obtain currency, or even be advanced on any plausible ground, until the law for the election of resident burgesses had gone into disuse.

Those who defended the existing law, forgetting, as is often the case with the defenders of existing laws, that it had lost its practical efficacy, urged that the inferior ranks using manual and mechanical arts ought, like the rest, to be regarded and consulted with on matters which concerned them, and of which strangers could less judge. "We," said a member, "who have never seen Berwick or St. Michael's Mount, can but blindly guess of them, albeit we look on the maps that come from thence, or see letters of instruction sent; some one whom observation, experience, and due consideration of that country hath taught, can more perfectly open what shall in question thereof grow, and more effectually reason thereupon, than the skilfullest otherwise whatsoever." But the greatest mischief resulting from an abandonment of their old constitution would be the interference of noblemen with elections: lords' letters, it was said, would from henceforth bear the sway; instances of which, so late as the days of Mary, were alleged, though no one cared to allude particularly to anything of a more recent date. Some proposed to impose a fine of forty pounds on any borough making its election on a peer's nomination. The bill was committed by a majority; but, as no further entry appears in the Journals, we may infer it to have dropped.[1]

It may be mentioned, as not unconnected with this subject, that in the same session a fine was imposed on the borough of Westbury for receiving a bribe of four pounds from Thomas Long, "being a very simple man and of small capacity to serve in that place;" and the mayor was ordered to repay the money. Long, however, does not seem to have been expelled. This is the earliest precedent on record for the punishment of bribery in elections.[2]

We shall find an additional proof that the house of com-

[1] D'Ewes, 168. [2] Journals, p. 88.

mons under the Tudor princes, and especially Elizabeth, was not so feeble and insignificant an assembly as has been often insinuated, if we look at their frequent assertion and gradual acquisition of those peculiar authorities and immunities which constitute what is called privilege of parliament. Of these, the first, in order of time if not of importance, was their exemption from arrest on civil process during their session. Several instances occurred under the Plantagenet dynasty where this privilege was claimed and admitted; but generally by means of a distinct act of parliament, or at least by a writ of privilege out of chancery. The house of commons for the first time took upon themselves to avenge their own injury in 1543, when the remarkable case of George Ferrers occurred. This is related in detail by Hollingshed, and is perhaps the only piece of constitutional information we owe to him. Without repeating all the circumstances, it will be sufficient here to mention that the commons sent their sergeant with his mace to demand the release of Ferrers, a burgess who had been arrested on his way to the house; that the jailers and sheriffs of London having not only refused compliance, but ill-treated the sergeant, they compelled them, as well as the sheriffs of London, and even the plaintiff who had sued the writ against Ferrers, to appear at the bar of the house, and committed them to prison; and that the king, in the presence of the judges, confirmed in the strongest manner this assertion of privilege by the commons. It was, however, so far at least as our knowledge extends, a very important novelty in constitutional practice; not a trace occurring in any former instance on record, either of a party being delivered from arrest at the mere demand of the sergeant, or of any one being committed to prison by the sole authority of the house of commons. With respect to the first, the "chancellor," says Hollingshed, "offered to grant them a writ of privilege, which they of the commons' house refused, being of a clear opinion that all commandments and other acts proceeding from the nether house were to be done and executed by their sergeant without writ, only by show of his mace, which was his warrant." It might naturally seem to follow from this position, if it were conceded, that the house had the same power of attachment for contempt, that is, of commit-

Assertion of privileges by commons.

Case of Ferrers under Henry VIII.

ting to prison persons refusing obedience to lawful process, which our law attributes to all courts of justice, as essential to the discharge of their duties. The king's behavior is worthy of notice: while he dexterously endeavors to insinuate that the offence was rather against him than the commons, Ferrers happening to be in his service, he displays that cunning flattery towards them in their moment of exasperation which his daughter knew so well how to employ.[1]

Other cases of privilege.

Such important powers were not likely to be thrown away, though their exertion might not always be thought expedient. The commons had sometimes recourse to a writ of privilege in order to release their members under arrest, and did not repeat the proceeding in Ferrers's case till that of Smalley, a member's servant in 1575, whom they sent their sergeant to deliver. And this was only "after sundry reasons, arguments, and disputations," as the journal informs us; and, what is more, after rescinding a previous resolution that they could find no precedents for setting at liberty any one in arrest, except by writ of privilege.[2] It is to be observed that the privilege of immunity extended to the menial servants of members, till taken away by the statute of George III. Several persons however were, at different times, under Mary and Elizabeth, committed by the house to the Tower, or to the custody of their own sergeant, for assaults on their members.[3] Smalley himself, above mentioned, it having been discovered that he had fraudulently procured this arrest, in order to get rid of the debt, was committed for a month, and ordered to pay the plaintiff one hundred pounds, which was possibly the amount of what he owed.[4] One also, who had served a subpœna out

[1] Hollingshed, vol. iii. p. 824. (4to. edit.) Hatsell's Precedents, vol. i. p. 53. Mr. Hatsell inclines too much, in my opinion, to depreciate the authority of this case, imagining that it was rather as the king's servant than as a member of the house that Ferrers was delivered. But, though Henry artfully endeavors to rest it chiefly on this ground, it appears to me that the commons claim the privilege as belonging to themselves, without the least reference to this circumstance. If they did not always assert it afterwards, this negative presumption is very weak, when we consider how common it was to overlook or recede from precedents before the constitution had been reduced into a system. Carte, vol. iii. p. 164, endeavors to discredit the case of Ferrers as an absolute fable; and certainly points out some inaccuracy as to dates; but it is highly improbable that the whole should be an invention. He returns to the subject afterwards, p. 541, and, with a folly almost inconceivable even in a Jacobite, supposes the puritans to have fabricated the tale, and prevailed on Hollingshed to insert it in his history.

[2] Journals, Feb. 22d and 27th.

[3] Hatsell, 73, 92, 119.

[5] Id. 90.

of the star-chamber on a member in the session of 1584, was not only put in confinement, but obliged to pay the party's expenses before they would discharge him, making his humble submission on his knees.[1] This is the more remarkable, inasmuch as the chancellor had but just before made answer to a committee deputed "to signify to him how, by the ancient liberties of the house, the members thereof are privileged from being served with subpœnas," that "he thought the house had no such privilege, nor would he allow any precedents for it, unless they had also been ratified in the court of chancery."[2] They continued to enforce this summary mode of redress with no objection, so far as appears by any other authority, till, before the end of the queen's reign, it had become their established law of privilege "that no subpœna or summons for the attendance of a member in any other court ought to be served, without leave obtained or information given to the house; and that the persons who procured or served such process were guilty of a breach of privilege, and were punishable by commitment or otherwise, by the order of the house."[3] The great importance of such a privilege was the security it furnished, when fully claimed and acted upon, against those irregular detentions and examinations by the council, and which, in despite of the promised liberty of speech, had, as we have seen, oppressed some of their most distinguished members. But it must be owned that, by thus suspending all civil and private suits against themselves, the commons gave too much encouragement to needy and worthless men who sought their walls as a place of sanctuary.

This power of punishment, as it were for contempt, assumed in respect of those who molested members of the commons by legal process, was still more naturally applicable to offences against established order committed by any of themselves. In the earliest record that is extant of their daily proceedings, the Commons' Journal of the first parliament of Edward VI., we find, on the 21st January, 1547–8, a short entry of an order that John Storie, one of the burgesses, shall be committed to the custody of the sergeant. The order is repeated the next day; on the next, articles of accusation are read against Storie. It is ordered on the fol-

[1] Hatsell, 97. [2] Id. 96. [3] Id. 119.

lowing day that he shall be committed prisoner to the Tower. His wife soon after presents a petition, which is ordered to be delivered to the protector. On the 20th of February letters from Storie in the Tower are read. These probably were not deemed satisfactory, for it is not till the 2d of March that we have an entry of a letter from Mr. Storie in the Tower with his submission. And an order immediately follows, that "the king's privy council in the nether house shall humbly declare unto the lord protector's grace that the resolution of the house is, that Mr. Storie be enlarged, and at liberty, out of prison; and to require the king's majesty to forgive him his offences in this case towards his majesty and his council."

Storie was a zealous enemy of the Reformation, and suffered death for treason under Elizabeth. His temper appears to have been ungovernable; even in Mary's reign he fell a second time under the censure of the house for disrespect to the speaker. It is highly probable that his offence in the present instance was some ebullition of virulence against the changes in religion; for the first entry concerning him immediately follows the third reading of the bill that established the English liturgy. It is also manifest that he had to atone for language disrespectful to the protector's government, as well as to the house. But it is worthy of notice that the commons by their single authority commit their burgess first to their own officer, and next to the Tower; and that upon his submission they inform the protector of their resolution to discharge him out of custody, recommending him to forgiveness as to his offence against the council, which, as they must have been aware, the privilege of parliament as to words spoken within its walls (if we are right in supposing such to have been the case) would extend to cover. It would be very unreasonable to conclude that this is the first instance of a member's commitment by order of the house, the earlier journals not being in existence. Nothing indicates that the course taken was unprecedented. Yet on the other hand we can as little infer that it rested on any previous usage; and the times were just such in which a new precedent was likely to be established. The right of the house indeed to punish its own members for indecent abuse of the liberty of speech may be thought to result naturally from the king's concession of that liberty; and its right to preserve order in debate is plainly incident to that of debating at all.

In the subsequent reign of Mary Mr. Copley incurred the displeasure of the house for speaking irreverent words of her majesty, and was committed to the sergeant-at-arms; but the despotic character of that government led the commons to recede in some degree from the regard to their own privileges they had shown in the former case. The speaker was directed to declare this offence to the queen, and to request her mercy for the offender. Mary answered that she would well consider that request, but desired that Copley should be examined as to the cause of his behavior. A prorogation followed the same day, and of course no more took place in this affair.[1]

A more remarkable assertion of the house's right to inflict punishment on its own members occurred in 1581, and, being much better known than those I have mentioned, has been sometimes treated as the earliest precedent. One Arthur Hall, a burgess for Grantham, was charged with having caused to be published a book against the present parliament, on account of certain proceedings in the last session, wherein he was privately interested, "not only reproaching some particular good members of the house, but also very much slanderous and derogatory to its general authority, power, and state, and prejudicial to the validity of its proceedings in making and establishing of laws." Hall was the master of Smalley, whose case has been mentioned above, and had so much incurred the displeasure of the house by his supposed privity to the fraud of his servant, that a bill was brought in and read a first time, the precise nature of which does not appear, but expressed to be against him and two of his servants. It seems probable, from these and some other passages in the entries that occur on this subject in the journal, that Hall in his libel had depreciated the house of commons as an estate of parliament, and especially in respect of its privileges, pretty much in the strain which the advocates of prerogative came afterwards to employ. Whatever share therefore personal resentment may have had in exasperating the house, they had a public quarrel to avenge against one of their members, who was led by pique to betray their an-

[1] Journals, 5th and 7th March, 1557-8.

cient liberties. The vengeance of popular assemblies is not easily satisfied. Though Hall made a pretty humble submission, they went on, by a unanimous vote, to heap every punishment in their power upon his head. They expelled him, they imposed a fine of five hundred marks upon him, they sent him to the Tower until he should make a satisfactory retraction. At the end of the session he had not been released; nor was it the design of the commons that his imprisonment should then terminate; but their own dissolution, which ensued, put an end to the business.[1] Hall sat in some later parliaments. This is the leading precedent, as far as records show, for the power of expulsion, which the commons have ever retained without dispute of those who would most curtail their privileges. But in 1558 it had been put to the vote whether one outlawed and guilty of divers frauds should continue to sit, and carried in his favor by a very small majority; which affords a presumption that the right of expulsion was already deemed to appertain to the house.[2] They exercised it with no small violence in the session of 1585 against the famous Dr. Parry, who, having spoken warmly against the bill inflicting the penalty of death on jesuits and seminary priests, as being cruel and bloody, the commons not only ordered him into the custody of the sergeant, for opposing a bill approved of by a committee, and directed the speaker to reprimand him upon his knees, but, on his failing to make a sufficient apology, voted him no longer a burgess of that house.[3] The year afterwards Bland, a currier, was brought to their bar for using what were judged contumelious expressions against the house for something they had done in a matter of little moment, and discharged on account of his poverty, on making submission, and paying a fine of twenty shillings.[4] In this case they

[1] D'Ewes, 291. Hatsell, 93. The latter says, "I cannot but suspect that there was some private history in this affair, some particular offence against the queen, with which we are unacquainted." But I believe the explanation I have given will be thought more to the purpose; and, so far from having offended the queen, Hall seems to have had a patron in lord Burleigh, to whom he wrote many letters, complaining of the commons, which are extant in the Lansdowne collection. He appears to have been a man of eccentric and unpopular character, and had already incurred the displeasure of the commons in the session of 1572, when he was ordered to be warned by the sergeant to appear at the bar, "to answer for sundry lewd speeches used as well in the house as elsewhere." Another entry records him to have been "charged with seven several articles, but, having humbly submitted himself to the house and confessed his folly, to have been upon the question released with a good exhortation from the speaker." D'Ewes, 207, 212.

[2] Hatsell, 80.

[3] D'Ewes, 341.

[4] Id. 366. This case, though of con-

perhaps stretched their power somewhat farther than in the case of Arthur Hall, who, as one of their body, might seem more amenable to their jurisdiction.

Privilege of determining contested elections claimed by the house.

The commons asserted in this reign, perhaps for the first time, another and most important privilege, the right of determining all matters relative to their own elections. Difficulties of this nature had in former times been decided in chancery, from which the writ issued, and into which the return was made. Whether no cases of interference on the part of the house had occurred it is impossible to pronounce, on account of the unsatisfactory state of the rolls and journals of parliament under Edward IV., Henry VII., and Henry VIII. One remarkable entry, however, may be found in the reign of Mary, when a committee is appointed "to inquire if Alexander Nowell, prebendary of Westminster, may be of the house;" and it is declared next day by them that "Alexander Nowell, being prebendary in Westminster, and thereby having voice in the convocation house, cannot be a member of this house; and so agreed by the house, and the queen's writ to be directed for another burgess in his place."[1] Nothing further appears on record till in 1586 the house appointed a committee to examine the state and circumstances of the returns for the county of Norfolk. The fact was, that the chancellor had issued a second writ for this county, on the ground of some irregularity in the first return, and a different person had been elected. Some notice having been taken of this matter in the commons, the speaker received orders to signify to them her majesty's displeasure that "the house had been troubled with a thing impertinent for them to deal with, and only belonging to the charge and office of the lord chancellor, whom she had appointed to confer with the judges about the returns for the county of Norfolk, and to act therein according to justice and right." The house, in spite of this peremptory inhibition, proceeded to nominate a committee to examine into and report the circumstances of these returns; who reported the whole case, with their opinion that those elected on the first writ should take their

siderable importance, is overlooked by Hatsell, who speaks of that of Hall as the only one, before the long parliament, wherein the commons have punished the authors of libels derogatory to their privileges, p. 127. Though he mentions only libels, certainly the punishment of words spoken is at least as strong an exercise of power.

[1] Journals, 1 Mary, p. 27.

seats, declaring further that they understood the chancellor and some of the judges to be of the same opinion; but that "they had not thought it proper to inquire of the chancellor what he had done, because they thought it prejudicial to the privilege of the house to have the same determined by others than such as were members thereof. And though they thought very reverently of the said lord chancellor and judges, and knew them to be competent judges in their places; yet in this case they took them not for judges in parliament in this house: and thereupon required that the members, if it were so thought good, might take their oaths and be allowed of by force of the first writ, as allowed by the censure of this house, and not as allowed of by the said lord chancellor and judges. Which was agreed unto by the whole house."[1] This judicial control over their elections was not lost. A committee was appointed, in the session of 1589, to examine into sundry abuses of returns, among which is enumerated that some are returned for new places.[2] And several instances of the house's deciding on elections occur in subsequent parliaments.

This tenaciousness of their own dignity and privileges was shown in some disagreements with the upper house. They complained to the lords in 1597 that they had received a message from the commons at their bar without uncovering or rising from their places. But the lords proved, upon a conference, that this was agreeable to usage in the case of messages; though, when bills were brought up from the lower house, the speaker of the lords always left his place, and received them at the bar.[3] Another remonstrance of the commons, against having amendments to bills sent down to them on paper instead of parchment, seems a little frivolous, but serves to indicate a rising spirit, jealous of the superiority that the peers had arrogated.[4] In one point more material, and in which they had more precedent on their side, the commons successfully vindicated their privilege. The lords sent them a message in the session of 1593, reminding them of the queen's want of a supply, and requesting that a committee of conference might be appointed. This was accordingly done, and sir Robert Cecil reported from it that the lords would consent to nothing less than a grant of

[1] D'Ewes, 393, &c. [2] Id. 430. [3] Id. 539. [4] Id. 596.

three entire subsidies, the commons having shown a reluctance to give more than two. But Mr. Francis Bacon said, "he yielded to the subsidy, but disliked that this house should join with the upper house in granting it. For the custom and privilege of this house hath always been, first to make offer of the subsidies from hence, then to the upper house; except it were that they present a bill unto this house, with desire of our assent thereto, and then to send it up again." But the house were now so much awakened to the privilege of originating money-bills, that, in spite of all the exertions of the court, the proposition for another conference with the lords was lost on a division by 217 to 128.[1] It was by this opposition to the ministry in this session that Bacon, who acted perhaps full as much from pique towards the Cecils, and ambitious attachment to Essex, as from any real patriotism, so deeply offended the queen, that, with all his subsequent pliancy, he never fully reinstated himself in her favor.[2]

The English constitution not admitted to be an absolute monarchy.

That the government of England was a monarchy bounded by law, far unlike the actual state of the principal kingdoms on the continent, appears to have been so obvious and fundamental a truth, that flattery itself did not venture directly to contravene it. Hume has laid hold of a passage in Raleigh's preface to his History of the World (written indeed a few years later than the age of Elizabeth), as if it fairly represented public opinion as to our form of government. Raleigh says that Philip II. "attempted to make himself not only an absolute monarch over the Netherlands, like unto the kings and sovereigns of England and France; but, Turk-like, to tread under his feet all their national and fundamental laws, privileges, and ancient rights." But who, that was really desirous of establishing the truth, would have brought Raleigh into court as an unexceptionable witness on such a question? Unscrupulous ambition taught men in that age, who sought to win or regain the crown's favor, to falsify all

[1] D'Ewes, 486. Another trifling circumstance may be mentioned to show the rising spirit of the age. In the session of 1601, sir Robert Cecil having proposed that the speaker should *attend* the lord keeper about some matter, sir Edward Hobby took up the word in strong language, as derogatory to their dignity; and the secretary, who knew, as later ministers have done, that the commons are never so unmanageable as on such points of honor, made a proper apology. Id. 627.

[2] Birch's Memoirs, i. 97, 120, 152, &c., ii. 129. Bacon's Works, ii. 416, 435.

law and fact in behalf of prerogative, as unblushingly as our modern demagogues exaggerate and distort the liberties of the people.[1] The sentence itself, if designed to carry the full meaning that Hume assigns to it, is little better than an absurdity. For why were the rights and privileges of the Netherlands more fundamental than those of England? and by what logic could it be proved more Turk-like to impose the tax of the twentieth penny, or to bring Spanish troops into those provinces, in contravention of their ancient charters, than to transgress the Great Charter of this kingdom, with all those unrescinded statutes and those traditional unwritten liberties which were the ancient inheritance of its subjects? Or could any one, conversant in the slightest degree with the two countries, range in the same class of absolute sovereigns the kings of France and England? The arbitrary acts of our Tudor princes, even of Henry VIII., were trifling in comparison of the despotism of Francis I. and Henry II., who forced their most tyrannical ordinances down the throats of the parliament of Paris with all the violence of military usurpers. No permanent law had ever been attempted in England, nor any internal tax imposed, without consent of the people's representatives. No law in France had ever received such consent; nor had the taxes, enormously burdensome as they were in Raleigh's time, been imposed, for one hundred and fifty years past, by any higher authority than a royal ordinance. If a few nobler spirits had protested against the excessive despotism of the house of Valois; if La Boetie had drunk at the springs of classical republicanism; if Hottoman had appealed to the records of their freeborn ancestry that surrounded the throne of Clovis; if Languet had spoken in yet a bolder tone of a

1 Raleigh's Dedication of his Prerogative of Parliaments to James I. contains terrible things. "The bonds of subjects to their kings should always be wrought out of iron, the bonds of kings unto subjects but with cobwebs." — "All binding of a king by law upon the advantage of his necessity makes the breach itself lawful in a king; his charters and all other instruments being no other than the surviving witnesses of his unconstrained will." The object, however, of the book is to persuade the king to call a parliament (about 1613), and we are not to suppose that Raleigh meant what he said. He was never very scrupulous about truth. In another of his tracts, entitled "The Prince; or, Thesaurus of State," he holds, though not without flattery towards James, a more reasonable language. "In every just state some part of the government is or ought to be imparted to the people; as, in a kingdom, a voice or suffrage in making laws; and sometimes also in levying of arms, if the charge be great and the prince be forced to borrow help of his subjects, the matter rightly may be propounded to a parliament, that the tax may seem to have proceeded from themselves."

rightful resistance to tyranny;[1] if the jesuits and partisans of the League had cunningly attempted to win men's hearts to their faction by the sweet sounds of civil liberty and the popular origin of politic rule; yet these obnoxious paradoxes availed little with the nation, which, after the wild fanaticism of a rebellion arising wholly from religious bigotry had passed away, relapsed at once into its patient loyalty, its self-complacent servitude. But did the English ever recognize, even by implication, the strange parallels which Raleigh has made for their government with that of France, and Hume with that of Turkey? The language adopted in addressing Elizabeth was always remarkably submissive. Hypocritical adulation was so much among the vices of that age, that the want of it passed for rudeness. Yet Onslow, speaker of the parliament of 1566, being then solicitor-general, in addressing the queen, says, "By our common law, although there be for the prince provided many princely prerogatives and royalties, yet it is not such as the prince can take money or other things, or do as he will at his own pleasure without order, but quietly to suffer his subjects to enjoy their own, without wrongful oppression; wherein other princes by their liberty do take as pleaseth them."[2]

1 Le Contre Un of La Boetie, the friend of Montaigne, is, as the title intimates, a vehement philippic against monarchy. It is subjoined to some editions of the latter's essays. The Franco-Gallia of Hottoman contains little more than extracts from Fredegarius, Aimoin, and other ancient writers, to prove the elective character and general freedom of the monarchy under the two first races. This made a considerable impression at the time, though the passages in question have been so often quoted since, that we are now almost surprised to find the book so devoid of novelty. Hubert Languet's Vindiciæ contra Tyrannos, published under the name of Junius Brutus, is a more argumentative discussion of the rights of governors and their subjects.

2 D'Ewes, p. 115.

I have already adverted to Gardiner's resolute assertion of the law against the prince's single will, as a proof that, in spite of Hume's preposterous insinuations to the contrary, the English monarchy was known and acknowledged to be limited. Another testimony may be adduced from the words of a great protestant churchman. Archbishop Parker, writing to Cecil to justify himself for not allowing the queen's right to grant some dispensation in a case of marriage, says, "he would not dispute of the queen's absolute power, or prerogative royal, how far her highness might go in following the Roman authority; but he yet doubted that, if any dispensation should pass from her authority, to any subject, not avouchable by laws of her realm, made and established by herself and her three estates, whether that subject be in surety at all times afterwards: especially seeing there be parliament laws precisely determining cases of dispensations." Strype's Parker, 177.

Perhaps, however, there is no more decisive testimony to the established principles of limited monarchy in the age of Elizabeth than a circumstance mentioned in Anderson's Reports, 154. The queen had granted to Mr. Richard Cavendish an office for issuing certain writs, and directed the judges to admit him to it, which they neglected (that is, did not think fit) to do. Cavendish hereupon obtained a letter from her majesty, expressing her surprise that he was not admitted according to her grant, and commanding them to sequester the profits of the office for his use, or that of any other to whom these

In the first months of Elizabeth's reign, Aylmer, afterwards bishop of London, published an answer to a book by John Knox, against female monarchy, or, as he termed it, "Blast of the Trumpet against the Monstrous Regiment of Women," which, though written in the time of Mary, and directed against her, was, of course, not acceptable to her sister. The answerer relies, among other arguments, on the nature of the English constitution, which, by diminishing the power of the crown, renders it less unfit to be worn by a woman. "Well," he says, "a woman may not reign in

might appear to be due, as soon as the controversy respecting the execution of the said office should be decided. It is plain that some other persons were in possession of these profits, or claimed a right therein. The judges conceived that they could not lawfully act according to the said letter and command, because through such a sequestration of the emoluments those who claimed a right to issue the writs would be disseised of their freehold. The queen, informed that they did not obey the letter, sent another, under the sign-manual, in more positive language, ending in these words: "We look that you and every of you should dutifully fulfil our commandment herein, and these our letters shall be your warrant." 21st April, 1587. This letter was delivered to the justices in the presence of the chancellor and lord Leicester, who were commissioned to hear their answer, telling them also that the queen had granted the patent on account of her great desire to provide for Cavendish. The judges took a little time to consult what should be said; and, returning to the lords, answered that they desired in all respects humbly to obey her majesty; but, as this case is, could not do so without perjury, which they well knew the queen would not require, and so went away. Their answer was reported to the queen, who ordered the chancellor, chief justice of the king's bench, and master of the rolls, to hear the judges' reasons, and the queen's council were ordered to attend; when the queen's sergeant began to show the queen's prerogative to grant the issuing of writs, and showed precedents. The judges protested in answer that they had every wish to assist her majesty to all her rights, but said that this manner of proceeding was out of course of justice; and gave their reasons, that the right of issuing these writs and fees incident to it was in the prothonotaries and others, who claimed it by freehold; who ought to be made to answer, and not the judges, being more interested therein. This was certainly a little feeble, but they soon recovered themselves. They were then charged with having neglected to obey these letters of the queen; which they confessed, but said that this was no offence or contempt towards her majesty, because the command was against the law of the land; in which case, they said, no one is bound to obey such command. When further pressed, they said the queen herself was sworn to keep the laws as well as they; and that they could not obey this command without going against the laws directly and plainly, against their oaths, and to the offence of God, her majesty, the country and commonwealth in which they were born and live: so that, if the fear of God were gone from them, yet the examples of others, and the punishment of those who had formerly transgressed the laws, would remind them and keep them from such an offence. Then they cited the Spensers, and Thorp, a judge under Edward III., and precedents of Richard II.'s time, and of Empson, and the statutes of Magna Charta, which show what a crime it is for judges to infringe the laws of the land; and thus, since the queen and the judges were sworn to observe them, they said that they would not act as was commanded in these letters.

All this was repeated to her majesty for her good allowance of the said reasons, and which her majesty, as I have heard, says the reporter, took well; but nothing further was heard of the business. Such was the law and the government, which Mr. Hume has compared to that of Turkey! It is almost certain that neither James nor Charles would have made so discreet a sacrifice of their pride and arbitrary temper; and in this self-command lay the great superiority of Elizabeth's policy.

England! Better in England than anywhere, as it shall well appear to him that without affection will consider the kind of regiment. While I compare ours with other, as it is in itself, and not maimed by usurpation, I can find none either so good or so indifferent. The regiment of England is not a mere monarchy, as some for lack of consideration think, nor a mere oligarchy nor democracy, but a rule mixed of all these, wherein each one of these have, or should have, like authority. The image whereof, and not the image but the thing indeed, is to be seen in the parliament-house, wherein you shall find these three estates — the king or queen which representeth the monarchy, the noblemen which be the aristocracy, and the burgesses and knights the democracy. If the parliament use their privileges, the king can ordain nothing without them: if he do, it is his fault in usurping it, and their fault in permitting it. Wherefore, in my judgment, those that in king Henry VIII.'s days would not grant him that his proclamations should have the force of a statute were good fathers of the country, and worthy commendation in defending their liberty. But to what purpose is all this? To declare that it is not in England so dangerous a matter to have a woman ruler as men take it to be. For first, it is not she that ruleth, but the laws, the executors whereof be her judges appointed by her, her justices, and such other officers. Secondly, she maketh no statutes or laws, but the honorable court of parliament; she breaketh none, but it must be she and they together, or else not. If, on the other part, the regiment were such as all hanged on the king's or queen's will, and not upon the laws written; if she might decree and make laws alone without her senate; if she judged offences according to her wisdom, and not by limitation of statutes and laws; if she might dispose alone of war and peace; if, to be short, she were a mere monarch and not a mixed ruler, you might peradventure make me to fear the matter the more, and the less to defend the cause."[1]

This passage affords a proof of the doctrine current among Englishmen in 1559, and may, perhaps, be the less suspected as it does not proceed from a legal pen. And the quotations

[1] Harborowe of True and faithful Subjects, 1559. Most of this passage is quoted by Dr. M'Crie, in his Life of Knox, vol. i. note BB, to whom I am indebted for pointing it out.

I have made in the last chapter from Hooker are evidence still more satisfactory, on account of the gravity and judiciousness of the writer, that the same theory of the constitution prevailed in the later period of Elizabeth's reign. It may be observed that those who speak of the limitations of the sovereign's power, and of the acknowledged liberties of the subject, use a distinct and intelligible language, while the opposite tenets are insinuated by means of vague and obscure generalities, as in the sentence above quoted from Raleigh. Sir Thomas Smith, secretary of state to Elizabeth, has bequeathed us a valuable legacy in his treatise on the commonwealth of England. But undoubtedly he evades, as far as possible, all great constitutional principles, and treats them, if at all, with a vagueness and timidity very different from the tone of Fortescue. He thus concludes his chapter on the parliament: "This is the order and form of the highest and most authentical court of England, by virtue whereof all these things be established whereof I spoke before, and no other means accounted available to make any new *forfeiture of life, members, or lands*, of any Englishman, where there was no law ordered for it before."[1] This leaves no small latitude for the authority of royal proclamations, which the phrase, I make no question, was studiously adopted in order to preserve.

Pretensions of the crown.

There was unfortunately a notion very prevalent in the cabinet of Elizabeth, though it was not quite so broadly or at least so frequently promulgated as in the following reigns, that, besides the common prerogatives of the English crown, which were admitted to have legal bounds, there was a kind of paramount sovereignty, which they denominated her absolute power, incident, as they pretended, to the abstract nature of sovereignty, and arising out of its primary office of preserving the state from destruction. This seemed analogous to the dictatorial power which might be said to reside in the Roman senate, since it could confer it upon an individual. And we all must, in fact, admit that self-preservation is the first necessity of commonwealths as well as persons, which may justify, in Montesquieu's poetical language, the veiling of the statues of liberty. Thus martial law is proclaimed during an invasion, and

[1] Commonwealth of England, b. ii. c. 3.

houses are destroyed in expectation of a siege. But few governments are to be trusted with this insidious plea of necessity, which more often means their own security than that of the people. Nor do I conceive that the ministers of Elizabeth restrained this pretended absolute power, even in theory, to such cases of overbearing exigency. It was the misfortune of the sixteenth century to see kingly power strained to the highest pitch in the two principal European monarchies. Charles V. and Philip II. had crushed and trampled the ancient liberties of Castile and Aragon. Francis I. and his successors, who found the work nearly done to their hands, had inflicted every practical oppression upon their subjects. These examples could not be without their effect on a government so unceasingly attentive to all that passed on the stage of Europe.[1] Nor was this effect confined to the court of Elizabeth. A king of England, in the presence of absolute sovereigns, or perhaps of their ambassadors, must always feel some degree of that humiliation with which a young man, in check of a prudent father, regards the careless prodigality of the rich heirs with whom he associates. Good sense and elevated views of duty may subdue the emotion; but he must be above human nature who is insensible to the contrast.

There must be few of my readers who are unacquainted with the animated sketch that Hume has delineated of the English constitution under Elizabeth. It has been partly the object of the present chapter to correct his exaggerated outline; and nothing would be more easy than to point at other mistakes into which he has fallen through prejudice, through carelessness, or through want of acquaintance with law. His capital and inexcusable fault in everything he has written on our constitution is to have sought for evidence upon one side only of the question. Thus the remonstrance of the judges against arbitrary imprisonment by the council is infinitely more conclusive to prove that the right of personal liberty existed than the fact of its infringement can be to prove that it did not. There is something fallacious in the

[1] Bodin says the English ambassador, M. Dail (Mr. Dale), had assured him, not only that the king may assent to or refuse a bill as he pleases, but that il ne laisse pas d'en ordonner à son plaisir, et contre la volonté des estats, comme on a vu Henry VIII. avoir toujours use de sa puissance souveraine. He admitted, however, that taxes could only be imposed in parliament. De la République, l. i. c. 8.

negative argument which he perpetually uses, that, because we find no mention of any umbrage being taken at certain strains of prerogative, they must have been perfectly consonant to law. For if nothing of this could be traced, which is not so often the case as he represents it, we should remember that, even when a constant watchfulness is exercised by means of political parties and a free press, a nation is seldom alive to the transgressions of a prudent and successful government. The character which on a former occasion I have given of the English constitution under the house of Plantagenet may still be applied to it under the line of Tudor, that it was a monarchy greatly limited by law, but retaining much power that was ill-calculated to promote the public good, and swerving continually into an irregular course, which there was no restraint adequate to correct. It may be added that the practical exercise of authority seems to have been less frequently violent and oppressive, and its legal limitations better understood, in the reign of Elizabeth than for some preceding ages; and that sufficient indications had become distinguishable before its close, from which it might be gathered that the seventeenth century had arisen upon a race of men in whom the spirit of those who stood against John and Edward was rekindled with a less partial and a steadier warmth.[1]

[1] The misrepresentations of Hume as to the English constitution under Elizabeth, and the general administration of her reign, have been exposed, since the present chapter was written, by Mr. Brodie, in his History of the British Empire from the accession of Charles I. to the Restoration, vol. i. c. 3. In some respects, Mr. B. seems to have gone too far in an opposite system, and to represent the practical course of government as less arbitrary than I can admit it to have been.

CHAPTER VI.

ON THE ENGLISH CONSTITUTION UNDER JAMES I.

Quiet Accession of James — Question of his Title to the Crown — Legitimacy of the Earl of Hertford's Issue — Early Unpopularity of the King — Conduct towards the Puritans — Parliament convoked by an irregular Proclamation — Question of Fortescue and Goodwin's Election — Shirley's Case of Privilege — Complaints of Grievances — Commons' Vindication of themselves — Session of 1605 — Union with Scotland debated — Continual Bickerings between the Crown and Commons — Impositions on Merchandise without Consent of Parliament — Remonstrances against these in Session of 1610 — Doctrine of King's absolute Power inculcated by Clergy — Articuli Cleri — Cowell's Interpreter — Renewed Complaints of the Commons — Negotiation for giving up the Feudal Revenue — Dissolution of Parliament — Character of James — Death of Lord Salisbury — Foreign Politics of the Government — Lord Coke's Alienation from the Court — Illegal Proclamations — Means resorted to in Order to avoid the Meeting of Parliament — Parliament of 1614 — Undertakers — It is dissolved without passing a single Act — Benevolences — Prosecution of Peacham — Dispute about the Jurisdiction of the Court of Chancery — Case of Commendams — Arbitrary Proceedings in Star Chamber — Arabella Stuart — Somerset and Overbury — Sir Walter Raleigh — Parliament of 1621 — Proceedings against Mompesson and Lord Bacon — Violence in the Case of Floyd — Disagreement between the King and Commons — Their Dissolution after a strong Remonstrance — Marriage Treaty with Spain — Parliament of 1624 — Impeachment of Middlesex.

Quiet accession of James.

IT might afford an illustration of the fallaciousness of political speculations to contrast the hopes and inquietudes that agitated the minds of men concerning the inheritance of the crown during Elizabeth's lifetime, while not less than fourteen titles were idly or mischievously reckoned up, with the perfect tranquillity which accompanied the accession of her successor.[1] The house of

[1] Father Persons, a subtle and lying jesuit, published in 1594, under the name of Doleman, a treatise entitled "Conference about the next Succession to the Crown of England." This book is dedicated to Lord Essex, whether from any hopes entertained of him, or, as was then supposed, in order to injure his fame and his credit with the queen. Sidney Papers, i. 357. Birch's Memoirs, i. 313. It is written with much art, to show the extreme uncertainty of the succession, and to perplex men's minds by multiplying the number of competitors. This however is but the second part of his Conference, the aim of the first being to prove the right of commonwealths to depose sovereigns, much more to exclude the right heir, especially for want of true religion. "I affirm and hold," he says, "that for any man to give his help, consent, or assistance towards the making of a king whom he judgeth or believeth to be faulty in religion, and consequently would advance either no religion, or the wrong, if he were in authority, is a most grievous and damnable sin to him that doth it, of what side soever the truth be, or how good or bad soever the party be that is preferred." P. 216. He pretends to have found very few who favor the king of Scots' title; an assertion by which we may appreciate his veracity. The protestant party, he tells us, was

Suffolk, whose claim was legally indisputable, if we admit the testament of Henry VIII. to have been duly executed, appear, though no public inquiry had been made into that fact, to have lost ground in popular opinion, partly through an unequal marriage of lord Beauchamp with a private gentleman's daughter, but still more from a natural disposition to favor the hereditary line rather than the capricious disposition of a sovereign long since dead, as soon as it became consistent with the preservation of the reformed faith. Leicester once hoped, it is said, to place his brother-in-law, the earl of Huntingdon, descended from the duke of Clarence, upon the throne; but this pretension had been entirely forgotten. The more intriguing and violent of the catholic party, after the death of Mary, entertaining little hope that the king of Scots would abandon the principles of his education, sought to gain support to a pretended title in the king of Spain, or his daughter the infanta, who afterwards married the archduke Albert, governor of the Netherlands. Others, abhorring so odious a claim, looked to Arabella Stuart, daughter of the earl of Lennox, younger brother of

wont to favor the house of Hertford, but of late have gone more towards Arabella, whose claim the lord Burleigh is supposed to countenance. P. 241. The drift of the whole is to recommend the infanta by means of perverted history and bad law, yet ingeniously contrived to ensnare ignorant persons. In his former and more celebrated treatise, Leicester's Commonwealth, though he harps much on the embarrassments attending the succession, Persons argues with all his power in favor of the Scottish title, Mary being still alive, and James's return to the faith not desperate. Both these works are full of the mendacity generally and justly ascribed to his order; yet they are worthy to be read by any one who is curious about the secret politics of the queen's reign.

Philip II. held out assurances that, if the English would aid him in dethroning Elizabeth, a free parliament should elect any catholic sovereign at their pleasure, not doubting that their choice would fall on the infanta. He promised also to enlarge the privileges of the people, to give the merchants a free trade to the Indies, with many other flattering inducements. Birch's Memoirs, ii. 308. But most of the catholic gentry, it is just to observe, would never concur in the invasion of the kingdom by foreigners, preferring the elevation of Arabella, according to the pope's project. This difference of opinion gave rise, among other causes, to the violent dissensions of that party in the latter years of Elizabeth's reign; dissensions that began soon after the death of Mary, in favor of whom they were all united, though they could never afterwards agree on any project for the succession. Winwood's Memorials, i. 57. Lettres du Cardinal d'Ossat, ii. 501.

For the life and character of the famous Father Persons, or Parsons, above mentioned, see Dodd's Church History, the Biographia Britannica, or Miss Aikin's James I., i. 360. Mr. Butler is too favorably inclined towards a man without patriotism or veracity. Dodd plainly thinks worse of him than he dares speak. [Several letters of considerable historical importance, relative to the catholic intrigues as to the succession, are lately published in Tierney's edition of Dodd's Church History, vol. iii. A considerable part of the catholics, especially those who had looked up to Mary personally as their rallying point, adhered to the Scottish title; and those of course were the best Englishmen. Persons and his Spanish faction, whose letters appear in the work above quoted, endeavor to depreciate them. I must add that Mr. T. does not by any means screen this last party. 1845.]

James's father, and equally descended from the stock of Henry VII., sustaining her manifest defect of primogeniture by her birth within the realm, according to the principle of law that excluded aliens from inheritance. But this principle was justly deemed inapplicable to the crown. Clement VIII., who had no other view than to secure the reëstablishment of the catholic faith in England, and had the judgment to perceive that the ascendency of Spain would neither be endured by the nation nor permitted by the French king, favored this claim of Arabella, who, though apparently of the reformed religion, was rather suspected at home of wavering in her faith, and entertained a hope of marrying her to the cardinal Farnese, brother of the duke of Parma.[1] Considerations of public interest, however, unequivocally pleaded for the Scottish line; the extinction of long sanguinary feuds, and the consolidation of the British empire. Elizabeth herself, though by no means on terms of sincere friendship with James, and harassing him by intrigues with his subjects to the close of her life, seems to have always designed that he should inherit her crown. And the general expectation of what was to follow, as well from conviction of his right as from the impracticability of any effectual competition, had so thoroughly paved the way that the council's proclamation of the king of Scots excited no more commotion than that of an heir apparent.[2]

[1] D'Ossat, ubi suprà. Clement had, some years before, indulged the idle hope that France and Spain might unite to conquer England, and either bestow the kingdom on some catholic prince, or divide it between themselves, as Louis XII. and Ferdinand had done with Naples in 1501; an example not very inviting to the French. D'Ossat, Henry's minister at Rome, pointed out the difficulties of such an enterprise, England being the greatest naval power in the world, and the people warlike. The pope only replied that the kingdom had been once conquered, and might be so again; and especially being governed by an old woman, whom he was ignorant enough to compare with Joanna II. of Naples. Vol. i. 399. Henry IV. would not even encourage the project of setting up Arabella, which he declared to be both unjust and chimerical. Mém. de Sully, l. 15. A knot of protestants were also busy about the interests of Arabella, or suspected of being so; Raleigh, Cobham, Northumberland, though perhaps the last was a catholic. Their intrigues occupy a great part of the letters of other intriguers, Cecil and lord Henry Howard, in the Secret Correspondence with king James, published by sir David Dalrymple, vol. i. passim.

[2] The explicit declaration on her deathbed, ascribed to her by Hume and most other writers, that her kinsman the king of Scots should succeed her, is not confirmed by Carey, who was there at the time. "She was speechless when the council proposed the king of Scots to succeed her, but put her hand to her head as if in token of approbation." E. of Monmouth's Memoirs, p. 176. But her uniform conduct shows her intentions. See, however, D'Israeli's Curiosities of Literature, iii. 107. [A remarkable account of Elizabeth's last days will be found in Dodd's Church History; it appears to have been written by lady Southwell, an eye-witness, who had been one of the queen's maids of honor. Tierney's edition of Dodd, vol. iii. p. 70. And this account is confirmed, so as to make it fully trustworthy, by a report

Question of his title to the crown.

The popular voice in favor of James was undoubtedly raised in consequence of a natural opinion that he was the lawful heir to the throne. But this was only according to vulgar notions of right which respect hereditary succession as something indefeasible. In point of fact, it is at least very doubtful whether James I. were a legitimate sovereign, according to the sense which that word ought properly to bear. The house of Stuart no more came in by a clear title than the house of Brunswick; by such a title, I mean, as the statute laws of this kingdom had recognized. No private man could have recovered an acre of land without proving a better right than they could make out to the crown of England. What, then, had James to rest upon? What renders it absurd to call him and his children usurpers? He had that which the flatterers of his family most affected to disdain — the will of the people; not certainly expressed in regular suffrage or declared election, but unanimously and voluntarily ratifying that which in itself could surely give no right, the determination of the late queen's council to proclaim his accession to the throne.

It is probable that what has been just said may appear rather paradoxical to those who have not considered this part of our history, yet it is capable of satisfactory proof. This proof consists of four propositions: 1. That a lawful king of England, with the advice and consent of parliament, may make statutes to limit the inheritance of the crown, as shall

from Beaumont, the French ambassador, published in Raumer's History of the 16th and 17th Centuries illustrated. London, 1835, vol. ii. p. 188.

The famous story of Essex's ring, delivered by the countess of Nottingham in her dying hours to the queen, has been rejected by modern writers, as only to be traced to some memoirs published in Holland eighty years afterwards. It may be considered, whether it derives any kind of confirmation from a passage in Raumer, ii. 166. — 1845.]

It is impossible to justify Elizabeth's conduct towards James in his own kingdom. What is best to be said for it is, that his indiscretion, his suspicious intrigues at Rome and Madrid, the dangerous influence of his favorites, and the evident purpose of the court of Spain to make him its tool, rendered it necessary to keep a very strict watch over his proceedings. If she excited the peers and presbyters of Scotland against their king, he was not behind her in some of the last years of her reign. It appears, by a letter from the Earl of Mar, in Dalrymple's Secret Correspondence, p. 2, that James had hopes of a rebellion in England in 1601, which he would have had no scruple in abetting. And in a letter from him to Tyrone, in the Lansdowne MSS. lxxxiv. 36, dated 22d Dec. 1597, when the latter was at least preparing for rebellion, though rather cautious, is full of expressions of favor, and of promises to receive his assistance thankfully at the queen's death. This letter, being found in the collection once belonging to sir Michael Hicks, must have been in lord Burleigh's and probably in Elizabeth's hands; it would not make her less inclined to instigate conspiracies across the Tweed. The letter is not an original, and may have been communicated by some one about the king of Scots in the pay of England.

seem fit; 2. That a statute passed in the 35th year of king Henry VIII. enabled that prince to dispose of the succession by his last will signed with his own hand; 3. That Henry executed such a will, by which, in default of issue from his children, the crown was entailed upon the descendants of his younger sister, Mary duchess of Suffolk, before those of Margaret queen of Scots; 4. That such descendants of Mary were living at the decease of Elizabeth.

Of these propositions, the two former can require no support; the first being one that it would be perilous to deny, and the second asserting a notorious fact. A question has, however, been raised with respect to the third proposition; for though the will of Henry, now in the chapter-house at Westminster, is certainly authentic, and is attested by many witnesses, it has been doubted whether the signature was made with his own hand, as required by the act of parliament. In the reign of Elizabeth it was asserted by the queen of Scots' ministers that, the king being at the last extremity, some one had put a stamp for him to the instrument.[1] It is true that he was in the latter part of his life accustomed to employ a stamp instead of making his signature. Many impressions of this are extant; but it is evi-

[1] See Burnet, vol. i. Appendix, 267, for secretary Lethington's letter to Cecil, where he tells a circumstantial story so positively, and so open, if false, to a contradiction it never received, that those who lay too much stress on this very equivocal species of presumption would, if the will had perished, have reckoned its forgery beyond question. The king's death approaching, he asserts, "some as well known to you as to me caused William Clarke, sometimes servant to Thomas Heneage, to sign the supposed will with a stamp, for otherwise signed it was never;" for which he appeals to an attestation of the late lord Paget in parliament, and requests the depositions of several persons now living to be taken. He proceeds to refer him "to the original will surmised to be signed with the king's own hand, that thereby, it may most clearly and evidently appear by some differences how the same was not signed with the king's hand, but stamped as aforesaid. And albeit it is used both as an argument and calumniation against my sovereign by some, that the said original hath been embezzled in queen Mary's time, I trust God will and hath reserved the same to be an instrument to relieve [prove] the truth, and to confound false surmises, that thereby the right may take place, notwithstanding the many exemplifications and transcripts, which, being sealed with the great seal, do run abroad in England." Lesley, bishop of Ross, repeats the same story with some additions. Bedford's Hereditary Right, p. 197. A treatise of Hales, for which he suffered imprisonment, in defence of the Suffolk title under the will, of which there is a manuscript in the British Museum, Harl. MSS. 537, and which is also printed in the appendix to the book last quoted, leads me to conjecture that the original will had been mislaid or rather concealed at that time. For he certainly argues on the supposition that it was not forthcoming, and had not himself seen it; but, "he has been informed that the king's name is evidently written with a pen, though some of the strokes are unseen, as if drawn by a weak and trembling hand." Every one who has seen the will must bear witness to the correctness of this information. The reappearance of this very remarkable instrument was, as I conceive, after the Revolution; for Collier mentions that he had heard it was in existence; and it is also described in a note to the Acta Regia.

dent on the first inspection not only that the presumed autographs in the will (for there are two) are not like these impressions, but that they are not the impressions of any stamp, the marks of the pen being very clearly discernible. It is more difficult to pronounce that they may not be feigned, but such is not the opinion of some who are best acquainted with Henry's handwriting;[1] and what is still more to the purpose, there is no pretence for setting up such a possibility, when the story of the stamp, as to which the partisans of Mary pretended to adduce evidence, appears so clearly to be a fabrication. We have, therefore, every reasonable ground to maintain that Henry did duly execute a will postponing the Scots line to that of Suffolk.

The fourth proposition is in itself undeniable. There were descendants of Mary duchess of Suffolk, by her two daughters, Frances, second duchess of Suffolk, and Eleanor countess of Cumberland. A story had, indeed, been circulated that Charles Brandon, duke of Suffolk, was already married to a lady of the name of Mortimer at the time of his union with the king's sister. But this circumstance seems to be sufficiently explained in the treatise of Hales.[2] It is somewhat more questionable from which of his two daughters we are to derive the hereditary stock. This depends on the legitimacy of lord Beauchamp, son of the earl of Hertford by Catherine Grey. I have mentioned in another place the process before a commission appointed by Elizabeth, which ended in declaring that their marriage was not proved, and that their cohabitation had been illicit. The parties alleged themselves to have been married clandestinely in the earl of Hertford's house by a minister whom they had never before seen, and of whose name they were ignorant, in the presence only of a sister of the earl then deceased. This entire absence of testimony, and the somewhat improbable nature of the story, at least in appearance, may still, perhaps, leave a shade of doubt as to the reality of the marriage. On the other hand, it was unquestionable that their object must have been a legitimate union; and such a hasty and furtive ceremony as they

Legitimacy of the earl of Hertford's issue.

[1] It is right to mention that some difference of opinion exists as to the genuineness of Henry's signature. But as it is attested by many witnesses, and cannot be proved a forgery, the legal presumption turns much in its favor.

[2] Bedford's (Harbin's) Hereditary Right Asserted, p. 204.

asserted to have taken place, while it would, if sufficiently proved, be completely valid, was necessary to protect them from the queen's indignation. They were examined separately upon oath to answer a series of the closest interrogatories, which they did with little contradiction, and a perfect agreement in the main; nor was any evidence worth mentioning adduced on the other side; so that, unless the rules of the ecclesiastical law are scandalously repugnant to common justice, their oaths entitled them to credit on the merits of the case.[1] The earl of Hertford, soon after the tranquil accession of James, having long abandoned all ambitious hopes, and seeking only to establish his children's legitimacy and the honor of one who had been the victim of their unhappy loves, petitioned the king for a review of the proceedings, alleging himself to have vainly sought this at the hands of Elizabeth. It seems probable, though I have not met with any more distinct proof of it than a story in Dugdale, that he had been successful in finding the person who solemnized the marriage.[2] A commission of delegates was accordingly appointed to investigate the allegations of the earl's petition. But the jealousy that had so long oppressed this unfortunate family was not yet at rest. Questions seem to have been raised as to the lapse of time and other technical difficulties, which served as a pretext for coming to no determination on the merits.[3] Hertford, or rather his son, not long after, endeavored indirectly to bring forward the main question by means of a suit for some lands against lord

[1] A manuscript in the Cottonian Library, Faustina, A. xi., written about 1562, in a very hostile spirit, endeavors to prove, from the want of testimony, and from some variances in their depositions (not very material ones), that their allegations of matrimony could not be admitted, and that they had incurred an ecclesiastical censure for fornication. But another, which I have also found in the Museum, Harl. MSS. 6286, contains the whole proceedings and evidence, from which I have drawn the conclusion in the text. Their ignorance of the clergyman who performed the ceremony is not perhaps very extraordinary; he seems to have been one of those vagabond ecclesiastics who till the marriage act of 1752 were always ready to do that service for a fee.

[2] "Hereupon I shall add, what I have heard related from persons of great credit, which is, that the validity of this marriage was afterwards brought to a trial at the common law; when the minister who married them being present, and other circumstances agreeing, the jury (whereof John Digby of Coleshill, in com. War., esquire, was the foreman) found it a good marriage." Baronage of England, part ii. 369. Mr. Luders doubts the accuracy of Dugdale's story; and I think it not unlikely that it is a confused account of what happened in the court of wards.

[3] I derive this fact from a Cotton MS. Vitellius, C. xvi. 412, &c.; but the volume is much burned, and the papers confused with others relative to Lord Essex's divorce. See as to the same suit, or rather perhaps that mentioned in the next note, Birch's Negotiations, p. 219, or Aikin's James the First, i. 225.

Monteagle. This is said to have been heard in the court of wards, where a jury was impanelled to try the fact. But the law officers of the crown interposed to prevent a verdict, which, though it could not have been legally conclusive upon the marriage, would certainly have given a sanction to it in public opinion.[1] The house of Seymour was now compelled to seek a renewal of its honors by another channel. Lord Beauchamp, as he had uniformly been called, took a grant of the barony of Beauchamp, and another of the earldom of Hertford, to take effect upon the death of the earl, who is not denominated his father in the patent.[2] But after the return of Charles II., in the patent restoring this lord Beauchamp's son to the dukedom of Somerset, he is recited to be heir male of the body of the first duke by his wife Anne, which establishes (if the recital of a private act of parliament can be said to establish anything) the validity of the disputed marriage.[3]

The descent from the younger daughter of Mary Brandon, Eleanor, who married the earl of Cumberland, is subject to no difficulties. She left an only daughter, married to the earl of Derby, from whom the claim devolved again upon females, and seems to have attracted less notice during the reign of Elizabeth than some others much inferior in plausibility. If any should be of opinion that no marriage was regularly contracted between the earl of Hertford and lady Catherine Grey, so as to make their children capable of inheritance, the title to the crown, resulting from the statute of 35 H. VIII. and the testament of that prince, will have descended at the death of Elizabeth on the issue of the countess

1 "The same day a great cause between the Lord Beauchamp and Monteagle was heard in the court of wards, the main point whereof was to prove the lawfulness of E. of Hertford's marriage. The court sat until five of the clock in the afternoon, and the jury had a week's respite for the delivery of their verdict." Letter of Sir E. Hoby to Sir T. Edmonds, Feb. 10, 1606. "For my lord of Hertford's cause, when the verdict was ready to be given up, Mr. Attorney interposed himself for the king, and said that the land that they both strove for was the king's, and, until his title were decided, the jury ought not to proceed; not doubting but the king will be gracious to both lords. But thereby both land and legitimation remain undecided." The same to the same, March 7. Sloane MSS. 4176.

2 Dugdale's Baronage. Luder's Essay on the Right of Succession to the Crown in the Reign of Elizabeth. This ingenious author is, I believe, the first who has taken the strong position as to the want of legal title to the house of Stuart which I have endeavored to support. In the entertaining letters of Joseph Mede on the news of the day, Harl. MSS. 389, it is said that the king had thought of declaring Hertford's issue by lady Catherine Grey illegitimate in the parliament of 1621, and that lord Southampton's commitment was for having searched for proofs of their marriage. June 30, 1622.

3 Luders, ubi suprà.

of Cumberland, the youngest daughter of the duchess of Suffolk, lady Frances Keyes, having died without issue.[1] In neither case could the house of Stuart have a lawful claim. But I may, perhaps, have dwelled too long on a subject which, though curious and not very generally understood, can be of no sort of importance, except as it serves to cast ridicule upon those notions of legitimate sovereignty and absolute right which it was once attempted to set up as paramount even to the great interests of a commonwealth.

There is much reason to believe that the consciousness of this defect in his parliamentary title put James on magnifying, still more than from his natural temper he was prone to do, the inherent rights of primogenitary succession as something indefeasible by the legislature; a doctrine which, however it might suit the schools of divinity, was in diametrical opposition to our statutes.[2] Through the servile spirit of those times, however, it made a rapid progress; and, interwoven by cunning and bigotry with religion, became a distinguishing tenet of the party who encouraged the Stuarts to subvert the liberties of this kingdom. In James's proclamation on ascending the throne he set forth his hereditary right in pompous and perhaps unconstitutional phrases. It was the first measure of parliament to pass an act of recognition, acknowledging that immediately on the decease of Elizabeth "the imperial crown of the realm of England did, by inherent birthright and lawful and undoubted succession, descend and come to his most excellent majesty, as being lineally, justly, and lawfully next and sole heir of the blood royal of this realm." [3] The will of Henry VIII. it was tacitly agreed by all parties to consign to oblivion: and this most wisely, not on the principles which seem rather too

[1] I have not adverted to one objection which some urged at the time, as we find by Persons's treatises, Leicester's Commonwealth, and The Conference. to the legitimacy of the Seymours. Catherine Grey had been betrothed, or perhaps married, to lord Herbert, son of the earl of Pembroke, during the brilliant days of her family, at the close of Edward's reign. But, on her father's fall, Pembroke caused a sentence of divorce to be pronounced, the grounds of which do not appear, but which was probably sufficient in law to warrant her subsequent union with Hertford. No advantage is taken of this in the proceedings, which seems to show that there was no legal bond remaining between the parties. Camden says she was divorced from lord Herbert, "being so far gone with child as to be very near her time." But, from her youth at the time, and the silence of all other writers, I conclude this to be unworthy of credit.

[2] Bolingbroke is of this opinion, considering the act of recognition as "the era of hereditary right, and of all those exalted notions concerning the power of prerogative of kings and the sacredness of their persons." Dissertation on Parties, Letter II.

[3] Stat. 1 Jac. c. 1.

much insinuated in this act of recognition, but on such substantial motives of public expediency as it would have shown an equal want of patriotism and of good sense for the descendants of the house of Suffolk to have withstood.

James left a kingdom where his authority was incessantly thwarted, and sometimes openly assailed, for one wherein the royal prerogative had for more than a century been strained to a very high pitch, and where there had not occurred for above thirty years the least appearance of rebellion, and hardly of tumult. Such a posture of the English commonwealth, as well as the general satisfaction testified at his accession, seemed favorable circumstances to one who entertained, with less disguise, if not with more earnestness, than most other sovereigns, the desire of reigning with as little impediment as possible to his own will. Yet some considerations might have induced a prince who really possessed the king-craft wherein James prided himself, to take his measures with caution. The late queen's popularity had remarkably abated during her last years.[1] It is a very common delusion of royal personages to triumph in the people's dislike of those into whose place they expect shortly to come, and to count upon the most transitory of possessions, a favor built on hopes that they cannot realize, and discontents that they will not assuage. If Elizabeth lost a great deal of that affection her subjects had entertained for her, this may be ascribed not so much to Essex's death, though that no doubt had its share, as to weightier taxation, to some oppressions of her government, and above all to her inflexible tenaciousness in every point of ecclesiastical discipline. It was the part of a prudent successor to preserve an undeviating economy, to remove without repugnance or delay the irritations of monopolies and purveyance, and to remedy those alleged abuses in the church against which the greater and stronger part of the nation had so long and so loudly raised its voice.

[1] This is confirmed by a curious little tract in the British Museum, Sloane MSS. 827, containing a short history of the queen's death and new king's accession. It affords a good contemporary illustration of the various feelings which influenced men at this crisis, and is written in a dispassionate manner. The author ascribes the loss of Elizabeth's popularity to the impoverishment of the realm, and to the abuses which prevailed. Carte says, "foreigners were shocked on James's arrival at the applause of the populace, who had professed to adore the late queen, but in fact she had no huzzas after Essex's execution. She was in four days' time as much forgot as if she had never existed, by all the world, and even by her own servants." Vol. iii. p. 707. This is exaggerated, and what Carte could not know; but there is no doubt that the generality were glad of a change.

The new king's character, notwithstanding the vicinity of Scotland, seems to have been little understood by the English at his accession. But he was not long in undeceiving them, if it be true that his popularity had vanished away before his arrival in London.[1] The kingdom was full of acute wits and skilful politicians, quick enough to have seen through a less unguarded character than that of James. It was soon manifest that he was unable to wield the sceptre of the great princess whom he ridiculously affected to despise, so as to keep under that rising spirit which might perhaps have grown too strong even for her control.[2] He committed an important error in throwing away the best opportunity that had offered itself for healing the wounds of the church of England. In his way to London the malecontent clergy presented to him what was commonly called the Millenary Petition, as if signed by 1000 ministers, though the real number was not so great.[3] This petition contained no de-

Early unpopularity of the king.

Conduct towards the puritans.

[1] Carte, no foe surely to the house of Stuart, says, "By the time he reached London the admiration of the intelligent world was turned into contempt." On this journey he gave a remarkable proof of his hasty temper and disregard of law, in ordering a pickpocket taken in the fact to be hanged without trial. The historian last quoted thinks fit to say, in vindication, that "all felonies committed within the verge of the court are cognizable in the court of the king's household," referring to 33 H. 8, c. 1. This act however contains no such thing; nor does any court appear to have been held. Though the man's notorious guilt might prevent any open complaint of so illegal a proceeding, it did not fail to excite observation. "I hear our new king," says sir John Harrington, "has hanged one man before he was tried; it is strangely done: now, if the wind bloweth thus, why may not a man be tried before he has offended?" Nugæ Antiquæ, vol. i. p. 180.

Birch and Carte tells us, on the authority of the French ambassador's despatches, that on this journey he expressed a great contempt for women, suffering them to be presented on their knees, and indiscreetly censuring his own wife; that he offended the military men by telling them they might sheathe their swords, since peace was his object; that he showed impatience of the common people, who flocked to see him while hunting, driving them away with curses, very unlike the affable manners of the late queen. This is confirmed by Wilson, in Kennet's Complete History, vol. ii. p. 667.

[It is also mentioned in the extracts from the reports of Beaumont, the French ambassador, published in Raumer's Illustrations of the History of the 16th and 17th Centuries. (Lord F. Egerton's translation, 1835, vol. ii. pp. 196, 202.) These extracts give a most unfavorable picture of the conduct of James at his accession, as those from other ambassadors do at a later period.]

[2] Sully, being sent over to compliment James on his accession, persisted in wearing mourning for Elizabeth, though no one had done so in the king's presence, and he was warned that it would be taken ill "dans une cour où il sembloit qu'on eût si fort affecté de mettre en oubli cette grande reine, qu'on n'y faisoit jamais mention d'elle, et qu'on évitoit même de prononcer son nom." Mém. de Sully, l. 14. James afterwards spoke slightingly to Sully of his predecessor, and said that he had long ruled England through her ministers.

[3] It was subscribed by 825 ministers from twenty-five counties. It states that neither as factious men desiring a popular party in the church, nor as schismatics aiming at the dissolution of the state ecclesiastical, they humbly desired the redress of some abuses. Their objections were chiefly to the cap and surplice, the cross in baptism, baptism by women, confirmation, the ring in marriage, the read-

mand inconsistent with the established hierarchy. James, however, who had not unnaturally taken an extreme disgust at the presbyterian clergy of his native kingdom, by whom his life had been perpetually harassed, showed no disposition to treat these petitioners with favor.[1] The bishops had promised him an obsequiousness to which he had been little accustomed, and a zeal to enhance his prerogative which they afterwards too well displayed. His measures towards the nonconformist party had evidently been resolved upon before he summoned a few of their divines to the famous conference at Hampton Court. In the accounts that we read of this meeting we are alternately struck with wonder at the indecent and partial behavior of the king, and at the abject baseness of the bishops, mixed, according to the custom of servile natures, with insolence towards their opponents.[2] It was easy for a monarch and eighteen churchmen to claim the victory, be the merits of their dispute what they might, over four abashed and intimidated adversaries.[3] A very few alterations were made in the church-service after this conference, but not of such moment as to reconcile probably a single minister to the established discipline.[4] The king soon afterwards put forth a proclamation requiring all ecclesiastical and civil officers to do their duty by enforcing conformity, and admonishing all men not to expect nor attempt any further alteration in the public service; for "he would

ing of the Apocrypha, bowing at the name of Jesus, &c.; to non-residence and incapable ministers, the commendams held by bishops, unnecessary excommunications, and other usual topics. Neal, p. 408; Fuller, part ii. p. 22.

[1] The puritans seem to have flattered themselves that James would favor their sect, on the credit of some strong assertions he had occasionally made of his adherence to the Scots kirk. Some of these were a good while before; but on quitting the kingdom he had declared that he left it in a state which he did not intend to alter. Neal, 406. James however was all his life rather a bold liar than a good dissembler. It seems strange that they should not have attended to his Basilicon Doron, printed three years before, though not for general circulation, wherein there is a passage quite decisive of his disposition towards the presbyterians and their scheme of polity. The Millenary Petition indeed did not go so far as to request anything of that kind.

[2] Strype's Whitgift, p. 571; Collier, p. 673; Neal, p. 411; Fuller, part ii. p. 7; State Trials, vol. ii. p. 69; Winwood, ii. 13. All these, except the last, are taken from an account of the conference published by Barlow, and probably more favorable to the king and bishops than they deserved. See what Harrington, an eye-witness, says in Nugæ Antiquæ, i. 181, which I would quote as the best evidence of James's behavior, were the passage quite decent.

[3] Reynolds, the principal disputant on the puritan side, was nearly, if not altogether, the most learned man in England. He was censured by his faction for making a weak defence; but the king's partiality and intemperance plead his apology. He is said to have complained of unfair representation in Barlow's account. Hist. and Ant. of Oxford, ii. 293. James wrote a conceited letter to one Blake, boasting of his own superior logic and learning. Strype's Whitgift, Append. 239.

[4] Rymer, xvi. 565.

neither let any presume that his own judgment, having determined in a matter of this weight, should be swayed to alteration by the frivolous suggestions of any light spirit, nor was he ignorant of the inconvenience of admitting innovation in things once settled by mature deliberation."[1] And he had already strictly enjoined the bishops to proceed against all their clergy who did not observe the prescribed order;[2] a command which Bancroft, who about this time followed Whitgift in the primacy, did not wait to have repeated. But the most enormous outrage on the civil rights of these men was the commitment to prison of ten among those who had presented the Millenary Petition; the judges having declared in the star-chamber that it was an offence finable at discretion, and very near to treason and felony, as it tended to sedition and rebellion.[3] By such beginnings did the house of Stuart indicate the course it would steer.

An entire year elapsed, chiefly on account of the unhealthiness of the season in London, before James summoned his first parliament. It might perhaps have been more politic to have chosen some other city; for the length of this interval gave time to form a disadvantageous estimate of his administration, and to alienate beyond recovery the puritanical party. Libels were already in circulation reflecting with a sharpness never before known on the king's personal behavior, which presented an extraordinary contrast to that of Elizabeth.[4] The nation, it is easy to perceive, cheated itself into a persuasion that it had borne that princess more affection than it had really felt, especially in her latter years; the sorrow of subjects for deceased mon-

1 Strype's Whitgift, 587. How desirous men not at all connected in faction with the puritans were of amendments in the church, appears by a tract of Bacon, written, as it seems, about the end of 1603, vol. i. p. 387. — He excepts to several matters of ceremony; the cap and surplice, the ring in marriage, the use of organs, the form of absolution, lay-baptism, &c. And inveighs against the abuse of excommunication, against non-residents and pluralities, the oath ex-officio, the sole exercise of ordination and jurisdiction by the bishop, conceiving that the dean and chapter should always assent, &c. And, in his predominant spirit of improvement, asks, "Why the civil state should be purged and restored by good and wholesome laws made every three or four years in parliament assembled, devising remedies as fast as time breedeth mischief; and contrariwise the ecclesiastical state should still continue upon the dregs of time, and receive no alteration now for these forty-five years or more?"

2 Strype's Whitgift, 587.

3 Neal, 432; Winwood, ii. 36.

4 See one of the Somers Tracts, vol. ii. p. 144, entitled "Advertisements of a Loyal Subject, drawn from the Observation of the People's Speeches." This appears to have been written before the meeting of parliament. The French ambassadors, Sully and La Boderie, thought most contemptibly of the king. Lingard, vol. ix. p. 107. His own courtiers, as their private letters show, disliked and derided him.

archs being often rather inspired by a sense of evil than a recollection of good. James, however, little heeded the popular voice, satisfied with the fulsome and preposterous adulation of his court, and intent on promulgating certain maxims concerning the dignity and power of princes, which he had already announced in his discourse on the True Law of Free Monarchies, printed some years before in Scotland. In this treatise, after laying it down that monarchy is the true pattern of divinity, and proving the duty of passive obedience, rather singularly, from that passage in the book of Samuel where the prophet so forcibly paints the miseries of absolute power, he denies that the kings of Scotland owe their crown to any primary contract, Fergus, their progenitor, having conquered the country with his Irish; and advances more alarming tenets, as that the king makes daily statutes and ordinances, enjoining such pains thereto as he thinks meet, without any advice of parliament or estates; that general laws made publicly in parliament may by the king's authority be mitigated or suspended upon causes only known to him; and that, "although a good king will frame all his actions to be according to the law, yet he is not bound thereto, but of his own will and for example-giving to his subjects."[1] These doctrines, if not absolutely novel, seem peculiarly indecent, as well as dangerous, from the mouth of a sovereign. Yet they proceeded far more from James's self-conceit and pique against the republican spirit of presbyterianism than from his love of power, which (in its exercise I mean, as distinguished from its possession) he did not feel in so eminent a degree as either his predecessor or his son.

In the proclamation for calling together his first parliament, the king, after dilating, as was his favorite practice, on a series of rather common truths in very good language, charges all persons interested in the choice of knights for the shire to select them out of the principal knights or gentlemen within the county; and for the burgesses that choice be made of men of sufficiency and discretion, without desire to please parents and friends that often speak for their children or kindred; avoiding persons noted in religion for their superstitious blindness one way, or for their turbulent humor

Parliament convoked by an irregular proclamation.

[1] King James's Works, p. 207.

other ways. We do command, he says, that no bankrupts or outlaws be chosen, but men of known good behavior and sufficient livelihood. The sheriffs are charged not to direct a writ to any ancient town being so ruined that there are not residents sufficient to make such choice, and of whom such lawful election may be made. All returns are to be filed in chancery, and if any be found contrary to this proclamation the same to be rejected as unlawful and insufficient, and the place to be fined for making it; and any one elected contrary to the purport, effect, and true meaning of this proclamation, to be fined and imprisoned.[1]

Question of Fortescue and Goodwin's election.

Such an assumption of control over parliamentary elections was a glaring infringement of those privileges which the house of commons had been steadily and successfully asserting in the late reign. An opportunity very soon occurred of contesting this important point. At the election for the county of Buckingham sir Francis Goodwin had been chosen in preference to sir John Fortescue, a privy councillor, and the writ returned into chancery. Goodwin having been some years before outlawed, the return was sent back to the sheriff, as contrary to the late proclamation; and, on a second election, sir John Fortescue was chosen. This matter, being brought under the consideration of the house of commons a very few days after the opening of the session, gave rise to their first struggle with the new king. It was resolved, after hearing the whole case, and arguments by members on both sides, that Goodwin was lawfully elected and returned, and ought to be received. The first notice taken of this was by the lords, who requested that this might be discussed in a conference between the two houses before any other matter should be proceeded in. The commons returned for answer that they conceived it not according to the honor of the house to give account of any of their proceedings. The lords replied, that, having acquainted his majesty with the matter, he desired there might be a conference thereon between the two houses. Upon this message the commons came to a resolution that the speaker with a numerous deputation of members should attend his majesty and report the reasons of their proceedings in Goodwin's case. In this conference with the king,

[1] Parl. Hist. i. 967.

as related by the speaker, it appears that he had shown some degree of chagrin, and insisted that the house ought not to meddle with returns, which could only be corrected by the court of chancery; and that, since they derived all matters of privilege from him and his grant, he expected they should not be turned against him. He ended by directing the house to confer with the judges. After a debate which seems from the minutes in the journals to have been rather warm, it was unanimously agreed not to have a conference with the judges; but the reasons of the house's proceeding were laid before the king in a written statement or memorial, answering the several objections that his majesty had alleged. This they sent to the lords, requesting them to deliver it to the king, and to be mediators in behalf of the house for his majesty's satisfaction; a message in rather a lower tone than they had previously taken. The king, sending for the speaker privately, told him that he was now distracted in judgment as to the merits of the case; and, for his further satisfaction, desired and commanded, as an absolute king, that there should be a conference between the house and the judges. Upon this unexpected message, says the journal, there grew some amazement and silence. But at last one stood up and said, "The prince's command is like a thunderbolt; his command upon our allegiance like the roaring of a lion. To his command there is no contradiction; but how or in what manner we should now proceed to perform obedience, that will be the question."[1] It was resolved to confer with the judges in presence of the king and council. In this second conference the king, after some favorable expressions towards the house, and conceding that it was a court of record, and judge of returns, though not exclusively of the chancery, suggested that both Goodwin and Fortescue should be set aside by issuing a new writ. This compromise was joyfully accepted by the greater part of the commons, after the dispute had lasted nearly three weeks.[2] They have been considered as victorious, upon the whole, in this contest, though they apparently fell short in

[1] Commons' Journals, i. 166.

[2] It appears that some of the more eager patriots were dissatisfied at the concession made by vacating Goodwin's seat, and said they had drawn on themselves the reproach of inconstancy and levity. "But the acclamation of the house was, that it was a testimony of our duty and no levity." It was thought expedient, however, to save their honor, that Goodwin should send a letter to the speaker expressing his acquiescence. Id. 168.

the result of what they had obtained some years before. But no attempt was ever afterwards made to dispute their exclusive jurisdiction.[1]

Shirley's case of privilege.

The commons were engaged during this session in the defence of another privilege, to which they annexed perhaps a disproportionate importance. Sir Thomas Shirley, a member, having been taken in execution on a private debt before their meeting, and the warden of the Fleet prison refusing to deliver him up, they were at a loss how to obtain his release. Several methods were projected; among which that of sending a party of members with the sergeant and his mace, to force open the prison, was carried on a division; but the speaker hinting that such a vigorous measure would expose them individually to prosecution as trespassers, it was prudently abandoned. The warden, though committed by the house to a dungeon in the Tower, continued obstinate, conceiving that by releasing his prisoner he should become answerable for the debt. They were evidently reluctant to solicit the king's interference; but, aware at length that their own authority was insufficient, "the vice-chamberlain," according to a memorandum in the journals, "was privately instructed to go to the king and humbly desire that he would be pleased to command the warden, on his allegiance, to deliver up sir Thomas; not as petitioned for by the house, but as if himself thought it fit, out of his own gracious judgment." By this stratagem, if we may so term it, they saved the point of honor and recovered their member.[2] The warden's apprehensions, however, of exposing himself to an action for the escape gave rise to a statute which empowers the creditor to sue out a new execution against any one who shall be delivered by virtue of his privilege of parliament, after that shall have expired, and discharges from liability those out of whose custody such persons shall be delivered. This is the first legislative recognition of privilege.[3] The most important part of the whole is a proviso subjoined to the act, "That nothing therein contained shall extend to

[1] Commons' Journals, 147, &c.; Parl. Hist. 997; Carte, iii. 780, who gives, on this occasion, a review of the earlier cases where the house had entered on matters of election. See also a rather curious letter of Cecil in Winwood's Memorials, ii. 18, where he artfully endeavors to treat the matter as of little importance.

[2] Commons' Journals, p. 155, &c.; Parl. Hist. 1028; Carte, 734.

[3] 1 Jac. I. c. 13.

the diminishing of any punishment to be hereafter, by censure in parliament, inflicted upon any person who hereafter shall make or procure to be made any such arrest as is aforesaid." The right of commitment, in such cases at least, by a vote of the house of commons, is here unequivocally maintained.

Complaints of grievances.

It is not necessary to repeat the complaints of ecclesiastical abuses preferred by this house of commons, as by those that had gone before them. James, by siding openly with the bishops, had given alarm to the reforming party. It was anticipated that he would go farther than his predecessor, whose uncertain humor, as well as the inclinations of some of her advisers, had materially counterbalanced the dislike she entertained of the innovators. A code of new canons had recently been established in convocation with the king's assent, obligatory perhaps upon the clergy, but tending to set up an unwarranted authority over the whole nation; imposing oaths and exacting securities in certain cases from the laity, and aiming at the exclusion of nonconformists from all civil rights.[1] Against these canons, as well as various other grievances, the commons remonstrated in a conference with the upper house, but with little immediate effect.[2] They made a more remarkable effort in attacking some public mischiefs of a temporal nature, which, though long the theme of general murmurs, were closely interwoven with the ancient and undisputed prerogatives of the crown. Complaints were uttered, and innovations projected, by the commons of 1604, which Elizabeth would have met with an angry message, and perhaps visited with punishment on the proposers. James, however, was not entirely averse to some of the projected alterations, from which he hoped to derive a pecuniary advantage. The two principal grievances were pur-

[1] By one of these canons, all persons affirming any of the thirty-nine articles to be erroneous are excommunicated *ipso facto*; consequently become incapable of being witnesses, of suing for their debts, &c. Neal, 428. But the courts of law disregarded these *ipso facto* excommunications.

[2] Somers Tracts, ii. 14; Journals, 199, 235, 238; Parl. Hist. 1067. It is here said that a bill restraining excommunications passed into a law, which does not appear to be true, though James himself had objected to their frequency. I cannot trace such a bill in the journals beyond the committee, nor is it in the statute-book. The fact is, that the king desired the house to confer on the subject with the convocation, which they justly deemed unprecedented, and derogatory to their privileges; but offered to confer with the bishops, as lords of parliament. Journals, 173.

veyance and the incidents of military tenure. The former had been restrained by not less than thirty-six statutes, as the commons assert in a petition to the king; in spite of which the impressing of carts and carriages, and the exaction of victuals for the king's use, at prices far below the true value, and in quantity beyond what was necessary, continued to prevail under authority of commissions from the board of green cloth, and was enforced, in case of demur or resistance, by imprisonment under their warrant. The purveyors, indeed, are described as living at free quarters upon the country, felling woods without the owners' consent, and commanding labor with little or no recompense.[1] Purveyance was a very ancient topic of remonstrance; but both the inadequate revenues of the crown, and a supposed dignity attached to this royal right of spoil, had prevented its abolition from being attempted. But the commons seemed still more to trench on the pride of our feudal monarchy when they proposed to take away guardianship in chivalry; that lucrative tyranny, bequeathed by Norman conquerors, the custody of every military tenant's estate until he should arrive at twenty-one, without accounting for the profits. This, among other grievances, was referred to a committee, in which Bacon took an active share. They obtained a conference on this subject with the lords, who refused to agree to a bill for taking guardianship in chivalry away, but offered to join in a petition for that purpose to the king, since it could not be called a wrong, having been patiently endured by their ancestors as well as themselves, and being warranted by the law of the land. In the end the lords advised to drop the matter for the present, as somewhat unseasonable in the king's first parliament.[2]

In the midst of these testimonies of dissatisfaction with the civil and ecclesiastical administration, the house of commons had not felt much willingness to greet the new sovereign with a subsidy. No demand had been made upon them, far less any proof given of the king's exigencies; and they doubtless knew by experience that an obstinate determination not to yield to any of their wishes would hardly be shaken by a liberal grant of money. They had even passed the usual bill granting tonnage and poundage for life, with

1 Bacon's Works, i. 624; Journals, 190, 215.
2 Commons' Journals, 150, &c.

certain reservations that gave the court offence, and which apparently they afterwards omitted. But there was so little disposition to do anything further, that the king sent a message to express his desire that the commons would not enter upon the business of a subsidy, and assuring them that he would not take unkindly their omission. By this artifice, which was rather transparent, he avoided the not improbable mortification of seeing the proposal rejected.[1]

Commons' vindication of themselves.

The king's discontent at the proceedings of this session, which he seems to have rather strongly expressed in some speech to the commons that has not been recorded,[2] gave rise to a very remarkable vindication, prepared by a committee at the house's command, and entitled "A Form of Apology and Satisfaction to be delivered to his Majesty," though such may not be deemed the most appropriate title. It contains a full and pertinent justification of all those proceedings at which James had taken umbrage, and asserts, with respectful boldness and in explicit language, the constitutional rights and liberties of parliament. If the English monarchy had been reckoned as absolute under the Plantagenets and Tudors as Hume has endeavored to make it appear, the commons of 1604 must have made a surprising advance in their notions of freedom since the king's accession. Adverting to what they call the misinformation openly delivered to his majesty in three things; namely, that their privileges were not of right, but of grace only, renewed every parliament on petition; that they are no court of record, nor yet a court that can command view of records; that the examination of the returns of writs for knights and burgesses is without their compass, and belonging to the chancery: assertions, they say, "tending directly and apparently to the utter overthrow of the very fundamental privileges of our house, and therein of the rights and liberties of the whole commons of your realm of England, which they and their ancestors, from time immemorial, have undoubtedly enjoyed under your majesty's most noble progenitors;" and against which they expressly protest, as derogatory in the highest degree to the true dignity and authority of parliament, desiring "that such their protestations might be recorded to all posterity;" they main-

[1] Commons' Journals, 246. [2] Ibid. 230.

tain, on the contrary, "1. That their privileges and liberties are their right and inheritance, no less than their very lands and goods; 2. That they cannot be withheld from them, denied, or impaired, but with apparent wrong to the whole state of the realm; 3. That their making request, at the beginning of a parliament, to enjoy their privilege, is only an act of manners, and does not weaken their right; 4. That their house is a court of record, and has been ever so esteemed; 5. That there is not the highest standing court in this land that ought to enter into competition, either for dignity or authority, with this high court of parliament, which, with his majesty's royal assent, gives law to other courts, but from other courts receives neither laws nor orders; 6. That the house of commons is the sole proper judge of return of all such writs, and the election of all such members as belong to it, without which the freedom of election were not entire." They aver that in this session the privileges of the house have been more universally and dangerously impugned than ever, as they suppose, since the beginnings of parliaments. That, "in regard to the late queen's sex and age, and much more upon care to avoid all trouble, which by wicked practice might have been drawn to impeach the quiet of his majesty's right in the succession, those actions were then passed over which they hoped in succeeding times to redress and rectify; whereas, on the contrary, in this parliament, not privileges, but the whole freedom of the parliament and realm, had been hewed from them." "What cause," they proceed, "we, your poor commons, have to watch over our privileges, is manifest in itself to all men. The prerogatives of princes may easily and do daily grow. The privileges of the subject are for the most part at an everlasting stand. They may be by good providence and care preserved; but, being once lost, are not recovered but with much disquiet." They then enter in detail on the various matters that had arisen during the session, — the business of Goodwin's election, of Shirley's arrest, and some smaller matters of privilege to which my limits have not permitted me to allude. "We thought not," speaking of the first, "that the judges' opinion, which yet in due place we greatly reverence, being delivered what the common law was, which extends only to inferior and standing courts, ought to bring any prejudice to this high court of parliament, whose power, being above the law, is not founded on the common law, but have their rights and privileges peculiar to themselves." They vindicate their endeavors to obtain redress of religious and public grievances: "Your majesty would be misinformed," they tell him, "if any man should deliver that the kings of England have any absolute power in themselves, either to alter religion, which God defend should be in the power of any mortal man whatsoever, or to make any laws concerning the same, otherwise than as in temporal causes, by consent of parliament. We have and shall at all times by our oaths acknowledge that your majesty is sovereign lord and supreme governor in both."[1] Such was the voice of the English commons in 1604, at the commencement of that great conflict for their liberties which is measured by the line of the house of Stuart. But it is not certain that this apology was ever delivered to the king, though he seems to allude to it in a letter written to one of his ministers about the same time.[2]

The next session, which is remarkable on account of the

[1] Parl. Hist. 1030, from Petyt's Jus Parliamentarium, the earliest book, as far as I know, where this important document is preserved. The entry on the Journals, p. 243, contains only the first paragraph. Hume and Carte have been ignorant of it. It is just alluded to by Rapin.

It was remarked that the attendance of members in this session was more frequent than had ever been known, so that fresh seats were required. Journals, 141.

[2] "My faithful 3, such is now my misfortune, as I must be for this time secretary to the devil in answering your letters directed unto him. That the entering now into the matter of the subsidy should be deferred until the council's next meeting with me, I think no ways convenient, especially for three reasons. First, ye see it has bin already longest delayd of any thing, and yet yee see the lower house are ever the longer the further from it; and (as in every thing that concerns mee) delay of time does never turn them towards mee, but, by the contrary, every hour breedeth a new trick of contradiction amongst them, and every day produces new matter of sedition, so fertile are their brains in ever buttering forth venome. Next, the Parlt. is now so very near an end, as this matter can suffer no longer delay. And thirdly, if this be not granted unto before they receive my answer unto their petition, it needs never to be moved, for the will of man or angel cannot devise a pleasing answer to their proposition, except I should pull the crown not only from my own head, but also from the head of all those that shall succeed unto mee, and lay it down at their feet. And that freedom of uttering my thoughts, which no extremity, strait, nor peril of my life could ever bereave mee of in time past, shall now remain with mee as long as the soul shall with the body. And as for the Reservations of the Bill of Tonnage and Poundage, yee of the Upper House must out of your Love and Discretion help it again, or otherwise they will in this, as in all things else that concern mee, wrack both mee and all my Posterity. Yee may impart this to little 10 and bigg Suffolk. And so Farewell from my Wildernesse, wch I had rather live in (as God shall judge mee) like an Hermite in this Forrest, then be a King over such a People as the pack of Puritans are that over-rules the lower-house.

J. R."

(MS. penes autorem.)

I cannot tell who is addressed in this letter by the numeral 3; perhaps the earl of Dunbar. By 10 we must doubtless understand Salisbury.

conspiracy of some desperate men to blow up both houses of parliament with gunpowder on the day of their meeting, did not produce much worthy of our notice. A bill to regulate, or probably to suppress, purveyance was thrown out by the lords. The commons sent up another bill to the same effect, which the upper house rejected without discussion, by a rule then perhaps first established, that the same bill could not be proposed twice in one session.[1] They voted a liberal subsidy, which the king, who had reigned three years without one, had just cause to require. For though he had concluded a peace with Spain soon after his accession, yet the late queen had left a debt of 400,000*l.*, and other charges had fallen on the crown. But the bill for this subsidy lay a good while in the house of commons, who came to a vote that it should not pass till their list of grievances was ready to be presented. No notice was taken of these till the next session, beginning in November, 1606, when the king returned an answer to each of the sixteen articles in which matters of grievance were alleged. Of these the greater part refer to certain grants made to particular persons in the nature of monopolies; the king either defending these in his answer, or remitting the parties to the courts of law to try their legality. The principal business of this third session, as it had been of the last, was James's favorite scheme of a perfect union between England and Scotland. It may be collected, though this was never explicitly brought forward, that his views extended to a legislative incorporation.[2] But in all the speeches on this

Session 1605.

Union with Scotland debated.

[1] Parl. Hist. Journals, 274, 278, &c. In a conference with the lords on this bill, Mr. Hare, a member, spoke so warmly as to give their lordships offence and to incur some reprehension. "You would have thought," says Sir Thomas Hoby, "that Hare and Hyde represented two tribunes of the people." Sloane MSS., 4161. But the commons resented this infringement on their privileges, and, after voting that Mr. Hare did not err in his employment in the committee with the lords, sent a message to inform the other house of their vote, and to request that they would "forbear hereafter any taxations and reprehensions in their conferences." Journals, Feb. 20 and 22.

[2] Journals, 316.

An acute historical critic doubts whether James aimed at an union of legislatures, though suggested by Bacon. Laing's Hist. of Scotland, iii. 17. It is certain that his own speeches on the subject do not mention this; nor do I know that it was ever distinctly brought forward by the government; yet it is hard to see how the incorporation could have been complete without it. Bacon not only contemplates the formation of a single parliament, but the alterations necessary to give it effect, vol. i. p. 638; suggesting that the previous commission of lords of articles might be adopted for some, though not for all, purposes. This of itself was a sufficient justification for the dilatoriness of the English parliament. Nor were the common lawyers who sat in the house much better pleased with Bacon's schemes for remodelling all our laws. See his speech, vol. i. p. 654, for naturalizing the ante-

subject, and especially his own, there is a want of distinctness as to the object proposed. He dwells continually upon the advantage of unity of laws, yet extols those of England as the best, which the Scots, as was evident, had no inclination to adopt. Wherefore then was delay to be imputed to our English parliament, if it waited for that of the sister kingdom? And what steps were recommended towards this measure that the commons can be said to have declined, except only the naturalization of the ante-nati, or Scots born before the king's accession to our throne, which could only have a temporary effect?[1] Yet Hume, ever prone to eulogize this monarch at the expense of his people, while he bestows merited praise on his speech in favor of the union, which is upon the whole a well-written and judicious performance, charges the parliament with prejudice, reluctance, and obstinacy. The code, as it may be called, of international hostility, those numerous statutes treating the northern inhabitants of this island as foreigners and enemies, were entirely abrogated. And if the commons, while both the theory of our own constitution was so unsettled, and its practice so full of abuse, did not precipitately give in to schemes that might create still further difficulty in all questions between the crown and themselves, schemes, too, which there was no imperious motive for carrying into effect at that juncture, we may justly consider it as an additional proof of their wisdom and public spirit. Their slow progress, however, in this fa-

nati. In this he asserts the kingdom not to be fully peopled; "the territories of France, Italy, Flanders, and some parts of Germany, do in equal space of ground bear and contain a far greater quantity of people, if they were mustered by the poll;" and even goes on to assert the population to have been more considerable under the heptarchy.

1 It was held by twelve judges out of fourteen, in Calvin's case, that the post-nati, or Scots born after the king's accession, were natural subjects of the king of England. This is laid down, and irresistibly demonstrated by Coke, then chief justice, with his abundant legal learning. State Trials, vol. ii. 559.

It may be observed that the high-flying creed of prerogative mingled itself intimately with this question of naturalization; which was much argued on the monarchical principle of personal allegiance to the sovereign, as opposed to the half-republican theory that lurked in the contrary proposition. "Allegiance," says lord Bacon, "is of a greater extent and dimension than laws or kingdoms, and cannot consist by the laws merely, because it began before laws; it continueth after laws, and it is in vigor when laws are suspended and have not had their force." Id. 596. So lord Coke: "Whatsoever is due by the law or constitution of man may be altered; but natural legiance or obedience of the subject to the sovereign cannot be altered; ergo, natural legiance or obedience to the sovereign is not due by the law or constitution of man." 652.

There are many doubtful positions scattered through the judgment in this famous case. Its surest basis is the long series of precedents, evincing that the natives of Jersey, Guernsey, Calais, and even Normandy and Guienne, while these countries appertained to the kings of England, though not in right of its crown, were never reputed aliens.

vorite measure, which, though they could not refuse to entertain it, they endeavored to defeat by interposing delays and impediments, gave much offence to the king, which he expressed in a speech to the two houses, with the haughtiness, but not the dignity, of Elizabeth. He threatened them to live alternately in the two kingdoms, or to keep his court at York; and alluded, with peculiar acrimony, to certain speeches made in the house, wherein probably his own fame had not been spared.[1] "I looked," he says, "for no such fruits at your hands, such personal discourses and speeches, which, of all other, I looked you should avoid, as not beseeming the gravity of your assembly. I am your king; I am placed to govern you, and shall answer for your errors; I am a man of flesh and blood, and have my passions and affections as other men; I pray you do not too far move me to do that which my power may tempt me unto." [2]

Continual bickerings between the crown and commons.

It is most probable, as experience had shown, that such a demonstration of displeasure from Elizabeth would have ensured the repentant submission of the commons. But, within a few years of the most unbroken tranquillity, there had been one of those changes of popular feeling which a government is seldom observant enough to watch. Two springs had kept in play the machine of her administration, affection and fear; attachment arising from the sense of dangers endured, and glory achieved, for her people, tempered, though not subdued, by the dread of her stern courage and vindictive rigor. For James not a particle of loyal affection lived in the hearts of the nation, while his easy and pusillanimous, though choleric, disposition had gradually diminished those sentiments of apprehension which royal frowns used to excite. The commons, after some angry speeches, resolved to make known to the king, through the speaker, their desire that he would listen

1 The house had lately expelled sir Christopher Pigott for reflecting on the Scots nation in a speech. Journals, 13th Feb. 1607.

2 Commons' Journals, 366.

The journals are full of notes of these long discussions about the union in 1604, 1606, 1607, and even 1610. It is easy to perceive a jealousy that the prerogative by some means or other would be the gainer. The very change of name to Great Britain was objected to. One said, we cannot legislate for Great Britain: p. 186. Another, with more astonishing sagacity, feared that the king might succeed, by what the lawyers call *remitter*, to the prerogatives of the British kings before Julius Cæsar, which would supersede Magna Charta: p. 185.

James took the title of King of Great Britain in the second year of his reign. Lord Bacon drew a well-written proclamation on that occasion. Bacon, i. 621; Rymer, xvi. 603. But it was, not long afterwards, abandoned.

to no private reports, but take his information of the house's meaning from themselves; that he would give leave to such persons as he had blamed for their speeches to clear themselves in his hearing; and that he would by some gracious message make known his intention that they should deliver their opinions with full liberty, and without fear. The speaker next day communicated a slight but civil answer he had received from the king, importing his wish to preserve their privileges, especially that of liberty of speech.[1] This, however, did not prevent his sending a message a few days afterwards, commenting on their debates, and on some clauses they had introduced into the bill for the abolition of all hostile laws.[2] And a petition having been prepared by a committee under the house's direction for better execution of the laws against recusants, the speaker, on its being moved that the petition be read, said that his majesty had taken notice of the petition as a thing belonging to himself, concerning which it was needless to press him. This interference provoked some members to resent it as an infringement of their liberties. The speaker replied that there were many precedents in the late queen's time where she had restrained the house from meddling in politics of divers kinds. This, as a matter of fact, was too notorious to be denied. A motion was made for a committee "to search for precedents of ancient as well as later times that do concern any messages from the sovereign magistrate, king or queen of this realm, touching petitions offered to the house of commons." The king now interposed by a second message, that, though the petition was such as the like had not been read in the house, and contained matter whereof the house could not properly take knowledge, yet, if they thought good to have it read, he was not against the reading. And the commons were so well satisfied with this concession, that no further proceedings were had; and the petition, says the Journal, was at length, with general liking, agreed to sleep. It contained some strong remonstrances against ecclesiastical abuses, and in favor of the deprived and silenced puritans, but such as the house had often before in various modes brought forward.[3]

The ministry betrayed, in a still more pointed manner,

1 Commons' Journals, p. 370. 2 P. 377. 3 P. 384.

their jealousy of any interference on the part of the commons with the conduct of public affairs in a business of a different nature. The pacification concluded with Spain in 1604, very much against the general wish,[1] had neither removed all grounds of dispute between the governments, nor allayed the dislike of the nations. Spain advanced in that age the most preposterous claims to an exclusive navigation beyond the tropic, and to the sole possession of the American continent; while the English merchants, mindful of the lucrative adventures of the queen's reign, could not be restrained from trespassing on the rich harvest of the Indies by contraband and sometimes piratical voyages. These conflicting interests led of course to mutual complaints of maritime tyranny and fraud; neither likely to be ill-founded, where the one party was as much distinguished for the despotic exercise of vast power, as the other by boldness and cupidity. It was the prevailing bias of the king's temper to keep on friendly terms with Spain, or rather to court her with undisguised and impolitic partiality.[2] But this so much thwarted the prejudices of his subjects, that no part, perhaps, of his administration had such a disadvantageous effect on his popularity. The merchants presented to the commons, in this session of 1607, a petition upon the grievances they sustained from Spain, entering into such a detail of alleged cruelties as was likely to exasperate that assembly. Nothing, however, was done for a considerable time, when, after receiving the report of a committee on the subject, the house prayed a conference with the lords. They, who acted in this and the preceding session as the mere agents of government, intimated in their reply that they thought it an unusual matter for the commons to enter upon, and took time to consider about a conference. After some delay this was granted, and sir Francis Bacon reported its result to the lower house. The earl of Salisbury

1 James entertained the strange notion that the war with Spain ceased by his accession to the throne. By a proclamation dated 23d June, 1603, he permits his subjects to keep such ships as had been captured by them before the 24th April, but orders all taken since to be restored to the owners. Rymer, xvi. 516. He had been used to call the Dutch rebels, and was probably kept with difficulty by Cecil from displaying his partiality still more outrageously. Carte, iii. 714. All the council, except this minister, are said to have been favorable to peace. Id. 938.

2 Winwood, vol. ii. p. 100, 152, &c.; Birch's Negotiations of Edmondes. If we may believe sir Charles Cornwallis, our ambassador at Madrid, "England never lost such an opportunity of winning honor and wealth as by relinquishing the war." The Spaniards were astonished how peace could have been obtained on such advantageous conditions. Winwood, p. 75.

managed the conference on the part of the lords. The tenor of his speech, as reported by Bacon, is very remarkable. After discussing the merits of the petition, and considerably extenuating the wrongs imputed to Spain, he adverted to the circumstance of its being presented to the commons. The crown of England was invested, he said, with an absolute power of peace and war; and inferred, from a series of precedents which he vouched, that petitions made in parliament, intermeddling with such matters, had gained little success; that great inconveniences must follow from the public debate of the king's designs, which, if they take wind, must be frustrated; and that, if parliaments have ever been made acquainted with matter of peace or war in a general way, it was either when the king and council conceived that it was material to have some declaration of the zeal and affection of the people, or else when they needed money for the charge of a war, in which case they should be sure enough to hear of it; that the lords would make a good construction of the commons' desire, that it sprang from a forwardness to assist his majesty's future resolutions, rather than a determination to do that wrong to his supreme power which haply might appear to those who were prone to draw evil inferences from their proceedings. The earl of Northampton, who also bore a part in this conference, gave as one reason among others why the lords could not concur in forwarding the petition to the crown, that the composition of the house of commons was in its first foundation intended merely to be of those that have their residence and vocation in the places for which they serve, and therefore to have a private and local wisdom according to that compass, and so not fit to examine or determine secrets of state which depend upon such variety of circumstances; and although he acknowledged that there were divers gentlemen in the house of good capacity and insight into matters of state, yet that was the accident of the person, and not the intention of the place; and things were to be taken in the institution, and not in the practice. The commons seem to have acquiesced in this rather contemptuous treatment. Several precedents indeed might have been opposed to those of the earl of Salisbury, wherein the commons, especially under Richard II. and Henry VI., had assumed a right of advising on matters of peace and war. But the more recent usage of the constitution did not warrant such an interference. It was, however, rather a bold assertion that they were not the proper channel through which public grievances, or those of so large a portion of the community as the merchants, ought to be represented to the throne.[1]

Impositions on merchandise without consent of parliament.

During the interval of two years and a half that elapsed before the commencement of the next session, a decision had occurred in the court of exchequer which threatened the entire overthrow of our constitution. It had always been deemed the indispensable characteristic of a limited monarchy, however irregular and inconsistent might be the exercise of some prerogatives, that no money could be raised from the subject without the consent of the estates. This essential principle was settled in England, after much contention, by the statute entitled Confirmatio Chartarum, in the 25th year of Edward I. More comprehensive and specific in its expression than the Great Charter of John, it abolishes all "aids, tasks, and prises, unless by the common assent of the realm, and for the common profit thereof, saving the ancient aids and prises due and accustomed;" the king explicitly renouncing the custom he had lately set on wool. Thus the letter of the statute and the history of the times conspire to prove that impositions on merchandise at the ports, to which alone the word prises was applicable, could no more be levied by the royal prerogative after its enactment, than internal taxes upon landed or movable property, known in that age by the appellations of aids and tallages. But as the former could be assessed with great ease, and with no risk of immediate resistance, and especially as certain ancient customs were preserved by the statute,[2] so that a train of fiscal

[1] Bacon, i. 663; Journals, p. 341. Carte says, on the authority of the French ambassador's despatches, that the ministry secretly put forward this petition of the commons in order to frighten the Spanish court into making compensation to the merchants, wherein they succeeded: iii. 766. This is rendered very improbable by Salisbury's behavior. It was Carte's mistake to rely too much on the despatches he was permitted to read in the Dépôt des Affaires Etrangères; as if an ambassador were not liable to be deceived by rumors in a country of which he has in general too little knowledge to correct them.

[2] There was a duty on wool, woolfels, and leather, called magna, or sometimes antiqua costuma, which is said in Dyer to have been by prescription, and by the barons in Bates's case to have been imposed by the king's prerogative. As this existed before the 25th Edward I., it is not very material whether it were so imposed or granted by parliament. During the discussion, however, which took place in 1610, a record was discovered of 3 Edw. I., proving it to have been granted par tous

officers, and a scheme of regulations and restraints upon the export and import of goods became necessary, it was long before the sovereigns of this kingdom could be induced constantly to respect this part of the law. Hence several remonstrances from the commons under Edward III. against the maletolts or unjust exactions upon wool, by which, if they did not obtain more than a promise of effectual redress, they kept up their claim, and perpetuated the recognition of its justice, for the sake of posterity. They became powerful enough to enforce it under Richard II., in whose time there is little clear evidence of illegal impositions; and from the accession of the house of Lancaster it is undeniable that they ceased altogether. The grant of tonnage and poundage for the king's life, which from the time of Henry V. was made in the first parliament of every reign, might perhaps be considered as a tacit compensation to the crown for its abandonment of these irregular extortions.

Henry VII., the most rapacious, and Henry VIII., the most despotic, of English monarchs, did not presume to violate this acknowledged right. The first who had again recourse to this means of enhancing the revenue was Mary, who, in the year 1557, set a duty upon cloths exported beyond seas, and afterwards another on the importation of French wines. The former of those was probably defended by arguing that there was already a duty on wool; and if cloth, which was wool manufactured, could pass free, there would be a fraud on the revenue. The merchants, however, did not acquiesce in this arbitrary imposition, and, as soon as Elizabeth's accession gave hopes of a restoration of English government, they petitioned to be released from this burden. The question appears, by a memorandum in Dyer's Reports, to have been extrajudicially referred to the judges, unless it were rather as assistants to the privy council that their opinion was demanded. This entry concludes abruptly, without any determination of the judges.[1] But we may presume that, if any such had been given in

les grauntz del realme, par la prière des comunes des marchants de tout Engleterre. Hale 146. The prisage of wines, or duty of two tuns from every vessel, is considerably more ancient; but how the crown came by this right does not appear.

[1] Dyer, fol. 165. An argument of the great lawyer Plowden in this case of the queen's increasing the duty on cloths is in the British Museum, Hargrave MSS. 32, and seems, as far as the difficult handwriting permitted me to judge, adverse to the prerogative.

favor of the crown, it would have been made public. And that the majority of the bench would not have favored this claim of the crown, we may strongly presume from their doctrine in a case of the same description, wherein they held the assessment of treble custom on aliens for violation of letters patent to be absolutely against the law.[1] The administration, however, would not release this duty, which continued to be paid under Elizabeth. She also imposed one upon sweet wines. We read of no complaint in parliament against this novel taxation; but it is alluded to by Bacon in one of his tracts during the queen's reign, as a grievance alleged by her enemies. He defends it, as laid only on a foreign merchandise, and a delicacy which might be forborne.[2] But, considering Elizabeth's unwillingness to require subsidies from the commons, and the rapid increase of foreign traffic during her reign, it might be asked why she did not extend these duties to other commodities, and secure to herself no trifling annual revenue. What answer can be given, except that, aware how little any unparliamentary levying of money could be supported by law or usage, her ministers shunned to excite attention to these innovations, which wanted hitherto the stamp of time to give them prescriptive validity?[3]

James had imposed a duty of five shillings per hundredweight on currants, over and above that of two shillings and sixpence, which was granted by the statute of tonnage and

[1] This case I have had the good fortune to discover in one of Mr. Hargrave's MSS. in the Museum, 132, fol. 66. It is in the handwriting of chief justice Hyde (temp. Car. I.), who has written in the margin, "This is the report of a case in my lord Dyer's written original, but is not in the printed books." The reader will judge for himself why it was omitted, and why the entry of the former case breaks off so abruptly. "Philip and Mary granted to the town of Southampton that all malmsy wines should be landed at that port under penalty of paying treble custom. Some merchants of Venice having landed wines elsewhere, an information was brought against them in the exchequer, 1 Eliz., and argued several times in the presence of all the judges. Eight were of opinion against the letters patent, among whom Dyer and Catlin, chief justices, as well for the principal matter of restraint in the landing of malmsies at the will and pleasure of the merchants, for that it was against the laws, statutes, and customs of the realm, Magna Charta, c. 30; 9 E. 3; 14 E. 3; 25 E. 3, c. 2; 27 E. 3; 28 E. 3; 2 R. 2, c. 1, and others; as also in the assessment of treble custom, *which is merely against the law;* also the prohibition above said was held to be private, and not public. But baron Lake e contra, and Browne J. censuit deliberandum. And after, at an after meeting the same Easter term at Sergeants' Inn, it was resolved as above. And after by parliament, 5 Eliz., the patent was confirmed and affirmed against aliens."

[2] Bacon, i. 521.

[3] Hale's Treatise on the Customs, part 3; in Hargrave's Collection of Law Tracts. See also the preface by Hargrave to Bates's case, in the State Trials, where this most important question is learnedly argued.

poundage.[1] Bates, a Turkey merchant, having refused payment, an information was exhibited against him in the exchequer. Judgment was soon given for the crown. The courts of justice, it is hardly necessary to say, did not consist of men conscientiously impartial between the king and the subject; some corrupt with hope of promotion, many more fearful of removal, or awe-struck by the frowns of power. The speeches of chief baron Fleming, and of baron Clark, the only two that are preserved in Lane's Reports, contain propositions still worse than their decision, and wholly subversive of all liberty. "The king's power," it was said, "is double — ordinary and absolute; and these have several laws and ends. That of the ordinary is for the profit of particular subjects, exercised in ordinary courts, and called common law, which cannot be changed in substance without parliament. The king's absolute power is applied to no particular person's benefit, but to the general safety; and this is not directed by the rules of common law, but more properly termed policy and government, varying according to his wisdom for the common good; and all things done within those rules are lawful. The matter in question is matter of state, to be ruled according to policy by the king's extraordinary power. All customs (duties so called) are the effects of foreign commerce; but all affairs of commerce and all treaties with foreign nations belong to the king's absolute power; he therefore who has power over the cause, must have it also over the effect. The seaports are the king's gates, which he may open and shut to whom he pleases." The ancient customs on wine and wool are asserted to have originated in the king's absolute power, and not in a grant of parliament; a point, whether true or not, of no great importance, if it were acknowledged that many statutes had subsequently controlled this prerogative. But these judges impugned the authority of statutes derogatory to their idol. That of 45 E. 3, c. 4, that no new imposition should be laid on wool or leather, one of them maintains, did not bind the king's successors; for the right to impose such duties was a principal part of the crown of England,

1 He had previously published letters patent, setting a duty of six shillings and eightpence a pound, in addition to twopence already payable, on tobacco; intended, no doubt, to operate as a prohibition of a drug he so much hated. Rymer, xvi. 602.

which the king could not diminish. They extolled the king's grace in permitting the matter to be argued, commenting at the same time on the insolence shown in disputing so undeniable a claim. Nor could any judges be more peremptory in resisting an attempt to overthrow the most established precedents than were these barons of king James's exchequer in giving away those fundamental liberties which were the inheritance of every Englishman.[1]

The immediate consequence of this decision was a book of rates, published in July, 1608, under the authority of the great seal, imposing heavy duties upon almost all merchandise.[2] But the judgment of the court of exchequer did not satisfy men jealous of the crown's encroachments. The imposition on currants had been already noticed as a grievance by the house of commons in 1606. But the king answered, that the question was in a course for legal determination; and the commons themselves, which is worthy of remark, do not appear to have entertained any clear persuasion that the impost was contrary to law.[3] In the session, however, which began in February, 1610, they had acquired new light by sifting the legal authorities, and, instead of submitting their opinions to the courts of law, which were in truth little worthy of such deference, were the more provoked to remonstrate against the novel usurpation those servile men had endeavored to prop up. Lawyers, as learned probably as most of the judges, were not wanting in their ranks. The illegality of impositions was shown in two elaborate speeches by Hakewill and Yelverton.[4] And the country gentlemen, who, though less deeply versed in precedents, had too good sense not to discern that the next step would be to levy taxes on their lands, were delighted to find that there had been an

Remonstrances against impositions in session of 1610.

1 State Trials, ii. 371.

2 Hale's Treatise on the Customs. These were perpetual, "to be forever hereafter paid to the king and his successors, on pain of his displeasure." State Trials, 481.

3 Journals, 295, 297.

4 Mr. Hakewill's speech, though long, will repay the diligent reader's trouble, as being a very luminous and masterly statement of this great argument. State Trials, ii. 407. The extreme inferiority of Bacon, who sustained the cause of prerogative, must be apparent to every one. Id. 345. Sir John Davis makes somewhat a better defence; his argument is, that the king may lay an embargo on trade, so as to prevent it entirely, and consequently may annex conditions to it. Id. 399. But to this it was answered, that the king can only lay a temporary embargo, for the sake of some public good, not prohibit foreign trade altogether.

As to the king's prerogative of restraining foreign trade, see extracts from Hale's MS. Treatise de Jure Coronæ, in Hargrave's Preface to Collection of Law Tracts, p. xxx., &c. It seems to have been chiefly as to exportation of corn.

old English constitution not yet abrogated, which would bear them out in their opposition. When the king therefore had intimated by a message, and afterwards in a speech, his command not to enter on the subject, couched in that arrogant tone of despotism which this absurd prince affected,[1] they presented a strong remonstrance against this inhibition; claiming "as an ancient, general, and undoubted right of parliament to debate freely all matters which do properly concern the subject; which freedom of debate being once foreclosed, the essence of the liberty of parliament is withal dissolved. For the judgment given by the exchequer, they take not on them to review it, but desire to know the reasons whereon it was grounded; especially as it was generally apprehended that the reasons of that judgment extended much farther, even to the utter ruin of the ancient liberty of this kingdom, and of the subjects' right of property in their lands and goods."[2] "The policy and constitution of this your kingdom (they say) appropriates unto the kings of this realm, with the assent of the parliament, as well the sovereign power of making laws, as that of taxing, or imposing upon the subjects' goods or merchandises, as may not, without their consents, be altered or changed. This is the cause that the people of this kingdom, as they ever showed themselves faithful and loving to their kings, and ready to aid them in all their just occasions with voluntary contributions, so have they been ever careful to preserve their own liberties and rights when anything hath been done to prejudice or impeach the same. And therefore, when their princes, occasioned either by their wars or their over-great bounty, or by any other necessity, have without consent of parliament set impositions, either within the land, or upon commodities either exported or imported by the merchants, they have, in open parliament, complained of it, in that it was done without their consents; and thereupon never failed to obtain a speedy and full redress, without any claim made by the kings, of

[1] Aikin's Memoirs of James I., i. 350. This speech justly gave offence. "The 21st of this present (May, 1610)," says a correspondent of sir Ralph Winwood, "he made another speech to both the houses, but so little to their satisfaction that I hear it bred generally much discomfort to see our monarchical power and royal prerogative strained so high, and made so transcendent every way, that, if the practice should follow the positions, we are not likely to leave to our successors that freedom we received from our forefathers; nor make account of anything we have longer than they list that govern." Winwood, iii. 175. The traces of this discontent appear in short notes of the debate. Journals, p. 430.

[2] Journals, 431.

any power or prerogative in that point. And though the law of property be original, and carefully preserved by the common laws of this realm, which are as ancient as the kingdom itself, yet these famous kings, for the better contentment and assurance of their loving subjects, agreed that this old fundamental right should be further declared and established by act of parliament. Wherein it is provided that no such charges should ever be laid upon the people without their common consent, as may appear by sundry records of former times. We, therefore, your majesty's most humble commons assembled in parliament, following the example of this worthy case of our ancestors, and out of a duty of those for whom we serve, finding that your majesty, without advice or consent of parliament, hath lately, in time of peace, set both greater impositions, and far more in number, than any your noble ancestors did ever in time of war, have, with all humility, presumed to present this most just and necessary petition unto your majesty, that all impositions set without the assent of parliament may be quite abolished and taken away; and that your majesty, in imitation likewise of your noble progenitors, will be pleased that a law be made during this session of parliament, to declare that all impositions set or to be set upon your people, their goods or merchandises, save only by common consent in parliament, are and shall be void."[1] They proceeded accordingly, after a pretty long time occupied in searching for precedents, to pass a bill taking away impositions; which, as might be anticipated, did not obtain the concurrence of the upper house.

Doctrine of king's absolute power inculcated by clergy.

The commons had reason for their apprehensions. This doctrine of the king's absolute power beyond the law had become current with all who sought his favor, and especially with the high church party. The convocation had in 1606 drawn up a set of canons, denouncing as erroneous a number of tenets hostile in their opinion to royal government. These canons, though never authentically published till a later age, could not have been secret. They consist of a series of propositions or paragraphs, to each of which an anathema of the opposite error is attached; deducing the origin of government from the patriarchal regimen of families, to the

[1] Somers Tracts, vol. ii. 159; in the Journals much shorter.

exclusion of any popular choice. In those golden days the functions both of king and priest were, as they term it, "the prerogatives of birthright," till the wickedness of mankind brought in usurpation, and so confused the pure stream of the fountain with its muddy runnels, that we must now look to prescription for that right which we cannot assign to primogeniture. Passive obedience in all cases without exception to the established monarch is inculcated.[1]

It is not impossible that a man might adopt this theory of the original of government, unsatisfactory as it appears on reflection, without deeming it incompatible with our mixed and limited monarchy. But its tendency was evidently in a contrary direction. The king's power was of God; that of the parliament only of man, obtained perhaps by rebellion; but out of rebellion what right could spring? Or were it even by voluntary concession, could a king alienate a divine gift, and infringe the order of Providence? Could his grants, if not in themselves null, avail against his posterity, heirs like himself under the great feoffment of creation? These consequences were at least plausible; and some would be found to draw them. And indeed if they were never explicitly laid down, the mere difference of respect with which mankind could not but contemplate a divine and human, a primitive or paramount, and a derivative authority, would operate as a prodigious advantage in favor of the crown.

The real aim of the clergy in thus enormously enhancing the pretensions of the crown was to gain its sanction and support for their own. Schemes of ecclesiastical jurisdiction, hardly less extensive than had warmed the imagination of Becket, now floated before the eyes of his successor Bancroft. He had fallen indeed upon evil days, and perfect independence on the temporal magistrate could no longer be

1 These canons were published in 1690, from a copy belonging to bishop Overall, with Sancroft's imprimatur. The title-page runs in an odd expression: —"Bishop Overall's Convocation-Book concerning the Government of God's Catholic Church and the Kingdoms of the whole World." The second canon is as follows: —"If any man shall affirm that men at the first ran up and down in woods and fields, &c., until they were taught by experience the necessity of government; and that therefore they chose some among themselves to order and rule the rest, giving them power and authority so to do; and that consequently all civil power, jurisdiction, and authority was first derived from the people and disordered multitude, or either is originally still in them, or else is deduced by their consent naturally from them, and is not God's ordinance, originally descending from him and depending upon him, he doth greatly err." P. 3.

attempted; but he acted upon the refined policy of making the royal supremacy over the church, which he was obliged to acknowledge, and professed to exaggerate, the very instrument of its independence upon the law. The favorite object of the bishops in this age was to render their ecclesiastical jurisdiction, no part of which had been curtailed in our hasty reformation, as unrestrained as possible by the courts of law. These had been wont, down from the reign of Henry II., to grant writs of prohibition whenever the spiritual courts transgressed their proper limits; to the great benefit of the subject, who would otherwise have lost his birthright of the common law, and been exposed to the defective, not to say iniquitous and corrupt, procedure of the ecclesiastical tribunals. But the civilians, supported by the prelates, loudly complained of these prohibitions, which seem to have been much more frequent in the latter years of Elizabeth and the reign of James than in any other period. Bancroft accordingly presented to the star-chamber, in 1605, a series of petitions in the name of the clergy, which lord Coke has denominated Articuli Cleri, by analogy to some similar representations of that order under Edward II.[1] In these it was complained that the courts of law interfered by continual prohibitions with a jurisdiction as established and as much derived from the king as their own, either in cases which were clearly within that jurisdiction's limits, or on the slightest suggestion of some matter belonging to the temporal court. It was hinted that the whole course of granting prohibitions was an encroachment of the king's bench and common pleas, and that they could regularly issue only out of chancery. To each of these articles of complaint, extending to twenty-five, the judges made separate answers, in a rough and, some might say, a rude style, but pointed and much to the purpose, vindicating in every instance their right to take cognizance of every collateral matter springing out of an ecclesiastical suit, and repelling the attack upon their power to issue prohibitions as a strange presumption. Nothing was done, nor, thanks to the firmness of the judges, could be done, by the council in this respect. For the clergy had begun by advancing that

Articuli Cleri.

1 Coke's 2d Institute, 601. Collier, 688. State Trials, ii. 131. See, too, an angry letter of Bancroft, written about 1611 (Strype's Life of Whitgift, Append. 227), wherein he inveighs against the common lawyers and the parliament.

the king's authority was sufficient to reform what was amiss in any of his own courts, all jurisdiction, spiritual and temporal, being annexed to his crown. But it was positively and repeatedly denied, in reply, that anything less than an act of parliament could alter the course of justice established by law. This effectually silenced the archbishop, who knew how little he had to hope from the commons. By the pretensions made for the church in this affair he exasperated the judges, who had been quite sufficiently disposed to second all rigorous measures against the puritan ministers, and aggravated that jealousy of the ecclesiastical courts which the common lawyers had long entertained.

Cowell's Interpreter.

An opportunity was soon given to those who disliked the civilians, that is, not only to the common lawyers, but to all the patriots and puritans in England, by an imprudent publication of a doctor Cowell. This man, in a law dictionary dedicated to Bancroft, had thought fit to insert passages of a tenor conformable to the new creed of the king's absolute or arbitrary power. Under the title King, it is said,—"He is above the law by his absolute power; and though for the better and equal course in making laws he do admit the three estates unto council, yet this in divers learned men's opinion is not of constraint, but of his own benignity, or by reason of the promise made upon oath at the time of his coronation. And though at his coronation he take an oath not to alter the laws of the land, yet, this oath notwithstanding, he may alter or suspend any particular law that seemeth hurtful to the public estate. Thus much in short, because I have heard some to be of opinion that the laws are above the king." And in treating of the parliament, Cowell observes, — "Of these two one must be true, either that the king is above the parliament, that is, the positive laws of his kingdom, or else that he is not an absolute king. And therefore, though it be a merciful policy, and also a politic mercy, not alterable without great peril, to make laws by the consent of the whole realm, because so no part shall have cause to complain of a partiality, yet simply to bind the prince to or by these laws were repugnant to the nature and constitution of an absolute monarchy." It is said again, under the title Prerogative, that "the king, by the custom of this kingdom, maketh no laws without the consent of the three estates, though he may quash any law concluded of by them;" and that he "holds it incontrollable that the king of England is an absolute king." [1]

Such monstrous positions from the mouth of a man of learning and conspicuous in his profession, who was surmised to have been instigated as well as patronized by the archbishop, and of whose book the king was reported to have spoken in terms of eulogy, gave very just scandal to the house of commons. They solicited and obtained a conference with the lords, which the attorney-general, sir Francis Bacon, managed on the part of the lower house; a remarkable proof of his adroitness and pliancy. James now discovered that it was necessary to sacrifice this too unguarded advocate of prerogative: Cowell's book was suppressed by proclamation, for which the commons returned thanks, with great joy at their victory.[2]

It is the evident policy of every administration, in dealing with the house of commons, to humor them in everything that touches their pride and tenaciousness of privilege, never attempting to protect any one who incurs their displeasure by want of respect. This seems to have been understood by the earl of Salisbury, the first English minister who, having long sat in the lower house, had become skilful in those arts of management which his successors have always reckoned so essential a part of their mystery. He wanted a considerable sum of money to defray the king's debts, which, on his coming into the office of lord treasurer after lord Buckhurst's death, he had found to amount to 1,300,000*l.*, about one third of which was still undischarged. The ordinary expense also surpassed the revenue by 81,000*l.* It was impossible that this could continue without involving the crown in such embarrassments as would leave it wholly at the mercy of parliament. Cecil therefore devised the scheme of obtaining a perpetual yearly revenue of 200,000*l.*, to be granted once for

[1] Cowell's Interpreter, or Law Dictionary; edit. 1607. These passages are expunged in the later editions of this useful book. What the author says of the writ of prohibition, and the statutes of præmunire, under these words, was very invidious towards the common lawyers, treating such restraints upon the ecclesiastical jurisdiction as necessary in former ages, but now become useless since the annexation of the supremacy to the crown.

[2] Commons' Journals, 339, and afterwards to 415. The authors of the Parliamentary History say there is no further mention of the business after the conference: overlooking the most important circumstance, the king's proclamation suppressing the book, which yet is mentioned by Rapin and Carte, though the latter makes a false and disingenuous excuse for Cowell. Vol. iii. p. 798. Several passages concerning this affair occur in Winwood's Memorials, to which I refer the curious reader. Vol. iii. pp. 125, 129, 131, 136, 137, 145.

all by parliament; and, the better to incline the house to this high and extraordinary demand, he promised in the king's name to give all the redress and satisfaction in his power for any grievances they might bring forward.[1]

This offer on the part of government seemed to make an opening for a prosperous adjustment of the differences which had subsisted ever since the king's accession. The commons, accordingly, postponing the business of a subsidy, to which the courtiers wished to give priority, brought forward a host of their accustomed grievances in ecclesiastical and temporal concerns. The most essential was undoubtedly that of impositions, which they sent up a bill to the lords, as above mentioned, to take away. They next complained of the ecclesiastical high commission court, which took upon itself to fine and imprison, powers not belonging to their jurisdiction, and passed sentences without appeal, interfering frequently with civil rights, and in all its procedure neglecting the rules and precautions of the common law. They dwelt on the late abuse of proclamations assuming the character of laws. "Amongst many other points of happiness and freedom," it is said, "which your majesty's subjects of this kingdom have enjoyed under your royal progenitors, kings and queens of this realm, there is none which they have accounted more dear and precious than this, to be guided and governed by the certain rule of the law, which giveth both to the head and members that which of right belongeth to them, and not by any uncertain or arbitrary form of government, which, as it hath proceeded from the original good constitution and temperature of this estate, so hath it been the principal means of upholding the same, in such sort as that their kings have been just, beloved, happy, and glorious, and the kingdom itself peaceable, flourishing, and durable so many ages. And the effect, as well of the contentment that the subjects of this kingdom have taken in this form of government, as also of the love, respect, and duty which they have by reason of the same rendered unto their princes, may appear in this, that they have, as occasion hath required, yielded more extraordinary and voluntary contribution to assist their kings than the subjects of any other known kingdom whatsoever.

Renewed complaints of the commons.

[1] Winwood, iii. 123.

Out of this root hath grown the indubitable right of the people of this kingdom, not to be made subject to any punishment that shall extend to their lives, lands, bodies, or goods, other than such as are ordained by the common laws of this land, or the statutes made by their common consent in parliament. Nevertheless, it is apparent, both that proclamations have been of late years much more frequent than heretofore, and that they are extended, not only to the liberty, but also to the goods, inheritances, and livelihood of men; some of them tending to alter some points of the law, and make a new; other some made, shortly after a session of parliament, for matter directly rejected in the same session; other appointing punishments to be inflicted before lawful trial and conviction; some containing penalties in form of penal statutes; some referring the punishment of offenders to courts of arbitrary discretion, which have laid heavy and grievous censures upon the delinquents; some, as the proclamation for starch, accompanied with letters commanding inquiry to be made against the transgressors at the quarter-sessions; and some vouching former proclamations to countenance and warrant the later, as by a catalogue here underwritten more particularly appeareth. By reason whereof there is a general fear conceived and spread amongst your majesty's people, that proclamations will, by degrees, grow up and increase to the strength and nature of laws; whereby not only that ancient happiness, freedom, will be much blemished (if not quite taken away), which their ancestors have so long enjoyed; but the same may also (in process of time) bring a new form of arbitrary government upon the realm; and this their fear is the more increased by occasion of certain books lately published, which ascribe a greater power to proclamations than heretofore had been conceived to belong unto them; as also of the care taken to reduce all the proclamations made since your majesty's reign into one volume, and to print them in such form as acts of parliament formerly have been, and still are used to be, which seemeth to imply a purpose to give them more reputation and more establishment than heretofore they have had." [1]

They proceed, after a list of these illegal proclamations, to enumerate other grievances, such as the delay of courts of

[1] Somers Tracts, ii. 162. State Trials, ii. 519.

law in granting writs of prohibition and habeas corpus, the jurisdiction of the council of Wales over the four bordering shires of Gloucester, Worcester, Hereford, and Salop,[1] some patents of monopolies, and a tax under the name of a license recently set upon victuallers. The king answered these remonstrances with civility, making, as usual, no concession with respect to the ecclesiastical commission, and evading some of their other requests; but promising that his proclamations should go no farther than was warranted by law, and that the royal licenses to victuallers should be revoked.

It appears that the commons, deeming these enumerated abuses contrary to law, were unwilling to chaffer with the crown for the restitution of their actual rights. There were, however, parts of the prerogative which they could not dispute, though galled by the burden — the incidents of feudal tenure and purveyance. A negotiation was accordingly commenced and carried on for some time with the court for abolishing both these, or at least the former. The king, though he refused to part with tenure by knight's service, which he thought connected with the honor of the monarchy, was induced, with some real or pretended reluctance, to give up its lucrative incidents, relief, primer seisin, and wardship, as well as the right of purveyance. But material difficulties recurred in the prosecution of this treaty. Some were apprehensive that the validity of a statute cutting off such ancient branches of prerogative might hereafter be called in question, especially if the root from which they sprung, tenure in capite, should still remain. The king's demands, too, seemed exorbitant.

Negotiation for giving up the feudal revenue.

[1] The court of the council of Wales was erected by statute 34 H. 8, c. 26, for that principality and its marches, with authority to determine such causes and matters as should be assigned to them by the king, "as heretofore had been accustomed and used;' which implies a previous existence of some such jurisdiction. It was pretended that the four counties of Hereford, Worcester, Gloucester, and Salop were included within their authority as marches of Wales. This was controverted in the reign of James by the inhabitants of these counties; and on reference to the twelve judges, according to lord Coke, it was resolved that they were ancient English shires, and not within the jurisdiction of the council of Wales; "and yet," he subjoins, "the commission was not after reformed in all points as it ought to have been." Fourth Inst. 242. An elaborate argument in defence of the jurisdiction may be found in Bacon, ii. 122. And there are many papers on this subject in Cotton MSS. Vitellius, C. i. The complaints of this enactment had begun in the time of Elizabeth. It was alleged that the four counties had been reduced from a very disorderly state to tranquillity by means of the council's jurisdiction. But if this were true, it did not furnish a reason for continuing to exclude them from the general privileges of the common law, after the necessity had ceased. The king, however, was determined not to concede this point. Carte, iii. 794.

He asked 200,000*l.* as a yearly revenue over and above 100,000*l.*, at which his wardships were valued, and which the commons were content to give. After some days' pause upon this proposition, they represented to the lords, with whom, through committees of conference, the whole matter had been discussed, that, if such a sum were to be levied on those only who had lands subject to wardship, it would be a burden they could not endure; and that, if it were imposed equally on the kingdom, it would cause more offence and commotion in the people than they could risk. After a good deal of haggling, Salisbury delivered the king's final determination to accept of 200,000*l.* per annum, which the commons voted to grant as a full composition for abolishing the right of wardship and dissolving the court that managed it, and for taking away all purveyance; with some further concessions, and particularly that the king's claim to lands should be bound by sixty years' prescription. Two points yet remained, of no small moment; namely, by what assurance they could secure themselves against the king's prerogative, so often held up by court lawyers as something uncontrollable by statute, and by what means so great an imposition should be levied; but the consideration of these was reserved for the ensuing session, which was to take place in October.[1] They were prorogued in July till that month, having previously granted a subsidy for the king's immediate exigencies. On their meeting again, the lords began the business by requesting a conference with the other house about the proposed contract. But it appeared that the commons had lost their disposition to comply. Time had been given them to calculate the disproportion of the terms, and the perpetual burden that lands held by knights' service must endure. They had reflected, too, on the king's prodigal humor, the rapacity of the Scots in his service, and the probability that this additional revenue would be wasted without sustaining the national honor, or preventing future applications for money. They saw that, after all the specious promises by which they had been led on, no redress was to be expected as to those grievances they had most at heart; that the ecclesiastical courts would not be suffered to lose a jot of their jurisdiction; that illegal customs were still

1 Commons' Journals for 1610, passim. Lords' Journals, 7th May, et post. Parl. Hist. 1124, et post. Bacon, i. 676. Winwood, iii. 119, et post.

to be levied at the outports; that proclamations were still to be enforced like acts of parliament. Great coldness accordingly was displayed in their proceedings, and in a short time this distinguished parliament, after sitting nearly seven years, was dissolved by proclamation.[1]

Dissolution of parliament.

It was now perhaps too late for the king, by any reform or concession, to regain that public esteem which he had forfeited. Deceived by an overweening opinion of his own learning, which was not inconsiderable, of his general abilities, which were far from contemptible, and of his capacity for government, which was very small, and confirmed in this delusion by the disgraceful flattery of his courtiers and bishops, he had wholly overlooked the real difficulties of his position — as a foreigner, rather distantly connected with the royal stock, and as a native of a hostile and hateful kingdom come to succeed the most renowned of sovereigns, and to grasp a sceptre which deep policy and long experience had taught her admirably to wield.[2] The people were proud of martial glory; he spoke only of the blessing of the peacemakers: they abhorred the court of Spain; he sought its friendship: they asked indulgence for scrupulous consciences; he would bear no deviation from conformity: they writhed under the yoke of the bishops, whose power he thought necessary to his own — they were animated by a persecuting temper towards the catholics; he was averse to extreme rigor: they had been used to the utmost frugality in dispensing the public treasure; he squandered it on unworthy favorites: they had seen at least exterior decency of morals prevail in the queen's court; they now heard only of its dissoluteness and extravagance:[3] they had imbibed an exclusive fondness for the

Character of James.

1 It appears by a letter of the king, in Murden's State Papers, p. 813, that some indecent allusions to himself in the house of commons had irritated him: — "Wherein we have misbehaved ourselves we know not, nor we can never yet learn; but sure we are we may say with Bellarmin in his book, that in all the lower houses these seven years past, especially these two last sessions, Ego pungor, ego carpor. Our fame and actions have been tossed like tennis-balls among them, and all that spite and malice durst do to disgrace and inflame us hath been used. To be short, this lower house by their behavior have perilled and annoyed our health, wounded our reputation, emboldened all ill-natured people, encroached upon many of our privileges, and plagued our people with their delays. It only resteth now that you labor all you can to do that you think best to the repairing of our estate."

2 "Your queen," says lord Thomas Howard, in a letter, "did talk of her subjects' love and good affection, and in good truth she aimed well; our king talketh of his subjects' fear and subjection, and herein I think he doth well too, as long as it holdeth good." Nugæ Antiquæ, i. 395.

3 The court of James I. was incom-

common law as the source of their liberties and privileges; his churchmen and courtiers, but none more than himself, talked of absolute power and the imprescriptible rights of monarchy.[1]

James lost in 1611 his son prince Henry, and in 1612 the lord treasurer Salisbury. He showed little regret for the former, whose high spirit and great popularity afforded a mortifying contrast, especially as the young prince had not taken sufficient pains to disguise his contempt for his father.[2] Salisbury was a very able man, to whom, perhaps, his contemporaries did some injustice. The ministers of weak and wilful monarchs are made answerable for the mischiefs they are compelled to suffer, and gain no credit for those which they prevent. Cecil had made personal enemies of those who had loved Essex or admired Raleigh, as well as those who looked invidiously on his elevation. It was believed that the desire shown by the house of commons to abolish the feudal wardships proceeded in a great measure from the circumstance that this obnoxious minister was master of the court of wards, an office both lucrative and productive of much influence. But he came into the scheme of abolishing it with a readiness that did him credit.

Death of lord Salisbury.

His chief praise, however, was his management of continental relations. The only minister of James's cabinet who had been trained in the councils of Elizabeth, he retained some of her jealousy of Spain and of her regard for the protestant interests. The court of Madrid, aware both of the king's pusillanimity and of his favorable disposi-

Foreign politics of the government.

parably the most disgraceful scene of profligacy which this country has ever witnessed; equal to that of Charles II. in the laxity of female virtue, and without any sort of parallel in some other respects. Gross drunkenness is imputed even to some of the ladies who acted in the court pageants, Nugæ Antiquæ, i. 348, which Mr. Gifford, who seems absolutely enraptured with this age and its manners, might as well have remembered. Life of Ben Jonson, p. 231, &c. The king's prodigality is notorious.

1 "It is atheism and blasphemy," he says, in a speech made in the star-chamber, 1616, "to dispute what God can do; good Christians content themselves with his will revealed in his word: so it is presumption and high contempt in a subject to dispute what a king can do, or say that a king cannot do this or that." King James's Works, p. 557.

It is probable that his familiar conversation was full of this rhodomontade, disgusting and contemptible from so wretched a pedant, as well as offensive to the indignant ears of those who knew and valued their liberties. The story of bishops Neile and Andrews is far too trite for repetition.

2 Carte, iii. 747. Birch's Life of P. Henry, 405. Rochester, three days after, directed sir Thomas Edmondes at Paris to commence a negotiation for a marriage between prince Charles and the second daughter of the late king of France; but the ambassador had more sense of decency, and declined to enter on such an affair at that moment.

tions, affected a tone in the conferences held in 1604 about a treaty of peace which Elizabeth would have resented in a very different manner.[1] On this occasion he not only deserted the United Provinces, but gave hopes to Spain that he might, if they persevered in their obstinacy, take part against them. Nor have I any doubt that his blind attachment to that power would have precipitated him into a ruinous connection, if Cecil's wisdom had not influenced his councils. During this minister's life our foreign politics seem to have been conducted with as much firmness and prudence as his master's temper would allow; the mediation of England was of considerable service in bringing about the great truce of twelve years between Spain and Holland in 1609; and in the dispute which sprang up soon afterwards concerning the succession to the duchies of Cleves and Juliers, a dispute which threatened to mingle in arms the catholic and protestant parties throughout Europe,[2] our councils were full of a vigor and promptitude unusual in this reign, nor did anything but the assassination of Henry IV. prevent the appearance of an English army in the Netherlands. It must at least be con-

1 Winwood, vol. ii. Carte, iii. 749. Watson's Hist. of Philip III., Appendix. In some passages of this negotiation Cecil may appear not wholly to have deserved the character I have given him for adhering to Elizabeth's principles of policy. But he was placed in a difficult position, not feeling himself secure of the king's favor, which, notwithstanding his great previous services, that capricious prince, for the first year after his accession, rather sparingly afforded; as appears from the Memoirs of Sully, i. 14, and Nugæ Antiquæ, i. 345. It may be said that Cecil was as little Spanish, just as Walpole was as little Hanoverian, as the partialities of their respective sovereigns would permit, though too much so in appearance for their own reputation. It is hardly necessary to observe that James and the kingdom were chiefly indebted to Cecil for the tranquillity that attended the accession of the former to the throne. I will take this opportunity of noticing that the learned and worthy compiler of the catalogue of the Lansdowne manuscripts in the Museum has thought fit not only to charge sir Michael Hicks with venality, but to add, — "It is certain that articles among these papers contribute to justify very strong suspicions that neither of the secretary's masters [lord Burleigh and lord Salisbury] was altogether innocent on the score of corruption." Lansd. Cat. vol. xci. p. 45. This is much too strong an accusation to be brought forward without more proof than appears. It is absurd to mention presents of fat bucks to men in power as bribes; and rather more so to charge a man with being corrupted because an attempt is made to corrupt him, as the catalogue-maker has done in this place. I would not offend this respectable gentleman; but by referring to many of the Lansdowne manuscripts I am enabled to say that he has travelled frequently out of his province, and substituted his conjectures for an analysis or abstract of the document before him.

2 A great part of Winwood's third volume relates to this business, which, as is well known, attracted a prodigious degree of attention throughout Europe. The question, as Winwood wrote to Salisbury, was "not of the succession of Cleves and Juliers, but whether the house of Austria and the church of Rome, both now on the wane, shall recover their lustre and greatness in these parts of Europe." P. 378. James wished to have the right referred to his arbitration, and would have decided in favor of the elector of Brandenburg, the chief protestant competitor.

fessed that the king's affairs, both at home and abroad, were far worse conducted after the death of the Earl of Salisbury than before.[1]

Lord Coke's alienation from the court.

The administration found an important disadvantage, about this time, in a sort of defection of sir Edward Coke (more usually called lord Coke), chief-justice of the king's bench, from the side of prerogative. He was a man of strong though narrow intellect; confessedly the greatest master of English law that had ever appeared, but proud and overbearing, a flatterer and tool of the court till he had obtained his ends, and odious to the nation for the brutal manner in which, as attorney-general, he had behaved towards sir Walter Raleigh on his trial. In raising him to the post of chief-justice the council had of course relied on finding his unfathomable stores of precedent subservient to their purposes. But, soon after his promotion, Coke, from various causes, began to steer a more independent course. He was little formed to endure a competitor in his own profession, and lived on ill terms both with the lord chancellor Egerton and with the attorney-general, sir Francis Bacon. The latter had long been his rival and enemy. Discountenanced by Elizabeth, who, against the importunity of Essex, had raised Coke over his head, that great and aspiring genius was now high in the king's favor. The chief-justice affected to look down on one as inferior to him in knowledge of our municipal law, as he was superior in all other learning and in all the philosophy of jurisprudence. And the mutual enmity of these illustrious men never ceased till each in his turn satiated his revenge by the other's fall. Coke was also much offended by the attempts of the bishops to emancipate their ecclesiastical courts from the civil jurisdiction. I have already mentioned the peremptory tone in which he repelled Bancroft's Articuli Cleri. But as the king and some of the council rather favored these episcopal pretensions, they were troubled by what they deemed his obstinacy, and discovered more and more that they had to deal with a most impracticable spirit.

1 Winwood, vols. ii. and iii. passim. Birch, that accurate master of this part of English history, has done justice to Salisbury's character. Negotiations of Edmondes, p. 347. Miss Aikin, looking to his want of constitutional principle, is more unfavorable, and in that respect justly: but what statesman of that age was ready to admit the new creed of parliamentary control over the executive government? Memoirs of James, i. 395.

It would be invidious to exclude from the motives that altered lord Coke's behavior in matters of prerogative his real affection for the laws of the land, which novel systems, broached by the churchmen and civilians, threatened to subvert.[1] In Bates's case, which seems to have come in some shape extrajudicially before him, he had delivered an opinion in favor of the king's right to impose at the outports; but so cautiously guarded, and bottomed on such different grounds from those taken by the barons of the exchequer, that it could not be cited in favor of any fresh encroachments.[2] He now performed a great service to his country.

Illegal proclamations.

The practice of issuing proclamations, by way of temporary regulation indeed, but interfering with the subject's liberty, in cases unprovided for by parliament, had grown still more usual than under Elizabeth. Coke was sent for to attend some of the council, who might perhaps have reason to conjecture his sentiments, and it was demanded whether the king, by his proclamation, might prohibit new buildings about London, and whether he might prohibit the making of starch from wheat. This was during the session of parliament in 1610, and with a view to what answer the king should make to the commons' remonstrance against these proclamations. Coke replied that it was a matter of great importance, on which he would confer with his brethren. "The chancellor said that every precedent had first a commencement, and he would advise the judges to maintain the power and prerogative of the king; and in cases wherein

[1] "On Sunday, before the king's going to Newmarket (which was Sunday last was a se'nnight), my lord Coke and all the judges of the common law were before his majesty to answer some complaints made by the civil lawyers for the general granting of prohibitions. I heard that the lord Coke, amongst other offensive speech, should say to his majesty that his highness was defended by his laws. At which saying, with other speech then used by the lord Coke, his majesty was very much offended, and told him he spoke foolishly, and said that he was not defended by his laws, but by God; and so gave the lord Coke, in other words, a very sharp reprehension, both for that and other things; and withal told him that sir Thomas Crompton [judge of the admiralty] was as good a man as Coke; my lord Coke having then, by way of exception, used some speech against sir Thomas Crompton. Had not my lord treasurer, most humbly on his knee, used many good words to pacify his majesty, and to excuse that which had been spoken, it was thought his highness would have been much more offended. In the conclusion, his majesty, by means of my lord treasurer, was well pacified, and gave a gracious countenance to all the other judges, and said he would maintain the common law." Lodge, iii. 364. This letter is dated 25th November, 1608, which shows how early Coke had begun to give offence by his zeal for the law.

[2] 12 Reports. In his Second Institute, p. 57, written a good deal later, he speaks in a very different manner of Bates's case, and declares the judgment of the court of exchequer to be contrary to law.

there is no authority and precedent, to leave it to the king to order in it according to his wisdom and for the good of his subjects, or otherwise the king would be no more than the duke of Venice; and that the king was so much restrained in his prerogative that it was to be feared the bonds would be broken. And the lord privy-seal (Northampton) said that the physician was not always bound to a precedent, but to apply his medicine according to the quality of the disease; and all concluded that it should be necessary at that time to confirm the king's prerogative with our opinions, although that there were not any former precedent or authority in law, for every precedent ought to have a commencement. To which I answered, that true it is that every precedent ought to have a commencement; but, when authority and precedent is wanting, there is need of great consideration before that anything of novelty shall be established, and to provide that this be not against the law of the land; for I said that the king cannot change any part of the common law, nor create any offence by his proclamation which was not an offence before, without parliament. But at this time I only desired to have a time of consultation and conference with my brothers." This was agreed to by the council and three judges, besides Coke, appointed to consider it. They resolved that the king, by his proclamation, cannot create any offence which was not one before; for then he might alter the law of the land in a high point; for if he may create an offence where none is, upon that ensues fine and imprisonment. It was also resolved that the king hath no prerogative but what the law of the land allows him. But the king, for the prevention of offences, may by proclamation admonish all his subjects that they keep the laws and do not offend them, upon punishment to be inflicted by the law; and the neglect of such proclamation, Coke says, aggravates the offence. Lastly, they resolved that, if an offence be not punishable in the star-chamber, the prohibition of it by proclamation cannot make it so. After this resolution, the report goes on to remark, no proclamation imposing fine and imprisonment was made.[1]

[1] 12 Reports. There were, however, several proclamations afterwards to forbid building within two miles of London, except on old foundations, and in that case only with brick or stone, under penalty of being proceeded against by the attorney-general in the star-chamber. Rymer, xvii. 107 (1618), 144 (1619), 607 (1624). London nevertheless increased rapidly, which was by means of licenses to build;

Means resorted to in order to avoid the meeting of parliament.

By the abrupt dissolution of parliament James was left nearly in the same necessity as before: their subsidy being by no means sufficient to defray his expenses, far less to discharge his debts. He had frequently betaken himself to the usual resource of applying to private subjects, especially rich merchants, for loans of money. These loans, which bore no interest, and for the repayment of which there was no security, disturbed the prudent citizens, especially as the council used to solicit them with a degree of importunity at least bordering on compulsion. The house of commons had in the last session requested that no one should be bound to lend money to the king against his will. The king had answered that he allowed not of any precedents from the time of usurping or decaying princes, or people too bold and wanton; that he desired not to govern in that commonwealth where the people should be assured of everything and hope for nothing, nor would he leave to posterity such a mark of weakness on his reign; yet, in the matter of loans, he would refuse no reasonable excuse.[1] Forced loans or benevolences were directly prohibited by an act of Richard III., whose laws, however the court might sometimes throw a slur upon his usurpation, had always been in the statute-book. After the dissolution of 1610, James attempted as usual to obtain loans; but the merchants, grown bolder with the spirit of the times, refused him the accommodation.[2] He had recourse to another method of raising money, unprecedented, I believe, before his reign, though long practised in France, the sale of honors. He sold several peerages for considerable sums,

the prohibition being in this, as in many other cases, enacted chiefly for the sake of the dispensations.

James made use of proclamations to infringe personal liberty in another respect. He disliked to see any country gentleman come up to London, where, it must be confessed, if we trust to what those proclamations assert and the memoirs of the age confirm, neither their own behavior, nor that of their wives and daughters, who took the worst means of repairing the ruin their extravagance had caused, redounded to their honor. The king's comparison of them to ships in a river and in the sea is well known. Still, in a constitutional point of view, we may be startled at proclamations commanding them to return to their country houses, and maintain hospitality, on pain of condign punishment. Rymer, xvi. 517 (1604); xvii. 417 (1622), 632 (1624).

I neglected, in the first chapter, the reference I had made to an important dictum of the judges in the reign of Mary which is decisive as to the legal character of proclamations even in the midst of the Tudor period. "The king, it is said, may make a proclamation, quoad terrorem populi, to put them in fear of his displeasure, but not to impose any fine, forfeiture, or imprisonment; for no proclamation can make a new law, but only confirm and ratify an ancient one." Dalison's Reports, 20.

1 Winwood, iii. 193.

2 Carte, iii. 805.

and created a new order of hereditary knights, called baronets, who paid 1000*l.* each for their patents.[1]

Such resources, however, being evidently insufficient and temporary, it was almost indispensable to try once more the temper of a parliament. This was strongly urged by Bacon, whose fertility of invention rendered him constitutionally sanguine of success. He submitted to the king that there were expedients for more judiciously managing a house of commons, than Cecil, upon whom he was too willing to throw blame, had done with the last; that some of those who had been most forward in opposing were now won over, such as Neville, Yelverton, Hyde, Crew, Dudley Digges; that much might be done by forethought towards filling the house with well-affected persons, winning or blinding the lawyers, whom he calls "the literæ vocales of the house," and drawing the chief constituent bodies of the assembly, the country gentlemen, the merchants, the courtiers, to act for the king's advantage; that it would be expedient to tender voluntarily certain graces and modifications of the king's prerogative, such as might with smallest injury be conceded, lest they should be first demanded, and in order to save more important points.[2] This advice was seconded by sir Henry Neville, an ambitious man, who had narrowly escaped in the queen's time for having tampered in Essex's conspiracy, and had much promoted the opposition in the late parliament, but was now seeking the post of secretary of state. He advised the king, in a very sensible memorial, to consider what had been demanded and what had been promised in the last session, granting the more reasonable of the commons' requests, and performing all his own promises; to avoid any speech likely to excite irritation; and to seem confident of the parliament's good affections, not waiting to be pressed for what he meant to do.[3] Neville, and others who, like him, professed to understand the temper of the

[1] The number of these was intended to be two hundred, but only ninety-three patents were sold in the first six years. Lingard, ix. 203, from Somers Tracts. In the first part of his reign he had availed himself of an old feudal resource, calling on all who held 40*l.* a year in chivalry (whether of the crown or not, as it seems) to receive knighthood, or to pay a composition. Rymer, xvi. 530. The object of this was of course to raise money from those who thought the honor troublesome and expensive, but such as chose to appear could not be refused; and this accounts for his having made many hundred knights in the first year of his reign. Harris's Life of James, 69.

[2] M.S. Penes autorem.

[3] Carte, iv. 17.

commons, and to facilitate the king's dealings with them, were called *undertakers*.[1] This circumstance, like several others in the present reign, is curious, as it shows the rise of a systematic parliamentary influence, which was one day to become the mainspring of government.

Under-takers.

Neville, however, and his associates, had deceived the courtiers with promises they could not realize. It was resolved to announce certain intended graces in the speech from the throne: that is, to declare the king's readiness to pass bills that might remedy some grievances and retrench a part of his prerogative. These proffered amendments of the law, though eleven in number, failed altogether of giving the content that had been fully expected. Except the repeal of a strange act of Henry VIII., allowing the king to make such laws as he should think fit for the principality of Wales without consent of parliament,[2] none of them could perhaps be reckoned of any constitutional importance. In all domanial and fiscal causes, and wherever the private interests of the crown stood in competition with those of a subject, the former enjoyed enormous and superior advantages, whereof what is strictly called its prerogative was principally composed. The terms of prescription that bound other men's right, the rules of pleading and procedure established for the sake of truth and justice, did not in general oblige the king. It was not by doing away a very few of these invidious and oppressive distinctions that the crown could be allowed to keep on foot still more momentous abuses.

Parliament of 1614.

The commons of 1614 accordingly went at once to the characteristic grievance of this reign, the customs at the outports. They had grown so confident in their cause by ransacking ancient records, that an unanimous vote passed against the king's right of imposition; not that there were no courtiers in the house, but the cry was too obstreperous to be withstood.[3] They demanded a conference on the subject with the lords, who preserved a kind of medi-

[1] Wilson, in Kennet, ii. 696.

[2] This act (34 H. VIII. c. 26) was repealed a few years afterwards. 21 J. I. c. 10.

[3] Commons' Journals, 466, 472, 481, 486. Sir Henry Wotton at length muttered something in favor of the prerogative of laying impositions, as belonging to hereditary, though not to elective, princes. Id. 493. This silly argument is only worth notice as a proof what erroneous notions of government were sometimes imbibed from an intercourse with foreign nations. Dudley Digges and Sandys answered him very properly.

ating neutrality throughout this reign.[1] In the course of their debate, Neyle, bishop of Lichfield, threw out some aspersion on the commons. They were immediately in a flame, and demanded reparation. This Neyle was a man of indifferent character, and very unpopular from the share he had taken in the earl of Essex's divorce, and from his severity towards the puritans; nor did the house fail to comment upon all his faults in their debate. He had, however, the prudence to excuse himself ("with many tears," as the Lords' Journals inform us), denying the most offensive words imputed to him; and the affair went no farther.[2] This ill-humor of the commons disconcerted those who had relied on the undertakers. But as the secret of these men had not been kept, their project considerably aggravated the prevailing discontent.[3] The king had positively denied in his first speech that there were any such undertakers; and Bacon, then attorney-general, laughed at the chimerical notion that private men should undertake for all the commons of England.[4] That some persons, however, had obtained that name at court, and held out such promises, is at present out of doubt; and indeed the king, forgetful of his former denial, expressly confessed it on opening the session of 1621.

Amidst these heats little progress was made; and no one took up the essential business of supply. The king at length sent a message requesting that a supply might be granted, with a threat of dissolving parliament unless it were done. But the days of intimidation were gone by. The house voted that they would first proceed with the business of impositions, and postpone supply till their grievances should be redressed.[5] Aware of the impossibility of conquering their resolution, the king carried his measure into effect by a dissolution.[6]

Dissolved without passing a single act

1 The judges, having been called upon by the house of lords to deliver their opinions on the subject of impositions, previous to the intended conference, requested, by the mouth of chief justice Coke, to be excused. This was probably a disappointment to lord chancellor Egerton, who moved to consult them, and proceeded from Coke's dislike to him and to the court. It induced the house to decline the conference. Lords' Journals, 23d May.

2 Lords' Journals, May 31. Commons' Journals, 496, 498.

3 Carte, iv. 23. Neville's memorial, above mentioned, was read in the house, May 14.

4 Carte, iv. 19, 20. Bacon, i. 695. C. J. 462.

5 C. J. 506. Carte, 23. This writer absurdly defends the prerogative of laying impositions on merchandise as part of the law of nations.

6 It is said that, previously to taking this step, the king sent for the commons, and tore all their bills before their faces in the banqueting-house at Whitehall. D'Israeli's Character of James, p. 158, on the authority of an unpublished letter.

They had sat about two months, and, what is perhaps unprecedented in our history, had not passed a single bill. James followed up this strong step by one still more vigorous. Several members, who had distinguished themselves by warm language against the government, were arrested after the dissolution, and kept for a short time in custody; a manifest violation of that freedom of speech, without which no assembly can be independent, and which is the stipulated privilege of the house of commons.[1]

It was now evident that James could never expect to be on terms of harmony with a parliament, unless by surrendering pretensions which not only were in his eyes indispensable to the lustre of his monarchy, but from which he derived an income that he had no means of replacing. He went on accordingly for six years, supplying his exigencies by such precarious resources as circumstances might furnish. He restored the towns mortgaged by the Dutch to Elizabeth on payment of 2,700,000 florins, about one third of the original debt. The enormous fines imposed by the star-chamber, though seldom, I believe, enforced to their utmost extent, must have considerably enriched the exchequer. It is said by Carte that some Dutch merchants paid fines to the amount of 133,000*l.* for exporting gold coin.[2] But still greater profit was hoped from the requisition of that more than half involuntary contribution, miscalled a benevolence. It began by a subscription of the nobility and principal persons about the court. Letters were sent written to the sheriffs and magistrates, directing them to call on people of ability. It had always been supposed doubtful whether the statute of Richard III. abrogating "exactions, called benevolences," should extend to voluntary gifts at the solicitation of the crown. The language used in that act certainly implies that the pretended benevolences of Edward's reign had been extorted against the subjects' will; yet if positive violence were not employed, it seems difficult to find a legal criterion by which to distinguish the effects of willing loyalty from those of fear or shame. Lord Coke is said to have at first declared that the king could not solicit a benevolence from his subjects, but to have afterwards retracted his opinion and pronounced in favor of its legality. To this second

Benevolences.

1 Carte. Wilson. Camden's Annals of James I. (in Kennet, ii. 643).
2 Carte, iv. 56.

opinion he adheres in his Reports.[1] While this business was pending, Mr. Oliver St. John wrote a letter to the mayor of Marlborough, explaining his reasons for declining to contribute, founded on the several statutes which he deemed applicable, and on the impropriety of particular men opposing their judgment to the commons in parliament, who had refused to grant any subsidy. This argument, in itself exasperating, he followed up by somewhat blunt observations on the king. His letter came under the consideration of the star-chamber, where the offence having been severely descanted upon by the attorney-general, Mr. St. John was sentenced to a fine of 5,000*l.* and to imprisonment during pleasure.[2]

Prosecution of Peacham.

Coke, though still much at the council-board, was regarded with increasing dislike on account of his uncompromising humor. This he had occasion to display in perhaps the worst and most tyrannical act of king James's reign, the prosecution of one Peacham, a minister in Somersetshire, for high treason. A sermon had been found in this man's study (it does not appear what led to the search), never preached, nor, if judge Coke is right, intended to be preached, containing such sharp censures upon the king, and invectives against the government, as, had they been published, would have amounted to a seditious libel. But common sense revolted at construing it into treason under the statute of Edward III., as a compassing of the king's death. James, however, took it up with indecent eagerness. Peacham was put to the rack, and examined upon various interrogatories, as it is expressed by secretary Winwood, "before torture, in torture, between torture, and after torture." Nothing could be drawn from him as to any accomplices, nor any explanation of his design in writing the sermon; which was probably but an intemperate effusion, so common among the puritan clergy. It was necessary therefore to rely on this as the overt act of treason. Aware of the difficulties that attended this course, the king directed Bacon previously to confer with the judges of the king's bench, one by one, in order to secure their determination for the crown. Coke objected that "such particular, and, as he called it, auricular taking of opinions was not according to

1 12 Reports, 119.

2 State Trials, ii. 889.

the custom of this realm."[1] The other three judges, having been tampered with, agreed to answer such questions concerning the case as the king might direct to be put to them; yielding to the sophism that every judge was bound by his oath to give council to his majesty. The chief-justice continued to maintain his objection to this separate closeting of judges; yet, finding himself abandoned by his colleagues, consented to give answers in writing, which seem to have been merely evasive. Peacham was brought to trial, and found guilty, but not executed, dying in prison a few months after.[2]

Dispute about the jurisdiction of the court of chancery.

It was not long before the intrepid chief-justice incurred again the council's displeasure. This will require, for the sake of part of my readers, some little previous explanation. The equitable jurisdiction, as it is called, of the court of chancery appears to have been derived from that extensive judicial power which, in early times, the king's ordinary council had exercised. The chancellor, as one of the highest officers of state, took a great share in the council's business; and when it was not sitting, he had a court of his own, with jurisdiction in many important matters, out of which process to compel appearance of parties might at any time emanate. It is not unlikely therefore that redress, in matters beyond the legal province of the chancellor, was occasionally given through the paramount authority of this court. We find the council and the chancery named together in many remonstrances of the commons against this interference with private rights, from the time of Richard II. to that of Henry VI. It was probably in the former reign that the chancellor began to establish systematically his peculiar restraining jurisdiction. This originated in the practice of feoffments to uses, by which the feoffee, who had legal seisin of the land, stood

1 There had, however, been instances of it, as in sir Walter Raleigh's case. Lodge, iii. 172, 173; and I have found proofs of it in the queen's reign; though I cannot at present quote my authority. In a former age the judges had refused to give an extrajudicial answer to the king. Lingard, v. 382, from the Year-book, Pasch. 1 H. VII. 15. Trin. 1.

2 State Trials, ii. 869. Bacon, ii. 483, &c. Dalrymple's Memorials of James I. vol. i. p. 56. Some other very unjustifiable constructions of the law of treason took place in this reign. Thomas Owen was indicted and found guilty, under the statute of Edward III., for saying that "the king, being excommunicated (*i. e.* if he should be excommunicated) by the pope, might be lawfully deposed and killed by any one, which killing would not be murder, being the execution of the supreme sentence of the pope;" a position very atrocious, but not amounting to treason. State Trials, ii. 879. And Williams, another papist, was convicted of treason, by a still more violent stretch of law, for writing a book predicting the king's death in the year 1621 Id. 1085.

bound by private engagement to suffer another, called the cestui que use, to enjoy its use and possession. Such fiduciary estates were well known to the Roman jurists, but inconsistent with the feudal genius of our law. The courts of justice gave no redress, if the feoffee to uses violated his trust by detaining the land. To remedy this, an ecclesiastical chancellor devised the writ of subpœna, compelling him to answer upon oath as to his trust. It was evidently necessary also to restrain him from proceeding, as he might do, to obtain possession; and this gave rise to injunctions, that is, prohibitions to sue at law, the violation of which was punishable by imprisonment as a contempt of court. Other instances of breach of trust occurred in personal contracts, and cases also wherein, without any trust, there was a wrong committed beyond the competence of the courts of law to redress; to all which the process of subpœna was made applicable. This extension of a novel jurisdiction was partly owing to a fundamental principle of our common law, that a defendant cannot be examined; so that, if no witness or written instrument could be produced to prove a demand, the plaintiff was wholly debarred of justice: but in a still greater degree to a strange narrowness and scrupulosity of the judges, who, fearful of quitting the letter of their precedents, even with the clearest analogies to guide them, repelled so many just suits, and set up rules of so much hardship, that men were thankful to embrace the relief held out by a tribunal acting in a more rational spirit. This error the common lawyers began to discover in time to resume a great part of their jurisdiction in matters of contract, which would otherwise have escaped from them. They made too an apparently successful effort to recover their exclusive authority over real property, by obtaining a statute for turning uses into possession; that is, for annihilating the fictitious estate of the feoffee to uses, and vesting the legal as well as equitable possession in the cestui que use. But this victory, if I may use such an expression (since it would have freed them, in a most important point, from the chancellor's control), they threw away by one of those timid and narrow constructions which had already turned so much to their prejudice; and they permitted trust estates, by the introduction of a few more words into a conveyance, to maintain their ground, contradistinguished from the legal seisin, under the protection and guarantee, as before, of the courts of equity.

The particular limits of this equitable jurisdiction were as yet exceedingly indefinite. The chancellors were generally prone to extend them; and being at the same time ministers of state in a government of very arbitrary temper, regarded too little that course of precedent by which the other judges held themselves too strictly bound. The cases reckoned cognizable in chancery grew silently more and more numerous; but with little overt opposition from the courts of law till the time of sir Edward Coke. That great master of the common law was inspired not only with the jealousy of this irregular and encroaching jurisdiction which most lawyers seem to have felt, but with a tenaciousness of his own dignity, and a personal enmity towards Egerton, who held the great seal. It happened that an action was tried before him, the precise circumstances of which do not appear, wherein the plaintiff lost the verdict in consequence of one of his witnesses being artfully kept away. He had recourse to the court of chancery, filing a bill against the defendant to make him answer upon oath, which he refused to do, and was committed for contempt. Indictments were upon this preferred, at Coke's instigation, against the parties who had filed the bill in chancery, their council and solicitors, for suing in another court after judgment obtained at law; which was alleged to be contrary to the statute of præmunire. But the grand jury, though pressed, as is said, by one of the judges, threw out these indictments. The king, already incensed with Coke, and stimulated by Bacon, thought this too great an insult upon his chancellor to be passed over. He first directed Bacon and others to search for precedents of cases where relief had been given in chancery after judgment at law. They reported that there was a series of such precedents from the time of Henry VIII.: and some where the chancellor had entertained suits even after execution. The attorney-general was directed to prosecute in the star-chamber those who had preferred the indictments; and as Coke had not been ostensibly implicated in the business, the king contented himself with making an order in the council-book, declaring the chancellor not to have exceeded his jurisdiction.[1]

[1] Bacon, ii. 500, 518, 522. Cro. Jac. 335, 343.

The chief-justice almost at the same time gave another provocation, which exposed him more directly to the court's resentment. A cause happened to be argued in the court of king's bench, wherein the validity of a particular grant of a benefice to a bishop to be held in commendam, that is, along with his bishopric, came into question; and the council at the bar, besides the special points of the case, had disputed the king's general prerogative of making such a grant. The king, on receiving information of this, signified to the chief-justice, through the attorney-general, that he would not have the court proceed to judgment till he had spoken with them. Coke requested that similar letters might be written to the judges of all the courts. This having been done, they assembled, and, by a letter subscribed with all their hands, certified his majesty that they were bound by their oaths not to regard any letters that might come to them contrary to law, but to do the law notwithstanding; that they held with one consent the attorney-general's letter to be contrary to law, and such as they could not yield to, and that they had proceeded according to their oath to argue the cause.

Case of commendams.

The king, who was then at Newmarket, returned answer that he would not suffer his prerogative to be wounded, under pretext of the interest of private persons; that it had already been more boldly dealt with in Westminster Hall than in the reigns of preceding princes, which popular and unlawful liberty he would no longer endure; that their oath not to delay justice was not meant to prejudice the king's prerogative; concluding that out of his absolute power and authority royal he commanded them to forbear meddling any further in the cause till they should hear his pleasure from his own mouth. Upon his return to London the twelve judges appeared as culprits in the council-chamber. The king set forth their misdemeanors, both in substance and in the tone of their letter. He observed that the judges ought to check those advocates who presume to argue against his prerogative; that the popular lawyers had been the men, ever since his accession, who had trodden in all parliaments upon it, though the law could never be respected if the king were not reverenced; that he had a double prerogative — whereof the one was ordinary, and had relation to his private interest, which might be and was every day disputed in Westminster

Hall; the other was of a higher nature, referring to his supreme and imperial power and sovereignty, which ought not to be disputed or handled in vulgar argument; but that of late the courts of common law are grown so vast and transcendent, as they did both meddle with the king's prerogative, and had encroached upon all other courts of justice. He commented on the form of the letter, as highly indecent; certifying him merely what they had done, instead of submitting to his princely judgment what they should do.

After this harangue the judges fell upon their knees, and acknowledged their error as to the form of the letter. But Coke entered on a defence of the substance, maintaining the delay required to be against the law and their oaths. The king required the chancellor and attorney-general to deliver their opinions; which, as may be supposed, were diametrically opposite to those of the chief-justice. These being heard, the following question was put to the judges: Whether, if at any time, in a case depending before the judges, his majesty conceived it to concern him either in power or profit, and thereupon required to consult with them, and that they should stay proceedings in the mean time, they ought not to stay accordingly? They all, except the chief-justice, declared that they would do so, and acknowledged it to be their duty; Hobart, chief-justice of the common-pleas, adding that he would ever trust the justice of his majesty's commandment. But Coke only answered that, when the case should arise, he would do what should be fit for a judge to do. The king dismissed them all with a command to keep the limits of their several courts, and not to suffer his prerogative to be wounded; for he well knew the true and ancient common law to be the most favorable to kings of any law in the world, to which law he advised them to apply their studies.[1]

The behavior of the judges in this inglorious contention was such as to deprive them of every shadow of that confidence which ought to be reposed in their integrity. Hobart, Doddridge, and several more, were men of much consideration for learning; and their authority in ordinary matters of law is still held high. But, having been induced by a sense of duty, or through the ascendency that Coke had acquired

[1] Bacon, ii. 517, &c. Carte, iv. 35. Biograph. Brit., art COKE. The king told the judges he thought his prerogative as much wounded if it be publicly disputed upon, as if any sentence were given against it.

over them, to make a show of withstanding the court, they behaved like cowardly rebels who surrender at the first discharge of cannon; and prostituted their integrity and their fame, through dread of losing their offices, or rather, perhaps, of incurring the unmerciful and ruinous penalties of the star-chamber.

The government had nothing to fear from such recreants; but Coke was suspended from his office, and not long afterwards dismissed.[1] Having, however, fortunately in this respect, married his daughter to a brother of the duke of Buckingham, he was restored in about three years to the privy council, where his great experience in business rendered him useful; and had the satisfaction of voting for an enormous fine on his enemy the earl of Suffolk, late high-treasurer, convicted in the star-chamber of embezzlement.[2] In the parliament of 1621, and still more conspicuously in that of 1628, he became, not without some honorable inconsistency of doctrine as well as practice, the strenuous asserter of liberty on the principles of those ancient laws, which no one was admitted to know so well as himself; redeeming, in an intrepid and patriotic old age, the faults which we cannot avoid perceiving in his earlier life.

Arbitrary proceedings of the star-chamber.

The unconstitutional and usurped authority of the star-chamber overrode every personal right, though an assembled parliament might assert its general privileges. Several remarkable instances in history illustrate its tyranny and contempt of all known laws and liberties. Two puritans, having been committed by the high commission court for refusing the oath ex-officio, employed Mr. Fuller, a bencher of Gray's Inn, to move for their habeas corpus; which he did on the ground that the high commissioners were not empowered to commit any of his majesty's subjects to prison. This being reckoned a heinous offence, he was himself committed, at Bancroft's instigation (whether by the king's personal warrant, or that of the council-board, does not appear), and lay in jail to the day of his death; the archbishop constantly opposing his discharge, for which he petitioned.[3] Whitelock, a barrister

[1] See D'Israeli, Character of James I. p. 125. He was too much affected by his dismissal from office.

[2] Camden's Annals of James I. in Kennet, vol. ii. Wilson, ibid. 704, 705. Bacon's Works, ii. 574. The fine imposed was 30,000*l.*; Coke voted for 100,000*l.*

[3] Fuller's Church Hist. 56. Neal, i. 435. Lodge, iii. 334.

and afterwards a judge, was brought before the star-chamber on the charge of having given a private opinion to his client, that a certain commission issued by the crown was illegal. This was said to be a high contempt and slander of the king's prerogative. But, after a speech from Bacon in aggravation of this offence, the delinquent was discharged on a humble submission.[1] Such, too, was the fate of a more distinguished person on a still more preposterous accusation. Selden, in his History of Tithes, had indirectly weakened the claim of divine right, which the high-church faction pretended, and had attacked the argument from prescription, deriving their legal institution from the age of Charlemagne, or even a later era. Not content with letting loose on him some stanch polemical writers, the bishops prevailed on James to summon the author before the council. This proceeding is as much the disgrace of England as that against Galileo nearly at the same time is of Italy. Selden, like the great Florentine astronomer, bent to the rod of power, and made rather too submissive an apology for entering on this purely historical discussion.[2]

Arabella Stuart.

Every generous mind must reckon the treatment of Arabella Stuart among the hard measures of despotism, even if it were not also grossly in violation of English law. Exposed by her high descent and ambiguous pretensions to become the victim of ambitious designs wherein she did not participate, that lady may be added to the sad list of royal sufferers who have envied the lot of humble birth. There is not, as I believe, the least particle of evidence that she was engaged in the intrigues of the catholic party to place her on the throne. It was, however, thought a necessary precaution to put her in confinement a short time before the queen's death.[3] At the trial of Raleigh she was present; and Cecil openly acquitted her of any share in the conspiracy.[4] She enjoyed afterwards a pension from the king, and might have died in peace and obscurity, had she not conceived an unhappy attachment for Mr. Seymour, grandson of that earl of Hertford, himself so memorable an example of the perils of ambitious love. They were privately married; but on the fact transpiring,

[1] State Trials, ii. 765.

[2] Collier, 712. 717. Selden's Life in Biographia Brit.

[3] Carte, iii. 698.

[4] State Trials, ii. 23. Lodge's Illustrations, iii. 217.

the council, who saw with jealous eyes the possible union of two dormant pretensions to the crown, committed them to the Tower.[1] They both made their escape, but Arabella was arrested and brought back. Long and hopeless calamity broke down her mind; imploring in vain the just privileges of an Englishwoman, and nearly in want of necessaries, she died in prison, and in a state of lunacy, some years afterwards.[2] And this through the oppression of a kinsman whose advocates are always vaunting his good nature! Her husband became the famous marquis of Hertford, the faithful counsellor of Charles I., and partaker of his adversity. Lady Shrewsbury, aunt to Arabella, was examined on suspicion of being privy to her escape; and for refusing to answer the questions put to her, or, in other words, to accuse herself, was sentenced to a fine of 20,000*l.*, and discretionary imprisonment.[3]

Somerset and Overbury.

Several events, so well known that it is hardly necessary to dwell on them, aggravated the king's unpopularity during this parliamentary interval. The murder of Overbury burst into light, and revealed to an indignant nation the king's unworthy favorite, the earl of Somerset, and the hoary pander of that favorite's vices, the earl of Northampton, accomplices in that deep-laid and de-

[1] Winwood, iii. 201, 279.

[2] Winwood, iii. 178. In this collection are one or two letters from Arabella, which show her to have been a lively and accomplished woman. It is said, in a manuscript account of circumstances about the king's accession, which seems entitled to some credit, that on its being proposed that she should walk at the queen's funeral, she answered with spirit that, as she had been debarred her majesty's presence while living, she would not be brought on the stage as a public spectacle after her death. Sloane MSS. 827.

Much occurs on the subject of this lady's imprisonment in one of the valuable volumes in Dr. Birch's handwriting, among the same MSS. 4161. Those have already assisted Mr. D'Israeli in his interesting memoir on Arabella Stuart, in the Curiosities of Literature, new series, vol. i. They cannot be read (as I should conceive) without indignation at James and his ministers. One of her letters is addressed to the two chief justices, begging to be brought before them by habeas corpus, being informed that it is designed to remove her far from those courts of justice where she ought to be tried and condemned, or cleared, to remote parts, whose courts she holds unfitted for her offence. "And if your lordships may not or will not grant unto me the ordinary relief of a distressed subject, then I beseech you become humble intercessors to his majesty that I may receive such benefit of justice as both his majesty by his oath hath promised, and the laws of this realm afford to all others, those of his blood not excepted. And though, unfortunate woman! I can obtain neither, yet I beseech your lordships retain me in your good opinion, and judge charitably, till I be proved to have committed any offence, either against God or his majesty, deserving so long restraint or separation from my lawful husband."

Arabella did not profess the Roman catholic religion, but that party seem to have relied upon her; and so late as 1610 she incurred some "suspicion of being collapsed." Winwood, ii. 117.

This had been also conjectured in the queen's lifetime. Secret Correspondence of Cecil with James I., p. 118.

[3] State Trials, ii. 769.

liberate atrocity. Nor was it only that men so flagitious should have swayed the councils of this country, and rioted in the king's favor. Strange things were whispered, as if the death of Overbury was connected with something that did not yet transpire, and which every effort was employed to conceal. The people, who had already attributed prince Henry's death to poison, now laid it at the door of Somerset; but for that conjecture, however highly countenanced at the time, there could be no foundation. The symptoms of the prince's illness, and the appearances on dissection, are not such as could result from any poison, and manifestly indicate a malignant fever, aggravated perhaps by injudicious treatment.[1] Yet it is certain that a mystery hangs over this scandalous tale of Overbury's murder. The insolence and menaces of Somerset in the Tower, the shrinking apprehensions of him which the king could not conceal, the pains taken by Bacon to prevent his becoming desperate, and, as I suspect, to mislead the hearers by throwing them on a wrong scent, are very remarkable circumstances to which, after a good deal of attention, I can discover no probable clue. But it is evident that he was master of some secret which it would have highly prejudiced the king's honor to divulge.[2]

[1] Sir Charles Cornwallis's Memoir of Prince Henry, reprinted in the Somers Tracts, vol. ii., and of which sufficient extracts may be found in Birch's Life, contains a remarkably minute detail of all the symptoms attending the prince's illness, which was an epidemic typhus fever. The report of his physicians after dissection may also be read in many books. Nature might possibly have overcome the disorder, if an empirical doctor had not insisted on continually bleeding him. He had no other murderer. We need not even have recourse to Hume's acute and decisive remark, that, if Somerset had been so experienced in this trade, he would not have spent five months in bungling about Overbury's death.

Carte says, vol. iv. 33, that the queen charged Somerset with designing to poison her, prince Charles, and the elector palatine, in order to marry the electress to lord Suffolk's son. But this is too extravagant, whatever Anne might have thrown out in passion against a favorite she hated. On Henry's death, the first suspicion fell of course on the papists. Winwood, iii. 410. Burnet doubts whether his aversion to popery did not hasten his death. And there is a remarkable letter from sir Robert Naunton to Winwood, in the note of the last reference, which shows that suspicions of some such agency were entertained very early. But the positive evidence we have of his disease outweighs all conjecture.

[2] The circumstances to which I allude are well known to the curious in English history, and might furnish materials for a separate dissertation, had I leisure to stray in these by-paths. Hume has treated them as quite unimportant; and Carte, with his usual honesty, has never alluded to them. Those who read carefully the new edition of the State Trials, and various passages in lord Bacon's Letters, may form for themselves the best judgment they can. A few conclusions may, perhaps, be laid down as established. 1. That Overbury's death was occasioned, not merely by lady Somerset's revenge, but by his possession of important secrets, which in his passion he had threatened Somerset to divulge. 2. That Somerset conceived himself to have a hold over the king by the possession of the same or some

Sir Walter Raleigh's execution was another stain upon the reputation of James I. It is needless to mention that he fell under a sentence passed fifteen years before, on a charge of high treason, in plotting to raise Arabella Stuart to the throne. It is very probable that this charge was, partly at least, founded in truth;[1] but his convic-

Sir Walter Raleigh.

other secrets, and used indirect threats of revealing them. 3. That the king was in the utmost terror at hearing of these measures; as is proved by a passage in Weldon's Memoirs, p. 115, which, after being long ascribed to his libellous spirit, has lately received the most entire confirmation by some letters from More, lieutenant of the Tower, published in the Archæologia, vol. xviii. 4. That Bacon was in the king's confidence, and employed by him so to manage Somerset's trial as to prevent him from making any imprudent disclosure, or the judges from getting any insight into that which it was not meant to reveal. See particularly a passage in his letter to Coke, vol. ii. 514, beginning, "This crime was second to none but the powder-plot."

Upon the whole, I cannot satisfy myself in any manner as to this mystery. Prince Henry's death, as I have observed, is out of the question; nor does a different solution, hinted by Harris and others, and which may have suggested itself to the reader, appear probable to my judgment on weighing the whole case. Overbury was an ambitious, unprincipled man; and it seems more likely than anything else that James had listened too much to some criminal suggestion from him and Somerset, — but of what nature I cannot pretend even to conjecture; and that, through apprehension of this being disclosed, he had pusillanimously acquiesced in the scheme of Overbury's murder.

It is a remarkable fact, mentioned by Burnet, and perhaps little believed, but which, like the former, has lately been confirmed by documents printed in the Archæologia, that James, in the last year of his reign, while dissatisfied with Buckingham, privately renewed his correspondence with Somerset, on whom he bestowed at the same time a full pardon, and seems to have given him hopes of being restored to his former favor. A memorial drawn up by Somerset, evidently at the king's command, and most probably after the clandestine interview reported by Burnet, contains strong charges against Buckingham. Archæologia, vol. xvii. 280. But no consequences resulted from this; James was either reconciled to his favorite before his death, or felt himself too old for a struggle. Somerset seems to have tampered a little with the popular party in the beginning of the next reign. A speech of sir Robert Cotton's, in 1625, Parl. Hist. ii. 145, praises him, comparatively at least with his successor in royal favor; and he was one of those against whom informations were brought in the star-chamber for dispersing sir Robert Dudley's famous proposal for bridling the impertinences of parliament. Kennet, iii. 62. The patriots, however, of that age had too much sense to encumber themselves with an ally equally unserviceable and infamous. There cannot be the slightest doubt of Somerset's guilt as to the murder, though some have thought the evidence insufficient (Carte, iv. 34); he does not deny it in his remarkable letter to James, requesting, or rather demanding, mercy, printed in the Cabala, and in Bacon's Works.

[1] Raleigh made an attempt to destroy himself on being committed to the Tower, which of course affords a presumption of his consciousness that something could be proved against him. Cayley's Life of Raleigh, vol. ii. p. 10. Hume says, it appears from Sully's Memoirs that he had offered his services to the French ambassador. I cannot find this in Sully; whom Raleigh, however, and his party seem to have aimed at deceiving by false information. Nor could there be any treason in making an interest with the minister of a friendly power. Carte quotes the despatches of Beaumont, the French ambassador, to prove the connection of the conspirators with the Spanish plenipotentiary. But it may be questioned whether he knew any more than the government gave out. If Raleigh had ever shown a discretion bearing the least proportion to his genius, we might reject the whole story as improbable. But it is to be remembered that there had long been a catholic faction, who fixed their hopes on Arabella; so that the conspiracy, though extremely injudicious, was not so perfectly unintelligible as it appears to a reader of Hume, who has overlooked the previous circumstances. It is also to be considered that

tion was obtained on the single deposition of lord Cobham, an accomplice, a prisoner, not examined in court, and known to have already retracted his accusation. Such a verdict was thought contrary to law, even in that age of ready convictions. It was a severe measure to detain for twelve years in prison so splendid an ornament of his country, and to confiscate his whole estate.[1] For Raleigh's conduct in the expedition of Guiana there is not much excuse to make. Rashness and want of foresight were always among his failings; else he would not have undertaken a service of so much hazard without obtaining a regular pardon for his former offence. But it might surely be urged that either his commission was absolutely null, or that it operated as a pardon; since a man attainted of treason is incapable of exercising that authority which is conferred upon him.[2] Be this as it may, no technical reasoning could overcome the moral sense that revolted at carrying the original sentence into execution. Raleigh might be amenable to punishment for the deception by which he had obtained a commission that ought never to have issued; but the nation could not help seeing in his death the sacrifice of the bravest and most renowned of Englishmen to the vengeance of Spain.[3]

This unfortunate predilection for the court of Madrid had

the king had shown so marked a prejudice against Raleigh on his coming to England, and the hostility of Cecil was so insidious and implacable, as might drive a man of his rash and impetuous courage to desperate courses. See Cayley's Life of Raleigh, vol. ii.; a work containing much interesting matter, but unfortunately written too much in the spirit of an advocate, which, with so faulty a client, must tend to an erroneous representation of facts.

1 This estate was Sherborn castle, which Raleigh had not very fairly obtained from the see of Salisbury. He settled this before his conviction upon his son; but an accidental flaw in the deed enabled the king to wrest it from him, and bestow it on the earl of Somerset. Lady Raleigh, it is said, solicited his majesty on her knees to spare it; but he only answered, "I mun have the land, I mun have it for Carr." He gave him, however, 12,000*l*. instead. But the estate was worth 5000*l*. per annum. This ruin of the prospects of a man, far too intent on aggrandizement, impelled him once more into the labyrinth of fatal and dishonest speculations. Cayley, 89, &c.; Somers Tracts, ii. 22, &c.; Curiosities of Literature, new series, vol. ii. It has been said that Raleigh's unjust conviction made him in one day the most popular, from having been the most odious, man in England. He was certainly such under Elizabeth. This is a striking, but by no means solitary, instance of the impolicy of political persecution.

2 Rymer, xvi. 789. He was empowered to name officers, to use martial law, &c.

3 James made it a merit with the court of Madrid that he had put to death a man so capable of serving him, merely to give them satisfaction. Somers Tracts, ii. 437. There is even reason to suspect that he betrayed the secret of Raleigh's voyage to Gondomar before he sailed. Hardwicke, State Papers, i. 398. It is said in Mr. Cayley's Life of Raleigh that his fatal mistake in not securing a pardon under the great seal was on account of the expense. But the king would have made some difficulty at least about granting it.

always exposed James to his subjects' jealousy. They connected it with an inclination at least to tolerate popery, and with a dereliction of their commercial interests. But from the time that he fixed his hopes on the union of his son with the infanta,[1] the popular dislike to Spain increased in proportion to his blind preference. If the king had not systematically disregarded the public wishes, he could never have set his heart on this impolitic match; contrary to the wiser maxim he had laid down in his own Basilicon Doron, never to seek a wife for his son except in a protestant family. But his absurd pride made him despise the uncrowned princes of Germany. This Spanish policy grew much more odious after the memorable events of 1619, the election of the king's son-in-law to the throne of Bohemia, his rapid downfall, and the conquest of the Upper Palatinate by Austria. If James had listened to some sanguine advisers, he would in the first instance have supported the pretensions of Frederic. But neither his own views of public law nor true policy dictated such an interference. The case was changed after the loss of his hereditary dominions, and the king was sincerely desirous to restore him to the Palatinate; but he unreasonably expected that he could effect this through the friendly mediation of Spain, while the nation, not perhaps less unreasonably, were clamorous for his attempting it by force of arms. In this agitation of the public mind he summoned the parliament that met in February, 1621.[2]

Parliament of 1621.

The king's speech on opening the session was, like all he had made on former occasions, full of hopes and promises, taking cheerfully his share of the blame as to past disagreements, and treating them as little likely to recur though all their causes were still in operation.[3] He

[1] This project began as early as 1605. Winwood, vol. ii. The king had hopes that the United Provinces would acknowledge the sovereignty of prince Henry and the infanta on their marriage; and Cornwallis was directed to propose this formally to the court of Madrid. Id. p. 201. But Spain would not cede the point of sovereignty; nor was this scheme likely to please either the states-general or the court of France.

In the later negotiation about the marriage of prince Charles, those of the council who were known or suspected catholics, Arundel, Worcester, Digby, Weston, Calvert, as well as Buckingham, whose connections were such, were in the Spanish party. Those reputed to be zealous protestants were all against it. Wilson in Kennet, ii. 725. Many of the former were bribed by Gondomar. Id., and Rushworth, i. 19.

[2] The proclamation for this parliament contains many of the unconstitutional directions to the electors, contained, as has been seen, in that of 1604, though shorter. Rymer, xvii. 270.

[3] "Deal with me as I shall desire at your hands," &c. "He knew not," he told them, "the laws and customs of the land when he first came, and was misled by the old councillors whom the old

displayed, however, more judgment than usual in the commencement of this parliament. Among the methods devised to compensate the want of subsidies, none had been more injurious to the subject than patents of monopoly, including licenses for exclusively carrying on certain trades. Though the government was principally responsible for the exactions they connived at, and from which they reaped a large benefit, the popular odium fell of course on the monopolists. Of these the most obnoxious was sir Giles Mompesson, who, having obtained a patent for gold and silver thread, sold it of baser metal. This fraud seems neither very extraordinary nor very important; but he had another patent for licensing inns and alehouses, wherein he is said to have used extreme violence and oppression. The house of commons proceeded to investigate Mompesson's delinquency. Conscious that the crown had withdrawn its protection, he fled beyond sea. One Michell, a justice of peace, who had been the instrument of his tyranny, fell into the hands of the commons, who voted him incapable of being in the commission of the peace and sent him to the Tower.[1] Entertaining however, upon second thoughts, as we must presume, some doubts about their competence to inflict this punishment, especially the former part of it, they took the more prudent course, with respect to Mompesson, of appointing Noy and Hakewill to search for precedents in order to show how far and for what offences their power extended to punish delinquents against the state as well as those who offended against that house. The result appears some days after, in a vote that "they must join with the lords for punishing sir Giles Mompesson; it being no offence against our particular house, nor any member of it, but a general grievance."[2]

Proceedings against Mompesson.

The earliest instance of parliamentary impeachment, or of a solemn accusation of any individual by the commons at the bar of the lords, was that of lord Latimer in the year

queen had left;" — he owns that at the last parliament there was "a strange kind of beast called undertaker," &c. Parl. Hist. i. 1180. Yet this coaxing language was oddly mingled with sallies of his pride and prerogative notions. It is evidently his own composition, not Bacon's. The latter, in granting the speaker's petitions, took the high tone so usual in this reign, and directed the house of commons like a schoolmaster. Bacon's Works, i 701.

[1] Debates of Commons in 1621, vol. i. p. 84. I quote the two volumes published at Oxford in 1766: they are abridged in the new Parliamentary History.

[2] Debates of Commons in 1621, vol. i. p. 103, 109.

1376. The latest hitherto was that of the duke of Suffolk in 1449; for a proceeding against the bishop of London in 1534, which has sometimes been reckoned an instance of parliamentary impeachment, does not by any means support that privilege of the commons.[1] It had fallen into disuse, partly from the loss of that control which the commons had obtained under Richard II. and the Lancastrian kings, and partly from the preference the Tudor princes had given to bills of attainder or of pains and penalties, when they wished to turn the arm of parliament against an obnoxious subject. The revival of this ancient mode of proceeding in the case of Mompesson, though a remarkable event in our constitutional annals, does not appear to have been noticed as an anomaly. It was not indeed conducted according to all the forms of an impeachment. The commons, requesting a conference with the other house, informed them generally of that person's offence, but did not exhibit any distinct articles at their bar. The lords took up themselves the inquiry; and, having become satisfied of his guilt, sent a message to the commons that they were ready to pronounce sentence. The speaker accordingly, attended by all the house, demanded judgment at the bar: when the lords passed as heavy a sentence as could be awarded for any misdemeanor; to which the king, by a stretch of prerogative which no one was then inclined to call in question, was pleased to add perpetual banishment.[2]

The impeachment of Mompesson was followed up by others against Michell, the associate in his iniquities; against sir John Bennet, judge of the prerogative court, for corruption in his office; and against Field, bishop of Llandaff, for being concerned in a matter of bribery.[3] The first of these was punished; but the prosecution of Bennet seems to have dropped in consequence of the adjournment, and that of the bishop ended in a slight censure. But the wrath of the commons was justly roused against that shameless corruption

[1] The commons in this session complained to the lords that the bishop of London (Stokesley) had imprisoned one Philips on suspicion of heresy. Some time afterwards they called upon him to answer their complaint. The bishop laid the matter before the lords, who all declared that it was unbecoming for any lord of Parliament to make answer to any one in that place; "quod non consentaneum fuit aliquem procerum prædictorum alicui in eo loco responsurum." Lords' Journals, i. 71. The lords, however, in 1701 (State Trials, xiv. 275), seem to have recognized this as a case of impeachment.

[2] Debates in 1621, p. 114, 228, 229

[3] Id. passim.

which characterizes the reign of James beyond every other in our history. It is too well known how deeply the greatest man of that age was tarnished by the prevailing iniquity.

Proceedings against lord Bacon.

Complaints poured in against the chancellor Bacon for receiving bribes from suitors in his court. Some have vainly endeavored to discover an excuse which he did not pretend to set up, and even ascribed the prosecution to the malevolence of sir Edward Coke.[1] But Coke took no prominent share in this business; and though some of the charges against Bacon may not appear very heinous, especially for those times, I know not whether the unanimous conviction of such a man, and the conscious pusillanimity of his defence, do not afford a more irresistible presumption of his misconduct than anything specially alleged. He was abandoned by the court, and had previously lost, as I rather suspect, Buckingham's favor; but the king, who had a sense of his transcendent genius, remitted the fine of 40,000*l.* imposed by the lords, which he was wholly unable to pay.[2]

1 Carte.

2 Clarendon speaks of this impeachment as an unhappy precedent, made to gratify a private displeasure. This expression seems rather to point to Buckingham than to Coke; and some letters of Bacon to the favorite at the time of his fall display a consciousness of having offended him. Yet Buckingham had much more reason to thank Bacon as his wisest counsellor than to assist in crushing him. In his Works, vol. i. p. 712, is a tract entitled "Advice to the Duke of Buckingham, containing instructions for his governance as Minister." These are marked by the deep sagacity and extensive observation of the writer. One passage should be quoted in justice to Bacon. "As far as it may lie in you, let no arbitrary power be intruded; the people of this kingdom love the laws thereof, and nothing will oblige them more than a confidence of the free enjoying of them; what the nobles upon an occasion once said in Parliament, 'Nolumus leges Angliæ mutari,' is imprinted in the hearts of all the people." I may add, that, with all Bacon's pliancy, there are fewer overstrained expressions about the prerogative in his political writings than we should expect. His practice was servile, but his principles were not unconstitutional. We have seen how strongly he urged the calling of parliament in 1614: and he did the same, unhappily for himself, in 1621. Vol. ii. p. 580. He refused also to set the great seal to an office intended to be erected for enrolling prentices, a speculation apparently of some monopolists; writing a very proper letter to Buckingham, that there was no ground of law for it. P. 555.

I am very loath to call Bacon, for the sake of Pope's antithesis, "the meanest of mankind." Who would not wish to believe the feeling language of his letter to the king, after the attack on him had already begun? "I hope I shall not be found to have the troubled fountain of a corrupt heart, in a depraved habit of taking rewards to pervert justice; howsoever I may be frail, and partake of the abuses of the times." P. 589. Yet the general disesteem of his contemporaries speaks forcibly against him. Sir Simon d'Ewes and Weldon, both indeed bitter men, give him the worst of characters. "Surely," says the latter, "never so many parts and so base and abject a spirit tenanted together in any one earthen cottage as in this man." It is a striking proof of the splendor of Bacon's genius that it was unanimously acknowledged in his own age amidst so much that should excite contempt. He had indeed ingratiated himself with every preceding parliament through his incomparable ductility; having taken an active part in their complaints of grievances in 1604, before he became attorney-general, and even on many occasions afterwards, while he held that office, having been

There was much to commend in the severity practised by the house towards public delinquents; such examples being far more likely to prevent the malversation of men in power than any law they could enact. But in the midst of these laudable proceedings they were hurried by the passions of the moment into an act of most unwarrantable violence. It came to the knowledge of the house that one Floyd, a gentleman confined in the Fleet prison, had used some slighting words about the elector palatine and his wife. It appeared, in aggravation, that he was a Roman catholic. Nothing could exceed the fury into which the commons were thrown by this very insignificant story. A flippant expression, below the cognizance of an ordinary court, grew at once into a portentous offence, which they ransacked their invention to chastise. After sundry novel and monstrous propositions, they fixed upon the most degrading punishment they could devise. Next day, however, the chancellor of the exchequer delivered a message, that the king, thanking them for their zeal, but desiring that it should not transport them to inconveniences, would have them consider whether they could sentence one who did not belong to them, nor had offended against the house or any member of it; and whether they could sentence a denying party, without the oath of witnesses; referring them to an entry on the rolls of parliament in the first year of Henry IV., that the judicial power of parliament does not belong to the commons. He would have them consider whether it would not be better to leave Floyd to him, who would punish him according to his fault.

This message put them into some embarrassment. They had come to a vote in Mompesson's case, in the very words employed in the king's message, confessing themselves to have no jurisdiction, except over offences against themselves. The warm speakers now controverted this proposition with such arguments as they could muster; Coke, though from the reported debates he seems not to have gone the whole

intrusted with the management of conferences on the most delicate subjects. In 1614 the commons, after voting that the attorney-general ought not to be elected to parliament, made an exception in favor of Bacon. Journals, p. 460. "I have been always gracious in the lower house," he writes to James in 1616, begging for the post of chancellor: "I have interest in the gentlemen of England, and shall be able to do some good effect in rectifying that body of parliament-men, which is cardo rerum." Vol. ii. p. 496.

I shall conclude this note by observing, that, if all lord Bacon's philosophy had never existed, there would be enough in his political writings to place him among the greatest men this country has produced.

length, contending that the house was a court of record, and that it consequently had power to administer an oath.[1] They returned a message by the speaker, excepting to the record in 1 H. IV., because it was not an act of parliament to bind them, and persisting, though with humility, in their first votes.[2] The king replied mildly; urging them to show precedents, which they were manifestly incapable of doing. The lords requested a conference, which they managed with more temper, and, notwithstanding the solicitude displayed by the commons to maintain their pretended right, succeeded in withdrawing the matter to their own jurisdiction.[3] This conflict of privileges was by no means of service to the unfortunate culprit: the lords perceived that they could not mitigate the sentence of the lower house without reviving their dispute, and vindicated themselves from all suspicion of indifference towards the cause of the Palatinate by augmented severity. Floyd was adjudged to be degraded from his gentility, and to be held an infamous person; his testimony not to be received; to ride from the Fleet to Cheapside on horseback without a saddle, with his face to the horse's tail, and the tail in his hand, and there to stand two hours in the pillory, and to be branded in the forehead with the letter K; to ride four days afterwards in the same manner to Westminster, and there to stand two hours more in the pillory, with words in a paper in his hat showing his offence; to be whipped at the cart's tail from the Fleet to Westminster Hall; to pay a fine of 5000*l.*, and to be a prisoner in Newgate during his life. The whipping was a few days after remitted on prince Charles's motion; but he seems to have undergone the rest of the sentence. There is surely no instance in the annals of our own, and hardly of

Violence in the case of Floyd.

1 Debates in 1621, vol. ii. p. 7.

2 Debates, p. 14.

3 In a former parliament of this reign, the commons having sent up a message, wherein they entitled themselves the knights, citizens, burgesses, and barons of the commons' court of parliament, the lords sent them word that they would never acknowledge any man that sitteth in the lower house to have the right or title of a baron of parliament; nor could admit the term of the commons' court of parliament: "because all your house together, without theirs, doth make no court of parliament." 4th March, 1606. Lord's Journals. Nevertheless the lords did not scruple, almost immediately afterwards, to denominate their own house a court, as appears by memoranda of 27th and 28th May; they even issued a habeas corpus, as from a court, to bring a servant of the earl of Bedford before them. So also in 1609, 16th and 17th of February; and on April 14th and 18th, 1614; and probably later, if search were made.

I need hardly mention that the barons mentioned above, as part of the commons, were the members for the cinque ports, whose denomination is recognized in several statutes.

any civilized country, where a trifling offence, if it were one, has been visited with such outrageous cruelty. The cold-blooded deliberate policy of the lords is still more disgusting than the wild fury of the lower house.[1]

This case of Floyd is an unhappy proof of the disregard that popular assemblies, when inflamed by passion, are ever apt to show for those principles of equity and moderation by which, however the sophistry of contemporary factions may set them aside, a calm-judging posterity will never fail to measure their proceedings. It has contributed at least, along with several others of the same kind, to inspire me with a jealous distrust of that indefinable, uncontrollable privilege of parliament, which has sometimes been asserted, and perhaps with rather too much encouragement from those whose function it is to restrain all exorbitant power. I speak only of the extent to which theoretical principles have been carried, without insinuating that the privileges of the house of commons have been practically stretched in late times beyond their constitutional bounds. Time and the course of opinion have softened down those high pretensions, which the dangers of liberty under James I., as well as the natural character of a popular assembly, then taught the commons to assume; and the greater humanity of modern ages has made us revolt from such disproportionate punishments as were inflicted on Floyd.[2]

Everything had hitherto proceeded with harmony between the king and parliament. His ready concurrence in their animadversion on Mompesson and Michell, delinquents who had acted at least with the connivance of government, and in the abolition of monopolies, seemed to remove all discontent.

[1] Debates in 1621, vol. i. p. 355, &c.; vol. ii. p. 5, &c. Mede writes to his correspondent on May 11, that the execution had not taken place; "but I hope it will." The king was plainly averse to it.

[2] The following observation on Floyd's case, written by Mr. Harley, in a manuscript account of the proceedings (Harl. MSS. 6274), is well worthy to be inserted. I copy from the appendix to the above-mentioned Debates of 1621. "The following collection," he has written at the top, "is an instance how far a zeal against popery and for one branch of the royal family, which was supposed to be neglected by king James, and consequently in opposition to him, will carry people against common justice and humanity." And again at the bottom: "For the honor of Englishmen, and indeed of human nature, it were to be hoped these debates were not truly taken, there being so many motions contrary to the laws of the land, the laws of parliament, and common justice. Robert Harley, July 14, 1702." It is remarkable that this date is very near the time when the writer of these just observations, and the party which he led, had been straining in more than one instance the privileges of the house of commons, not certainly with such violence as in the case of Floyd, but much beyond what can be deemed their legitimate extent.

The commons granted two subsidies early in the session without alloying their bounty with a single complaint of grievances. One might suppose that the subject of impositions had been entirely forgotten, not an allusion to them occurring in any debate.[1] It was voted indeed, in the first days of the session, to petition the king about the breach of their privilege of free speech, by the imprisonment of sir Edwin Sandys, in 1614, for words spoken in the last parliament; but the house did not prosecute this matter, contenting itself with some explanation by the secretary of state.[2] They were going on with some bills for reformation of abuses, to which the king was willing to accede, when they received an intimation that he expected them to adjourn over the summer. It produced a good deal of dissatisfaction to see their labor so hastily interrupted; especially as they ascribed it to a want of sufficient sympathy on the court's part with their enthusiastic zeal for the elector palatine.[3] They were adjourned by the king's commission, after an unanimous declaration (" sounded forth," says one present, " with the voices of them all, withal lifting up their hats in their hands so high as they could hold them, as a visible testimony of their unanimous consent, in such sort that the like had scarce ever been seen in parliament") of their resolution to spend their lives and fortunes for the defence of their own religion and of the Palatinate. This solemn protestation and pledge was entered on record in the journals.[4]

They met again after five months, without any change in their views of policy. At a conference of the two houses, lord Digby, by the king's command, explained all that had occurred in his embassy to Germany for the restitution of

1 In a much later period of the session, when the commons had lost their good humor, some heat was very justly excited by a petition from some brewers, complaining of an imposition of fourpence on the quarter of malt. The courtiers defended this as a composition in lieu of purveyance. But it was answered that it was compulsory, for several of the principal brewers had been committed and lay long in prison for not yielding to it. One said that impositions of this nature overthrew the liberty of all the subjects of this kingdom; and if the king may impose such taxes, then are we but villains, and lose all our liberties. It produced an order that the matter be examined before the house, the petitioners to be heard by counsel, and all the lawyers of the house to be present. Debates of 1621, vol. ii. 252. Journals, p. 652. But nothing farther seems to have taken place, whether on account of the magnitude of the business which occupied them during the short remainder of the session, or because a bill which passed their house to prevent illegal imprisonment, or restraint on the lawful occupation of the subject, was supposed to meet this case. It is a remarkable instance of arbitrary taxation, and preparatory to an excise.

2 Debates of 1621, p. 14. Hatsell's Precedents, i. 133.

3 Debates, p. 114, et alibi, passim.

4 Vol. ii. p. 170, 172.

the Palatinate; which, though absolutely ineffective, was as much as James could reasonably expect without a war.[1] He had in fact, though, according to the laxity of those times, without declaring war on any one, sent a body of troops under sir Horace Vere, who still defended the Lower Palatinate. It was necessary to vote more money, lest these should mutiny for want of pay. And it was stated to the commons in this conference, that to maintain a sufficient army in that country for one year would require 900,000*l.*; which was left to their consideration.[2] But now it was seen that men's promises to spend their fortunes in a cause not essentially their own are written in the sand. The commons had no reason perhaps to suspect that the charge of keeping 30,000 men in the heart of Germany would fall much short of the estimate. Yet after long haggling they voted only one subsidy, amounting to 70,000*l.*; a sum manifestly insufficient for the first equipment of such a force.[3] This parsimony could hardly be excused by their suspicion of the king's unwillingness to undertake the war, for which it afforded the best justification.

Disagreement between the king and commons.

James was probably not much displeased at finding so good a pretext for evading a compliance with their martial humor; nor had there been much appearance of dissatisfaction on either side (if we except some murmurs at the commitment of one of their most active members, sir Edwin Sandys, to the Tower, which were tolerably appeased by the secretary Calvert's declaration that he had not been committed for any parliamentary matter[4]) till the commons drew up a petition and remonstrance against the growth of popery; suggesting,

1 Journals, vol. ii. p. 186.

2 P. 189. Lord Cranfield told the commons there were three reasons why they should give liberally. 1. That lands were now a third better than when the king came to the crown. 2. That wools, which were then 20*s.*, were now 30*s.* 3. That corn had risen from 26*s.* to 36*s.* the quarter. Ibid. There had certainly been a very great increase of wealth under James, especially to the country gentlemen; of which their style of building is an evident proof. Yet in this very session complaints had been made of the want of money and fall in the price of lands, vol. i. p. 16; and an act was proposed against the importation of corn, vol. ii. p. 87. In fact, rents had been enormously enhanced in this reign, which the country gentlemen of course endeavored to keep up. But corn, probably through good seasons, was rather lower in 1621 than it had been — about 30*s.* a quarter.

3 P. 242, &c.

4 Id. 174, 200. Compare also p. 151. Sir Thomas Wentworth appears to have discountenanced the resenting this as a breach of privilege. Doubtless the house showed great and even excessive moderation in it; for we can hardly doubt that Sandys was really committed for no other cause than his behavior in parliament. It was taken up again afterwards; p. 259.

among other remedies for this grievance, that the prince should marry one of our own religion, and that the king would direct his efforts against that power (meaning Spain) which first maintained the war in the Palatinate. This petition was proposed by sir Edward Coke. The courtiers opposed it as without precedent; the chancellor of the duchy observing that it was of so high and transcendent a nature, he had never known the like within those walls. Even the mover defended it rather weakly, according to our notions, as intended only to remind the king, but requiring no answer. The scruples affected by the courtiers, and the real novelty of the proposition, had so great an effect, that some words were inserted declaring that the house "did not mean to press on the king's most undoubted and royal prerogative."[1] The petition, however, had not been presented, when the king, having obtained a copy of it, sent a peremptory letter to the speaker, that he had heard how some fiery and popular spirits had been emboldened to debate and argue on matters far beyond their reach or capacity, and directing him to acquaint the house with his pleasure that none therein should presume to meddle with anything concerning his government or mysteries of state; namely, not to speak of his son's match with the princess of Spain, nor to touch the honor of that king, or any other of his friends and confederates. Sandys' commitment, he bade them be informed, was not for any misdemeanor in parliament. But, to put them out of doubt of any question of that nature that may arise among them hereafter, he let them know that he thought himself very free and able to punish any man's misdemeanors in parliament, as well during their sitting as after, which he meant not to spare upon occasion of any man's insolent behavior in that place. He assured them that he would not deign to hear their petition if it touched on any of those points which he had forbidden.[2]

The house received this message with unanimous firmness, but without any undue warmth. A committee was appointed to draw up a petition, which, in the most decorous language and with strong professions of regret at his majesty's displeasure, contained a defence of their former proceedings, and hinted very gently that they could not conceive his

[1] Journals, vol. ii. p. 261, &c.

[2] P. 284.

honor and safety, or the state of the kingdom, to be matters at any time unfit for their deepest consideration in time of parliament. They adverted more pointedly to that part of the king's message which threatened them for liberty of speech, calling it their ancient and undoubted right, and an inheritance received from their ancestors, which they again prayed him to confirm.[1] His answer, though considerably milder than what he had designed, gave indications of a resentment not yet subdued. He dwelt at length on their unfitness for entering on matters of government, and commented with some asperity even on their present apologetical petition. In the conclusion he observed that, "although he could not allow of the style calling their privileges an undoubted right and inheritance, but could rather have wished that they had said that their privileges were derived from the grace and permission of his ancestors and himself (for most of them had grown from precedent, which rather shows a toleration than inheritance), yet he gave them his royal assurance that, as long as they contained themselves within the limits of their duty, he would be as careful to maintain their lawful liberties and privileges as he would his own prerogative, so that their house did not touch on that prerogative, which would enforce him or any just king to retrench their privileges."[2]

This explicit assertion that the privileges of the commons existed only by sufferance, and conditionally upon good behavior, exasperated the house far more than the denial of their right to enter on matters of state. In the one they were conscious of having somewhat transgressed the boundaries of ordinary precedents; in the other their individual security, and their very existence as a deliberative assembly, were at stake. Calvert, the secretary, and the other ministers, admitted the king's expressions to be incapable of defence, and called them a slip of the pen at the close of a long answer.[3] The commons were not to be diverted by any such excuses from their necessary duty of placing on record a solemn claim of right. Nor had a letter from the king, addressed to Calvert, much influence; wherein, while he reiterated his assurances of respecting their privileges, and tacitly withdrew the menace that rendered them precarious, he

[1] Journals, vol. ii. p. 289. [2] P. 317. [3] P. 330.

said that he could not with patience endure his subjects to use such anti-monarchical words to him concerning their liberties as "ancient and undoubted right and inheritance, without subjoining that they were granted by the grace and favor of his predecessors."[1] After a long and warm debate they entered on record in the Journals their famous protestations of December 18th, 1621, in the following words: —

"The commons now assembled in parliament, being justly occasioned thereunto, concerning sundry liberties, franchises, privileges, and jurisdictions of parliament, amongst others not herein mentioned, do make this protestation following: — That the liberties, franchises, privileges, and jurisdictions of parliament are the ancient and undoubted birthright and inheritance of the subjects of England; and that the arduous and urgent affairs concerning the king, state, and the defence of the realm, and of the church of England, and the making and maintenance of laws, and redress of mischiefs and grievances which daily happen within this realm, are proper subjects and matter of counsel and debate in parliament; and that in the handling and proceeding of those businesses every member of the house hath, and of right ought to have, freedom of speech to propound, treat, reason, and bring to conclusion the same; that the commons in parliament have like liberty and freedom to treat of those matters in such order as in their judgments shall seem fittest: and that every such member of the said house hath like freedom from all impeachment, imprisonment, and molestation (other than by the censure of the house itself), for or concerning any bill, speaking, reasoning, or declaring of any matter or matters touching the parliament or parliament business; and that, if any of the said members be complained of and questioned for anything said or done in parliament, the same is to be showed to the king by the advice and assent of all the commons assembled in parliament, before the king give credence to any private information."[2]

This protestation was not likely to pacify the king's anger. He had already pressed the commons to make an end of the business before them, under pretence of wishing to adjourn them before Christmas, but probably looking to a dissolution. They were

Dissolution of the commons after a strong remonstrance.

[1] Journals, vol. ii. p. 339.

[2] P. 359.

not in a temper to regard any business, least of all to grant a subsidy, till this attack on their privileges should be fully retracted. The king therefore adjourned, and, in about a fortnight after, dissolved them. But in the interval, having sent for the journal-book, he erased their last protestation with his own hand, and published a declaration of the causes which had provoked him to this unusual measure, alleging the unfitness of such a protest, after his ample assurance of maintaining their privileges, the irregular manner in which, according to him, it was voted, and its ambiguous and general wording, which might serve in future times to invade most of the prerogatives annexed to the imperial crown. In his proclamation for dissolving the parliament James recapitulated all his grounds of offences; but finally required his subjects to take notice that it was his intention to govern them as his progenitors and predecessors had done, and to call a parliament again on the first convenient occasion.[1] He immediately followed up this dissolution of parliament by dealing his vengeance on its most conspicuous leaders: sir Edward Coke and sir Robert Philips were committed to the Tower; Mr. Pym and one or two more to other prisons; sir Dudley Digges, and several who were somewhat less obnoxious than the former, were sent on a commission to Ireland, as a sort of honorable banishment.[2] The earls of Oxford and Southampton underwent an examination before the council, and the former was committed to the Tower on pretence of having spoken words against the king. It is worthy of observation that, in this session, a portion of the upper house had united in opposing the court. Nothing of this kind is noticed in former parliaments, except perhaps a little on the establishment of the Reformation. In this minority were considerable names: Essex, Southampton, Warwick, Oxford, Say, Spencer. Whether a sense of public wrongs or their particular resentments influenced these noblemen, their opposition must be reckoned an evident sign of the change that was at work in the spirit of the nation, and by which no rank could be wholly unaffected.[3]

[1] Rymer, xvii. 344; Parl. Hist.; Carte, 93; Wilson.

[2] Besides the historians, see Cabala, part ii. p. 155 (4to. edit.); D'Israeli's Character of James I., p. 125; and Mede's Letters, Harl. MSS. 389.

[3] Wilson's History of James I., in Kennet, ii. 247, 749. Thirty-three peers, Mr. Joseph Mede tells us in a letter of Feb. 24, 1621 (Harl. MSS. 389), "signed a petition to the king which they refused to deliver to the council, as he desired, nor even to

James, with all his reputed pusillanimity, never showed any signs of fearing popular opinion. His obstinate adherence to the marriage treaty with Spain was the height of political rashness in so critical a state of the public mind. But what with elevated notions of his prerogative and of his skill in government on the one hand, what with a confidence in the submissive loyalty of the English on the other, he seems constantly to have fancied that all opposition proceeded from a small troublesome faction, whom if he could any way silence, the rest of his people would at once repose in a dutiful reliance on his wisdom. Hence he met every succeeding parliament with as sanguine hopes as if he had suffered no disappointment in the last. The nation was however wrought up at this time to an alarming pitch of discontent. Libels were in circulation about 1621, so bitterly malignant in their censures of his person and administration, that two hundred years might seem, as we read them, to have been mistaken in their date.[1] Heedless, however, of this growing odium,

Marriage treaty with Spain.

the prince, unless he would say he did not receive it as a councillor; whereupon the king sent for Lord Oxford, and asked him for it: he, according to previous agreement, said he had it not: then he sent for another, who made the same answer; at last they told him they had resolved not to deliver it, unless they were admitted all together. Whereupon his majesty, wonderfully incensed, sent them all away, re infectâ, and said that he would come into parliament himself, and bring them all to the bar." This petition, I believe, did not relate to any general grievances, but to a question of their own privileges, as to their precedence of Scots peers. Wilson, ubi suprà. But several of this large number were inspired by more generous sentiments; and the commencement of an aristocratic opposition deserves to be noticed. In another letter, written in March, Mede speaks of the good understanding between the king and parliament; he promised they should sit as long as they like, and hereafter he would have a parliament every three years. "Is not this good if it be true? . . . . . But certain it is that the lords stick wonderful fast to the commons, and all take great pains."

The entertaining and sensible biographer of James has sketched the characters of these Whig peers. Aikin's James I., ii. 238.

[1] One of these may be found in the Somers Tracts, ii. 470, entitled Tom Tell-truth, a most malignant ebullition of disloyalty, which the author must have risked his neck as well as ears in publishing. Some outrageous reflections on the personal character of the king could hardly be excelled by modern licentiousness. Proclamations about this time against excess of lavish speech in matters of state, Rymer, xvii. 275, 514, and against printing or uttering seditious and scandalous pamphlets, id. 522, 616, show the tone and temper of the nation. [See also the extracts from the reports of Tillières, the French ambassador, in Raumer's History of 16th and 17th Centuries illustrated, vol. ii. p. 246, et alibi. Nothing can be more unfavorable to James in every respect than these reports; but his leaning towards Spanish connections might inspire some prejudice into a French diplomatist. At a considerably earlier period, 1606, if we may trust the French ambassador, the players brought forward "their own king and all his favorites in a very strange fashion. They made him curse and swear because he had been robbed of a bird, and beat a gentleman because he had called off the hounds from the scent. They represent him as drunk at least once a day, &c. He has upon this made order that no play shall be henceforth acted in London; for the repeal of which order they have

James continued to solicit the affected coyness of the court of Madrid. The circumstances of that negotiation belong to general history.[1] It is only necessary to remind the reader that the king was induced, during the residence of prince Charles and the duke of Buckingham in Spain, to swear to certain private articles, some of which he had already promised before their departure, by which he bound himself to suspend all penal laws affecting the catholics, to permit the exercise of their religion in private houses, and to procure from parliament if possible a legal toleration. This toleration, as preliminary to the entire reëstablishment of popery, had been the first great object of Spain in the treaty. But that court, having protracted the treaty for years, in order to extort more favorable terms, and interposed a thousand pretences, became the dupe of its own artifices; the resentment of a haughty minion overthrowing with ease the painful fabric of this tedious negotiation.

Parliament of 1624.

Buckingham obtained a transient and unmerited popularity by thus averting a great public mischief, which rendered the next parliament unexpectedly peaceable. The commons voted three subsidies and three fifteenths, in value about 300,000*l.*;[2] but with a condition,

already offered 100,000 livres. Perhaps the permission will be again granted, but upon condition that they represent no recent history, nor speak of the present time." Raumer, ii. 219. If such an order was ever issued, it was speedily repealed; for there is no year to which new plays are not referred by those who have written the history of our drama. But the offence which provoked it is extraordinary, and hardly credible; though, coming on the authority of a resident ambassador, we cannot set it aside. The satire was, of course, conveyed under the character of a fictitious king; for otherwise the players themselves would have been punished. The time seems to have been in March, 1606. The recent story of the Duc de Biron had been also brought on the stage, which seems much less wonderful. 1845.]

[1] The letters on this subject published by lord Hardwicke, State Papers, vol. i., are highly important; and, being unknown to Carte and Hume, render their narratives less satisfactory. Some pamphlets of the time, in the second volume of the Somers Tracts, may be read with interest; and Howell's Letters, being written from Madrid during the prince of Wales's residence, deserve notice. See also Wilson in Kennet, p. 750, et post. Dr. Lingard has illustrated the subject lately, ix. 271.

[2] Hume, and many other writers on the side of the crown, assert the value of a subsidy to have fallen from 70,000*l.*, at which it had been under the Tudors, to 55,000*l.*, or a less sum. But, though I will not assert a negative too boldly, I have no recollection of having found any good authority for this; and it is surely too improbable to be lightly credited. For, admit that no change was made in each man's rate according to the increase of wealth and diminution of the value of money, the amount must at least have been equal to what it had been; and to suppose the contributors to have prevailed on the assessors to underrate them is rather contrary to common fiscal usage. In one of Mede's letters, which of course I do not quote as decisive, it is said that the value of a subsidy was *not above* 80,000*l.*; and that the assessors were directed (this was in 1621) not to follow former books, but value every man's estate according to their knowledge, and not his own confession.

proposed by the king himself, that, in order to insure its application to naval and military armaments, it should be paid into the hands of treasurers appointed by themselves, who should issue money only on the warrant of the council of war. He seemed anxious to tread back the steps made in the former session, not only referring the highest matters of state to their consideration, but promising not to treat for peace without their advice. They, on the other hand, acknowledged themselves most bound to his majesty for having been pleased to require their humble advice in a case so important, not meaning, we may be sure, by these courteous and loyal expressions, to recede from what they had claimed in the last parliament as their undoubted right.[1]

Impeachment of Middlesex.

The most remarkable affair in this session was the impeachment of the earl of Middlesex, actually lord treasurer of England, for bribery and other misdemeanors. It is well known that the prince of Wales and duke of Buckingham instituted this prosecution, to gratify the latter's private pique, against the wishes of the king, who warned them they would live to have their fill of parliamentary impeachment. It was conducted by managers on the part of the commons in a very regular form, except that the depositions of witnesses were merely read by the clerk; that fundamental rule of English law which insists on the vivâ voce examination being as yet unknown, or dispensed with in political trials. Nothing is more worthy of notice in the proceedings upon this impeachment than what dropped from sir Edwin Sandys, in speaking upon one of the charges. Middlesex had laid an imposition of *3l.* per ton on French wines, for taking off which he received a gratuity. Sandys commenting on this offence, protested, in the name of the commons, that they intended not to question the power of imposing claimed by the king's prerogative: this they touched not upon now; they continued only their claim, and when they should have occasion to dispute it would do so with all due regard to his majesty's state and revenue.[2] Such cautious and temperate language, far from indicating any dispo-

1 Parl. Hist. 1383, 1388, 1390; Carte, 119. The king seems to have acted pretty fairly in this parliament, bating a gross falsehood in denying the intended toleration of papists. He wished to get further pledges of support from parliament before he plunged into a war, and was very right in doing so. On the other hand, the prince and duke of Buckingham behaved in public towards him with great rudeness. Parl. Hist. 1396.

2 Parl. Hist. 1421.

sition to recede from their pretensions, is rather a proof of such united steadiness and discretion as must insure their success. Middlesex was unanimously convicted by the peers.[1] His impeachment was of the highest moment to the commons, as it restored forever that salutary constitutional right which the single precedent of lord Bacon might have been insufficient to establish against the ministers of the crown.

The two last parliaments had been dissolved without passing a single act, except the subsidy bill of 1621. An interval of legislation for thirteen years was too long for any civilized country. Several statutes were enacted in the present session, but none so material as that for abolishing monopolies for the sale of merchandise, or for using any trade.[2] This is of a declaratory nature, and recites that they are already contrary to the ancient and fundamental laws of the realm. Scarce any difference arose between the crown and the commons. This singular calm might probably have been interrupted, had not the king put an end to the session. They expressed some little dissatisfaction at this step,[3] and presented a list of grievances, one only of which is sufficiently considerable to deserve notice; namely, the proclamations already mentioned in restraint of building about London, whereof they complain in very gentle terms, considering their obvious illegality and violation of private right.[4]

The commons had now been engaged for more than twenty years in a struggle to restore and to fortify their own and their fellow-subjects' liberties. They had obtained in this period but one legislative measure of importance, the late declaratory act against monopolies. But they had rescued from disuse their ancient right of impeachment. They had placed on record a protestation of their claim to debate all matters of public concern. They had remonstrated against the usurped prerogatives of binding the subject by proclamation and of levying customs at the outports. They had

1 Clarendon blames the impeachment of Middlesex for the very reason which makes me deem it a fortunate event for the constitution, and seems to consider him as a sacrifice to Buckingham's resentment. Hacket also, the biographer of Williams, takes his part. Carte, however, thought him guilty, p. 116; and the unanimous vote of the peers is much against him, since that house was not wholly governed by Buckingham. See too the Life of Nicholas Farrar in Wordsworth's Ecclesiastical Biography, vol. iv., where it appears that that pious and conscientious man was one of the treasurer's most forward accusers, having been deeply injured by him. It is difficult to determine the question from the printed trial.

2 21 Jac. I. c. 3. See what lord Coke says on this act, and on the general subject of monopolies, 3 Inst. 181.

3 P. H. 1483.

4 Id. 1488.

secured beyond controversy their exclusive privilege of determining contested elections of their members. Of these advantages some were evidently incomplete, and it would require the most vigorous exertions of future parliaments to realize them. But such exertions the increased energy of the nation gave abundant cause to anticipate. A deep and lasting love of freedom had taken hold of every class except perhaps the clergy, from which, when viewed together with the rash pride of the court and the uncertainty of constitutional principles and precedents, collected through our long and various history, a calm by-stander might presage that the ensuing reign would not pass without disturbance, nor perhaps end without confusion.

CHAPTER VII.

ON THE ENGLISH CONSTITUTION FROM THE ACCESSION OF CHARLES I. TO THE DISSOLUTION OF HIS THIRD PARLIAMENT.

Parliament of 1625 — Its Dissolution — Another Parliament called — Prosecution of Buckingham — Arbitrary Proceedings towards the Earls of Arundel and Bristol — Loan demanded by the King — Several committed for refusal to contribute — They sue for a Habeas Corpus — Arguments on this Question, which is decided against them — A Parliament called in 1628 — Petition of Right — King's Reluctance to grant it — Tonnage and Poundage disputed — King dissolves Parliament — Religious Differences — Prosecution of Puritans by Bancroft — Growth of High Church Tenets — Differences as to the Observance of Sunday — Arminian Controversy — State of Catholics under James — Jealousy of the Court's Favor towards them — Unconstitutional Tenets promulgated by the High Church Party — General Remarks.

CHARLES I. had much in his character very suitable to the times in which he lived, and to the spirit of the people he was to rule; a stern and serious deportment, a disinclination to all licentiousness, and a sense of religion that seemed more real than in his father.[1] These qualities we might suppose to have raised some expectation of him, and to have procured at his accession some of that popularity which is rarely withheld from untried princes. Yet it does not appear that he enjoyed even this first transient sunshine of his subjects' affection. Solely intent on retrenching the excesses of prerogative, and well aware that no sovereign would voluntarily recede from the possession of power, they seem to have dreaded to admit into their bosoms any sentiments of personal loyalty which might enervate their resolution. And Charles took speedy means to convince them that they had not erred in withholding their confidence.

Elizabeth in her systematic parsimony, James in his averse-

[1] The general temperance and chastity of Charles, and the effect those virtues had in reforming the outward face of the court, are attested by many writers, and especially by Mrs. Hutchinson, whose good word he would not have undeservedly obtained. Mem. of Col. Hutchinson, p. 65. I am aware that he was not the perfect saint as well as martyr which his panegyrists represent him to have been; but it is an unworthy office, even for the purpose of throwing ridicule on exaggerated praise, to turn the microscope of history on private life.

ness to war, had been alike influenced by a consciousness that want of money alone could render a parliament formidable to their power. None of the irregular modes of supply were ever productive enough to compensate for the clamor they occasioned; after impositions and benevolences were exhausted, it had always been found necessary, in the most arbitrary times of the Tudors, to fall back on the representatives of the people. But Charles succeeded to a war, at least to the preparation of a war, rashly undertaken through his own weak compliance, the arrogance of his favorite, and the generous or fanatical zeal of the last parliament. He would have perceived it to be manifestly impossible, if he had been capable of understanding his own position, to continue this war without the constant assistance of the house of commons, or to obtain that assistance without very costly sacrifices of his royal power. It was not the least of this monarch's imprudences, or rather of his blind compliances with Buckingham, to have not only commenced hostilities against Spain which he might easily have avoided,[1] and persisted in them for four years, but entered on a fresh war with France, though he had abundant experience to demonstrate the impossibility of defraying its charges.

Parliament of 1625.

The first parliament of this reign has been severely censured on account of the penurious supply it doled out for the exigencies of a war in which its predecessors had involved the king. I will not say that this reproach is wholly unfounded. A more liberal proceeding, if it did not obtain a reciprocal concession from the king, would have put him more in the wrong. But, according to the common practice and character of all such assemblies, it was preposterous to expect subsidies equal to the occasion until a foundation of confidence should be laid between the crown and parliament. The commons had begun probably to repent of their hastiness in the preceding year, and to discover that Buckingham and his pupil, or master (which shall we say?), had conspired to deceive them.[2] They were not to

1 War had not been declared at Charles's accession, nor at the dissolution of the first parliament. In fact, he was much more set upon it than his subjects. Hume and all his school kept this out of sight.

2 Hume has disputed this, but with little success, even on his own showing. He observes, on an assertion of Wilson that Buckingham lost his popularity after Bristol arrived, because he proved that the former, while in Spain, had professed himself a papist, — that it is false, and *was never said by Bristol*. It is singular that Hume should know so positively what Bristol did not say in 1624,

forget that none of the chief grievances of the last reign were yet redressed, and that supplies must be voted slowly and conditionally if they would hope for reformation. Hence they made their grant of tonnage and poundage to last but for a year instead of the king's life, as had for two centuries been the practice; on which account the upper house rejected the bill.[1] Nor would they have refused a further supply, beyond the two subsidies (about 140,000*l.*) which they had granted, had some tender of redress been made by the crown; and were actually in debate upon the matter when interrupted by a sudden dissolution.[2]

Its dissolution.

Nothing could be more evident, by the experience of the late reign as well as by observing the state of public spirit, than that hasty and premature dissolutions or prorogations of parliament served but to aggravate the crown's embarrassments. Every successive house of commons inherited the feelings of its predecessor, without which it would have ill represented the prevalent humor of the nation. The same men, for the most part, came again to parliament more irritated and desperate of reconciliation with the sovereign than before. Even the politic measure, as it was fancied to be, of excluding some of the most active members from seats in the new assembly, by nominating them sheriffs for the year, failed altogether of the expected success; as it naturally must in an age when all ranks partook in a common enthusiasm.[3] Hence the prosecution against Buckingham, to avert which Charles had dissolved his first parliament, was commenced with redoubled vigor in the second. It was too late, after the precedents of Bacon and Middlesex, to dispute the right of the commons to impeach a minister of state. The king, however, anticipating their resolutions, after some sharp speeches only had been uttered against his favorite, sent a message

when it is notorious that he said in parliament what nearly comes to the same thing in 1626. See a curious letter in Cabala, p. 224, showing what a combination had been formed against Buckingham, of all descriptions of malecontents.

1 Parl. Hist. vol. ii. p. 6.

2 Id. 33.

3 The language of lord-keeper Coventry in opening the session was very ill-calculated for the spirit of the commons: "If we consider aright, and think of that incomparable distance between the supreme height and majesty of a mighty monarch and the submissive awe and lowliness of loyal subjects, we cannot but receive exceeding comfort and contentment in the frame and constitution of this highest court, wherein not only the prelates, nobles, and grandees, but the commons of all degrees, have their part; and wherein that high majesty doth descend to admit, or rather to invite, the humblest of his subjects to conference and counsel with him," &c. He gave them a distinct hint afterwards that they must not expect to sit long. Parl. Hist. 39.

that he would not allow any of his servants to be questioned among them, much less such as were of eminent place and near unto him. He saw, he said, that some of them aimed at the duke of Buckingham, whom, in the last parliament of his father, all had combined to honor and respect, nor did he know what had happened since to alter their affections; but he assured them that the duke had done nothing without his own special direction and appointment. This haughty message so provoked the commons, that, having no express testimony against Buckingham, they came to a vote that common fame is a good ground of proceeding either by inquiry or presenting the complaint to the king or lords; nor did a speech from the lord-keeper, severely rating their presumption, and requiring on the king's behalf that they should punish two of their members who had given him offence by insolent discourses in the house, lest he should be compelled to use his royal authority against them, — nor one from the king himself, bidding them "remember that parliaments were altogether in his power for their calling, sitting, and dissolution; therefore, as he found the fruits of them good or evil, they were to continue to be or not to be,"[1] — tend to pacify or to intimidate the assembly. They addressed the king in very decorous language, but asserting "the ancient, constant, and undoubted right and usage of parliaments to question and complain of all persons, of what degree soever, found grievous to the commonwealth, in abusing the power and trust committed to them by their sovereign." The duke was accordingly impeached at the bar of the house of peers on eight articles, many of them probably well founded; yet, as the commons heard no evidence in support of them, it was rather unrea-

Prosecution of Buckingham.

[1] Parl. Hist. 60. I know of nothing under the Tudors of greater arrogance than this language. Sir Dudley Carleton, accustomed more to foreign negotiations than to an English house of commons, gave very just offence by descanting on the misery of the people in other countries. "He cautioned them not to make the king out of love with parliaments by encroaching on his prerogative; for in his messages he had told them that he must then use new councils. In all Christian kingdoms there were parliaments anciently, till the monarchs, seeing their turbulent spirits, stood upon their prerogatives, and overthrew them all, except with us. In foreign countries the people look not like ours, with store of flesh on their backs, but like ghosts, being nothing but skin and bones, with some thin cover to their nakedness, and wearing wooden shoes on their feet — a misery beyond expression, and that we are yet free from; and let us not lose the repute of a free-born nation by our turbulency in parliament." Rushworth.

This was a hint, in the usual arrogant style of courts, that the liberties of the people depended on favor, and not on their own determination to maintain them.

sonable in them to request that he might be committed to the Tower.

In the conduct of this impeachment, two of the managers, sir John Eliot and sir Dudley Digges, one the most illustrious confessor in the cause of liberty whom that time produced, the other a man of much ability and a useful supporter of the popular party, though not free from some oblique views towards promotion, gave such offence by words spoken, or alleged to be spoken, in derogation of his majesty's honor, that they were committed to the Tower. The commons of course resented this new outrage. They resolved to do no more business till they were righted in their privileges. They denied the words imputed to Digges; and, thirty-six peers asserting that he had not spoken them, the king admitted that he was mistaken, and released both their members.[1] He had already broken in upon the privileges of the house of lords by committing the earl of Arundel to the Tower during the session; not upon any political charge, but, as was commonly surmised, on account of a marriage which his son had made with a lady of royal blood. Such private offences were sufficient in those arbitrary reigns to expose the subject to indefinite imprisonment, if not to an actual sentence in the star-chamber. The lords took up this detention of one of their body, and, after formal examination of precedents by a committee, came to a resolution, "that no lord of parliament, the parliament sitting, or within the usual times of privilege of parliament, is to be imprisoned or restrained without sentence or order of the house, unless it be for treason or felony, or for refusing to give surety for the peace." This assertion of privilege was manifestly warranted by the coextensive liberties of the commons. After various messages between the king and lords, Arundel was ultimately set at liberty.[2]

Arbitrary proceedings towards the earls of Arundel

This infringement of the rights of the peerage was accom-

1 Parl. Hist. 119; Hatsell, i. 147; Lords' Journals. A few peers refused to join in this.

Dr. Lingard has observed that the opposition in the house of lords was headed by the earl of Pembroke, who had been rather conspicuous in the late reign, and whose character is drawn by Clarendon in the first book of his history. He held ten proxies in the king's first parliament, as Buckingham did thirteen. Lingard, ix. 328. In the second, Pembroke had only five, but the duke still came with thirteen. Lords' Journals, p. 491. This enormous accumulation of suffrages in one person led to an order of the house, which is now its established regulation, that no peer can hold more than two proxies. Lords' Journals, p. 507.

2 Parl. Hist. 125; Hatsell, 141

panied by another not less injurious, the refusal of a writ of summons to the earl of Bristol. The lords were justly tenacious of this unquestionable privilege of their order, without which its constitutional dignity and independence could never be maintained. Whatever irregularities or uncertainty of legal principle might be found in earlier times as to persons summoned only by writ without patents of creation, concerning whose hereditary peerage there is much reason to doubt, it was beyond all controversy that an earl of Bristol holding his dignity by patent was entitled of right to attend parliament. The house necessarily insisted upon Bristol's receiving his summons, which was sent him with an injunction not to comply with it by taking his place. But the spirited earl knew that the king's constitutional will expressed in the writ ought to outweigh his private command, and laid the secretary's letter before the house of lords. The king prevented any further interference in his behalf by causing articles of charge to be exhibited against him by the attorney-general, whereon he was committed to the Tower. These assaults on the pride and consequence of an aristocratic assembly, from whom alone the king could expect effectual support, display his unfitness not only for the government of England, but of any other nation. Nor was his conduct towards Bristol less oppressive than impolitic. If we look at the harsh and indecent employment of his own authority, and even testimony, to influence a criminal process against a man of approved and untainted worth,[1] and his sanction of charges which, if Bristol's defence be as true as it is now generally admitted to be, he must have known to be unfounded, we shall hardly concur with those candid persons who believe that Charles would have been an excellent prince in a more absolute monarchy. Nothing, in truth, can be more preposterous than to maintain, like Clarendon and Hume, the integrity and innocence of lord Bristol, together with the sincerity and humanity of Charles I. Such inconsistencies betray a determination in the historian to speak of men according to his preconceived affec-

and Bristol.

[1] Mr. Brodie has commented rather too severely on Bristol's conduct, vol. ii. p. 109. That he was "actuated merely by motives of self-aggrandizement" is surely not apparent; though he might be more partial to Spain than we may think right, or even though he might have some bias towards the religion of Rome. The last, however, is by no means proved; for the king's word is no proof in my eyes.

tion or prejudice, without so much as attempting to reconcile these sentiments to the facts which he can neither deny nor excuse.[1]

Though the lords petitioned against a dissolution, the king was determined to protect his favorite, and rescue himself from the importunities of so refractory a house of commons.[2] Perhaps he had already taken the resolution of governing without the concurrence of parliaments, though he was induced to break it the ensuing year. For, the commons having delayed to pass a bill for the five subsidies which they had voted in this session till they should obtain some satisfaction for their complaints, he was left without any regular supply. This was not wholly unacceptable to some of his councillors, and probably to himself, as affording a pretext for those unauthorized demands which the advocates of arbitrary prerogative deemed more consonant to the monarch's honor. He had issued letters of privy seal, after the former parliament, to those in every county whose names had been returned by the lord lieutenant as most capable, mentioning the sum they were required to lend, with a promise of repayment in

Loan demanded by the king.

[1] See the proceedings on the mutual charges of Buckingham and Bristol in Rushworth, or the Parliamentary History. Charles's behavior is worth noticing. He sent a message to the house, desiring that they would not comply with the earl's request of being allowed counsel; and yielded ungraciously when the lords remonstrated against the prohibition. Parl. Hist. 97, 132. The attorney-general exhibited articles against Bristol as to facts depending in great measure on the king's sole testimony. Bristol petitioned the house "to take into consideration of what consequence such a precedent might be; and thereon most humbly to move his majesty for the declining, at least, of his majesty's accusation and testimony." Id. 98. The house ordered two questions on this to be put to the judges: 1. Whether, in case of treason or felony, the king's testimony was to be admitted or not? 2. Whether words spoken to the prince, who is after king, make any alteration in the case? They were ordered to deliver their opinions three days afterwards. But when the time came, the chief justice informed the house that the attorney-general had communicated to the judges his majesty's pleasure that they should forbear to give an answer. Id. 103, 106.

Hume says, "Charles himself was certainly deceived by Buckingham when he corroborated his favorite's narrative by his testimony." But no assertion can be more gratuitous; the supposition indeed is impossible.

[2] Parl. Hist. 193. If the following letter is accurate, the privy council themselves were against this dissolution: — "Yesterday the lords sitting in council at Whitehall, to argue whether the parliament should be dissolved or not, were all with one voice against the dissolution of it; and to-day, when the lord-keeper drew out the commission to have read it, they sent four of their own body to his majesty to let him know how dangerous this abruption would be to the state, and beseech him the parliament might sit but two days—he answered, Not a minute." 15 June, 1626. Mede's Letters, ubi suprà. The author expresses great alarm at what might be the consequence of this step. Mede ascribes this to the council; but others, perhaps more probably, to the house of peers. The king's expression, "not a minute," is mentioned by several writers.

eighteen months.[1] This specification of a particular sum was reckoned an unusual encroachment, and a manifest breach of the statute against arbitrary benevolences; especially as the names of those who refused compliance were to be returned to the council. But the government now ventured on a still more outrageous stretch of power. They first attempted to persuade the people that, as subsidies had been voted in the house of commons, they should not refuse to pay them, though no bill had been passed for that purpose. But a tumultuous cry was raised in Westminster-hall from those who had been convened, that they would pay no subsidy but by authority of parliament.[2] This course, therefore, was abandoned for one hardly less unconstitutional. A general loan was demanded from every subject, according to the rate at which he was assessed in the last subsidy. The commissioners appointed for the collection of this loan received private instructions to require not less than a certain proportion of each man's property in lands or goods, to treat separately with every one, to examine on oath such as should refuse, to certify the names of refractory persons to the privy council, and to admit of no excuse for abatement of the sum required.[3]

This arbitrary taxation (for the name of loan could not

1 Rushworth, Kennet.

2 Mede's Letters. — "On Monday the judges sat in Westminster-hall to persuade the people to pay subsidies; but there arose a great tumultuous shout amongst them: 'A parliament! a parliament! else no subsidies!' The levying of the subsidies, verbally granted in parliament, being propounded to the subsidy-men in Westminster, all of them, saving some thirty among five thousand (and they all the king's servants), cried, 'A parliament! a parliament!' &c. The same was done in Middlesex on Monday also, in five or six places; but far more are said to have refused the grant. At Hicks's-hall, the men of Middlesex assembled there, when they had heard a speech for the purpose, made their obeisance; and so went out without any answer affirmative or negative. In Kent the whole county denied, saying that subsidies were matters of too high a nature for them to meddle withal, and that they durst not deal therewith, lest hereafter they might be called in question." July 22, et post. In Harleian MSS. vol. xxxvii. fol. 192, we find a letter from the king to the deputy-lieutenants and justices of every county, informing them that he had dissolved the last parliament because the disordered passion of some members of that house, contrary to the good inclination of the greater and wiser sort of them, had frustrated the grant of four subsidies and three fifteenths, which they had promised; he therefore enjoins the deputy lieutenants to cause all the troops and bands of the county to be mustered, trained, and ready to march, as he is threatened with invasion; that the justices do divide the county into districts, and appoint in each able persons to collect and receive moneys, promising the parties to employ them in the common defence; to send a list of those who contribute and those who refuse, "that we may hereby be informed who are well-affected to our service, and who are otherwise." July 7, 1626. It is evident that the pretext of invasion, which was utterly improbable, was made use of in order to shelter the king's illegal proceedings.

3 Rushworth's Abr. i. 270.

disguise the extreme improbability that the money would be repaid), so general and systematic as well as so weighty, could not be endured without establishing a precedent that must have shortly put an end to the existence of parliaments. For, if those assemblies were to meet only for the sake of pouring out stupid flatteries at the foot of the throne, of humbly tendering such supplies as the ministry should suggest, or even of hinting at a few subordinate grievances which touched not the king's prerogative and absolute control in matters of state — functions which the Tudors and Stuarts were well pleased that they should exercise — if every remonstrance was to be checked by a dissolution, and chastised by imprisonment of its promoters, every denial of subsidy to furnish a justification for extorted loans, our free-born, highminded gentry would not long have brooked to give their attendance in such an ignominious assembly, and an English parliament would have become as idle a mockery of national representation as the cortes of Castile. But this kingdom was not in a temper to put up with tyranny. The king's advisers were as little disposed to recede from their attempt. They prepared to enforce it by the arm of power.[1] The common people who refused to contribute were impressed to serve in the navy. The gentry were bound by recognizance to appear at the council-table, where many of them were committed to prison.[2] Among these were five knights,

Several committed for refusal to contribute.

[1] The 321st volume of Hargrave MSS., p. 300, contains minutes of a debate at the council-table during the interval between the second and third parliaments of Charles, taken by a councillor. It was proposed to lay an excise on beer; others suggested that it should be on malt, on account of what was brewed in private houses. It was then debated "how to overcome difficulties, whether by persuasion or force. Persuasion, it was thought, would not gain it; and for judicial courses, it would not hold against the subject that would stand upon the right of his own property, and against the fundamental constitutions of the kingdom. The last resort was to a proclamation; for in star-chamber it might be punishable, and thereupon it rested." There follows much more: it seemed to be agreed that there was such a necessity as might justify the imposition; yet a sort of reluctance is visible even among these timid councillors. The king pressed it forward much. In the same volume, p. 393, we find other proceedings at the council-table, whereof the subject was the censuring or punishing of some one who had refused to contribute to the loan of 1626, on the ground of its illegality. The highest language is held by some of the conclave in this debate.

Mr. D'Israeli has collected from the same copious reservoir, the manuscripts of the British Museum, several more illustrations both of the arbitrary proceedings of the council and of the bold spirit with which they were resisted. Curiosities of Literature, new series, iii. 381. But this ingenious author is too much imbued with "the monstrous faith of many made for one," and sets the private feelings of Charles for an unworthy and dangerous minion above the liberties and interests of the nation.

[2] Rushworth, Kennet.

Darnel, Corbet, Earl, Heveningham, and Hampden, who sued the court of king's bench for their writ of habeas corpus. The writ was granted; but the warden of the Fleet made return that they were detained by a warrant from the privy council, informing him of no particular cause of imprisonment, but that they were committed by the special command of his majesty. This gave rise to a most important question, whether such a return was sufficient in law to justify the court in remitting the parties to custody. The fundamental immunity of English subjects from arbitrary detention had never before been so fully canvassed; and it is to the discussion which arose out of the case of these five gentlemen that we owe its continual assertion by parliament, and its ultimate establishment in full practical efficacy by the statute of Charles II. It was argued with great ability by Noy, Selden, and other eminent lawyers, on behalf of the claimants, and by the attorney-general Heath for the crown.

They sue for a habeas corpus.

The counsel for the prisoners grounded their demand of liberty on the original basis of Magna Charta, the twenty-ninth section of which, as is well known, provides that "no free man shall be taken or imprisoned unless by lawful judgment of his peers, or the law of the land." This principle having been frequently transgressed by the king's privy council in earlier times, statutes had been repeatedly enacted, independently of the general confirmations of the charter, to redress this material grievance. Thus in the 25th of Edward III. it is provided that "no one shall be taken by petition or suggestion to the king or his counsel, unless it be (*i. e.* but only) by indictment or presentment, or by writ original at the common law." And this is again enacted three years afterwards, with little variation, and once again in the course of the same reign. It was never understood, whatever the loose language of these old statutes might suggest, that no man could be kept in custody upon a criminal charge before indictment, which would have afforded too great security to offenders. But it was the regular practice that every warrant of commitment, and every return by a jailer to the writ of habeas corpus, must express the nature of the charge, so that it might appear whether it were no legal offence, in which case the party must be instantly set at liberty; or one for which bail ought to be

Arguments on this question.

taken ; or one for which he must be remanded to prison. It appears also to have been admitted without controversy, though not perhaps according to the strict letter of law, that the privy council might commit to prison on a criminal charge, since it seemed preposterous to deny that power to those intrusted with the care of the commonwealth which every petty magistrate enjoyed. But it was contended that they were as much bound as every petty magistrate to assign such a cause for their commitments as might enable the court of king's bench to determine whether it should release or remand the prisoner brought before them by habeas corpus.

The advocates for this principle alleged several precedents from the reign of Henry VII. to that of James, where persons committed by the council generally, or even by the special command of the king, had been admitted to bail on their habeas corpus. "But I conceive," said one of these, "that our case will not stand upon precedent, but upon the fundamental laws and statutes of this realm; and though the precedents look one way or the other, they are to be brought back unto the laws by which the kingdom is governed." He was aware that a pretext might be found to elude most of his precedents. The warrant had commonly declared the party to be charged on *suspicion* of treason or of felony; in which case he would of course be bailed by the court. Yet in some of these instances the words "by the king's special command" were inserted in the commitment; so that they served to repel the pretension of an arbitrary right to supersede the law by his personal authority. Ample proof was brought from the old law-books that the king's command could not excuse an illegal act. "If the king command me," said one of the judges under Henry VI., "to arrest a man, and I arrest him, he shall have an action of false imprisonment against me, though it was done in the king's presence." "The king," said chief-justice Markham to Edward IV., "cannot arrest a man upon suspicion of felony or treason, as any of his subjects may; because, if he should wrong a man by such arrest, he can have no remedy against him." No verbal order of the king, nor any under his sign manual or privy signet, was a command, it was contended by Selden, which the law would recognize as sufficient to arrest or detain any of his subjects, a writ duly issued under the seal of a court being the only language in which he could signify his will. They urged further that, even if the first commitment by the king's command were lawful, yet, when a party had continued in prison for a reasonable time, he should be brought to answer, and not be indefinitely detained — liberty being a thing so favored by the law that it will not suffer any man to remain in confinement for any longer time than of necessity it must.

To these pleadings for liberty, Heath, the attorney-general, replied in a speech of considerable ability, full of those high principles of prerogative which, trampling as it were on all statute and precedent, seemed to tell the judges that they were placed there to obey rather than to determine. "This commitment," he says, "is not in a legal and ordinary way, but by the special command of our lord the king, which implies not only the fact done, but so extraordinarily done, that it is notoriously his majesty's immediate act and will that it should be so." He alludes afterwards, though somewhat obscurely, to the king's absolute power, as contradistinguished from that according to law — a favorite distinction, as I have already observed, with the supporters of despotism. "Shall we make inquiries," he says, "whether his commands are lawful? — who shall call in question the justice of the king's actions, who is not to give account for them?" He argues, from the legal maxim that the king can do no wrong, that a cause must be presumed to exist for the commitment though it be not set forth. He adverts with more success to the number of papists and other state-prisoners detained for years in custody for mere political jealousy. "Some there were," he says, "in the Tower who were put in it when very young; should they bring a habeas corpus, would the court deliver them?" Passing next to the precedents of the other side, and condescending to admit their validity, however contrary to the tenor of his former argument, he evades their application by such distinctions as I have already mentioned.

Which is decided against them.

The judges behaved during this great cause with apparent moderation and sense of its importance to the subject's freedom. Their decision, however, was in favor of the crown; and the prisoners were remanded to custody. In pronouncing this judgment the chief justice, sir Nicholas Hyde, avoiding the more extravagant tenets of absolute monarchy, took the narrower line of denying the application of those precedents which had been alleged to show the practice of the court in bailing persons committed by the king's special command. He endeavored also to prove that, where no cause had been expressed in the warrant, except such command as in the present instance, the judges had always remanded the parties; but with so little success, that I cannot perceive more than one case mentioned by him, and that above a hundred years old, which supports this doctrine. The best authority on which he had to rely was the resolution of the judges in the 34th of Elizabeth, published in Anderson's Reports.[1] For, though this is not grammatically worded, it seems impossible to doubt that it acknowledges the special command of the king, or the authority of the privy council as a body, to be such sufficient warrant for a commitment as to require no further cause to be expressed, and to prevent the judges from discharging the party from custody, either absolutely or upon bail. Yet it was evidently the consequence of this decision that every statute from the time of Magna Charta, designed to protect the personal liberties of Englishmen, became a dead letter, since the insertion of four words in a warrant (per speciale mandatum regis), which might become matter of form, would control their remedial efficacy. And this wound was the more deadly in that the notorious cause of these gentlemen's imprisonment was their withstanding an illegal exaction of money. Everything that distinguished our constitutional laws, all that rendered the name of England valuable, was at stake in this issue. If the judgment in the case of ship-money was more flagrantly iniquitous, it was not so extensively destructive as the present.[2]

Neither these measures, however, of illegal severity towards the uncompliant, backed as they were by a timid court of justice, nor the exhortations of a more prostitute and shameless band of churchmen, could divert the nation from its cardinal point of faith in its own prescriptive franchises.

[1] See above, in chap. v. Coke himself, while chief justice, had held that one committed by the privy council was not bailable by any court in England. Parl. Hist. 310. He had nothing to say, when pressed with this in the next parliament, but that he had misgrounded his opinion upon a certain precedent, which being nothing to the purpose, he was now assured his opinion was as little to the purpose. Id. 325. State Trials, iii. 81.

[2] State Trials, iii. 1-234; Parl. Hist. 246, 259, &c.; Rushworth.

A parliament called in 1628.

To call another parliament appeared the only practicable means of raising money for a war in which the king persisted with great impolicy, or rather blind trust in his favorite. He consented to this with extreme unwillingness.[1] Previously to its assembling he released a considerable number of gentlemen and others who had been committed for their refusal of the loan. These were in many cases elected to the new parliament, coming thither with just indignation at their country's wrongs, and pardonable resentment of their own. No year, indeed, within the memory of any one living had witnessed such violations of public liberty as 1627. Charles seemed born to carry into daily practice those theories of absolute power which had been promulgated from his father's lips. Even now, while the writs were out for a new parliament, commissioners were appointed to raise money "by impositions or otherwise, as they should find most convenient in a case of such inevitable necessity, wherein form and circumstance must be dispensed with rather than the substance be lost and hazarded;"[2] and the levying of ship-money was already debated in the council. Anticipating, as indeed was natural, that this house of commons would correspond as ill to the king's wishes as their predecessors, his advisers were preparing schemes more congenial, if they could be rendered effective, to the spirit in which he was to govern. A contract was entered into for transporting some troops and a considerable quantity of arms from Flanders into England, under circumstances at least highly suspicious, and which, combined with all the rest that appears of the court policy at that time, leaves no great doubt on the mind that they were designed to keep under the people while the business of contribution was going forward.[3] Shall it be imputed as a reproach to the Cokes, the Seldens, the Glanvils, the Pyms, the Eliots, the Philipses of this famous parliament, that they endeavored to devise more effectual restraints than the law had hitherto imposed on a prince who had snapped like bands of tow the ancient statutes of the land, to remove from his presence counsellors to have been misled by whom was his best apology, and to sub-

1 At the council-table, some proposing a parliament, the king said he did abominate the name. Mede's Letters, 30th Sept. 1626.

2 Rushworth; Mede's Letters in Harl. MSS. passim.

3 Rushworth's Abr. i. 304; Cabala, part ii. 217. See what is said of this by Mr. Brodie, ii. 158.

ject him to an entire dependence on his people for the expenditure of government, as the surest pledge of his obedience to the laws?

The principal matters of complaint taken up by the commons in this session were, the exaction of money under the name of loans; the commitment of those who refused compliance, and the late decision of the king's bench remanding them upon a habeas corpus; the billeting of soldiers on private persons, which had occurred in the last year, whether for convenience or for purposes of intimidation and annoyance; and the commissions to try military offenders by martial law — a procedure necessary within certain limits to the discipline of an army, but unwarranted by the constitution of this country, which was little used to any regular forces, and stretched by the arbitrary spirit of the king's administration beyond all bounds.[1] These four grievances or abuses form the foundation of the Petition of Right, presented by the commons in the shape of a declaratory statute. Charles had recourse to many subterfuges in hopes to elude the passing of this law; rather perhaps through wounded pride, as we may judge from his subsequent conduct, than much apprehension that it would create a serious impediment to his despotic schemes. He tried to persuade them to acquiesce in his royal promise not to arrest any one without just cause, or in a simple confirmation of the Great Charter and other statutes in favor of liberty. The peers, too pliant in this instance to his wishes, and half receding from the patriot banner they had lately joined, lent him their aid by proposing amendments (insidious in those who suggested them, though not in the body of the house), which the commons firmly rejected.[2] Even when the bill was tendered to him for that

Petition of Right.

The king's reluctance to grant it.

[1] A commission addressed to lord Wimbleton, 28th Dec. 1625, empowers him to proceed against soldiers, or dissolute persons joining with them, who should commit any robberies, &c., which by martial law ought to be punished with death, by such summary course as is agreeable to martial law, &c. Rymer, xviii. 254. Another, in 1626, may be found, p. 763. It is unnecessary to point out how unlike these commissions are to our present mutiny bills.

[2] Bishop Williams, as we are informed by his biographer, though he promoted the Petition of Right, stickled for the additional clause adopted by the lords, reserving the king's sovereign power; which very justly exposed him to suspicion of being corrupted. For that he was so is most evident by what follows; where we are told that he had an interview with the duke of Buckingham, when they were reconciled; and "his grace had the bishop's consent, with a little asking, that he would be his grace's faithful servant in the next session of parliament, and was allowed to hold up a seeming enmity, and his own popular estimation, that he might the sooner do the work." Hackett's Life of Williams,

assent which it had been necessary for the last two centuries that the king should grant or refuse in a word, he returned a long and equivocal answer, from which it could only be collected that he did not intend to remit any portion of what he had claimed as his prerogative. But on an address from both houses for a more explicit answer, he thought fit to consent to the bill in the usual form. The commons, of whose harshness towards Charles his advocates have said so much, immediately passed a bill for granting five subsidies, about 350,000*l.* — a sum not too great for the wealth of the kingdom or for his exigencies, but considerable according to the precedents of former times, to which men naturally look.[1]

The sincerity of Charles in thus according his assent to the Petition of Right may be estimated by the following very remarkable conference which he held on the subject with his judges. Before the bill was passed he sent for the two chief justices, Hyde and Richardson, to Whitehall, and propounded certain questions, directing that the other judges should be assembled in order to answer them. The first question was, "Whether in no case whatsoever the king may not commit a subject without showing cause?" To which the judges gave an answer the same day under their hands, which was the next day presented to his majesty by the two chief justices, in these words: "We are of opinion that, by the general rule of law, the cause of commitment by his majesty ought to be shown; yet some cases may require such secrecy, that the king may commit a subject without showing the cause for a convenient time." The king then delivered them a second question, and required them to keep it very secret, as the former: "Whether, in case a habeas corpus be brought, and a warrant from the king without any general or special cause returned, the judges ought to deliver him before they understand the cause from the king?" Their

p. 77, 80. With such instances of baseness and treachery in the public men of this age, surely the distrust of the commons was not so extravagant as the school of Hume pretend.

1 The debates and conferences on this momentous subject, especially on the article of the habeas corpus, occupy near two hundred columns in the New Parliamentary History, to which I refer the reader.

In one of these conferences the lords, observing what a prodigious weight of legal ability was arrayed on the side of the petition, very fairly determined to hear counsel for the crown. One of these, serjeant Ashley, having argued in behalf of the prerogative in a high tone, such as had been usual in the late reign, was ordered into custody; and the lords assured the other house that he had no authority from them for what he had said. Id. 327. A remarkable proof of the rapid growth of popular principles!

answer was as follows: "Upon a habeas corpus brought for one committed by the king, if the cause be not specially or generally returned, so as the court may take knowledge thereof, the party ought by the general rule of law to be delivered. But, if the case be such that the same requireth secrecy, and may not presently be disclosed, the court in discretion may forbear to deliver the prisoner for a convenient time, to the end the court may be advertised of the truth thereof." On receiving this answer, the king proposed a third question: "Whether, if the king grant the commons' petition, he doth not thereby exclude himself from committing or restraining a subject for any time or cause whatsoever without showing a cause?" The judges returned for answer to this important query: "Every law, after it is made, hath its exposition, and so this petition and answer must have an exposition as the case in the nature thereof shall require to stand with justice; which is to be left to the courts of justice to determine, which cannot particularly be discovered until such case shall happen. And although the petition be granted, there is no fear of conclusion as is intimated in the question." [1]

The king, a very few days afterwards, gave his *first* answer to the Petition of Right. For even this indirect promise of compliance which the judges gave him did not relieve him from apprehensions that he might lose the prerogative of arbitrary commitment. And though, after being beaten from this evasion, he was compelled to accede in general terms to the petition, he had the insincerity to circulate one thousand five hundred copies of it through the country, after the prorogation, with his first answer annexed—an attempt to deceive without the possibility of success.[2] But instances of such ill faith, accumulated as they are through the life of Charles, render the assertion of his sincerity a proof either of historical ignorance, or of a want of moral delicacy.

The Petition of Right, as this statute is still called, from its not being drawn in the common form of an act of parliament, after reciting the various laws which have established certain essential privileges of the subject, and enumerating the violations of them which had recently occurred, in the four points of illegal exactions, arbitrary commitments, quartering of

[1] Hargrave MSS. xxxii. 97.

[2] Parl. Hist. 436.

soldiers or sailors, and infliction of punishment by martial law, prays the king, "That no man hereafter be compelled to make or yield any gift, loan, benevolence, tax, or such-like charge, without common consent by act of parliament; and that none be called to answer or take such oath, or to give attendance, or be confined or otherwise molested or disquieted concerning the same, or for refusal thereof; and that no freeman in any such manner as is before mentioned be imprisoned or detained; and that your majesty would be pleased to remove the said soldiers and marines, and that your people may not be so burthened in time to come; and that the aforesaid commissions for proceeding by martial law may be revoked and annulled; and that hereafter no commissions of the like nature may issue forth to any person or persons whatever, to be executed as aforesaid, lest by color of them any of your majesty's subjects be destroyed or put to death contrary to the laws and franchises of the land." [1]

It might not unreasonably be questioned whether the language of this statute were sufficiently general to comprehend duties charged on merchandise at the outports as well as internal taxes and exactions, especially as the former had received a sort of sanction, though justly deemed contrary to law, by the judgment of the court of exchequer in Bates's case. The commons however were steadily determined not to desist till they should have rescued their fellow-subjects from a burden as unwarrantably imposed as those specifically enumerated in their Petition of Right. Tonnage and poundage, the customary grant of every reign, had been taken by the present king without consent of parliament; the lords having rejected, as before mentioned, a bill that limited it to a single year. The house now prepared a bill to grant it, but purposely delayed its passing, in order to remonstrate with the king against his unconstitutional anticipation of their consent. They declared "that there ought not any imposition to be laid upon the goods of merchants, exported or imported, without common consent by act of parliament;" that tonnage and poundage, like other subsidies, sprung from the free grant of the people; that, "when impositions had been laid on the subjects'

Tonnage and poundage disputed.

[1] Stat. 3 Car. I. c. 1. Hume has printed in a note the whole statute with the preamble, which I omit for the sake of brevity, and because it may be found in so common a book.

goods and merchandises without authority of law, which had very seldom occurred, they had, on complaint in parliament, been forthwith relieved; except in the late king's reign, who, through evil counsel, had raised the rates and charges to the height at which they then were." They conclude, after repeating their declaration that the receiving of tonnage and poundage and other impositions not granted by parliament is a breach of the fundamental liberties of this kingdom, and contrary to the late Petition of Right, with most humbly beseeching his majesty to forbear any further receiving of the same, and not to take it in ill part from those of his loving subjects who should refuse to make payment of any such charges without warrant of law.[1]

The king anticipated the delivery of this remonstrance by proroguing parliament. Tonnage and poundage, he told them, was what he had never meant to give away, nor could possibly do without. By this abrupt prorogation while so great a matter was unsettled, he trod back his late footsteps, and dissipated what little hopes might have arisen from his tardy assent to the Petition of Right. During the interval before the ensuing session, those merchants, among whom Chambers, Rolls, and Vassal are particularly to be remembered with honor, who gallantly refused to comply with the demands of the custom-house, had their goods distrained, and, on suing writs of replevin, were told by the judges that the king's right, having been established in the case of Bates, could no longer be disputed.[2] Thus the commons reassembled, by no means less inflamed against the king's administration than at the commencement of the preceding session. Their proceedings were conducted with more than usual warmth.[3] Buckingham's death, which had occurred since the prorogation, did not allay their resentment against the advisers of the crown. But the king, who had very much lowered his tone in speaking of tonnage and poundage, and would have been content to receive it as their grant, perceiving that they were bent on a full statutory recognition of the illegality of impositions without their consent, and that they had opened a fresh battery on another side, by mingling

1 Parl. Hist. 431.
2 Rushworth, Abr. i. 409.
3 Parl. Hist. 441, &c.

in certain religious disputes in order to attack some of his favorite prelates, took the step, to which he was always inclined, of dissolving this third parliament.

The king dissolves the parliament.

The religious disputes to which I have just alluded are chiefly to be considered, for the present purpose, in their relation to those jealousies and resentments springing out of the ecclesiastical administration, which during the reigns of the two first Stuarts furnished unceasing food to political discontent. James having early shown his inflexible determination to restrain the puritans, the bishops proceeded with still more rigor than under Elizabeth. No longer thwarted, as in her time, by an unwilling council, they succeeded in exacting a general conformity to the ordinances of the church. It had been solemnly decided by the judges in the queen's reign, and in 1604, that, although the statute establishing the high-commission court did not authorize it to deprive ministers of their benefices, yet, this law being only in affirmation of the queen's inherent supremacy, she might, by virtue of that, regulate all ecclesiastical matters at her pleasure, and erect courts with such powers as she should think fit. Upon this somewhat dangerous principle archbishop Bancroft deprived a considerable number of puritan clergymen;[1] while many more, finding that the interference of the commons in their behalf was not regarded, and that all schemes of evasion were come to an end, were content to submit to the obnoxious discipline. But their affections being very little conciliated by this coercion, there remained a large party within the bosom of the established church prone to watch for and magnify the errors of their spiritual rulers. These men preserved the name of puritans. Austere in their lives, while many of the others were careless or ir-

Religious differences.

Prosecution of puritans by Bancroft.

[1] Cawdrey's Case, 5 Reports; Cro. Jac. 37; Neal, p. 432. The latter says above three hundred were deprived; but Collier reduces them to forty-nine, p. 687. The former writer states the nonconformist ministers at this time in twenty-four counties to have been 754; of course the whole number was much greater: p. 434. This minority was considerable; but it is chiefly to be noticed that it contained the more exemplary portion of the clergy; no scandalous or absolutely illiterate incumbent, of whom there was a very large number, being a nonconformist. This general enforcement of conformity, however it might compel the majority's obedience, rendered the separation of the incompliant more decided. Neal, 446. Many retired to Holland, especially of the Brownist or Independent denomination. Id. 436. And Bancroft, like his successor Laud, interfered to stop some who were setting out for Virginia. Id. 454.

regular, learned as a body comparatively with the opposite party, implacably averse to everything that could be construed into an approximation to popery, they acquired a degree of respect from grave men which would have been much more general had they not sometimes given offence by a moroseness and even malignity of disposition, as well as by a certain tendency to equivocation and deceitfulness; faults, however, which so frequently belong to the weaker party under a rigorous government that they scarcely afford a marked reproach against the puritans. They naturally fell in with the patriotic party in the house of commons, and kept up throughout the kingdom a distrust of the crown, which has never been so general in England as when connected with some religious apprehensions.

Growth of high-church tenets.

The system pursued by Bancroft and his imitators, bishops Neile and Laud, with the approbation of the king, far opposed to the healing councils of Burleigh and Bacon, was just such as low-born and little-minded men, raised to power by fortune's caprice, are ever found to pursue. They studiously aggravated every difference, and irritated every wound. As the characteristic prejudice of the puritans was so bigoted an abhorrence of the Romish faith that they hardly deemed its followers to deserve the name of Christians, the prevailing high-church party took care to shock that prejudice by somewhat of a retrograde movement, and various seeming, or indeed real, accommodations of their tenets to those of the abjured religion. They began by preaching the divine right, as it is called, or absolute indispensability, of episcopacy; a doctrine of which the first traces, as I apprehend, are found about the end of Elizabeth's reign.[1] They insisted on the necessity of

[1] Lord Bacon, in his advertisement respecting the Controversies of the Church of England, written under Elizabeth, speaks of this notion as newly broached. "Yea, and some indiscreet persons have been bold in open preaching to use dishonourable and derogatory speech and censure of the churches abroad; and that so far as some of our men ordained in foreign parts have been pronounced to be no lawful ministers." Vol. i. p. 382. It is evident, by some passages in Strype, attentively considered, that natives regularly ordained abroad in the presbyterian churches were admitted to hold preferment in England; the first bishop who objected to them seems to have been Aylmer. Instances, however, of foreigners holding preferment without any re-ordination, may be found down to the civil wars. Annals of Reformation, ii. 522, and Appendix, 116; Life of Grindal, 271; Collier, ii. 594; Neal, i. 258. The cases of laymen, such as Casaubon holding prebends by dispensation, are not in point.

The divine right of episcopacy is said to have been laid down by Bancroft, in his famous sermon at Paul's Cross in 1588. But I do not find anything in it to

episcopal succession regularly derived from the apostles. They drew an inference from this tenet, that ordinations by presbyters were in all cases null. And as this affected all the reformed churches in Europe except their own, the Lutherans not having preserved the succession of their bishops, while the calvinists had altogether abolished that order, they began to speak of them not as brethren of the same faith, united in the same cause, and distinguished only by differences little more material than those of political commonwealths (which had been the language of the church of England ever since the Reformation), but as aliens, to whom they were not at all related, and schismatics, with whom they held no communion; nay, as wanting the very essence of a Christian society. This again brought them nearer by irresistible consequence to the disciples of Rome, whom, with becoming charity, but against the received creed of the puritans, and perhaps against their own articles, they all acknowledged to be a part of the catholic church, while they were withholding that appellation, expressly or by inference, from Heidelberg and Geneva.

Differences as to the observance of Sunday.

The founders of the English Reformation, after abolishing most of the festivals kept before that time, had made little or no change as to the mode of observance of those they retained. Sundays and holidays stood much on the same footing, as days on which no work except for good cause was to be performed, the service of the church was to be attended, and any lawful amusement might be indulged in.[1] A just distinction however soon grew up; an industrious people could spare time for very few holidays; and the more scrupulous party,

that effect. It is however pretty distinctly asserted, if I mistake not the sense, in the canons of 1606. Overall's Convocation Book, 179, &c. Yet Laud had been reproved by the university of Oxford, in 1664, for maintaining, in his exercise for bachelor of divinity, that there could be no true church without bishops, which was thought to cast a bone of contention between the church of England and the reformed upon the Continent. Heylin's Life of Laud, 54.

Cranmer, and some of the original founders of the Anglican church, far from maintaining the divine and indispensable right of episcopal government, held bishops and priests to be the same order.

[A learned and candid Oxford writer (Cardwell's Annals of the Church, vol. ii. p. 5) has supposed me to have overlooked a passage in Bancroft's Sermon at Paul's Cross, p. 97, where he asserts the divine right of episcopacy. But, on referring again to this passage, it is perfectly evident that he says nothing about what is commonly meant by the *jure divino* doctrine, the perpetual and indispensable government by bishops, confining himself to an assertion of the fact, and that in no strong terms. 1845.]

[1] See the queen's injunctions of 1559, Somers Tracts, i. 65; and compare preamble of 5 & 6 of Edw. VI. c. 3.

while they slighted the church-festivals as of human appointment, prescribed a stricter observance of the Lord's day. But it was not till about 1595 that they began to place it very nearly on the footing of the Jewish sabbath, interdicting not only the slightest action of worldly business, but even every sort of pastime and recreation; a system which, once promulgated, soon gained ground as suiting their atrabilious humor, and affording a new theme of censure on the vices of the great.[1] Those who opposed them on the high-church side not only derided the extravagance of the Sabbatarians, as the others were called, but pretended that, the commandment having been confined to the Hebrews, the modern observance of the first day of the week as a season of rest and devotion was an ecclesiastical institution, and in no degree more venerable than that of the other festivals or the season of Lent, which the puritans stubbornly despised.[2] Such a

[1] The first of these Sabbatarians was a Dr. Bound, whose sermon was suppressed by Whitgift's order. But some years before, one of Martin Mar-prelate's charges against Aylmer was for playing at bowls on Sundays; and the word sabbath, as applied to that day, may be found occasionally under Elizabeth, though by no means so usual as afterwards; it is even recognized in the Homilies. One of Bound's recommendations was that no feasts should be given on that day, "except by lords, knights, and persons of quality;" for which unlucky reservation his adversaries did not forget to deride him. Fuller's Church History, p. 227. This writer describes, in his quaint style, the abstinence from sports produced by this new doctrine; and remarks, what a slight acquaintance with human nature would have taught archbishop Laud, that "the more liberty people were offered, the less they used it; it was sport for them to refrain from sport." See also Collier, 643; Neal, 386; Strype's Whitgift, 530; May's Hist. of Parliament, 16.

[2] Heylin's Life of Laud, 15; Fuller, part ii. p. 76.

The regulations enacted at various times since the Reformation for the observance of abstinence in as strict a manner, though not ostensibly on the same grounds, as it is enjoined in the church of Rome, may deserve some notice. A statute of 1548 (2 and 3 Edward VI. c. 19), after reciting that one day or one kind of meat is not more holy, pure, or clean than another, and much else to the same effect, yet, "forasmuch as divers of the king's subjects, turning their knowledge therein to gratify their sensuality, have of late more than in times past broken and contemned such abstinence, which hath been used in this realm upon the Fridays and Saturdays, the embering days, and other days commonly called vigils, and in the time commonly called Lent, and other accustomed times; the king's majesty, considering that due and godly abstinence is a mean to virtue and to subdue men's bodies to their soul and spirit, and considering also especially that fishers and men using the trade of fishing in the sea may thereby the rather be set on work, and that by eating of fish much flesh shall be saved and increased," enacts, after repealing all existing laws on the subject, that such as eat flesh at the forbidden seasons shall incur a penalty of ten shillings, or ten days' imprisonment, *without flesh*, and a double penalty for the second offence.

The next statute relating to abstinence is one (5th Eliz. c. 5) entirely for the increase of the fishery. It enacts, § 15, &c., that no one, unless having a license, shall eat flesh on fish-days, or on Wednesdays, now made an additional fish-day, under a penalty of 3*l*., or three months' imprisonment. Except that every one having three dishes of sea-fish at his table, might have one of flesh also. But, "because no manner of person shall misjudge of the intent of this statute," it is enacted that whosoever shall notify that any eating of fish or forbearing of flesh mentioned therein is of any necessity for the saving of the soul of man, or

controversy might well have been left to the usual weapons. But James I., or some of the bishops to whom he listened, bethought themselves that this might serve as a test of puritan ministers. He published accordingly a declaration to be read in churches, permitting all lawful recreations on Sunday after divine service, such as dancing, archery, May-games, and morrice-dances, and other usual sports but with a prohibition of bear-baiting and other unlawful games. No recusant, or any one who had not attended the

that it is the service of God, otherwise than as other politic laws are and be; that then such persons shall be punished as spreaders of false news, § 39 and 40. The act 27th Eliz. c. 11, repeals the prohibition as to Wednesday; and provides that no victuallers shall vend flesh in Lent, nor upon Fridays or Saturdays, under a penalty. The 35th Eliz. c. 7, § 22, reduces the penalty of 3*l.*, or three months' imprisonment, enacted by 5th of Eliz., to one third. This is the latest statute that appears on the subject.

Many proclamations appear to have been issued in order to enforce an observance so little congenial to the propensities of Englishmen. One of those in the first year of Edward was before any statute; and its very words respecting the indifference of meats in a religious sense were adopted by the legislature the next year. (Strype's Eccles. Memor. ii. 81.) In one of Elizabeth's, A. D. 1572, as in the statute of Edward, the political motives of the prohibition seem in some measure associated with the superstition it disclaims; for eating in the season of Lent is called "licentious and carnal disorder, in contempt of God and man, and only to the satisfaction of devilish and carnal appetite;" and butchers, &c., "ministering to such foul lust of the flesh," were severely mulcted. Strype's Annals, ii. 208. But in 1576 another proclamation to the same effect uses no such hard words, and protests strongly against any superstitious interpretation of its motives. Life of Grindal, p. 226. So also in 1579, Strype's Annals, ii. 608, and, as far as I have observed, in all of a later date, the encouragement of the navy and fishery is set forth as their sole ground. In 1596, Whitgift, by the queen's command, issued letters to the bishops of his province to take order that the fasting-days, Wednesday and Friday, should be kept, and no suppers eaten, especially on Friday evens. This was on account of the great dearth of that and the preceding year. Strype's Whitgift, p. 490. These proclamations for the observance of Lent continued under James and Charles, as late, I presume, as the commencement of the civil war. They were diametrically opposed to the puritan tenets; for, notwithstanding the pretext about the fishery, there is no doubt that the dominant ecclesiastics maintained the observance of Lent as an ordinance of the church. But I suspect that little regard was paid to Friday and Saturday as days of weekly fast. Rymer, xvii. 131, 134, 349; xviii. 268, 282, 961.

This abstemious system, however, was only compulsory on the poor. Licenses were easily obtained by others from the privy council in Edward's days, and afterwards from the bishop. They were empowered, with their guests, to eat flesh on all fasting-days for life. Sometimes the number of guests was limited. Thus the marquis of Winchester had permission for twelve friends; and John Sandford, draper of Gloucester, for two. Strype's Memorials, ii. 82. The act above mentioned for encouragement of the fishery, 5th Eliz. c. 5, provides that 1*l.* 6*s.* 8*d.* shall be paid for granting every license, and 6*s.* 8*d.* annually afterwards, to the poor of the parish. But no license was to be granted for eating beef at any time of the year, or veal from Michaelmas to the 1st of May. A melancholy privation to our countrymen! but, I have no doubt, little regarded. Strype makes known to us the interesting fact that Ambrose Potter, of Gravesend, and his wife, had permission from archbishop Whitgift "to eat flesh and white meats in Lent during their lives; so that it was done soberly and frugally, cautiously, and avoiding public scandal as much as might be, and giving 6*s.* 8*d.* annually to the poor of the parish." Life of Whitgift, 246.

The civil wars did not so put an end to the compulsory observance of Lent and fish-days, but that similar proclamations are found after the Restoration, I know not how long. Kennet's Register, p. 367 and 558.

church-service, was entitled to this privilege, which might consequently be regarded as a bounty on devotion. The severe puritan saw it in no such point of view. To his cynical temper May-games and morrice-dances were hardly tolerable on six days of the week; they were now recommended for the seventh. And this impious license was to be promulgated in the church itself. It is indeed difficult to explain so unnecessary an insult on the precise clergy but by supposing an intention to harass those who should refuse compliance.[1] But this intention, from whatever cause, perhaps through the influence of Archbishop Abbot, was not carried into effect, nor was the declaration itself enforced till the following reign.

The house of commons displayed their attachment to the puritan maxims, or their dislike of the prelatical clergy, by bringing in bills to enforce a greater strictness in this respect. A circumstance that occurred in the session of 1621 will serve to prove their fanatical violence. A bill having been brought in "for the better observance of the Sabbath, usually called Sunday," one Mr. Shepherd, sneering at the puritans, remarked that, as Saturday was dies Sabbati, this might be entitled a bill for the observance of Saturday, commonly called Sunday. This witticism brought on his head the wrath of that dangerous assembly. He was reprimanded on his knees, expelled the house, and, when he saw what befell poor Floyd, might deem himself cheaply saved from their fangs with no worse chastisement.[2] Yet when the upper house sent down their bill with "the Lord's day" substituted for "the Sabbath," observing "that people do now much incline to words of Judaism," the commons took no exception.[3] The use of the word Sabbath instead of Sunday became in that age a distinctive mark of the puritan party.

1 Wilson, 709.

2 Debates in Parliament, 1621, vol. i. p. 45, 52. The king requested them not to pass this bill, being so directly against his proclamation. Id. 60. Shepherd's expulsion is mentioned in Mede's Letters, Harl. MSS., 389.

3 Vol. ii. 97. Two acts were passed, 1 Car. I. c. 1, and 3 Car. I. c. 2, for the better observance of Sunday; the former of which gave great annoyance, it seems, to the orthodox party. "Had any such bill," says Heylin, "been offered in king James's time, it would have found a sorry welcome; but this king, being under a necessity of compliance with them, resolved to grant them their desires in that particular, to the end that they might grant his also in the aid required, when that obstruction was removed. The Sabbatarians took the benefit of this opportunity for the obtaining of this grant, the first that ever they obtained by all their strugglings, which of what consequence it was we shall see hereafter." Life of Laud, p. 129. Yet this statute permits the people lawful sports and pastimes on Sundays within their own parishes.

Arminian controversy.

A far more permanent controversy sprang up about the end of the same reign, which afforded a new pretext for intolerance, and a fresh source of mutual hatred. Every one of my readers is acquainted more or less with the theological tenets of original sin, free-will, and predestination, variously taught in the schools, and debated by polemical writers for so many centuries; and few can be ignorant that the articles of our own church, as they relate to these doctrines, have been very differently interpreted, and that a controversy about their meaning has long been carried on with a pertinacity which could not have continued on so limited a topic, had the combatants been merely influenced by the love of truth. Those who have no bias to warp their judgment will not perhaps have much hesitation in drawing their line between, though not at an equal distance between, the conflicting parties. It appears, on the one hand, that the articles are worded on some of these doctrines with considerable ambiguity; whether we attribute this to the intrinsic obscurity of the subject, to the additional difficulties with which it had been entangled by theological systems, to discrepancy of opinion in the compilers, or to their solicitude to prevent disunion by adopting formularies which men of different sentiments might subscribe. It is also manifest that their framers came, as it were, with averted eyes to the Augustinian doctrine of predestination, and wisely reprehended those who turned their attention to a system so pregnant with objections, and so dangerous, when needlessly dwelt upon, to all practical piety and virtue. But, on the other hand, this very reluctance to inculcate the tenet is so expressed as to manifest their undoubting belief in it; nor is it possible either to assign a motive for inserting the seventeenth article, or to give any reasonable interpretation to it, upon the theory which at present passes for orthodox in the English church. And upon other subjects intimately related to the former, such as the penalty of original sin and the depravation of human nature, the articles, after making every allowance for want of precision, seem totally irreconcilable with the scheme usually denominated Arminian.

The force of those conclusions which we must, in my judgment deduce from the language of these articles, will be materially increased by that appeal to contemporary and other early authorities to which recourse has been had in order to invalidate them. Whatever doubts may be raised as to the Calvinism of Cranmer and Ridley, there can surely be no room for any as to the chiefs of the Anglican church under Elizabeth. We find explicit proofs that Jewell, Nowell, Sandys, Cox, professed to concur with the reformers of Zurich and Geneva in every point of doctrine.[1] The works of Calvin and Bullinger became text-books in the English universities.[2] Those who did not hold the predestinarian theory were branded with reproach by the names of free-willers and Pelagians.[3] And when the opposite tenets came to be advanced, as they were at Cambridge about 1590, a clamor was raised as if some unusual heresy had been broached. Whitgift, with the concurrence of some other prelates, in order to withstand its progress, published what were called the Lambeth articles, containing the broadest and most repulsive declaration of all the Calvinistic tenets. But, lord Burleigh having shown some disapprobation, these articles never obtained any legal sanction.[4]

These more rigorous tenets, in fact, especially when so crudely announced, were beginning to give way. They had been already abandoned by the Lutheran church. They had long been opposed in that of Rome by the Franciscan order, and latterly by the Jesuits. Above all, the study of the Greek fathers, with whom the first reformers had been little conversant, taught the divines of a more learned age that men of as high a name as Augustin, and whom they were prone to overvalue, had entertained very different sentiments.[5] Still the novel opinions passed for heterodox, and were promulgated with much vacillation and indistinctness. When they were published in unequivocal propositions by Arminius and his school, James declared himself with vehemence against this heresy.[6] He not only sent English

[1] Without loading the page with too many references on a subject so little connected with this work, I mention Strype's Annals, vol. i. p. 118, and a letter from Jewell to P. Martyr, in Burnet, vol. iii., Appendix, 275.

[2] Collier, 568.

[3] Strype's Annals, i. 207, 294.

[4] Strype's Whitgift, 434-472.

[5] It is admitted on all hands that the Greek fathers did not inculcate the predestinarian system. Elizabeth having begun to read some of the fathers, bishop Cox writes of it with some disapprobation, adverting especially to the Pelagianism of Chrysostom and the other Greeks. Strype's Annals, i. 324.

[6] Winwood, iii. 293. The intemperate and even impertinent behavior of James, in pressing the states of Holland to inflict some censure or punishment on Vorstius, is well known. But though Vorstius was an Arminian, it was not precisely on account of those opinions that he incurred the king's peculiar displeasure, but for certain propositions as to the nature of the Deity, which James called atheistical, but which were in fact

divines to sit in the synod of Dort, where the Calvinistic system was fully established, but instigated the proceedings against the remonstrants with more of theological pedantry than charity or decorum.[1] Yet this inconsistent monarch within a very few years was so wrought on by one or two favorite ecclesiastics, who inclined towards the doctrines condemned in that assembly, that openly to maintain the Augustinian system became almost a sure means of exclusion from preferment in our church. This was carried to its height under Charles. Laud, his sole counsellor in ecclesiastical matters, advised a declaration enjoining silence on the controverted points; a measure by no means unwise if it had been fairly acted upon. It is alleged, however, that the preachers on one side only were silenced, the printers of books on one side censured in the star-chamber, while full scope was indulged to the opposite sect.[2]

Arian. The letters on this subject in Winwood are curious. Even at this time the king is said to have spoken moderately of predestination as a dubious point (p. 452), though he had treated Arminius as a mischievous innovator for raising a question about it; and this is confirmed by his letter to the States in 1613. Brandt, iii. 129, and see p. 138. See Collier, p. 711, for the king's sentiments in 1616; also Brandt, iii. 313.

[1] Sir Dudley Carleton's Letters and Negotiations, passim. Brandt's History of Reformation in Low Countries, vol. iii. The English divines sent to this synod were decidedly inclined to Calvinism, but they spoke of themselves as deputed by the king, not by the church of England, which they did not represent.

[2] There is some obscurity about the rapid transition of the court from Calvinism to the opposite side. It has been supposed that the part taken by James at the synod of Dort was chiefly political, with a view to support the house of Orange against the party headed by Barnevelt. But he was so much more of a theologian than a statesman, that I much doubt whether this will account satisfactorily for his zeal in behalf of the Gomarists. He wrote on the subject with much polemical bitterness, but without reference, so far as I have observed, to any political faction; though sir Dudley Carleton's letters show that *he* contemplated the matter as a minister ought to do. Heylin intimates that the king grew "more moderate afterwards, and into a better liking of those opinions which he had laboured to condemn at the synod of Dort." Life of Laud, 120. The court language, indeed, shifted so very soon after this, that Antonio de Dominis, the famous half-converted archbishop of Spalato, is said to have invented the name of doctrinal puritans for those who distinguished themselves by holding the Calvinistic tenets. Yet the synod of Dort was in 1618, while De Dominis left England not later than 1622. Buckingham seems to have gone very warmly into Laud's scheme of excluding the Calvinists. The latter gave him a list of divines on Charles's accession, distinguishing their names by O. and P., for orthodox and puritan; including several tenets in the latter denomination, besides those of the quinquarticular controversy, such as the indispensable observance of the Lord's day, the indiscrimination of bishops and presbyters, &c. Life of Laud, 119. The influence of Laud became so great, that to preach in favor of Calvinism, though commonly reputed to be the doctrine of the church, incurred punishment in any rank. Davenant, bishop of Salisbury, one of the divines sent to Dort, and reckoned among the principal theologians of that age, was reprimanded on his knees before the privy council for this offence. Collier, p. 750. But in James's reign the university of Oxford was decidedly Calvinistic. A preacher, about 1623, having used some suspicious expressions, was compelled to recant them, and to maintain the following theses in the divinity school: Decretum prædestinationis non est conditionale — Gracia sufficiens ad

The house of commons, especially in their last session, took up the increase of Arminianism as a public grievance. It was coupled in their remonstrances with popery, as a new danger to religion, hardly less terrible than the former. This bigoted clamor arose in part from the nature of their own Calvinistic tenets, which, being still prevalent in the kingdom, would, independently of all political motives, predominate in any popular assembly. But they had a sort of excuse for it in the close, though accidental and temporary, connection that subsisted between the partisans of these new speculative tenets and those of arbitrary power; the churchmen who receded most from Calvinism being generally the zealots of prerogative. They conceived also that these theories, conformable in the main to those most countenanced in the church of Rome, might pave the way for that restoration of her faith which from so many other quarters appeared to threaten them. Nor was this last apprehension so destitute of all plausibility as the advocates of the two first Stuarts have always pretended it to be.

State of catholics under James.

James, well instructed in the theology of the reformers, and inured himself to controversial dialectics, was far removed in point of opinion from any bias towards the Romish creed. But he had, while in Scotland, given rise to some suspicions at the court of Elizabeth by a little clandestine coquetry with the pope, which he fancied to be a political means of disarming enmity.[1] Some knowledge of this, probably, as well as his

salutem non conceditur omnibus. Wood, ii. 348. And I suppose it continued so in the next reign, so far as the university's opinions could be manifested. But Laud took care that no one should be promoted, as far as he could help it, who held these tenets.

[1] Winwood, vol. i. p. 1, 52, 388; Lettres d'Ossat, i. 221; Birch's Negotiations of Edmondes, p. 36. These references do not relate to the letter said to have been forged in the king's name and addressed to Clement VIII. by lord Balmerino. But Laing, Hist. of Scotland, iii. 59, and Birch's Negotiations, &c., 177, render it almost certain that this letter was genuine, which indeed has been generally believed by men of sense. James was a man of so little consistency or sincerity, that it is difficult to solve the problem of this clandestine intercourse. But it might very likely proceed from his dread of being excommunicated, and, in consequence, assassinated. In a proclamation, commanding all jesuits and priests to quit the realm, dated in 1603, he declares himself personally "so much beholden to the new bishop of Rome for his kind office and private temporal carriage towards us in many things, as we shall ever be ready to requite the same towards him as bishop of Rome in state and condition of a secular prince." Rymer, xvi. 573. This is explained by a passage in the Memoirs of Sully (l. 15). Clement VIII., though before Elizabeth's death he had abetted the project of placing Arabella on the throne, thought it expedient, after this design had failed, to pay some court to James, and had refused to accept the dedication of a work written against him, besides, probably, some other courtesies. There is a letter from the king addressed to the pope, and

avowed dislike of sanguinary persecution, and a foolish reliance on the trifling circumstance that one if not both of his parents had professed their religion, led the English catholics to expect a great deal of indulgence, if not support, at his hands. This hope might receive some encouragement from his speech on opening the parliament of 1604, wherein he intimated his design to revise and explain the penal laws, "which the judges might perhaps," he said, "in times past, have too rigorously interpreted. But the temper of those he addressed was very different. The catholics were disappointed by an act inflicting new penalties on recusants, and especially debarring them from educating their children according to their consciences.[1] The administration took a sudden turn towards severity; the prisons were filled, the penalties exacted, several suffered death,[2] and the general helplessness of their condition impelled a few persons (most of whom had belonged to what was called the Spanish party in the last reign) to the gunpowder conspiracy, unjustly imputed to the majority of catholics, though perhaps extending beyond those who appeared in it.[3] We cannot wonder that a parliament so nar-

Jealousy of the court's favor towards them.

probably written in 1603, among the Cottonian MSS., Nero, B. vi. 9, which shows his disposition to coax and coquet with the Babylonian, against whom he so much inveighs in his printed works. It seems that Clement had so far presumed as to suggest that the prince of Wales should be educated a catholic, which the king refuses, but not in so strong a manner as he should have done. I cannot recollect whether this letter has been printed, though I can scarcely suppose the contrary. Persons himself began to praise the works of James, and show much hope of what he would do. Cotton, Jul. B. vi. 77.

The severities against catholics seem at first to have been practically mitigated. Winwood, ii. 78. Archbishop Hutton wrote to Cecil, complaining of the toleration granted to papists, while the puritans were severely treated. Id. p. 40. Lodge, iii. 251. "The former," he says, "partly by this round dealing with the puritans, and partly by some extraordinary favor, had grown mightily in number, courage, and influence." — "If the gospel shall quail, and popery prevail, it will be imputed principally unto your great counsellors, who either procure or yield to grant toleration to some." James told some gentlemen who petitioned for toleration that the utmost they could expect was connivance. Carte, iii. 711. This seems to have been what he intended through his reign, till importuned by Spain and France to promise more.

[1] 1 Jac. I. c. 4. The penalties of recusancy were particularly hard upon women, who, as I have observed in another place, adhered longer to the old religion than the other sex; and still more so upon those who had to pay for their scruples. It was proposed in parliament, but with the usual fate of humane suggestions, that husbands going to church should not be liable for their wives' recusancy. Carte, 754. But they had the alternative afterwards, by 7 Jac. I. c. 6, of letting their wives lie in prison or paying 10*l.* a month.

[2] Lingard, ix. 41. 55.

[3] From comparing some passages in sir Charles Cornwallis's despatches, Winwood, vol. ii. p. 143, 144, 153, with others in Birch's account of sir Thomas Edmondes's negotiations, p. 233, et seq., it appears that the English catholics were looking forward at this time to some crisis in their favor, and that even the court of Spain was influenced by their hopes. A letter from sir Thomas Parry to Edmondes, dated at Paris, 10 Oct.

rowly rescued from personal destruction endeavored to draw the cord still tighter round these dangerous enemies. The statute passed on this occasion is by no means more harsh than might be expected. It required not only attendance on worship, but participation in the communion, as a test of conformity, and gave an option to the king of taking a penalty of 20*l.* a month from recusants, or two thirds of their lands. It prescribed also an oath of allegiance, the refusal of which incurred the penalties of a præmunire. This imported that,

1605, is remarkable: "Our priests are very busy about petitions to be exhibited to the king's majesty at this parliament, and some further designs upon refusal. These matters are secretly managed by intelligence with their colleagues in those parts where you reside, and with the two nuncios. I think it were necessary for his majesty's service that you found means to have privy spies amongst them, to discover their negotiations. Something is at present in hand amongst these desperate hypocrites, which I trust God shall divert by the vigilant care of his majesty's faithful servants and friends abroad, and prudence of his council at home." Birch, p. 233. There seems indeed some ground for suspicion that the nuncio at Brussels was privy to the conspiracy; though this ought not to be asserted as an historical fact. Whether the offence of Garnet went beyond misprision of treason has been much controverted. The catholic writers maintain that he had no knowledge of the conspiracy, except by having heard it in confession. But this rests altogether on his word; and the prevarication of which he has been proved to be guilty (not to mention the damning circumstance that he was taken at Hendlip in concealment along with the other conspirators) makes it difficult for a candid man to acquit him of a thorough participation in their guilt. Compare Townsend's Accusations of History against the Church of Rome (1825), p. 247, containing extracts from some important documents in the State Paper Office, not as yet published, with State Trials, vol. ii.; and see Lingard, ix. 160, &c. Yet it should be kept in mind that it was easy for a few artful persons to keep on the alert by indistinct communications a credulous multitude whose daily food was rumor; and the general hopes of the English Romanists at the moment are not evidence of their privity to the gunpowder-treason, which was probably contrived late, and imparted to very few. But to deny that there was such a plot, or, which is the same thing, to throw the whole on the contrivance and management of Cecil, as has sometimes been done, argues great effrontery in those who lead, and great stupidity in those who follow. The letter to lord Monteagle, the discovery of the powder, the simultaneous rising in arms in Warwickshire, are as indisputable as any facts in history. What then had Cecil to do with the plot, except that he hit upon the clue to the dark allusions in the letter to Monteagle, of which he was courtier enough to let the king take the credit? James's admirers have always reckoned this, as he did himself, a vast proof of sagacity; yet there seems no great acuteness in the discovery, even if it had been his own. He might have recollected the circumstances of his father's catastrophe, which would naturally put him on the scent of gunpowder. In point of fact, however, the happy conjecture appears to be Cecil's. Winwood, ii. 170. But had he no previous hint? See Lodge, iii. 301.

The earl of Northumberland was not only committed to the Tower on suspicion of privity in the plot, but lay fourteen years there, and paid a fine of 11,000*l.* (by composition for 30,000*l.*), before he was released. Lingard, ix. 89. It appears almost incredible that a man of his ability, though certainly of a dangerous and discontented spirit, and rather destitute of religion than a zealot for popery, which he did not. I believe, openly profess, should have mingled in so flagitious a design. There is indeed a remarkable letter in Winwood, vol. iii. p. 287, which tends to corroborate the suspicions entertained of him. But this letter is from Salisbury, his inveterate enemy. Every one must agree that the fine imposed on this nobleman was preposterous. Were we even to admit that suspicion might justify his long imprisonment, a participation in one of the most atrocious conspiracies recorded in history was, if proved, to be more severely punished; if unproved, not at all.

notwithstanding any sentence of deprivation or excommunication by the pope, the taker would bear true allegiance to the king, and defend him against any conspiracies which should be made by reason of such sentence or otherwise, and do his best endeavor to disclose them; that he from his heart abhorred, detested, and abjured as impious and heretical the damnable doctrine and position that princes excommunicated or deprived by the pope may be deposed or murdered by their subjects, or any other whatsoever; and that he did not believe that the pope or any other could absolve him from this oath.[1]

Except by cavilling at one or two words, it seemed impossible for the Roman catholics to decline so reasonable a test of loyalty, without justifying the worst suspicions of protestant jealousy. Most of the secular priests in England, asking only a connivance in the exercise of their ministry, and aware how much the good work of reclaiming their apostate countrymen was retarded by the political obloquy they incurred, would have willingly acquiesced in the oath. But the court of Rome, not yet receding an inch from her proudest claims, absolutely forbade all catholics to abjure her deposing power by this test, and employed Bellarmine to prove its unlawfulness. The king stooped to a literary controversy with this redoubted champion, and was prouder of no exploit of his life than his answer to the cardinal's book, by which he incurred the contempt of foreign courts and of all judicious men.[2] Though neither the murderous conspiracy of 1605, nor this refusal to abjure the principles on which it was founded, could dispose James to persecution, or even render the papist so obnoxious in his eyes as the puritan, yet he was long averse to anything like a general remission of the penal laws. In sixteen instances after this time the sanguinary enactments of his predecessor were enforced, but only perhaps against priests who refused the oath;[3] the catholics enjoyed on the whole somewhat more

[1] 3 Jac. I. c. 4, 5.

[2] Carte, iii. 782; Collier, 690; Butler's Memoirs of Catholics; Lingard, vol. ix. 97; Aikin, i. 319. It is observed by Collier, ii. 695, and indeed by the king himself, in his Apology for the Oath of Allegiance, edit. 1619, p. 46, that Bellarmine plainly confounds the oath of allegiance with that of supremacy. But this cannot be the whole of the case: it is notorious that Bellarmine protested against any denial of the pope's deposing power.

[3] Lingard, ix. 215. Drury, executed in 1607, was one of the twelve priests who, in 1602, had signed a declaration of the queen's right to the crown, notwithstanding her excommunication. But,

indulgence than before in respect to the private exercise of their religion; at least enough to offend narrow-spirited zealots, and furnish pretext for the murmurs of a discontented parliament, but under condition of paying compositions for recusancy — a regular annual source of revenue, which, though apparently trifling in amount, the king was not likely to abandon, even if his notions of prerogative and the generally received prejudices of that age had not determined him against an express toleration.[1]

In the course, however, of that impolitic negotiation, which exposed him to all eyes as the dupe and tool of the court of Madrid, James was led on to promise concessions for which his protestant subjects were ill prepared. That court had wrought on his feeble mind by affected coyness about the infanta's marriage, with two private aims: to secure his neutrality in the war of the Palatinate, and to obtain better terms for the English catholics. Fully successful in both ends, it would probably have at length permitted the union to take place, had not Buckingham's rash insolence broken off the treaty; but I am at a loss to perceive the sincere and even generous conduct which some have found in the Spanish council during this negotiation.[2] The king acted

though he evidently wavered, he could not be induced to say as much now in order to save his life. State Trials, ii. 358.

[1] Lord Bacon, wise in all things, always recommended mildness towards recusants. In a letter to Villiers, in 1616, he advises that the oath of supremacy should by no means be tendered to recusant magistrates in Ireland; "the new plantation of protestants," he says, "must mate the other party in time." Vol. ii. p. 530. This has not indeed proved true; yet as much, perhaps, for want of following Bacon's advice, as for any other cause. He wished for a like toleration in England. But the king, as Buckingham lets him know, was of a quite contrary opinion; for, "though he would not by any means have a more severe course held than his laws appoint in that case, yet there are many reasons why there should be no mitigation above that which h s laws have exerted, and his own conscience telleth him to be fit." He afterwards professes "to account it a baseness in a prince to show such a desire of the match [this was in 1617] as to slack anything in his course of government, much more in propagation of the religion he professeth, for fear of giving hinderance to the match thereby." Page 562. What a contrast to the behavior of this same king six years afterwards! The commons were always dissatisfied with lenity, and complained that the lands of recusants were undervalued, as they must have been, if the king got only 6000*l*. per annum by the compositions. Debates in 1621, vol. i. p. 24, 91. But he valued those in England and Ireland at 36,000*l*. Lingard, 215, from Hardwicke Papers.

[2] The absurd and highly blamable conduct of Buckingham has created a prejudice in favor of the court of Madrid. That they desired the marriage is easy to be believed; but that they would have ever sincerely coöperated for the restoration of the Palatinate, or even withdrawn the Spanish troops from it, is neither rendered probable by the general policy of that government, nor by the conduct it pursued in the negotiation. Compare Hardwicke State Papers, vol. i.; Cabala, 1, et post; Howell's Letters; Clarendon State Papers, vol. i. ad initium, especially p. 13.

A very curious paper in the latter collection, p. 14, may be thought, perhaps,

with such culpable weakness as even in him excites our astonishment. Buckingham, in his first eagerness for the marriage, on arriving in Spain, wrote to ask if the king would acknowledge the pope's spiritual supremacy, as the surest means of success. James professed to be shocked at this, but offered to recognize his jurisdiction as patriarch of the west, to whom ecclesiastical appeals might ultimately be made: a concession as incompatible with the code of our protestant laws as the former. Yet with this knowledge of his favorite's disposition, he gave the prince and him a written promise to perform whatever they should agree upon with the court of Madrid.[1] On the treaty being almost concluded, the king, prince, and privy council swore to observe certain stipulated articles, by which the infanta was not only to have the exercise of her religion, but the education of her children till ten years of age. But the king was also sworn to private articles: that no penal laws should be put in force against the catholics, that there should be a perpetual toleration of their religion in private houses, that he and his son would

to throw a light on Buckingham's projects, and account in some measure for his sudden enmity to Spain. During his residence at Madrid in 1623, a secretary who had been dissatisfied with the court revealed to him a pretended secret discovery of gold-mines in a part of America, and suggested that they might be easily possessed by any association that could command seven or eight hundred men; and that, after having made such a settlement, it would be easy to take the Spanish flotilla and attempt the conquest of Jamaica and St. Domingo. This made so great an impression on the mind of Buckingham, that long afterwards, in 1628, he entered into a contract with Gustavus Adolphus, who bound himself to defend him against all opposers in the possession of these mines, as an absolute prince and sovereign, on condition of receiving one tenth of the profits; promising especially his aid against any puritans who might attack him from Barbadoes or elsewhere, and to furnish him with four thousand men and six ships of war, to be paid out of the revenue of the mines.

This is a very strange document, if genuine. It seems to show that Buckingham, aware of his unpopularity in England, and that sooner or later he must fall, and led away, as so many were by the expectation of immense wealth in America, had contrived this arrangement, which was probably intended to take place only in the event of his banishment from England. The share that Gustavus appears to have taken in so wild a plan is rather extraordinary, and may expose the whole to some suspicion. It is not clear how this came among the Clarendon papers; but the endorsement runs — "Presented, and the design attempted and in some measure attained by Cromwell, anno 1652." I should conjecture therefore that some spy of the king's procured the copy from Cromwell's papers.

I have since found that Harte had seen a sketch of this treaty, but he does not tell us by what means. Hist. Gust. Adolph. i. 130. But that prince, in 1627, laid before the diet of Sweden a plan for establishing a commerce with the West Indies; for which sums of money were subscribed. Id. 143.

[1] Hardwicke Papers, p. 402, 411, 417. The very curious letters in this collection relative to the Spanish match are the vouchers for my text. It appears by one of Secretary Conway's, since published, Ellis, iii. 154, that the king was in great distress at the engagement for a complete immunity from penal laws for the catholics, entered into by the prince and Buckingham; but on full deliberation in the council, it was agreed that he must adhere to his promise. This rash promise was the cause of his subsequent prevarications.

use their authority to make parliament confirm and ratify these articles, and revoke all laws (as it is with strange latitude expressed) containing anything repugnant to the Roman catholic religion, and that they would not consent to any new laws against them. The prince of Wales separately engaged to procure the suspension or abrogation of the penal laws within three years, and to lengthen the term for the mother's education of their children from ten to twelve years, if it should be in his own power. He promised also to listen to catholic divines whenever the infanta should desire it.[1]

These secret assurances, when they were whispered in England, might not unreasonably excite suspicion of the prince's wavering in his religion, which he contrived to aggravate by an act as imprudent as it was reprehensible. During his stay at Madrid, while his inclinations were still bent on concluding the marriage, the sole apparent obstacle being the pope's delay in forwarding the dispensation, he wrote a letter to Gregory XV., in reply to one received from him, in language evidently intended to give an impression of his favorable dispositions towards the Roman faith. The whole tenor of his subsequent life must have satisfied every reasonable inquirer into our history of Charles's real attachment to the Anglican church; nor could he have had any other aim than to facilitate his arrangements with the court of Rome by this deception. It would perhaps be uncandid to judge severely a want of ingenuousness which youth, love, and bad counsels may extenuate; yet I cannot help remarking that the letter is written with the precautions of a veteran in dissimulation; and while it is full of what might raise expectation, contains no special pledge that he could be called on to redeem. But it was rather presumptuous to hope that he could foil the subtlest masters of artifice with their own weapons.[2]

1 Hardwicke Papers; Rushworth.

2 Hardwicke Papers, p. 452, where the letter is printed in Latin. The translation, in Wilson, Rushworth, and Cabala, p. 214, is not by any means exact, going in several places much beyond the original. If Hume knew nothing but the translation, as is most probable, we may well be astonished at his way of dismissing this business; that, "the prince having received a very civil letter from the pope, he was induced to return a very civil answer." Clarendon saw it in a different light: Clar. State Papers, ii. 337.

Urban VIII. had succeeded Gregory XV. before the arrival of Charles's letter. He answered it of course in a style of approbation, and so as to give the utmost meaning to the prince's compliments, expressing his satisfaction, "cum pontificem Romanum ex officii genere colere princeps Britannus inciperet, &c. Rushworth, vol. i. p. 98.

James, impatient for this ill-omened alliance, lost no time in fulfilling his private stipulations with Spain. He published a general pardon of all penalties already incurred for recusancy. It was designed to follow this up by a proclamation prohibiting the bishops, judges, and other magistrates to execute any penal statute against the catholics. But the lord-keeper, bishop Williams, hesitated at so unpopular a stretch of power.[1] And, the rupture with Spain ensuing almost immediately, the king, with a singular defiance of all honest men's opinions, though the secret articles of the late treaty had become generally known, declared, in his first speech to parliament in 1624, that "he had only thought good sometimes to wink and connive at the execution of some penal laws, and not to go on so rigorously as at other times, but not to dispense with any, or to forbid or alter any, that concern religion; he never permitted or yielded, he never did think it with his heart, nor spoke it with his mouth."[2]

When James, soon after this, not yet taught by experience to avoid a Romish alliance, demanded the hand of Henrietta Maria for his son, Richelieu thought himself bound by policy and honor as well as religion to obtain the same or greater advantages for the English catholics than had been promised in the former negotiation. Henrietta was to have the education of her children till they reached the age of twelve; thus were added two years, at a time of life when the mind becomes susceptible of lasting impressions, to the term at which, by the treaty with Spain, the mother's superintendence was to cease.[3] Yet there is the strongest reason to believe that this condition was merely inserted for the honor of the French crown, with a secret understanding that it should never be executed.[4] In fact, the royal children were

It is said by Howell, who was then on the spot, that the prince never used the service of the church of England while he was at Madrid, though two chaplains, church-plate, &c., had been sent over. Howell's Letters, p. 140. Bristol and Buckingham charged each other with advising Charles to embrace the Romish religion; and he himself, in a letter to Bristol, Jan. 21, 1625-6, imputes this to him in the most positive terms. Cabala, p. 17, 4to. edit. As to Buckingham's willingness to see this step taken, there can, I presume, be little doubt.

[1] Rushworth; Cabala, p. 19.

[2] Parl. Hist. 1375. Both houses, however, joined in an address that the laws against recusants might be put in execution. Id. 1408. And the commons returned again to the charge afterwards. Idem, 1484.

[3] Rushworth.

[4] See a series of letters from lord Kensington (better known afterwards as earl of Holland), the king's ambassador at Paris for this marriage treaty; in the appendix to Clarendon State Papers, vol. ii. p. v. viii. ix.

placed at a very early age under protestant governors of the king's appointment; nor does Henrietta appear to have ever insisted on her right. That James and Charles should have incurred the scandal of this engagement, since the articles, though called private, must be expected to transpire, without any real intentions of performing it, is an additional instance of that arrogant contempt of public opinion which distinguished the Stuart family. It was stipulated in the same private articles that prisoners on the score of religion should be set at liberty, and that none should be molested in future.[1] These promises were irregularly fulfilled, according

1 Hardwicke Papers, i. 536. Birch, in one of those volumes given by him to the British Museum (and which ought to be published according to his own intention), has made several extracts from the MS. despatches of Tillieres, the French ambassador, which illustrate this negotiation. The pope, it seems, stood off from granting the dispensation, requiring that the English catholic clergy should represent to him their approbation of the marriage. He was informed that the cardinal had obtained terms much more favorable for the catholics than in the Spanish treaty. In short, they evidently fancied themselves to have gained a full assurance of toleration; nor could the match have been effected on any other terms. The French minister writes to Louis XIII. from London, October 6, 1624, that he had obtained a supersedeas of all prosecutions, more than themselves expected, or could have believed possible; en somme, un acte très publique, et qui fut résolu en plein conseil, le dit roi l'ayant assemblé exprès pour cela le jour d'hier." The pope agreed to appoint a bishop for England, nominated by the king of France. Oct. 22. The oath of allegiance, however, was a stumbling-block; the king could not change it by his own authority and establish another in parliament, "où la faction des puritains prédomine, de sorte qu'ils peuvent ce qu'ils veulent." Buckingham however promised "de nous faire obtenir l'assurance que votre majesté désire tant, que les catholiques de ce pais ne seront jamais inquiétés pour la raison du serment de fidélité, du quel votre majesté a si souvent oui parler." Dec. 22. He speaks the same day of an audience he had of king James, who promised never to persecute his catholic subjects, nor desire of them any oath which spoke of the pope's spiritual authority, "mais seulement un acte de la reconnoissance de la domination temporelle que Dieu lui a donnée, et qu'ils auroient en considération de votre majesté, et de la confiance que vous prenez en sa parole, beaucoup plus de liberté qu'ils n'auroient eu en vertu des articles du traité d'Espagne." The French advised that no parliament should be called till Henrietta should come over, "de qui la présence serviroit de bride aux puritains." It is not wonderful, with all this good-will on the part of their court, that the English catholics should now send a letter to request the granting of the dispensation. A few days after, Dec. 26, the ambassador announces the king's letter to the archbishops, directing them to stop the prosecution of catholics, the enlargement of prisoners on the score of religion, and the written promises of the king and prince to let the catholics enjoy more liberty than they would have had by virtue of the treaty with Spain. On the credit of this Louis wrote on the 23d of January, to request six or eight ships of war to employ against Soubise, the chief of the Hugonots; with which, as is well known, Charles complied in the ensuing summer.

The king's letter above mentioned does not, I believe, appear. But his ambassadors, Carlisle and Holland, had promised in his name that he would give a written promise, on the word and honor of a king, which the prince and a secretary of state should also sign, that all his Roman catholic subjects should enjoy more freedom as to their religion than they could have had by any articles agreed on with Spain; not being molested in their persons or property for their profession and exercise of their religion, provided they used their liberty with moderation, and rendered due submission to the king, who would not force them to any oath contrary to their religion. This was signed 18th Nov. Hardw. Pap. 546.

Yet after this concession on the king's part the French cabinet was encouraged by it to ask for a "direct and public

to the terms on which Charles stood with his brother-in-law. Sometimes general orders were issued to suspend all penal laws against papists; again, by capricious change of policy, all officers and judges are directed to proceed in their execution; and this severity gave place in its turn to a renewed season of indulgence. If these alternations were not very satisfactory to the catholics, the whole scheme of lenity displeased and alarmed the protestants. Tolerance, in any extensive sense, of that proscribed worship, was equally abhorrent to the prelatist and the puritan; though one would have winked at its peaceable and domestic exercise, which the other was zealous to eradicate. But, had they been capable of more liberal reasoning upon this subject, there was enough to justify their indignation at this attempt to sweep away the restrictive code established by so many statutes, and so long deemed essential to the security of their church, by an unconstitutional exertion of the prerogative, prompted by no more worthy motive than compliance with a foreign power, and tending to confirm suspicions of the king's wavering between the two religions, or his indifference to either. In the very first months of his reign, and while that parliament was sitting which has been reproached for its parsimony, he sent a fleet to assist the French king in blocking up the port of Rochelle; and, with utter disregard of the national honor, ordered the admiral, who reported that the sailors would not fight against protestants, to sail to Dieppe, and give up his ships into the possession of France.[1] His subsequent alliance with the Hugonot party in consequence merely of Buckingham's unwarrantable hostility to France,

toleration, not by connivance, promise, or écrit secret, but by a public notification to all the Roman catholics, and that of all his majesty's kingdoms whatsoever, confirmed by his majesty's and the prince's oath, and attested by a public act, whereof a copy to be delivered to the pope or his minister, and the same to bind his majesty and the prince's successors forever." Id. p. 552. The ambassadors expressed the strongest indignation at this proposal, on which the French did not think fit to insist. In all this wretched negotiation James was as much the dupe as he had been in the former, expecting that France would assist in the recovery of the Palatinate, towards which, in spite of promises, she took no steps. Richelieu had said, "Donnez-nous des prêtres, et nous vous donnerons des colonels." Id. p. 538. Charles could hardly be expected to keep his engagements as to the catholics, when he found himself so grossly outwitted.

It was during this marriage-treaty of 1624 that the archbishop of Embrun, as he relates himself, in the course of several conferences with the king on that subject, was assured by him that he was desirous of reëntering the fold of the church. Wilson in Kennet, p. 786, note by Wellwood. I have not seen the original passage; but Dr. Lingard puts by no means so strong an interpretation on the king's words, as related by the archbishop: vol. ix. 323.

[1] Kennet, p. vi.; Rushworth; Lingard, ix. 353: Cabala, p. 144.

founded on the most extraordinary motives, could not redeem, in the eyes of the nation, this instance of lukewarmness, to say the least, in the general cause of the reformation. Later ages have had means of estimating the attachment of Charles the First to protestantism, which his contemporaries in that early period of his reign did not enjoy; and this has led some to treat the apprehensions of parliament as either insincere or preposterously unjust. But can this be fairly pretended by any one who has acquainted himself with the course of proceedings on the Spanish marriage, the whole of which was revealed by the earl of Bristol to the house of lords? Was there nothing, again, to excite alarm in the frequent conversions of persons of high rank to popery, in the more dangerous partialities of many more, in the evident bias of certain distinguished churchmen to tenets rejected at the Reformation? The course pursued with respect to religious matters after the dissolution of parliament in 1629, to which I shall presently advert, did by no means show the misgivings of that assembly to have been ill-founded.

Unconstitutional tenets promulgated by the high-church party.

It was neither, however, the Arminian opinions of the higher clergy, nor even their supposed leaning towards those of Rome, that chiefly rendered them obnoxious to the commons. They had studiously inculcated that resistance to the commands of rulers was in every conceivable instance a heinous sin; a tenet so evidently subversive of all civil liberty that it can be little worth while to argue about right and privilege, wherever it has obtained a real hold on the understanding and conscience of a nation. This had very early been adopted by the Anglican reformers, as a barrier against the disaffection of those who adhered to the ancient religion, and in order to exhibit their own loyalty in a more favorable light. The homily against wilful disobedience and rebellion was written on occasion of the rising of the northern earls in 1569, and is full of temporary and even personal allusions.[1]

1 "God alloweth (it is said in this homily, among other passages to the same effect) neither the dignity of any person, nor the multitude of any people, nor the weight of any cause, as sufficient for the which the subjects may move rebellion against their princes." The next sentence contains a bold position. "Turn over and read the histories of all nations, look over the chronicles of our own country, call to mind so many rebellions of old time, and some yet fresh in memory; ye shall not find that God ever prospered any rebellion against their natural and lawful prince, but contrariwise, that the rebels were overthrown and slain, and such as were taken prisoners dreadfully executed." They il-

But the same doctrine is enforced in others of those compositions, which enjoy a kind of half authority in the English church. It is laid down in the canons of convocation in 1606. It is very frequent in the writings of English divines, those especially who were much about the court. And an unlucky preacher at Oxford, named Knight, about 1622, having thrown out some intimation that subjects oppressed by their prince on account of religion might defend themselves by arms, that university, on the king's highly resenting such heresy, not only censured the preacher (who had the audacity to observe that the king by then sending aid to the French Hugonots of Rochelle, as was rumored to be designed, had sanctioned his position), but pronounced a solemn decree that it is in no case lawful for subjects to make use of force against their princes, nor to appear offensively or defensively in the field against them. All persons promoted to degrees were to subscribe this article, and to take an oath that they not only at present detested the opposite opinion, but would at no future time entertain it. A ludicrous display of the folly and despotic spirit of learned academies! [1]

Those however who most strenuously denied the abstract right of resistance to unlawful commands were by no means obliged to maintain the duty of yielding them an active obedience. In the case of religion, it was necessary to admit that God was rather to be obeyed than man. Nor had it been pretended, except by the most servile churchmen, that subjects had no positive rights, in behalf of which they might decline compliance with illegal requisitions. This however was openly asserted in the reign of Charles. Those who re-

lustrate their doctrine by the most preposterous example I have ever seen alleged in any book: that of the Virgin Mary, who, "being of the royal blood of the ancient natural kings of Jewry, obeyed the proclamation of Augustus to go to Bethlehem. This obedience of this most noble and most virtuous lady to a foreign and pagan prince doth well teach us, who in comparison of her are both base and vile, what ready obedience we do owe to our natural and gracious sovereign."

In another homily, entitled "On Obedience," the duty of non-resistance, even in defence of religion, is most decidedly maintained; and in such a manner as might have been inconvenient in case of a popish successor. Nor was this theory very consistent with the aid and countenance given to the United Provinces. Our learned churchmen, however, cared very little for the Dutch. They were more puzzled about the Maccabees. But that knot is cut in bishop Overall's Convocation Book by denying that Antiochus Epiphanes had lawful possession of Palestine — a proposition not easy to be made out.

1 Collier, 724. Neal, 495. Wood's History of the University of Oxford, ii. 341. Knight was sent to the Gatehouse prison, where he remained two years. Laud was the chief cause of this severity, if we may believe Wood; and his own diary seems to confirm this.

fused the general loan of 1626 had to encounter assaults from very different quarters, and were not only imprisoned, but preached at. Two sermons by Sibthorp and Mainwaring excited particular attention. These men, eager for preferment, which they knew the readiest method to attain, taught that the king might take the subject's money at his pleasure, and that no one might refuse his demand, on penalty of damnation. "Parliaments," said Mainwaring, "were not ordained to contribute any right to the king, but for the more equal imposing and more easy exacting of that which unto kings doth appertain by natural and original law and justice, as their proper inheritance annexed to their imperial crowns from their birth."[1] These extravagances of rather obscure men would have passed with less notice if the government had not given them the most indecent encouragement. Abbot, archbishop of Canterbury, a man of integrity, but upon that account, as well as for his Calvinistic partialities, long since obnoxious to the courtiers, refused to license Sibthorp's sermon, alleging some unwarrantable passages which it contained. For no other cause than this, he was sequestered from the exercise of his archiepiscopal jurisdiction, and confined to a country house in Kent.[2] The house of commons, after many complaints of those ecclesiastics, finally proceeded against Mainwaring by impeachment at the bar of the lords. He was condemned to pay a fine of 1000*l.*,

[1] Parl. Hist. 877, 395, 410, &c. Kennet, p. 30. Collier, 740, 743. This historian, though a nonjuror, is Englishman enough to blame the doctrines of Sibthorp and Mainwaring, and, consistently with his high-church principles, is displeased at the suspension of Abbot by the king's authority.

[2] State Trials, ii. 1449. A few years before this, Abbot had the misfortune, while hunting deer in a nobleman's park, to shoot one of the keepers with his crossbow. Williams and Laud, who then acted together, with some others, affected scruples at the archbishop's continuance in his function, on pretence that, by some old canon, he had become irregular in consequence of this accidental homicide; and Spelman disgraced himself by writing a treatise in support of this doctrine. James, however, had more sense than the antiquary, and less ill-nature than the churchmen; and the civilians gave no countenance to Williams's hypocritical scruples. Hacket's Life of Williams, p. 651. Biograph. Britann., art. ABBOT. Spelman's Works, part 2, p. 3. Aikin's James I., ii. 259. Williams's real object was to succeed the archbishop on his degradation.

It may be remarked that Abbot, though a very worthy man, had not always been untainted by the air of a court. He had not scrupled grossly to flatter the king (see his article in Biograph. Brit., and Aikin, i. 368); and tells us himself that he introduced Villiers in order to supplant Somerset; which, though well meant, did not become his function. Even in the delicate business of promising toleration to the catholics by the secret articles of the treaty with Spain, he gave satisfaction to the king (Hardwicke Papers, i. 428), which could only be by compliance. This shows that the letter in Rushworth, ascribed to the archbishop, deprecating all such concessions, is not genuine. In Cabala, p. 13, it is printed with the name of the archbishop of York, Mathews.

to be suspended for three years from his ministry, and to be incapable of holding any ecclesiastical dignity. Yet the king almost immediately pardoned Mainwaring, who became in a few years a bishop, as Sibthorp was promoted to an inferior dignity.[1]

General remarks.

There seems on the whole to be very little ground for censure in the proceedings of this illustrious parliament. I admit that, if we believe Charles I. to have been a gentle and beneficent monarch, incapable of harboring any design against the liberties of his people, or those who stood forward in defence of their privileges, wise in the choice of his counsellors, and patient in listening to them, the commons may seem to have carried their opposition to an unreasonable length. But, if he had shown himself possessed with such notions of his own prerogative, no matter how derived, as could bear no effective control from fixed law, or from the nation's representatives; if he was hasty and violent in temper, yet stooping to low arts of equivocation and insincerity; whatever might be his estimable qualities in other respects, they could act, in the main, no otherwise than by endeavoring to keep him in the power of parliament, lest his power should make parliament but a name. Every popular assembly, truly zealous in a great cause, will display more heat and passion than cool-blooded men after the lapse of centuries may wholly approve.[2] But so far were they from encroaching, as our Tory writers pretend, on the just powers of a limited monarch, that they do not appear to have conceived, they at least never hinted at, the securities without which all they had obtained or at-

1 The bishops were many of them mere sycophants of Buckingham. Besides Laud, Williams, and Neile, one Field, bishop of Llandaff, was an abject courtier. See a letter of his in Cabala, p. 118, 4to. edit. Mede says, (27th May, 1626), "I am sorry to hear they (the bishops) are so habituated to flattery that they seem not to know of any other duty that belongs to them." See Ellis's Letters, iii. 228, for the account Mede gives of the manner in which the heads of houses forced the election of Buckingham as chancellor of Cambridge, while the impeachment was pending against him. The junior masters of arts, however, made a good stand; so that it was carried against the earl of Berkshire only by three voices.

2 Those who may be inclined to dissent from my text will perhaps bow to their favorite Clarendon. He says that in the three first parliaments, though there were "several distempered speeches of particular persons, not fit for the reverence due to his majesty," yet he "does not know any formed act of either house (for neither the remonstrance nor votes of the last day were such) that was not agreeable to the wisdom and justice of great courts upon those extraordinary occasions; and whoever considers the acts of power and injustice in the intervals of parliament will not be much scandalized at the warmth and vivacity of those meetings." Vol. i. p. 8, edit. 1826.

tempted would become ineffectual. No one member of that house, in the utmost warmth of debate, is recorded to have suggested the abolition of the court of star-chamber, or any provision for the periodical meeting of parliament. Though such remedies for the greatest abuses were in reality consonant to the actual unrepealed law of the land, yet, as they implied, in the apprehension of the generality, a retrenchment of the king's prerogative, they had not yet become familiar to their hopes. In asserting the illegality of arbitrary detention, of compulsory loans, of tonnage and poundage levied without consent of parliament, they stood in defence of positive rights won by their fathers, the prescriptive inheritance of Englishmen. Twelve years more of repeated aggressions taught the Long Parliament what a few sagacious men might perhaps have already suspected, that they must recover more of their ancient constitution from oblivion, that they must sustain its partial weakness by new securities, that, in order to render the existence of monarchy compatible with that of freedom, they must not only strip it of all it had usurped, but of something that was its own.

END OF THE FIRST VOLUME.

www.ingramcontent.com/pod-product-compliance
Lightning Source LLC
LaVergne TN
LVHW020106110826
845151LV00001B/80

* 9 7 8 1 4 2 5 5 4 4 1 7 1 *